20-MINUTE RECIPES 500

Fabulous, fast dishes for every occasion from breakfasts, soups, appetizers and snacks to main courses and desserts, shown in over 500 tempting photographs

Make life simple with this fantastic collection of delicious, fuss-free recipes that can all be prepared, cooked and put on the table in 20 minutes or less

CONTRIBUTING EDITOR: JENNI FLEETWOOD

JG PRESS

Published by World Publications Group, Inc.
140 Laurel Street
East Bridgewater, MA 02333
www.wrldpub.net

Produced by Anness Publishing Ltd
Hermes House
88–89 Blackfriars Road
London SE1 8HA
tel. 020 7401 2077; fax 020 7633 9499

www.annesspublishing.com

If you like the images in this book and would like to investigate using them
for publishing, promotions or advertising, please visit our website
www.practicalpictures.com for more information.

Publisher: Joanna Lorenz
Editorial Director: Helen Sudell
Editor: Elizabeth Woodland
Recipes: Pepita Aris, Catherine Atkinson, Mridula Baljekar, Jane Bamforth,
Ghillie basan, Judy Bastyra, Steve Baxter, Michelle Berriedale-Johnson, Angela
Boggiano, Janet Brinkworth, Kathy Brown, Georgina Campbell, Carla
Capalbo, Kit Chan, Jacqueline Clarke, Maxine Clarke, Carole Clements, Trish
Davies, Roz Denny, Patrizia Diemling, Matthew Drennen, Coralie Dorman,
Joanna Farrow, Valerie Ferguson, Rafi Fernandez, Maria Filippelli, Jenni
Fleetwood, Christine France, Silvano Franco, Sarah Gates, Shirley Gill, Brian
Glover, Nicola Graimes, Rosamund Grant, Carole Handslip, Juliet Harbutt,
Simona Hill, Shehzad Husain, Deh-Ta Hsiung, Christine Ingram, Becky
Johnson, Bridget Jones, Peter Jordan, Manisha Kanani, Soheila Kimberley,
Masaki Ko, Lucy Knox, Elisabeth Lambert Ortiz, Ruby Le Bois, Clare Lewis,
Sara Lewis, Gilly Love, Lesley Mackley, Norma MacMillan, Sue Maggs, Kathy
Man, Sally Mansfield, Elizabeth Martin, Norma Miller, Jane Milton, Sallie
Morris, Annie Nichols, Suzannah Olivier, Maggie Pannell, Katherine
Richmond, Keith Richmond, Rena Salaman, Anne Sheasby, Jennie Shapter,
Ysanne Spevack Marlena Spieler, Jenny Stacey, Liz Trigg, Linda Tubby, Sunil
Vijayakar, Hilaire Walden, Stuart Walton, Laura Washburn, Steven Wheeler,
Kate Whiteman, Jenny White, Biddy White-Lennon, Rosemary Wilkinson,
Elizabeth Wolf-Cohen, Jeni Wright, Annette Yates
Photography: Karl Adamson, Edward Allwright, Peter Anderson, David
Armstrong, Tim Auty, Caroline Barty, Steve Baxter, Martin Brigdale, Nicki
Dowey, James Duncan, Gus Filgate, John Freeman, Ian Garlick, Michelle
Garrett, Amanda Heywood, Peter Henley, John Heseltine, Ferguson Hill,
Janine Hosegood, David Jordan, Maria Kelly, Dave King, Don Last, William
Lingwood, Patrick McLeavey, Michael Michaels,
Norma Miller, Craig Robertson, Steve Moss, Thomas Odulate, Sam Stowell,
Simon Smith and Stuart Walton.
Design: SMI and Diane Pullen
Cover Design: Nigel Partridge
Editorial Reader: Molly Perham
Production Manager: Steve Lang

ISBN-10: 1-57215-600-7
ISBN-13: 978-1-57215-600-5

Printed and bound in China

ETHICAL TRADING POLICY
Because of our ongoing ecological investment program, you, as our
customer, can have the pleasure and reassurance of knowing that a tree is
being cultivated on your behalf to naturally replace the materials used to
make the book you are holding. For further information about this scheme,
go to www.annesspublishing.com/trees

PUBLISHER'S NOTE
Although the advice and information in this book are believed to be
accurate and true at the time of going to press, neither the authors nor
the publisher can accept any legal responsibility or liability for any errors or
omissions that may be made.

Main front cover image shows Duck & Sesame Stir-fry
– for recipe, see page 154

Notes
Bracketed terms are intended for American readers.
For all recipes, quantities are given in both metric and
imperial measures and, where appropriate, in standard
cups and spoons.

Follow one set of measures, but not a mixture, because
they are not interchangeable.

Standard spoon and cup measures are level.
1 tsp = 5ml, 1 tbsp = 15ml, 1 cup = 250ml/8fl oz.
Australian standard tablespoons are 20ml.
Australian readers should use 3 tsp in place of 1 tbsp
for measuring small quantities.
American pints are 16fl oz/2 cups. American readers
should use 20fl oz/2.5 cups in place of 1 pint
when measuring liquids.

Electric oven temperatures in this book are for
conventional ovens. When using a fan oven, the
temperature will probably need to be reduced by about
10–20°C/20–40°F. Since ovens vary, you should check with
your manufacturer's instruction book for guidance.

The nutritional analysis given for each recipe is calculated
per portion (i.e. serving or item), unless otherwise stated.

If the recipe gives a range, such as Serves 4–6, then the
nutritional analysis will be for the smaller portion size,
i.e. 6 servings.

Measurements for sodium do not include salt
added to taste.
Medium (US large) eggs are used unless otherwise stated.

Contents

Introduction

Twenty minutes isn't very long. You can easily spend that amount of time puzzling over a crossword clue, or trying to telephone a company determined to leave you on hold, or having a

cup of coffee in a busy restaurant. So can you cook a meal in twenty minutes? Yes you can, and this is the book to tell you how to do it.

Time: we never seem to have enough of it. Whether you are a student trying to balance study with a hectic social life, a single person trying to carve out a career, or a parent with a different but equally pressing set of priorities, time is a precious luxury. We're all riding the rollercoaster, rushing from home to work to

home to sport to parents' evening to home to sleep. Putting good food on the table should be in there somewhere, but sometimes it is difficult to achieve. That's why this book takes a pragmatic approach. Preparing your own vegetables is ideal, but if buying a bag of shake-it-out salad or some ready-trimmed beans means you can eat well and still get to your night class, go for it. Look out for quick-cook versions of favourite ingredients such as polenta and rice, and don't be afraid of mixing bought items like pesto or tapenade with home-cooked pasta.

When you want great food fast, what you need in your repertoire are easy, no-fuss recipes: breakfasts you can blitz in a blender; lunches you can prepare and pack in next to no time; and

suppers that raise your spirits without sapping any of the energy you have left at the end of the day. If you are entertaining, you want to do so in style, but without missing more than a few moments of your guests' company.

You can achieve these aims – after a fashion – by frequenting the ready meal section of your favourite supermarket. Some days you'll do just that, but it is more rewarding and nutritious to serve something you've cooked yourself.

The aim of this book is to provide a wide-ranging selection of recipes that can be cooked in 20 minutes or less. That's assuming the cook is reasonably experienced. If you've never chopped

an onion in your life, it is likely to take you a little longer. Efficient cooking is all about organization, so do read through your chosen recipe carefully, assemble your ingredients and give some thought to strategy. Recipe methods reflect this, but you need to work within the bounds of your own ability and the confines of your own kitchen. If a recipe calls for a slotted spoon and you need to rummage under the sink for one, you could lose valuable time, so be as

well prepared as possible. If you are inexperienced, the best way to start is by choosing the shortest recipes of 10 minutes or less, or opt for something that needs no cooking at all, such as a salad. Also, enlist aid when you can. Something as simple as getting a partner to line up ingredients can be a huge help.

Some of the recipes in this book require some advance preparation – for example, marinating, soaking or chilling. The timeline at the top of the recipe will make it clear when this is required and there will probably be some mention of the fact in the recipe introduction, so do watch out for this. The recipes still won't take more than 20 minutes in all, but the preparation will be in

stages and not all at the same time. There are times when advance preparation can be a great advantage, such as when you want to get some food for a dinner party out of the way beforehand, for instance.

When you have extra time on your hands, consider making stock or a few sauces that can be frozen for later use. Then, when you are in a rush, you'll have the means to make a simple, speedy meal that tastes great.

Vitality Juice

The clue is in the name. This speedy juice really does put a spring in your step. Watercress has a slightly peppery flavour when eaten on its own, but blending it with pear, wheatgerm and yogurt tames the taste while boosting your morning energy levels.

Serves 4

25g/1oz watercress
1 large ripe pear
30ml/2 tbsp wheatgerm
150ml/¼ pint/⅔ cup natural (plain) yogurt
15ml/1 tbsp linseeds (flax seeds)
10ml/2 tsp lemon juice
mineral water (optional)
ice cubes

Preparation: 4 minutes; Cooking: 0 minutes

1 Roughly chop the watercress (you do not need to remove the tough stalks). Peel, core and roughly chop the pear.

2 Put the watercress and pear in a blender or food processor with the wheatgerm and blend until smooth. Scrape the mixture down from the side of the bowl, if necessary.

3 Add the yogurt, seeds and lemon juice and blend until combined. Thin with a little mineral water if too thick.

4 Put several ice cubes in the bottom of a tall glass. Fill the glass to just below the brim with the Vitality Juice, leaving enough room to decorate with a few sprigs of chopped watercress on top.

Variations
• *For a non-dairy version of this delicious, refreshing drink, use yogurt made from goat's milk, sheep's milk or soya.*
• *A large apple can be used instead of the pear.*
• *Linseeds are a very useful addition to this juice, as they have abundant levels of omega-3 and omega-6 fatty acids, which are good for strengthening immunity and easing digestive problems. However, they are not to everyone's taste, and three walnuts could be used instead.*

Pineapple, Ginger & Carrot Juice

You're never too busy for breakfast when you have recipes like this one in your repertoire. Ginger adds a zing to the sweet, scented mixture of fresh pineapple and carrot.

Makes 1 glass

½ small pineapple
25g/1oz fresh root ginger
1 carrot
ice cubes

Preparation: 5 minutes; Cooking: 0 minutes

1 Using a sharp knife, cut away the skin from the pineapple, then cut it into quarters and remove the core from each piece. Roughly slice the pineapple flesh and then chop into portions small enough to fit in the juicer.

2 Thinly peel the ginger, using a sharp knife or vegetable peeler, then chop the flesh roughly. Scrape or peel the carrot and cut it into rounds or chunks. Push the carrot, ginger and pineapple through a juicer and pour into a glass. Add ice cubes and serve.

Raspberry & Oatmeal Smoothie

Just a spoonful or so of oatmeal gives substance to this tangy, invigorating drink, providing slow-release carbohydrates to balance the fruit.

Makes 1 large glass

25ml/1½ tbsp medium oatmeal
150g/5oz/scant 1 cup raspberries
45ml/3 tbsp natural (plain) yogurt

Preparation: 2 minutes; Cooking: 0 minutes

1 Put the oats in a blender and add all but two or three of the raspberries, and about 30ml/2 tbsp of the yogurt. Blend until smooth, scraping down the side of the blender if necessary. Pour in 120ml/4fl oz/½ cup very cold water. Blend briefly. Pour the raspberry and oatmeal smoothie into a large glass, swirl in the remaining yogurt and top with the reserved raspberries.

Vitality Juice Energy 287kcal/1207kJ; Protein 17.8g; Carbohydrate 39.8g, of which sugars 31.2g; Fat 7.6g, of which saturates 1.6g; Cholesterol 2mg; Calcium 394mg; Fibre 8.8g; Sodium 144mg.
Pineapple Juice Energy 108kcal/462kJ; Protein 1.3g; Carbohydrate 26.1g, of which sugars 25.8g; Fat 0.6g, of which saturates 0.1g; Cholesterol 0mg; Calcium 55mg; Fibre 4.2g; Sodium 23mg.
Raspberry Smoothie Energy 186kcal/793kJ; Protein 7.5g; Carbohydrate 34.6g, of which sugars 16.4g; Fat 3.1g, of which saturates 0.4g; Cholesterol 1mg; Calcium 137mg; Fibre 5.4g; Sodium 51mg.

Muesli Smoothie

This divinely smooth drink has all the goodness but none of the lumpy bits.

Serves 2

50g/2oz/¼ cup ready-to-eat dried apricots

1 piece preserved stem ginger, plus 30ml/2 tbsp syrup from the ginger jar

40g/1½oz/scant ½ cup natural muesli (granola)

about 200ml/7fl oz/scant 1 cup semi-skimmed (low-fat) milk

Preparation: 4 minutes; Cooking: 0 minutes

1 Using a sharp knife, chop the dried apricots into slices or chunks. Chop the preserved ginger.

2 Put the apricots and ginger in a blender or food processor and add the syrup from the ginger jar with the muesli and milk. Process until smooth, adding more milk if necessary, to make a creamy drink. Serve in wide glasses.

Breakfast in a Glass

This energizing blend is simply bursting with goodness – just what you need when you wake up.

Serves 2

250g/9oz firm tofu

200g/7oz/1¾ cups strawberries

45ml/3 tbsp pumpkin or sunflower seeds, plus extra for sprinkling

30–45ml/2–3 tbsp clear honey

juice of 2 large oranges

juice of 1 lemon

Preparation: 5 minutes; Cooking: 0 minutes

1 Roughly chop the tofu, then hull and roughly chop the strawberries. Reserve a few strawberry chunks.

2 Put all the ingredients in a blender or food processor and blend until completely smooth, scraping the mixture down from the side of the bowl, if necessary. Pour into tumblers and sprinkle with extra seeds and strawberry chunks.

Big Breakfast

Easy to prepare, this energy-packed smoothie makes a great start to the day. Bananas and sesame seeds provide slow-release carbohydrate that will keep you going all morning.

Makes 2 glasses

½ mango

1 banana

1 large orange

30ml/2 tbsp wheatbran

15ml/1 tbsp sesame seeds

10–15ml/2–3 tsp honey

Preparation: 6 minutes; Cooking: 0 minutes

1 Using a small, sharp knife, skin the mango, then slice the flesh off the stone (pit). Peel the banana and break it into lengths, then place it in a blender or food processor with the mango.

2 Squeeze the juice from the orange and add to the blender or food processor along with the bran, sesame seeds and honey. Whizz until smooth and creamy, then pour into glasses.

Golden Wonder

Vitamin-rich and energizing, this drink is sure to set you up for the day. Passion fruit has a lovely tangy flavour which goes very well with banana.

Makes 1 large glass

2 passion fruit

2 yellow plums

1 small banana

about 15ml/1 tbsp lemon juice

Preparation: 3 minutes; Cooking: 0 minutes

1 Halve the passion fruit and, using a teaspoon, scoop the pulp into a blender or food processor. Using a small, sharp knife, halve and stone (pit) the plums and add to the blender or food processor.

2 Add the banana and lemon juice and blend the mixture until smooth, scraping the mixture down from the side of the bowl, if necessary. Pour into a large glass and check the sweetness. Add a little more lemon juice, if you like.

Muesli Smoothie Energy 204kcal/865kJ; Protein 6.6g; Carbohydrate 39.1g, of which sugars 28.8g; Fat 3.4g, of which saturates 1.4g; Cholesterol 6mg; Calcium 150mg; Fibre 3.1g; Sodium 97mg.
Breakfast in a Glass Energy 259kcal/1087kJ; Protein 13.3g; Carbohydrate 30.4g, of which sugars 28.2g; Fat 10.2g, of which saturates 1.1g; Cholesterol 0mg; Calcium 671mg; Fibre 1.8g; Sodium 19mg.
Big Breakfast Energy 172kcal/726kJ; Protein 4.9g; Carbohydrate 27.6g, of which sugars 23.1g; Fat 5.5g, of which saturates 0.9g; Cholesterol 0mg; Calcium 102mg; Fibre 8.5g; Sodium 11mg.
Golden Wonder Energy 108kcal/461kJ; Protein 2.1g; Carbohydrate 25.6g, of which sugars 23.7g; Fat 0.4g, of which saturates 0.1g; Cholesterol 0mg; Calcium 16mg; Fibre 2.8g; Sodium 8mg.

Vanilla Caffe Latte

This luxurious vanilla and chocolate version of the classic coffee drink can be served at any time of day topped with whipped cream. Serve in mugs or heatproof glasses, with cinnamon sticks to stir and flavour the coffee.

Serves 2
700ml/24fl oz/scant 3 cups milk
250ml/8fl oz/1 cup espresso or
  very strong coffee
45ml/3 tbsp vanilla sugar, plus
  extra to taste
115g/4oz dark (bittersweet)
  chocolate, grated

Preparation: 3 minutes; Cooking: 8 minutes

1 Pour the milk into a small pan and bring to the boil, then remove from the heat.

2 Mix the espresso or very strong coffee with 500ml/16fl oz/ 2 cups of the boiled milk in a large heatproof jug (pitcher). Sweeten with vanilla sugar to taste.

3 Return the remaining boiled milk in the pan to the heat and add the 45ml/3 tbsp vanilla sugar. Stir constantly until dissolved. Bring to the boil, then reduce the heat.

4 Add the dark chocolate and continue to heat, stirring constantly until all the chocolate has melted and the mixture is smooth and glossy.

5 Pour the chocolate milk into the jug of coffee and whisk thoroughly. Serve in mugs or glasses.

> **Variation**
> The fun thing about this drink is that the taste can be varied, depending on what type of chocolate you buy. Orange, peppermint, hazelnut, almond – the choice is as wide as the selection on the supermarket shelf. Echo the coffee flavour with espresso chocolate or try a more unusual offering, such as pistachio chocolate or a crème brûlée flavour. Grate more chocolate on top for extra pleasure.

Banana & Maple Flip

This satisfying drink is packed with so much goodness that it makes a complete breakfast in a glass. It takes only moments to make so is the perfect way to start a busy day.

Serves 1
1 small banana, peeled
  and halved
50ml/2fl oz/¼ cup thick Greek
  (US strained plain) yogurt
1 egg
30ml/2 tbsp maple syrup

Preparation: 4 minutes; Cooking: 0 minutes

1 Put the peeled and halved banana, thick Greek yogurt, egg and maple syrup in a food processor or blender. Add 30ml/2 tbsp chilled water or an ice cube.

2 Process the ingredients constantly for about 2 minutes, or until the mixture turns a really pale, creamy colour and has a nice frothy texture. Pour the drink into a tall, chilled glass and serve immediately.

> **Warning**
> The very young, the elderly and pregnant women are advised against consuming raw eggs or drinks containing raw eggs.

Frothy Hot Chocolate

Make this with the best chocolate you can afford, whisked in hot milk until really frothy. Use an electric frother for best results.

Serves 4
1 litre/1¾ pints/4 cups milk
1 vanilla pod (bean)
50–115g/2–4oz dark
  (bittersweet) chocolate, grated

Preparation: 3 minutes; Cooking: 4 minutes

1 Pour the milk into a pan. Split the vanilla pod lengthways using a sharp knife to reveal the seeds, and add it to the milk; the vanilla seeds and the pod will flavour the milk. Add the chocolate. The amount to use depends on personal taste – start with a smaller amount if you are unsure of the flavour and taste at the beginning of step 2, adding more if necessary.

2 Heat the chocolate milk gently, stirring until all the chocolate has melted and the mixture is smooth, then whisk with a wire whisk until the mixture boils. Remove the vanilla pod from the pan and divide the drink among four mugs or heatproof glasses. Serve immediately.

> **Variation**
> You could use Mexican chocolate, which is flavoured with almonds, cinnamon and vanilla, and sweetened with sugar. All the ingredients are crushed together in a special mortar, and heated over coals. The powdered mixture is then shaped into discs, which can be bought in specialist stores.

Vanilla Caffe Latte Energy 545Kcal/2299kJ; Protein 15g; Carbohydrate 77g, of which sugars 76g; Fat 22g, of which saturates 13g; Cholesterol 24mg; Calcium 445mg; Fibre 1.4g; Sodium 200mg.
Banana and Maple Flip Energy 376Kcal/1573kJ; Protein 12g; Carbohydrate 58g, of which sugars 52g; Fat 12g, of which saturates 5g; Cholesterol 240mg; Calcium 141mg; Fibre 0.9g; Sodium 100mg.
Frothy Hot Chocolate Energy 223Kcal/942kJ; Protein 10g; Carbohydrate 25g, of which sugars 25g; Fat 10g, of which saturates 6g; Cholesterol 16mg; Calcium 307mg; Fibre 0.5g; Sodium 100mg.

Thick Banana Smoothie with Rich Chocolate Sauce

The secret of a good smoothie is to serve it ice-cold and whizzing it up with ice is the perfect way to ensure this. Keep an ice tray of frozen orange juice at the ready for drinks like these.

Serves 2 generously
For the smoothie
3 ripe bananas
200ml/7fl oz/scant 1 cup natural (plain) yogurt

30ml/2 tbsp mild honey
350ml/12fl oz/1½ cups orange juice ice cubes, crushed

For the hot chocolate sauce
175g/6oz plain (semisweet) chocolate with more than 60% cocoa solids
60ml/4 tbsp water
15ml/1 tbsp golden (light corn) syrup
15g/½oz/1 tbsp butter

Preparation: 5 minutes; Cooking: 10–12 minutes

1 Peel and chop the bananas, put them in a bowl, then mash them with a fork.

2 For the sauce, break up the chocolate and put into a bowl over a pan of barely simmering water. Leave undisturbed for 10 minutes until the chocolate has melted, then add the water, syrup and butter and stir until smooth.

3 Place the mashed bananas, yogurt, honey and orange ice cubes in a blender or food processor and blend until smooth, operating the machine in short bursts or pulsing for best results.

4 Pour into large, tall glasses, then pour in some chocolate sauce from a height. The sauce will swirl around the glasses to give a marbled effect. Serve with long-handled spoons.

> **Cook's Tip**
> Pouring chocolate sauce like this cools it slightly on the way down, so that it thickens on contact with the cold smoothie.

Cantaloupe Melon Salad

Lightly caramelized ripe strawberries look pretty and taste divine in this simplest of salads. Serve it for a special occasion brunch.

Serves 4
115g/4oz/1 cup strawberries
15ml/1 tbsp icing (confectioners') sugar, plus extra for dusting
½ cantaloupe melon

Preparation: 3 minutes; Cooking: 4–5 minutes

1 Preheat the grill (broiler) to high. Hull the strawberries and cut them in half. Arrange the fruit in a single layer, cut side up, on a baking sheet or in an ovenproof dish and dust with the icing sugar.

2 Grill (broil) the strawberries for 4–5 minutes, or until the sugar starts to bubble and turn golden.

3 Meanwhile, scoop out the seeds from the half melon using a spoon. Using a sharp knife, remove the skin, then cut the flesh into wedges. Arrange the melon wedges attractively on a serving plate and sprinkle the lightly caramelized strawberries on top. Dust the salad with icing sugar and serve immediately.

Zingy Papaya Fruit Salad

This refreshing, fruity salad makes a lovely light breakfast, perfect for the summer months when meals tend to be light.

Serves 4
2 large ripe papayas
juice of 1 fresh lime
2 pieces preserved stem ginger, finely sliced

Preparation: 5 minutes; Cooking: 0 minutes

1 Cut the papayas in half lengthways. Scoop out the seeds, using a teaspoon. With a sharp knife, cut the flesh into neat, thin slices. Arrange the papaya slices on a platter. Squeeze the lime juice over the papaya and sprinkle with the sliced stem ginger. Serve immediately.

Smoothie Energy 901kcal/3790kJ; Protein 13.2g; Carbohydrate 148.1g, of which sugars 142.2g; Fat 32.5g, of which saturates 19.4g; Cholesterol 23mg; Calcium 253mg; Fibre 4.9g; Sodium 176mg.
Cantaloupe Melon Energy 34kcal/144kJ; Protein 0.7g; Carbohydrate 8g, of which sugars 8g; Fat 0.1g, of which saturates 0g; Cholesterol 0mg; Calcium 21mg; Fibre 1.1g; Sodium 8mg.
Zingy Papaya Energy 112kcal/475kJ; Protein 1.6g; Carbohydrate 27.3g, of which sugars 27.3g; Fat 0.3g, of which saturates 0g; Cholesterol 0mg; Calcium 72mg; Fibre 6.8g; Sodium 16mg.

Cranachan Crunch

This tasty breakfast dish is based on a traditional Scottish recipe. The toasted cereal tastes delicious with yogurt and a generous drizzle of heather honey.

Serves 4

75g/3oz crunchy oat cereal
600ml/1 pint/2½ cups Greek (US strained plain) yogurt
250g/9oz/1½ cups raspberries

Preparation: 2 minutes; Cooking: 3–4 minutes

1 Preheat the grill (broiler) to high. Spread the oat cereal on a baking sheet and place under the hot grill for 3–4 minutes until lightly toasted, stirring regularly. Set aside to cool.

2 When the oat cereal has cooled completely, fold it into the Greek yogurt, then gently fold in 200g/7oz/generous 1 cup of the raspberries, being careful not to crush the berries too much.

3 Spoon the yogurt mixture into four serving glasses or dishes, top with the remaining raspberries and serve immediately.

Classic Porridge

Porridge remains a favourite way to start the day, especially on chilly winter mornings.

Serves 4

750ml/1¼ pints/3 cups water
115g/4oz/1 cup rolled oats
good pinch of salt

Preparation: 1–2 minutes; Cooking: 7–8 minutes

1 Put the water, rolled oats and salt into a heavy pan and bring to the boil over a medium heat, stirring with a wooden spatula to prevent sticking.

2 Simmer for about 5 minutes, stirring frequently, then spoon into bowls.

3 Serve hot with cold milk and extra salt, if required.

Cinnamon Toast

This is an old-fashioned snack that is warming and comforting on a cold autumnal morning. Cinnamon toast is perfect with a spicy hot chocolate drink or with a few slices of fresh fruit such as peaches, plums, nectarines or mango.

Serves 2

75g/3oz/6 tbsp butter, softened
10ml/2 tsp ground cinnamon
30ml/2 tbsp caster (superfine) sugar, plus extra to serve
4 slices bread
prepared fresh fruit

Preparation: 2 minutes; Cooking: 2–3 minutes

1 Place the softened butter in a bowl. Beat with a spoon until soft and creamy, then mix in the ground cinnamon and most of the sugar.

2 Toast the bread on both sides. Spread with the butter and sprinkle with a little remaining sugar. Serve at once, with pieces of fresh fruit, if you like.

Variations
You can use any type of bread for cinnamon toast. Wholewheat or granary adds a nuttiness that goes well with fruit like apricots, peaches or mangoes. A fruit loaf or halved hot cross buns would taste delicious, and for a seasonal treat around Christmas time, try this with panettone. For a special treat, serve a generous dollop of thick, creamy yogurt on the side, or a spoonful of crème fraîche.

Cook's Tip
To round off this winter warmer, serve a quick cardamom hot chocolate with the cinnamon toast. Put 900ml/1½ pints/ 3¾ cups milk in a pan with two bruised cardamom pods and bring to the boil. Add 200g/7oz plain (semisweet) chocolate and whisk until melted. Using a slotted spoon, remove the cardamom pods just before serving.

Cranachan Crunch Energy 222kcal/935kJ; Protein 10.1g; Carbohydrate 23g, of which sugars 13.3g; Fat 10.7g, of which saturates 6.7g; Cholesterol 21mg; Calcium 250mg; Fibre 3g; Sodium 236mg.
Classic Porridge Energy 460kcal/1952kJ; Protein 14.4g; Carbohydrate 83.6g, of which sugars 0g; Fat 10g, of which saturates 0g; Cholesterol 0mg; Calcium 64mg; Fibre 8g; Sodium 1216mg.
Cinnamon Toast Energy 461kcal/1921kJ; Protein 4.7g; Carbohydrate 41.6g, of which sugars 17.3g; Fat 31.8g, of which saturates 19.6g; Cholesterol 80mg; Calcium 72mg; Fibre 0.8g; Sodium 499mg.

Griddled Tomatoes on Soda Bread

Nothing could be simpler than this basic brunch dish, transformed into something special by adding a drizzle of olive oil, balsamic vinegar and shavings of Parmesan cheese to griddled tomatoes and serving them on toast.

Serves 4
olive oil, for brushing and drizzling
6 tomatoes, thickly sliced
4 thick slices soda bread
balsamic vinegar, for drizzling
salt and ground black pepper
shavings of Parmesan cheese,
  to serve

Preparation: 2 minutes; Cooking: 4–6 minutes

1 Brush a griddle pan with olive oil and heat. Add the tomato slices and cook for 4–6 minutes, turning once, until softened and slightly blackened. Alternatively, heat a grill (broiler) to high and line the rack with foil. Grill (broil) the tomato slices for 4–6 minutes, turning once, until softened.

2 While the tomatoes are cooking, lightly toast the soda bread. Place the tomatoes on top of the toast and drizzle each portion with a little olive oil and vinegar. Season to taste and serve immediately with thin shavings of Parmesan.

Variation
A dish like this one tastes perfect on its own, but if you prefer something slightly more substantial, add slices of bacon, grilled (broiled) until crisp, or some herby sausage. When cooking the sausage, don't prick it first, as this allows juices to flow out and tends to make the sausage dry. If you grill the sausage under low to medium heat, and turn it often, it will be unlikely to burst.

Cook's Tip
Using a griddle pan reduces the amount of oil required for cooking the tomatoes and gives them a barbecued flavour. The ridges on the pan brand the tomatoes, which gives them an attractive appearance.

Mushrooms on Spicy Toast

Dry-panning is a quick way of cooking mushrooms that makes the most of their flavour. It works well with large, flat mushrooms. The juices run when they are heated, so they become really moist and tender.

Serves 4
8–12 large flat field (portabello)
  mushrooms
50g/1oz/2 tbsp butter
5ml/1 tsp curry paste
salt
4 slices thickly sliced white bread,
  toasted, to serve

Preparation: 2–3 minutes; Cooking: 4–5 minutes

1 Preheat the oven to 200°C/400°F/Gas 6. Peel the field mushrooms, if necessary, and remove the stalks. Heat a dry frying pan until very hot.

2 Place the mushrooms in the hot frying pan, with the gills on top. Using half the butter, add a piece the size of a hazelnut to each one, then sprinkle all the mushrooms lightly with salt. Cook over a medium heat until the butter begins to bubble and the mushrooms are juicy and tender.

3 Meanwhile, mix the remaining butter with the curry paste. Spread on the toasted bread. Bake in the oven for 10 minutes, pile the mushrooms on top and serve.

Variations
Using a flavoured butter makes these mushrooms even more special. Try one of the following.
• **Herb butter** Mix softened butter with chopped fresh herbs such as parsley and thyme, or marjoram and chopped chives.
• **Olive butter** Mix softened butter with diced green olives and spring onions (scallions).
• **Tomato butter** Mix softened butter with sun-dried tomato purée (paste).
• **Garlic butter** Mix softened butter with finely chopped garlic.
• **Pepper and paprika butter** Mix softened butter with 2.5ml/½ tsp paprika and 2.5ml/½ tsp black pepper.

Griddled Tomatoes Energy 178kcal/751kJ; Protein 4.2g; Carbohydrate 26.3g, of which sugars 6.9g; Fat 7g, of which saturates 1g; Cholesterol 0mg; Calcium 66mg; Fibre 2.7g; Sodium 175mg.
Mushrooms Energy 230kcal/966kJ; Protein 6.1g; Carbohydrate 25.1g, of which sugars 1.6g; Fat 12.5g, of which saturates 6.7g; Cholesterol 27mg; Calcium 63mg; Fibre 1.9g; Sodium 341mg.

Croque Monsieur

This classic French toastie is delicious served at any time of day, but with a double espresso or a foaming cup of milky coffee it makes a particularly enjoyable breakfast or brunch dish.

Serves 4
8 slices white bread
softened butter
4 large lean ham slices
175g/6oz Gruyère or
*   mild Cheddar cheese*
ground black pepper

Preparation: 5 minutes; Cooking: 5 minutes

1 Preheat the grill (broiler) to the highest setting. Arrange the bread on the grill rack and toast four slices on both sides and the other four slices on one side only.

2 Slice the cheese thinly. Butter the slices of bread that have been toasted on both sides and top with the ham, then the cheese. Season with plenty of ground black pepper. Transfer the topped bread slices to the grill pan.

3 Lay the remaining, half-toasted bread slices on top of the cheese, with the untoasted side uppermost. Grill (broil) the tops of the sandwiches until golden brown, then cut them in half using a sharp knife and serve.

Variations
Using Gruyère can make this rather an expensive dish, so look out for cheeses that are similarly tasty, but do not cost quite so much. Jarlsberg is a good alternative, or try Emmenthal.

Cook's Tip
To slice the cheese thinly, use a cheese parer, which looks like a spatula with a slot cut in the head. This stands slightly proud of the utensil, and has a cutting edge. If you draw it across the face of the cheese, it is possible to slice the cheese very thinly. For slightly thicker slices, press down harder.

Cheese Toasties

Also known as bubbly cheese toast, because of the way the egg and cheese mixture puffs up during baking, this is a nutritious and easy snack that everyone enjoys. It goes down well with children, especially if you swap the mustard for sweet pickle.

Serves 4
2 eggs
175–225g/6–8oz/1½–2 cups
*   grated Cheddar cheese*
5–10ml/1–2 tsp wholegrain
*   mustard*
4 slices bread, buttered
2–4 halved tomatoes (optional)
ground black pepper
watercress or fresh parsley,
*   to serve (optional)*

Preparation: 3–4 minutes; Cooking: 10–15 minutes

1 Preheat the oven to 230°C/450°F/Gas 8 (the top oven of a range-type stove is ideal for this recipe). Whisk the eggs lightly and stir in the grated cheese, mustard and pepper.

2 Lay the buttered bread face down in a shallow baking dish. Divide the cheese mixture among the slices of bread, spreading it out evenly.

3 Bake in the oven for 10–15 minutes, or until well risen and golden brown, adding the halved tomatoes for a few minutes, if using. Serve immediately, with the tomatoes, and garnish with sprigs of watercress or parsley.

Variation
Any cheese that can be grated can be used for these toasties, and this is a good way of using up leftovers from a cheeseboard.

Cook's Tips
• For the best flavour, use a mature (sharp) Cheddar cheese or a mixture of Cheddar and Leicester.
• To save time, buy packets of ready-grated cheese.

Croque Monsieur Energy 336kcal/1409kJ; Protein 20.3g; Carbohydrate 26.9g, of which sugars 1.7g; Fat 16.2g, of which saturates 9.8g; Cholesterol 57mg; Calcium 385mg; Fibre 0.8g; Sodium 897mg.
Cheese Toasties Energy 357kcal/1484kJ; Protein 16.6g; Carbohydrate 13.4g, of which sugars 0.8g; Fat 25.8g, of which saturates 15.5g; Cholesterol 159mg; Calcium 369mg; Fibre 0.4g; Sodium 552mg.

Bacon Sandwich

The secret of making the perfect bacon sandwich is to use quality bacon.

Makes 1
4 best bacon rashers (strips), dry-cured if possible

a large, soft morning roll or 2 thick slices fresh white, crusty bread
softened butter
sauce of your choice, such as tomato or brown sauce

Preparation: 2 minutes; Cooking: 6 minutes

1 Grill (broil) the bacon rashers to your liking, then put on a dinner plate, cover, and keep them warm. While the bacon is grilling, warm a bread roll, if using, underneath the grill pan.

2 Toast the bread after you have grilled the bacon. Butter both pieces of the bread or toast, or split and butter the roll. Top the bread or toast with the bacon, or fill the roll. Add the sauce and top with the remaining slice of bread or toast. Serve at once.

Kidney & Mushroom Toasts

Meltingly tender lamb's kidneys are a traditional breakfast treat. Cooking them with mushrooms in mustard butter flatters their flavour and they taste great on toast, making a delightful hot breakfast. Buy the kidneys from a reputable butcher and cook them as soon as possible after purchase. If they smell a bit strong, soak them in milk before cooking.

Serves 2–4
4 large flat field (portabello) mushrooms, stalks trimmed
75g/3oz/6 tbsp butter, softened
10ml/2 tsp wholegrain mustard
15ml/1 tbsp chopped fresh parsley
4 lamb's kidneys, skinned, halved and cored
4 thick slices of brown bread, cut into rounds and toasted
sprig of parsley, to garnish
tomato wedges, to serve

Preparation: 5 minutes; Cooking: 4–6 minutes

1 Wash the mushrooms, pat dry with kitchen paper and remove the stalks.

2 Mix the butter, wholegrain mustard and fresh parsley together in a small bowl.

3 Rinse the prepared lamb's kidneys well under cold running water and pat dry with kitchen paper.

4 Melt about two-thirds of the butter mixture in a large frying pan and fry the mushrooms and kidneys for 2–3 minutes on each side. Spoon the butter over occasionally.

5 When the kidneys are cooked to your liking, spread them with the remaining herb butter. Pile on the hot toast and serve with the tomato, garnished with parsley.

Panettone French Toast

Thickly sliced stale white bread is usually used for French toast, but the slightly dry texture of panettone makes a great alternative. Serve with fresh summer berries or an apricot or peach compote.

Serves 4
2 large (US extra large) eggs
50g/2oz/¼ cup butter or 30ml/2 tbsp sunflower oil
4 large slices panettone, halved
30ml/2 tbsp caster (superfine) sugar
fresh berries, to serve

Preparation: 2 minutes; Cooking: 4–6 minutes

1 Break the eggs into a bowl and whisk lightly, then tip them into a shallow dish. Heat the butter or oil in a large non-stick frying pan. Dip the panettone slices in the egg and fry for 2–3 minutes on each side, until golden brown. Drain, dust with sugar and serve with the berries.

> **Cook's Tips**
> • Kidneys are best served when they are still pink in the centre. If overcooked, they will become tough.
> • Serve the mixture on halved, warm scones, if you prefer.

Kidney Toasts Energy 379kcal/1580kJ; Protein 20.1g; Carbohydrate 14.9g, of which sugars 1g; Fat 27.1g, of which saturates 15.9g; Cholesterol 353mg; Calcium 59mg; Fibre 1.7g; Sodium 560mg.
Bacon Sandwich Energy 416kcal/1738kJ; Protein 21.1g; Carbohydrate 26.7g, of which sugars 1.5g; Fat 25.7g, of which saturates 11.4g; Cholesterol 74mg; Calcium 66mg; Fibre 0.8g; Sodium 1881mg.
Panettone Energy 369kcal/1550kJ; Protein 9.2g; Carbohydrate 47.4g, of which sugars 19.9g; Fat 17.3g, of which saturates 8.7g; Cholesterol 123mg; Calcium 103mg; Fibre 1.7g; Sodium 349mg.

Pancakes with Caramelized Pears

If you can find them, use
Williams pears for this
recipe because they are so
juicy. For a really indulgent
breakfast, top with a
spoonful of crème fraîche
or fromage frais. Or serve
with yogurt – low fat or
rich and creamy.

Serves 4
8 ready-made pancakes
50g/2oz/¼ cup butter
4 ripe pears, peeled, cored and
   thickly sliced
30ml/2 tbsp light muscovado
   (brown) sugar
crème fraîche or fromage frais,
   to serve

Preparation: 5 minutes; Cooking: 6 minutes

1 Preheat the oven to 150°C/300°F/Gas 2. Tightly wrap the
pancakes in foil and place in the oven to warm through.

2 Meanwhile, heat the butter in a large frying pan and add the
pears. Fry for 2–3 minutes, until the undersides are golden. Turn
the pears over and sprinkle with sugar. Cook for a further
2–3 minutes, or until the sugar dissolves and the pan juices
become sticky.

3 Remove the pancakes from the oven and take them out
of the foil. Divide the pears among them, placing them in
one quarter. Fold each pancake in half over the filling, then
into quarters and place two folded pancakes on each plate.
Drizzle the pan juices over and serve with crème fraîche or
fromage frais.

Cook's Tip
*Look out for ready-made pancakes in the chiller cabinet at the
supermarket. They freeze well and are handy for breakfasts and
desserts. Alternatively, make your own: sift 115g/4oz/1 cup
plain (all-purpose) flour into a bowl and add a pinch of salt.
Make a well in the centre and add 1 beaten egg and
120ml/4fl oz/½ cup each of milk and water. Beat the liquids
and incorporate the flour to make a smooth batter. Cook in a
greased 18cm/7in frying pan. Makes eight.*

Light Pancakes

These pancakes are
sweetened with sugar and
should be kept small,
otherwise they can be
difficult to turn. They need a
well-buttered or oiled
surface for cooking. Aim for
pancakes with one side that
is smooth and golden
brown, and the other full of
holes and lightly browned.
Eat them warm with butter,
maybe with fresh soft fruit
such as raspberries.

Makes 12–14
125g/4½ oz/1 cup plain
   (all-purpose) flour
1.25ml/¼ tsp bicarbonate of
   soda (baking soda)
pinch of salt
75g/3oz/⅔ cup caster
   (superfine) sugar
1 egg
about 90ml/6 tbsp buttermilk
   or milk
butter for greasing

Preparation: 3 minutes; Cooking: 12–15 minutes

1 Preheat a large bakestone or heavy frying pan over
medium heat.

2 Sift the flour, bicarbonate of soda and salt into a bowl and
stir in the sugar.

3 With a whisk beat the egg into the flour, and then add
enough milk to make a batter.

4 Butter the hot bakestone or pan. Drop spoonfuls of batter
on the surface to make pancakes about 7.5–10cm/3–4in in
diameter, allowing space between.

5 Cook for a minute or two until the underside is golden
brown and small bubbles have risen to the top surface and
burst open. With a metal spatula, carefully flip the pancakes
over and briefly cook the second side until light golden brown
and set. Lift off and keep warm on a warm dish.

6 Repeat with the remaining pancake batter to make
12–14 pancakes. They are best served warm and certainly
should be eaten on the day they are made.

Pear Pancakes Energy 544kcal/2274kJ; Protein 7.7g; Carbohydrate 64.9g, of which sugars 42.4g; Fat 29.9g, of which saturates 6.5g; Cholesterol 27mg; Calcium 155mg; Fibre 4.3g; Sodium 144mg.
Light Cakes Energy 60kcal/254kJ; Protein 1.5g; Carbohydrate 12.8g, of which sugars 6g; Fat 0.6g, of which saturates 0.2g; Cholesterol 14mg; Calcium 25mg; Fibre 0.3g; Sodium 8mg.

Buttermilk Pancakes

It is traditional to have these plump pancakes on their own, with honey, but they also taste good American-style, with crisp fried bacon and a generous drizzle of maple syrup. In Yorkshire, they might be enjoyed with raspberry vinegar, while South Africans would add a drizzle of golden (light corn) syrup. However you serve them, they are delicious.

Makes about 12
*225g/8oz/2 cups plain
    (all-purpose) flour
7.5ml/1½ tsp bicarbonate of
    soda (baking soda)
25–50g/1–2oz/2–4 tbsp sugar
1 egg
about 300ml/½ pint/1¼ cups
    buttermilk
butter and oil, mixed, or white
    vegetable fat (shortening),
    for frying
honey, to serve*

Preparation: 2 minutes; Cooking: 12–18 minutes

1 In a food processor or a large mixing bowl, mix together the plain flour, the bicarbonate of soda and enough sugar to taste.

2 Add the egg, blend or stir to mix, then gradually pour in just enough of the buttermilk to make a thick, smooth batter.

3 Heat a heavy pan and add the butter and oil, or fat. Place spoonfuls of the batter into the hot pan and cook for 2–3 minutes until bubbles rise to the surface.

4 Flip the pancakes over and cook for a further 2–3 minutes. You will need to cook the pancakes in batches, so keep them warm on a low oven temperature, tightly wrapped in foil. Serve warm with honey.

Variation
Buttermilk is not always easy to locate. As a substitute, use milk that has been soured by the addition of 5ml/1 tsp vinegar. Skimmed milk is better than whole or full cream milk, as it most closely resembles buttermilk. If you have time, leave the batter to stand for about an hour before using it.

Oatmeal Pancakes with Bacon

Wrap an oatmeal pancake around a crisp slice of best bacon and sample a new taste sensation with your traditional cooked breakfast. It makes a great egg dipper, too. If you don't like fried egg, serve these filled pancakes with sliced grilled (broiled) tomatoes or a home-made tomato sauce.

Makes 4 pancakes
*50g/2oz/½ cup fine wholemeal
    (whole-wheat) flour
30ml/2 tbsp fine pinhead oatmeal
pinch of salt
1 egg
about 150ml/¼ pint/⅔ cup
    buttermilk or milk
butter or oil, for greasing
4 rashers (strips) bacon*

Preparation: 2–3 minutes; Cooking: 12 minutes

1 Mix the flour, oatmeal and salt in a bowl, beat in the egg and add enough buttermilk or milk to make a creamy batter of the same consistency as that used for ordinary pancakes.

2 Thoroughly heat a griddle or cast-iron frying pan over a medium-hot heat. When very hot, grease the surface lightly with butter or oil.

3 Pour in the batter, about a ladleful at a time. Tilt the frying pan to spread the batter evenly and cook the pancake for about 2 minutes until set and the underside is browned. Turn over and cook for 1 minute until browned.

4 Keep the pancake warm while you cook the others and fry the bacon. Roll the pancakes around the bacon to serve.

Cook's Tip
The oatmeal in the batter gives it texture, so these pancakes are firmer than conventional crêpes. You can easily double or treble the mixture and even make it ahead of time. It will thicken on standing, though, so thin it with buttermilk or milk before use. Ladle the batter into the frying pan or – if you are good at judging the right amount to use – pour it in from a jug (pitcher).

Buttermilk Pancakes Energy 90kcal/380kJ; Protein 3.2g; Carbohydrate 18.7g, of which sugars 4.4g; Fat 0.8g, of which saturates 0.2g; Cholesterol 17mg; Calcium 61mg; Fibre 0.6g; Sodium 18mg.
Oatmeal Pancakes Energy 148kcal/621kJ; Protein 9.7g; Carbohydrate 13.1g, of which sugars 2g; Fat 6.7g, of which saturates 2.2g; Cholesterol 64mg; Calcium 62mg; Fibre 1.5g; Sodium 469mg.

American Pancakes with Bacon

These small, thick, buttery pancakes will be eaten in seconds, so make plenty. The batter can be made the night before.

Makes about 20
175g/6oz/1½ cups plain
  (all-purpose) flour, sifted
pinch of salt

15ml/1 tbsp caster (superfine) sugar
2 large eggs
150ml/¼ pint/⅔ cup milk
5ml/1 tsp bicarbonate of soda
  (baking soda)
10ml/2 tsp cream of tartar
oil, for cooking
butter
maple syrup
crisp bacon, to serve

Preparation: 3–4 minutes; Cooking: 12 minutes

1 To make the batter, mix together the flour, salt and sugar. In a separate bowl, beat the eggs and milk together, then gradually stir into the flour, beating to a smooth, thick consistency.

2 Add the bicarbonate of soda and cream of tartar, mix well, then cover and chill until ready to cook. When you are ready to cook the pancakes, beat the batter again. Heat a little oil in a heavy-based frying pan or griddle.

3 Drop dessertspoonfuls of the mixture into the pan, spaced well apart, and cook over a fairly high heat until the batter sets, bubbles appear on the surface of the pancakes and the undersides become golden brown.

4 Carefully turn the pancakes over with a fish slice or metal spatula and cook briefly until golden underneath, then transfer them to a heated serving dish.

5 Top each pancake with a little butter and drizzle with maple syrup. Serve with grilled bacon.

> **Cook's Tip**
> Make bitesize pancakes in advance and freeze for parties or children's teas.

Lox with Bagels & Cream Cheese

This sophisticated dish is perfect for a weekend breakfast or brunch with friends. Lox is the Jewish word for smoked salmon and this deli classic is so easy that anyone can make it at home.

Serves 2
2 bagels
115–175g/4–6oz/½–¾ cup
  full-fat cream cheese
150g/5oz sliced best
  smoked salmon
ground black pepper
lemon wedges, to serve

Preparation: 3 minutes; Cooking: 4–5 minutes

1 Preheat the oven to 200°C/400°F/Gas 6. Put the bagels on a large baking sheet and warm them in the oven for 4–5 minutes.

2 Remove the bagels from the oven, split them in two and spread each half generously with cream cheese. Pile the salmon on top of the bagel bases and grind over plenty of black pepper.

3 Squeeze over some lemon juice, then add the bagel tops, placing them at a jaunty angle.

4 Place on serving plates with the lemon wedges. If you have time, wrap each lemon wedge in a small square of muslin (cheesecloth), tie with fine string and put it on the plate.

> **Cook's Tip**
> It is essential to be generous with the smoked salmon and to use the best cream cheese you can find.

Eggs Benedict

Using a good-quality bought hollandaise for this recipe saves time and makes all the difference to the end result. Eggs Benedict are delicious served on toasted English muffins.

Serves 4
4 large (US extra large) eggs
4 lean ham slices
60ml/4 tbsp warm
  hollandaise sauce
2 English muffins, split
salt and ground black pepper

Preparation: 2–3 minutes; Cooking: 4–6 minutes

1 Pour cold water into a medium pan to a depth of about 5cm/2in and bring to a gentle simmer. Crack an egg into a saucer. Swirl the water in the pan with a spoon, then slide the egg carefully into the centre of the swirl.

2 Add the second egg to the pan. Simmer both eggs for 2–3 minutes, until the whites are set, but the yolks are still soft.

3 Meanwhile, toast the muffin halves. Place on four serving plates and arrange the ham slices on top. Remove the eggs from the pan using a slotted spoon and place on top of the ham on two of the plates. Poach two more eggs and top the remaining muffins.

Pancakes Energy 496kcal/2068kJ; Protein 25.9g; Carbohydrate 28.9g, of which sugars 3.3g; Fat 31.6g, of which saturates 17.7g; Cholesterol 81mg; Calcium 71mg; Fibre 1.2g; Sodium 1858mg.
Bagels Energy 276kcal/1154kJ; Protein 14.9g; Carbohydrate 15.9g, of which sugars 1.6g; Fat 17.7g, of which saturates 3.7g; Cholesterol 258mg; Calcium 81mg; Fibre 0.7g; Sodium 520mg.
Eggs Benedict Energy 553kcal/2304kJ; Protein 19.8g; Carbohydrate 31.6g, of which sugars 2.2g; Fat 39.7g, of which saturates 18.9g; Cholesterol 427mg; Calcium 148mg; Fibre 1.3g; Sodium 635mg.

Egg Crostini with Rouille

Crostini are extremely quick to make so are perfect for breakfast or brunch. The rouille gives them a hint of Mediterranean flavour. Traditionally, rouille is served with thick fish soup, but here it provides the perfect complement to lightly fried eggs.

Serves 4
4 slices of ciabatta bread
extra virgin olive oil
45ml/3 tbsp home-made
  mayonnaise
5ml/1 tsp harissa
4 eggs
4 small slices smoked ham
watercress, to serve

Preparation and cooking: 10 minutes

1 Preheat the oven to 200°C/400°F/Gas 6. Use a pastry brush to lightly brush each slice of ciabatta bread with a little olive oil.

2 Place the bread on a baking sheet and bake for 10 minutes or until crisp and turning golden brown.

3 Meanwhile, make the rouille. Mix together the mayonnaise and harissa. Then fry the eggs lightly in a very little oil in a non-stick pan.

4 Top the baked bread with the ham, eggs and a small spoonful of rouille. Serve immediately with watercress.

Cook's Tip
Harissa is a fiery North African chilli paste made from dried red chillies, cumin, garlic, coriander, caraway and olive oil. It adds a sweet spicy taste to dips, sauces and stews, and makes a great addition to mayonnaise for serving with meat or fish dishes. It is usually sold in glass jars or tubes. In this recipe, home-made mayonnaise is specified, but if you do not have time to make your own, or are serving this to someone for whom a raw egg product is not recommended, it is perfectly acceptable to use a good quality bought mayonnaise for mixing with the harissa.

Bacon & Egg Muffins Hollandaise

This tasty breakfast is ideal for days when you want to treat family or friends to an extra-special start to the day.

4 eggs
4 English muffins
butter, for spreading
ground black pepper

Serves 4
350g/12oz rindless back (lean)
  bacon rashers (strips)
dash of white wine vinegar

For the hollandaise sauce
2 egg yolks
5ml/1 tsp white wine vinegar
75g/3oz/6 tbsp butter

Preparation: 5 minutes; Cooking: 8–12 minutes

1 Preheat the grill (broiler) and cook the bacon for 5–8 minutes, turning once, or until crisp on both sides. Keep warm.

2 Fill a large frying pan with water and bring to the boil. Add the vinegar and regulate the heat so that the water simmers. Crack the eggs into the water and poach them for 3–4 minutes, or slightly longer for firm eggs.

3 Meanwhile, make the hollandaise sauce. Process the egg yolks and white wine vinegar in a blender or food processor. Melt the butter. With the motor still running, very gradually add the hot melted butter through the feeder tube. The hot butter will cook the yolks to make a thick, glossy sauce. Switch off the machine as soon as all the butter has been added and the sauce has thickened. Season to taste.

4 Split and toast the muffins. Spread with butter and place on warmed plates. Arrange the bacon on the muffins and add a poached egg to each. Top with a spoonful of sauce and grind over some black pepper. Serve immediately.

Variations
• Replace the bacon with smoked salmon for a special treat.
• Add some sliced grilled (broiled) mushrooms for a more filling breakfast or brunch.

Egg Crostini Energy 259kcal/1083kJ; Protein 15.8g; Carbohydrate 13.6g, of which sugars 1.3g; Fat 16.3g, of which saturates 3.4g; Cholesterol 220mg; Calcium 62mg; Fibre 0.6g; Sodium 705mg.
Muffins Energy 612Kcal/2549kJ; Protein 32.6g; Carbohydrate 30.2g, of which sugars 2.4g; Fat 41.1g, of which saturates 18.3g; Cholesterol 429mg; Calcium 143mg; Fibre 1.3g; Sodium 1880mg.

Scrambled Eggs with Asparagus

Delightfully tender fresh asparagus and sweet peas make perfect partners to lightly cooked eggs. The secret of successful scrambling is to keep the heat under the pan fairly low and serve the eggs while they are still creamy.

Serves 4
1 bunch thin asparagus
30–45ml/2–3 tbsp tiny raw
    mangetout (snow peas)
8 large (US extra large) eggs
30ml/2 tbsp milk
50g/2oz/¼ cup butter
salt and ground black pepper
sweet paprika, for dusting

Preparation: 3–4 minutes; Cooking: 13–15 minutes

1 Prepare the asparagus. Using a large sharp knife, cut off and discard any hard stems. Cut the stems into short lengths, keeping the tips separate. Shell some of the fatter mangetout pods, to extract the tiny peas.

2 Tip the stems into a pan of boiling water and simmer for 4 minutes. Add the asparagus tips, and cook for another 6 minutes. If including some pea pod strips, cook them for 2 minutes.

3 Break the eggs into a bowl. Add the milk, salt and black pepper and beat with a whisk until well combined.

4 Melt the butter in a large frying pan and pour in the eggs, scrambling them by pulling the cooked outsides to the middle with a wooden spoon.

5 When the eggs are almost cooked, drain the asparagus and pea pod strips, if using, and stir into the eggs. Sprinkle the peas over the top, and dust lightly with paprika. Serve immediately.

Variation
Replace the asparagus with mangetouts. String 150g/5oz mangetouts, then slice them diagonally into two or three pieces. Cook in boiling water for 2 minutes.

Chive Scrambled Eggs in Brioches

These creamy scrambled eggs are delicious at any time of day, but when served with France's favourite breakfast bread, they become the ultimate breakfast or brunch treat. Set the brioches at an angle so some filling spills on to the plate.

Serves 4
4 individual brioches
6 eggs, beaten
45ml/3 tbsp chopped fresh
    chives, plus extra to serve
25g/1oz/2 tbsp butter
45ml/3 tbsp cottage cheese
60–75ml/4–5 tbsp double
    (heavy) cream
salt and ground black pepper

Preparation: 6 minutes; Cooking: 7 minutes

1 Preheat the oven to 180°C/350°F/Gas 4. Cut the tops off the brioches and set to one side. Carefully scoop out the centre of each brioche, leaving a bread case. Put the brioche cases and lids on a baking sheet and bake in the oven for 5 minutes until they are hot and crisp.

2 Meanwhile, beat the eggs lightly and season to taste. Add about one-third of the chopped chives. Heat the butter in a medium pan until it begins to foam, then add the eggs and cook, stirring constantly with a wooden spoon until semi-solid.

3 Stir in the cottage cheese, cream and half the remaining chives. Cook for 1–2 minutes more, making sure that the eggs remain soft and creamy.

4 To serve, put the crisp brioche shells on individual plates, spoon in the creamy scrambled egg and sprinkle with the remaining chives. Top with the lids.

Variation
If you do not happen to have brioches to hand, these wonderful herby eggs taste delicious on top of thick slices of toasted bread. Try them piled high on warm focaccia, or on toasted ciabatta, Granary (whole-wheat) bread or muffins.

Eggs with Asparagus Energy 252kcal/1045kJ; Protein 13.8g; Carbohydrate 1.3g, of which sugars 1.2g; Fat 21.7g, of which saturates 9.7g; Cholesterol 408mg; Calcium 78mg; Fibre 0.6g; Sodium 219mg.
Eggs in Brioches Energy 414kcal/1731kJ; Protein 16.2g; Carbohydrate 32.5g, of which sugars 10.5g; Fat 25.5g, of which saturates 12g; Cholesterol 322mg; Calcium 154mg; Fibre 1.9g; Sodium 374mg.

Scrambled Eggs with Smoked Salmon & Roe

For a luxury breakfast, or a special brunch, you can't beat this delicious combination. Serve it with Buck's Fizz: champagne mixed with equal parts of freshly squeezed orange juice.

Serves 4
4 slices of pumpernickel or wholemeal (whole-wheat)

bread, crusts trimmed
50g/2oz/¼ cup butter
115g/4oz thinly sliced smoked salmon
6 eggs
105ml/7 tbsp crème fraîche or sour cream
salt and ground black pepper
generous 60ml/4 tbsp salmon roe or lumpfish roe
sprigs of dill, to garnish

Preparation: 3 minutes; Cooking: 3–5 minutes

1 Spread the slices of pumpernickel or wholemeal bread with half of the butter and arrange the smoked salmon on top. Cut each slice in half, place two halves on each serving plate and set aside while you make the scrambled eggs.

2 Lightly beat the eggs in a bowl and season with salt and freshly ground pepper. Melt the remaining butter in a pan until sizzling, then quickly stir in the beaten eggs. Stir constantly until the eggs begin to thicken. Just before they have finished cooking, remove the pan from the heat and stir in the crème fraîche or sour cream. Return to the heat briefly to finish cooking, if required.

3 Spoon the scrambled eggs on to the smoked salmon. Top each serving with a spoonful of salmon roe or lumpfish roe and serve garnished with sprigs of dill.

Variation
If you are lucky enough to have a truffle, another treat is to grate a little into the scrambled eggs. Serve them on toast, topped with a little chopped fresh chervil.

Scrambled Eggs with Anchovies

Lifting the spirits on the dullest of days, scrambled eggs are true comfort food. This version combines with anchovies, whose salty tang is superb with the egg. The flavour of anchovies is echoed in the paste.

Serves 2
2 slices bread
40g/1½ oz/3 tbsp butter, plus extra for spreading

anchovy paste, such as Gentleman's Relish, for spreading
2 eggs and 2 egg yolks, beaten
60–90ml/4–6 tbsp single (light) cream or milk
ground black pepper
anchovy fillets, cut into strips, and paprika, to garnish

Preparation: 2–3 minutes; Cooking: 7 minutes

1 Toast the bread, spread with butter and anchovy paste, then remove the crusts and cut into triangles. Place on a plate and keep warm under a low grill (broiler).

2 Melt the rest of the butter in a medium non-stick pan, then stir in the beaten eggs, cream or milk, and a little ground pepper. Heat very gently, stirring constantly, until the mixture begins to thicken.

3 Remove the pan from the heat and continue to stir until the mixture becomes very creamy, but do not allow it to harden.

4 Divide the scrambled eggs among the triangles of toast and garnish each one with strips of anchovy fillet and a generous sprinkling of paprika. Serve immediately, while the scrambled eggs are still hot and have not had time to set firm.

Cook's Tip
These creamy scrambled eggs are delicious in baked potatoes instead of on toast. Serve with a salad and a glass of crisp white wine for a tasty brunch or light lunch.

Eggs with Salmon Energy 369kcal/1535kJ; Protein 18.7g; Carbohydrate 13.3g, of which sugars 1.5g; Fat 27.4g, of which saturates 15.2g; Cholesterol 259mg; Calcium 78mg; Fibre 1.5g; Sodium 837mg.
Eggs with Anchovies Energy 405kcal/1680kJ; Protein 12.6g; Carbohydrate 14.1g, of which sugars 1.5g; Fat 33.7g, of which saturates 17.2g; Cholesterol 451mg; Calcium 112mg; Fibre 0.4g; Sodium 350mg.

Scrambled Eggs with Prawns

The Spanish are particular about eggs, distinguishing between a revuelto, which uses softly set scrambled eggs, and the more solid tortilla that is cooked until set. This revuelto de gambas is an economical way of using a few shellfish and tastes delicious with crusty bread or toast.

Serves 4
1 bunch spring onions (scallions)
25g/1oz/2 tbsp butter
30ml/2 tbsp oil
150g/5oz shelled prawns (shrimp)
8 large (US extra large) eggs
30ml/2 tbsp milk
45ml/3 tbsp chopped
   fresh parsley
salt and ground black pepper
crusty bread, to serve

Preparation: 3 minutes; Cooking: 4–6 minutes

1 Chop the spring onions, keeping the white section separate from the green. Put the white pieces in a bowl and 30ml/2 tbsp of the chopped green pieces in another bowl.

2 Heat the butter and oil in a large frying pan. Add the spring onion white and cook briefly. Add the prawns and heat through. (If the prawns are raw, cook them for 2 minutes or until they turn pink. Do not overcook them or they will toughen.)

3 In a bowl, beat the eggs with the milk and then season with plenty of salt and pepper. Turn the heat to medium-high and pour the egg mixture over the prawns. Cook for about 2 minutes, stirring with a wooden spoon.

4 Sprinkle the creamy scrambled eggs and prawn mixture with parsley and spring onion greens. Divide among four plates and serve immediately with crusty bread.

> **Variation**
> The green shoots from garlic bulbs are another very popular spring ingredient for this type of dish and can be used in place of the spring onions (scallions). Called ajetes in Spain, they lend a delicate flavour to scrambled eggs or tortillas.

Smoked Salmon & Chive Omelette

The addition of a generous portion of chopped smoked salmon gives a really luxurious finish to this simple, classic dish, which is an ideal quick lunch for two people. The chives add colour and extra flavour.

Serves 2
4 eggs
15ml/1 tbsp chopped fresh chives
   or spring onions (scallions)
a knob (pat) of butter
50g/2oz smoked salmon,
   roughly chopped
salt and ground black pepper

Preparation: 2–3 minutes; Cooking: 5–6 minutes

1 Break the eggs into a bowl. Beat with a fork until just combined, then stir in the chopped fresh chives or spring onions. Season with salt and a generous sprinkling of freshly ground black pepper, and set aside.

2 Heat the butter in a medium frying pan until foamy. Pour in the eggs and cook over a medium heat for 3–4 minutes, drawing the cooked egg from around the edge into the centre of the pan from time to time.

3 At this stage, you can either leave the top of the omelette slightly soft or finish it off under the grill (broiler), depending on how you like your omelette. Top with the smoked salmon, fold the omelette over and cut in half to serve.

> **Variations**
> • Use smoked trout instead of smoked salmon. The colour ranges from rose pink to reddish brown and it has very good flavour, especially when it has been hot smoked over oak or birch chippings.
> • Add a little rocket (arugula) or watercress when folding the omelette. Both have peppery leaves, so use slightly less pepper to season the scrambled egg.
> • A little crème fraîche or fromage frais, served on the side, makes a good addition. For an extra special occasion, top this with salmon or trout roe.

Eggs with Prawns Energy 287kcal/1191kJ; Protein 20.1g; Carbohydrate 1.9g, of which sugars 1.9g; Fat 22.4g, of which saturates 7.4g; Cholesterol 468mg; Calcium 126mg; Fibre 0.9g; Sodium 258mg.
Omelette Energy 221kcal/920kJ; Protein 19g; Carbohydrate 0.2g, of which sugars 0.2g; Fat 16.4g, of which saturates 5.9g; Cholesterol 400mg; Calcium 65mg; Fibre 0.1g; Sodium 641mg.

Sweet Breakfast Omelette

For a hearty start to a day when you know you're going to be too rushed to have much more than an apple for lunch, try this sweet omelette with a spoonful of jam or a good fruit compote.

Serves I
3 eggs
10ml/2 tsp caster (superfine) sugar
5ml/1 tsp plain (all-purpose) flour
10g/¼ oz/½ tbsp unsalted (sweet) butter
bread and jam, to serve

Preparation: 3 minutes; Cooking: 5 minutes

I Break the eggs into a large bowl, add the sugar and flour and beat until really frothy.

2 Heat the butter in an omelette pan until it begins to bubble, then pour in the egg mixture and cook, without stirring, until it begins to set on top and is golden brown underneath.

3 Run a wooden spatula around the edge of the omelette, then carefully turn it over and cook the second side for 1–2 minutes until golden. Serve hot or warm with thick slices of fresh bread and a bowlful of fruity jam.

Cook's Tips
• Although this recipe is stated to serve one, it is substantial enough for two not-very-hungry people. Omelettes are best eaten the moment they emerge from the pan, so if you are cooking for a crowd, get each guest to make his or her own and eat breakfast in relays.
• This tastes good with a plum or nectarine compote. Buy fruit that is ripe, but still slightly on the firm side. Cut the fruit in half and either remove the stones (pits) or cut around the stones to remove the flesh in neat slices. Mix 60ml/4 tbsp sugar with 120ml/4fl oz/½ cup water in a shallow pan. Bring to the boil, stirring until the sugar dissolves to form a syrup. Add the fruit, with a cinnamon stick and some cloves if you like, and simmer until it is tender. Serve warm or cold.

Omelette Arnold Bennett

This smoked haddock soufflé omelette is delicious.

Serves 2
175g/6oz smoked haddock fillet (preferably undyed if available)
50g/2oz/4 tbsp butter, diced

175ml/6fl oz/¾ cup whipping or double (heavy) cream
4 eggs, separated
40g/1½ oz/⅓ cup mature (sharp) Cheddar cheese, grated
ground black pepper
watercress, to garnish

Preparation: 2 minutes; Cooking: 12 minutes

I Put the haddock in a shallow pan with water to cover and poach over a medium heat for 8–10 minutes. Drain well. Remove the skin and any bones and flake the flesh.

2 Melt half the butter with 60ml/4 tbsp of the cream in a pan, add the flaked fish and stir together. Preheat the grill (broiler).

3 Mix the egg yolks with 15ml/1 tbsp of the cream. Season with pepper, then stir into the fish. Mix the cheese and the remaining cream. Whisk the egg whites until stiff, then fold into the mixture. Heat the remaining butter in an omelette pan, add the fish mixture and cook until browned. Pour the cheese mixture over and grill (broil) until bubbling. Garnish and serve.

Jugged Kippers

The demand for naturally smoked kippers is ever increasing. They are most popular for breakfast, with butter and lemon.

Serves 4
4 kippers (smoked herrings)
25g/1oz/2 tbsp butter
ground black pepper
lemon wedges, to serve

Preparation: 2–3 minutes; Cooking: 5–6 minutes

I If the heads are still on the kippers, remove them. Put into a jug, tails up. Cover with boiling water. Leave for 5 minutes, until tender. Drain well and serve with butter and the lemon wedges.

Omelette Energy 351kcal/1465kJ; Protein 19.3g; Carbohydrate 14.4g, of which sugars 10.6g; Fat 24.9g, of which saturates 9.9g; Cholesterol 592mg; Calcium 100mg; Fibre 0.2g; Sodium 271mg.
Arnold Bennett Energy 821kcal/3396kJ; Protein 36.1g; Carbohydrate 2.6g, of which sugars 2.6g; Fat 74g, of which saturates 42.6g; Cholesterol 577mg; Calcium 280mg; Fibre 0g; Sodium 1123mg.
Jugged Kippers Energy 248kcal/1025kJ; Protein 15.9g; Carbohydrate 0g, of which sugars 0g; Fat 20.4g, of which saturates 5.8g; Cholesterol 68mg; Calcium 49mg; Fibre 0g; Sodium 776mg.

Chilled Tomato Soup with Rocket Pesto

This soup takes hardly any time to make, but must be chilled, so bear that in mind when planning your menu. Whizz it up when you wake, and make the pesto just before serving.

Serves 4
225g/8oz cherry tomatoes, halved
225g/8oz baby plum
  tomatoes, halved
225g/8oz vine-ripened
  tomatoes, halved
2 shallots, roughly chopped

25ml/1½ tbsp sun-dried tomato
  purée (paste)
600ml/1 pint/2½ cups
  vegetable stock
salt and ground black pepper
ice cubes, to serve

For the rocket pesto
15g/½ oz rocket
  (arugula) leaves
75ml/5 tbsp olive oil
15g/½ oz/2 tbsp pine nuts
1 garlic clove
25g/1oz/⅓ cup freshly grated
  Parmesan or Romano cheese

Preparation: 10 minutes; Cooking: 4–5 minutes; Chilling ahead

1 Purée all the tomatoes and the shallots in a food processor or blender. Add the sun-dried tomato paste and process until smooth. Press the purée through a sieve (strainer) into a pan.

2 Add the vegetable stock and heat gently for 4–5 minutes. Season well. Pour into a bowl, leave to cool, then chill for at least 4 hours.

3 For the rocket pesto, put the rocket, oil, pine nuts and garlic in a food processor or blender and process to form a paste. Transfer to a bowl and stir in the Parmesan cheese. (This can also be prepared using a mortar and pestle. Pound the rocket leaves, chopped pine nuts and crushed garlic together, then add the oil a little at a time, continuing to pound the mixture. Add the Parmesan and work it in.)

4 Ladle the soup into bowls and add a few ice cubes to each. Spoon some of the rocket pesto into the centre of each portion and serve.

Gazpacho

Probably the most famous chilled soup in the world, this originated in Spain but now appears on menus everywhere. It is perfect for a summer lunch.

Serves 6
900g/2lb ripe tomatoes, peeled
  and seeded
1 cucumber, peeled and
  roughly chopped
2 red (bell) peppers, seeded and
  roughly chopped
2 garlic cloves, crushed
1 large onion, roughly chopped
30ml/2 tbsp white wine vinegar
120ml/4fl oz/½ cup olive oil

250g/9oz/4½ cups fresh
  white breadcrumbs
450ml/¾ pint/scant 2 cups
  iced water
salt and ground black pepper
ice cubes, to serve

For the garnish
30–45ml/2–3 tbsp olive oil
4 thick slices bread, crusts
  removed, cut into small cubes
2 tomatoes, peeled, seeded and
  finely diced
1 small green (bell) pepper,
  seeded and finely diced
1 small onion, very finely sliced
a small bunch of fresh flat leaf
  parsley, chopped

Preparation: 12 minutes; Cooking: 5–6 minutes; Chilling ahead

1 In a large bowl, mix the tomatoes, cucumber, peppers, garlic and onion. Stir in the vinegar, oil, breadcrumbs and water until well mixed.

2 Purée the mixture in a food processor or blender until almost smooth, and pour into a large bowl. Stir in salt and pepper to taste and chill for at least 4 hours.

3 To make the garnish, heat the oil in a frying pan and add the bread cubes.

4 Fry over a medium heat for 5–6 minutes, stirring occasionally to brown evenly. Lift out the cubes with a slotted spoon, drain on kitchen paper and put into a small bowl. Place the remaining garnishing ingredients in separate bowls or on a serving plate.

5 Ladle the gazpacho into bowls and add ice cubes to each portion. Serve at once with the garnishing ingredients.

Tomato Soup Energy 218kcal/902kJ; Protein 4.8g; Carbohydrate 7.5g, of which sugars 7.2g; Fat 19g, of which saturates 3.6g; Cholesterol 6mg; Calcium 100mg; Fibre 2.2g; Sodium 104mg.
Gazpacho Energy 412kcal/1730kJ; Protein 9.1g; Carbohydrate 55.6g, of which sugars 14.7g; Fat 18.6g, of which saturates 2.6g; Cholesterol 0mg; Calcium 109mg; Fibre 5g; Sodium 431mg.

Avogolemono

The name of this popular Greek soup means 'egg and lemon', the two key ingredients. It is a light soup made with orzo, a Greek rice-shaped pasta, but you can use any very small pasta shape in its place.

Serves 4–6
1.75 litres/3 pints/7½ cups chicken stock
115g/4oz/½ cup orzo pasta
3 eggs
juice of 1 large lemon
salt and ground black pepper
lemon slices, to garnish

Preparation: 2–3 minutes; Cooking: 7 minutes

1 Pour the stock into a large pan and bring to the boil. Add the pasta and cook for 5 minutes.

2 Beat the eggs until frothy, then add the lemon juice and 15ml/1 tbsp cold water.

3 Stir in a ladleful of the hot chicken stock, then add 1–2 more. Return this mixture to the pan, off the heat, and stir well. Season with salt and pepper, ladle into warmed bowls and serve at once, garnished with lemon slices.

Cook's Tips
• *To make your own chicken stock, place a chicken carcass in a large pan with 1 onion, 1 carrot, 1 celery stick, 1 garlic clove and a bouquet garni, cover with water and bring to the boil. Simmer for 2 hours, skimming occasionally. Strain the stock and use as required. If you do not need the stock immediately, cool it quickly by pouring it into a large jug (pitcher) and standing this in a sink of iced water. As soon as it is cold, put the jug in the refrigerator (or, briefly, in the freezer), until the fat solidifies on the surface and can be lifted off. Defatted stock freezes well and can be thawed at room temperature or in the microwave for use in soups and stews and for making risotto.*
• *Do not allow the soup to boil once the eggs have been added or they will curdle.*

Cauliflower Cream Soup

This delicately flavoured, thick winter soup is enriched at the last minute with chopped hard-boiled eggs and crème fraîche. Use broccoli in place of the cauliflower to equal effect.

Serves 4
1 cauliflower, cut into large pieces
1 large onion, roughly chopped
1 large garlic clove, chopped
bouquet garni
5ml/1 tsp ground coriander
pinch of mustard powder
900ml/1½ pints/3¾ cups vegetable or chicken stock
5–10ml/1–2 tsp cornflour (cornstarch)
150ml/¼ pint/⅔ cup milk
45ml/3 tbsp crème fraîche
2 eggs, hard-boiled and roughly chopped
15ml/1 tbsp chopped fresh coriander (cilantro)
salt and ground black pepper

Preparation: 5 minutes; Cooking: 13–15 minutes

1 Place the cauliflower in a large pan with the onion, garlic, bouquet garni, coriander, mustard, salt and pepper and stock. Simmer for 10–15 minutes until the cauliflower is tender. Remove from the heat and leave to cool slightly.

2 Remove the garlic and bouquet garni, then blend the cauliflower and onion with some of the cooking liquid in a food processor, or press through a sieve (strainer) for a really smooth result. Return to the pan along with the rest of the liquid.

3 Blend the cornflour with a little of the milk, then add to the soup with the rest of the milk. Return to the heat and cook until thickened, stirring all the time. Season to taste and, just before serving, turn off the heat and blend in the crème fraîche. Stir in the chopped egg and coriander and serve at once.

Cook's Tip
Garlic croûtons would make a delicious accompaniment. Cut white bread into cubes. Heat a mixture of butter and oil in a frying pan, fry 1 crushed garlic clove gently to flavour it, then remove the garlic and fry the bread cubes until crisp.

Avogolemono Energy 104kcal/440kJ; Protein 5.6g; Carbohydrate 14.3g, of which sugars 0.7g; Fat 3.3g, of which saturates 0.8g; Cholesterol 95mg; Calcium 20mg; Fibre 0.6g; Sodium 171mg.
Cauliflower Soup Energy 169kcal/711kJ; Protein 7.4g; Carbohydrate 27.7g, of which sugars 10.8g; Fat 4g, of which saturates 1.1g; Cholesterol 3mg; Calcium 111mg; Fibre 4g; Sodium 55mg.

Fresh Tomato Soup

The combination of intensely flavoured sun-ripened and fresh tomatoes needs little embellishment in this tasty Italian soup.

Serves 6
1.3–1.6kg/3–3½lb ripe tomatoes
400ml/14fl oz/1⅔ cups chicken
 or vegetable stock
45ml/3 tbsp sun-dried tomato
 purée (paste)
30–45ml/2–3 tbsp balsamic
 vinegar
10–15ml/2–3 tsp sugar
a small handful of fresh basil
 leaves, plus extra to garnish
salt and ground black pepper
toasted cheese croûtes and crème
 fraîche, to serve

Preparation: 5–6 minutes; Cooking: 14 minutes

1 Plunge the tomatoes into boiling water for 30 seconds, then refresh in cold water. Peel off the skins and cut the tomatoes into quarters.

2 Put the tomatoes in a large pan and pour over the chicken or vegetable stock. Bring just to the boil, reduce the heat, cover and simmer gently for 10 minutes until the tomatoes are pulpy.

3 Stir in the tomato purée, vinegar, sugar and basil. Season with salt and pepper, then cook gently, stirring, for 2 minutes.

4 Process the soup in a blender or food processor, then return to a clean pan and reheat gently. Serve in bowls, topped with one or two toasted cheese croûtes and a spoonful of crème fraîche, garnished with basil leaves.

Cook's Tips
• *Use a sharp knife to cut a cross in the base of each tomato before plunging it into the boiling water. The skin will then peel back easily from the crosses.*
• *To make the toasted cheese croûtes, slice a loaf of French bread thinly. Spread out the slices in a grill (broiler) pan and top each with finely grated Cheddar or Parmesan cheese. Grill (broil) until the cheese has melted and browned slightly.*

Avocado Soup

This delicious soup has a fresh, delicate flavour and a wonderful colour. For added zest, add a squeeze of lime or lemon juice just before serving. Serve the soup in white bowls if possible, to show off the pretty green hue to best advantage.

Serves 4
2 large ripe avocados
300ml/½ pint/1¼ cups
 sour cream
1 litre/1¾ pints/4 cups
 well-flavoured chicken stock
a small bunch of fresh coriander
 (cilantro) or flat leaf parsley,
 chopped
salt and ground black pepper

Preparation: 3 minutes; Cooking: 3–4 minutes

1 Cut the avocados in half, remove the peel and lift out the stones (pits). Chop the flesh coarsely and place it in a food processor with 45–60ml/3–4 tbsp of the sour cream. Process until smooth.

2 Heat the chicken stock in a pan. When it is hot, but still below simmering point, add the rest of the sour cream and stir gently to mix.

3 Gradually stir the avocado mixture into the hot stock. Heat gently but do not let the mixture approach boiling point. Add salt to taste.

4 Ladle the soup into heated bowls and sprinkle each portion with chopped coriander or flat leaf parsley and black pepper. Serve immediately, as it will discolour on standing.

Cook's Tip
Choose ripe avocados for this soup – they should feel soft when gently pressed. Keep very firm avocados at room temperature for 3–4 days until they soften. To speed ripening, place the avocados in a brown paper bag with a ripe banana or an apple. Look out for 'ready to eat' avocados at the supermarket – expensive but handy for dishes like these.

Fresh Tomato Soup Energy 52Kcal/225kJ; Protein 1.9g; Carbohydrate 10.4g, of which sugars 10.4g; Fat 0.7g, of which saturates 0.2g; Cholesterol 0mg; Calcium 19mg; Fibre 2.4g; Sodium 38mg.
Avocado Soup Energy 343kcal/1416kJ; Protein 4.4g; Carbohydrate 5.1g, of which sugars 3.6g; Fat 33.9g, of which saturates 13.4g; Cholesterol 45mg; Calcium 106mg; Fibre 4g; Sodium 41mg.

Butter Bean & Sun-dried Tomato Soup

This soup is quick and easy to make. The key is to use a good-quality home-made or bought fresh stock with plenty of pesto and sun-dried tomato purée. Only partly blending the soup gives it great texture.

Serves 4

2 x 400g/14oz cans butter (lima) beans, drained and rinsed
900ml/1½ pints/3¾ cups chicken or vegetable stock
60ml/4 tbsp sun-dried tomato purée (paste)
75ml/5 tbsp pesto

Preparation: 2 minutes; Cooking: 12 minutes

1 Put the butter beans in a pan. Pour in the stock and bring to the boil over a medium heat, stirring once or twice.

2 Stir in the tomato purée and pesto. Lower the heat and cook gently for 5 minutes.

3 Transfer six ladlefuls of the soup to a blender or food processor, scooping up plenty of the beans. Process until smooth, then return the purée to the pan.

4 Heat gently, stirring frequently, for 5 minutes, then season if necessary. Ladle into four warmed soup bowls and serve with warm crusty bread or breadsticks.

Cook's Tips
• *For the busy cook, good-quality bought stocks are a blessing. Most large supermarkets now sell fresh stock in tubs or packets. Another good product is concentrated liquid stock, sold in bottles. Varieties include beef, chicken and vegetable. However, if you cannot find any of the above, a good-quality stock cube will do the job.*
• *Swirl a little extra pesto on top of each portion of soup for an attractive finish, or garnish with one or two small fresh basil leaves to echo the pesto flavour.*

Pea Soup with Garlic

This delicious green pea and garlic soup has a wonderfully sweet taste and smooth texture, and is great served with crusty bread and garnished with fresh garden mint.

Serves 4

25g/1oz/2 tbsp butter
1 garlic clove, crushed
900g/2lb/8 cups frozen peas
1.2 litres/2 pints/5 cups chicken stock
salt and ground black pepper

Preparation: 3–4 minutes; Cooking: 8–10 minutes

1 Heat the butter in a large pan and add the garlic. Fry gently for 2–3 minutes, until softened, then add the peas. Cook for 1–2 minutes more, then pour in the stock.

2 Bring the soup to the boil, then reduce the heat to a simmer. Cover and cook for 5–6 minutes, until the peas are tender.

3 Leave to cool slightly, then transfer the mixture to a food processor and process until smooth (you may have to do this in two batches).

4 Return the soup to the pan and heat through gently. Season with salt and pepper to taste.

Variation
To make Pea and Leek Soup with Garlic, slice a leek in half, then slice it thinly. Add to the pan with the garlic. Cook over low heat for about 5 minutes until softened, then add the peas and proceed as in the recipe.

Cook's Tip
If you keep a bag of frozen peas in the freezer, you can rustle up this soup at very short notice. When processing the peas cooked in the soup, keep a few back and float them on each portion as an additional garnish.

Butter Bean Energy 269kcal/1130kJ; Protein 15.6g; Carbohydrate 28.3g, of which sugars 4.5g; Fat 11.2g, of which saturates 2.5g; Cholesterol 6mg; Calcium 111mg; Fibre 9.7g; Sodium 944mg.
Pea Soup Energy 233Kcal/965kJ; Protein 15.6g; Carbohydrate 25.5g, of which sugars 5.2g; Fat 8.5g, of which saturates 3.9g; Cholesterol 13mg; Calcium 49mg; Fibre 10.6g; Sodium 40mg.

Stilton & Watercress Soup

A good creamy Stilton
cheese and plenty of
peppery watercress bring
maximum flavour to this
rich, smooth soup, which
is superlative in small
portions and very quick to
prepare. It is ideal for a
dinner party.

Serves 4–6
600ml/1 pint/2½ cups chicken
   or vegetable stock
225g/8oz watercress
150g/5oz Stilton or other
   blue cheese
150ml/¼ pint/⅔ cup single
   (light) cream

Preparation: 6 minutes; Cooking: 8 minutes

1 Pour the stock into a pan and bring almost to the boil.
Remove and discard any very large stalks from the watercress.
Add the watercress to the pan and simmer gently for
2–3 minutes, until tender.

2 Crumble the cheese into the pan and simmer for 1 minute
more, until the cheese has started to melt. Process the soup in
a blender or food processor, in batches if necessary, until very
smooth. Return the soup to the pan.

3 Stir in the cream and check the seasoning. The soup will
probably not need any extra salt, as the blue cheese is already
quite salty. Heat the soup gently, without boiling, then ladle it
into warm bowls.

> **Variations**
> • Rocket (arugula) can be used as an alternative to watercress
> – both leaves are an excellent source of iron. When choosing
> any salad leaves, look for crisp, fresh leaves and reject any
> wilted or discoloured greens.
> • Stilton is the classic cheese for this soup, but there are plenty
> of other options. Gorgonzola and Roquefort can be used, but
> they have punchy flavours and you may need to use slightly
> less. Milder options include Bleu de Bresse, Irish Cashel Blue
> or Cambozola.

Egg & Cheese Soup

In this classic Roman soup,
eggs and cheese are beaten
into hot soup, producing the
slightly scrambled texture that
is characteristic of this dish.
The texture isn't to everyone's
taste, but aficionados rave
about it. The trick is to
remove the soup from the
heat when the eggs have
thickened but not curdled it.

Serves 6
3 eggs
45ml/3 tbsp fine semolina
90ml/6 tbsp freshly grated
   Parmesan cheese
pinch of nutmeg
1.5 litres/2½ pints/6¼ cups cold
   meat or chicken stock
salt and ground black pepper
12 rounds of country bread or
   ciabatta, to serve

Preparation: 2–3 minutes; Cooking: 6–7 minutes

1 Beat the eggs in a bowl, then beat in the semolina and the
cheese. Add the nutmeg and beat in 250ml/8fl oz/1 cup of the meat
or chicken stock. Pour the mixture into a measuring jug (pitcher).
Pour the remaining stock into a large pan, heat the stock and
bring to a gentle simmer.

2 A few minutes before you are ready to serve the soup, whisk
the egg mixture into the hot stock. Raise the heat slightly, and
bring it barely to the boil. Season and cook for 3–4 minutes.

3 To serve, toast the rounds of country bread or ciabatta, place
two in each soup plate and ladle on the hot soup. Serve at once.

> **Variation**
> If Parmesan is a bit expensive, use Pecorino Romano. It has a
> slightly milder flavour, which works very well in this soup.

> **Cook's Tip**
> Once added to the hot soup, the egg will begin to cook and the
> soup will become less smooth. Try not to overcook the soup at
> this stage because it may cause the egg to curdle.

Stilton and Watercress Energy 162Kcal/671kJ; Protein 8g; Carbohydrate 1g, of which sugars 1g; Fat 14g, of which saturates 9g; Cholesterol 38mg; Calcium 169mg; Fibre 0.6g; Sodium 400mg.
Egg and Cheese Energy 245kcal/1030kJ; Protein 14.1g; Carbohydrate 27.5g, of which sugars 1.3g; Fat 9.4g, of which saturates 4.1g; Cholesterol 110mg; Calcium 246mg; Fibre 1.1g; Sodium 424mg.

Egg Flower Soup

This simple, healthy soup is flavoured with fresh root ginger and Chinese five-spice powder. It is quick and delicious and can be made at the last minute.

Serves 4

1.2 litres/2 pints/5 cups fresh chicken or vegetable stock
10ml/2 tsp peeled, grated fresh root ginger
10ml/2 tsp light soy sauce
5ml/1 tsp sesame oil
5ml/1 tsp Chinese five-spice powder
15–30ml/1–2 tbsp cornflour (cornstarch)
2 eggs
salt and ground black pepper
1 spring onion (scallion), very finely sliced diagonally and 15ml/ 1 tbsp roughly chopped coriander (cilantro) or flat leaf parsley, to garnish

Preparation: 3–4 minutes; Cooking: 16 minutes

1 Put the chicken or vegetable stock into a large pan with the ginger, soy sauce, oil and five-spice powder. Bring to the boil and allow to simmer gently for about 10 minutes.

2 Blend the cornflour in a measuring jug (cup) with 60–75ml/ 4–5 tbsp water and stir into the stock. Cook, stirring constantly, until slightly thickened. Season to taste with salt and pepper.

3 In a jug, beat the eggs together with 30ml/2 tbsp cold water until the mixture becomes frothy.

4 Bring the soup back just to the boil and drizzle in the egg mixture, stirring vigorously with chopsticks until the egg begins to solidify. Serve at once, sprinkled with the sliced spring onions and chopped coriander or parsley.

Cook's Tip
This soup is a good way of using up leftover egg yolks or whites, which have been stored in the freezer and then thawed. When adding the egg to the soup, use a jug with a fine spout to form a very thin drizzle.

Hot & Sweet Vegetable Soup

This soothing, nutritious soup takes only minutes to make as the spinach and silken tofu are simply placed in bowls and covered with the richly flavoured hot vegetable stock.

Serves 4

1.2 litres/2 pints/5 cups vegetable stock
5–10ml/1–2 tsp Thai red curry paste
2 kaffir lime leaves, torn
40g/1½ oz/3 tbsp palm sugar or light muscovado (brown) sugar
30ml/2 tbsp soy sauce
juice of 1 lime
1 carrot, cut into thin batons
50g/2oz baby spinach leaves, any coarse stalks removed
225g/8oz block silken tofu, diced

Preparation: 4 minutes; Cooking: 7–12 minutes

1 Heat the stock in a large pan, then add the red curry paste. Stir constantly over a medium heat until the paste has dissolved. Add the lime leaves, sugar and soy sauce and bring to the boil. Add the lime juice and carrot to the pan. Reduce the heat and simmer for 5–10 minutes. Place the spinach and tofu in four individual serving bowls and pour the hot vegetable stock on top to serve.

Miso Broth with Mushrooms

Shiitake mushrooms give this soup superb flavour.

Serves 4

1.2 litres/2 pints/5 cups boiling water
3 tbsp light miso paste
3 fresh shiitake mushrooms, sliced
115g/4 oz tofu, diced
1 spring onion (scallion), green part only, sliced

Preparation: 4 minutes; Cooking: 5 minutes

1 Mix the boiling water and miso in a pan. Add the mushrooms and simmer for 5 minutes. Divide the tofu among four warmed soup bowls, ladle in the soup, scatter with sliced spring onions and serve.

Egg Flower Soup Energy 58kcal/244kJ; Protein 3.3g; Carbohydrate 3.8g, of which sugars 0.3g; Fat 3.6g, of which saturates 0.9g; Cholesterol 95mg; Calcium 16mg; Fibre 0g; Sodium 304mg.
Hot & Sweet Soup Energy 105Kcal/439kJ; Protein 5.3g; Carbohydrate 13.2g, of which sugars 12.8g; Fat 3.8g, of which saturates 0.5g; Cholesterol 0mg; Calcium 320mg; Fibre 0.7g; Sodium 559mg.
Miso Broth Energy 25kcal/103kJ; Protein 2.4g; Carbohydrate 2.6g, of which sugars 2.4g; Fat 0.6g, of which saturates 0.1g; Cholesterol 0mg; Calcium 107mg; Fibre 1.6g; Sodium 882mg.

Japanese-style Noodle Soup

This delicate, fragrant soup, flavoured with a hint of chilli, makes a delicious light lunch or first course.

Serves 4
45ml/3 tbsp miso
200g/7oz/scant 2 cups udon noodles, soba noodles or Chinese noodles
30ml/2 tbsp sake or dry sherry
15ml/1 tbsp rice or wine vinegar

45ml/3 tbsp Japanese soy sauce
115g/4oz asparagus tips or mangetouts (snow peas), thinly sliced diagonally
50g/2oz/scant 1 cup shiitake mushrooms, stalks removed and thinly sliced
1 carrot, sliced into julienne strips
3 spring onions (scallions), thinly sliced diagonally
salt and ground black pepper
5ml/1 tsp dried chilli flakes, to serve

Preparation: 8 minutes; Cooking: 10 minutes

1 Bring 1 litre/1¾ pints/4 cups water to the boil in a large pan. Pour 150ml/¼ pint/⅔ cup of the boiling water over the miso and stir until dissolved, then set aside.

2 Meanwhile, bring another large pan of lightly salted water to the boil, add the noodles and cook according to the packet instructions until just tender.

3 Drain the noodles in a colander. Rinse under cold running water, then drain again.

4 Add the sake or sherry, rice or wine vinegar and soy sauce to the boiling water remaining in the first pan. Boil gently for 3 minutes then reduce the heat to a simmer and stir in the miso mixture.

5 Add the asparagus or mangetouts, mushrooms, carrot and spring onions, and simmer for about 2 minutes until the vegetables are just tender. Season to taste.

6 Divide the noodles among four warm bowls and pour the soup over the top. Serve immediately, sprinkled with the dried chilli flakes.

Chinese Crab & Corn Soup

There's no denying the delightful combination of shellfish and corn in this Chinese favourite, but dressing the crab does increase the preparation time somewhat. Using frozen white crab meat will work just as well.

Serves 4
600ml/1 pint/2½ cups fish or chicken stock
2.5cm/1in piece fresh root ginger, peeled and very finely sliced

400g/14oz can creamed corn
150g/5oz cooked fresh white crab meat or frozen crab, thawed and drained
15ml/1 tbsp arrowroot or cornflour (cornstarch)
15ml/1 tbsp rice wine or dry sherry
15–30ml/1–2 tbsp light soy sauce
1 egg white
salt and ground white pepper
shredded spring onions (scallions) or finely chopped fresh chives, to garnish

Preparation: 6 minutes; Cooking: 10 minutes

1 Put the stock and ginger in a large pan and bring to the boil. Stir in the creamed corn and bring back to the boil.

2 Switch off the heat and add the crab meat. Put the arrowroot or cornflour in a cup and stir in the rice wine or sherry to make a smooth paste.

3 Stir the paste into the soup. Cook over a low heat for about 4 minutes until the soup has thickened and is slightly glutinous in consistency. Add soy sauce, salt and white pepper to taste.

4 In a bowl, whisk the egg white to a stiff foam. Gradually fold it into the soup. Ladle the soup into heated bowls, garnish each portion with spring onions and serve.

> **Cook's Tip**
> This soup is sometimes made with whole kernel corn, but creamed corn gives a better texture. If you can't find it in a can, use thawed frozen creamed corn.

Noodle Soup Energy 254kcal/1076kJ; Protein 10.2g; Carbohydrate 48.1g, of which sugars 4.9g; Fat 3.6g, of which saturates 0.1g; Cholesterol 0mg; Calcium 37mg; Fibre 3.4g; Sodium 814mg.
Crab Soup Energy 194kcal/821kJ; Protein 10.5g; Carbohydrate 30.1g, of which sugars 9.7g; Fat 3.9g, of which saturates 0.6g; Cholesterol 27mg; Calcium 50mg; Fibre 1.4g; Sodium 494mg.

Cucumber & Salmon Soup with Salsa

Charred salmon brings a hint of heat to the refreshing flavours of this chilled soup. Good-looking and beautifully light, it makes the perfect opener for an al fresco meal.

Serves 4
3 medium cucumbers
300ml/½ pint/1¼ cups Greek (US strained plain) yogurt
250ml/8fl oz/1 cup vegetable stock, chilled
120ml/4fl oz/½ cup crème fraîche
15ml/1 tbsp chopped fresh chervil
15ml/1 tbsp chopped fresh chives
15ml/1 tbsp chopped fresh flat leaf parsley
1 small fresh red chilli, seeded and very finely chopped
a little oil, for brushing
225g/8oz salmon fillet, skinned and cut into eight thin slices
salt and ground black pepper
fresh chervil or chives, to garnish

Preparation: 8–10 minutes; Cooking: 2–4 minutes

1 Peel two of the cucumbers and halve them lengthways. Scoop out and discard the seeds, then roughly chop the flesh. Purée the chopped flesh in a food processor or blender.

2 Add the yogurt, stock, crème fraîche, chervil, chives and seasoning, and process until smooth. Pour the mixture into a bowl, cover and chill.

3 Peel, halve and seed the remaining cucumber. Cut the flesh into small neat dice. Mix with the chopped parsley and chilli in a bowl. Cover the salsa and chill until required.

4 Brush a griddle or frying pan with oil and heat until very hot. Add the salmon slices and sear them for 1–2 minutes, then turn over carefully and sear the other side until tender and charred.

5 Ladle the chilled soup into soup bowls. Top each portion with two slices of salmon, then pile a portion of salsa in the centre. Garnish with the chervil or chives and serve.

Malaysian Laksa

This spicy prawn and noodle soup tastes just as good when made with fresh crab meat or any flaked cooked fish. If you are short of time, buy ready-made laksa paste, which is available from most Asian stores.

Serves 2–3
15ml/1 tbsp vegetable or groundnut (peanut) oil
115g/4oz rice vermicelli or stir-fry rice noodles
600ml/1 pint/2½ cups fish stock
400ml/14fl oz/1⅔ cups thin coconut milk
30ml/2 tbsp Thai fish sauce
¼ lime
16–24 cooked peeled prawns (shrimp)
salt and cayenne pepper
60ml/4 tbsp fresh coriander (cilantro) sprigs and leaves, chopped, to garnish

For the spicy laksa paste
2 lemon grass stalks, finely chopped
2 fresh red chillies, seeded and chopped
2.5cm/1in piece fresh root ginger, peeled and sliced
2.5ml/½ tsp shrimp paste
2 garlic cloves, chopped
2.5ml/½ tsp ground turmeric
30ml/2 tbsp tamarind paste

Preparation: 8 minutes; Cooking: 9–10 minutes

1 To make the spicy paste, place all the ingredients in a mortar and pound with a pestle. Alternatively, use a food processor.

2 Heat the vegetable or groundnut oil in a large pan, add the spicy paste and cook, stirring occasionally, for a few moments.

3 Meanwhile, cook the rice vermicelli or noodles in a large pan of boiling salted water according to the instructions on the packet. Tip into a large colander, rinse, drain and keep warm.

4 Add the fish stock and coconut milk to the spicy paste and bring to the boil. Stir in the Thai fish sauce, then simmer for 5 minutes. Season with salt and cayenne to taste, adding a squeeze of lime. Add the prawns and heat through briefly.

5 Divide the noodles among two or three soup plates. Pour over the soup, garnish and serve piping hot.

Malaysian Laksa Energy 436kcal/1830kJ; Protein 36.9g; Carbohydrate 55.2g, of which sugars 10.1g; Fat 7.6g, of which saturates 1.2g; Cholesterol 341mg; Calcium 239mg; Fibre 0.8g; Sodium 562mg.
Cucumber and Salmon Energy 314Kcal/1299kJ; Protein 17.8g; Carbohydrate 3.9g, of which sugars 3.7g; Fat 26.1g, of which saturates 13.1g; Cholesterol 62mg; Calcium 183mg; Fibre 1.2g; Sodium 92mg.

Snapper, Tamarind & Noodle Soup

Red snapper is a popular fish throughout South-east Asia, and tamarind gives this light, fragrant noodle soup a slightly sour taste.

Serves 4
2 litres/3½ pints/8 cups water
1kg/2¼lb red snapper or other
  red fish such as mullet
1 onion, sliced
50g/2oz tamarind pods
15ml/1 tbsp Thai fish sauce
15ml/1 tbsp sugar

30ml/2 tbsp vegetable oil
2 garlic cloves, finely chopped
2 lemon grass stalks, very
  finely chopped
4 ripe tomatoes, roughly chopped
30ml/2 tbsp yellow bean paste
225g/8oz rice vermicelli, soaked
  in warm water until soft
115g/4oz/1⅓ cups beansprouts
8–10 fresh basil or mint sprigs
25g/1oz roasted peanuts, ground
salt and ground black pepper

Preparation: 4–5 minutes; Cooking: 15 minutes

1 Bring the water to the boil in a pan. Lower the heat and add the fish and onion, with 2.5ml/½ tsp salt. Simmer gently until the fish is cooked through.

2 Remove the fish from the stock and set aside. Add the tamarind, fish sauce and sugar to the stock. Cook for 5 minutes, then strain the stock into a large jug (pitcher) or bowl. Carefully remove all of the bones from the fish, keeping the flesh in large pieces rather than small chunks. Keep hot.

3 Heat the oil in a large frying pan. Add the garlic and lemon grass and fry for a few seconds. Stir in the tomatoes and bean paste. Cook gently for 5–7 minutes, until the tomatoes are soft. Add the reserved flavoured fish stock, bring back to a simmer and adjust the seasoning.

4 Drain the vermicelli. Plunge it into a pan of boiling water for a few minutes, drain and divide among individual serving bowls. Add the beansprouts, fish, basil or mint, and sprinkle the ground peanuts on top. Top up each bowl by pouring in the hot soup. If there is any soup left over, pour it into a jug and place it on the table so guests can top up their bowls as needed.

Pork & Sichuan Pickle Noodle Soup

Noodle soup can taste a bit bland, but not when Sichuan hot pickle is one of the ingredients. This tasty soup makes a great winter warmer.

Serves 4
1 litre/1¾ pints/4 cups
  chicken stock
350g/12oz egg noodles
15ml/1 tbsp dried shrimp, soaked
  in water

30ml/2 tbsp vegetable oil
225g/8oz lean pork, such
  as fillet (tenderloin),
  finely shredded
15ml/1 tbsp yellow bean paste
15ml/1 tbsp soy sauce
115g/4oz Sichuan hot pickle,
  rinsed, drained and shredded
pinch of sugar
salt and ground black pepper
2 spring onions (scallions), finely
  sliced, to garnish

Preparation: 5 minutes; Cooking: 12 minutes

1 Bring the stock to the boil in a large pan. Add the noodles and cook until almost tender. Drain the dried shrimp, rinse them under cold water, drain again and add to the stock. Lower the heat and simmer for a further 2 minutes. Keep hot.

2 Heat the oil in a frying pan or wok. Add the pork and stir-fry over a high heat for about 3 minutes.

3 Add the bean paste and soy sauce to the pork and stir-fry the mixture for 1 minute more. Add the hot pickle with a pinch of sugar. Stir-fry for 1 minute more.

4 Divide the noodles and soup among individual serving bowls. Spoon the pork mixture on top, then sprinkle with the spring onions and serve immediately.

Cook's Tip
Sichuan hot pickle, also known as Szechuan (or Sichuan) preserved vegetables, is a pickle made from the stems of mustard cabbage, which are dried in the sun and then pickled in brine with chillies and spices.

Snapper, Tamarind Energy 495kcal/2079kJ; Protein 43.1g; Carbohydrate 55.5g, of which sugars 9.1g; Fat 11.4g, of which saturates 1.9g; Cholesterol 65mg; Calcium 108mg; Fibre 2.4g; Sodium 165mg.
Pork and Sichuan Energy 218kcal/911kJ; Protein 24.5g; Carbohydrate 7.8g, of which sugars 0.9g; Fat 9.7g, of which saturates 3g; Cholesterol 74mg; Calcium 90mg; Fibre 0.8g; Sodium 454mg.

Chicken & Soba Noodle Soup

Soba noodles are widely enjoyed in Japan. They are usually served in hot seasoned broth with a mixture of chicken, fish, seafood or vegetables.

Serves 4
225g/8oz skinless, boneless chicken breast portions
120ml/4fl oz/½ cup soy sauce
15ml/1 tbsp sake
1 litre/1¾ pints/4 cups chicken stock
2 young leeks, cut into 2.5cm/1in pieces
175g/6oz spinach leaves
300g/11oz soba noodles
sesame seeds, toasted, to garnish

Preparation: 5 minutes; Cooking: 13 minutes

1 Slice the chicken diagonally into bitesize pieces. Combine the soy sauce and sake in a pan. Bring to a simmer. Add the chicken and cook gently for about 3 minutes until it is tender. Keep hot.

2 Bring the stock to the boil in a pan. Add the leek and simmer for 3 minutes, then add the spinach. Keep the mixture warm.

3 Cook the noodles in a large pan of boiling water until just tender, following the directions on the packet. Drain the noodles and divide among individual serving bowls. Ladle the hot soup into the bowls, then add a portion of chicken to each. Serve immediately, sprinkled with sesame seeds.

> **Cook's Tip**
> Home-made chicken stock makes the world of difference to noodle soup. Put about 1.3–1.6kg/3–3½lb meaty chicken bones into a large pan, add 3 litres/5 pints/12 cups water and gradually bring to the boil, skimming off any foam that rises to the top. Add 2 slices fresh root ginger, 2 garlic cloves, 2 celery sticks, 4 spring onions (scallions), a handful of coriander (cilantro) stalks and about 10 peppercorns, crushed. Reduce the heat and simmer the stock for 2–2½ hours. Remove from the heat and leave to cool, uncovered and undisturbed. Strain the stock and remove any fat that congeals on top.

Chiang Mai Noodle Soup

A signature dish of the Thai city of Chiang Mai, this delicious noodle soup has Burmese origins and is the Thai equivalent of the Malaysian laksa.

Serves 4–6
600ml/1 pint/2½ cups coconut milk
30ml/2 tbsp red curry paste
5ml/1 tsp ground turmeric
450g/1lb boneless chicken thighs, cut into bitesize chunks
600ml/1 pint/2½ cups chicken stock
60ml/4 tbsp Thai fish sauce
15ml/1 tbsp dark soy sauce
juice of ½–1 lime
450g/1lb fresh egg noodles
salt and ground black pepper

For the garnish
3 spring onions (scallions), chopped
4 red chillies, chopped
4 shallots, chopped
60ml/4 tbsp sliced pickled mustard leaves, rinsed
30ml/2 tbsp fried sliced garlic
coriander (cilantro) leaves
4–6 fried noodle nests (optional)

Preparation: 5–6 minutes; Cooking: 13 minutes

1 Pour about one-third of the coconut milk into a large pan and bring to the boil over medium heat, stirring frequently with a wooden spoon until it separates.

2 Add the curry paste and ground turmeric, stir to mix completely and cook until fragrant.

3 Add the chicken and stir-fry for about 2 minutes, ensuring that all the chunks are coated with the paste.

4 Add the remaining coconut milk, chicken stock, fish sauce and soy sauce. Season with salt and pepper to taste. Simmer gently for 7–10 minutes. Remove from the heat and stir in the lime juice, a little at a time.

5 Cook the noodles in a large pan of boiling water until just tender, following the directions on the packet. Drain and divide among individual bowls. Divide the chicken among the bowls and ladle in the hot soup. Serve with the garnishes in separate bowls so guests can add the toppings of their choice.

Chiang Mai Energy 453kcal/1915kJ; Protein 28.8g; Carbohydrate 59.1g, of which sugars 6.7g; Fat 12.9g, of which saturates 3.7g; Cholesterol 120mg; Calcium 63mg; Fibre 2.3g; Sodium 513mg.
Chicken and Soba Energy 373kcal/1563kJ; Protein 20.1g; Carbohydrate 65.7g, of which sugars 4g; Fat 1.3g, of which saturates 0.3g; Cholesterol 39mg; Calcium 103mg; Fibre 2g; Sodium 2241mg.

Tapas of Almonds, Olives & Cheese

Serving a few choice nibbles with drinks is the perfect way to get an evening off to a good start, and when you can get everything ready ahead of time, life's easier all round.

Serves 6–8
For the marinated olives
2.5ml/½ tsp coriander seeds
2.5ml/½ tsp fennel seeds
2 garlic cloves, crushed
5ml/1 tsp chopped fresh rosemary
10ml/2 tsp chopped fresh parsley
15ml/1 tbsp sherry vinegar
30ml/2 tbsp olive oil
115g/4oz/⅔ cup black olives
115g/4oz/⅔ cup green olives

For the marinated cheese
150g/5oz Manchego or other firm cheese
90ml/6 tbsp olive oil
15ml/1 tbsp white wine vinegar
5ml/1 tsp black peppercorns
1 garlic clove, sliced
fresh thyme or tarragon sprigs
fresh flat leaf parsley or tarragon sprigs, to garnish (optional)

For the salted almonds
1.5ml/¼ tsp cayenne pepper
30ml/2 tbsp sea salt
25g/1oz/2 tbsp butter
60ml/4 tbsp olive oil
200g/7oz/1¾ cups blanched almonds

Preparation: 10–15 minutes; Cooking: 5 minutes; Make ahead

1 To make the marinated olives, crush the coriander and fennel seeds in a mortar with a pestle. Work in the garlic, then add the rosemary, parsley, vinegar and olive oil. Mix well. Put the olives in a small bowl and pour over the marinade. Cover with clear film (plastic wrap) and chill for up to 1 week.

2 To make the marinated cheese, cut the Manchego or other firm cheese into bitesize pieces, removing any rind, and put in a small bowl. Combine the oil, vinegar, peppercorns, garlic, thyme or tarragon and pour over the cheese. Cover with clear film and chill for up to 3 days.

3 To make the salted almonds, combine the cayenne pepper and salt in a bowl. Melt the butter with the oil in a frying pan. Add the almonds and fry them, stirring, for 5 minutes. Tip the almonds into the salt mixture and toss until they are coated. Leave to cool, then store in an airtight container for up to 1 week. Serve the almonds, olives, and cheese in separate dishes.

Guacamole

Serve this tangy avocado dip with tortilla chips or crudités as scoops.

Serves 4
2 ripe avocados, peeled
2 tomatoes, peeled, seeded and chopped

6 spring onions (scallions), finely chopped
30ml/2 tbsp fresh lime juice
15ml/1 tbsp chopped fresh coriander (cilantro)
salt and ground black pepper
fresh coriander (cilantro) sprigs to garnish

Preparation: 5 minutes; Cooking: 0 minutes

1 Mash the avocado flesh with a fork and add the remaining ingredients. Season with salt and pepper and mix well. Garnish with sprigs of coriander.

Hummus

This classic Middle Eastern dish is made from cooked chickpeas, ground to a paste and flavoured with garlic, lemon juice, tahini, olive oil and cumin. Serve with pitta wedges or on toast fingers. Hummus also makes a good filling for hollowed-out cocktail tomatoes.

Serves 4–6
400g/14oz can chickpeas, drained
60ml/4 tbsp tahini
2–3 garlic cloves, chopped
juice of ½–1 lemon
cayenne pepper to taste
small pinch to 1.5ml/¼ tsp ground cumin, or more to taste
salt and ground black pepper

Preparation: 5 minutes; Cooking: 0 minutes

1 Using a potato masher or food processor, coarsely mash the chickpeas. If you prefer a smoother purée, process them in a food processor or blender until smooth.

2 Mix the tahini into the chickpeas, then stir in the garlic, lemon juice, cayenne, cumin and salt and pepper to taste. If needed, add a little water. Serve at room temperature.

Tapas Energy 383kcal/1580kJ; Protein 10.3g; Carbohydrate 1.8g, of which sugars 1.1g; Fat 36.8g, of which saturates 8.9g; Cholesterol 25mg; Calcium 217mg; Fibre 2.7g; Sodium 1051mg.
Guacamole Energy 156kcal/645kJ; Protein 2.1g; Carbohydrate 3.7g, of which sugars 2.5g; Fat 14.7g, of which saturates 3.1g; Cholesterol 0mg; Calcium 26mg; Fibre 3.5g; Sodium 11mg.
Hummus Energy 140kcal/586kJ; Protein 6.9g; Carbohydrate 11.2g, of which sugars 0.4g; Fat 7.8g, of which saturates 1.1g; Cholesterol 0mg; Calcium 97mg; Fibre 3.6g; Sodium 149mg.

Chopped Eggs & Onions

Quick and easy to make, this is a speedy lunch. You could even pack it up and take it to work, although the aroma of eggs and onion might not prove irresistible to everyone. This makes great picnic fare. Pack it in a polybox, exclude the air, and transport it in a chiller bag with a selection of rolls and a bag of washed leaves.

Serves 4–6
8–10 eggs
6–8 spring onions (scallions)
    and/or 1 yellow or white onion,
    very finely chopped, plus extra
    to garnish
60–90ml/4–6 tbsp mayonnaise
mild French wholegrain mustard,
    to taste (optional)
15ml/1 tbsp chopped
    fresh parsley
salt and ground black pepper
rye toasts or crackers, to serve

Preparation: 3–4 minutes; Cooking: 12 minutes

1 Put the eggs in a large pan and pour in cold water to cover. Heat the water. When it boils, reduce the heat and simmer the eggs for 10 minutes. Stir the eggs twice so they cook evenly but don't let them become cracked or the contents will escape and cloud the water.

2 Drain the eggs, hold them under cold running water, then remove the shells, dry the eggs and chop roughly.

3 Place the chopped eggs in a large bowl. Add the onions, season with salt and pepper and mix well. Add enough mayonnaise to bind the mixture together.

4 Stir in the mustard, if using, and the chopped parsley, or sprinkle the parsley on top to garnish. If you have time, chill the mixture before serving with rye toasts or crackers.

> **Cook's Tip**
> Holding a freshly boiled egg under cold running water helps to prevent the yolk from acquiring a greenish tinge where it meets the white. Shell the eggs as soon as possible.

Spiced Feta with Chilli Seeds & Olives

What could be handier than jars of flavoured feta kept in the refrigerator? Chilli seeds flavour the marinated cubes of cheese spiked with spices and olives. Spoon the cheese cubes over green leaves and serve with warm bread as an appetizer.

Makes 4–5 small jars
500g/1¼ lb feta cheese
50g/2oz/½ cup stuffed olives
10ml/2 tsp coriander seeds
10ml/2 tsp whole peppercorns
5ml/1 tsp chilli seeds
few sprigs fresh rosemary or thyme
750ml/1¼ pints/3 cups virgin
    olive oil

Preparation: 15 minutes; Cooking: 0 minutes; Make ahead

1 Drain the feta cheese, discarding the liquid surrounding it, dice it and put it in a bowl. Slice the olives.

2 Using a pestle, crush the coriander seeds and peppercorns in a mortar and add them to the cheese with the olives, chilli seeds and rosemary or thyme leaves. Toss lightly.

3 Sterilize 4–5 small, clean glass jars by heating them in the oven at 150°C/300°F/Gas 2 for 15 minutes.

4 Spoon the cheese into the warm, dry sterilized jars and top up with olive oil, making sure that the cheese is well covered by the oil. Close the jars tightly and store them in the refrigerator for up to 3 weeks.

> **Cook's Tips**
> • The glass jars can also be sterilized by putting them through a hot wash in a dishwasher. As soon as the cycle is finished, while the jars are still warm, fill them with the cheese and oil. To ring the changes, use a garlic-infused oil, or try basil or chilli oil.
> • Seal the jars with screw-topped or clip-down lids. The jars need to be totally airtight to keep the cheese fresh.

Chopped Eggs Energy 170kcal/706kJ; Protein 8.7g; Carbohydrate 0.5g, of which sugars 0.5g; Fat 15.1g, of which saturates 3.2g; Cholesterol 261mg; Calcium 48mg; Fibre 0.3g; Sodium 140mg.
Spiced Feta Energy 440kcal/1818kJ; Protein 15.7g; Carbohydrate 1.5g, of which sugars 1.5g; Fat 41.3g, of which saturates 16.7g; Cholesterol 70mg; Calcium 366mg; Fibre 0.3g; Sodium 1665mg.

Chilli Yogurt Cheese in Olive Oil

Yogurt, hung in muslin to drain off the whey, makes a superb soft cheese. Here it is bottled in olive oil with chilli and herbs, ready for serving on toast as a summer snack.

Fills 2 x 450g/1lb jars
800g/1¾lb/about 4 cups Greek (US strained, plain) yogurt
2.5ml/½ tsp salt

10ml/2 tsp crushed dried chillies or chilli powder
15ml/1 tbsp chopped fresh rosemary
15ml/1 tbsp chopped fresh thyme or oregano
about 300ml/½ pint/1¼ cups olive oil, preferably garlic-flavoured
lightly toasted country bread, to serve

Preparation: 2 minutes; Cooking: 18 minutes; Make ahead

1 Sterilize a 30cm/12in square of muslin (cheesecloth) by steeping it in boiling water. Drain and lay over a large plate. Mix the yogurt with the salt and tip on to the centre of the cloth. Bring up the sides of the cloth and tie firmly.

2 Hang the bag from a kitchen cabinet handle or in any convenient, cool position that allows a bowl to be placed underneath to catch the whey. Leave for 2–3 days until the yogurt stops dripping.

3 Sterilize two 450g/1lb clean glass preserving or jam jars by heating them in the oven at 150°C/300°F/Gas 2 for about 15 minutes or put them through a hot wash in a dishwasher.

4 Mix the dried chillies and herbs in a bowl. Take teaspoonfuls of the cheese and roll into balls between the palms of your hands. Lower into jars, sprinkling each layer with the herb and chilli mixture.

5 Pour the oil over the cheese until the balls are completely covered. Close the jars tightly and store in the refrigerator for up to 3 weeks. To serve the cheese, spoon out of the jars with a little of the flavoured olive oil and spread on to fresh or lightly toasted farmhouse bread.

Vegetarian Chopped Liver

This mixture of browned onions, chopped vegetables, hard-boiled egg and walnuts looks and tastes surprisingly like chopped liver but is lighter and fresher.

Serves 6
90ml/6 tbsp vegetable oil, plus extra if necessary

3 onions, chopped
175–200g/6–7oz/1½–scant 1¾ cups frozen peas
115–150g/4–5oz/1 cup green beans, roughly chopped
15 walnuts, shelled (30 halves)
3 eggs
salt and ground black pepper
slices of rye bread or crisp matzos, to serve

Preparation: 7–8 minutes; Cooking: 10 minutes

1 Boil the eggs in a pan of water for 10 minutes. Drain, plunge into cold water and leave until cold, then shell.

2 Meanwhile, heat the oil in a pan, add the onions and fry until softened and lightly browned. Add the peas and beans and season with salt and pepper to taste. Continue to cook until the vegetables are tender and the beans are no longer bright green but look fairly pale.

3 Put the vegetables in a food processor, add the walnuts and eggs and process until the mixture forms a thick paste. Taste for seasoning and, if the mixture seems a bit dry, add a little more oil and mix in thoroughly. Serve the nutty vegetable mixture with slices of rye bread or matzos.

Cook's Tips
If you are serving this to vegetarians, you might want to change the name, since even mentioning the words 'chopped liver' could put them off. This would be a shame, as the dish is really tasty and nutritious. The walnuts add fibre and flavour, with the added bonus that they are a good source of omega-3 fatty acids, which help to keep the heart healthy. Walnuts are also a valuable source of potassium, magnesium, iron, zinc, copper and selenium.

Chilli Yogurt Energy 1331kcal/5488kJ; Protein 24g; Carbohydrate 7.5g, of which sugars 7.5g; Fat 138.2g, of which saturates 33.8g; Cholesterol 0mg; Calcium 563mg; Fibre 0g; Sodium 758mg.
Chopped Liver Energy 309kcal/1277kJ; Protein 9g; Carbohydrate 11.1g, of which sugars 6.2g; Fat 25.9g, of which saturates 3.4g; Cholesterol 95mg; Calcium 64mg; Fibre 3.6g; Sodium 39mg.

Tapenade with Quail's Eggs & Crudités

This olive-based spread or dip makes a sociable start to a meal for friends.

Serves 6
225g/8oz/2 cups pitted
    black olives
2 large garlic cloves, peeled
15ml/1 tbsp salted capers, rinsed
6 canned or bottled anchovy
    fillets, drained
50g/2oz good-quality canned tuna
5–10ml/1–2 tsp Cognac
    (optional)
5ml/1 tsp chopped fresh thyme
30ml/2 tbsp chopped fresh
    parsley
30–60ml/2–4 tbsp extra virgin
    olive oil

a dash of lemon juice
30ml/2 tbsp crème fraîche or
    fromage frais (optional)
12–18 quail's eggs
ground black pepper

For the crudités
bunch of spring onions (scallions),
    halved if large
bunch of radishes, trimmed
bunch of baby fennel, trimmed
    and halved if large, or 1 large
    fennel bulb, cut into thin
    wedges

To serve
French bread
unsalted (sweet) butter or olive oil
    and sea salt to dip

Preparation: 10 minutes; Cooking: 3–4 minutes

1 Process the olives, garlic cloves, capers, anchovies and tuna in a food processor or blender. Transfer to a mixing bowl and stir in the Cognac, if using, the thyme, parsley and enough olive oil to make a paste. Season to taste with pepper and a dash of lemon juice. Stir in the crème fraîche or fromage frais, if using, and transfer to a serving bowl.

2 Place the quail's eggs in a pan of cold water and bring to the boil. Cook for only 2 minutes, then immediately drain and plunge the eggs into iced water to stop them from cooking any further and to help make them easier to shell. When the eggs are cold, carefully part-shell them.

3 Serve the tapenade with the eggs and crudités and offer French bread, unsalted butter or oil and sea salt alongside.

White Beans in a Spicy Dressing

Tender white beans are delicious in this spicy sauce with the bite of fresh, crunchy green pepper and the flavour of juicy tomatoes. It is perfect for preparing ahead of time.

Serves 4
750g/1⅔lb tomatoes, diced
1 onion, finely chopped
½–1 mild fresh chilli, finely
    chopped

1 green (bell) pepper, seeded
    and chopped
pinch of sugar
4 garlic cloves, chopped
400g/14oz can cannellini
    beans, drained
45–60ml/3–4 tbsp olive oil
grated rind and juice of 1 lemon
15ml/1 tbsp cider vinegar or
    wine vinegar
salt and ground black pepper
chopped fresh parsley or
    coriander (cilantro), to garnish

Preparation: 7 minutes; Cooking: 0 minutes; Chilling: 2–3 hours

1 Put the tomatoes, onion, chilli, green pepper, sugar, garlic, cannellini beans, salt and plenty of ground black pepper in a large bowl and toss together until well combined.

2 Add the olive oil, grated lemon rind, lemon juice and vinegar to the salad and toss lightly to combine.

3 Cover and chill for 2–3 hours if time permits. Garnish the bean salad with chopped parsley or coriander and serve with toasted pitta breads.

> **Variations**
> • Substitute flageolets (small cannellini), or try using haricots (navy beans). They will all taste and look attractive.
> • Instead of serving the salad with toasted pitta bread, it could be used as a filling for pitta pockets. Warm 4 large pitta breads under a medium grill (broiler). Alternatively, place them between sheets of kitchen paper and warm them in a microwave on High for 1–2 minutes. Cut the breads in half through the middle and open each half up to make 8 pitta pockets. Spoon the salad into each pitta pocket.

Tapenade Energy 157kcal/665kJ; Protein 6.3g; Carbohydrate 28.4g, of which sugars 1.8g; Fat 2.8g, of which saturates 0.6g; Cholesterol 37mg; Calcium 76mg; Fibre 1.5g; Sodium 522mg.
White Beans Energy 391kcal/1654kJ; Protein 24g; Carbohydrate 53.8g, of which sugars 11.8g; Fat 10.4g, of which saturates 1.6g; Cholesterol 0mg; Calcium 120mg; Fibre 18.5g; Sodium 37mg.

Sweet & Sour Cucumber with Dill

This dish is half pickle, half salad, and totally delicious served as a brunch or appetizer. Serve with thin slices of pumpernickel or other coarse, dark, full-flavoured bread. Some people find cucumber skin indigestible, so peel them if you prefer. The dill will provide plenty of colour.

Serves 4
1 large or 2 small cucumbers, thinly sliced
3 onions, thinly sliced
45ml/3 tbsp sugar
75–90ml/5–6 tbsp white wine vinegar or cider vinegar
30–45ml/2–3 tbsp water
30–45ml/2–3 tbsp chopped fresh dill
salt

Preparation: 10–12 minutes; Cooking: 0 minutes; Chilling ahead

1 In a bowl, mix together the sliced cucumber and onion, season with salt and toss together until thoroughly combined. Leave to stand in a cool place for 5–10 minutes. Add the sugar, vinegar, water and chopped dill to the cucumber mixture. Toss together until well combined, then chill for a few hours, or until ready to serve.

Spinach & Mushroom Salad

This nutritious salad goes well with strongly flavoured dishes like chilli chicken.

Serves 4
10 baby corn cobs

2 tomatoes
115g/4oz/1½ cups mushrooms
1 onion, cut into rings
20 small spinach leaves
25g/1oz salad cress (optional)
salt and ground black pepper

Preparation: 5 minutes; Cooking: 0 minutes

1 Halve the baby corn cobs lengthwise and slice the tomatoes. Trim the mushrooms and cut them into thin slices.

2 Arrange all the salad ingredients attractively in a large bowl. Season with salt and pepper and serve.

Pears with Blue Cheese & Walnuts

Succulent pears filled with blue cheese and walnut cream look pretty on colourful leaves and make a great appetizer.

Serves 6
115g/4oz fresh cream cheese
75g/3oz Stilton or other mature blue cheese, such as Roquefort
30–45ml/2–3 tbsp single (light) cream
115g/4oz/1 cup roughly chopped walnuts

6 ripe pears
15ml/1 tbsp lemon juice
mixed salad leaves, such as frisée, oakleaf lettuce and radicchio
6 cherry tomatoes
sea salt and ground black pepper
walnut halves and sprigs of fresh flat leaf parsley, to garnish

For the dressing
juice of 1 lemon
a little finely grated lemon rind
a pinch of caster (superfine) sugar
60ml/4 tbsp olive oil

Preparation: 8–10 minutes; Cooking: 0 minutes

1 Mash the cream cheese and blue cheese together in a mixing bowl with a good grinding of black pepper, then blend in the cream to make a smooth mixture. Add 25g/1oz/¼ cup of the chopped walnuts and mix to distribute evenly.

2 Peel and halve the pears and scoop out the core from each. Put the pears into a bowl of water with the 15ml/1 tbsp lemon juice to prevent them from browning. Make the dressing by whisking the ingredients together in a small bowl, and then add salt and pepper to taste.

3 Arrange a bed of salad leaves on six plates – shallow soup plates are ideal – add a cherry tomato to each and sprinkle over the remaining chopped walnuts.

4 Drain the pears well and pat dry with kitchen paper, then turn them in the prepared dressing and arrange, hollow side up, on the salad leaves.

5 Divide the blue cheese filling among the 12 pear halves and spoon the dressing over the top. Garnish each filled pear half with a walnut half and a sprig of flat leaf parsley before serving.

Cucumber Energy 89kcal/375kJ; Protein 2g; Carbohydrate 20.7g, of which sugars 18.3g; Fat 0.4g, of which saturates 0g; Cholesterol 0mg; Calcium 63mg; Fibre 2.3g; Sodium 9mg.
Spinach Energy 21kcal/89kJ; Protein 2g; Carbohydrate 2.4g, of which sugars 2.2g; Fat 0.5g, of which saturates 0.1g; Cholesterol 0mg; Calcium 29mg; Fibre 1.5g; Sodium 309mg
Pears Energy 322kcal/1332kJ; Protein 5.1g; Carbohydrate 15.7g, of which sugars 15.7g; Fat 26.9g, of which saturates 10.2g; Cholesterol 30mg; Calcium 109mg; Fibre 3.7g; Sodium 218mg.

Salad Leaves with Gorgonzola

Crispy fried pancetta makes a tasty addition and contrasts well in texture and flavour with the softness of mixed salad leaves and the sharp taste of Gorgonzola.

Serves 4

225g/8oz pancetta rashers (strips), any rinds removed, coarsely chopped
2 large garlic cloves, roughly chopped
75g/3oz rocket (arugula) leaves
75g/3oz radicchio leaves or mixed baby salad leaves
50g/2oz/½ cup walnuts, roughly chopped
115g/4oz Gorgonzola cheese
60ml/4 tbsp olive oil
15ml/1 tbsp balsamic vinegar
salt and ground black pepper

Preparation: 5 minutes; Cooking: 5 minutes

1 Put the chopped pancetta and garlic in a non-stick or heavy frying pan and heat gently, stirring constantly, until the pancetta fat runs.

2 Increase the heat and fry until the pancetta and garlic are crisp. Try not to let the garlic brown or it will acquire a bitter flavour. Remove the pancetta and garlic with a slotted spoon and drain on kitchen paper. Leave the pancetta fat in the pan, but take it off the heat.

3 Tear the rocket and radicchio or mixed baby salad leaves into a salad bowl. Sprinkle over the walnuts, pancetta and garlic. Add salt and pepper and toss to mix. Crumble the Gorgonzola cheese on top.

4 Return the frying pan to medium heat and add the oil and balsamic vinegar to the pancetta fat. Stir until sizzling, then pour over the salad. Serve at once, to be tossed at the table.

> **Variation**
> If pancetta is not available, use unsmoked streaky (fatty) bacon instead. You could also try chorizo, cut thinly, for extra flavour.

Prawn Cocktail

There is no nicer starter than a good, fresh prawn cocktail, with firm, juicy prawns, crisp lettuce and a piquant sauce. This recipe shows just how good a prawn cocktail can be.

Serves 6

60ml/4 tbsp double (heavy) cream, lightly whipped
60ml/4 tbsp mayonnaise
60ml/4 tbsp tomato ketchup
5–10ml/1–2 tsp Worcestershire sauce
juice of 1 lemon
½ cos lettuce or other crisp lettuce
450g/1lb cooked peeled prawns (shrimp)
salt, ground black pepper and paprika
6 large whole cooked prawns (shrimp) in the shell, to garnish (optional)
thinly sliced brown bread and butter and lemon wedges, to serve

Preparation: 6–7 minutes; Cooking: 0 minutes

1 Place the lightly whipped cream, mayonnaise and tomato ketchup in a small bowl and whisk lightly to combine. Add Worcestershire sauce to taste, then whisk in enough of the lemon juice to make a really tangy sauce.

2 Finely shred the lettuce and spoon it into six individual glasses, filling them about one-third full.

3 Stir the prawns into the sauce, then check the seasoning and spoon the prawn mixture generously over the lettuce. If you like, drape a whole cooked prawn over the edge of each glass and sprinkle each of the cocktails with ground black pepper and/or paprika. Serve immediately, with thinly sliced brown bread and butter and lemon wedges.

> **Cook's Tip**
> Partly peeled prawns make a pretty garnish. To prepare, carefully peel the body shell from the prawns and leave the tail fan for decoration.

Salad Leaves Energy 448Kcal/1850kJ; Protein 17.7g; Carbohydrate 1g, of which sugars 0.9g; Fat 41.4g, of which saturates 12.4g; Cholesterol 58mg; Calcium 219mg; Fibre 1.2g; Sodium 1113mg.
Prawn Cocktail Energy 194kcal/805kJ; Protein 13.9g; Carbohydrate 4.2g, of which sugars 4g; Fat 13.6g, of which saturates 4.6g; Cholesterol 167mg; Calcium 80mg; Fibre 0.4g; Sodium 384mg.

Crab Salad with Rocket

This colourful and fresh-tasting appetizer is an interesting way to use crab meat. The capers and peppery rocket leaves add a zing to the dish.

Serves 6

white and brown meat from
    4 small fresh dressed crabs,
    about 450g/1lb
1 small red (bell) pepper, seeded
    and finely chopped
1 small red onion, finely chopped
30ml/2 tbsp drained capers
30ml/2 tbsp chopped fresh
    coriander (cilantro)
grated rind and juice of 2 lemons
Tabasco sauce, to taste
salt and ground black pepper
lemon rind strips, to garnish

**For the rocket (arugula)
salad**
40g/1½oz rocket leaves
30ml/2 tbsp sunflower oil
15ml/1 tbsp fresh lime juice

Preparation: 6–7 minutes; Cooking: 0 minutes

1 Put the white and brown crab meat, red pepper, onion, capers and chopped coriander in a bowl. Add the lemon rind and juice and toss gently to mix together. Season with a few drops of Tabasco sauce, according to taste, and a little salt and ground black pepper.

2 Divide the rocket leaves among four plates. Mix together the oil and lime juice in a small bowl. Dress the rocket leaves, then pile the crab salad on top and serve garnished with lemon rind.

Variation
Sweet red piquant peppers in oil would make a great addition to this salad. Drain 4–6 of the peppers, chop them roughly and add with the red (bell) pepper.

Cook's Tip
If the dressed crabs are really small, pile the salad back into the shells to serve. This looks very pretty.

Amanida

This salad is simple to make, because it combines small quantities of ready-to-eat ingredients.

Serves 6
1 lolla green lettuce
50g/2oz cured, sliced chorizo or
    in a piece, skinned and diced
4 thin slices Serrano ham
130g/4½oz can sardines
    in oil, drained
130g/4½oz can albacore tuna
    steak in oil, drained
8 canned white asparagus
    spears, drained
2–3 canned palm hearts, drained
115g/4oz/⅔ cup tiny
    arbequina olives
115g/4oz/⅔ cup big gordas or
    queen olives, preferably
    purplish ones
10 medium red tomatoes
15ml/1 tbsp chopped fresh
    parsley, to garnish

For the vinaigrette
1 garlic clove, split lengthways
30ml/2 tbsp sherry vinegar
30ml/2 tbsp red wine vinegar
60ml/4 tbsp olive oil
60ml/4 tbsp extra virgin olive oil
salt and ground black pepper

Preparation: 20 minutes; Cooking: 0 minutes

1 Make the vinaigrette. Wipe the cut side of the garlic round a bowl, then discard.

2 Whisk the sherry vinegar, red wine vinegar, olive oil and extra virgin olive oil together in the bowl, then season with salt and black pepper. Tip the vinaigrette into a small jug (pitcher) and set aside.

3 Choose a large serving plate. Select eight lettuce leaves, to make small bunches round it. Break off the stem ends. Tip the leaves into the vinaigrette bowl and toss to coat in a little dressing. Arrange them around the serving plate.

4 Position the chorizo slices on one side of the plate. Roll the ham and arrange opposite. Drain and blot the canned fish and arrange the sardines and tuna across the plate, in a cross.

5 Arrange the asparagus, spears outwards, and the palm hearts (split lengthways), on opposite sides of the plate. Pile the two types of olive in the remaining spaces.

6 Put the tomatoes in a bowl and pour over boiling water. Leave to stand for 10 minutes, then drain. Peel and quarter two-thirds of the tomatoes and cut out the centres.

7 Arrange the tomatoes, round side up, in the centre of the plate, just touching all the prepared sections. Prepare more tomatoes as they are needed.

8 Arrange them in a flower shape, each new ring just overlapping the previous one. The final ring, in the centre of the pile, should make a flower shape.

9 Brush vinaigrette dressing over the tomatoes, palm hearts and asparagus spears and season lightly with salt and black pepper. Sprinkle parsley very discreetly on the tomatoes and white vegetables. Serve at room temperature. (Refrigerate if you must, while waiting to serve.)

Crab Salad Energy 106kcal/443kJ; Protein 14.2g; Carbohydrate 2.1g, of which sugars 2g; Fat 4.6g, of which saturates 0.6g; Cholesterol 54mg; Calcium 114mg; Fibre 0.7g; Sodium 431mg.
Amanida Energy 304Kcal/1264kJ; Protein 14.7g; Carbohydrate 7.5g, of which sugars 6.8g; Fat 24.2g, of which saturates 4.4g; Cholesterol 37mg; Calcium 169mg; Fibre 3.4g; Sodium 878mg.

Rice Triangles

These rice shapes – onigiri – are very popular in Japan. You can put anything you like in the rice, so you could invent your own onigiri.

Serves 4
1 salmon steak
15ml/1 tbsp salt

450g/1lb/4 cups freshly cooked sushi rice
1/4 cucumber, seeded and cut into matchsticks
1/2 sheet yaki-nori seaweed, cut into four equal strips
white and black sesame seeds, for sprinkling on the salmon onigiri before serving

Preparation: 12 minutes; Cooking: 6 minutes

1 Grill (broil) the salmon steaks on each side, until the flesh flakes easily when tested with the tip of a sharp knife. Set aside to cool while you make other onigiri. When the salmon is cold, flake it, discarding any skin and bones.

2 Put the salt in a bowl. Spoon an eighth of the warm cooked rice into a small rice bowl. Make a hole in the middle of the rice and put in a few cucumber matchsticks. Smooth the rice over to cover the cucumber completely.

3 Wet the palms of both hands with cold water, then rub the salt evenly on to your palms.

4 Empty the rice and cucumbers from the bowl onto one hand. Use both hands to shape the rice into a triangular shape, using firm but not heavy pressure, and making sure that the cucumber is encased by the rice. Make three more rice triangles the same way.

5 Mix the flaked salmon into the remaining rice, then shape it into triangles as before.

6 Wrap a strip of yaki-nori around each of the cucumber triangles. Sprinkle sesame seeds on the salmon triangles.

7 Arrange the onigiri on a plate, with alternate triangles inverted for best presentation. Serve at once.

Smoked Fish Platter

A wide variety of smoked fish is available today – trout, salmon and mackerel feature in this simple appetizer – but any smoked fish can be used.

Serves 4
1/2 Charentais melon
1/2 cantaloupe melon
50g/2oz rocket (arugula)

75g/3oz hot-smoked trout fillets
75g/3oz smoked salmon
75g/3oz smoked mackerel with peppercorns

For the dressing
75ml/5 tbsp extra virgin olive oil
15ml/1 tbsp white wine vinegar
5ml/1 tsp wholegrain mustard
5ml/1 tsp clear honey
salt and ground black pepper

Preparation: 8 minutes; Cooking: 0 minutes

1 Scoop out and discard all the seeds from the Charentais and cantaloupe melons and cut each melon into four or eight slices, leaving the skin on. Divide the melon slices among four small serving plates, placing the slices neatly to one side.

2 Add a quarter of the rocket leaves to each plate, placing them opposite the melon.

3 Make the honey dressing by combining all the ingredients in a small jug (pitcher). Add plenty of salt and black pepper and whisk with a fork until emulsified.

4 Divide the smoked fish into four portions, breaking or cutting the trout fillets and smoked salmon into bitesize pieces. Peel the skin from the mackerel, then break up the flesh.

5 Arrange the trout fillets, smoked salmon and mackerel over the rocket and melon on each platter. Drizzle the dressing over and serve immediately.

> **Variation**
> As long as the total amount of smoked fish is 250g/9oz, any varieties can be used. Try smoked eel for a change.

Rice Triangles Energy 342kcal/1427kJ; Protein 10.5g; Carbohydrate 29.8g, of which sugars 1.9g; Fat 20.7g, of which saturates 7.8g; Cholesterol 37mg; Calcium 140mg; Fibre 1.1g; Sodium 38mg.
Fish Platter Energy 312kcal/1298kJ; Protein 14.8g; Carbohydrate 15.2g, of which sugars 15.2g; Fat 21.7g, of which saturates 3.5g; Cholesterol 33mg; Calcium 66mg; Fibre 1.3g; Sodium 961mg.

Chilled Soba Noodles with Nori

Nori is familiar as the seaweed sheets that are used for wrapping sushi, but it is often crumbled or sliced and used as a flavourful topping for Japanese dishes. Nori is widely available in supermarkets, but you will find a greater selection in Asian supermarkets.

Serves 4
350g/12oz dried soba noodles
1 sheet nori seaweed

For the dipping sauce
300ml/½ pint/1¼ cups
    bonito stock
120ml/4fl oz/½ cup dark
    soy sauce
60ml/4 tbsp mirin
5ml/1 tsp sugar
10g/¼oz loose bonito flakes

To serve
4 spring onions (scallions),
    finely chopped
30ml/2 tbsp grated daikon
wasabi paste
4 egg yolks (optional)

Preparation: 6 minutes; Cooking: 10–12 minutes

1 Make the dipping sauce. Combine the stock, soy sauce, mirin and sugar in a pan. Bring rapidly to the boil, add the bonito flakes, then remove from the heat. When cool, strain the sauce into a bowl and cover. (This can be done in advance and the sauce kept chilled for up to a week.)

2 Cook the soba noodles in a pan of lightly salted boiling water for 6–7 minutes or until just tender, following the manufacturer's directions on the packet.

3 Drain and rinse the noodles under cold running water, agitating them gently to remove the excess starch. Drain well, tip into a bowl and set aside.

4 Toast the nori over a high gas flame or under a hot grill (broiler), then place on a board and cut into thin strips.

5 Divide the noodles among four serving dishes and top with the nori. Serve each portion with an individual bowl of dipping sauce and offer the spring onions, daikon and wasabi paste separately. An egg yolk can be added to each portion if liked.

Cheese Fritters in Wonton Wrappers

These crisp fritters owe their inspiration to Italy although the wrappers are strictly Chinese – a fine example of fusion food. A note of caution – do be careful not to burn your mouth when you take your first bite, as the soft, rich cheese filling will be very hot and the fritters are so irresistible that waiting for them to cool down is well nigh impossible.

Makes 16
115g/4oz/½ cup
    ricotta cheese
50g/2oz/½ cup grated
    fontina cheese
25g/1oz/⅓ cup finely grated
    Parmesan cheese
pinch of cayenne pepper
1 egg, beaten, plus a little extra
    to seal the wontons
16 wonton wrappers
vegetable oil, for deep-frying

Preparation: 6–8 minutes; Cooking: 12 minutes

1 Line a large baking sheet with baking parchment or sprinkle it lightly with flour. Set aside. Combine the cheeses in a bowl, then add the cayenne and beaten egg and mix well.

2 Place one wonton wrapper at a time on a board. Brush the edges with egg. Spoon a little filling in the centre. Pull the top corner down to the bottom corner, to make a triangle.

3 Transfer the filled wontons to the prepared baking sheet.

4 Heat the oil in a deep-fryer or large pan. Slip in as many wontons at one time as can be accommodated without overcrowding. Fry them for 2–3 minutes on each side or until the fritters are golden. Remove with a slotted spoon and keep warm while you make the remaining fritters. Drain well on kitchen paper and serve immediately.

> **Cook's Tip**
> *The optimum temperature for frying wontons is 190°C/375°F. If you do not have a thermometer, drop a cube of stale bread into the oil; it should brown in 30–40 seconds.*

Soba Noodles Energy 353kcal/1479kJ; Protein 5.5g; Carbohydrate 75.7g, of which sugars 4.1g; Fat 0.2g, of which saturates 0g; Cholesterol 0mg; Calcium 23mg; Fibre 0.2g; Sodium 2150mg.
Cheese Fritters Energy 112kcal/467kJ; Protein 3.5g; Carbohydrate 8.7g, of which sugars 0.4g; Fat 7.2g, of which saturates 2.3g; Cholesterol 20mg; Calcium 59mg; Fibre 0.3g; Sodium 44mg.

Fried Black Pudding

Spanish morcilla – black pudding – is very popular throughout Spain. It is flavoured with spices and herbs, usually including garlic and oregano, and has a wonderfully rich, spicy taste.

Serves 4
15ml/1 tbsp olive oil
1 onion, thinly sliced
2 garlic cloves, thinly sliced
5ml/1 tsp dried oregano
5ml/1 tsp paprika
225g/8oz black pudding
   (blood sausage), cut into
   12 thick slices
1 thin French stick, sliced into 12
30ml/2 tbsp fino sherry
sugar, to taste
salt and ground black pepper
chopped fresh oregano, to garnish

Preparation: 5 minutes; Cooking: 15 minutes

1 Heat the olive oil in a large frying pan and fry the sliced onion, garlic, oregano and paprika for about 7–8 minutes until the onion is softened and has turned golden brown.

2 Add the slices of black pudding, then increase the heat and cook them for 3 minutes, without stirring. Turn them over carefully with a spatula and cook for a further 3 minutes until the slices of black pudding are crisp.

3 Arrange the rounds of bread on a large serving plate and top each with a slice of black pudding.

4 Stir the sherry into the onions and add a little sugar to taste. Heat, swirling the mixture around the pan until bubbling, then season with salt and black pepper.

5 Spoon a little of the onion mixture on top of each slice of black pudding. Scatter the oregano over and serve.

> **Cook's Tip**
> If you can find real morcilla, serve it neat: simply fry the slices in olive oil and use to top little rounds of bread. If you cannot find black pudding, you can use red chorizo instead.

Walnut & Goat's Cheese Bruschetta

The combination of toasted walnuts and melting goat's cheese is lovely in this simple lunchtime snack, which can be served with a dressed salad if the occasion calls for it.

Serves 4
50g/2oz/½ cup walnut pieces
4 thick slices walnut bread
120ml/4fl oz/½ cup French
   dressing
200g/7oz chèvre or other
   semi-soft goat's cheese

Preparation: 5 minutes; Cooking: 3–5 minutes

1 Preheat the grill (broiler). Spread out the walnut pieces on a baking sheet. Lightly toast them, shaking the baking sheet once or twice so that they cook evenly, then remove and set them aside, leaving them to cool on the baking sheet.

2 Put the walnut bread on a foil-lined grill rack and lightly toast on one side. Turn the slices over and drizzle the untoasted side of each with 15ml/1 tbsp of the French dressing so that it soaks in a little.

3 Cut the goat's cheese into 12 slices and place three on each piece of bread. Grill (broil) under medium heat for about 3 minutes, until the cheese is melting and beginning to brown and bubble on the surface.

4 Transfer the bruschetta to serving plates, sprinkle with the toasted walnuts and drizzle with the remaining French dressing. Serve the bruschetta immediately with salad leaves.

> **Cook's Tip**
> Walnut bread is sold in most large supermarkets and makes an interesting alternative to ordinary crusty bread, although a freshly baked loaf of the latter is fine if speciality breads are not available. If using crusty bread, try to find a slender loaf to slice, so that the portions are not too wide. If you can only buy a large loaf, cut the slices in half to make neat, chunky pieces, perfect for making bruschetta.

Black Pudding Energy 506kcal/2137kJ; Protein 18.4g; Carbohydrate 77.8g, of which sugars 4.7g; Fat 14.8g, of which saturates 5.2g; Cholesterol 38mg; Calcium 171mg; Fibre 3.1g; Sodium 1422mg.
Bruschetta Energy 558kcal/2321kJ; Protein 16.7g; Carbohydrate 25.6g, of which sugars 2.2g; Fat 37.2g, of which saturates 12.7g; Cholesterol 47mg; Calcium 137mg; Fibre 1.2g; Sodium 841mg.

Rice Tortitas

Like miniature tortillas, these little rice pancakes are good served hot, either plain or with tomato sauce for dipping. They make an excellent scoop for any soft vegetable mixture or dip – a very Spanish way of eating.

Serves 4
30ml/2 tbsp olive oil
115g/4oz/1 cup cooked long
   grain white rice
1 potato, grated

4 spring onions (scallions),
   thinly sliced
1 garlic clove, finely chopped
15ml/1 tbsp chopped
   fresh parsley
3 large (US extra large)
   eggs, beaten
2.5ml/½ tsp paprika
salt and ground black pepper

Preparation: 6–7 minutes; Cooking: 11–12 minutes

1 Heat half the olive oil in a large frying pan and stir-fry the rice, with the potato, spring onions and garlic, over a high heat for 3 minutes until golden.

2 Tip the rice and vegetable mixture into a bowl and stir in the parsley and eggs, with the paprika and plenty of salt and pepper. Mix well.

3 Heat the remaining oil in the frying pan and drop in large spoonfuls of the rice mixture, leaving room for spreading. Cook the tortitas for 1–2 minutes on each side.

4 Drain the tortitas on kitchen paper and keep hot while cooking the remaining mixture. Pile the cooked tortitas on a serving platter or on individual plates and serve hot.

Cook's Tip
These tortitas can be used as a base, for example for cooked chicken livers, instead of the usual sliced bread. Children like them as they are, with a puddle of tomato ketchup for dipping.

Deep-fried Onion Rings

These are a very popular accompaniment for grilled meats, especially steaks and burgers. They also provide a crisp contrast when served with sliced hard-boiled eggs or fried mushrooms.

Serves 4
2 Spanish onions, thickly sliced
1 large egg white, lightly beaten
60ml/4 tbsp plain
   (all-purpose) flour
groundnut oil for deep-frying
salt and ground black pepper

Preparation: 4 minutes; Cooking: 6 minutes

1 Separate the onion slices into rings. Dip them into the egg white and stir to coat on all sides.

2 Season the flour with salt and pepper, then dip the onion rings into it, one at a time, until evenly coated.

3 Heat the oil for deep-frying to 190°C/375°F, or until a cube of day-old bread browns in 30–40 seconds. Fry the onion rings for 3–4 minutes, until browned and crisp. Drain on kitchen paper and serve immediately.

Variations
• *For corn-crusted onion rings, soak red onion rings in milk for about 30 minutes. Drain, then dip into coarse cornmeal (polenta), mixed with a pinch each of dried red chilli flakes, paprika and ground toasted cumin seeds. Deep-fry.*
• *For spicy onion rings, mix 90ml/6 tbsp chick-pea flour (besan or gram flour) with 2.5ml/½ tsp each of ground cumin, ground coriander, chilli powder and garam masala. Season and add 1 chopped green chilli and 30ml/2 tbsp chopped fresh coriander (cilantro). Mix with 45–60ml/3–4 tbsp cold water to make a fairly thick batter. Dip the onion rings into the batter, then deep-fry until crisp.*
• *For onion tempura, beat 2 egg yolks with 150ml/¼ pint/ ⅔ cup iced sparkling water. Lightly mix in 115g/4oz sifted self-raising (self-rising) flour and a pinch of salt, leaving the batter lumpy. Dip onion rings into the batter and deep-fry.*

Onion Rings Energy 214kcal/880kJ; Protein 1.4g; Carbohydrate 8.9g, of which sugars 6.3g; Fat 19.5g, of which saturates 2.3g; Cholesterol 0mg; Calcium 28mg; Fibre 1.6g; Sodium 4mg.
Rice Tortitas Energy 185kcal/776kJ; Protein 6.8g; Carbohydrate 17.6g, of which sugars 1.2g; Fat 10.4g, of which saturates 2.1g; Cholesterol 143mg; Calcium 56mg; Fibre 1.3g; Sodium 63mg.

Toasted Ciabatta with Tomatoes, Cheese & Marjoram Flowers

Here is a very simple but tasty method of using marjoram flowers. The combination of cheese, tomato and marjoram is popular, but lots of extras can be added, such as capers, olives, anchovies or slices of roasted peppers.

Serves 2
1 ciabatta loaf
4 tomatoes
115g/4oz mozzarella or
   Cheddar cheese
15ml/1 tbsp olive oil
15ml/1 tbsp marjoram flowers
salt and ground black pepper

Preparation: 4 minutes; Cooking: 4–5 minutes

1 Preheat the grill (broiler) to high. Cut the loaf in half lengthwise and toast very lightly under the grill until it has turned a pale golden brown.

2 Meanwhile, skin the tomatoes by plunging them in boiling water for 30 seconds, then refreshing them in cold water. Peel and cut into thick slices.

3 Slice or grate the mozzarella or Cheddar cheese. Lightly drizzle the olive oil over the bread and top with the tomato slices and sliced or grated cheese. Season with salt and pepper and scatter the marjoram flowers over the top. Drizzle with a little more olive oil.

4 Place under the hot grill until the cheese bubbles and is just starting to brown. Serve immediately.

Cook's Tip
Add marjoram flowers to your favourite pizza topping. Sprinkle over 7.5–15ml/½–1 tbsp flowers or flowering tops and add a few of the leaves. The flavours are strong, so marjoram flowers should be used with care, especially if you haven't tried them before. The amount you use will depend on your own palate.

Tomato & Mozzarella Toasts

These resemble mini pizzas and are good with drinks before a dinner party. You can prepare them several hours in advance and pop them in the oven just as your guests arrive. Ring the changes as regards toppings to satisfy meat-eaters and vegetarians alike.

Serves 6–8
3 sfilatini (thin ciabatta)
about 250ml/8 fl oz/1 cup
   sun-dried tomato purée (paste)
3 x 150g/5oz packets mozzarella
   cheese, drained and chopped
about 10ml/2 tsp dried oregano
   or mixed herbs
30–45ml/2–3 tbsp olive oil
ground black pepper

Preparation: 3 minutes; Cooking: 7 minutes

1 Preheat the oven to 220°C/425°F/Gas 7. Also preheat the grill (broiler). Cut each sfilatino on the diagonal into 12–15 slices, discarding the ends.

2 Grill (broil) until lightly toasted on both sides. Spread sun-dried tomato purée on one side of each slice of toast. Arrange the mozzarella over the tomato purée.

3 Put the toasts on baking sheets, sprinkle with herbs and pepper to taste and drizzle with oil. Bake for 5 minutes, or until the mozzarella has melted and is bubbling. Leave the toasts to cool for a few minutes before serving.

Variations
These tasty toast treats are capable of infinite variation. Instead of sun-dried tomato purée or paste, try spreading them with a fruity chutney, a mild piquant pepper ketchup or even Dijon mustard. Toppings could include anchovies, olives or even figs.

Cook's Tip
Mozzarella can also be bought as tiny balls. If you prefer to use these, just halve them and place on top of the tomato purée.

Ciabatta Energy 502kcal/2113kJ; Protein 22.3g; Carbohydrate 58.2g, of which sugars 9.3g; Fat 21.7g, of which saturates 9.5g; Cholesterol 33mg; Calcium 343mg; Fibre 4.3g; Sodium 783mg.
Toasts Energy 227kcal/947kJ; Protein 13.3g; Carbohydrate 10.9g, of which sugars 4.8g; Fat 14.8g, of which saturates 8.2g; Cholesterol 33mg; Calcium 230mg; Fibre 1.2g; Sodium 365mg.

Fried Rice Balls Stuffed with Mozzarella

These deep-fried balls are very popular snacks, which is hardly surprising as they are quite delicious.

Serves 4

1 quantity risotto with Parmesan cheese or mushroom risotto

3 eggs
breadcrumbs and plain (all-purpose) flour, to coat
115g/4oz/⅔ cup mozzarella cheese, cut into small cubes
oil, for deep-frying
dressed curly endive and cherry tomatoes, to serve

Preparation: 5 minutes; Cooking: 6–9 minutes

1 Put the risotto in a bowl and allow it to cool completely. Beat two of the eggs, and stir them into the bowl of cold risotto until the ingredients are well mixed.

2 Use your hands to form the rice mixture into balls the size of a large egg. If the mixture is too moist to hold its shape well, stir in a few tablespoons of breadcrumbs.

3 Poke a hole in the centre of each ball with your finger, then fill it with a few small cubes of mozzarella, and close the hole over again with the rice mixture.

4 Heat the oil for deep-frying in a wok or deep-fryer to a temperature of 190°C/375°F or until a small piece of bread sizzles as soon as it is dropped in.

5 Spread some flour on a plate. Beat the remaining egg in a shallow bowl. Sprinkle another plate with breadcrumbs. Roll the balls in the flour, then in the egg, and finally in the breadcrumbs, making sure they are coated all over.

6 Fry the coated rice balls a few at a time in the hot oil until golden and crisp. Drain on kitchen paper while the remaining balls are being fried. Pile on to a serving platter and serve hot, with a simple salad of dressed curly endive leaves and cherry tomatoes.

Mozzarella & Tomato Skewers

Stacks of flavour – layers of oven-baked mozzarella, tomatoes, basil and bread. These colourful kebabs will be popular with adults and children alike.

Serves 4

12 slices white country bread, each about 1cm/½in thick

45ml/3 tbsp olive oil
225g/8oz mozzarella cheese, cut into 5mm/¼ in slices
3 ripe plum tomatoes, cut into 5mm/¼ in slices
15g/½oz/½ cup fresh basil leaves, plus extra to garnish
salt and ground black pepper
30ml/2 tbsp chopped fresh flat leaf parsley, to garnish

Preparation: 3 minutes; Cooking: 13–15 minutes

1 Preheat the oven to 220°C/425°F/Gas 7. Trim the crusts from the bread and cut each slice into four equal squares. Arrange on a baking sheet and brush with half the olive oil. Bake for 3–5 minutes until the squares are a pale golden colour.

2 Remove the bread squares from the oven and place them on a chopping board with the sliced mozzarella and tomatoes and the fresh basil leaves.

3 Make 16 stacks, each starting with a square of bread, then a slice of mozzarella topped with a slice of tomato and a basil leaf. Sprinkle with salt and pepper, then repeat, ending with a piece of bread. Push a skewer through each stack and place on the baking sheet.

4 Drizzle the kebabs with the remaining oil and bake for 10–12 minutes until the cheese begins to melt. Garnish with basil and flat leaf parsley.

> **Cook's Tips**
> • If you use wooden skewers, soak them in water first, to prevent them from scorching during the cooking time.
> • The bread for these skewers needs to be quite robust, so don't be tempted to use slices from a soft white sandwich loaf.

Rice Balls Energy 670kcal/2792kJ; Protein 23.8g; Carbohydrate 73.8g, of which sugars 1.5g; Fat 31.2g, of which saturates 18.2g; Cholesterol 192mg; Calcium 383mg; Fibre 0.7g; Sodium 621mg.
Skewers Energy 472kcal/1981kJ; Protein 20g; Carbohydrate 47.2g, of which sugars 5g; Fat 24g, of which saturates 10g; Cholesterol 36mg; Calcium 341mg; Fibre 2.4g; Sodium 726mg.

Chinese-steamed Prawns

This is a wonderfully simple dish, widely eaten in China but equally popular in other parts of the world.

Serves 4
350–450g/12oz–1lb large raw
  prawns (shrimp)
soy sauce, to serve

Preparation: 0 minutes; Cooking: 2–3 minutes

1 Place the raw prawns in a large bamboo steamer. Steam over a high heat for 2–3 minutes, or until the prawns have turned pink. Pile the prawns on plates and serve immediately with the soy sauce for dipping.

Garlic Prawns

For this simple Spanish tapas dish, you really need fresh raw prawns which absorb the flavours of the garlic and chilli as they fry. Have everything ready for last-minute cooking so you can take it to the table while it is still sizzling.

Serves 4
350–450g/12oz–1lb large raw
  prawns (jumbo shrimp)
2 fresh red chillies
75ml/5 tbsp olive oil
3 garlic cloves, crushed
salt and ground black pepper

Preparation: 5 minutes; Cooking: 3 minutes

1 Remove the heads and shells from the prawns, leaving the tails intact. Devein the prawns.

2 Halve each chilli lengthways and discard the seeds. Heat the oil in a flameproof pan, suitable for serving. (Alternatively, use a frying pan and have a warmed serving dish ready in the oven.)

3 Add all the prawns, chilli and garlic to the pan and cook over a high heat for about 3 minutes, stirring until the prawns turn pink. Season lightly with salt and pepper and serve immediately.

Aromatic Tiger Prawns

There is no elegant way to eat these aromatic prawns – just hold them by the tails, pull them off the sticks with your fingers and pop them into your mouth.

Serves 4
16 raw tiger prawns (shrimp) or
  scampi (extra large shrimp) tails
2.5ml/½ tsp chilli powder
5ml/1 tsp fennel seeds
5 Sichuan or black peppercorns
1 star anise, broken into segments
1 cinnamon stick, broken into
  pieces
30ml/2 tbsp groundnut (peanut)
  or sunflower oil
2 garlic cloves, chopped
2cm/¾in piece fresh root ginger,
  peeled and finely chopped
1 shallot, chopped
30ml/2 tbsp water
30ml/2 tbsp rice vinegar
30ml/2 tbsp soft brown or palm
  (jaggery) sugar
salt and ground black pepper
lime slices and chopped spring
  onion (scallions), to garnish

Preparation: 5 minutes; Cooking: 15 minutes

1 Thread the prawns or scampi tails in pairs on 8 wooden cocktail sticks. Set aside.

2 Heat a frying pan over medium heat, put in all the chilli powder, fennel seeds, Sichuan or black peppercorns, star anise and cinnamon stick and dry-fry for 1–2 minutes to release the flavours. Leave to cool, then grind coarsely in a grinder or tip into a mortar and crush with a pestle.

3 Heat the groundnut or sunflower oil in a shallow pan, add the garlic, ginger and chopped shallot and then fry gently until very lightly coloured. Add the crushed spices and seasoning and cook the mixture gently for 2 minutes. Pour in the water and simmer, stirring constantly, for 5 minutes more.

4 Add the rice vinegar and soft brown or palm sugar, stir until dissolved, then add the prawns or scampi tails. Cook for about 3–5 minutes, until the seafood has turned pink, but is still very juicy. Serve hot, garnished with lime slices and spring onion.

Chinese Prawns Energy 67kcal/281kJ; Protein 15.4g; Carbohydrate 0g, of which sugars 0g; Fat 0.5g, of which saturates 0.1g; Cholesterol 171mg; Calcium 69mg; Fibre 0g; Sodium 166mg.
Garlic Prawns Energy 118kcal/495kJ; Protein 17.9g; Carbohydrate 3g, of which sugars 3g; Fat 3.9g, of which saturates 0.5g; Cholesterol 195mg; Calcium 83mg; Fibre 0.4g; Sodium 234mg.
Tiger Prawns Energy 142kcal/593kJ; Protein 13.4g; Carbohydrate 9g, of which sugars 8.7g; Fat 6g, of which saturates 0.7g; Cholesterol 146mg; Calcium 67mg; Fibre 0.2g; Sodium 144mg.

Prawn & Sesame Toasts

These attractive little toast triangles are ideal for serving with pre-dinner drinks and are always a favourite hot snack at parties. They are surprisingly easy to prepare and you can cook them in your wok for just a few minutes. Serve them with a sweet chilli sauce for dipping.

Serves 4

225g/8oz peeled raw
    prawns (shrimp)
15ml/1 tbsp sherry
15ml/1 tbsp soy sauce
30ml/2 tbsp cornflour (cornstarch)
2 egg whites
4 slices white bread
115g/4oz/1/2 cup sesame seeds
oil, for deep-frying
sweet chilli sauce, to serve

Preparation: 6 minutes; Cooking: 6–9 minutes

1 Put the prawns, sherry, soy sauce and cornflour in a food processor. Pulse until the ingredients are processed to a rough paste which retains some texture.

2 In a grease-free bowl, whisk the egg whites until stiff. Fold them into the prawn and cornflour mixture.

3 Cut each slice of bread into four triangular quarters. Spread out the sesame seeds on a large plate. Spread the prawn paste over one side of each bread triangle, then press the coated sides into the sesame seeds so that they stick and cover the prawn paste.

4 Heat the oil in a wok or deep-fryer, to 190°C/375°F or until a cube of bread, added to the oil, browns in about 45 seconds. Add the toasts, a few at a time, prawn side down, and deep-fry for 2–3 minutes, then turn the toasts over carefully and fry on the other side until golden.

5 Drain on kitchen paper and serve hot with sweet chilli sauce.

> **Variation**
> *Crabmeat can be used instead of peeled raw prawns (shrimp). Use fresh crab if you can get it, or thawed frozen crabmeat.*

Sweet Potato, Pumpkin & Prawn Cakes

This unusual Asian combination makes a delicious dish which needs only a fish sauce or soy sauce to dip into. Serve with noodles or fried rice for a lovely light meal.

Serves 4

200g/7oz/1 2/3 cups strong white
    bread flour
2.5ml/1/2 tsp salt
2.5ml/1/2 tsp dried yeast
175ml/6fl oz/3/4 cup warm water
1 egg, beaten
200g/7oz raw prawns (shrimp)
225g/8oz pumpkin, peeled,
    seeded and grated
150g/5oz sweet potato, grated
2 spring onions (scallions),
    chopped
50g/2oz water chestnuts,
    chopped
2.5ml/1/2 tsp chilli sauce
1 garlic clove, crushed
juice of 1/2 lime
vegetable oil, for deep-frying
lime wedges, to serve

Preparation: 8 minutes; Cooking: 12 minutes

1 Sift together the flour and salt into a large bowl and make a well in the centre. In a separate container dissolve the yeast in the water until creamy, then pour into the centre of the flour and salt mixture. Pour in the egg and set aside for a few minutes until bubbles appear. Mix to form a smooth batter.

2 Peel the prawns, if necessary, then place in a pan with just enough boiling water to cover. Simmer for about 2 minutes or until the prawns have turned pink. Drain, rinse in cold water and drain again well. Coarsely chop the prawns, then place in a bowl with the pumpkin and sweet potato.

3 Add the spring onions, water chestnuts, chilli sauce, garlic and lime juice and mix well. Fold into the batter mixture carefully until evenly mixed.

4 Heat a 1cm/1/2 in layer of oil in a large frying pan until really hot. Spoon in the batter in heaps, leaving space between each one, and cook until golden on both sides. Drain on kitchen paper and serve with the lime wedges.

Sesame Toasts Energy 392Kcal/1634kJ; Protein 19.1g; Carbohydrate 21.1g, of which sugars 1.2g; Fat 25.8g, of which saturates 3.4g; Cholesterol 110mg; Calcium 270mg; Fibre 2.7g; Sodium 557mg.
Prawn Cakes Energy 317kcal/1346kJ; Protein 18.2g; Carbohydrate 57.6g, of which sugars 9.1g; Fat 3.2g, of which saturates 0.9g; Cholesterol 145mg; Calcium 216mg; Fibre 6g; Sodium 383mg.

Oysters on the Half-shell

Ireland is famous for oysters. The best native ones come from the Galway area on the west coast and, every September, festivals are held in Galway and Clarenbridge to celebrate the beginning of the new season. Whatever the source of the oysters you buy, enjoy them with freshly made brown soda bread and butter, and a cool glass of Guinness or white wine.

Serves 2–4
24 Galway oysters, in the shell
crushed ice and dulse or dillisk
(soaked if dried), to garnish
soda bread and butter, and lemon
wedges, to serve

Preparation: 14 minutes; Cooking: 0 minutes

1 Use a blunt-ended oyster knife to shuck the oysters: insert the end of the knife between the shells near the hinge and work it until you cut through the muscle that holds the shells together. Catch the oyster liquid in a bowl.

2 When the oysters are all open, discard the flat shells. Divide the oysters, in the deep halves, among four serving plates lined with crushed ice and soaked dulse. Strain the reserved liquid over the oysters. Serve immediately with the lemon wedges for squeezing over each portion.

> **Cook's Tips**
> • *Although they were once plentiful, Galway oysters are now a rare delicacy and should be eaten raw – buy them with their shells tightly clamped together, showing that they are still alive. The edible seaweed, dulse, or dillisk as it is also known, is an appropriate garnish for oysters.*
> • *If you want oysters for a cooked dish, look for the widely cultivated, larger Pacific oysters, which are available all year round, unlike the native oyster which is found only when there's an 'r' in the month. In Britain, native oysters are named after their place of origin, such as the Irish Galway and the English Whitstable, Helford and Colchester; and in America the best known of the eastern and Atlantic oysters is the Blue Point.*

Scallops with Bacon & Sage

Many people consider scallops the finest of all seafood, with their tender flesh and pure, sweet flavour. This dish adds bacon for a contrasting taste. Samphire, a salty asparagus-like plant that grows on sea margins around England, goes very well with the scallops. It can be obtained from fishmongers in summer.

Serves 4
15ml/1 tbsp olive oil
4 streaky (fatty) bacon rashers (strips), cut into 2.5cm/1in strips
2–3 fresh sage leaves, chopped
small piece of butter
8 large or 16 small scallops
15ml/1 tbsp fresh lemon juice
100ml/3½ fl oz dry cider or white wine

Preparation: 4 minutes; Cooking: 6 minutes

1 Heat a frying pan and add the oil, bacon and sage. Cook over medium heat, stirring occasionally, until the bacon is golden brown. Lift out and keep warm.

2 Add the butter to the pan and when hot add the scallops. Cook for about 1 minute on each side until browned. Lift out and keep warm with the bacon.

3 Add the lemon juice and cider to the pan and, scraping up any sediment, bring just to the boil. Continue bubbling gently until the mixture has reduced to a few tablespoons of syrupy sauce that barely covers the bottom of the pan.

4 Serve the scallops and bacon with the sauce drizzled over.

> **Cook's Tips**
> • *Scallops that are particularly large can be sliced in half so that they form two discs before cooking (cut off the corals and cook these separately in the pan).*
> • *To prepare samphire (glasswort), wash it and pick off the soft fleshy branches, discarding the thicker woody stalks. Drop it into boiling water for just 1 minute before draining and serving.*

Scallops Energy 179kcal/745kJ; Protein 15.6g; Carbohydrate 1.9g, of which sugars 0.2g; Fat 10.4g, of which saturates 3.3g; Cholesterol 42mg; Calcium 19mg; Fibre 0g; Sodium 414mg.
Oysters Energy 78Kcal/330kJ; Protein 13g; Carbohydrate 3.3g, of which sugars 0g; Fat 1.6g, of which saturates 0.3g; Cholesterol 68mg; Calcium 168mg; Fibre 0g; Sodium 612mg.

Sautéed Mussels with Garlic & Herbs

These mussels are served without their shells, in a delicious paprika-flavoured sauce. Eat them with cocktail sticks.

Serves 4
900g/2lb fresh mussels
1 lemon slice
90ml/6 tbsp olive oil
2 shallots, finely chopped
1 garlic clove, finely chopped
15ml/1 tbsp chopped
   fresh parsley
2.5ml/½ tsp sweet paprika
1.5ml/¼ tsp dried chilli flakes
parsley sprigs, to garnish

Preparation: 4 minutes; Cooking: 4–6 minutes

1 Scrub the mussels, discarding any damaged ones as well as any that are open and which do not close when tapped with the back of a knife.

2 Put the mussels in a large pan with 250ml/8fl oz/1 cup water and the slice of lemon. Bring to the boil and cook for 3–4 minutes, removing the mussels with a slotted spoon as they open and putting them in a bowl.

3 Discard any that remain closed. Using a sharp knife, cut the mussels out of the shells and drain on kitchen paper.

4 Heat the oil in a sauté pan, add the mussels and cook, stirring, for a minute. Remove from the pan.

5 Add the shallots and garlic and cook, covered, over a low heat, for about 5 minutes, until soft and tender. Stir in the parsley, paprika and chilli, then add the mussels with any juices. Cook briefly.

6 Remove the pan from the heat, cover and leave for 1–2 minutes to let the flavours mingle.

7 Pile the mussels into a large warmed bowl or spoon into individual bowls, garnish with parsley and serve immediately.

Fried Squid with Salt & Pepper

Cooking squid couldn't be simpler. Salt and pepper are used to season, and that's it. A Chinese tradition for all sorts of fish and shellfish, this is a Vietnamese and Cambodian favourite, too. Ideal snack and finger food, the tender squid can be served on its own, with noodles or – as it is in the streets of Saigon – with baguette and chillies. Those who like chilli can replace the black pepper with chopped dried chilli or chilli powder. Butterflied prawns, with the shells removed, are also delicious cooked in this way. To butterfly prawns, cut down the backs and open them out.

Serves 4
450g/1lb baby or medium squid
30ml/2 tbsp coarse salt
15ml/1 tbsp ground black pepper
50g/2oz/½ cup rice flour or
   cornflour (cornstarch)
vegetable oil, for deep-frying
2 limes, halved

Preparation: 8 minutes; Cooking: 6 minutes

1 Prepare the squid by pulling the head away from the body. Sever the tentacles from the rest and trim them. Reach inside the body sac and pull out the backbone, then clean the squid inside and out, removing any skin. Rinse well in cold water.

2 Using a sharp knife, slice the squid into rings and pat them dry with kitchen paper. Put them in a dish with the tentacles.

3 Combine the salt and pepper with the rice flour or cornflour, add it to the squid and toss well, making sure that all the pieces are evenly coated.

4 Heat the oil for deep-frying in a wok or heavy pan. Cook the squid in batches, until the rings turn crisp and golden. Drain on kitchen paper and serve with limes to squeeze over.

> **Variation**
> Use chopped dried chillies or chilli powder instead of black pepper, or flavour the flour with ground coriander or cumin.

Sautéed Mussels Energy 214kcal/888kJ; Protein 12g; Carbohydrate 1.3g, of which sugars 0.9g; Fat 17.9g, of which saturates 2.6g; Cholesterol 27mg; Calcium 145mg; Fibre 0.4g; Sodium 144mg.
Fried Squid Energy 339Kcal/1405kJ; Protein 14g; Carbohydrate 5g, of which sugars 0g; Fat 29g, of which saturates 4g; Cholesterol 146mg; Calcium 70mg; Fibre 0g; Sodium 140mg.

Fish Cakes

A well-made fishcake is always a treat and they can be made with salmon or any fresh or smoked white fish. This dish makes a little fish go a long way, but don't stretch it beyond equal quantities of fish and potato. Parsley sauce is the traditional accompaniment, but for a change, try mushroom sauce or a rich tomato sauce. A cold sauce such as tzatziki would also go well with the fish cakes.

Serves 4
450g/1lb fresh salmon or smoked white fish
wedge of lemon
small bay leaf and a few fresh parsley stalks
25g/1oz/2 tbsp butter
1 onion, finely chopped
450g/1lb potatoes, cooked and mashed
30ml/2 tbsp chopped fresh parsley
pinhead oatmeal, to coat
butter and oil, for frying
ground black pepper

Preparation: 5–6 minutes; Cooking: 14 minutes

1 Rinse the fish and cut it into medium-sized pieces. Put it into a pan with the lemon, bay leaf and parsley stalks and enough cold water to cover. Bring slowly to the boil, then reduce the heat and simmer gently for 5–7 minutes. Remove the fish and drain well.

2 When cool enough to handle, flake the flesh and discard the skin and bones. Melt the butter in a large pan, add the onion and cook gently for a few minutes until softened but not coloured. Add the flaked fish, potato and parsley. Season to taste with pepper.

3 Turn the mixture on to a work surface generously covered with pinhead oatmeal. Divide in half, and then quarter each piece. Form into eight flat cakes and coat them evenly with the oatmeal on all sides.

4 Heat a little butter and an equal quantity of oil in a heavy frying pan, add the fishcakes (in batches, if necessary) and fry until golden on both sides. Drain on kitchen paper and serve immediately with your favourite sauce.

Thai-style Fish Cakes

These light fish cakes are scented with the exotic flavours of sesame, lime and ginger. They make a tempting appetizer served simply with a wedge of lime for squeezing over, but are also perfect for a light lunch or supper, served with a crunchy, refreshing salad.

Makes 25
500g/1¼lb salmon fillet, skinned and boned

45ml/3 tbsp dried breadcrumbs
30ml/2 tbsp mayonnaise
30ml/2 tbsp sesame seeds
30ml/2 tbsp light soy sauce
finely grated rind of 2 limes
10ml/2 tsp finely grated fresh root ginger
4 spring onions (scallions), finely sliced
vegetable oil, for frying
salt and ground black pepper
spring onions (scallions), to garnish
lime wedges, to serve

Preparation: 5 minutes; Cooking: 12–15 minutes; Chilling: 2 hours

1 Finely chop the salmon and place in a bowl. Add the breadcrumbs, mayonnaise, sesame seeds, soy sauce, lime rind, ginger and spring onions and use your fingers to mix well.

2 With wet hands, divide the mixture into 25 portions and shape each into a small round cake. Place the cakes on a baking sheet lined with baking parchment, cover and chill for at least two hours. They can be left overnight.

3 When you are ready to cook the fish cakes, heat about 5cm/2in vegetable oil in a wok and fry the fish cakes in batches, over a medium heat, for 2–3 minutes on each side.

4 Drain the fish cakes well on kitchen paper and serve warm or at room temperature, garnished with spring onion slivers and plenty of lime wedges for squeezing over.

> **Cook's Tip**
> When chopping the salmon, look out for stray bones and pick these out with tweezers.

Fish Cakes Energy 380Kcal/1584kJ; Protein 25.3g; Carbohydrate 20.5g, of which sugars 3.3g; Fat 22.4g, of which saturates 8.6g; Cholesterol 83mg; Calcium 49mg; Fibre 1.8g; Sodium 138mg.
Thai-style Fish Cakes Energy 83Kcal/343kJ; Protein 4.6g; Carbohydrate 1.6g, of which sugars 0.2g; Fat 6.5g, of which saturates 0.9g; Cholesterol 11mg; Calcium 16mg; Fibre 0.2g; Sodium 117mg.

Tuna & Corn Fish Cakes

Definitely one for younger members of the family who like the sweet taste of corn. The children may even enjoy helping you make some fishy-shaped cakes.

Serves 4
300g/11oz mashed potatoes
200g/7oz can tuna in soya
  oil, drained

115g/4oz/³⁄₄ cup canned or
  frozen corn
30ml/2 tbsp chopped
  fresh parsley
50g/2oz/1 cup fresh white or
  brown breadcrumbs
60ml/4 tbsp sunflower oil
salt and ground black pepper

Preparation: 6 minutes; Cooking: 12 minutes

1 Place the mashed potatoes in a large bowl. Flake the tuna with a fork and stir it into the potatoes with the corn and chopped fresh parsley.

2 Season the mixture to taste with salt and black pepper and mix together thoroughly, then shape into eight patty shapes.

3 Lightly coat the fish cakes in the breadcrumbs, pressing to adhere, then place on a baking sheet.

4 Heat the oil in a large frying pan and cook the fish cakes until crisp and golden brown on both sides, turning once. Serve hot.

Cook's Tip
For extra colour on the plate, add peas, broad (fava) beans or lightly cooked green beans. Broccoli would also be suitable.

Variation
For simple variations, try using canned sardines, red or pink salmon or smoked mackerel in place of the tuna, and instant mash when you're in a real hurry.

Fried Whitebait with Sherry Salsa

Small freshly fried fish are offered in every tapas bar in Spain. Black-backed anchovies taste the best, but whitebait are often easier to come by. They cook very quickly, in less than two minutes.

Serves 4
225g/8oz whitebait
30ml/2 tbsp seasoned plain
  (all-purpose) flour
60ml/4 tbsp olive oil
60ml/4 tbsp sunflower oil

For the salsa
1 shallot, finely chopped
2 garlic cloves, finely chopped
4 ripe tomatoes, roughly chopped
1 small red chilli, seeded and
  finely chopped
30ml/2 tbsp olive oil
60ml/4 tbsp sweet oloroso sherry
30–45ml/2–3 tbsp chopped
  mixed fresh herbs, such as
  parsley or basil
25g/1oz/¹⁄₂ cup stale white
  breadcrumbs
salt and ground black pepper

Preparation: 5–6 minutes; Cooking: 14 minutes

1 To make the salsa, place the chopped shallot, garlic, tomatoes, chilli and olive oil in a pan. Cover with a lid and cook gently for about 10 minutes.

2 Pour the sherry into the pan and season with salt and pepper to taste. Stir in the herbs and breadcrumbs, then cover and keep the salsa hot until the whitebait are ready.

3 Preheat the oven to 150°C/300°F/Gas 2. Wash the whitebait thoroughly, drain well and dry on kitchen paper, then dust in the seasoned flour.

4 Heat the oils together in a heavy frying pan and cook the fish in batches for 1–2 minutes until crisp and golden. Drain on kitchen paper and place in a bowl. Keep warm in the oven until all the fish are cooked. Serve at once with the salsa.

Cook's Tip
The trick when frying whitebait is not to crowd the pan, or the fish will simply clump together in a soggy and unattractive mass.

Fish Cakes Energy 231kcal/976kJ; Protein 17.5g; Carbohydrate 29.8g, of which sugars 4.4g; Fat 5.5g, of which saturates 0.9g; Cholesterol 25mg; Calcium 53mg; Fibre 2.1g; Sodium 330mg.
Whitebait Energy 406kcal/1683kJ; Protein 12.5g; Carbohydrate 12.4g, of which sugars 4.4g; Fat 32.6g, of which saturates 0.9g; Cholesterol 0mg; Calcium 502mg; Fibre 1.2g; Sodium 186mg.

Devilled Whitebait

This is the classic way of cooking whitebait, juvenile fish that are fried and eaten whole. In the UK whitebait are herring, but other types of fish are used elsewhere. Serve with lemon wedges and thinly sliced brown bread and butter, and eat them with your fingers.

Serves 4
oil for deep-frying
150ml/¼ pint/⅔ cup milk
115g/4oz/1 cup plain
(all-purpose) flour
450g/1lb whitebait, thawed if frozen and dried thoroughly on kitchen paper
salt, freshly ground black pepper and cayenne pepper

Preparation: 3 minutes; Cooking: 6–9 minutes

1 Heat the oil in a large pan or deep-fryer. Put the milk in a shallow bowl and spoon the flour into a plastic bag. Season the flour with salt, pepper and a little cayenne.

2 Dip a handful of the whitebait into the bowl of milk, drain well, then pop them into the paper bag. Shake gently to coat them evenly in the seasoned flour. Repeat until all the fish have been coated. This is the easiest method of flouring whitebait, but don't add too many at once, or they will stick together.

3 Heat the oil to 190°C/375°F or until a cube of stale bread, dropped into the oil, browns in 20 seconds. Add a batch of whitebait, preferably in a chip basket, and fry for 2–3 minutes, until crisp and golden brown. Drain and keep hot while you fry the rest. Sprinkle with more cayenne and serve very hot.

Cook's Tip
Devilled whitebait is traditionally served with tartare sauce. To make this, press 2 hard-boiled egg yolks through a sieve (strainer) into a bowl. Stir in 2 fresh egg yolks. Season to taste, then mix in 15ml/1 tbsp white wine vinegar. Add 300ml/½ pint/ 1¼ cups olive oil, trickling it in gradually while whisking the mixture as when making mayonnaise. Flavour with capers, chopped gherkin, chopped parsley and chives.

Surtido de Pescado

The Spanish enjoy and make the most of preserved fish. This is a very pretty dish, which uses whatever is easily available, and it makes an ideal party starter.

Serves 4
6 eggs
cos or romaine lettuce leaves
75–90ml/5–6 tbsp mayonnaise
90g/3½oz jar Avruga herring roe

2 x 115g/4oz cans sardines in oil
2 x 115g/4oz cans mackerel fillets in oil
2 x 150g/5oz jars cockles (small clams) in brine, drained
2 x 115g/4oz cans mussels or scallops in tomato sauce
fresh flat leaf parsley or dill sprigs, to garnish
lemon or lime wedges or slices, to serve

Preparation: 3–4 minutes; Cooking: 12 minutes

1 Put the eggs in a pan with enough water to cover and bring to the boil. Turn down the heat and simmer for 10 minutes. Drain immediately, then cover with cold water and set aside until completely cool. Peel the eggs and slice in half.

2 Arrange the lettuce leaves on a large serving platter, with the tips pointing outwards. (You may need to break off the bottom end of each leaf if the leaves are large.)

3 Place a teaspoonful or so of mayonnaise on the flat side of each halved egg and top with a spoonful of fish caviar. Carefully arrange in the centre of the dish. Arrange the sardines and mackerel fillets at four points on the plate. Spoon the pickled cockles into two of the gaps, opposite each other, and the mussels in sauce in the remaining gaps. Garnish with parsley sprigs or dill. Serve with lemon or lime.

Cook's Tip
Smoked salmon, kippers (smoked herrings) and rollmops (pickled herring fillets) can also be included on the platter. Try to maintain a balance between fish or shellfish pickled in brine or vinegar, with those in oil or sauce.

Devilled Whitebait Energy 656kcal/2718kJ; Protein 24.4g; Carbohydrate 6.6g, of which sugars 0.1g; Fat 59.4g, of which saturates 0g; Cholesterol 0mg; Calcium 1075mg; Fibre 0.3g; Sodium 288mg.
Surtido de Pescado Energy 622kcal/2588kJ; Protein 56.1g; Carbohydrate 2.7g, of which sugars 0.7g; Fat 43.2g, of which saturates 8.8g; Cholesterol 482mg; Calcium 373mg; Fibre 0.2g; Sodium 661mg.

Smoked Mackerel Pâté

A delicious dish that is simple to make.

Serves 6
4 smoked mackerel fillets, skinned
225g/8oz/1 cup cream cheese

1–2 garlic cloves, finely chopped
juice of 1 lemon
30ml/2 tbsp chopped fresh
    chervil, parsley or chives
15ml/1 tbsp Worcestershire sauce
salt and cayenne pepper

Preparation: 3 minutes; Cooking: 0 minutes; Make ahead

1 Break up the mackerel and put it in a food processor. Add the cream cheese, garlic, lemon juice and herbs. Process the mixture. Add Worcestershire sauce, salt and cayenne pepper to taste. Whizz to mix, then spoon the pâté into a dish, cover with clear film (plastic wrap) and chill.

Chicken Liver & Brandy Pâté

This pâté tastes so much better than anything you can buy in the supermarkets.

Serves 4
50g/2oz/¼ cup butter

350g/12oz chicken livers,
    trimmed and roughly chopped
30ml/2 tbsp brandy
30ml/2 tbsp double (heavy)
    cream
salt and ground black pepper

Preparation: 3 minutes; Cooking: 5–6 minutes; Make ahead

1 Heat the butter in a large frying pan. Add the chicken livers. Cook over a medium heat for 3–4 minutes, or until browned and cooked through. Add the brandy and allow to bubble for a few minutes. Let the mixture cool slightly, then place in a food processor with the cream and some salt and pepper.

2 Process the mixture until smooth and spoon into ramekin dishes. Level the surface and chill overnight to set. If making more than 1 day ahead, seal the surface of each portion with a layer of melted butter. Serve garnished with sprigs of parsley to add a little colour.

Figs with Prosciutto & Roquefort

In this easy, stylish dish, figs and honey balance the richness of the ham and cheese. Serve with warm bread for a simple appetizer before any rich main course.

Serves 4
8 fresh figs
75g/3oz prosciutto
45ml/3 tbsp clear honey
75g/3oz Roquefort cheese
ground black pepper

Preparation: 2–3 minutes; Cooking: 4–5 minutes

1 Preheat the grill (broiler). Quarter the figs and place on a foil-lined grill rack. Tear each slice of prosciutto into two or three pieces. Crumple the pieces of prosciutto and place them on the foil beside the figs. Brush the figs with 15ml/1 tbsp of the clear honey and cook under the grill until lightly browned.

2 Crumble the Roquefort cheese and divide among four plates, setting it to one side. Add the honey-grilled figs and ham and pour over any cooking juices caught on the foil. Drizzle the remaining honey over the figs, ham and cheese, and serve seasoned with plenty of ground black pepper.

Variations
• Any thinly sliced cured ham can be used instead of prosciutto: Westphalian, Bayonne, Culatello or Serrano.
• The figs could be replaced with fresh pears. Slice 2 ripe but firm dessert pears in quarters and remove the cores. Toss in olive oil and cook on a hot ridged grill or griddle pan for 2 minutes on each side. Drizzle balsamic vinegar over and cook for 1 minute more until nicely coloured.

Cook's Tip
Fresh figs are a delicious treat, whether you choose dark purple, yellow green or green-skinned varieties. When they are ripe, you can split them open with your fingers to reveal the soft, sweet flesh full of edible seeds. They also taste great stuffed with goat's cheese.

Mackerel Pâté Energy 344kcal/1421kJ; Protein 10.7g; Carbohydrate 0.5g, of which sugars 0.4g; Fat 33.3g, of which saturates 14.3g; Cholesterol 88mg; Calcium 57mg; Fibre 0.1g; Sodium 518mg.
Chicken Liver Pâté Energy 227kcal/942kJ; Protein 15.7g; Carbohydrate 0.2g, of which sugars 0.2g; Fat 16.3g, of which saturates 9.6g; Cholesterol 369mg; Calcium 13mg; Fibre 0g; Sodium 144mg.
Figs Energy 326kcal/1378kJ; Protein 10.7g; Carbohydrate 57.4g, of which sugars 57.4g; Fat 7.5g, of which saturates 3.8g; Cholesterol 25mg; Calcium 324mg; Fibre 6.9g; Sodium 512mg.

Chorizo in Olive Oil

Spanish chorizo sausage has a deliciously pungent taste; its robust seasoning of garlic, chilli and paprika flavours the ingredients it is cooked with. Frying chorizo with onions and olive oil is one of its simplest and most delicious uses.

Serves 4
75ml/5 tbsp extra virgin olive oil
350g/12oz chorizo sausage, sliced
1 large onion, thinly sliced
roughly chopped flat leaf parsley,
  to garnish

Preparation: 2 minutes; Cooking: 5 minutes

1 Heat the oil in a frying pan and fry the chorizo sausage over a high heat until beginning to colour. Remove from the pan with a slotted spoon.

2 Add the onion to the pan and fry until coloured. Return the sausage slices to the pan and heat through for 1 minute.

3 Tip the mixture into a shallow serving dish and scatter with the parsley. Serve with warm bread.

Variations
• Peppers go well with chorizo. Add slices of fresh red (bell) pepper or drained canned pimiento when frying the onion.
• A little fresh chilli would be a good addition, but don't overdo it as the chorizo already contains this seasoning. Choose mild fresnos or jalapenos, and remove the seeds.
• For those who prefer not to go for the burn, substitute sun-dried tomatoes. Use the ones that come packed in oil, so that you can drain off a little of the oil for frying the chorizo.

Cook's Tip
Chorizo is usually available in large supermarkets or delicatessens. Other similarly rich, spicy sausages can be used as a substitute.

Chicken Lettuce Parcels

Known as sang choy in Hong Kong, this is a popular assemble-it-yourself treat. The filling is served with crisp lettuce leaves, which are used as wrappers.

Serves 6
2 chicken breast fillets, total
  weight about 350g/12oz
4 dried Chinese mushrooms,
  soaked for 30 minutes in warm
  water to cover
30ml/2 tbsp vegetable oil
2 garlic cloves, crushed
6 drained canned water
  chestnuts, thinly sliced
30ml/2 tbsp light soy sauce
5ml/1 tsp Sichuan peppercorns,
  dry-fried and crushed
4 spring onions (scallions),
  finely chopped
5ml/1 tsp sesame oil
vegetable oil, for deep-frying
50g/2oz cellophane noodles
salt and ground black pepper
  (optional)
1 crisp lettuce, divided into leaves,
  and 60ml/4 tbsp hoisin sauce,
  to serve

Preparation: 8 minutes; Cooking: 10 minutes

1 Remove the skin from the chicken breast fillets, pat dry and set aside. Chop the chicken into thin strips. Drain the soaked mushrooms. Cut off and discard the mushroom stems; slice the caps finely and set aside.

2 Heat the oil in a wok or large frying pan. Add the garlic, then add the chicken. Stir-fry until the pieces are cooked through. Add the sliced mushrooms, water chestnuts, soy sauce and peppercorns. Toss for 2–3 minutes, then season. Stir in half the spring onions, then the sesame oil. Set aside.

3 Cut the chicken skin into strips, deep fry in hot oil until very crisp and drain on kitchen paper. Deep fry the noodles until crisp. Drain on kitchen paper.

4 Crush the noodles and put in a serving dish. Top with the chicken skin, chicken mixture and the remaining spring onions. Arrange the lettuce leaves on a platter. Toss the chicken and noodles to mix. Invite guests to take a lettuce leaf, spread the inside with hoisin sauce and add a spoonful of filling, turning in the sides of the leaf and rolling it into a parcel before eating it.

Chorizo Energy 408kcal/1689kJ; Protein 9.2g; Carbohydrate 15.2g, of which sugars 5.1g; Fat 35g, of which saturates 10.7g; Cholesterol 35mg; Calcium 58mg; Fibre 1.3g; Sodium 711mg.
Lettuce Parcels Energy 237kcal/984kJ; Protein 15.3g; Carbohydrate 7.6g, of which sugars 1.1g; Fat 16.1g, of which saturates 2g; Cholesterol 41mg; Calcium 24mg; Fibre 0.6g; Sodium 41mg.

Sweet & Salty Vegetable Crisps

The Spanish love new and colourful snacks. Try these brightly coloured crisps, which make an appealing alternative to potato crisps (US potato chips). Serve them with a bowl of creamy, garlicky mayonnaise, and use the crisps to scoop it up.

Serves 4
1 small fresh beetroot (beet)
caster (superfine) sugar and fine salt, for sprinkling
olive oil, for frying
coarse sea salt, to serve

Preparation: 3–4 minutes; Cooking: 6–8 minutes

1 Peel the beetroot and, using a mandolin or a vegetable peeler, cut it into very thin slices.

2 Lay the slices on kitchen paper and sprinkle them with sugar and fine salt.

3 Pour oil into a deep pan to a depth of 5cm/2in. Heat to 180°C/350°F or until a bread cube, added to the hot oil, turns golden in 1 minute. Cook the slices in batches, until they float to the surface and turn golden at the edges. Drain on kitchen paper and sprinkle with sea salt when cool.

Cook's Tip
Don't fry too many beetroot (beet) slices at once, or they will not become crisp. If you use a chip basket, it will be easy to lift the cooked crisps out so they can be drained on kitchen paper. Keep each batch hot while cooking the remainder.

Variation
Beetroot crisps are particularly flavoursome, but other naturally sweet root vegetables, such as carrots and sweet potato, also taste delicious when cooked in this way. You might like to make several different varieties and serve them heaped in separate small bowls.

Popcorn with Lime & Chilli

If the only popcorn you've had came out of a carton at the movies, try this Mexican speciality. The lime juice and chilli powder are inspired additions, and the snack is quite a healthy choice to serve with drinks.

Makes 1 large bowl
30ml/2 tbsp vegetable oil
225g/8oz/1¼ cups corn kernels for popcorn
10ml/2 tsp chilli powder
juice of 2 limes

Preparation: 0 minutes; Cooking: 5–6 minutes

1 Heat the oil in a large, heavy frying pan until it is very hot. Add the popcorn and immediately cover the pan tightly with a lid and reduce the heat.

2 After a few minutes the corn should start to pop. Resist the temptation to lift the lid to check. Shake the pan occasionally so that all the corn will be cooked and browned.

3 When the sound of popping corn has stopped, quickly remove the pan from the heat and allow to cool slightly. Take off the lid and with a spoon lift out and discard any corn kernels that have not popped. The uncooked corn will have fallen to the bottom of the pan and is completely inedible.

4 Add the chilli powder. Shake the pan again and again to make sure that all of the corn is covered with a colourful dusting of chilli.

5 Tip the popcorn into a large bowl and keep warm. Add a squeeze of lime juice immediately before serving.

Variation
Instead of tossing popcorn with chilli powder and lime juice, simply add salt and pepper, with a little butter to help the coating stick, if you like. For an unusual variation, try tossing popcorn with a little green or red pesto.

Vegetable Crisps Energy 113kcal/466kJ; Protein 0.4g; Carbohydrate 3.2g, of which sugars 3.1g; Fat 11g, of which saturates 1.6g; Cholesterol 0mg; Calcium 6mg; Fibre 0.5g; Sodium 508mg.
Popcorn Energy 1334kcal/5553kJ; Protein 13.9g; Carbohydrate 109.6g, of which sugars 2.5g; Fat 96.3g, of which saturates 9.7g; Cholesterol 0mg; Calcium 23mg; Fibre 0g; Sodium 9mg.

Roasted Coconut Cashew Nuts

Serve these wok-fried hot and sweet cashew nuts in paper or cellophane cones at parties.

Serves 6–8
15ml/1 tbsp groundnut (peanut) oil
30ml/2 tbsp clear honey

250g/9oz/2 cups cashew nuts
115g/4oz/1⅓ cups desiccated
  (dry unsweetened shredded)
  coconut
2 small fresh red chillies, seeded
  and finely chopped
salt and ground black pepper

Preparation: 2 minutes; Cooking: 3–4 minutes

1 Heat the oil in a wok or large frying pan and then stir in the honey. After a few seconds add the nuts and coconut and stir-fry until both are golden brown. Add the chillies, with salt and pepper to taste. Toss until all the ingredients are well mixed. Serve warm or cooled in paper cones or on saucers.

Raw Vegetable Platter

A colourful selection of raw vegetables, or crudités, makes a quick and easy accompaniment to drinks or before lunch.

Serves 6–8
2 red and yellow (bell) peppers,
  sliced lengthways
225g/8oz fresh baby corn,
  blanched
1 chicory (Belgian endive) head

(red or white), trimmed and
  leaves separated
175–225g/6–8oz thin asparagus,
  trimmed and blanched
small bunch radishes with small
  leaves attached, washed
175g/6oz cherry tomatoes,
  washed
12 quail's eggs, boiled for
  3 minutes, drained, refreshed
  and peeled
aioli or tapenade, for dipping

Preparation: 10 minutes; Cooking: 0 minutes

1 Arrange a selection of prepared vegetables, such as those above, on a serving plate. Cover with a damp dish towel until ready to serve.

Spiced Noodle Pancakes

The delicate rice noodles puff up in the hot oil to give a fabulous crunchy bite that melts in the mouth. For maximum enjoyment, serve the golden pancakes as soon as they are cooked and savour the subtle blend of spices and wonderfully crisp texture.

Serves 4
150g/5oz dried thin rice noodles
1 fresh red chilli, finely diced

10ml/2 tsp garlic salt
5ml/1 tsp ground ginger
¼ small red onion, very
  finely diced
5ml/1 tsp finely chopped
  lemon grass
5ml/1 tsp ground cumin
5ml/1 tsp ground coriander
large pinch of ground turmeric
salt
vegetable oil, for frying
sweet chilli sauce or sweet
  piquant pepper ketchup,
  for dipping

Preparation: 4 minutes; Cooking: 4–0 minutes

1 Roughly break up the noodles and place in a large bowl. Pour over enough boiling water to cover, and soak for 4–5 minutes. Drain and rinse under cold water. Dry on kitchen paper.

2 Transfer the noodles to a bowl and add the chilli, garlic salt, ground ginger, red onion, lemon grass, ground cumin, coriander and turmeric. Toss well to mix, and season with salt.

3 Heat 5–6cm/2–2½in oil in a wok. Working in batches, drop tablespoonfuls of the noodle mixture into the oil. Flatten using the back of a skimmer and cook for 1–2 minutes on each side until crisp and golden. Lift out from the wok.

4 Drain the noodle pancakes on kitchen paper and carefully transfer to a plate or a deep bowl. Serve immediately with the chilli sauce or sweet piquant pepper ketchup for dipping.

> **Cook's Tip**
> For deep-frying, choose very thin rice noodles. These can be cooked dry, but here are soaked and seasoned first.

Cashew Nuts Energy 301Kcal/1247kJ; Protein 7.2g; Carbohydrate 9.7g, of which sugars 5.5g; Fat 26.2g, of which saturates 11.1g; Cholesterol 0mg; Calcium 14mg; Fibre 3g; Sodium 95mg.
Vegetable Platter Energy 67kcal/281kJ; Protein 4.8g; Carbohydrate 6.6g, of which sugars 5.7g; Fat 2.8g, of which saturates 0.8g; Cholesterol 71mg; Calcium 33mg; Fibre 2.3g; Sodium 353mg.
Noodle Pancakes Energy 190Kcal/791kJ; Protein 2g; Carbohydrate 31.8g, of which sugars 0.9g; Fat 5.6g, of which saturates 0.7g; Cholesterol 0mg; Calcium 9mg; Fibre 0.2g; Sodium 496mg.

Spiced Plantain Chips

Plantains are more starchy than the bananas to which they are related, and must be cooked before being eaten. In Latin America the fruit is used much as a potato would be. This snack has a lovely sweet taste, which is balanced by the heat from the chilli powder and sauce. Cook the chips just before you plan to serve them.

Serves 4
2 large plantains
oil, for shallow frying
2.5ml/½ tsp chilli powder
5ml/1 tsp ground cinnamon
hot chilli sauce, to serve

Preparation: 2 minutes; Cooking: 6 minutes

1 Peel the plaintains. Cut off and throw away the ends, then slice the fruit into rounds, cutting slightly on the diagonal to give larger, flatter slices.

2 Pour the oil for frying into a small frying pan, to a depth of about 1cm/½in. Heat the oil until it is very hot, watching it closely all the time. It should register 190°C/375°F on a sugar thermometer. Test by carefully adding a slice of plantain; it should float and the oil should immediately bubble up around it.

3 Fry the plantain slices in small batches or the temperature of the oil will drop. When they are golden brown remove from the oil with a slotted spoon and drain on kitchen paper. Keep hot while cooking successive batches.

4 Mix the chilli powder with the cinnamon. Put the plantain chips on a serving plate, sprinkle them with the chilli and cinnamon mixture and serve immediately, with a small bowl of hot chilli sauce for dipping.

Cook's Tip
Plantain skins are very dark, almost black, when the fruit is ready to eat. If they are green when you buy them, allow them to ripen at room temperature for a few days before use.

Mozzarella in Carozza with Fresh Tomato Salsa

The title of this delectable Italian snack translates as cheese 'in a carriage'. The recipe is similar to croque monsieur, except that it contains mozzarella and is dipped in egg and fried.

Serves 4
200g/7oz mozzarella cheese, thinly sliced
8 thin slices of bread, crusts removed
a little dried oregano
30ml/2 tbsp freshly grated Parmesan cheese
3 eggs, beaten
olive oil, for frying
salt and ground black pepper
fresh herbs, to garnish

For the salsa
4 ripe plum tomatoes, peeled, seeded and finely chopped
15ml/1 tbsp chopped fresh parsley
5ml/1 tsp balsamic vinegar
15ml/1 tbsp extra virgin olive oil

Preparation: 7 minutes; Cooking: 8 minutes; Standing: 5–10 minutes

1 Arrange the mozzarella on four slices of the bread. Season with salt and pepper and sprinkle with a little dried oregano and the Parmesan. Top with the other bread slices and press them firmly together.

2 Pour the beaten eggs into a large shallow dish and season with salt and pepper. Add the cheese sandwiches, two at a time, pressing them into the egg with a fish slice or metal spatula until they are well coated. Repeat with the remaining sandwiches, then leave them to stand for 5–10 minutes.

3 To make the salsa, put the chopped tomatoes in a bowl and add the parsley. Stir in the vinegar and the extra virgin olive oil. Season well with salt and pepper and set aside.

4 Heat olive oil to a depth of 5mm/¼in in a large frying pan. Carefully add the sandwiches in batches and cook for about 2 minutes on each side until golden and crisp. Drain well on kitchen paper. Cut in half and serve garnished with fresh herbs and accompanied by the salsa.

Plantain Chips Energy 193kcal/806kJ; Protein 1.1g; Carbohydrate 22.7g, of which sugars 4.3g; Fat 11.5g, of which saturates 1.4g; Cholesterol 0mg; Calcium 23mg; Fibre 1.6g; Sodium 14mg.
Mozzarella Energy 472kcal/1968kJ; Protein 21.7g; Carbohydrate 27g, of which sugars 3.6g; Fat 31.7g, of which saturates 11.6g; Cholesterol 179mg; Calcium 353mg; Fibre 1.5g; Sodium 599mg.

Corn Fritters

Sometimes it is the simplest dishes that taste the best. These tasty fritters, packed with corn, are easy to prepare and go well with everything from gammon to nut rissoles.

Makes 12

3 corn cobs, total weight about
   250g/9oz
1 garlic clove, crushed
a small bunch of fresh coriander
   (cilantro), chopped
1 small fresh red or green chilli,
   seeded and finely chopped
1 spring onion (scallion),
   finely chopped
15ml/1 tbsp soy sauce
75g/3oz/¾ cup rice flour or plain
   (all-purpose) flour
2 eggs, lightly beaten
60ml/4 tbsp water
oil, for shallow-frying
salt and ground black pepper
sweet chilli sauce or tomato
   ketchup, to serve

Preparation: 5 minutes; Cooking: 8 minutes

1 Using a sharp knife, slice the kernels from the cobs using downward strokes. Rinse to remove any clinging debris from the cob. Place all the kernels in a bowl.

2 Add the garlic, chopped coriander, red or green chilli, spring onion, soy sauce, flour, beaten eggs and water to the corn and mix well. Season with salt and pepper to taste and mix again. The mixture should be firm enough to hold its shape, but not so stiff that it is unworkable.

3 Heat the oil in a large frying pan. Add spoonfuls of the corn mixture, gently spreading each one out with the back of the spoon to make a roundish fritter. Cook for 1–2 minutes on each side, turning carefully with a spatula.

4 Drain the first batch of fritters on kitchen paper and keep hot on a foil-covered dish while frying more. Serve the fritters hot with sweet chilli sauce or tomato ketchup – arrange on a large plate around the sauce, if you like. Alternatively, serve the fritters on individual plates, giving each guest their own bowl of dipping sauce. An egg cup makes a novel container for this, or use one of the miniature Chinese bowls intended for soy sauce.

Cheese Aigrettes

These choux buns, flavoured with mature Gruyère and dusted with grated Parmesan, are a bit fiddly to make, but the dough can be prepared ahead and then deep fried.

Makes 30

100g/3¾oz/scant 1 cup strong
   plain (all-purpose) flour
2.5ml/½ tsp paprika
2.5ml/½ tsp salt
75g/3oz/6 tbsp cold butter, diced
200ml/7fl oz/scant 1 cup water
3 eggs, beaten
75g/3oz/¾ cup coarsely grated
   mature Gruyère cheese
corn or vegetable oil, for
   deep frying
50g/2oz piece of Parmesan
   cheese, finely grated
ground black pepper
sprigs of flat leaf parsley,
   to garnish

Preparation: 8 minutes; Cooking: 9–12 minutes

1 Sift the flour, paprika and salt on to a large sheet of foil or baking parchment. Add a generous grinding of black pepper.

2 Put the butter and water into a medium pan and heat gently. As soon as the butter has melted and the liquid starts to boil, tip in all the seasoned flour at once and beat hard with a wooden spoon until the dough forms a ball and comes away from the sides of the pan.

3 Remove the pan from the heat and cool the paste for 5 minutes. This step is important if the aigrettes are to rise well. Gradually beat in enough of the beaten egg to give a stiff dropping consistency that still holds a shape on the spoon. Mix in the Gruyère.

4 Heat the oil for deep frying to 180°C/350°F or until a cube of bread, added to the hot oil, browns in about 1 minute. Take a teaspoonful of the choux paste and use a second spoon to slide it into the oil. Make more aigrettes in the same way. Fry for 3–4 minutes until golden brown. Drain on kitchen paper and keep warm while cooking successive batches.

5 To serve, pile the aigrettes on a warmed serving dish, sprinkle with Parmesan and garnish with sprigs of parsley.

Cheese Aigrettes Energy 84kcal/348kJ; Protein 2.2g; Carbohydrate 2.4g, of which sugars 0.1g; Fat 7.3g, of which saturates 2.7g; Cholesterol 28mg; Calcium 46mg; Fibre 0.1g; Sodium 58mg.
Corn Fritters Energy 76kcal/314kJ; Protein 2.1g; Carbohydrate 7.6g, of which sugars 0.5g; Fat 4.1g, of which saturates 0.7g; Cholesterol 32mg; Calcium 14mg; Fibre 0.6g; Sodium 102mg.

Courgette Rissoles

This is an ingenious way of transforming bland-tasting courgettes into a dish that captivates everyone who tries it.

Serves 3–4
500g/1¼lb courgettes (zucchini)
120ml/4fl oz/½ cup extra virgin olive oil
1 large onion, finely chopped
2 spring onions (scallions), green and white parts finely chopped
1 garlic clove, crushed
3 medium slices proper bread (not from a pre-sliced loaf)
2 eggs, lightly beaten
200g/7oz feta cheese, crumbled
50g/2oz/½ cup freshly grated Greek Graviera or Italian Parmesan cheese
45–60ml/3–4 tbsp finely chopped fresh dill or 5ml/1 tsp dried oregano
50g/2oz/½ cup plain (all-purpose) flour
salt and ground black pepper
lemon wedges, to serve

Preparation: 5–6 minutes; Cooking: 14 minutes

1 Slice the courgettes into 4cm/1½in lengths and cook in a pan of boiling salted water for 10 minutes, until very soft. Drain in a colander and set aside until cool enough to handle.

2 Heat 45ml/3 tbsp of the oil in a frying pan and sauté the onion and spring onions until transparent. Add the garlic, cook for 1 minute, then remove from the heat and set aside.

3 Squeeze the courgettes to remove as much liquid as possible, then tip into a large bowl. Stir in the onion mixture and mix well.

4 Toast the bread, remove the crusts and crumb it in a food processor. Add to the courgette and onion mixture, then stir in the eggs, feta and grated cheese.

5 Stir in the herbs, with salt and pepper to taste. Mix well, adding a little flour if needed. Shape the mixture into 6–8 rissoles and coat them lightly in flour.

6 Heat the remaining oil in a large frying pan and fry the rissoles until crisp and brown all over. Drain on kitchen paper and serve hot, with lemon wedges for squeezing.

Golden Gruyère & Basil Tortillas

Tortilla flip-overs are a great invention. Once you've tried this recipe, you'll want to experiment with lots of different fillings, and leftovers will never go to waste again.

Serves 2
15ml/1 tbsp olive oil
2 soft flour tortillas
115g/4oz Gruyère cheese, thinly sliced
a handful of fresh basil leaves
salt and ground black pepper

Preparation: 1–2 minutes; Cooking: 4 minutes

1 Heat the oil in a frying pan over a medium heat. Add one of the tortillas, and heat through for 1 minute.

2 Arrange the Gruyère cheese slices and basil leaves on top of the tortilla and season with salt and pepper.

3 Place the remaining tortilla on top to make a sandwich and flip the whole thing over with a metal spatula. Cook for a few minutes, until the underneath is golden.

4 Slide the tortilla sandwich on to a chopping board or plate and cut into wedges. Serve immediately.

> **Variations**
> • If you have a few slices of ham or salami in the refrigerator, add these to the tortillas – or simply prepare a mixture of the two to satisfy a range of palates.
> • Other filling ingredients that would go well with the cheese might include cooked chicken, and if you have some leftover stuffing from a roast bird, try spreading that on top of the tortilla before adding the chicken and cheese.
> • If you've been cooking pasta and have made too much bolognese sauce, this recipe is a perfect way of using the surplus.
> • Instead of Gruyère, use Parmesan cheese or Pecorino Romano.
> • For vegetarians, a cheese and onion tortilla is a good choice: cook onion rings in water until tender, then drain and sandwich with the cheese.

Rissoles Energy 528kcal/2194kJ; Protein 22g; Carbohydrate 28.8g, of which sugars 7.9g; Fat 36.9g, of which saturates 13g; Cholesterol 143mg; Calcium 436mg; Fibre 3g; Sodium 1001mg.
Tortillas Energy 354kcal/1474kJ; Protein 16.4g; Carbohydrate 15g, of which sugars 0.4g; Fat 24.6g, of which saturates 13.3g; Cholesterol 56mg; Calcium 453mg; Fibre 0.6g; Sodium 486mg.

Molettes

This is the Mexican version of beans on toast. Sold by street traders around mid-morning, they make the perfect snack for those who have missed breakfast. A nourishing and sustaining snack, it would taste good at any time.

Serves 4
4 crusty finger rolls
50g/2oz/1/4 cup butter, softened
225g/8oz/1 1/3 cups refried beans
150g/5oz/1 1/4 cups grated
    medium Cheddar cheese
green salad leaves, to garnish
120ml/4fl oz/1/2 cup classic
    tomato salsa, to serve

Preparation: 2 minutes; Cooking: 7 minutes

1 Cut the rolls in half, then take a sliver off the base so that they lie flat. Remove a little of the crumbs. Spread them lightly with enough butter to cover.

2 Arrange them on a baking sheet and grill (broil) for about 5 minutes, or until they are crisp and golden. Meanwhile, heat the refried beans over a low heat in a small pan.

3 Scoop the beans into the rolls, then sprinkle the grated cheese on top. Pop back under the grill until the cheese melts. Serve with the tomato salsa and garnish with salad leaves.

Cook's Tips
• Refried beans can be made at home, but the process is quite a lengthy one – not really suitable for a book that aims to save you time. Fortunately the product now comes in cans, so look out for them in the Mexican aisle at the supermarket.
• To make the salsa, roast 3 Serrano chillies over the flame of a gas burner until they char. Place them in a plastic bag for 20 minutes so that the steam softens them, then skin them, remove the seeds and chop the flesh. Chop 1 onion and soak it in the juice of 2 limes. Peel and dice 8 firm but ripe tomatoes. Chop a large bunch of fresh coriander (cilantro). Mix all these ingredients in a bowl and add a generous pinch each of sugar and salt. Chill before serving if possible.

Samosas

Throughout the East, they are sold by street vendors, and eaten at any time of day.

Makes about 20
1 packet 25cm/10in square
    spring roll wrappers, thawed
    if frozen
30ml/2 tbsp plain (all-purpose)
    flour, mixed to a paste
    with water
vegetable oil, for deep frying
coriander (cilantro) leaves,
    to garnish

For the filling
25g/1oz/2 tbsp ghee or
    unsalted butter

1 small onion, finely chopped
1cm/1/2 in piece fresh root ginger,
    peeled and chopped
1 garlic glove, crushed
2.5ml/1/2 tsp chilli powder
1 large potato, about 225g/8oz,
    cooked until just tender and
    finely diced
50g/2oz/1/2 cup cauliflower
    florets, lightly cooked, chopped
    into small pieces
50g/2oz/1/2 cup frozen
    peas, thawed
5–10ml/1–2 tsp garam masala
15ml/1 tbsp chopped fresh
    coriander (leaves and stems)
squeeze of lemon juice
salt

Preparation: 8 minutes; Cooking: 12 minutes

1 Heat the ghee or butter in a large frying pan and fry the onion, ginger and garlic for 5 minutes until the onion has softened but not browned. Add the chilli powder and cook for 1 minute, then stir in the potato, cauliflower and peas. Sprinkle with garam masala and set aside to cool. Stir in the chopped coriander, lemon juice and salt.

2 Cut the spring roll wrappers into three strips (or two for larger samosas). Brush the edges with a little of the flour paste. Place a small spoonful of filling about 2cm/3/4in in from the edge of one strip. Fold one corner over the filling to make a triangle and continue this folding until the entire strip has been used and a triangular pastry has been formed. Seal any open edges with more flour and water paste.

3 Heat the oil for deep frying to 190°C/375°F and fry the samosas, a few at a time, until golden and crisp. Drain well on kitchen paper and serve hot garnished with coriander leaves.

Goat's Cheese & Trout Toasties

These little rounds are packed full of flavour – the goat's cheese and trout combine beautifully to make a delicious snack suitable for any time of the day.

Serves 4

8 thick slices of white bread
30ml/2 tbsp olive oil
5ml/1 tsp fresh thyme leaves
20ml/4 tsp pesto
50g/2oz smoked trout slices
4 round goat's cheese slices, each about 50g/2oz
salt and ground black pepper
cherry tomatoes and fresh basil, to serve

Preparation: 2 minutes; Cooking: 14 minutes

1 Preheat the oven to 200°C/400°F/Gas 6. Using a pastry cutter that is slightly larger than the goat's cheese rounds, cut a circle from each slice of bread.

2 Brush the bread rounds with a little olive oil, scatter with a few thyme leaves and season well. Place the bread rounds on a baking sheet and bake for 5 minutes or until crisp and a light golden colour, turning over once.

3 Remove the bread from the oven and spread 5ml/1 tsp pesto over half the rounds. Divide the smoked trout among the pesto-topped bread, top with the cheese rounds and season well with black pepper. Top the cheese with the remaining bread circles, sandwich-style.

4 Bake the toasties in the oven for 5 minutes more, until the cheese has just started to soften slightly. Remove from the oven, transfer to a platter and serve immediately with the cherry tomatoes and basil leaves.

> **Variation**
> Thyme goes particularly well with goat's cheese but other strong herbs can be substituted. Try oregano, marjoram or sage for a completely different taste.

Welsh Rarebit

The Welsh have always loved roasted cheese. In its simplest form Welsh Rarebit, Caws wedi pobi, would traditionally have consisted of a slice of bread and a large slice of hard cheese, each toasted in front of the open fire. Just before the cheese had a chance to soften too much, it was laid on top of the crisp bread and served.

Serves 2

2 thick slices bread
soft butter, for spreading
10ml/2 tsp ready-made mustard of your choice
100g/3¾oz Cheddar-style cheese such as Llanboidy, or crumbly cheese such as Caerphilly, sliced
ground black pepper
pinch of paprika or cayenne pepper
tomato wedges and basil leaves, to garnish (optional)

Preparation: 2 minutes; Cooking: 4–5 minutes

1 Put the bread on the rack of a grill (broiler) pan and put the pan under a hot grill until both sides are lightly toasted.

2 Spread one side of each slice of toast with butter and then a little mustard (or to taste). Top with cheese slices.

3 Put under the hot grill until the cheese is soft and bubbling and beginning to turn golden brown.

4 Sprinkle with a little black pepper and paprika or cayenne and serve immediately, garnished with tomato wedges and basil leaves (if using).

> **Variations**
> • As an alternative method, use a mixture of cheeses, grated and stirred together with the butter and mustard before spreading them on the toast and grilling (broiling).
> • For another topping, melt 25g/1oz butter and stir in 15ml/1 tbsp plain (all-purpose) flour. After 1 minute, stir in 45ml/3 tbsp milk and 30ml/2 tbsp ale. Add 175g/6oz grated hard cheese and allow it to melt.

Toasties Energy 402kcal/1685kJ; Protein 21.7g; Carbohydrate 30.1g, of which sugars 2.1g; Fat 22.6g, of which saturates 11.4g; Cholesterol 58mg; Calcium 225mg; Fibre 0.9g; Sodium 929mg.
Rarebit Energy 386kcal/1611kJ; Protein 18.4g; Carbohydrate 25.8g, of which sugars 1.4g; Fat 23.7g, of which saturates 13.5g; Cholesterol 59mg; Calcium 442mg; Fibre 0.8g; Sodium 652mg.

Grilled Aubergine

The combination of hot, spicy, sweet and fruity flavours in this Moroccan dish will have everyone asking for the recipe. Serve as an appetizer or for a light second course. This is a good dish for vegetarian guests who are bored with always being given the ubiquitous pasta with pesto.

Serves 4

2 aubergines (eggplants)
olive oil, for frying
2–3 garlic cloves, crushed
5cm/2in piece fresh root ginger, peeled and grated
5ml/1 tsp ground cumin
5ml/1 tsp harissa
75ml/5 tbsp clear honey
juice of 1 lemon
salt

Preparation: 2 minutes; Cooking: 15 minutes

1 Preheat the grill (broiler) or a griddle pan. Cut the aubergines lengthways into thick slices.

2 Brush each aubergine slice with olive oil and cook in a pan under the grill or in a griddle pan. Turn the slices so that they are lightly browned on both sides.

3 Meanwhile, in a wide frying pan, fry the garlic in a little olive oil for a few seconds, then stir in the ginger, cumin, harissa, honey and lemon juice.

4 Add enough water to thin the mixture, then add the aubergine slices. Cook for about 10 minutes, or until they have absorbed all the sauce.

5 Add a little extra water if necessary, season to taste with salt, and serve at room temperature, with chunks of fresh bread to mop up the juices.

> **Cook's Tip**
> Grilled (broiled) blood oranges make an excellent quick accompaniment to this dish. Dip the halves or quarters in icing (confectioners') sugar and grill until just about to blacken.

Green Curry Puffs

Shrimp paste and green curry sauce, used judiciously, give these puffs their distinctive spicy, savoury flavour, and the addition of chilli steps up the heat.

Makes 24

24 small wonton wrappers, about 8cm/3¼in square, thawed if frozen
15ml/1 tbsp cornflour (cornstarch), mixed to a paste with 30ml/2 tbsp water
oil, for deep-frying

For the filling

1 small potato, about 115g/4oz, boiled and mashed
25g/1oz/3 tbsp cooked petits pois (baby peas)
25g/1oz/3 tbsp cooked corn
few sprigs fresh coriander (cilantro), chopped
1 small fresh red chilli, seeded and finely chopped
½ lemon grass stalk, finely chopped
15ml/1 tbsp soy sauce
5ml/1 tsp shrimp paste or fish sauce
5ml/1 tsp Thai green curry paste

Preparation: 3 minutes; Cooking: 17 minutes

1 Combine the mashed potato, peas, corn, coriander, chilli and lemon grass in a bowl. Stir in the soy sauce, shrimp paste or fish sauce and Thai green curry paste. Lay out one wonton wrapper on a board or clean work surface and place a teaspoon of the filling in the centre.

2 Brush a little of the cornflour paste along two sides of the square. Fold the other two sides over to meet them, then press together to make a triangular pastry and seal in the filling. Make more pastries in the same way.

3 Heat the oil in a wok to 190°C/375°F or until a cube of bread, added to the oil, browns in about 45 seconds. Add the pastries to the oil, a few at a time, and fry them for about 5 minutes, until golden brown.

4 Remove from the wok and drain on kitchen paper. If you intend serving the puffs hot, place them in a single layer on a serving plate in a low oven while cooking successive batches. The puffs also taste good cold.

Grilled Aubergine Energy 168kcal/701kJ; Protein 1g; Carbohydrate 16.5g, of which sugars 16.3g; Fat 11.4g, of which saturates 1.7g; Cholesterol 0mg; Calcium 11mg; Fibre 2g; Sodium 4mg.
Green Curry Puffs Energy 69Kcal/291kJ; Protein 1.4g; Carbohydrate 9.9g, of which sugars 0.4g; Fat 3g, of which saturates 0.4g; Cholesterol 1mg; Calcium 22mg; Fibre 0.5g; Sodium 58mg.

Thai Spring Rolls

Crunchy spring rolls are as popular in Thailand as in China. Everyone loves them.

Makes 24
4–6 Chinese dried mushrooms, soaked for 30 minutes
50g/2oz cellophane noodles
30ml/2 tbsp vegetable oil
2 garlic cloves, chopped
2 fresh red chillies, seeded and chopped
225g/8oz minced (ground) pork
50g/2oz cooked prawns (shrimp)
30ml/2 tbsp Thai fish sauce
5ml/1 tsp sugar
ground black pepper
1 carrot, grated
50g/2oz drained canned bamboo shoots, chopped
50g/2oz/1 cup beansprouts
2 spring onions (scallions), finely chopped
15ml/1 tbsp chopped fresh coriander (cilantro)
24 x 15cm/6in square spring roll wrappers
flour and water paste, for sealing rolls
vegetable oil, for deep-frying
Thai sweet chilli dipping sauce, to serve (optional)

Preparation: 10 minutes; Cooking: 10 minutes

1 Drain the mushrooms, discard the stems and chop the caps finely. Soak the noodles in boiling water for 10 minutes. Drain the noodles and chop them into 5cm/2in lengths.

2 Heat the oil in a wok, add the garlic and chillies and stir-fry for 30 seconds. Transfer to a plate. Add the pork to the wok and stir-fry until browned. Add the noodles, mushrooms and prawns. Stir in the fish sauce and sugar; season with pepper.

3 Tip the noodle mixture into a bowl and stir in the carrot, bamboo shoots, beansprouts, spring onions and chopped coriander together with the reserved chilli mixture.

4 Unwrap the spring roll wrappers. Place a spoonful of filling in the centre of each wrapper, turn up the bottom edge, fold in the sides, then roll up and seal with flour and water paste.

5 Heat the oil and fry the spring rolls until crisp and golden brown. Drain on kitchen paper and keep hot while cooking successive batches. Serve hot, with the sauce, if you like.

Breaded Sole Batons

Crisp, crumbed fish strips are almost as speedy as fish fingers, but much smarter.

Serves 4
275g/10oz lemon sole fillets, skinned
2 eggs
115g/4oz/2 cups fine fresh breadcrumbs
75g/3oz/3/4 cup plain (all-purpose) flour
salt and ground black pepper
oil, for frying
lemon wedges and tartare sauce, to serve

Preparation: 10–12 minutes; Cooking: 6–7 minutes

1 Cut the fish fillets into long diagonal strips each measuring about 2cm/3/4in wide.

2 Break the eggs into a shallow dish and beat well with a fork. Place the fresh breadcrumbs in another shallow dish. Put the flour in a large plastic bag and season with plenty of salt and ground black pepper. Shake to mix.

3 Dip the fish strips in the egg, turning to coat well. Place on a plate and then shake a few at a time in the bag of seasoned flour.

4 Dip the fish strips in the egg again and then in the breadcrumbs, turning to coat well. Place on a tray in a single layer, making sure that none of the breaded strips touches its neighbour. Let the coating set for at least 5 minutes.

5 Heat 1cm/1/2in oil in a large frying pan over medium-high heat. When the oil is hot (a cube of bread will sizzle) fry the fish strips in batches for about 2–2½ minutes, turning once, taking care not to overcrowd the pan. Drain on kitchen paper and keep warm. Serve the fish on a platter, with the tartare sauce and lemon wedges.

Variation
Instead of lemon sole, use fillets of plaice (flounder) or cod. Pollock would also work well.

Thai Spring Rolls Energy 74kcal/310kJ; Protein 3.1g; Carbohydrate 7.2g, of which sugars 0.7g; Fat 3.8g, of which saturates 0.7g; Cholesterol 10mg; Calcium 13mg; Fibre 0.4g; Sodium 12mg.
Breaded Sole Batons Energy 334kcal/1405kJ; Protein 20.2g; Carbohydrate 36.9g, of which sugars 1g; Fat 12.9g, of which saturates 2.1g; Cholesterol 136mg; Calcium 90mg; Fibre 1.2g; Sodium 320mg.

Crab Dim Sum with Chinese Chives

These delectable Chinese-style dumplings have a wonderfully sticky texture and make a perfect appetizer. You can make these in advance, storing them in the refrigerator until ready to cook. Steam them just before serving, then enjoy the sensation as your teeth sink through the soft wrapper into the savoury crab filling.

Serves 4
150g/5oz fresh white crab meat
115g/4oz minced (ground) pork
30ml/2 tbsp chopped Chinese
 chives
15ml/1 tbsp finely chopped red
 (bell) pepper
30ml/2 tbsp sweet chilli sauce
30ml/2 tbsp hoisin sauce
24 fresh dumpling wrappers
 (available from Asian stores)
Chinese chives, to garnish
chilli oil and soy sauce, to serve

Preparation: 8 minutes; Cooking: 8–10 minutes

1 Place the crab meat, pork and chopped chives in a bowl. Add the red pepper and mix well, then pour in the sweet chilli and hoisin sauces. Stir until thoroughly combined.

2 Working with 2–3 wrappers at a time, put a spoonful of the mixture on to each wrapper. Brush the edges of a wrapper with water and fold over to form a half-moon shape. Press and pleat the edges to seal, and flatten. Cover with a clean, damp dish towel and make the rest.

3 Arrange the dumplings on three lightly oiled plates and fit inside three tiers of a bamboo steamer. Alternatively, use a stainless steel steamer or an electric steamer.

4 Cover the bamboo steamer and place over a wok of simmering water (making sure the water does not touch the steamer). Steam for 8–10 minutes, or until the dumplings are cooked through and become slightly translucent. If using an electric steamer follow the manufacturer's instructions.

5 Divide the dumplings among four plates. Garnish with Chinese chives and serve immediately with chilli oil and soy sauce for dipping.

Salmon & Scallop Brochettes

With their delicate colours and superb flavour, these salmon and scallop skewers are the perfect choice for a sophisticated al fresco lunch in the summer.

½ yellow (bell) pepper, seeded
 and cut into 8 squares
25g/1oz/2 tbsp butter
juice of ½ lemon
salt, ground white pepper
 and paprika

Serves 4
8 lemon grass stalks
225g/8oz salmon fillet, skinned
8 queen scallops, with their corals
 if possible
8 baby (pearl) onions, peeled
 and blanched

For the sauce
30ml/2 tbsp dry vermouth
50g/2oz/¼ cup butter
5ml/1 tsp chopped fresh tarragon

Preparation: 8 minutes; Cooking: 7–10 minutes

1 Preheat the grill (broiler) to medium-high. Cut off the top 7.5–10cm/3 4in of each lemon grass stalk. Reserve the bulb ends for another dish.

2 Cut the salmon into 12 x 2cm/¾in cubes. Thread the salmon, scallops, corals if available, onions and pepper squares on to the lemon grass and arrange the brochettes in a grill pan.

3 Melt the butter in a small pan, add the lemon juice and a pinch of paprika and then brush all over the brochettes. Grill (broil) the skewers for about 2–3 minutes on each side, turning and basting the brochettes every minute, until the fish and scallops are just cooked, but are still very juicy. Transfer to a platter and keep hot while you make the tarragon butter sauce.

4 Pour the dry vermouth and all the leftover cooking juices from the brochettes into a small pan and boil quite fiercely to reduce by half.

5 Add the butter and melt, stirring constantly. Stir in the chopped fresh tarragon and add salt and ground white pepper to taste. Pour the butter sauce over the brochettes and serve.

Crab Dim Sum Energy 166kcal/700kJ; Protein 14.7g; Carbohydrate 20.5g, of which sugars 1.4g; Fat 3.3g, of which saturates 1.1g; Cholesterol 46mg; Calcium 83mg; Fibre 0.8g; Sodium 287mg.
Brochettes Energy 333kcal/1384kJ; Protein 23.9g; Carbohydrate 7.4g, of which sugars 4.4g; Fat 22.5g, of which saturates 11.1g; Cholesterol 92mg; Calcium 45mg; Fibre 1.1g; Sodium 232mg.

Whitefish Salad with Toasted Bagels

A traditional deli favourite, smoked whitefish makes a superb salad. If you can't find it, use smoked halibut, but don't pass up the bagels, which are the perfect accompaniment.

Serves 4–6
1 smoked whitefish or halibut, skinned and boned
2 celery sticks, chopped
½ red, white or yellow onion or 3–5 spring onions (scallions), chopped
45ml/3 tbsp mayonnaise
45ml/3 tbsp sour cream
juice of ½–1 lemon
1 round lettuce
ground black pepper
5–10ml/1–2 tsp chopped fresh parsley, to garnish
toasted bagels, to serve

Preparation: 8–10 minutes; Cooking: 0 minutes

1 Break the smoked fish into bitesize pieces. In a bowl, combine the chopped celery, onion or spring onion, mayonnaise and sour cream, and add lemon juice to taste.

2 Fold the fish into the mixture and season with pepper. Arrange the lettuce leaves on serving plates, then spoon the smoked fish salad on top. Sprinkle with parsley and serve with the toasted bagels.

Cook's Tip
Smoked whitefish is a product you are more likely to come across in the United States or Canada than in the UK. The fish is related to char and grayling and is a member of the salmon family. The flesh is soft and oily, with a mild flavour. As the introduction to the recipe suggests, smoked halibut can be used instead, or you could substitute smoked trout. Mackerel would have too dominant a flavour and is not as suitable. If buying smoked fish direct from the smokehouse, use it as quickly as possible; if you have purchased it at the supermarket in a vacuum pack, check the use-by date. Smoked fish can be frozen in the original packaging for up to 1 month.

Tuna Melt Muffins

Take a tip from the Americans and try this delicious and nutritious snack consisting of wholemeal muffins topped with tuna and hot bubbling cheese. Use wholemeal toast in place of the muffins, if you like.

Serves 2
200g/7oz can tuna, drained and flaked
1 spring onion (scallion), chopped
1 small celery stick, chopped
15ml/1 tbsp chopped canned pimiento or 1 medium tomato, chopped
30ml/2 tbsp mayonnaise
generous pinch of dried oregano or marjoram
2 wholemeal muffins, split
65g/2½ oz mature Monterey Jack or Cheddar cheese, coarsely grated or sliced
8 pimiento- or anchovy-stuffed olives, sliced
salt and ground black pepper

Preparation: 6 minutes; Cooking: 3–4 minutes

1 Mix the tuna with the spring onion, celery, pimiento or tomato, mayonnaise and oregano or marjoram. Stir in salt and pepper to taste, then set aside.

2 Preheat the grill (broiler) and toast the cut side of the muffins until they are golden and slightly crisp.

3 Spoon a quarter of the tuna mixture on to each muffin half, then top with the cheese and stuffed olive slices. Grill (broil) until the cheese has melted and is bubbling. There is no need to brown the cheese. Serve hot, sprinkled with more pepper.

Variations
• *Melts have become increasingly popular and often feature on snack bar menus. In this version, muffins form the base, but baps or bread rolls, split in half, could be used instead.*
• *Tuna is frequently used for the topping, but cooked chicken or turkey also make a good melt. Use the white breast meat only, and cut it into bitesize pieces before mixing it with the mayonnaise and flavouring ingredients.*

Whitefish Salad Energy 108kcal/450kJ; Protein 7.8g; Carbohydrate 1.6g, of which sugars 1.3g; Fat 7.9g, of which saturates 1.9g; Cholesterol 22mg; Calcium 29mg; Fibre 0.4g; Sodium 64mg.
Tuna Muffins Energy 567kcal/2356kJ; Protein 22.3g; Carbohydrate 23.3g, of which sugars 1.6g; Fat 42.8g, of which saturates 15.5g; Cholesterol 96mg; Calcium 231mg; Fibre 3.2g; Sodium 832mg.

Salmon Tortilla Cones

Whether you're snuggling up
on the sofa to watch a late-
night movie or catering for
a crowd, these simple yet
sophisticated wraps are
irresistible.

Serves 4
115g/4oz/½ cup soft white
   (farmer's) cheese
30ml/2 tbsp roughly chopped
   fresh dill

juice of 1 lemon
1 small red onion
15ml/1 tbsp drained bottled
   capers
30ml/2 tbsp extra virgin olive oil
30ml/2 tbsp roughly chopped
   fresh flat leaf parsley
115g/4oz smoked salmon
8 small or 4 large wheat
   flour tortillas
salt and ground black pepper
lemon wedges, for squeezing

Preparation: 8–10 minutes; Cooking: 0 minutes

1 Place the soft cheese in a small bowl and mix in half the
chopped dill. Add a little salt and pepper and just a dash of the
lemon juice to taste. Put the remaining lemon juice in a fairly
large bowl and set it aside.

2 Finely chop the red onion. Add the chopped onion, drained
capers and olive oil to the lemon juice in the bowl. Add the
chopped flat leaf parsley and the remaining dill and stir gently.
Set aside for 5 minutes to give the ingredients a chance to
infuse. The lemon will soften the onion a little.

3 Cut the smoked salmon into short, thin strips, and add to
the red onion mixture. Toss to mix. Season to taste with plenty
of pepper.

4 If using small tortillas, leave them whole, but large ones need
to be cut in half so that they can be rolled into cones. Spread a
little of the soft cheese mixture on each piece of tortilla and
top with the smoked salmon mixture.

5 Roll up the tortillas into cones and secure with wooden
cocktail sticks (toothpicks). Arrange on a serving plate and add
some lemon wedges, for squeezing. Serve immediately. The
tortillas are eaten in the hand; supply wipes for sticky fingers.

Anchovy & Quail's Egg Bruschetta

Quail's eggs taste marvellous
with the anchovies and mild
red onion slices, especially
when the mixture is piled
on toasted ciabatta which
has been rubbed with fresh
garlic to add flavour.

Serves 4–6
50g/2oz anchovy fillets in salt
milk, for soaking

12 quail's eggs
2–3 garlic cloves
1 ciabatta or similar loaf
coarse salt
1 red onion, halved and
   thinly sliced
10–15ml/2–3 tsp cumin seeds,
   roasted and ground
a small bunch of flat leaf parsley,
   roughly chopped
30–45ml/2–3 tbsp olive oil

Preparation: 15 minutes; Cooking: 3–5 minutes

1 Soak the anchovies in a shallow bowl of milk for 15 minutes
to reduce the salty flavour.

2 Meanwhile, put the quail's eggs in a pan of cold water. Bring
to the boil and cook for 2 minutes, then drain and plunge into
cold water.

3 Remove the skin from the garlic cloves, halve, and crush
using a pestle and mortar.

4 Preheat the grill (broiler) on the hottest setting. Slice the
loaf of bread horizontally in half and toast the cut sides
until golden.

5 Rub the toasted bread all over with the crushed garlic and
sprinkle with a little salt. Don't overdo this, as the anchovies will
be quite salty.

6 Cut each piece of bread into four or six equal pieces. Drain
the quail's eggs, shell them and cut them in half. Drain the
anchovy fillets.

7 Pile the onion slices, quail's egg halves and anchovy fillets on
the pieces of bread. Sprinkle liberally with the ground roasted
cumin and chopped parsley and serve immediately.

Tortilla Cones Energy 374kcal/1576kJ; Protein 16.6g; Carbohydrate 53.2g, of which sugars 3g; Fat 12g, of which saturates 3.6g; Cholesterol 22mg; Calcium 128mg; Fibre 2.9g; Sodium 783mg.
Bruschetta Energy 181kcal/761kJ; Protein 8.8g; Carbohydrate 18.2g, of which sugars 1.7g; Fat 8.6g, of which saturates 1.6g; Cholesterol 100mg; Calcium 87mg; Fibre 1g; Sodium 543mg.

Focaccia with Sardines & Roast Tomatoes

Fresh sardines have a lovely flavour and texture, are cheap to buy and cook quickly.

Serves 4
20 cherry tomatoes
45ml/3 tbsp herb-infused olive oil
12 fresh sardine fillets
1 focaccia loaf
salt and ground black pepper

Preparation: 3–4 minutes; Cooking: 15 minutes

1 Preheat the oven to 190°C/375°F/Gas 5. Put the cherry tomatoes in a small roasting pan and drizzle 30ml/2 tbsp of the herb-infused olive oil over the top.

2 Season the tomatoes with salt and pepper and roast for 10–15 minutes, shaking the pan gently once or twice so that the tomatoes cook evenly on all sides. When they are tender and slightly charred, remove from the oven and set aside.

3 While the tomatoes are cooking, preheat the grill (broiler) to high. Brush the sardine fillets with the remaining oil and lay them on a baking sheet. Grill (broil) for 4–5 minutes on each side, until cooked through.

4 Split the focaccia in half horizontally and cut each piece in half to give four equal pieces. Toast the cut side under the grill. Top with the sardines and tomatoes and an extra drizzle of oil. Season with black pepper and serve.

> **Variations**
> • This rather sumptuous topping tastes great on focaccia, but a split French stick would work just as well.
> • Slice some cold boiled potatoes and fry them quickly in oil while the sardines are cooking. Abandon the bread and pile the sardines and tomatoes on the potatoes.

Roast Chicken Pitta Pockets

Families often have to eat in relays: a parent is going to be home late; one child has a music lesson; another is off to the skate park. This serve-anytime snack will suit the lot.

Makes 6
1 small cucumber, peeled and diced
3 tomatoes, peeled, seeded and chopped
2 spring onions (scallions), chopped
30ml/2 tbsp olive oil
a small bunch of flat leaf parsley, finely chopped
a small bunch of mint, finely chopped
1/2 preserved lemon, finely chopped
45–60ml/3–4 tbsp tahini
juice of 1 lemon
2 garlic cloves, crushed
6 pitta breads
1/2 small roast chicken or 2 large roast chicken breasts, cut into strips
salt and ground black pepper

Preparation: 12–14 minutes; Cooking: 2 minutes

1 Place the cucumber in a sieve (strainer) over a bowl, sprinkle with a little salt and leave for 5 minutes to drain. Rinse well and drain, then place in a bowl with the tomatoes and spring onions. Stir in the olive oil, parsley, mint and preserved lemon. Season well.

2 In a small bowl, mix the tahini with the lemon juice, then thin the mixture down with a little water to the consistency of thick double (heavy) cream. Beat in the garlic and season.

3 Preheat the grill (broiler) to hot. Lightly toast the pitta breads well away from the heat source until they puff up. (Alternatively, lightly toast the breads in a toaster.) Open the breads and stuff them liberally with the chicken and salad. Drizzle tahini sauce into each one and serve with any extra salad.

> **Cook's Tip**
> The chicken in these pitta breads can be hot or cold — either roast a small bird specially or use up the leftovers from a large roast chicken.

Focaccia Energy 301kcal/1262kJ; Protein 15.8g; Carbohydrate 27.6g, of which sugars 3.1g; Fat 15g, of which saturates 2.9g; Cholesterol 0mg; Calcium 106mg; Fibre 1.7g; Sodium 334mg.
Pitta Pockets Energy 337kcal/1419kJ; Protein 21g; Carbohydrate 43.5g, of which sugars 4.4g; Fat 9.9g, of which saturates 1.5g; Cholesterol 35mg; Calcium 182mg; Fibre 3.5g; Sodium 369mg.

Pork on Lemon Grass Sticks

These make a substantial snack, either on their own or as part of a barbecue menu. The lemon grass sticks not only add a subtle flavour but are also a good talking point.

Serves 4
300g/11oz/1½ cups minced (ground) pork
4 garlic cloves, crushed
4 fresh coriander (cilantro) roots, finely chopped
2.5ml/½ tsp granulated white sugar
15ml/1 tbsp soy sauce or kecap manis
salt and ground black pepper
8 x 10cm/4in lengths lemon grass stalk
sweet chilli sauce, to serve

Preparation: 6 minutes; Cooking: 6–8 minutes

1 Place the minced pork, crushed garlic, chopped coriander root, sugar and soy sauce or kecap manis in a large bowl. Season with salt and pepper to taste and mix well.

2 Divide into eight portions and mould each one into a ball. It may help to dampen your hands before shaping the mixture to prevent it from sticking.

3 Stick a length of lemon grass halfway into each ball, then press the meat mixture around the lemon grass to make a shape like a chicken leg

4 Cook the pork sticks under a hot grill (broiler) for 3–4 minutes on each side, until golden and cooked through.

5 Serve with chilli sauce or sambal for dipping.

> **Variations**
> • *Slimmer versions of these pork sticks are perfect for parties. The mixture will be enough for 12 lemon grass sticks if you use it sparingly.*
> • *Sweet and sour sauce can be used instead of sweet chilli sauce, or try a peach chutney.*

Dates Stuffed with Chorizo

This is a delicious combination from Spain, using fresh dates and spicy chorizo sausage, wrapped in bacon and encased in breadcrumbs so that all the flavour is sealed in. When the snacks are fried, the coating becomes crisp and crunchy; a lovely contrast to the squidgy dates inside.

Serves 4–6
50g/2oz chorizo sausage
12 fresh dates, stoned
6 streaky (fatty) bacon slices
oil, for frying
plain (all-purpose) flour, for dusting
1 egg, beaten
50g/2oz/1 cup fresh breadcrumbs

Preparation: 6 minutes; Cooking: 2–4 minutes

1 Trim the ends of the chorizo sausage and then peel away the skin. Cut into three 2cm/¾in slices. Cut these in half lengthways, then into quarters, giving 12 pieces.

2 Stuff each date with a piece of chorizo, closing the date around it. Stretch the bacon, by running the back of a knife along the rasher.

3 Cut each rasher in half, widthways. Wrap a piece of bacon around each date and hold in place securely with a wooden cocktail stick (toothpick).

4 In a deep pan, heat 1cm/½in of oil. Dust the dates with flour, dip them in the beaten egg, then coat in breadcrumbs. Fry the dates in the hot oil, turning them, until golden. Remove the dates with a draining spoon, and drain on kitchen paper. Serve at once.

> **Variation**
> *For a vegetarian version of this tasty snack, omit the chorizo and stuff the dates with pecan nuts or brazil nuts (halved lengthways if necessary). Omit the bacon – just coat the stuffed dates in egg and breadcrumbs and fry them as detailed in the recipe. This is good with pre-dinner drinks.*

Dates with Chorizo Energy 204kcal/851kJ; Protein 6g; Carbohydrate 17.9g, of which sugars 10.8g; Fat 12.6g, of which saturates 3.1g; Cholesterol 46mg; Calcium 29mg; Fibre 0.8g; Sodium 355mg.
Pork Sticks Energy 132kcal/552kJ; Protein 14.7g; Carbohydrate 2g, of which sugars 1.6g; Fat 7.3g, of which saturates 2.7g; Cholesterol 50mg; Calcium 10mg; Fibre 0.2g; Sodium 317mg.

Steak Ciabatta with Hummus

Packed with garlicky hummus and a mustard-seasoned dressing on the crunchy salad, these steak sandwiches are just right for lunch on the patio.

Serves 4
3 garlic cloves, crushed to a
   paste with enough salt to
   season the steaks
30ml/2 tbsp extra virgin olive oil
4 sirloin steaks, 2.5cm/1in thick,
   total weight about 900g/2lb
2 romaine lettuce hearts
4 small ciabatta breads
salt and ground black pepper

For the dressing
10ml/2 tsp Dijon mustard
5ml/1 tsp cider or white
   wine vinegar
15ml/1 tbsp olive oil

For the hummus
400g/14oz can chickpeas,
   drained and rinsed
45ml/3 tbsp tahini
2 garlic cloves, crushed
juice of 1 lemon
30ml/2 tbsp water

Preparation: 5 minutes; Cooking: 6–9 minutes

1 To make the hummus, place the chickpeas in a large bowl and mash to a paste. Add the tahini, garlic, lemon juice, salt and pepper. Stir in the water. Mash together well.

2 Make a dressing by mixing the mustard and vinegar in a jar. Add the oil and season to taste. Shake well.

3 Mix the garlic and oil in a dish. Add the steaks and rub the mixture into both surfaces.

4 Preheat the grill (broiler). Cook the steaks on a rack in a grill pan. For rare meat, allow 2 minutes on one side and 3 minutes on the second side. For medium steaks, allow 4 minutes on each side. Transfer to a plate, cover and set aside to rest for 2 minutes.

5 Dress the lettuce. Split each ciabatta and heat on the grill rack for a minute. Fill with hummus, the steaks and leaves. Cut each in half and serve immediately, just as they are.

Mexican Tortas

The greatest thing about hollowing out a bread roll is that you can pack in more filling. This Mexican snack uses roast pork and refried beans but any other fillings can be used.

Serves 4
2 fresh jalapeño chillies
juice of ½ lime

2 French bread rolls or 2 pieces
   French bread
75g/3oz/⅔ cup canned
   refried beans
150g/5oz roast pork
2 small tomatoes, sliced
115g/4oz Cheddar or Monterey
   Jack cheese, sliced
a small bunch of fresh
   coriander (cilantro)
30ml/2 tbsp crème fraîche

Preparation: 5–6 minutes; Cooking: 0 minutes

1 Cut the chillies in half, scrape out the seeds, then cut the flesh into thin strips. Put it in a bowl and pour in the lime juice.

2 If using rolls, slice them in half and remove some of the crumbs so that they are slightly hollowed. If using French bread, slice each piece in half lengthways.

3 Set the top of each piece of bread or roll aside and spread the bottom halves with a nice thick layer of the refried beans. Make sure the paste is evenly spread, as it will help to hold the next layer in place.

4 Cut the pork into thin shreds and put these on top of the refried beans. Top with the tomato slices. Drain the jalapeño strips and put them on top of the tomato slices. Add the cheese and sprinkle with coriander leaves.

5 Turn the top halves of the bread or rolls over so that the cut sides are uppermost, and spread these with crème fraîche. Sandwich back together again and serve.

> **Variation**
> Use sliced gammon or honey-glazed ham instead of roast pork.

Tortas Energy 307kcal/1285kJ; Protein 22.8g; Carbohydrate 18.2g, of which sugars 2.9g; Fat 15.8g, of which saturates 9.4g; Cholesterol 78mg; Calcium 271mg; Fibre 2g; Sodium 485mg.
Ciabatta Energy 765kcal/3210kJ; Protein 69.8g; Carbohydrate 55.2g, of which sugars 2.8g; Fat 30.8g, of which saturates 7.4g; Cholesterol 115mg; Calcium 222mg; Fibre 6.7g; Sodium 783mg.

Mexican Tacos

Ready-made taco shells make perfect edible containers for shredded salad, meat fillings, grated cheese and sour cream. This is an excellent choice for a quick supper.

Serves 4
15ml/1 tbsp olive oil
250g/9oz lean minced (ground)
  beef or turkey
2 garlic cloves, crushed
5ml/1 tsp ground cumin
5–10ml/1–2 tsp mild
  chilli powder
8 ready-made taco shells
½ small iceberg lettuce, shredded
1 small onion, thinly sliced
2 tomatoes, chopped in chunks
1 avocado, stoned (pitted)
  and sliced
60ml/4 tbsp sour cream
125g/4oz/1 cup crumbled
  queso blanco or anejado, or
  grated Cheddar or Monterey
  Jack cheese
salt and ground black pepper

Preparation: 8 minutes; Cooking: 8 minutes

1 Heat the oil in a frying pan. Add the meat, with the garlic and spices, and brown over medium heat, stirring frequently to break up any lumps. Season with salt and ground black pepper; cook for 5 minutes, then set aside to cool slightly.

2 Meanwhile, warm the taco shells according to the instructions on the packet. Do not let them get too crisp.

3 Spoon the lettuce, onion, tomatoes and avocado slices into the taco shells. Top with the sour cream followed by the minced beef or turkey mixture.

4 Sprinkle the crumbled or grated cheese into the tacos and serve immediately. Tacos are eaten with the fingers, so have plenty of paper napkins to hand, and wipes or finger bowls filled with warm water.

> **Cook's Tip**
> Stir-fried strips of turkey, chicken or pork are excellent instead of the minced (ground) beef or turkey.

Steak & Blue Cheese on Ciabatta

Many people prefer their steaks cooked quite rare in the centre, but they are still delicious if cooked a little longer. Add a couple of minutes to the cooking time If necessary but do not let the meat dry out.

Serves 2
1 part-baked ciabatta bread
2 ribeye steaks, about
  200g/7oz each
15ml/1 tbsp olive oil
115g/4oz Gorgonzola
  cheese, sliced
salt and ground black pepper

Preparation: 2–3 minutes; Cooking: 12–14 minutes

1 Bake the ciabatta according to the instructions on the packet. Remove from the oven, wrap in foil to keep warm, and leave to rest while you cook the steak.

2 Heat a griddle pan until hot. Brush the steaks with the olive oil and lay them on the griddle pan. Cook for 2–3 minutes on each side, depending on the thickness of the steaks.

3 Remove the steaks and set them aside to rest. Meanwhile, cut the loaf in half and split each half horizontally.

4 Cut the steaks in half lengthways so each is only half as thick as before. Moisten the bread with the pan juices then make into sandwiches using the steak and cheese. Season well and serve on a platter or individual plates.

> **Variation**
> Gorgonzola is particularly good in this ciabatta sandwich, but St Agur would also work well. For a milder flavour, use Cambozola.

> **Cook's Tip**
> Part-baked bread cooks in about 8 minutes in a hot oven, but if even that is too long, just warm a regular baked ciabatta or French stick.

Steak Energy 767kcal/3221kJ; Protein 66g; Carbohydrate 52g, of which sugars 3.1g; Fat 34.2g, of which saturates 15.8g; Cholesterol 161mg; Calcium 410mg; Fibre 2.3g; Sodium 1360mg.
Mexican Tacos Energy 497Kcal/2067kJ; Protein 25.4g; Carbohydrate 19.4g, of which sugars 3.8g; Fat 35.1g, of which saturates 14.3g; Cholesterol 74mg; Calcium 305mg; Fibre 3.6g; Sodium 511mg.

Grilled Swordfish Skewers

This delicious skewered and grilled swordfish dish is cooked with olive oil, garlic and oregano. In Greece it is known as souvlakia.

Serves 4
2 red onions, quartered
2 red or green (bell) peppers, quartered and seeded

20–24 thick cubes of swordfish, 675–800g/1½–1¾lb in total
lemon wedges, to garnish

For the basting sauce
75ml/5 tbsp extra virgin olive oil
1 garlic clove, crushed
large pinch of dried oregano or marjoram
salt and ground black pepper

Preparation: 10 minutes; Cooking: 8–10 minutes

1 Carefully separate the onion quarters into pieces, each composed of two or three layers. Slice each pepper quarter in half widthways, or into thirds if you have very large peppers.

2 Make the souvlakia by threading five or six pieces of swordfish on to each of four long metal skewers, alternating with pieces of the pepper and onion. Lay the souvlakia across a grill (broiling) pan and set aside while you make the sauce.

3 Whisk the olive oil, crushed garlic and oregano or marjoram in a bowl. Add salt and pepper, and whisk again. Brush the souvlakia generously on all sides with the basting sauce.

4 Preheat the grill (broiler) to the highest setting, or prepare a barbecue. Slide the grill pan or roasting tray underneath the grill or transfer the skewers to the barbecue, making sure that they are not too close to the heat.

5 Cook for 8–10 minutes, turning the skewers several times and brushing them with the basting sauce to increase the flavours, until the fish is cooked and the peppers and onions have begun to scorch around the edges.

6 Serve the souvlakia immediately with a salad of cucumber, red onion and fresh olives and garnished with one or two wedges of lemon.

Griddled Swordfish with Tomatoes

Slow-roasting the tomatoes is a great technique when you are entertaining as they need no last-minute attention, but a much quicker way is simply to grill them instead.

Serves 4
1kg/2¼lb large vine or plum tomatoes, peeled, halved and seeded
5–10ml/1–2 tsp ground cinnamon

a pinch of saffron threads
15ml/1 tbsp orange flower water
60ml/4 tbsp olive oil
45–60ml/3–4 tbsp caster (superfine) sugar
4 x 225g/8oz swordfish steaks
rind of ½ preserved lemon, finely chopped
a small bunch of fresh coriander (cilantro), finely chopped or 15ml/1 tbsp chopped fresh dill
a handful of blanched almonds
a knob (pat) of butter
salt and ground black pepper

Preparation: 4 minutes; Cooking: 12 minutes

1 Sprinkle the halved tomatoes with the cinnamon, saffron and orange flower water. Trickle half the oil over, being sure to moisten every tomato half, and sprinkle with sugar. Place under a medium grill (broiler) for 10 minutes.

2 Brush the remaining olive oil over the swordfish steaks and season with salt and pepper.

3 Lightly oil a pre-heated cast-iron griddle and cook the steaks for 3–4 minutes on each side. Sprinkle the chopped preserved lemon and chopped coriander or dill over the steaks towards the end of the cooking time. Do not let the herbs char.

4 In a separate pan, fry the almonds in the butter until golden and sprinkle them over the tomatoes. Serve the steaks immediately with the tomatoes.

> **Variation**
> For slow-roasted tomatoes, preheat the oven to 110°C/225°F/ Gas ¼. Place the tray in the bottom of the oven and cook the tomatoes for about 3 hours, then leave them to cool.

Skewers Energy 363Kcal/1,511kJ; Protein 32.2g; Carbohydrate 11.5g, of which sugars 9.6g; Fat 21.2g, of which saturates 3.6g; Cholesterol 69mg; Calcium 33mg; Fibre 2.5g; Sodium 225mg.
Griddled Swordfish Energy 405kcal/1696kJ; Protein 42.3g; Carbohydrate 7.8g, of which sugars 7.8g; Fat 23g, of which saturates 5.2g; Cholesterol 98mg; Calcium 27mg; Fibre 2.5g; Sodium 330mg.

Warm Swordfish & Rocket Salad

Swordfish is robust enough to take the sharp flavours of rocket and Pecorino cheese. The fish can be dry, so don't skip the marinating stage unless you're really pushed.

Serves 4
4 swordfish steaks, about 175g/6oz each

75ml/5 tbsp extra virgin olive oil, plus extra for serving
juice of 1 lemon
30ml/2 tbsp finely chopped fresh parsley
115g/4oz rocket (arugula) leaves, stalks removed
115g/4oz Pecorino cheese
salt and ground black pepper

Preparation: 7 minutes; Cooking: 8–12 minutes

1 Lay the swordfish steaks in a shallow dish. Mix 60ml/4 tbsp of the olive oil with the lemon juice. Pour over the fish. Season, sprinkle with parsley and turn the fish to coat. Cover the dish and leave to marinate for 5 minutes.

2 Heat a ridged griddle pan or the grill (broiler) until very hot. Take the fish out of the marinade and pat it dry with kitchen paper.

3 Grill (broil) two steaks at a time for 2–3 minutes on each side until the swordfish is just cooked, but still juicy.

4 Meanwhile, put the rocket leaves in a bowl and season with a little salt and plenty of pepper. Add the remaining 15ml/1 tbsp olive oil and toss well.

5 Place the swordfish steaks on four individual plates and arrange a little pile of salad on each steak. Shave the Pecorino over the top. Serve extra olive oil separately so it can be drizzled over the swordfish.

Variation
Tuna, shark or marlin steaks would be equally good in this delicious fish salad, with its sophisticated flavours.

Swordfish Tacos

It is important not to overcook swordfish, or it can be tough and dry. Cooked correctly, however, it is absolutely delicious and makes a great change from beef or chicken as a taco filling. The mixture is also very good in warmed pitta breads. Slit them and open them out to make pockets, place a little shredded lettuce in each and fill with the swordfish mixture.

Serves 6
3 swordfish steaks
30ml/2 tbsp vegetable oil
2 garlic cloves, crushed
1 small onion, chopped
3 fresh green chillies, seeded and chopped
3 tomatoes
small bunch of fresh coriander (cilantro), chopped
6 fresh corn tortillas
½ iceberg lettuce, shredded
salt and ground black pepper
lemon wedges, to serve (optional)

Preparation: 7–10 minutes; Cooking: 10–13 minutes

1 Preheat the grill (broiler). Put the swordfish on an oiled rack over a grill pan and grill (broil) for 2–3 minutes on each side. When cool enough to handle, remove the skin and flake the fish into a bowl.

2 Heat the oil in a pan. Add the garlic, onion and chillies and fry for 5 minutes or until the onion is soft and translucent. Do not let the onion burn or it will taste bitter.

3 Cut a cross in the base of each tomato and pour over boiling water. After 3 minutes lift out the tomatoes and plunge them into cold water. Remove the skins and seeds and chop the flesh into 1cm/½in dice.

4 Add the tomatoes and swordfish to the onion mixture. Cook for 5 minutes over a low heat. Add the coriander and cook for 1–2 minutes. Season to taste.

5 Wrap the tortillas in foil and steam on a plate over boiling water until pliable. Place some shredded lettuce and fish mixture on each tortilla. Fold in half and serve with lemon wedges, if you like.

Warm Salad Energy 452kcal/1880kJ; Protein 43.6g; Carbohydrate 0.5g, of which sugars 0.4g; Fat 30.6g, of which saturates 9.5g; Cholesterol 101mg; Calcium 401mg; Fibre 0.6g; Sodium 581mg.
Tacos Energy 293kcal/1236kJ; Protein 22.7g; Carbohydrate 33.2g, of which sugars 3.7g; Fat 8.6g, of which saturates 1.4g; Cholesterol 41mg; Calcium 77mg; Fibre 2.1g; Sodium 276mg.

Red Snapper Burritos

Fish makes a great filling for a tortilla, especially when it is succulent red snapper.	1 pasilla or similar dried chilli, seeded and ground
	75g/3oz/³⁄₄ cup slivered almonds
	200g/7oz can chopped tomatoes in tomato juice
Serves 6	150g/5oz/1¼ cups grated
3 red snapper fillets	Monterey Jack or mild
90g/3½ oz/½ cup long grain	Cheddar cheese
white rice	8 x 20cm/8in wheat flour tortillas
30ml/2 tbsp vegetable oil	fresh flat-leaf parsley to garnish
1 small onion, finely chopped	lime wedges (optional)
5ml/1 tsp ground achiote seed (annatto powder)	

Preparation: 4–5 minutes; Cooking: 14 minutes

1 Preheat the grill (broiler). Grill the fish on an oiled rack for about 5 minutes, turning once. When cool, remove the skin and flake the fish into a bowl. Set it aside.

2 Meanwhile, put the rice in a pan, cover with cold water, cover and bring to the boil. Drain, rinse and drain again.

3 Heat the oil in a pan and fry the onion until soft and translucent. Stir in the ground achiote (annatto powder) and the chilli and cook for 5 minutes.

4 Add the rice, stir well, then stir in the fish and almonds. Add the tomatoes, with their juice. Cook over a moderate heat until the juice is absorbed and the rice is tender. Stir in the cheese and remove from the heat.

5 Wrap the tortillas in foil and warm them in a low oven, or wrap them in a clean dish towel, separating the individual tortillas with clear film (plastic wrap) and warm the package in the microwave. They will take about 1 minute on High.

6 Divide the filling among the tortillas and fold them to make neat parcels. Garnish with fresh parsley and serve with lime wedges, if liked. A green salad makes a good accompaniment.

Red Snapper with Fresh Coriander & Almonds

Fried almonds are a standard accompaniment for trout but are equally good with red snapper, a fish that is very popular.	salt and ground black pepper
	75g/3oz/6 tbsp butter
	15ml/1 tbsp vegetable oil
	75g/3oz/³⁄₄ cup flaked (sliced) almonds
	grated rind and juice of 1 lime
Serves 4	small bunch of fresh coriander (cilantro), finely chopped
75g/3oz/³⁄₄ cup plain (all-purpose) flour	boiled rice and warm wheat flour tortillas, to serve
4 red snapper fillets	

Preparation: 4 minutes; Cooking: 8–10 minutes

1 Preheat the oven to 140°C/275°F/Gas 1. Spread out the flour in a shallow dish and add seasoning. Dry the fish fillets with kitchen paper, then coat each fillet in the seasoned flour.

2 Heat the butter and oil in a frying pan. Add the snapper fillets, in batches if necessary, and cook for 2 minutes. Turn the fillets over carefully and cook the other side until golden.

3 Using a fish slice, carefully transfer the fillets to a shallow dish and keep them warm in the oven. Add the almonds to the fat remaining and fry them for 3–4 minutes, until golden.

4 Add the lime rind, juice and coriander to the almonds in the frying pan and stir well. Heat through for 1–2 minutes, then pour the mixture over the fish. Serve with a bowl of rice or with warm wheat flour tortillas.

> **Cook's Tip**
> Warm the tortillas by wrapping them in foil and steaming them on a plate over boiling water for a few minutes. Alternatively, wrap them in microwave-safe film and heat them in a microwave on full power for about 1 minute.

Burritos Energy 224kcal/935kJ; Protein 17.1g; Carbohydrate 11.3g, of which sugars 1.7g; Fat 11.9g, of which saturates 4.6g; Cholesterol 41mg; Calcium 172mg; Fibre 1.1g; Sodium 178mg.
Red Snapper Energy 433kcal/1803kJ; Protein 25.4g; Carbohydrate 16g, of which sugars 1.2g; Fat 30.2g, of which saturates 11.3g; Cholesterol 77mg; Calcium 115mg; Fibre 2g; Sodium 194mg.

Seared Tuna with Watercress Salad

Tuna steaks are wonderful seared and served slightly rare with a punchy sauce and watercress salad.

Serves 4
30ml/2 tbsp olive oil
5ml/1 tsp harissa
5ml/1 tsp clear honey
4 x 200g/7oz tuna steaks
salt and ground black pepper
lemon wedges, to serve

For the salad
30ml/2 tbsp olive oil
a little butter
25g/1oz fresh root ginger, peeled and thinly sliced
2 garlic cloves, finely sliced
2 fresh green chillies, seeded and thinly sliced
6 spring onions (scallions), cut into bitesize pieces
2 large handfuls watercress
1 lemon, cut into 4 wedges

Preparation: 6 minutes; Cooking: 10 minutes

1 Mix the olive oil, harissa, honey and salt, and rub it over the tuna steaks.

2 Heat a frying pan, grease it with a little oil and sear the tuna steaks for about 2 minutes on each side. They should still be pink on the inside.

3 Keep the tuna warm while you quickly prepare the salad: heat the olive oil and butter in a heavy pan. Stir in the ginger, garlic, chillies and spring onions, cook until the mixture begins to colour, then add the watercress. As soon as the watercress begins to wilt, toss in the lemon juice and season well with salt and plenty of ground black pepper.

4 Tip the warm salad on to a serving dish or individual plates. Slice the tuna steaks and arrange on top of the salad. Serve immediately with lemon wedges for squeezing over.

Cook's Tip
Harissa is a North African spice paste based on chillies, garlic, coriander and cumin seeds. It is sold in tubes, like tomato purée (paste), or jars, or can be made fresh.

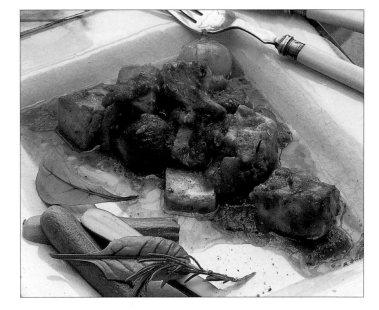

Fresh Tuna & Tomato Stew

A deliciously simple Italian recipe that relies on good basic ingredients: fresh fish, tomatoes and herbs. For an authentic flavour, serve with polenta or pasta.

Serves 4
12 baby (pearl) onions, peeled
900g/2lb ripe tomatoes
675g/1½lb tuna
45ml/3 tbsp olive oil

2 garlic cloves, crushed
45ml/3 tbsp chopped fresh herbs
2 bay leaves
2.5ml/½ tsp caster (superfine) sugar
30ml/2 tbsp sun-dried tomato purée (paste)
150ml/¼ pint/⅔ cup dry white wine
salt and ground black pepper
baby courgettes (zucchini) and fresh herbs, to garnish

Preparation: 4–5 minutes; Cooking: 15 minutes

1 Leave the onions whole and cook in a pan of boiling water for 4 minutes until softened. Drain. Plunge the tomatoes into boiling water for 30 seconds, then refresh in cold water. Peel off the skins and chop roughly.

2 Cut the tuna into 2.5cm/1in chunks. Heat the oil in a large frying or sauté pan and quickly fry the tuna until the surface has browned. Lift the chunks out of the pan and drain.

3 Stir in the onions, garlic, tomatoes, chopped herbs, bay leaves, sugar, tomato purée and wine, and bring to the boil, breaking up the tomatoes with a wooden spoon.

4 Reduce the heat and simmer the sauce gently for 5 minutes. Return the fish to the pan and cook for a further 4 minutes. Season, and serve hot, garnished with the baby courgettes and a selection of fresh herbs.

Variation
Two large mackerel make a more readily available alternative to the tuna. Simply lay the whole fish over the sauce and cook, covered with a lid, until the mackerel is cooked through.

Seared Tuna Energy 389kcal/1630kJ; Protein 49.2g; Carbohydrate 1.6g, of which sugars 1.6g; Fat 20.8g, of which saturates 4.2g; Cholesterol 56mg; Calcium 123mg; Fibre 1g; Sodium 120mg.
Tuna Stew Energy 393kcal/1648kJ; Protein 42.8g; Carbohydrate 13.8g, of which sugars 12.4g; Fat 16.8g, of which saturates 3.4g; Cholesterol 47mg; Calcium 64mg; Fibre 3.4g; Sodium 121mg.

Salmon & Tuna Parcels

You need fairly large smoked salmon slices for this dish, as they are wrapped around a light tuna mixture before being served on a vibrant tomato salad.

Serves 4
30ml/2 tbsp natural (plain) yogurt
15ml/1 tbsp tomato purée (paste)
5ml/1 tsp wholegrain honey
    mustard
grated rind and juice of 1 lime
200g/7oz can tuna in brine,
    drained

12–16 large slices of
    smoked salmon
salt and ground black pepper
fresh mint leaves, to garnish

For the salad
3 ripe vine tomatoes, sliced
2 kiwi fruit, peeled and sliced
¼ cucumber, cut into
    julienne sticks
15ml/1 tbsp chopped fresh mint
7.5ml/1½ tsp white wine vinegar
45ml/3 tbsp olive oil
2.5ml/½ tsp mustard

Preparation: 10–12 minutes; Cooking: 0 minutes

1 Put the yogurt, tomato purée and mustard in a bowl and mix well with a wooden spoon until all the tomato purée has been incorporated. Stir in the grated lime rind and juice. Add the tuna, with black pepper to taste, and mix well.

2 Spread out the salmon slices on a chopping board and spoon some of the tuna mixture on to each piece.

3 Roll up or fold the smoked salmon into neat parcels. Carefully press the edges together to seal.

4 Make the salad. Arrange the tomato and kiwi slices on four serving plates. Sprinkle over the cucumber sticks.

5 In a bowl, whisk the chopped mint, white wine vinegar, oil, mustard and a little seasoning together and spoon some over each salad to moisten.

6 Arrange 3–4 salmon parcels on each plate, placing them so that they form a rough triangle on top of the tomato and kiwi slices. Garnish with the fresh mint leaves and serve immediately.

Salmon Fish Cakes

The secret of a good fish cake is to make it with freshly prepared fish and potatoes, home-made breadcrumbs and plenty of fresh herbs, such as dill and parsley or tarragon.

Serves 4
450g/1lb cooked salmon fillet
450g/1lb freshly cooked
    potatoes, mashed
25g/1oz/2 tbsp butter, melted or
    30ml/2 tbsp olive oil
10ml/2 tsp wholegrain mustard

15ml/1 tbsp each chopped fresh
    dill and chopped fresh parsley
    or tarragon
grated rind and juice of ½ lemon
15g/½oz/2 tbsp wholemeal
    (whole-wheat) flour
1 egg, lightly beaten
150g/5oz/2 cups dried
    breadcrumbs
60ml/4 tbsp sunflower oil
sea salt and ground black pepper
rocket (arugula) leaves and
    chives, to garnish
lemon wedges, to serve

Preparation: 5 minutes; Cooking: 8–10 minutes

1 Flake the cooked salmon, discarding any skin and bones. Put it in a bowl with the mashed potato, melted butter or oil and wholegrain mustard, and mix well. Stir in the herbs and the lemon rind and juice. Season to taste with plenty of sea salt and ground black pepper.

2 Divide the mixture into eight portions and shape each into a ball, then flatten into a thick disc. Dip the fish cakes first in flour, then in egg and finally in breadcrumbs, making sure that they are evenly coated with crumbs.

3 Heat the oil in a frying pan until it is very hot. Fry the fish cakes in batches until golden brown and crisp all over. As each batch is ready, drain on kitchen paper and keep hot. Garnish with rocket and chives and serve with lemon wedges.

> **Cook's Tip**
> *Any fresh white or hot-smoked fish is suitable. Always buy organically farmed fish, or sustainably caught wild fish.*

Parcels Energy 309kcal/1295kJ; Protein 38.8g; Carbohydrate 8.5g, of which sugars 8.4g; Fat 13.5g, of which saturates 2.2g; Cholesterol 61mg; Calcium 56mg; Fibre 1.6g; Sodium 2064mg.
Fish Cakes Energy 586kcal/2453kJ; Protein 29.8g; Carbohydrate 49.9g, of which sugars 3.2g; Fat 31g, of which saturates 7.2g; Cholesterol 117mg; Calcium 79mg; Fibre 1.3g; Sodium 266mg.

Salmon with Green Peppercorns

Salmon benefits from being served with a piquant accompaniment. Lemon and lime are the obvious choices, but capers and green peppercorns also serve to counter the rich taste of the fish.

Serves 4
15g/½oz/1 tbsp butter
2–3 shallots, finely chopped
15ml/1 tbsp brandy (optional)
60ml/4 tbsp white wine
90ml/6 tbsp fish or chicken stock
120ml/4fl oz/½ cup whipping cream
30–45ml/2–3 tbsp green peppercorns in brine, rinsed
15–30ml/1–2 tbsp vegetable oil
4 pieces salmon fillet, each about 175g/6oz
salt and ground black pepper
fresh parsley, to garnish

Preparation: 3–4 minutes; Cooking: 13–15 minutes

1 Melt the butter in a heavy pan over a medium heat. Add the shallots and cook over low to medium heat for 1–2 minutes, until just softened but not coloured.

2 Add the brandy, if using, then pour in the white wine and stock. Bring to the boil. Boil vigorously to reduce by three-quarters, stirring occasionally.

3 Reduce the heat, then add the cream and half the peppercorns, crushing them slightly against the sides of the pan with the back of a spoon. Cook very gently for 4–5 minutes, until the sauce has thickened slightly.

4 Strain the sauce into a clean pan and stir in the remaining peppercorns. Keep the sauce warm over a very low heat, stirring occasionally, while you cook the salmon fillets.

5 Heat the oil in a large, heavy frying pan over a medium-high heat. Lightly season the salmon. When the oil is very hot, add the salmon. Sear the fillets on both sides, then lower the heat and cook for 4–6 minutes, until the flesh is opaque throughout.

6 Arrange the fish on warmed plates and pour over the sauce. Garnish with parsley and serve.

Salmon with Whisky & Cream

This dish combines two of the finest flavours of Scotland – salmon and whisky. It takes very little time to make, so cook it at the last moment. Serve quite plainly.

Serves 4
4 thin pieces of salmon fillet, about 175g/6oz each
5ml/1 tsp chopped fresh thyme leaves
50g/2oz/¼ cup butter
75ml/5 tbsp whisky
150ml/¼ pint/⅔ cup double (heavy) cream
juice of ½ lemon (optional)
salt and ground black pepper
fresh dill sprigs, to garnish

Preparation: 2 3 minutes; Cooking: 12–16 minutes

1 Season the salmon with salt, pepper and thyme. Melt half the butter in a frying pan large enough to hold two pieces of salmon side by side.

2 When the butter is foaming, fry the first two pieces of salmon for 2–3 minutes on each side, until they are golden on the outside and just cooked through.

3 Pour in 30ml/2 tbsp of the whisky and ignite it. When the flames have died down, carefully transfer the salmon to a plate and keep it hot. Heat the remaining butter in the frying pan. Scrape the base to incorporate any sediment, and cook the second two pieces of salmon in the same way. Add them to the plate with the other pieces of salmon, cover with foil and continue to keep the fish hot while you make the sauce.

4 Pour the cream into the pan and bring to the boil, stirring constantly and scraping up the cooking juices from the base of the pan. Allow to bubble until reduced and slightly thickened, then season and add the last of the whisky and a squeeze of lemon, if you like.

5 Place the salmon pieces on individual warmed plates, pour the sauce over and garnish with dill. New potatoes and crisp green beans are good with this.

With Peppercorns Energy 526kcal/2180kJ; Protein 36.3g; Carbohydrate 2.9g, of which sugars 2.3g; Fat 40g, of which saturates 13.5g; Cholesterol 127mg; Calcium 63mg; Fibre 0.4g; Sodium 110mg.
With Whisky Energy 667kcal/2760kJ; Protein 36.1g; Carbohydrate 0.8g, of which sugars 0.8g; Fat 53g, of which saturates 24.5g; Cholesterol 174mg; Calcium 61mg; Fibre 0g; Sodium 164mg.

Salmon with Lemon & Tofu Sauce

The elegant simplicity of this dish makes it an ideal choice for a dinner party. Moreover, it is very quick and easy to prepare while looking and tasting wonderful.

Serves 2
2 salmon steaks or fillets, each
    weighing about
    130–150g/4 1/2–5oz
5cm/2in piece fresh root ginger,
    cut into thin sticks
2 garlic cloves, finely chopped

1 small red chilli, seeded and
    finely chopped
bunch of fresh dill, parsley or
    coriander (cilantro), tough
    stems removed
sea salt and ground black pepper
15ml/1 tbsp sesame seeds,
    toasted, to garnish

For the sauce
175g/6oz silken tofu
grated rind and juice of 1 lemon
50ml/3 1/2 tbsp water

Preparation: 8 minutes; Cooking: 5–10 minutes

1 Line a bamboo steaming basket or metal steaming tray with baking parchment, then arrange the salmon steaks or fillets on top. Pile the ginger, garlic and chilli, and half of the dill, parsley or coriander on top of the fish and season with salt and pepper, then cover and steam for 5–10 minutes, or until the fish is opaque and just cooked through.

2 Meanwhile, make the sauce by blending all the ingredients and the remaining herbs in a blender or food processor until smooth. Transfer to a small pan and gently warm through, stirring frequently.

3 Serve the fish with the sauce spooned over the top and garnished with the toasted sesame seeds.

Cook's Tip
Steaming is a wonderful way of cooking fish, ensuring that the maximum flavour is retained. If you like, the water beneath the steamer can be scented by the addition of some lemon grass or a strip of pared lemon rind.

Baked Salmon with a Guava Sauce

Guavas have a creamy flesh with a citrus tang, which makes them perfect to serve with salmon.

Serves 4
6 ripe guavas
45ml/3 tbsp vegetable oil

1 small onion, finely chopped
120ml/4fl oz/1/2 cup well-
    flavoured chicken stock
10ml/2 tsp hot pepper sauce
4 salmon steaks
salt and ground black pepper
strips of red (bell) pepper
    to garnish

Preparation: 4 minutes; Cooking: 12–14 minutes

1 Cut each guava in half. Scoop the seeded soft flesh into a sieve (strainer) placed over a bowl. Press it through the sieve, discard the seeds and skin and set the pulp aside.

2 Heat 30ml/2 tbsp of the oil in a frying pan. Fry the chopped onion for about 4 minutes over a moderate heat until softened and translucent.

3 Stir in the guava pulp, with the chicken stock and hot pepper sauce. Cook, stirring, until the sauce thickens. Keep it warm.

4 Brush the salmon steaks on one side with a little of the remaining oil. Season them with salt and pepper. Heat a griddle or ridged grill pan until very hot and add the salmon steaks, oiled side down. Cook for 2–3 minutes, until the underside is golden, then brush the surface with oil, turn each salmon steak over and cook the other side until the fish is cooked and flakes easily when tested with the tip of a sharp knife.

5 Transfer each steak to a warmed plate. Serve, garnished with strips of red pepper on a pool of sauce. A fresh green salad is a good accompaniment.

Cook's Tip
Ripe guavas have yellow skin and succulent flesh that ranges in colour from white to deep pink or salmon red.

Salmon with Lemon Energy 387kcal/1612kJ; Protein 39.5g; Carbohydrate 1.4g, of which sugars 0.9g; Fat 24.9g, of which saturates 3.9g; Cholesterol 75mg; Calcium 578mg; Fibre 1.9g; Sodium 81mg.
Baked Salmon Energy 389kcal/1621kJ; Protein 31.7g; Carbohydrate 8.7g, of which sugars 8.2g; Fat 25.5g, of which saturates 3.8g; Cholesterol 75mg; Calcium 55mg; Fibre 5.8g; Sodium 76mg.

Hot Smoked Salmon

This is a fantastic way of smoking salmon on a barbecue in no time at all. The mojo makes a mildly spicy companion.

Serves 6
6 salmon fillets, each about
 175g/6oz, with skin
15ml/1 tbsp sunflower oil
salt and ground black pepper
2 handfuls hickory wood chips,
 soaked in cold water for as
 much time as you have
 available, preferably 30 minutes

For the mojo
1 ripe mango, diced
4 drained canned pineapple
 slices, diced
1 small red onion, finely chopped
1 fresh long mild red chilli, seeded
 and finely chopped
15ml/1 tbsp good-quality sweet
 chilli sauce
grated rind and juice of 1 lime
leaves from 1 small lemon basil
 plant or 45ml/3 tbsp fresh
 coriander (cilantro) leaves,
 shredded or chopped

Preparation: 5 minutes; Cooking: 11–13 minutes, plus soaking

1 First, make the mojo by putting the mango and diced pineapple in a bowl. Add the chopped onion and seeded and chopped chilli, and stir to mix. Add the chilli sauce, lime rind and juice, and the herb leaves. Stir to mix well. Cover tightly with clear film (plastic wrap) and leave in a cool place until needed.

2 Rinse the salmon fillets and pat dry, then brush each with a little oil. Place the fillets skin side down on a lightly oiled grill (broiler) rack over medium-hot coals. Cover the barbecue with a lid or tented heavy-duty foil and cook the fish for 3–5 minutes.

3 Drain the hickory chips into a colander and sprinkle about a third of them as evenly as possible over the coals. Carefully drop them through the slats in the grill racks, taking care not to scatter the ash as you do so.

4 Replace the barbecue cover and continue cooking for a further 8 minutes, adding a small handful of hickory chips twice more during this time. Serve the salmon hot or cold, with the mango and pineapple mojo.

Filo-wrapped Salmon

Select a chunky variety of tomato sauce for this simple but delicious recipe. When working with filo pastry, keep it covered with clear film (plastic wrap) or a damp dish towel, as once it's exposed to air it dries out quickly and becomes brittle and difficult to handle.

Serves 3–4
about 130g/4½oz filo pastry
 (6–8 large sheets)
about 30ml/2 tbsp olive oil,
 for brushing
450g/1lb salmon fillets
550ml/18fl oz/2½ cups fresh
 tomato sauce

Preparation: 4–5 minutes; Cooking: 10–15 minutes

1 Preheat the oven to 200°C/400°F/Gas 6. Take a sheet of filo pastry, brush with a little olive oil and cover with a second sheet of pastry. Place a piece of fish on top of the pastry, towards the bottom edge, then top with 1–2 spoonfuls of the tomato sauce, spreading it in an even layer.

2 Roll the fish in the pastry, taking care to enclose the filling completely. Brush with a little olive oil. Place on a baking sheet and repeat with the remaining fish and pastry, placing each parcel on the baking sheet but keeping them apart. You should have about half the sauce remaining, to serve with the fish.

3 Bake for 10–15 minutes, or until golden. Meanwhile, reheat the remaining sauce. Serve the filo-wrapped salmon immediately with the remaining tomato sauce.

Cook's Tip
To save time, use a bottled tomato sauce in this dish. There is a vast selection these days and a quick trawl through the pasta sauces at the supermarket will offer a wide choice. A simple tomato and basil sauce, or one including mushrooms, would work well. Alternatively, try puttanesca sauce, which includes black olives, chilli, garlic and anchovies. It has a robust flavour but if you use it sparingly it will not overwhelm the flavour of the salmon.

Filo-wrapped Salmon Energy 460kcal/1924kJ; Protein 28.1g; Carbohydrate 31.3g, of which sugars 5.9g; Fat 25.8g, of which saturates 5.5g; Cholesterol 70mg; Calcium 85mg; Fibre 2.7g; Sodium 519mg.
Hot Smoked Salmon Energy 364kcal/1519kJ; Protein 35.9g; Carbohydrate 7.8g, of which sugars 7.4g; Fat 21.2g, of which saturates 3.6g; Cholesterol 88mg; Calcium 58mg; Fibre 1.3g; Sodium 82mg.

Creamy Penne with Smoked Salmon

No supper dish could be simpler. Freshly cooked pasta is tossed with cream, smoked salmon and thyme to make a lovely, light dish that looks as good as it tastes and goes down well with guests of all ages.

Serves 4
350g/12oz/3 cups dried penne
115g/4oz thinly sliced
   smoked salmon
2–3 fresh thyme sprigs
25g/1oz/2 tbsp butter
150ml/¼ pint/²⁄₃ cup double
   (heavy) cream
salt and ground black pepper

Preparation: 2 minutes; Cooking: 10–12 minutes

1 Cook the pasta in a large pan of lightly salted boiling water for 10–12 minutes, until tender but still firm to the bite.

2 Meanwhile, using kitchen scissors or a small, sharp knife, cut the smoked salmon into thin strips, each about 5mm/¼ in wide, and place on a plate. Strip the leaves from the thyme sprigs.

3 Melt the butter in a large pan. Stir in the cream with a quarter of the salmon and thyme leaves, then season with pepper. Heat gently for 3–4 minutes, stirring constantly. Do not allow the sauce to boil. Taste for seasoning.

4 Drain the pasta and toss it in the cream and salmon sauce. Divide among four warmed bowls and top with the remaining salmon and thyme leaves.

> **Cook's Tip**
> For a healthier, low-fat version of this dish, use low-fat crème fraîche in place of the double (heavy) cream.

> **Variation**
> Substitute low-fat cream cheese for half the cream in the sauce for a less rich mixture that still tastes very good.

Lemon & Salmon Pappardelle

This is a fantastic all-in-one supper dish that tastes great and is made in just a few minutes – ideal for when you're really hungry but haven't much time. Serve it with a rocket salad dressed with extra virgin olive oil, balsamic vinegar and black pepper. Add some baby plum tomatoes for extra colour, if you like, and some slices of orange or green (bell) pepper for crunch.

Serves 4
500g/1¼lb fresh pappardelle
   or tagliatelle
300ml/½ pint/1¼ cups single
   (light) cream
grated rind and juice of 2 lemons
225g/8oz smoked salmon pieces
2.5ml/½ tsp grated nutmeg
60ml/4 tbsp chopped fresh parsley
salt and ground black pepper
fresh Parmesan cheese shavings,
   to garnish
rocket (arugula) salad, to serve

Preparation: 2 minutes; Cooking: 6–7 minutes

1 Bring a large pan of lightly salted water to the boil and cook the pappardelle or tagliatelle for 3–5 minutes, or according to the instructions on the packet, until risen to the surface of the boiling water and just tender. Drain well.

2 Add the cream, lemon rind and juice to the pan and heat through gently until piping hot. Return the cooked pappardelle to the pan and stir thoroughly to coat the pasta with the creamy mixture.

3 Add the salmon pieces, grated nutmeg, chopped parsley and plenty of ground black pepper to the sauce in the pan and stir well to combine.

4 Divide the pasta among four warmed serving plates and top with the fresh Parmesan shavings. Serve immediately with the rocket salad.

> **Cook's Tip**
> Smoked salmon freezes well in its original packaging. It thaws quickly, ready for simple suppers and breakfasts.

Penne Energy 573kcal/2403kJ; Protein 18.5g; Carbohydrate 65.5g, of which sugars 3.6g; Fat 28.2g, of which saturates 16.2g; Cholesterol 75mg; Calcium 47mg; Fibre 2.6g; Sodium 589mg.
Pappardelle Energy 657kcal/2773kJ; Protein 32.2g; Carbohydrate 94.6g, of which sugars 6.1g; Fat 19.3g, of which saturates 9.8g; Cholesterol 61mg; Calcium 134mg; Fibre 4.3g; Sodium 1087mg.

Tagliatelle with Smoked Salmon

The light texture of the cucumber perfectly complements the smoked salmon and the pastel colours look very attractive against the creamy swirls of tagliatelle.

Serves 4

350g/12oz/3 cups dried or
   fresh tagliatelle
½ cucumber
75g/3oz/6 tbsp butter
grated rind of 1 orange
30ml/2 tbsp chopped fresh dill
300ml/½ pint/1¼ cups single
   (light) cream
15ml/1 tbsp orange juice
115g/4oz smoked salmon,
   skinned
salt and ground black pepper

Preparation: 2 minutes; Cooking: 6–16 minutes

1 Bring a large pan of lightly salted water to the boil and add the pasta. If using dried pasta, cook for about 12 minutes or for the time recommended on the packet. If using fresh pasta, cook for 2–3 minutes, or until just tender but still firm to the bite.

2 Using a sharp knife, cut the cucumber in half lengthways, then use a small spoon to scoop out and discard the cucumber seeds. Turn the cucumber on to the flat side and slice it thinly in crescent shapes.

3 Melt the butter in a heavy pan, add the grated orange rind and fresh dill and stir well. Add the cucumber and cook over a low heat for about 2 minutes, stirring from time to time with a wooden spoon.

4 Stir in the cream and orange juice, with salt and pepper to taste. Reduce the heat to the lowest setting and cook gently for 1 minute, stirring constantly with a wooden spoon.

5 Cut the salmon into thin strips. Stir these into the sauce and heat through gently. Do not let the sauce boil.

6 Drain the pasta thoroughly and return it to the pan. Add the sauce and toss to combine. Spoon into a dish or into individual shallow pasta plates and serve.

Farfalle with Smoked Salmon & Dill

This quick, luxurious sauce for pasta has become very fashionable in Italy, but wherever you have it, it will taste delicious. Dill is the classic herb for cooking with fish, but if you don't like its aniseed flavour, substitute parsley or a little fresh tarragon. The fresher the herbs, the better the taste, so it is always worth growing some in pots or in the garden.

Serves 4

6 spring onions (scallions), sliced
50g/2oz/¼ cup butter
90ml/6 tbsp dry white wine
   or vermouth
450ml/¾ pint/scant 2 cups
   double (heavy) cream
freshly grated nutmeg
225g/8oz smoked salmon
30ml/2 tbsp chopped fresh dill
freshly squeezed lemon juice
450g/1lb/4 cups fresh farfalle
salt and ground black pepper
fresh dill sprigs, to garnish

Preparation: 4 minutes; Cooking: 8–10 minutes

1 Using a sharp cook's knife, slice the spring onions finely. Melt the butter in a large pan and fry the spring onions for about 1 minute, stirring occasionally, until softened.

2 Add the wine or vermouth and boil hard to reduce to about 30ml/2 tbsp. Stir in the cream and add salt, pepper and nutmeg to taste. Bring to the boil, then simmer for 2–3 minutes until slightly thickened.

3 Cut the smoked salmon into 2.5cm/1in squares and stir into the sauce, together with the dill. Add lemon juice to taste.

4 Cook the pasta in a large pan of boiling salted water for 2–3 minutes, or until it rises to the surface of the liquid. Drain well. Toss with the sauce. Spoon into serving bowls and serve immediately, garnished with sprigs of dill.

Cook's Tip
If you can't locate fresh pasta, use dried, and cook in boiling water for 12 minutes or according to package instructions.

Tagliatelle Energy 626kcal/2624kJ; Protein 20.4g; Carbohydrate 66.9g, of which sugars 5g; Fat 32.6g, of which saturates 19.3g; Cholesterol 91mg; Calcium 98mg; Fibre 2.6g; Sodium 679mg.
Farfalle Energy 1162kcal/4846kJ; Protein 30g; Carbohydrate 86.5g, of which sugars 6.8g; Fat 77.4g, of which saturates 46.1g; Cholesterol 206mg; Calcium 104mg; Fibre 3.5g; Sodium 1180mg.

Buckwheat Noodles with Smoked Salmon

Young pea sprouts are available for only a short time. You can substitute watercress, mustard cress, young leeks or your favourite green vegetable or herb in this dish, but don't choose anything too robust in terms of texture or flavour. Mangetouts, sliced lengthways, pencil-thin green beans or young asparagus spears would be ideal.

Serves 4
225g/8oz buckwheat or
  soba noodles
15ml/1 tbsp oyster sauce
juice of ½ lemon
30–45ml/2–3 tbsp light olive oil
115g/4oz smoked salmon, cut
  into fine strips
115g/4oz young pea sprouts
2 ripe tomatoes, peeled, seeded
  and cut into strips
15ml/1 tbsp snipped chives
salt and ground black pepper

Preparation: 8–10 minutes; Cooking: 6–7 minutes

1 Cook the buckwheat or soba noodles in a large pan of boiling water, following the directions on the packet. Drain, then tip into a colander and rinse under cold running water. Drain well, shaking the colander to extract any remaining water.

2 Tip the noodles into a large bowl. Add the oyster sauce and lemon juice and season with pepper to taste. Moisten with the olive oil.

3 Add the smoked salmon, pea sprouts, tomatoes and chives. Mix well and serve at once.

Variations
• *To keep the cost of this dish down, use a packet of smoked salmon trimmings instead of cutting up more expensive slices. It will taste just the same.*
• *Instead of buckwheat or soba noodles, use fresh tagliatelle or pappardelle, cooked in salted boiling water for 2–3 minutes. The pasta is ready when it rises to the surface of the liquid.*

Smoked Trout Pasta Salad

Choose hollow pasta shapes, such as shells or penne, which trap the creamy filling, creating tasty mouthfuls of trout, fennel and spring onion. The addition of dill is not only attractive, but also gives this salad a distinctive aniseed flavour.

Serves 8
15g/½oz/1 tbsp butter
1 bulb fennel, finely chopped

8 spring onions (scallions),
  2 very finely chopped and
  4 thinly sliced
225g/8oz smoked trout fillets,
  skinned and flaked
45ml/3 tbsp chopped fresh dill
120ml/4fl oz/½ cup mayonnaise
10ml/2 tsp lemon juice
30ml/2 tbsp whipping cream
450g/1lb small fresh pasta
  shapes, such as shells
salt and ground black pepper
fresh dill sprigs, to garnish

Preparation: 8–10 minutes; Cooking: 5–8 minutes

1 Melt the butter in a small frying pan. Add the fennel and finely chopped spring onions and fry over a medium heat for 3–5 minutes. Transfer to a large bowl and leave to cool.

2 Add the sliced spring onions, trout, dill, mayonnaise, lemon juice and cream to the bowl with the fennel. Season lightly with salt and pepper and mix gently until well blended.

3 Bring a large pan of lightly salted water to the boil. Add the pasta. Cook for 2–3 minutes until al dente. Drain thoroughly in a colander and leave to cool.

4 Add the pasta to the vegetable and trout mixture and toss to coat evenly. Taste for seasoning. Serve the salad lightly chilled or at room temperature. It looks good on a shallow dish, garnished with the sprigs of dill.

Variation
This pasta salad works well with any type of fresh, cooked fish fillets, including salmon. Alternatively, you can use a 200g/7oz can of tuna in water in place of the trout.

Noodles Energy 341kcal/1437kJ; Protein 16.2g; Carbohydrate 47.6g, of which sugars 3.6g; Fat 10.9g, of which saturates 1.2g; Cholesterol 10mg; Calcium 28mg; Fibre 3.5g; Sodium 547mg.
Pasta Salad Energy 369kcal/1548kJ; Protein 14.5g; Carbohydrate 42.7g, of which sugars 2.8g; Fat 16.8g, of which saturates 4g; Cholesterol 29mg; Calcium 31mg; Fibre 2.3g; Sodium 613mg.

Fusilli with Smoked Trout

With its creamy sauce, smoked trout blends beautifully with the crisp but tender vegetables in this classic pasta dish.

Serves 4–6

2 carrots, cut into matchsticks
1 leek, cut into matchsticks
2 celery sticks, cut into matchsticks
150ml/¼ pint/⅔ cup vegetable stock
225g/8oz smoked trout fillets, skinned and cut into strips
200g/7oz cream cheese
150ml/¼ pint/⅔ cup medium sweet white wine or fish stock
15ml/1 tbsp chopped fresh dill or fennel
225g/8oz/2 cups fresh fusilli or other pasta shapes
salt and ground black pepper
fresh dill sprigs, to garnish

Preparation: 5 minutes; Cooking: 10–12 minutes

1 Put the carrot, leek and celery matchsticks into a pan and add the stock. Bring to the boil and cook quickly for 4–5 minutes, until most of the stock has evaporated. Remove from the heat and add the smoked trout.

2 Put the cream cheese and wine or fish stock into a pan over a medium heat, and whisk until smooth. Add the dill or fennel and salt and pepper.

3 Cook the fusilli in a pan of salted boiling water for 2–3 minutes, or until it rises to the surface. When the pasta is tender, but still firm to the bite, drain it thoroughly, and return to the pan.

4 Add the sauce, toss lightly and transfer to a serving bowl. Top with the cooked vegetables and trout. Serve immediately, garnished with the dill sprigs.

Variation
Cream cheese now comes in a variety of flavours. A herb variety would be ideal in this dish, or you could use smoked salmon-flavoured cheese, and substitute salmon for the trout.

Trout with Almonds

Some people regard this dish as a cliché, but if that's true, it's one that has endured for a long time. The reason is simple: this combination works extremely well.

Serves 2

2 trout, each about 350g/12oz, cleaned
40g/1½oz/⅓ cup plain (all-purpose) flour
50g/2oz/¼ cup butter
25g/1oz/¼ cup flaked (sliced) almonds
30ml/2 tbsp dry white wine
salt and ground black pepper
new potatoes and mixed green salad, to serve

Preparation: 2 minutes; Cooking: 14–16 minutes

1 Rinse the trout and pat dry. Put the flour in a large plastic bag and season with salt and pepper. Place the trout, one at a time, in the bag and shake to coat with flour. Shake off the excess flour from the fish and discard the remaining flour.

2 Melt half the butter in a large frying pan over a medium heat. When it is foamy, add the trout and cook for 6 minutes.

3 Turn the trout over and cook for 3 minutes more until the skin is golden brown and the flesh next to the bone is opaque. Transfer the fish to warmed plates and cover to keep warm.

4 Add the remaining butter to the pan and cook the almonds, shaking the pan frequently, until just lightly browned.

5 Add the white wine to the pan and boil for 1 minute, stirring constantly, until the sauce is slightly syrupy. Pour or spoon the sauce and almonds over each fish and serve immediately with boiled new potatoes and a green salad.

Variation
Other nuts can be used instead of almonds. Hazelnuts are particularly good with trout. The nuts swiftly brown and go crisp, so watch them closely to prevent them burning.

Fusilli Energy 348kcal/1455kJ; Protein 15.9g; Carbohydrate 31.4g, of which sugars 4.5g; Fat 18.5g, of which saturates 10.3g; Cholesterol 45mg; Calcium 74mg; Fibre 2.8g; Sodium 822mg.
Trout Energy 475kcal/1978kJ; Protein 39.2g; Carbohydrate 7.6g, of which sugars 0.8g; Fat 32.2g, of which saturates 12.4g; Cholesterol 187mg; Calcium 101mg; Fibre 1.2g; Sodium 249mg.

Ham-wrapped Trout

Serrano ham is used to stuff and wrap trout for this unusual recipe from Spain, ensuring a succulent flavour. One of the beauties of this method is that the skins come off in one piece, leaving the succulent, moist flesh to be eaten with the crisped, salty ham.

Serves 4

*4 brown or rainbow trout, about
    250g/9oz each, cleaned
16 thin slices Serrano ham,
    about 200g/7oz
50g/2oz/¼ cup melted butter,
    plus extra for greasing
salt and ground black pepper
buttered potatoes, to
    serve (optional)*

Preparation: 10–12 minutes; Cooking: 8 minutes

1 Extend the belly cavity of each trout, cutting up one side of the backbone. Slip a knife behind the rib bones to loosen them (sometimes just flexing the fish makes them pop up). Snip these off from both sides with scissors, and season the fish well inside.

2 Fold a piece of ham into each belly. Use smaller or broken bits of ham for this, and reserve the eight best slices.

3 Prepare the barbecue. Position a lightly oiled grill (broiler) rack over the hot coals. Brush each trout with a little butter, seasoning the outside lightly with salt and pepper. Wrap two ham slices round each one, crossways, tucking the ends into the belly.

4 Put the fish into oiled hinged wire fish baskets or directly on to the grill rack. The combined grilling time should be 4 minutes on each side, though it is wise to turn the fish every 2 minutes to ensure that the ham does not become charred.

5 Serve the trout hot, with the butter spooned over the top. Diners should open the trout on their plates, and eat them from the inside, pushing the flesh off the skin.

> **Cook's Tip**
> *The trout can be cooked under a conventional grill (broiler).*

Classic Fish & Chips

Quintessentially English, this is fish and chips as it should be cooked, with tender flakes of fish in a crisp batter, and home-made chips.

Serves 4

*450g/1lb potatoes
groundnut (peanut) oil,
    for deep-frying*

*4 x 175g/6oz cod fillets, skinned
    and any tiny bones removed*

For the batter

*75g/3oz/⅔ cup plain
    (all-purpose) flour
1 egg yolk
10ml/2 tsp oil
175ml/6fl oz/¾ cup water
salt*

Preparation: 5 minutes; Cooking: 14–15 minutes

1 To make the chips (French fries), cut the potatoes into 5mm/¼in thick slices. Then cut the slices into 5mm/¼in fingers. Rinse thoroughly, drain well and then dry in a clean dish towel.

2 Heat the oil in a deep fat fryer to 180°C/350°F. Add the chips in the basket to the fryer and cook for 3 minutes. Lift out and shake off excess fat.

3 To make the batter, sift the flour into a bowl. Add a pinch of salt. Make a well in the middle of the flour and add the egg yolk, oil and a little of the water. Mix the yolk with the liquid, then add the remaining water and incorporate the surrounding flour to make a smooth batter. Cover and set aside.

4 Reheat the oil in the fryer and cook the chips again for about 5 minutes, until they are golden and crisp. Drain on kitchen paper and season with salt. Keep hot in a low oven.

5 Dip the pieces of fish fillet into the batter and turn them to make sure they are evenly coated. Allow any excess batter to drip off before carefully lowering the fish into the hot oil.

6 Cook the fish for 5 minutes, turning once, if necessary, so that the batter browns evenly. The batter should be crisp and golden. Drain on kitchen paper. Serve at once, with lemon wedges and the chips.

Trout Energy 369kcal/1546kJ; Protein 48g; Carbohydrate 0.6g, of which sugars 0.6g; Fat 19.4g, of which saturates 8.8g; Cholesterol 216mg; Calcium 66mg; Fibre 0g; Sodium 821mg.
Fish and Chips Energy 645kcal/2700kJ; Protein 32.6g; Carbohydrate 54.3g, of which sugars 0.7g; Fat 34.5g, of which saturates 4.2g; Cholesterol 0mg; Calcium 130mg; Fibre 3.4g; Sodium 294mg.

Roasted Cod with Tomato Sauce

Really fresh cod has a sweet, delicate flavour and a pure white flaky flesh. Served with an aromatic tomato sauce, it makes a delicious meal and is so satisfying that it is not necessary to serve potatoes alongside. Crisp green beans are the best option.

Serves 4
350g/12oz ripe plum tomatoes
75ml/5 tbsp olive oil
2.5ml/½ tsp sugar
2 strips of pared orange rind
1 fresh thyme sprig
6 fresh basil leaves
900g/2lb fresh cod fillet, skin on
salt and ground black pepper
steamed green beans, to serve

Preparation: 3–4 minutes; Cooking: 14 minutes

1 Preheat the oven to 230°C/450°F/Gas 8. Using a sharp knife, chop the tomatoes roughly.

2 Heat 15ml/1 tbsp of the olive oil in a heavy pan, add the tomatoes, sugar, orange rind, thyme and basil, and simmer for 5 minutes until the tomatoes are soft.

3 Press the mixture through a fine sieve (strainer), discarding the solids that remain in the sieve. Pour into a pan and warm.

4 Scale the cod fillet and cut on the diagonal into four pieces. Season with plenty of salt and pepper.

5 Heat the remaining oil in a heavy frying pan and fry the cod, skinside down, until the skin is crisp. Place the fish on a greased baking sheet, skinside up, and roast in the oven for 8–10 minutes until the fish is cooked through. Serve the fish on the steamed green beans with the tomato sauce.

Cook's Tip
Cod is becoming increasingly rare and expensive. You can substitute any firm white fish fillets in this dish. Try haddock, pollock, or that excellent and underrated fish, coley. When raw, coley flesh looks grey, but it turns white on cooking.

Fried Sole with Lime

Simple dishes like this one capitalize on the delicious flavour of good fish.

Serves 4
75g/3oz/¾ cup plain (all-purpose) flour
10ml/2 tsp garlic salt

5ml/1 tsp ground black pepper
4 sole fillets
oil, for frying
juice of 2 limes
small bunch of fresh parsley, chopped, plus extra sprigs, to garnish
fresh salsa, to serve

Preparation: 5 minutes; Cooking: 4–8 minutes

1 Mix the flour, garlic salt and pepper together. Spread out the seasoned flour mixture in a shallow dish. Pat the sole fillets dry with kitchen paper, then turn them in the seasoned flour until they are evenly coated.

2 Pour oil into a wide frying pan to a depth of 2.5cm/1in. Heat it until a cube of bread added to the oil rises to the surface and browns in 45–60 seconds.

3 Add the fish, in batches if necessary, and fry for 3–4 minutes. Lift each fillet out and drain it on kitchen paper. Transfer to a heated serving dish.

4 Squeeze the juice of half a lime over each piece of fish and sprinkle with the chopped parsley. Serve immediately, with a fresh salsa to complement the fish. Garnish with parsley sprigs. New potatoes would also go well.

Cook's Tip
A sweet pepper salsa would taste good with this dish. Roast 2 red (bell) peppers under a hot grill (broiler) until the skins blacken and blister. Put them in a plastic bag until the skin softens, then peel them and remove the seeds. Process the flesh in a food processor with 1 seeded and chopped red chilli, 30ml/2 tbsp coriander (cilantro) leaves, 30ml/2 tbsp olive oil and 15ml/1 tbsp red wine vinegar. Season to taste.

Roasted Cod Energy 294kcal/1229kJ; Protein 41.8g; Carbohydrate 2.7g, of which sugars 2.7g; Fat 12.8g, of which saturates 1.9g; Cholesterol 104mg; Calcium 26mg; Fibre 0.9g; Sodium 143mg.
Fried Sole Energy 254kcal/1066kJ; Protein 21.5g; Carbohydrate 25.6g, of which sugars 0.8g; Fat 7.9g, of which saturates 0.7g; Cholesterol 50mg; Calcium 100mg; Fibre 1.6g; Sodium 105mg.

Cajun Blackened Fish with Salsa

This is an excellent way of cooking fillets of snapper or cod, leaving the fish moist in the middle and crisp and spicy on the outside.

Serves 4

5ml/1 tsp black peppercorns
5ml/1 tsp cumin seeds
5ml/1 tsp white mustard seeds
10ml/2 tsp paprika
5ml/1 tsp chilli powder
5ml/1 tsp dried oregano
10ml/2 tsp dried thyme

4 skinned fish fillets,
  225g/8oz each
50g/2oz/¼ cup butter, melted
salt
lime wedges and coriander
  (cilantro) sprigs, to garnish

For the papaya salsa
1 papaya
1 fresh red chilli
½ small red onion, diced
45ml/3 tbsp chopped fresh
  coriander (cilantro)
grated rind and juice of 1 lime

Preparation: 8–10 minutes; Cooking: 4 minutes

1 Start by making the salsa. Cut the papaya in half and scoop out the seeds. Remove the skin, cut the flesh into small dice and place it in a bowl. Slit the chilli, remove and discard the seeds and finely chop the flesh.

2 Add the onion, chilli, coriander, lime rind and juice to the papaya. Season with salt to taste. Mix well and set aside.

3 Dry-fry the peppercorns, cumin and mustard seeds in a pan, then grind them to a fine powder. Add the paprika, chilli powder, oregano, thyme and 5ml/1 tsp salt. Grind again and spread on a plate.

4 Preheat a large heavy frying pan over a medium heat. Brush the fish fillets with the melted butter then dip them in the mixture of spices until well coated.

5 Place the fish fillets in the hot pan and cook for 1–2 minutes on each side until blackened.

6 Transfer the fish to individual heated plates and garnish with lime wedges and coriander sprigs. Serve at once, with the salsa.

Mediterranean Fish Cutlets with Aniseed Tomato Sauce

This attractive dish is perfect for a dinner party, as the white flesh of the fish contrasts with the striking red of the sauce. The pastis in the sauce adds a surprise to the range of flavours, and will give your guests a meal to remember.

Serves 4
4 white fish cutlets, about
  150g/5oz each
150ml/¼ pint/⅔ cup fish
  stock and/or dry white
  wine, for poaching
1 bay leaf

a few black peppercorns
a strip of pared lemon rind
fresh parsley and lemon wedges,
  to garnish

For the tomato sauce
400g/14oz can chopped
  tomatoes
1 garlic clove
15ml/1 tbsp sun-dried tomato
  purée (paste)
15ml/1 tbsp pastis or other
  aniseed flavoured liqueur
15ml/1 tbsp drained capers
12–16 pitted black olives
salt and ground black pepper

Preparation: 3–4 minutes; Cooking: 12 minutes

1 Make the sauce. Heat the chopped tomatoes in a pan with the whole garlic clove. Stir in the sun-dried tomato purée until it has been absorbed completely.

2 Measure the pastis or other liqueur into the pan, then add the capers and olives. Season with salt and black pepper. Heat all the ingredients together for 10 minutes, stirring occasionally, to blend the flavours.

3 Meanwhile, place the fish in a frying pan, pour over the stock and/or wine and add the flavourings. Cover and simmer for 10 minutes or until the fish flakes easily.

4 Using a slotted spoon, transfer the fish to a heated dish. Strain the stock into the sauce and boil to reduce slightly. Season the sauce, pour it over the fish and serve immediately, with parsley and lemon wedges.

Cajun Blackened Fish Energy 295kcal/1228kJ; Protein 32.7g; Carbohydrate 3g, of which sugars 2.9g; Fat 16.9g, of which saturates 10g; Cholesterol 120mg; Calcium 31mg; Fibre 0.9g; Sodium 222mg.
Mediterranean Fish Energy 187kcal/783kJ; Protein 28.7g; Carbohydrate 3.6g, of which sugars 3.6g; Fat 5.5g, of which saturates 0.9g; Cholesterol 69mg; Calcium 45mg; Fibre 2.2g; Sodium 952mg.

Fish Moolie

Choose a firm-textured fish like snapper so that the pieces stay intact during the brief cooking process.

Serves 4

500g/1¼lb firm-textured fish
fillets, skinned and cut into
2.5cm/1in cubes
2.5ml/½ tsp salt
50g/2oz/⅔ cup desiccated (dry
unsweetened shredded) coconut
6 shallots, roughly chopped

6 blanched almonds
2–3 garlic cloves, roughly chopped
2.5cm/1in piece fresh root ginger,
peeled and sliced
2 lemon grass stalks, trimmed
10ml/2 tsp ground turmeric
45ml/3 tbsp vegetable oil
2 x 400ml/14fl oz cans
coconut milk
1–3 fresh red or green chillies,
seeded and sliced
salt and ground black pepper
fresh chives, to garnish

Preparation: 8 minutes; Cooking: 10 minutes

1 Spread out the pieces of fish in a shallow dish and sprinkle them with the salt. Dry-fry the coconut in a wok over medium to low heat, tip it into a food processor and process to an oily paste. Scrape into a bowl and reserve.

2 Add the shallots, almonds, garlic and ginger to the food processor. Cut off the lower 5cm/2in of the lemon grass stalks, chop them roughly and add them to the mixture. Process to a paste. Bruise the remaining lemon grass and set the stalks aside. Add the ground turmeric to the mixture in the processor and process briefly to mix.

3 Heat the oil in the clean wok. Add the onion mixture and cook for a few minutes without browning. Stir in the coconut milk and bring to the boil, stirring constantly.

5 Add the cubes of fish, most of the sliced chillies and the bruised lemon grass stalks. Cook for 3–4 minutes. Stir in the coconut paste and cook for 2 minutes. Season.

6 Remove the lemon grass stalks. Spoon the moolie on to a hot serving dish and sprinkle with the remaining slices of chilli. Garnish with chives and serve.

Poached Fish in Spicy Tomato Sauce

A selection of white fish fillets are used in this Middle Eastern dish: cod, haddock, hake or halibut are all good. Serve with flat breads, such as pitta, and serve a spicy tomato relish or some pickled lemons on the side.

Serves 8

600ml/1 pint/2½ cups fresh
tomato sauce
2.5–5ml/½–1 tsp harissa
60ml/4 tbsp chopped fresh
coriander (cilantro) leaves
1.5kg/3¼lb mixed white fish
fillets, cut into chunks
salt and ground black pepper

Preparation: 2 minutes; Cooking: 10 minutes

1 Heat the tomato sauce with the harissa and coriander in a large pan. Add seasoning to taste and bring to the boil. Remove the pan from the heat.

2 Add the fish to the hot sauce. Return to the heat and bring the sauce to the boil again.

3 Reduce the heat and simmer very gently for about 5 minutes, or until the fish flakes easily when tested with the tip of a sharp knife. Taste the sauce and adjust the seasoning, adding more harissa if necessary. Serve hot or warm.

Cook's Tips

• Harissa is a chilli paste spiced with cumin, garlic and coriander. It is fiery and should be used with care until you are familiar with the flavour. Start by adding a small amount and then add more after tasting the sauce.

• Pickled lemons are often served with Middle Eastern dishes like this one, in the same way as fresh lemons are the classic accompaniment in the West. Look out for pickled lemons at delicatessens. It is possible – and easy – to make your own, but the ones in jars are convenient, and because very thin-skinned lemons are used, they tend to be of good quality.

Fish Moolie Energy 287kcal/1204kJ; Protein 21.3g; Carbohydrate 13g, of which sugars 12.3g; Fat 17.2g, of which saturates 8.2g; Cholesterol 18mg; Calcium 79mg; Fibre 2.1g; Sodium 493mg.
Poached Fish Energy 219kcal/923kJ; Protein 36.2g; Carbohydrate 6.7g, of which sugars 3.2g; Fat 5.5g, of which saturates 1.5g; Cholesterol 94mg; Calcium 46mg; Fibre 1.4g; Sodium 370mg.

Escabeche

This dish originated in Spain, but is now popular the world over.

Serves 6
900g/2lb white fish fillets
45–60ml/3–4 tbsp seasoned flour
vegetable oil, for shallow frying
spring onions (scallions), finely
    shredded, to garnish (optional)
boiled long grain rice, to serve

For the sauce
30ml/2 tbsp vegetable oil
2.5cm/1in piece fresh root ginger,
    peeled and thinly sliced

2–3 garlic cloves, crushed
1 onion, cut into thin rings
1/2 large green (bell) pepper,
    seeded and cut in squares
1/2 large red (bell) pepper, seeded
    and cut in squares
2 small fresh chillies, seeded and
    finely sliced
1 carrot, cut into matchsticks
25ml/1 1/2 tbsp cornflour
    (cornstarch)
450ml/3/4 pint/scant 2 cups water
45–60ml/3–4 tbsp cider vinegar
15ml/1 tbsp light soft brown sugar
5–10ml/1–2 tsp Thai fish sauce
salt and ground black pepper

Preparation: 8 minutes; Cooking: 8–10 minutes

1 Wipe the fish fillets. Leave them whole, or cut them into serving portions, if you prefer. Pat dry on kitchen paper then dust lightly with seasoned flour.

2 Heat the oil for shallow frying in a frying pan and fry the fish fillets or portions in batches until golden and almost cooked. Transfer to an ovenproof dish and keep warm.

3 Make the sauce in a wok. Heat the oil and fry the ginger, garlic and onion until the onion rings have softened. Add the pepper squares with half the chilli slices and all the carrot. Stir-fry for 1 minute. Put the cornflour in a bowl and stir in a little of the water to make a paste. Stir in the remaining water, the vinegar and the sugar. Pour the cornflour mixture over the vegetables in the wok and stir until the sauce boils and thickens a little. Season with fish sauce, and salt and pepper.

4 Add the fried fish to the sauce and reheat briefly. Transfer to a warmed platter. Garnish with the remaining chilli and shredded spring onions, if using. Serve with rice.

Hoki Stir-fry

Any firm white fish, such as monkfish, hake or cod, can be used for this stir-fry. Vary the vegetables according to what is available.

Serves 4–6
675g/1 1/2 lb hoki fillet, skinned
salt and ground black pepper
pinch of five-spice powder
115g/4oz/1 cup small
    mangetouts (snow peas)
4 spring onions (scallions)

45ml/3 tbsp groundnut
    (peanut) oil
2 garlic cloves, finely chopped
2.5cm/1in piece fresh root ginger,
    peeled and cut into thin slivers
300g/11oz beansprouts
2 carrots, cut diagonally into slices
    as thin as mangetouts
115g/4oz asparagus spears,
    trimmed and cut in half
    crossways
8–12 small baby corn cobs
15–30ml/1–2 tbsp light soy sauce

Preparation: 7–8 minutes; Cooking: 9–10 minutes

1 Cut the hoki into thin strips, removing any stray bones with tweezers. Put the salt, pepper and five-spice powder in a strong plastic bag, add the strips of fish and shake the bag gently to coat them evenly all over.

2 Trim the mangetouts. Trim the spring onions and cut the green and white parts diagonally into 2cm/3/4in pieces. Keep the green and white parts separate.

3 Heat a wok, then pour in the oil. As soon as it is hot, add the garlic and ginger. Stir-fry for 1 minute, then add the white parts of the spring onions and cook for 1 minute more.

4 Add the hoki strips and stir-fry for 2–3 minutes, until all the pieces of fish are opaque. Add the beansprouts. Toss them around to coat them in the oil, then put in the carrots, mangetouts, asparagus and corn.

5 Continue to stir-fry for 3–4 minutes, by which time the fish should be cooked, but all the vegetables will still be crunchy. Add soy sauce to taste, toss everything quickly together, then stir in the green parts of the spring onions. Spoon into a heated bowl and serve immediately.

Escabeche Energy 414kcal/1721kJ; Protein 41.9g; Carbohydrate 1.3g, of which sugars 1g; Fat 26.7g, of which saturates 3.2g; Cholesterol 104mg; Calcium 30mg; Fibre 0.2g; Sodium 137mg.
Hoki Stir-fry Energy 183kcal/764kJ; Protein 22.4g; Carbohydrate 5g, of which sugars 3.8g; Fat 8.2g, of which saturates 1.1g; Cholesterol 0mg; Calcium 49mg; Fibre 2.3g; Sodium 295mg.

Grilled Hake with Lemon & Chilli

Nothing could be simpler than perfectly grilled fish with a dusting of chilli and lemon rind. This is an ideal meal for those occasions when something light is called for.

Serves 4
4 hake fillets, each 150g/5oz
30ml/2 tbsp olive oil
finely grated rind and juice
    of 1 lemon
15ml/1 tbsp crushed chilli flakes
salt and ground black pepper

Preparation: 2 minutes; Cooking: 6–8 minutes

1 Preheat the grill (broiler) to high. Brush the hake fillets with the olive oil and place them skin side up on a baking sheet.

2 Grill (broil) the fish for 4–5 minutes, until the skin is crispy, then carefully turn the fillets over in the pan, using a metal spatula or two spoons.

3 Sprinkle the fillets with the lemon rind and chilli flakes and season with salt and ground black pepper.

4 Grill the fillets for a further 2–3 minutes, or until the hake is cooked through. (Test using the point of a sharp knife; the flesh should flake.) Transfer the fillets of hake to individual plates and squeeze over the lemon juice just before serving.

> **Cook's Tip**
> A pastry brush is the ideal implement for coating fish with oil, but keep one specifically for the purpose, unless you want your apple pie to taste slightly fishy. Draw a fish on the handle with a marker pen to distinguish it from your pastry brush.

> **Variation**
> Any firm white fish can be cooked in this simple, low-fat way. Try cod, halibut or hoki. If you haven't got any chilli flakes, brush the fish with chilli oil instead of olive oil.

Hake & Potato Salad

Hake is a meaty fish that is excellent served cold in a salad, and the flavour is enhanced here with a piquant dressing.

Serves 4
450g/1lb hake fillets
150ml/¼ pint/⅔ cup fish stock
1 onion, thinly sliced
1 bay leaf
450g/1lb cooked baby new
    potatoes, halved unless tiny
1 red (bell) pepper, seeded
    and diced
115g/4oz/1 cup petits pois
    (baby peas), cooked

2 spring onions (scallions), sliced
½ cucumber, unpeeled and diced
4 large red lettuce leaves
salt and ground black pepper

For the dressing
150ml/¼ pint/⅔ cup Greek
    (US strained plain) yogurt
30ml/2 tbsp olive oil
juice of ½ lemon
15–30ml/1–2 tbsp capers

To garnish
2 hard-boiled eggs, finely chopped
15ml/1 tbsp finely chopped fresh
    flat leaf parsley
15ml/1 tbsp finely chopped chives

Preparation: 8 minutes; Cooking: 11 minutes

1 Put the hake in a shallow pan with the fish stock, onion slices and bay leaf. Bring to the boil over a medium heat. Lower the heat and poach the fish gently for 10 minutes, until it flakes easily when tested with the tip of a sharp knife. Leave it to cool.

2 Remove and discard the skin and any remaining bones from the fish, and separate the flesh into large flakes.

3 Put the baby new potatoes in a bowl with the red pepper, petits pois, spring onions and cucumber. Gently stir in the flaked hake and season to taste with salt and pepper.

4 Make the dressing by stirring all the ingredients together in a bowl or jug (pitcher). Season and spoon or pour over the salad. Toss gently with salad servers or two spoons.

5 Place a lettuce leaf on each plate and spoon the salad over it. Mix the finely chopped hard-boiled eggs for the garnish with the parsley and chives. Sprinkle the mixture over each salad.

Grilled Hake Energy 188kcal/786kJ; Protein 27g; Carbohydrate 0.1g, of which sugars 0.1g; Fat 8.8g, of which saturates 1.2g; Cholesterol 35mg; Calcium 22mg; Fibre 0g; Sodium 150mg.
Hake Salad Energy 373kcal/1561kJ; Protein 31.2g; Carbohydrate 29.1g, of which sugars 8.8g; Fat 15.8g, of which saturates 4.2g; Cholesterol 121mg; Calcium 129mg; Fibre 4.3g; Sodium 192mg.

Kedgeree

Impress house guests by rustling up this delectable dish in less time than it takes them to take a shower. Kedgeree is an Anglo-Indian dish, made popular in England by memsahibs returning from overseas postings.

Serves 4

350g/12oz/1½ cups
   basmati rice
225g/8oz undyed smoked
   haddock fillet
4 eggs
25g/1oz/2 tbsp butter
30ml/2 tbsp garam masala
ground black pepper

Preparation: 2–3 minutes; Cooking: 16 minutes

1 Preheat the grill (broiler) to medium. Place the smoked haddock on a baking sheet and grill (broil) for 10 minutes, or until cooked through.

2 Meanwhile, place the eggs in a pan of cold water and bring to the boil. Cook for 6–7 minutes. At the same time as the eggs and haddock are cooking, cook the rice in a pan of boiling water for 10–12 minutes.

3 When the eggs are cooked, drain and place under cold running water until cool enough to handle. Shell the eggs and cut into halves or quarters.

4 Remove the baking sheet from under the grill and transfer the smoked haddock to a board. Remove the skin when cool enough to handle.

5 Using a fork, ease the flesh apart so that it separates into large flakes. Remove any remaining bones.

6 Drain the rice and tip it into a bowl. Melt the butter in a pan, stir in the garam masala and add the fish. When it has warmed through, add it to the rice with the smoked fish and eggs. Mix gently, taking care not to mash the eggs. Carefully transfer to a warmed serving dish, taste and season. The dish will probably not need much salt, since the smoked haddock will be quite salty, but be generous with the pepper. Serve immediately.

Haddock in Cider Sauce

First-class fish doesn't need elaborate treatment. The cider sauce served with the haddock is based on the poaching liquid, enriched by just a whisper of cream. If the amount of cider seems excessive, use equal parts of water and fish stock or vegetable stock.

Serves 4

675g/1½lb haddock fillet
1 medium onion, thinly sliced
1 bay leaf
2 parsley sprigs
10ml/2 tsp lemon juice
450ml/¾ pint/2 cups dry
   (hard) cider
25g/1oz/¼ cup cornflour
   (cornstarch)
30ml/2 tbsp single (light) cream
salt and ground black pepper

Preparation: 2 minutes; Cooking: 13 minutes

1 Cut the haddock fillet into four equal portions and place in a pan big enough to hold them neatly in a single layer. Add the onion, bay leaf, parsley and lemon. Season with salt.

2 Pour in most of the cider, reserving 30ml/2 tbsp for the sauce. Cover and bring to the boil, reduce the heat and simmer for 10 minutes, or until the fish is just cooked.

3 Strain 300ml/½ pint/1¼ cups of the cooking liquid into a measuring jug (cup). Cover the pan containing the fish and remove from the heat.

4 In a small pan, mix the cornflour with the 30ml/2 tbsp cider reserved earlier, then gradually whisk in the measured cooking liquid and bring to the boil. Whisk over the heat until the mixture is smooth and thick.

5 Whisk in more of the cooking liquid, if necessary, to make a pouring sauce. Remove the pan from the heat, stir in the cream and season to taste with salt and ground black pepper.

6 To serve, remove any skin from the fish, arrange on individual hot serving plates and pour the sauce over. Serve with a selection of vegetables.

Kedgeree Energy 480kcal/2006kJ; Protein 23.5g; Carbohydrate 69.9g, of which sugars 0g; Fat 11.5g, of which saturates 4.9g; Cholesterol 224mg; Calcium 59mg; Fibre 0g; Sodium 536mg.
Haddock in Cider Sauce Energy 216kcal/918kJ; Protein 32.5g; Carbohydrate 9.4g, of which sugars 3.5g; Fat 2.5g, of which saturates 1.1g; Cholesterol 65mg; Calcium 43mg; Fibre 0.1g; Sodium 127mg.

Sea Bass with Parsley & Lime Butter

The delicate but firm, sweet flesh of sea bass goes beautifully with citrus flavours. Serve with roast fennel and sautéed diced potatoes or, for a summer lunch, with new potatoes and salad.

Serves 6
50g/2oz/¼ cup butter
6 sea bass fillets, about
   150g/5oz each
grated rind and juice of
   1 large lime
30ml/2 tbsp chopped fresh parsley
salt and ground black pepper

Preparation: 2–3 minutes; Cooking: 9–10 minutes

1 Heat the butter in a large frying pan and add three of the sea bass fillets, skin side down. Cook for 3–4 minutes, or until the skin is crisp and golden. Flip the fish over and cook for a further 2–3 minutes, or until cooked through.

2 Remove the fillets from the pan with a metal spatula. Place each on a serving plate and keep them warm. Cook the remaining fish in the same way and transfer to serving plates.

3 Add the lime rind and juice to the pan with the parsley, and season with salt and black pepper. Allow to bubble for 1–2 minutes, then pour a little over each fish portion and serve immediately.

Variation
Instead of serving this with sautéed diced potatoes, offer fat home-made oven chips (french fries) with fresh herbs and a little lime to echo the flavouring used in the butter for the fish. Slice 4 large waxy potatoes thickly and spread them in a single layer in a roasting pan. Sprinkle with 30ml/2 tbsp chopped fresh herbs and the finely grated rind of 1 lime. Drizzle with 30ml/2 tbsp olive oil and dot with the same quantity of butter. Cover with foil and bake at 200°C/400°F/Gas 6 for 1–1¼ hours, removing the foil after 30 minutes and stirring the chips at least twice.

Skate with Bitter Salad Leaves

This dish is popular in Spain, which is famous for both its skate and its watercress. Skate has a delicious sweet flavour, enhanced here by orange. It contrasts well with any bitter leaves – buy a bag of mixed salad leaves for contrasting textures, colours and flavours.

Serves 4
800g/1¾lb skate wings
15ml/1 tbsp white wine vinegar
4 black peppercorns

1 fresh thyme sprig
175g/6oz bitter salad leaves,
   such as frisée, rocket (arugula),
   radicchio, escarole, lamb's lettuce
   (mâche) and watercress
1 orange
2 tomatoes, peeled, seeded and diced

For the dressing
15ml/1 tbsp white wine vinegar
45ml/3 tbsp extra virgin olive oil
1 bunch spring onions (scallions),
   whites finely chopped
salt, paprika and black pepper
crusty bread, to serve

Preparation: 5 minutes; Cooking: 8–10 minutes

1 Put the skate wings into a large shallow pan, cover with cold water and add the vinegar, peppercorns and thyme. Bring to the boil, then poach gently for 8–10 minutes, until the flesh comes away easily from the bones.

2 Make the dressing. Whisk together the vinegar, oil and spring onions and season with salt, paprika and pepper.

3 Put the salad leaves in a large bowl, pour over the dressing and toss well. Remove the rind from the orange using a zester, then peel it, removing all the pith. Slice into thin rounds.

4 Flake the fish, discarding the bones, and add to the salad. Add a pinch of zest, the orange slices and tomatoes, toss gently and serve with bread.

Cook's Tip
Skate is a fine-flavoured fish with creamy flesh. Once it is cooked, it comes away from the bone very easily.

Sea Bass Energy 213Kcal/890kJ; Protein 29g; Carbohydrate 0g, of which sugars 0g; Fat 11g, of which saturates 5g; Cholesterol 138mg; Calcium 199mg; Fibre 0.1g; Sodium 200mg.
Skate Energy 230kcal/965kJ; Protein 31.6g; Carbohydrate 4.8g, of which sugars 4.8g; Fat 9.5g, of which saturates 1.3g; Cholesterol 0mg; Calcium 118mg; Fibre 1.5g; Sodium 247mg.

Skate with Black Butter

Skate can be quite inexpensive and this classic dish is perfect for a family supper. The sweet flesh is easily removed from the unthreatening soft bones, and it is a good choice for children as well as senior members of the family. Serve it with steamed leeks and plain boiled potatoes.

Serves 4
4 skate wings, about
 225g/8oz each
60ml/4 tbsp red wine vinegar
 or malt vinegar
30ml/2 tbsp drained capers in
 vinegar, chopped if large
30ml/2 tbsp chopped
 fresh parsley
150g/5oz/⅔ cup butter
salt and ground black pepper

Preparation: 2 minutes; Cooking: 15–17 minutes

1 Put the skate wings in a large, shallow pan, cover with cold water and add a pinch of salt and 15ml/1 tbsp of the red wine or malt vinegar.

2 Bring to the boil, skim the surface, then lower the heat and simmer gently for about 10–12 minutes, until the skate flesh comes away from the bone easily. Carefully drain the skate and peel off the skin.

3 Transfer the skate to a warmed serving dish, season with salt and pepper and sprinkle over the capers and parsley. Keep hot.

4 In a small pan, heat the butter until it foams and turns a rich nutty brown. Pour it over the skate. Pour the remaining vinegar into the pan and boil until reduced by about two-thirds. Drizzle over the skate and serve.

> **Cook's Tips**
> • *Don't be put off by the faint ammonia smell of skate. It vanishes when the fish is cooked.*
> • *Despite the title of the recipe, the butter should be a rich golden brown. It should never be allowed to blacken, or it will taste unpleasantly bitter.*

Halibut with Sauce Vierge

Sauce vierge can be served either at room temperature or, as in this popular fish dish, slightly warm.

Serves 2
3 large ripe beefsteak tomatoes, peeled, seeded and chopped
2 shallots or 1 small red onion, finely chopped
1 garlic clove, crushed
90ml/6 tbsp chopped mixed fresh herbs, such as parsley, coriander (cilantro), basil, tarragon, chervil or chives
120ml/4fl oz/½ cup extra virgin olive oil, plus extra for greasing
4 halibut fillets or steaks (175–200g/6–7oz each)
salt and ground black pepper
green salad, to serve

Preparation: 4 minutes; Cooking: 5–6 minutes

1 To make the sauce vierge, mix together the tomatoes, shallots or onion, garlic and herbs in a bowl. Stir in the oil and season with salt and ground black pepper. Cover the bowl with clear film (plastic wrap) and leave the sauce to stand at room temperature while you grill the fish.

2 Preheat the grill (broiler). Line a grill (broiling) pan with foil and brush the foil lightly with oil.

3 Season the fish with salt and pepper. Place the fish on the foil and brush with a little extra oil. Grill (broil) for 5–6 minutes until the flesh is opaque and the top lightly browned.

4 Meanwhile, transfer the sauce to a pan and heat it gently for a few minutes. Serve the fish with the sauce and a salad.

> **Cook's Tips**
> • *To peel the tomatoes, put a cross in the base of each one. Place them in a heatproof bowl and cover with boiling water. After 30 seconds, lift them out and plunge them into a bowl of cold water. Drain, then remove the skins.*
> • *If time permits, leave the sauce to stand for up to an hour before heating it to serve with the fish.*

Skate Energy 411kcal/1709kJ; Protein 30.8g; Carbohydrate 0.6g, of which sugars 0.5g; Fat 31.8g, of which saturates 19.5g; Cholesterol 80mg; Calcium 112mg; Fibre 0.6g; Sodium 472mg.
Halibut Energy 791kcal/3311kJ; Protein 89.3g; Carbohydrate 10.6g, of which sugars 9.7g; Fat 43.9g, of which saturates 6.5g; Cholesterol 140mg; Calcium 230mg; Fibre 4.9g; Sodium 276mg.

Griddled Halibut

Any thick white fish fillets can be cooked in this versatile dish, but the flavoursome sauce of tomatoes, capers, anchovies and herbs also gives humbler fish such as cod, haddock or hake a real lift.

Serves 4
2.5ml/½ tsp fennel seeds
2.5ml/½ tsp celery seeds
5ml/1 tsp mixed peppercorns
105ml/7 tbsp olive oil
5ml/1 tsp chopped fresh thyme leaves
5ml/1 tsp chopped fresh rosemary leaves
5ml/1 tsp chopped fresh oregano

675–800g/1½–1¾ lb middle cut of halibut, about 3cm/1¼ in thick, cut into 4 pieces
coarse sea salt

For the sauce
105ml/7 tbsp extra virgin olive oil
juice of 1 lemon
1 garlic clove, finely chopped
2 tomatoes, peeled, seeded and diced
5ml/1 tsp small capers
2 drained canned anchovy fillets, chopped
5ml/1 tsp chopped fresh chives
15ml/1 tbsp chopped fresh basil leaves
15ml/1 tbsp chopped fresh chervil

Preparation: 7 minutes; Cooking: 6–8 minutes

1 Prepare the barbecue. Heat a griddle on the grill rack over the hot coals. Mix the fennel and celery seeds with the peppercorns in a mortar. Crush with a pestle, and then stir in coarse sea salt to taste. Spoon into a shallow dish large enough to hold the fish in one layer and stir in the herbs and oil.

2 Add the halibut pieces to the olive oil mixture, turning them to coat them thoroughly, then arrange them with the dark skin uppermost in the griddle. Cook for about 6–8 minutes, or until the fish is cooked all the way through and the skin has browned.

3 Combine all the sauce ingredients except the fresh herbs in a pan and heat gently on the grill rack until warm but not hot. Stir in the chives, basil and chervil.

4 Place the halibut on four warmed plates. Spoon the sauce around and over the fish and serve immediately.

Grilled Sole with Chive Butter

The very best way of transforming simple grilled fish into a luxury dish is by topping it with a flavoured butter, as in this recipe.

Serves 4
115g/4oz/½ cup unsalted (sweet) butter, softened, plus extra, melted
5ml/1 tsp diced lemon grass

pinch of finely grated lime rind
1 kaffir lime leaf, very finely shredded (optional)
45ml/3 tbsp chopped chives or chopped chive flowers, plus extra chives or chive flowers to garnish
2.5–5ml/½–1 tsp Thai fish sauce
4 sole, skinned
salt and ground black pepper
lemon or lime wedges, to serve

Preparation: 3–4 minutes; Cooking: 10 minutes

1 Put the butter in a bowl and cream it with a wooden spoon. Add the lemon grass, lime rind, lime leaf, if using, and chives or chive flowers. Mix well, making sure all the ingredients are thoroughly combined, then season to taste with Thai fish sauce, salt and pepper.

2 Chill the butter mixture to firm it a little, then form it into a roll and wrap in foil or clear film (plastic wrap). Chill until firm. Preheat the grill (broiler).

3 Brush the fish with melted butter. Place it on the grill rack and season. Grill (broil) for about 5 minutes, then carefully turn the pieces of fish over and grill the other side for 4–5 minutes, until firm and just cooked.

4 Meanwhile, cut the chilled butter into thin slices. Put the fish on individual plates and top with the butter. Garnish with chives and serve with lemon or lime wedges.

> **Cook's Tips**
> • Finer white fish fillets, such as plaice, can be cooked in this way, but reduce the cooking time slightly.
> • The flavoured butter can be made ahead and frozen.

Griddled Halibut Energy 363kcal/1513kJ; Protein 37.4g; Carbohydrate 1.9g, of which sugars 1.8g; Fat 22.9g, of which saturates 3.3g; Cholesterol 60mg; Calcium 82mg; Fibre 1.1g; Sodium 169mg.
Grilled Sole Energy 349kcal/1447kJ; Protein 27.4g; Carbohydrate 0.5g, of which sugars 0.5g; Fat 26.3g, of which saturates 15g; Cholesterol 136mg; Calcium 49mg; Fibre 0g; Sodium 591mg.

Pan-fried Sole with Lemon Butter Sauce

The delicate flavour and texture of sole is brought out in this classic recipe, which uses just a simple sauce to complement the fish.

45ml/3 tbsp olive oil
50g/2oz/¼ cup butter
60ml/4 tbsp lemon juice
30ml/2 tbsp rinsed bottled capers
salt and ground black pepper

Serves 2
30–45ml/2–3 tbsp plain
   (all-purpose) flour
4 lemon or Dover sole fillets
   (see Cook's Tip)

For the garnish
fresh flat leaf parsley
lemon wedges

Preparation: 2–3 minutes; Cooking: 9 minutes

1 Season the flour with salt and pepper. Coat the sole fillets evenly on both sides. Heat the oil with half the butter in a large shallow pan until foaming. Add two sole fillets and fry over a medium heat for 2–3 minutes on each side.

2 Lift out the sole fillets with a fish slice or metal spatula and place on a warmed serving platter. Keep hot. Fry the remaining sole fillets in the same way, then add them to the platter.

3 Remove the pan from the heat and add the lemon juice and remaining butter. Return the pan to a high heat and stir vigorously until the pan juices are sizzling and beginning to turn golden brown. Remove from the heat and stir in the capers.

4 Arrange the sole fillets on two plates and pour the pan juices over them. Sprinkle with salt and pepper to taste. Garnish with the parsley and lemon wedges. Serve at once.

Cook's Tip
Lemon sole is used here because it is often easier to obtain and less expensive than Dover sole.

Fried Plaice with Tomato Sauce

This simple dish is perennially popular with children. It works equally well with lemon sole or dabs, which do not need skinning, or fillets of haddock or whiting.

25g/1oz/2 tbsp butter
30ml/2 tbsp sunflower oil
salt and ground black pepper
fresh basil leaves, to garnish
1 lemon, quartered, to serve

Serves 4
25g/1oz/¼ cup plain
   (all-purpose) flour
2 eggs, beaten
75g/3oz/¾ cup dried
   breadcrumbs, preferably
   home-made
4 small plaice or flounder, skinned

For the tomato sauce
30ml/2 tbsp olive oil
1 red onion, finely chopped
1 garlic clove, finely chopped
400g/14oz can chopped
   tomatoes
15ml/1 tbsp tomato
   purée (paste)
15ml/1 tbsp torn fresh
   basil leaves

Preparation: 5 minutes; Cooking: 14 minutes

1 First make the tomato sauce. Heat the olive oil in a large pan, add the finely chopped onion and garlic and cook for about 2–3 minutes, until softened. Stir in the chopped tomatoes and tomato purée and simmer for 10 minutes, or until the fish is ready to be served, stirring occasionally.

2 Spread out the flour in a shallow dish, pour the beaten eggs into another and spread out the breadcrumbs in a third.

3 Season the fish with salt and pepper. Hold a fish in your left hand and dip it first in flour, then in egg and finally in the breadcrumbs, patting the crumbs on with your dry right hand. Aim for an even coating that is not too thick. Shake off any excess crumbs and set aside while you prepare the frying pans.

4 Heat the butter and oil in two large frying pans until foaming. Fry the fish for about 5 minutes on each side, until golden brown and cooked through. Drain on kitchen paper. Season the tomato sauce, stir in the basil and serve with the fish, garnished with basil leaves. Offer lemon wedges separately.

Pan-fried Sole Energy 535kcal/2222kJ; Protein 35.9g; Carbohydrate 7.9g, of which sugars 0.3g; Fat 40.2g, of which saturates 15.8g; Cholesterol 173mg; Calcium 53mg; Fibre 0.3g; Sodium 342mg.
Fried Plaice Energy 417kcal/1738kJ; Protein 28.1g; Carbohydrate 17.7g, of which sugars 4.9g; Fat 26.4g, of which saturates 3.1g; Cholesterol 0mg; Calcium 113mg; Fibre 1.6g; Sodium 349mg.

Mackerel with Mustard & Lemon

Mackerel must be really fresh to be enjoyed. Look for bright, firm-looking fish.

Serves 4
4 fresh mackerel, about 275g/10oz
   each, gutted and cleaned
175–225g/6–8oz young
   spinach leaves

*For the mustard and
lemon butter*
115g/4oz/½ cup butter
30ml/2 tbsp wholegrain mustard
grated rind of 1 lemon
30ml/2 tbsp lemon juice
*45ml/3 tbsp chopped
   fresh parsley*
salt and ground black pepper

Preparation: 5 minutes; Cooking: 10–12 minutes

1 Place the mackerel on a board. Cut off the mackerel heads just behind the gills, using a sharp knife, then slit the belly so that each fish can be opened out flat.

2 Place the fish skinside up. With the heel of your hand, press along the backbone to loosen it.

3 Turn the fish the right way up and pull the bone away. Cut off the tail and cut each fish in half lengthways. Wash all the mackerel quickly under cold running water, drain and pat dry.

4 Turn the mackerel over again. Using a sharp knife, score the skin three or four times then season the fish with salt and ground black pepper.

5 To make the mustard and lemon butter, heat the butter in a small pan until it has melted, then stir in the wholegrain mustard, grated lemon rind and juice, with the parsley and salt and pepper to taste.

6 Place the mackerel on a grill (broiling) pan. Brush a little of the butter over the mackerel and grill (broil) for 5 minutes each side, basting occasionally, until cooked through.

7 Arrange the spinach leaves around a large plate. Place the mackerel on top. Heat the remaining flavoured butter until sizzling and pour over the mackerel. Serve at once.

Herring Fillets in Oatmeal with Apples

Fresh herrings make an inexpensive and tasty supper fish. Coating them in oatmeal before frying gives them a crisp outer edge that contrasts well with the tender flesh and the sweet fruitiness of the fried apples.

Serves 4
8 herring fillets
seasoned flour, for coating
1 egg, beaten
115g/4oz/1 cup fine pinhead
   oatmeal or oatflakes
oil, for frying
2 eating apples
25g/1oz/2 tbsp butter

Preparation: 3–4 minutes; Cooking: 6 minutes

1 Wash the fish and pat dry with kitchen paper. Skin the fillets and check that all bones have been removed.

2 Toss the herring fillets in the seasoned flour, then dip them in the beaten egg and roll them in the pinhead oatmeal or oatflakes until evenly coated.

3 Heat a little oil in a heavy frying pan and fry the fillets, a few at a time, until golden brown. Drain on kitchen paper, transfer to a serving platter and keep warm.

4 Core the apples, but do not peel. Slice them quite thinly. In another pan, melt the butter and fry the apple slices gently until just softened. Serve the apple with the coated fish fillets.

> **Variations**
> • *Mackerel fillets can be cooked in the same way.*
> • *A fruit sauce – apple, gooseberry or rhubarb – could be served instead of the sliced apples. Cook 225g/8oz of your preferred fruit with 90ml/6 tbsp cold water until just softened. Purée and serve with the fish.*
> • *Poached nectarine slices would also be a good accompaniment.*

Mackerel Energy 785kcal/3253kJ; Protein 49.8g; Carbohydrate 1.2g, of which sugars 1.1g; Fat 64.5g, of which saturates 23.3g; Cholesterol 194mg; Calcium 116mg; Fibre 1.3g; Sodium 502mg.
Herring Energy 566kcal/2361kJ; Protein 35.6g; Carbohydrate 24.3g, of which sugars 3.4g; Fat 37g, of which saturates 9.9g; Cholesterol 146mg; Calcium 128mg; Fibre 2.6g; Sodium 270mg.

Fillets of Brill in Red Wine Sauce

Forget the old maxim that red wine and fish do not go well together. The robust sauce adds colour and richness to this excellent and unusual fish dish.

Serves 4

4 fillets of brill, each about
175g/6oz each, skinned

150g/5oz/10 tbsp chilled butter,
plus extra for greasing
115g/4oz shallots, thinly sliced
200ml/7fl oz/scant 1 cup robust
red wine
200ml/7fl oz/scant 1 cup
fish stock
salt and ground white pepper
fresh chervil or flat leaf parsley
leaves, to garnish

Preparation: 3–4 minutes; Cooking: 12–14 minutes

1 Preheat the oven to 180°C/350°F/Gas 4. Season the fish on both sides with a little salt and plenty of pepper. Generously butter a flameproof dish, which is large enough to take all the brill fillets in a single layer without overlapping. Spread the shallots over the base and lay the fish fillets on top. Season the fish generously with salt and ground black pepper.

2 Pour in the red wine and fish stock, cover the dish and bring the liquid to just below boiling point. Transfer the dish to the oven and bake for 6–8 minutes, or until the brill is just cooked. It should flake readily if tested with the tip of a sharp knife.

3 Using a fish slice, carefully lift the fish and shallots on to a serving dish, cover with foil and keep hot.

4 Transfer the dish to the hob and bring the cooking liquid to the boil over a high heat. Cook until it has reduced by half.

5 Lower the heat and whisk in the chilled butter or margarine, one piece at a time, to make a smooth, shiny sauce. Season the sauce with salt and ground white pepper, remove from the heat and cover to keep hot.

6 Divide the shallots among four warmed plates and lay the brill fillets on top. Pour the sauce over and around the fish and garnish with the chervil or flat leaf parsley.

Monkfish with Pimiento & Cream

This recipe comes from Spain's Rioja country, where a special horned red pepper is used to make a spicy sauce. Here, red peppers are used with a little chilli, while cream makes a mellow pink sauce. To drink, choose a Marqués de Cáceres white Rioja.

Serves 4

2 large red (bell) peppers
1kg/2¼lb monkfish tail
or 900g/2lb halibut

plain (all-purpose) flour,
for dusting
30ml/2 tbsp olive oil
25g/1oz/2 tbsp butter
120ml/4fl oz/½ cup white Rioja
or dry vermouth
½ dried chilli, seeded
and chopped
8 raw prawns (shrimp),
in the shell
150ml/¼ pint/⅔ cup double
(heavy) cream
salt and ground black pepper
fresh flat leaf parsley, to garnish

Preparation: 4 minutes; Cooking: 12–14 minutes

1 Preheat the grill (broiler) to high and cook the peppers for 6–8 minutes, turning occasionally, until they are soft, and the skins blackened. Leave, covered, until cool enough to handle. Skin and discard the stalks and seeds. Put the flesh into a blender, strain in the juices and purée.

2 Cut the monkfish or halibut into eight steaks (freeze the bones for stock). Season well and dust with flour.

3 Heat the oil and butter in a large frying pan and fry the fish for 3 minutes on each side. Remove to a warm dish.

4 Add the wine or vermouth and chilli to the pan and stir to deglaze the pan. Add the prawns and cook them briefly, then lift out with a slotted spoon and reserve in a bowl.

5 Boil the sauce to reduce by half, then strain into a small jug (pitcher). Add the cream to the pan and boil briefly to reduce. Return the sauce to the pan, stir in the puréed peppers and check the seasonings. Pour the sauce over the fish and serve garnished with the cooked prawns and parsley.

Fillets of Brill Energy 511kcal/2123kJ; Protein 35.7g; Carbohydrate 1.3g, of which sugars 1.3g; Fat 36.7g, of which saturates 19.5g; Cholesterol 156mg; Calcium 97mg; Fibre 0.4g; Sodium 454mg.
Monkfish Energy 518kcal/2163kJ; Protein 50.2g; Carbohydrate 10.8g, of which sugars 10.3g; Fat 27.4g, of which saturates 13.7g; Cholesterol 140mg; Calcium 74mg; Fibre 2.3g; Sodium 115mg.

Spicy Squid

This aromatically spiced squid dish is simple yet delicious. Gone are the days when cleaning squid was such a chore: today they can be bought ready-cleaned from fish stores, market stalls and the fish counters of large supermarkets.

Serves 3–4
675g/1½lb squid, cleaned
45ml/3 tbsp groundnut oil

1 onion, finely chopped
2 garlic cloves, crushed
1 beefsteak tomato, peeled and chopped
15ml/1 tbsp dark soy sauce
2.5ml/½ tsp freshly grated nutmeg
6 cloves
150ml/¼ pint/⅔ cup water
juice of ½ lemon or lime
salt and ground black pepper
fresh coriander (cilantro) leaves and shredded spring onion (scallion), to garnish

Preparation: 6 minutes; Cooking: 9–11 minutes

1 Rinse and drain the squid, then slice lengthways along one side and open it out flat. Score the inside of the squid in a lattice pattern, using the blunt side of a knife blade, then cut it crossways into long thin strips.

2 Heat a wok and add 15ml/1 tbsp of the oil. When hot, toss in the squid strips and stir-fry for 2–3 minutes, by which time the squid will have curled into attractive shapes or into firm rings. Lift out and set aside.

3 Wipe out the wok, add the remaining oil and heat it. Stir-fry the onion and garlic until soft and beginning to brown. Stir in the tomato, soy sauce, nutmeg, cloves, water and lemon or lime juice. Bring to the boil, lower the heat and add the squid with seasoning to taste.

4 Cook the mixture gently for a further 3–5 minutes, stirring occasionally to prevent it from sticking. Take care not to overcook the squid.

5 Spoon the spicy squid on to warm plates. Garnish with coriander leaves and shredded spring onions and serve.

Stir-fried Squid with Ginger

There's an ancient belief that a well-loved wok holds the memory of all the dishes that have ever been cooked in it. Give yours something to think about by introducing it to this classic combination of baby squid in soy sauce, ginger and lemon juice. Chopped spring onions add a crunchy texture that is very welcome.

Serves 2
4 ready-prepared baby squid, total weight about 250g/9oz
15ml/1 tbsp vegetable oil
2 garlic cloves, finely chopped
30ml/2 tbsp soy sauce
2.5cm/1in piece fresh root ginger, peeled and finely chopped
juice of ½ lemon
5ml/1 tsp granulated (white) sugar
2 spring onions (scallions), chopped

Preparation: 2–3 minutes; Cooking: 2 minutes

1 Rinse the squid well and pat dry with kitchen paper. Place on a board and use a sharp knife to cut the bodies into rings. Halve the tentacles, if necessary.

2 Heat the oil in a wok or frying pan and cook the garlic until golden brown, but do not let it burn. Add the squid and stir-fry for 30 seconds over a high heat.

3 Add the soy sauce, ginger, lemon juice, sugar and spring onions. Stir-fry for a further 30 seconds, then spoon into individual heated bowls and serve.

Cook's Tip
Squid has an undeserved reputation for being rubbery in texture. This is always a result of overcooking it.

Variation
This dish is often prepared with fresh galangal rather than ginger and works well with most kinds of seafood, including prawns (shrimp) and scallops.

Spicy Squid Energy 310kcal/1301kJ; Protein 35.8g; Carbohydrate 8.6g, of which sugars 4.7g; Fat 15.1g, of which saturates 3g; Cholesterol 506mg; Calcium 46mg; Fibre 1.2g; Sodium 610mg.
Stir-fried Squid Energy 165Kcal/694kJ; Protein 19.7g; Carbohydrate 4.8g, of which sugars 3.2g; Fat 7.6g, of which saturates 1.2g; Cholesterol 281mg; Calcium 20mg; Fibre 0g; Sodium 1206mg.

Prawn Salad

In Mexico, this salad would form the fish course in a formal meal, but it is so good that you'll want to serve it on all sorts of occasions. It is perfect for a buffet lunch.

Serves 4
450g/1lb cooked peeled
   prawns (shrimp)
juice of 1 lime
3 tomatoes
1 ripe but firm avocado
30ml/2 tbsp hot chilli sauce
5ml/1 tsp sugar
150ml/¼ pint/⅔ cup sour cream
2 Little Gem (Bibb) lettuces,
   separated into leaves
salt and ground black pepper
fresh basil leaves and strips of
   green pepper to garnish

Preparation: 10 minutes; Cooking: 0 minutes

1 Put the prawns in a large bowl, add the lime juice and salt and pepper. Toss lightly, then cover and leave to marinate while you prepare the tomatoes and avocado.

2 Cut a cross in the base of each tomato. Place them in a heatproof bowl and pour over boiling water to cover.

3 After 3 minutes, lift the tomatoes out on a slotted spoon and plunge them into a bowl of cold water. Drain. The skins will have begun to peel back easily from the crosses.

4 Skin the tomatoes completely, then cut them in half and squeeze out the seeds. Chop the flesh into 1cm/¼ in cubes and add it to the prawns.

5 Cut the avocado in half, remove the skin and seed, then slice the flesh into 1cm/½ in chunks. Add it to the prawn and tomato mixture.

6 Mix the hot chilli sauce, sugar and soured cream in a bowl. Fold into the prawn mixture. Line a bowl with the lettuce leaves, then top with the prawn mixture. The salad can be served immediately, but will have a better flavour if covered and chilled for at least 1 hour. Garnish with fresh basil and strips of green pepper. Crusty bread makes a perfect accompaniment.

Salt & Pepper Prawns

These succulent shellfish beg to be eaten with the fingers, so provide finger bowls or hot wipes for all your guests.

Serves 3–4
15–18 large raw prawns
   (shrimp), in the shell,
   about 450g/1lb
vegetable oil, for deep-frying
3 shallots or 1 small onion,
   very finely chopped
2 garlic cloves, crushed
1cm/½in piece fresh root ginger,
   peeled and very finely grated
1–2 fresh red chillies, seeded
   and finely sliced
2.5ml/½ tsp caster (superfine)
   sugar or to taste
3–4 spring onions (scallions),
   shredded, to garnish

For the fried salt
10ml/2 tsp salt
5ml/1 tsp Sichuan peppercorns

Preparation: 7–8 minutes; Cooking: 4–5 minutes

1 Make the fried salt by dry-frying the salt and peppercorns in a heavy frying pan over medium heat until the peppercorns begin to release their aroma. Cool the mixture, then tip into a mortar and crush with a pestle.

2 Carefully remove the heads and legs from the raw prawns and discard. Leave the body shells and the tails in place. Pat the prepared prawns dry with sheets of kitchen paper.

3 Heat the oil for deep frying to 190°C/375°F. Fry the prawns for 1 minute, then lift them out and drain thoroughly on kitchen paper. Spoon 30ml/2 tbsp of the hot oil into a large frying pan, leaving the rest of the oil to one side to cool.

4 Heat the oil in the frying pan. Add the fried salt, with the shallots or onion, garlic, ginger, chillies and sugar. Toss all the ingredients in the pan together for 1 minute.

5 Add the prawns and toss them over the heat for about 1 minute more until they are coated and the shells are pleasantly impregnated with the seasonings. Spoon the shellfish mixture into heated serving bowls and garnish with the shredded spring onions.

Prawn Salad Energy 221kcal/920kJ; Protein 21.8g; Carbohydrate 3.8g, of which sugars 3.5g; Fat 13.2g, of which saturates 5.9g; Cholesterol 242mg; Calcium 141mg; Fibre 1.3g; Sodium 232mg.
Salt & Pepper Prawns Energy 122kcal/514kJ; Protein 20.1g; Carbohydrate 2.7g, of which sugars 2.4g; Fat 3.5g, of which saturates 0.5g; Cholesterol 219mg; Calcium 97mg; Fibre 0.3g; Sodium 1197mg.

Prawns in Garlic Butter

This quick and easy dish is perfect for serving to friends who don't mind getting their hands dirty. Provide a plate for the prawn shells and offer warm tortillas or chunks of crusty farmhouse bread for mopping up the delectable juices. Clean plates are guaranteed with this superb seafood recipe.

Serves 6
900g/2lb large raw tiger prawns
    (jumbo shrimp), in their shells,
    thawed if frozen
115g/4oz/½ cup butter
15ml/1 tbsp vegetable oil
6 garlic cloves, crushed
grated rind and juice of 2 limes
small bunch of fresh coriander
    (cilantro), chopped
warm tortillas, to serve
lemon slices, for the finger bowls

Preparation: 8 minutes; Cooking: 6–7 minutes

1 Rinse the prawns in a colander, remove their heads and leave them to drain. Heat the butter and oil in a large frying pan, add the garlic and fry over a low heat for 2–3 minutes.

2 Add the lime rind and juice. Cook, stirring constantly, for 1 minute more.

3 Add the prawns and cook them for 2–3 minutes until they turn pink. Remove from the heat, sprinkle with coriander and serve with the warm tortillas. Give each guest a finger bowl filled with water and a slice of lemon, for cleaning their fingers after shelling the prawns, and provide paper napkins.

Cook's Tips
• *Frozen prawns (shrimp) should be put in a colander and thawed for 5–8 hours in the refrigerator or 2–3 hours at room temperature. Set the colander over a bowl. For faster thawing, run cold water over the prawns or defrost them in the microwave, following the instructions in your handbook.*
• *Cook the prawns in a large frying pan or cast iron flameproof dish that can be taken directly to the table, so that they retain their heat until they are served.*

Sizzling Prawns

When you splash out and buy a luxury item like these large prawns, you want to be sure they taste great. This recipe is swift, simple and always a sure-fire success. Serve these for a celebration lunch.

Serves 4
1–2 dried chillies (to taste)
60ml/4 tbsp olive oil
3 garlic cloves, finely chopped
16 large raw prawns (jumbo
    shrimp), in the shell
salt and ground black pepper
French bread, to serve

Preparation: 2–3 minutes; Cooking: 5 minutes

1 Split the chillies lengthways and discard the seeds. It is best to do this with a knife and fork, because the seeds, in particular, contain hot capsaicin, which can be very irritating to the eyes, nose and mouth.

2 Heat the oil in a large frying pan and stir-fry the garlic and chilli for 1 minute, until the garlic begins to turn brown.

3 Add the whole prawns and stir-fry for 3–4 minutes, coating them well with the flavoured oil.

4 Remove from the heat and divide the prawns among four dishes. Spoon over the flavoured oil and serve immediately. (Remember to provide a plate for the heads and shells, plus plenty of napkins for messy fingers.)

Variations
• *Another great way to serve the prawns (shrimp) is in a warm lime and sweet chilli dressing. Use garlic to flavour the oil, but remove it before frying the prawns (shrimp). Let the oil for frying cool slightly, then whisk in fresh lime juice and a little sweet chilli sauce. Spoon over the prawns.*
• *An alternative to using fresh chillies is simply to use chilli oil for frying the garlic and prawns, or, if you prefer to avoid chillies altogether, substitute sun-dried tomatoes for the chillies and use a little of the oil from the jar for frying.*

Prawns in Garlic Energy 223kcal/924kJ; Protein 13.3g; Carbohydrate 0.3g, of which sugars 0.3g; Fat 18.8g, of which saturates 10.5g; Cholesterol 87mg; Calcium 103mg; Fibre 0.4g; Sodium 1034mg.
Sizzling Prawns Energy 124kcal/511kJ; Protein 5.7g; Carbohydrate 0g, of which sugars 0g; Fat 11.2g, of which saturates 1.6g; Cholesterol 63mg; Calcium 26mg; Fibre 0g; Sodium 62mg.

Stir-fried Prawns with Tamarind

Fresh tamarind pods can be bought, but it is much simpler and easier to use tamarind paste either in block form or packed in a jar.

Serves 4–6
6 dried red chillies
30ml/2 tbsp vegetable oil
30ml/2 tbsp chopped onion
30ml/2 tbsp palm sugar (jaggery) or light muscovado (brown) sugar
30ml/2 tbsp chicken stock or water
15ml/1 tbsp Thai fish sauce
90ml/6 tbsp tamarind juice, made by mixing tamarind paste with warm water
450g/1lb raw prawns (shrimp), peeled (see Cook's Tip)
15ml/1 tbsp fried chopped garlic
30ml/2 tbsp fried sliced shallots

Preparation: 8 minutes; Cooking: 10–12 minutes

1 Heat a wok or large frying pan, but do not add any oil at this stage. Add the dried chillies and dry-fry them by pressing them against the surface of the wok or pan with a spatula, turning them occasionally. Do not let them burn. Lift them out of the pan and set them aside on a plate to cool slightly.

2 Add the oil to the wok or pan and reheat. Add the chopped onion and cook over medium heat, stirring occasionally, for 2–3 minutes, until softened and golden brown.

3 Add the sugar, stock or water, fish sauce, dry-fried red chillies and the tamarind juice, stirring constantly until the sugar has dissolved. Bring to the boil over high heat, then lower the heat slightly.

4 Add the prawns, garlic and shallots to the wok or pan. Toss over the heat for 3–4 minutes, until the prawns are cooked. Transfer to a warmed dish or individual bowls.

Cook's Tip
Leave a few prawns (shrimp) in their shells for a garnish, if you like. Fry them on their own until they turn pink.

Fragrant Tiger Prawns with Dill

This elegant dish has a fresh, light flavour and is equally good served as a simple supper or for a dinner party. It takes only minutes to make, so you can spend more time with your guests. The delicate texture of fresh prawns goes really well with mild cucumber and fragrant dill, and all you need is some rice or noodles to serve.

Serves 4–6
500g/1¼lb raw tiger prawns (jumbo shrimp), heads and shells removed but tails left on
500g/1¼lb cucumber
30ml/2 tbsp butter
15ml/1 tbsp olive oil
15ml/1 tbsp finely chopped garlic
45ml/3 tbsp chopped fresh dill
juice of 1 lemon
salt and ground black pepper
steamed rice or noodles, to serve

Preparation: 3–4 minutes; Cooking: 5–7 minutes

1 Using a small, sharp knife, carefully make a shallow slit along the back of each prawn and use the point of the knife to remove the black vein. Set the prawns aside.

2 Peel the cucumber and slice in half lengthways. Using a small teaspoon, gently scoop out all the seeds and discard. Cut the cucumber into 4 x 1cm/1½ x ½in sticks.

3 Heat a wok over a high heat, then add the butter and oil. When the butter has melted, add the cucumber and garlic and fry over a high heat for 2–3 minutes, stirring continuously.

4 Add the prepared prawns to the wok and continue to stir-fry over a high heat for 3–4 minutes, or until the prawns turn pink and are just cooked through, then remove from the heat.

5 Add the fresh dill and lemon juice to the wok and toss to combine. Season well with salt and ground black pepper and serve immediately with steamed rice or noodles.

Cook's Tip
The best rice to use is jasmine, also known as Thai fragrant rice.

Stir-fried Prawns Energy 112kcal/469kJ; Protein 13.4g; Carbohydrate 5.5g, of which sugars 5.2g; Fat 4.1g, of which saturates 0.5g; Cholesterol 146mg; Calcium 65mg; Fibre 0.2g; Sodium 321mg.
Fragrant Prawns Energy 192Kcal/798kJ; Protein 23.2g; Carbohydrate 2.5g, of which sugars 1.9g; Fat 9.8g, of which saturates 4.4g; Cholesterol 260mg; Calcium 123mg; Fibre 0.9g; Sodium 287mg.

King Prawns in Crispy Batter

A huge range of prawns is enjoyed in Spain, each with its appropriate cooking method. Langostinos are deep-water prawns, often with tiger stripes, and can be among the biggest of the crustaceans. The best way to enjoy them is dipped in a simple batter and deep-fried.

Serves 4
120ml/4fl oz/½ cup water
1 large egg (US extra large)
115g/4oz/1 cup plain
  (all-purpose) flour
5ml/1 tsp cayenne pepper
12 raw king prawns (jumbo
  shrimp), in the shell
vegetable oil, for deep frying
flat leaf parsley, to garnish
lemon wedges, to serve (optional)

Preparation: 5–8 minutes; Cooking: 2–3 minutes

1 In a large bowl, whisk together the water and the egg. Whisk in the flour and cayenne pepper until smooth.

2 Peel the prawns, leaving just the tails intact. Make a shallow cut down the back of each prawn.

3 Using the tip of the knife, pull out and discard the dark intestinal tract.

4 Heat the oil in a large pan or deep-fat fryer, until a cube of bread dropped into the oil browns in 1 minute.

5 Holding the prawns by their tails, dip them into the batter, one at a time, shaking off any excess. Carefully drop each prawn into the oil and fry for 2–3 minutes until crisp and golden. Drain on kitchen paper, garnish with parsley and serve with lemon wedges, if you like.

> **Variation**
> *If you have any batter left over, use it to coat thin strips of vegetables such as sweet potato, beetroot (beet), carrot or (bell) pepper, or use small broccoli florets or whole baby spinach leaves. Deep-fry the vegetables until golden.*

Butterflied Prawns in Hot Chocolate Sauce

This comes from Spain, where, as in Mexico, there is a long tradition of cooking savoury food – even shellfish – with chocolate.

Serves 4
8 large raw prawns (shrimp),
  in the shell
15ml/1 tbsp seasoned plain
  (all-purpose) flour

15ml/1 tbsp pale dry sherry
juice of 1 large orange
15g/½oz dark (bittersweet)
  chocolate, chopped
30ml/2 tbsp olive oil
2 garlic cloves, finely chopped
2.5cm/1in piece fresh root ginger,
  finely chopped
1 small dried chilli, seeded
  and chopped
salt and ground black pepper

Preparation: 10 minutes; Cooking: 8–9 minutes

1 Peel the prawns, leaving just the tail sections intact. Make a shallow cut down the back of each one and carefully pull out and discard the dark intestinal tract.

2 Turn the prawns over so that the undersides are uppermost, and then carefully slit them open from tail to top, using a small sharp knife, cutting them almost, but not quite, through to the central back line. Press the prawns down firmly to flatten them out. Coat with the seasoned flour and set aside.

3 Gently heat the sherry and orange juice in a small pan. When warm, remove from the heat and stir in the chopped chocolate until melted.

4 Heat the oil in a frying pan. Add the garlic, ginger and chilli and cook for 2 minutes until golden. Remove with a slotted spoon and reserve. Add the prawns, cut side down, and cook for 2–3 minutes until golden brown with pink edges. Turn the prawns and cook for a further 2 minutes.

5 Return the garlic mixture to the pan and pour the chocolate sauce over. Cook for 1 minute, turning the prawns to coat them in the glossy sauce. Season to taste and serve hot.

Butterflied Prawns Energy 125kcal/520kJ; Protein 8.5g; Carbohydrate 6.5g, of which sugars 3.6g; Fat 6.9g, of which saturates 1.5g; Cholesterol 88mg; Calcium 44mg; Fibre 0.2g; Sodium 88mg.
King Prawns Energy 253kcal/1061kJ; Protein 13.1g; Carbohydrate 22.4g, of which sugars 0.4g; Fat 13.1g, of which saturates 1.8g; Cholesterol 145mg; Calcium 87mg; Fibre 0.9g; Sodium 113mg.

Hot & Spicy Prawns with Coriander

This is a quick, easy and low-fat way of preparing prawns for an appetizer. If you increase the quantities, it can be served as a main course. Scallops and mussels are also delicious cooked in this way. Serve the prawns with bread to mop up the tasty juices. Lemon is traditionally squeezed over the prawns but lime juice could be used instead. Lime juice goes well with coriander.

Serves 4
20ml/4 tsp olive oil
2–3 garlic cloves, chopped
25g/1oz fresh root ginger, peeled and grated
1 fresh chilli, seeded and chopped
5ml/1 tsp cumin seeds
5ml/1 tsp paprika
450g/1lb fresh raw king prawns (jumbo shrimp), peeled
bunch of fresh coriander (cilantro), chopped
salt, to taste
1 lemon, cut into wedges, to serve

Preparation: 3–4 minutes; Cooking: 4–6 minutes

1 In a large, heavy, non-stick frying pan, heat the oil with the garlic. Stir in the ginger, chilli and cumin seeds.

2 Cook briefly, until the ingredients give off a lovely aroma, then add the paprika and toss in the prawns.

3 Fry the prawns over a fairly high heat, turning them frequently, for 3–5 minutes, or until just cooked. Season to taste with salt and add the coriander.

4 Spoon the prawns on to a large plate and serve immediately, with lemon wedges for squeezing over the prawns.

Cook's Tip
Unless you cook Thai or Chinese dishes frequently, the chances are that you will waste a lot of root ginger through using a little and leaving the remainder in the refrigerator to soften and ultimately spoil. Freeze the root in a plastic bag instead. It can be grated from frozen and will thaw almost instantly.

Prawns on Crisp Noodle Cake

The contrast between the crisp noodle cake and the shellfish mixture works well.

Serves 4
300g/11oz thin dried egg noodles
60ml/4 tbsp vegetable oil
500g/1¼lb medium raw king prawns (jumbo shrimp), peeled and deveined
2.5ml/½ tsp ground coriander
15ml/1 tbsp ground turmeric
2 garlic cloves, finely chopped
2 slices fresh root ginger, finely chopped
tender parts of 2 lemon grass stalks, finely chopped
2 shallots, finely chopped
15ml/1 tbsp tomato purée (paste)
250ml/8fl oz/1 cup coconut milk
15–30ml/1–2 tbsp lime juice
15–30ml/1–2 tbsp Thai fish sauce
1 cucumber, peeled, seeded and cut into 5cm/2in batons
1 tomato, seeded and cut into strips
2 fresh red chillies, seeded and finely sliced in rings
salt and ground black pepper
2 spring onions (scallions), finely sliced, and a few coriander (cilantro) sprigs, to garnish

Preparation: 10 minutes; Cooking: 10 minutes

1 Cook the noodles as directed on the packet. Drain, rinse and drain well again. Heat 15ml/1 tbsp of the oil in a large frying pan. Add the noodles in an even layer. Fry for 4–5 minutes until they form a crisp, golden cake. Turn over and fry the other side.

2 In a bowl, toss the prawns with the ground coriander, garlic, ginger, turmeric, and lemon grass. Add salt and pepper to taste.

3 Heat the remaining oil in a large frying pan. Fry the shallots for 1 minute, then add the prawns and fry for 2 minutes more. Remove the prawns. Stir the tomato purée, coconut milk, lime juice and fish sauce into the pan. Bring the sauce to a simmer, gently stir in the prawns, then add the cucumber. Simmer until the prawns are cooked and the sauce has a coating consistency.

4 Add the tomato, stir until warmed, then add the chillies. Serve the prawns in the sauce on the noodle cake, and garnish with the sliced spring onions and coriander sprigs.

Hot & Spicy Prawns Energy 382kcal/1590kJ; Protein 40.8g; Carbohydrate 1g, of which sugars 0.9g; Fat 23.8g, of which saturates 3.4g; Cholesterol 439mg; Calcium 254mg; Fibre 1.9g; Sodium 440mg.
Prawns on Noodle Cake Energy 134kcal/560kJ; Protein 21.2g; Carbohydrate 2.4g, of which sugars 0.5g; Fat 4.4g, of which saturates 0.6g; Cholesterol 219mg; Calcium 116mg; Fibre 1.1g; Sodium 219mg.

Prawn Rice Vermicelli

Chillies add a hint of heat to this tasty mixture of vegetables, shellfish and rice vermicelli – perfect for a midweek supper.

Serves 4
60ml/4 tbsp vegetable oil
I large onion, finely sliced
2–4 dried red chillies,
    finely ground
30ml/2 tbsp yellow bean paste
2 garlic cloves, finely chopped
30ml/2 tbsp soy sauce
225g/8oz cooked prawns
    (shrimp), peeled
6 fried beancurd (tofu)
    blocks, sliced
225g/8oz/2⅔ cups beansprouts
115g/4oz garlic chives, chopped
350g/12oz rice vermicelli,
    soaked in warm water
    until soft, drained
2 hard-boiled eggs, cut into
    wedges, to garnish
salt and ground black pepper

Preparation: 8–10 minutes; Cooking: 6–7 minutes

1 Heat the oil in a wok. Fry the onion with the ground chillies until soft. Stir in the yellow bean paste, garlic and soy sauce. Fry for 1–2 minutes.

2 Add the prawns, beancurd slices, beansprouts and garlic chives. Stir to mix, then fry for 1–2 minutes more.

3 Add the vermicelli to the mixture and fry, stirring gently until it is evenly heated through. Taste for seasoning, adding more soy sauce if required. Pile onto a heated platter and serve immediately, garnished with the hard-boiled egg wedges.

Cook's Tip
Rice vermicelli noodles are extremely thin, almost hair-like. It is easy to confuse them with bean thread noodles, especially as the latter are also called vermicelli noodles. The difference lies in the source: bean thread vermicelli noodles are made from ground mung beans. Both are prepared in a similar fashion, by being soaked in warm water. Rice vermicelli noodles require 5–10 minutes for this process, and can then be drained and used as indicated in recipes.

Sun-dried Tomato & Prawn Stir-fry

The Mediterranean flavour of sun-dried tomatoes combined with glossy Japanese noodles – East meets West.

Serves 4
350g/12oz somen noodles
45ml/3 tbsp olive oil
20 uncooked king prawns (jumbo
    shrimp), peeled and deveined
2 garlic cloves, finely chopped
45–60ml/3–4 tbsp sun-dried
    tomato paste
salt and ground black pepper

For the garnish
handful of fresh basil leaves
30ml/2 tbsp sun-dried
    tomatoes in oil, drained
    and cut into strips

Preparation: 4–5 minutes; Cooking: 9–11 minutes

1 Cook the noodles in a large pan of boiling water until tender, following the directions on the packet. Drain.

2 Heat half the oil in a large frying pan. Add the prawns and garlic and fry them over a medium heat for 3–5 minutes, until the prawns turn pink and are firm to the touch.

3 Stir in 15ml/1 tbsp of the sun-dried tomato paste and mix well. Using a slotted spoon, transfer to a bowl and keep hot.

4 Reheat the oil remaining in the pan. Stir in the rest of the oil with the remaining sun-dried tomato paste. You may need to add a spoonful of water if the mixture is very thick. When the mixture starts to sizzle, toss in the noodles. Add salt and pepper to taste and mix well.

5 Return the prawns to the pan and toss to combine. Serve immediately garnished with the basil and sun-dried tomatoes.

Cook's Tip
Ready-made sun-dried tomato paste is readily available, but you can make your own simply by processing bottled sun-dried tomatoes with their oil.

Vermicelli Energy 546kcal/2279kJ; Protein 25.2g; Carbohydrate 78.4g, of which sugars 6.8g; Fat 14.6g, of which saturates 1.7g; Cholesterol 110mg; Calcium 408mg; Fibre 3.3g; Sodium 665mg.
Stir-fry Energy 481kcal/2026kJ; Protein 19.2g; Carbohydrate 67.4g, of which sugars 2.9g; Fat 16.8g, of which saturates 1.6g; Cholesterol 98mg; Calcium 62mg; Fibre 2.8g; Sodium 99mg.

Seafood Pancakes

English pancakes can be traced back as far as the 15th century, when a simple batter would have been made with eggs, flour and water.

Serves 4

For the pancakes
115g/4oz/1 cup plain
   (all-purpose) flour
pinch of salt
1 egg
300ml/½ pint/1¼ cups milk
15ml/1 tbsp melted butter
oil or melted butter, for cooking

For the filling
300ml/½ pint/1¼ cups milk,
   preferably semi-skimmed
   (low-fat)
150ml/¼ pint/⅔ cup fish stock
25g/1oz/2 tbsp plain
   (all-purpose) flour
25g/1oz/2 tbsp butter
350g/12oz skinless fish fillets,
   such as haddock and salmon,
   cut into bitesize pieces
115g/4oz peeled prawns (shrimp)
large handful of baby
   spinach leaves
50g/2oz cheese, such as Cheddar
   or Lancashire, grated

Preparation: 3–4 minutes; Cooking: 15 minutes

1 To make the pancakes, sift the flour and salt into a bowl and break the egg into it. Gradually beat in the milk to make a smooth batter and then stir in 15ml/1 tbsp melted butter.

2 Put a 20cm/8in non-stick frying pan over a medium heat and brush with oil or butter. When hot, add 45ml/3 tbsp batter, tilting to cover the surface. Cook until the underside is golden brown then flip over and briefly cook the other side. Repeat with the remaining batter to make eight pancakes. Keep warm.

3 To make the filling, put the milk, stock, flour and butter into a pan. Bring to the boil, whisking continuously, until the sauce thickens. Add the fish pieces and simmer gently for 3 minutes or until the fish is just cooked. Stir in the prawns and spinach.

4 Cook until the prawns are heated through and the spinach is wilted. Stir in the cheese. Remove from the heat. Spoon the fish mixture into the centre of the pancakes and roll up or fold into triangles. Serve immediately.

Seafood Risotto

Risotto is one of Italy's most popular rice dishes and it is made with everything from pumpkin to squid ink. On the Mediterranean shores, fresh seafood is the most obvious addition.

Serves 4
60ml/4 tbsp sunflower oil
1 onion, chopped
2 garlic cloves, crushed

225g/8oz/generous 1 cup
   arborio rice
105ml/7 tbsp white wine
1.5 litres/2½ pints/6 cups hot
   fish stock
350g/12oz mixed seafood, such
   as raw prawns (shrimp),
   mussels, squid rings or clams
grated rind of ½ lemon
30ml/2 tbsp tomato purée (paste)
15ml/1 tbsp chopped
   fresh parsley
salt and ground black pepper

Preparation: 2 minutes; Cooking: 18 minutes

1 Heat the oil in a heavy-based pan, add the onion and garlic and cook until soft. Add the rice and stir to coat the grains with oil. Add the wine and cook over a moderate heat, stirring, for a few minutes until absorbed.

2 Add 150ml/¼ pint/⅔ cup of the hot stock and cook, stirring constantly, until the liquid is absorbed by the rice. Continue stirring and adding stock in 150ml/¼ pint/⅔ cup quantities, until half is left. This should take about 10 minutes.

3 Stir in the seafood and cook for 2–3 minutes. Add the remaining stock as before, until the rice is cooked. It should be quite creamy and the grains al dente.

4 Stir in the lemon rind, tomato purée and parsley. Season with salt and pepper and serve warm.

Cook's Tip
Stirring the rice constantly produces a beautifully creamy risotto. Although this means that the cook must stand over the stove the whole time, the action is incredibly therapeutic.

Seafood Pancakes Energy 393kcal/1647kJ; Protein 26.7g; Carbohydrate 25.4g, of which sugars 5.7g; Fat 21.2g, of which saturates 11.9g; Cholesterol 203mg; Calcium 273mg; Fibre 0.8g; Sodium 513mg.
Seafood Risotto Energy 404kcal/1693kJ; Protein 28.1g; Carbohydrate 56.3g, of which sugars 1.1g; Fat 3.9g, of which saturates 1.9g; Cholesterol 228mg; Calcium 200mg; Fibre 0.2g; Sodium 301mg.

Garlicky Scallops & Prawns

Scallops and prawns provide a healthy meal in next to no time. This particular recipe comes from France and is popular in Provence. It is very quick and easy to make and is perfect for a summer lunch or a quick meal before a trip to the theatre, as it is lovely and light, and easily digested.

Serves 2–4
6 large shelled scallops
6–8 large raw prawns (jumbo
  shrimp), peeled
plain (all-purpose) flour, for dusting
30–45ml/2–3 tbsp olive oil
1 garlic clove, finely chopped
15ml/1 tbsp chopped fresh basil
30–45ml/2–3 tbsp lemon juice
salt and ground black pepper

Preparation: 1 minute; Cooking: 4–5 minutes

1 Rinse the scallops under cold running water to remove any sand or grit. Drain, then pat dry using kitchen paper. Cut them in half crossways.

2 Season the scallops and prawns with salt and pepper and dust lightly with flour. Heat the oil in a large frying pan over high heat and add the scallops and prawns.

3 Reduce the heat slightly and cook for 2 minutes, then turn the scallops and prawns and add the garlic and basil, shaking the pan to distribute them evenly.

4 Cook for a further 2 minutes, until the scallops are golden and just firm to the touch. Sprinkle over the lemon juice and toss to blend. Spoon into a heated dish or on to individual plates and serve at once.

> **Cook's Tips**
> • *Like oysters, scallops are traditionally best when there is an 'r' in the month. Frozen scallops are available, but their quality is not as good as the fresh ones.*
> • *Scallops should be cooked for the shortest possible time, as they become leathery when overcooked. The bright red corals require even less time than the nuggets of white flesh.*

Seafood Conchiglie

This is a very special modern dish – a warm salad composed of scallops, pasta and fresh rocket flavoured with roasted pepper, chilli and balsamic vinegar.

Serves 4
8 large fresh scallops
300g/11oz/2¾ cups
  dried conchiglie
15ml/1 tbsp olive oil
15g/½ oz/1 tbsp butter
120ml/4fl oz/½ cup dry
  white wine

90g/3½ oz rocket (arugula)
  leaves, stalks trimmed
salt and ground black pepper

For the vinaigrette
60ml/4 tbsp extra virgin olive oil
15ml/1 tbsp balsamic vinegar
1 piece bottled roasted pepper,
  drained and finely chopped
1–2 fresh red chillies, seeded
  and chopped
1 garlic clove, crushed
5–10ml/1 2 tsp clear honey,
  to taste

Preparation: 8 minutes; Cooking: 10–12 minutes

1 Cut each scallop into 2–3 pieces. If the corals are attached, pull them off and cut each piece in half. Season the scallops and corals with salt and pepper.

2 To make the vinaigrette, put all the ingredients in a measuring jug (cup) and whisk well.

3 Cook the pasta in a large pan of lightly salted boiling water for 10–12 minutes.

4 Meanwhile, heat the oil and butter in a non-stick frying pan until sizzling. Add half the scallops and toss over a high heat for 2 minutes. Remove with a slotted spoon and keep warm. Cook the remaining scallops in the same way.

5 Add the wine to the liquid remaining in the pan and stir over a high heat until the mixture has reduced to a few tablespoons. Remove from the heat and keep warm. Drain the pasta and tip it into a warmed bowl. Add the rocket, scallops, the reduced cooking juices and the vinaigrette and toss well to combine. Serve immediately.

Garlicky Scallops Energy 159kcal/664kJ; Protein 16.4g; Carbohydrate 2.9g, of which sugars 0.2g; Fat 9.2g, of which saturates 1.4g; Cholesterol 72mg; Calcium 51mg; Fibre 0.4g; Sodium 140mg.
Seafood Conchiglie Energy 485kcal/2039kJ; Protein 18.4g; Carbohydrate 59.3g, of which sugars 4.9g; Fat 18.9g, of which saturates 4.3g; Cholesterol 26mg; Calcium 72mg; Fibre 2.7g; Sodium 126mg.

Scallops with Garlic & Coriander

Shellfish is often best when cooked very simply. This recipe comes from Mexico, where hot chilli sauce and lime are popular ingredients in many fish recipes. The dish packs quite a punch, so use just enough sauce to give the intensity of flavour you prefer.

Serves 4
20 scallops
2 courgettes (zucchini)
75g/3oz/6 tbsp butter
15ml/1 tbsp vegetable oil
4 garlic cloves, chopped
30ml/2 tbsp hot chilli sauce
juice of 1 lime
small bunch of fresh coriander
  (cilantro), finely chopped

Preparation: 10 minutes; Cooking: 5–6 minutes

1 If you have bought scallops in their shells, open them. Hold a scallop shell in the palm of your hand, with the flat side uppermost. Insert the blade of a knife close to the hinge that joins the shells and prise them apart.

2 Run the blade of the knife across the inside of the flat shell to cut away the scallop. Only the white adductor muscle and the orange coral are eaten, so pull away and discard all other parts. Rinse the scallops under cold running water.

3 Cut the courgettes in half, then into four pieces. Heat the butter with the oil in a large frying pan. Add the courgettes and fry until soft. Remove from the pan. Add the garlic and fry until golden. Stir in the hot chilli sauce.

4 Add the scallops to the sauce. Cook, stirring constantly, for 1–2 minutes only. Stir in the lime juice, chopped coriander and the courgette pieces. Serve immediately on heated plates.

> **Cook's Tip**
> *Hot chilli sauces vary hugely, from relatively mild mixtures to ones with paint-blistering potential. If using something like Tabasco sauce, reduce the quantity considerably unless you have a cast-iron constitution.*

Herb- & Chilli-seared Scallops

Tender, succulent scallops taste simply divine when marinated in fresh chilli, fragrant mint and aromatic basil, then quickly seared in a piping hot wok. If you can't find king scallops for this recipe, use twice the quantity of smaller queen scallops or use a mixture of prawns and scallops.

Serves 4
20–24 king scallops, cleaned
120ml/4fl oz/¾ cup olive oil
finely grated rind and juice
  of 1 lemon
30ml/2 tbsp finely chopped mixed
  fresh mint and basil
1 fresh red chilli, seeded and
  finely chopped
salt and ground black pepper
500g/1¼lb pak choi (bok choy)

Preparation: 3 minutes; Cooking: 5 minutes

1 Place the scallops in a shallow, non-metallic bowl in a single layer. In a clean bowl, mix together half the oil, the lemon rind and juice, chopped herbs and chilli, and spoon over the scallops. Season well with salt and black pepper, cover and set aside.

2 Using a sharp knife, cut each pak choi lengthways into four pieces. Place on a plate and set aside.

3 Heat a wok over a high heat. When hot, drain the scallops (reserving the marinade) and add to the wok. Cook for 1 minute on each side, or until cooked to your liking. Don't overcook the scallops or they will toughen.

4 Pour the marinade over the scallops and remove the wok from the heat. Transfer the scallops and juices to a platter and keep warm. Wipe out the wok with a piece of kitchen paper.

5 Place the wok over a high heat. When all traces of moisture have evaporated, add the remaining oil. When the oil is hot add the pak choi and stir-fry over a high heat for 2–3 minutes, until the leaves wilt.

6 Divide the greens among four warmed serving plates, then top with the reserved scallops. Spoon the lemon, herb and chilli pan juices over the scallops and serve immediately.

Scallops with Garlic Energy 291kcal/1213kJ; Protein 24.2g; Carbohydrate 4.4g, of which sugars 1g; Fat 19.8g, of which saturates 10.5g; Cholesterol 87mg; Calcium 45mg; Fibre 0.5g; Sodium 294mg.
Chilli-seared Scallops Energy 410Kcal/1714kJ; Protein 44.5g; Carbohydrate 8.3g, of which sugars 2.1g; Fat 22.3g, of which saturates 3.5g; Cholesterol 82mg; Calcium 286mg; Fibre 3.2g; Sodium 494mg.

Scallops with Lime Butter

Chargrilling fennel releases its aniseed flavour, which tastes great with sweet and rich scallops. These wonderful shellfish are ideal for the barbecue because they have firm flesh that cooks quickly – simply toss in lime juice before cooking.

Serves 4
1 head fennel
2 limes
12 large scallops, cleaned
1 egg yolk
90ml/6 tbsp melted butter
olive oil for brushing
salt and ground black pepper

Preparation: 5 minutes; Cooking: 6–8 minutes

1 Trim any feathery leaves from the fennel and reserve them. Slice the rest lengthways into thin wedges.

2 Cut one lime into wedges. Finely grate the rind and squeeze the juice of the other lime and toss half the juice and rind on to the scallops. Season well with salt and ground black pepper to taste.

3 Place the egg yolk and remaining lime rind and juice in a small bowl and whisk until pale and smooth.

4 Gradually whisk in the melted butter and continue whisking until thick and smooth. Finely chop the reserved fennel leaves and stir them in, with seasoning.

5 Prepare the barbecue. Position a lightly oiled grill (broiler) rack over the hot coals. Brush the fennel wedges with olive oil and cook them over high heat for 3–4 minutes, turning once.

6 Add the scallops and cook for a further 3–4 minutes, turning once. Serve with the lime butter and the lime wedges.

Cook's Tip
Thread small scallops on to metal or bamboo skewers to make turning them easier. If using bamboo, soak in water first.

Scallops with Bacon

In the 19th century, scallops were dredged in large numbers along England's Sussex coast. Today, they are fished off the Isle of Man. Like oysters, scallops are often believed to be an aphrodisiac. They are best when cooked quickly and briefly, and go well with bacon.

Serves 4
15ml/1 tbsp olive oil
4 streaky bacon (fatty)
   rashers (strips), cut into
   2.5cm/1in pieces
2–3 fresh sage leaves, chopped
small piece of butter
8 large or 16 small scallops
15ml/1 tbsp fresh lemon juice
100ml/3¾fl oz dry (hard) cider
   or dry white wine

Preparation: 3–4 minutes; Cooking: 4 minutes

1 Heat the oil in a frying pan. Add the bacon and sage and cook, stirring occasionally, until the bacon is golden brown. Lift out and keep warm.

2 Add the butter to the pan and when hot add the scallops. Cook quickly for about 1 minute on each side until browned. Lift out and keep warm.

3 Add the lemon juice and cider or wine to the pan and, scraping up any sediment remaining in the pan, bring just to the boil. Continue bubbling gently until the mixture has reduced to just a few tablespoons of syrupy sauce.

4 Serve the scallops and bacon on heated individual plates with the cider or wine sauce drizzled over.

Cook's Tip
In summer, some fishmongers sell marsh samphire (glasswort), which grows around the coast of England and makes a good accompaniment to this dish. To prepare samphire, wash it well and pick off the soft fleshy branches, discarding the thicker woody stalks. Drop it into boiling water for just 1 minute before draining and serving.

Scallops with Butter Energy 232kcal/961kJ; Protein 10g; Carbohydrate 2.2g, of which sugars 0.9g; Fat 20.5g, of which saturates 12.3g; Cholesterol 116mg; Calcium 31mg; Fibre 1.1g; Sodium 211mg.
Scallops with Bacon Energy 208kcal/867kJ; Protein 15.6g; Carbohydrate 2.4g, of which sugars 0.7g; Fat 14.5g, of which saturates 5.9g; Cholesterol 53mg; Calcium 19mg; Fibre 0g; Sodium 445mg.

Sautéed Scallops

Scallops go well with all
sorts of sauces, but simple
cooking is the best way to
enjoy their delicate, fresh-
from-the-sea flavour. For this
recipe they are served with
a vermouth sauce.

Serves 2
450g/1lb shelled scallops
25g/1oz/2 tbsp butter
30ml/2 tbsp dry white vermouth
15ml/1 tbsp finely chopped
    fresh parsley
salt and ground black pepper

Preparation: 1 minute; Cooking: 5 minutes

1 Rinse the scallops under cold running water to remove any
sand or grit. Drain them well and pat dry using kitchen paper.
Spread them out and season them lightly with salt and pepper.

2 In a frying pan large enough to hold the scallops in one layer,
heat half the butter until it begins to colour.

3 Sauté the scallops for 3–5 minutes, turning until golden
brown on both sides and just firm to the touch. Remove to a
serving platter and cover with foil to keep hot.

4 Add the vermouth to the hot frying pan, swirl in the
remaining butter, stir in the parsley and pour the sauce over
the scallops. Serve immediately.

Variation
*An impressive way of serving these scallops is in puff pastry
boxes. It isn't necessary to make your own puff pastry as the
bought product is very good. Roll out the pastry and cut out
two squares, each measuring about 10cm/4in across. Then,
using a sharp knife, mark out an inner square on each piece of
pastry, about 2cm/¾in in from the edge and about half the
depth of the pastry. Put the pastry squares on a baking sheet
and bake in a preheated oven at 220°C/425°F/Gas 7 for
20 minutes until well risen and golden. Remove the inner lid
from each box and scoop out the soft inside, then pile in the
scallop filling and replace the lid at an angle.*

Mussels in Garlic Butter

Garlic and herb butter is a
classic treatment for snails
in Burgundy, but became
very popular in the 1960s
with mussels, and makes a
delicious first course.

Serves 4
2kg/4½lb mussels, scrubbed
2 large shallots, finely chopped
200ml/7fl oz/scant 1 cup dry
    white wine

115g/4oz/½ cup unsalted
    (sweet) butter, softened
2–3 garlic cloves, finely chopped
grated rind of 1 lemon
60ml/4 tbsp finely chopped mixed
    herbs, such as parsley, chervil,
    tarragon and chives
115g/4oz/1 cup fresh white
    breadcrumbs
salt and ground black pepper
lemon wedges, to serve

Preparation: 6–7 minutes; Cooking: 10 minutes

1 Check that all the mussels are closed after cleaning and
discard any that remain open when sharply tapped. Place the
shallots and wine in a large pan and bring to the boil. Throw
in the mussels and cover tightly. Cook over a high heat for
4–5 minutes, shaking the pan vigorously 2–3 times.

2 The mussels should be cooked and gaping open. Discard any
that do not open after 5 minutes' cooking. Drain, reserving the
cooking liquid. Discard the top (empty) half of each shell. Place
the mussels in a roasting pan.

3 Pour the cooking liquid into a clean pan and boil it vigorously
until reduced to about 45ml/3 tbsp. Remove the pan from the
heat and set it aside to cool.

4 Cream the butter with the shallots from the reduced liquid,
the garlic, lemon rind and herbs. Season well and set aside.

5 Distribute the flavoured butter among the mussels. Sprinkle
with the cooking liquid, then scatter the breadcrumbs over.

6 Preheat the grill (broiler) and position the shelf 10cm/4in below
the heat. Grill (broil) the mussels until the butter is bubbling
and the breadcrumbs are golden and crisp. Serve with lemon.

Scallops Energy 378kcal/1588kJ; Protein 52.5g; Carbohydrate 8.4g, of which sugars 0.7g; Fat 13.5g, of which saturates 7.4g; Cholesterol 132mg; Calcium 84mg; Fibre 0.4g; Sodium 485mg.
Mussels Energy 494kcal/2068kJ; Protein 26.3g; Carbohydrate 28.5g, of which sugars 2.1g; Fat 27.7g, of which saturates 15.5g; Cholesterol 141mg; Calcium 121mg; Fibre 0.9g; Sodium 875mg.

Mussels in Cider

Mussels are delicious when steamed and lifted out of their shells, and quickly fried with bacon. Here they are cooked with a broth of cider, garlic and cream. Serve the mussels in large shallow bowls with a chunk of bread to mop up the juices. Don't forget to provide finger bowls for cleaning sticky fingers.

Serves 4
1.8kg/4lb mussels in their shells
40g/1½oz/3 tbsp butter
1 leek, washed and finely chopped
1 garlic clove, finely chopped
150ml/¼ pint/⅔ cup dry (hard) cider
30–45ml/2–3 tbsp double (heavy) cream
a handful of fresh parsley, chopped
ground black pepper

Preparation: 5–6 minutes; Cooking: 8–10 minutes

1 Scrub the mussels and scrape off any barnacles. Discard those with broken shells or that refuse to close when given a sharp tap with a knife. Pull off the hairy beards with a sharp tug.

2 Melt the butter in a very large pan and add the leek and garlic. Cook over medium heat for about 5 minutes, stirring frequently, until very soft but not browned. Season with pepper.

3 Add the cider and immediately tip in the mussels. Cover with a lid and cook quickly, shaking the pan occasionally, until the mussels have just opened (take care not to overcook and toughen them).

4 Remove the lid, add the cream and parsley and bubble gently for a minute or two. Serve immediately in shallow bowls.

Cook's Tip
Eat mussels the fun way! Use an empty shell as pincers to pick out the mussels from the other shells. Don't try to eat any whose shells have not opened during cooking or you risk food poisoning. Provide an empty bowl for the mussel shells.

Thai Steamed Mussels in Coconut Milk

An ideal dish for informal entertaining, mussels steamed in coconut milk and fresh aromatic herbs are quick and easy to prepare and great for a relaxed dinner with friends.

Serves 4
1.6kg/3½lb mussels
15ml/1 tbsp sunflower oil
6 garlic cloves, roughly chopped
15ml/1 tbsp finely chopped fresh root ginger
2 large red chillies, seeded and finely sliced
6 spring onions (scallions), finely chopped
400ml/14fl oz/1⅔ cups coconut milk
45ml/3 tbsp light soy sauce
2 limes
5ml/1 tsp caster (superfine) sugar
a large handful of chopped coriander (cilantro)
salt and ground black pepper

Preparation: 10 minutes; Cooking: 6–7 minutes

1 Scrub the mussels in cold water. Scrape off any barnacles with a knife, then pull out and discard the fibrous beard visible between the hinge on any of the shells. Discard any mussels that are not tightly closed, or that fail to close when tapped sharply.

2 Heat a wok over a high heat and then add the oil. Stir in the garlic, ginger, chillies and spring onions and stir-fry over medium to high heat for 30 seconds.

3 Grate the rind of the limes into the ginger mixture, then squeeze both fruit and add the juice to the wok with the coconut milk, soy sauce and sugar. Stir to mix.

4 Bring the mixture to the boil, then add the mussels. Return to the boil, cover and cook briskly for 5–6 minutes, or until all the mussels have opened. Discard any unopened mussels.

5 Remove the wok from the heat and stir in the chopped coriander. Season the mussels well with salt and pepper. Ladle into warmed bowls and serve immediately.

Mussels in Cider Energy 261kcal/1092kJ; Protein 21.1g; Carbohydrate 6.5g, of which sugars 2.1g; Fat 15.6g, of which saturates 8.2g; Cholesterol 104mg; Calcium 82mg; Fibre 1g; Sodium 498mg.
Thai Steamed Mussels Energy 160kcal/679kJ; Protein 21.5g; Carbohydrate 6.7g, of which sugars 6.7g; Fat 5.5g, of which saturates 1g; Cholesterol 48mg; Calcium 272mg; Fibre 0.2g; Sodium 630mg.

Mouclade of Mussels

This recipe is quite similar to moules marinière but has the additional flavouring of fennel and mild curry. Traditionally the mussels are shelled and piled into scallop shells, but nothing beats a bowlful of steaming hot, garlicky mussels, served in their own shells.

Serves 6
1.75kg/4½lb fresh mussels
250ml/8fl oz/1 cup dry
   white wine
good pinch of grated nutmeg
3 thyme sprigs
2 bay leaves
1 small onion, finely chopped
50g/2oz/¼ cup butter
1 fennel bulb, thinly sliced
4 garlic cloves, crushed
2.5ml/½ tsp curry paste
   or powder
30ml/2 tbsp plain
   (all-purpose) flour
150ml/¼ pint/⅔ cup double
   (heavy) cream
ground black pepper
chopped fresh dill, to garnish

Preparation: 2–3 minutes; Cooking: 14 minutes

1 Scrub the mussels, discarding any that are damaged or open ones that do not close when tapped with a knife.

2 Put the wine, nutmeg, thyme, bay leaves and onion in a large pan and bring just to the boil. Tip in the mussels and cover with a lid. Cook for 4–5 minutes until the mussels have opened.

3 Drain the mussels, reserving all the juices. Discard any mussels that remain closed.

4 Melt the butter in a large clean pan and gently fry the fennel slices and garlic for about 5 minutes until softened.

5 Stir in the curry paste or powder and flour and cook for 1 minute. Remove from the heat and gradually blend in the cooking juices from the mussels. Return to the heat and cook, stirring, for 2 minutes.

6 Stir in the cream and a little pepper. Add the mussels to the pan and heat through for 2 minutes. Serve hot, garnished with chopped fresh dill.

Mussels & Clams with Lemon Grass

Fresh lemon grass has an incomparable flavour and is excellent used with seafood. If you cannot find clams, use extra mussels instead.

Serves 6
1.8–2kg/4–4½lb mussels
450g/1lb baby clams, washed
120ml/4fl oz/½ cup dry
   white wine
1 bunch spring onions
   (scallions), chopped
2 lemon grass stalks, chopped
6 kaffir lime leaves, chopped
10ml/2 tsp Thai green curry paste
200ml/7fl oz/scant 1 cup
   coconut cream
30ml/2 tbsp chopped fresh
   coriander (cilantro)
salt and ground black pepper
whole garlic chives, to garnish

Preparation: 5 minutes; Cooking: 10 minutes

1 Clean the mussels. Pull off the beards and scrub the shells. Discard any that are broken or stay open when tapped.

2 Put the wine, spring onions, lemon grass, lime leaves and curry paste in a pan. Simmer until the wine almost evaporates.

3 Add the mussels and clams to the pan, cover tightly and steam the shellfish over a high heat for 5–6 minutes, until they open. Shake the pan frequently.

4 Using a slotted spoon, transfer the mussels and clams to a warmed serving bowl and keep hot. Discard any shellfish that remain closed. Strain the cooking liquid into a clean pan and then simmer to reduce the amount to about 250ml/8fl oz/1 cup.

5 Stir in the coconut cream and coriander, with salt and pepper to taste. Heat through. Pour over the seafood and serve, garnished with garlic chives.

> **Cook's Tip**
> *Buy extra mussels in case any have to be discarded because of damage or because they are permanently closed.*

Mouclade of Mussels Energy 314kcal/1308kJ; Protein 16.6g; Carbohydrate 6g, of which sugars 1.9g; Fat 22.2g, of which saturates 13g; Cholesterol 87mg; Calcium 207mg; Fibre 1.1g; Sodium 246mg.
Mussels and Clams Energy 237kcal/993kJ; Protein 22.5g; Carbohydrate 2.8g, of which sugars 1.7g; Fat 13.8g, of which saturates 10.3g; Cholesterol 58mg; Calcium 238mg; Fibre 0.9g; Sodium 606mg.

Spiced Clams

Spanish clams, especially in the north, are much larger than clams found elsewhere, and have more succulent bodies. This modern recipe uses Arab spicing to make a hot dip or sauce. Serve with plenty of fresh bread to mop up the delicious juices.

Serves 3–4

1 small onion, finely chopped
1 celery stick, sliced
2 garlic cloves, finely chopped
2.5cm/1in piece fresh root
　ginger, grated
30ml/2 tbsp olive oil
1.5ml/¼ tsp chilli powder
5ml/1 tsp ground turmeric
30ml/2 tbsp chopped fresh
　parsley
500g/1¼lb small clams, in the shell
30ml/2 tbsp dry white wine
salt and ground black pepper
celery leaves, to garnish
fresh bread, to serve

Preparation: 4 minutes; Cooking: 9–12 minutes

1 Place the onion, celery, garlic and ginger in a large pan, add the olive oil, spices and chopped parsley and stir-fry for about 5 minutes. Add the clams to the pan and cook for 2 minutes.

2 Add the wine, then cover and cook gently for 2–3 minutes, shaking the pan occasionally. Season. Discard any clams whose shells remain closed. Pile the remainder on a heated platter and serve, garnished with the celery leaves.

Cook's Tips
• There are many different varieties of clam. One of the best is the almeja fina (the carpet shell clam), which is perfect used in this dish. These attractive shellfish have grooved brown shells with a yellow lattice pattern.
• Before cooking the clams, check that all the shells are closed. Any clams that do not open after cooking should be discarded.
• When buying the ginger, visit a shop or market with a rapid turnover. Much of the fresh ginger in the shops has been around for such a long time that it has dried out and developed a musty flavour. Fresh ginger should feel firm and smooth to the touch.

Lemon, Chilli & Herb Steamed Razor Clams

Razor clams have beautiful striped gold and brown tubular shells and make a wonderful and unusual appetizer. Here they are lightly steamed and tossed in a fragrant Italian-style dressing of chilli, lemon, garlic and parsley. Serve with plenty of crusty bread for mopping up the delicious pan juices. For a main course, make double the quantity.

Serves 4

12 razor clams
90–120ml/6–8 tbsp extra virgin
　olive oil
finely grated rind and juice of
　1 small lemon
2 garlic cloves, very finely grated
1 red chilli, seeded and very
　finely chopped
60ml/4 tbsp chopped flat
　leaf parsley
salt and ground black pepper
mixed salad leaves and crusty
　bread, to serve

Preparation: 5 minutes; Cooking: 3–4 minutes

1 Wash the razor clams well in plenty of cold running water. Drain and arrange half the clams in a steamer, placing them side by side, with the hinge side down.

2 Pour 5cm/2in water into a wok and bring to the boil. Carefully balance the steamer over the water and cover tightly. Steam for 3–4 minutes until the clams have opened. Discard any clams that remain closed.

3 Remove the clams from the wok and keep warm while you steam the remaining clams in the same way.

4 Pour the olive oil into a small bowl. Add the grated lemon rind and juice, stir well, then add the garlic, red chilli and flat leaf parsley. Mix thoroughly.

5 Season the dressing well with salt and pepper. Spoon the steamed razor clams on to plates and spoon the dressing over. Serve immediately with a crisp mixed-leaf salad and crusty bread.

Spiced Clams Energy 126kcal/526kJ; Protein 12.5g; Carbohydrate 4.5g, of which sugars 2.2g; Fat 6g, of which saturates 0.9g; Cholesterol 50mg; Calcium 69mg; Fibre 0.6g; Sodium 906mg.
Razor Clams Energy 188Kcal/775kJ; Protein 6.1g; Carbohydrate 2.9g, of which sugars 0.5g; Fat 16.9g, of which saturates 2.4g; Cholesterol 20mg; Calcium 47mg; Fibre 1.1g; Sodium 364mg.

Oysters Rockefeller

This is the perfect dish for those who prefer to eat their oysters lightly cooked. As a cheaper alternative, for those who are not as rich as Rockefeller, give mussels or clams the same treatment; they will also taste delicious.

Serves 6
450g/1lb/3 cups coarse sea salt, plus extra to serve
24 oysters, opened
115g/4oz/½ cup butter

2 shallots, finely chopped
500g/1¼lb spinach leaves, finely chopped
60ml/4 tbsp chopped fresh parsley
60ml/4 tbsp chopped celery leaves
90ml/6 tbsp fresh white or wholemeal (whole-wheat) breadcrumbs
10–20ml/2–4 tsp vodka
cayenne pepper
sea salt and ground black pepper
lemon or lime wedges, to serve

Preparation: 6–7 minutes; Cooking: 12–13 minutes

1 Preheat the oven to 220°C/425°F/Gas 7. Make a bed of coarse salt on two large baking sheets. Set the oysters in the half-shell in the bed of salt to keep them steady. Set aside.

2 Melt the butter in a large frying pan. Add the chopped shallots and cook them over a low heat for 2–3 minutes until they are softened. Stir in the spinach and let it wilt.

3 Add the parsley, celery leaves and breadcrumbs to the pan and fry gently for 5 minutes. Season with salt, pepper and cayenne pepper.

4 Divide the stuffing among the oysters. Drizzle a few drops of vodka over each oyster, then bake for about 5 minutes until bubbling and golden brown. Serve on a heated platter on a shallow salt bed with lemon or lime wedges.

Cook's Tip
Frozen chopped spinach can be used. Thaw it in a colander over a bowl and press out as much liquid as possible.

Crab Meat in Vinegar

A refreshing summer tsumami (a Japanese dish that accompanies alcoholic drinks). For the dressing, use a Japanese or Greek cucumber, if possible – they are about one-third of the size of ordinary salad cucumbers and contain less water.

Serves 4
½ red (bell) pepper, seeded

pinch of salt
275g/10oz cooked white crab meat, or 2 x 165g/ 5½oz cans white crab meat, drained
about 300g/11oz Japanese, Greek or salad cucumber

For the vinegar mixture
15ml/1 tbsp rice vinegar
10ml/2 tsp caster (superfine) sugar
10ml/2 tsp awakuchi shoyu

Preparation: 15 minutes; Cooking: 0 minutes

1 Slice the red pepper into thin strips lengthways. Sprinkle with a little salt and leave for about 10 minutes. Rinse well and drain.

2 For the vinegar mixture, combine the rice vinegar, sugar and awakuchi shoyu in a small bowl.

3 Loosen the crab meat and mix it with the sliced red pepper in a mixing bowl. Divide among four small bowls.

4 If you use salad cucumber, scoop out the seeds. Finely grate the cucumber with a fine-toothed grater or use a food processor. Drain in a fine-meshed sieve (or strainer).

5 Mix the cucumber with the vinegar mixture, and pour a quarter on to the crab meat mixture in each bowl. Serve cold immediately, before the cucumber loses its colour.

Variation
The vinegar mixture is best made using awakuchi shoyu, but ordinary soy sauce can be used instead. It will make a darker dressing, however.

Oysters Energy 210kcal/867kJ; Protein 6.4g; Carbohydrate 3.4g, of which sugars 2.1g; Fat 17g, of which saturates 10.1g; Cholesterol 60mg; Calcium 211mg; Fibre 2.3g; Sodium 406mg.
Crab Meat in Vinegar Energy 82kcal/345kJ; Protein 13.3g; Carbohydrate 5.6g, of which sugars 5.4g; Fat 0.8g, of which saturates 0.1g; Cholesterol 50mg; Calcium 100mg; Fibre 0.9g; Sodium 560mg.

Soft-shell Crabs with Chilli & Salt

If fresh soft-shell crabs are unavailable, you can buy frozen ones in Oriental supermarkets. Allow two small crabs per serving, or one if they are large.

Serves 4

8 small soft-shell crabs, thawed
    if frozen
50g/2oz/½ cup plain
    (all-purpose) flour
60ml/4 tbsp groundnut (peanut)
    or vegetable oil

2 large fresh red chillies, or 1 green
    and 1 red chilli, seeded and
    thinly sliced
4 spring onions (scallions) or
    a small bunch of garlic
    chives, chopped
sea salt and ground black
    pepper

To serve

shredded lettuce, mooli (daikon)
    and carrot
light soy sauce, for dipping

Preparation: 6 minutes; Cooking: 6–14 minutes

1 Pat the crabs dry with kitchen paper. Season the flour with pepper and coat the crabs lightly with the mixture.

2 Heat the oil in a shallow pan until very hot, then put in the crabs (you may need to do this in two batches). Fry for 2–3 minutes on each side, until the crabs are golden brown but still juicy in the middle. Drain the cooked crabs on kitchen paper and keep hot.

3 Add the sliced chillies and spring onions or garlic chives to the oil remaining in the pan and cook gently for about 2 minutes. Sprinkle over a generous pinch of salt, then spread the chilli and onion mixture on to the crabs.

4 Mix the shredded lettuce, mooli and carrot together. Arrange on plates, top each portion with two crabs and serve, with a bowl of light soy sauce for dipping.

> **Cook's Tip**
> If you can't locate any mooli, use celeriac instead.

Stir-fried Noodles in Seafood Sauce

This Chinese-style pasta dish makes a perfect appetizer or main course, combining noodles, vegetables and crab meat in a colourful, tasty and quick dish.

Serves 4

225g/8oz Chinese egg noodles
8 spring onions (scallions),
    trimmed
8 asparagus spears, plus extra
    steamed asparagus spears,
    to serve (optional)

30ml/2 tbsp vegetable oil
5cm/2in piece fresh root
    ginger, peeled and cut into
    very fine matchsticks
3 garlic cloves, chopped
60ml/4 tbsp oyster sauce
450g/1lb cooked crab meat (all
    white, or two-thirds white and
    one-third brown)
30ml/2 tbsp rice wine vinegar
15–30ml/1–2 tbsp light soy
    sauce, to taste

Preparation: 10–12 minutes; Cooking: 6–7 minutes

1 Put the noodles in a large pan, cover with lightly salted boiling water, place a lid on top and leave for 3–4 minutes, or for the time suggested on the packet. Drain in a colander, then separate the strands with a fork. Spoon the noodles into a bowl and set aside.

2 Cut off the green spring onion tops and slice them thinly. Set aside. Cut the white parts into 2cm/¾in lengths and quarter them lengthways. Cut the asparagus spears on the diagonal into 2cm/¾in pieces.

3 Heat the oil in a pan or wok until very hot, then add the ginger, garlic and white spring onion batons. Stir-fry over high heat for 1 minute.

4 Add the oyster sauce, crab meat, rice wine vinegar and soy sauce to taste. Stir-fry over medium to high heat for about 2 minutes, until the crab and sauce are hot.

5 Add the noodles and toss until heated through. At the last moment, toss in the spring onion tops and serve with a few extra asparagus spears, if you like.

Soft-shell Crabs Energy 306kcal/1280kJ; Protein 37.6g; Carbohydrate 10g, of which sugars 0.5g; Fat 13g, of which saturates 1.5g; Cholesterol 144mg; Calcium 262mg; Fibre 0.5g; Sodium 1101mg.
Stir-fried Noodles Energy 192kcal/811kJ; Protein 14.3g; Carbohydrate 23g, of which sugars 3.2g; Fat 5.5g, of which saturates 1.1g; Cholesterol 49mg; Calcium 83mg; Fibre 1.2g; Sodium 617mg.

Thai-style Beef & Mango Salad

Rare beef and juicy mangoes – a marriage made in heaven. Come down to earth by serving the salad with a mixture of slightly bitter salad leaves in a lemon and oil dressing.

Serves 4
450g/1lb sirloin steak
45ml/3 tbsp garlic-infused olive oil
45ml/3 tbsp soy sauce
2 mangoes, peeled, stoned (pitted) and finely sliced
ground black pepper

Preparation: 2 minutes; Cooking: 18 minutes

1 Put the steak in a shallow, non-metallic dish and pour over the oil and soy sauce. Season with pepper and turn the steaks to coat them in the marinade. Marinate for at least 10 minutes; longer if you can spare the time. Two hours in a covered bowl in the refrigerator would be ideal.

2 Heat a griddle or ridged grill pan until hot. Remove the steak from the marinade and place on the griddle. Cook for 3–5 minutes on each side, moving the steak halfway through if you want a criss-cross pattern on the surface.

3 Transfer the steak to a board and leave to rest for 2 minutes. Meanwhile, heat the marinade in a pan. Cook for a few seconds, then remove from the heat. Slice the steak thinly and arrange on four serving plates with the mangoes. Drizzle over the pan juices and serve with some salad leaves dressed with lemon and oil.

Cook's Tips
• This is a simplified version of the classic Thai beef salad, which usually comes with a vast array of chopped vegetables. If you want to add a complement to this delicious no-fuss version, set out little bowls of fresh coriander (cilantro) leaves, chopped spring onions (scallions) and peanuts, for sprinkling.
• Instead of using garlic-infused olive oil in the marinade for the steak, use oil infused with basil, chilli or lemon. Flavoured oils are readily available in bottles in most supermarkets and are useful for adding flavour to cooked dishes and salads.

Home-made Burgers with Relish

Making your own burgers means you control what goes into them. These are full of flavour and always prove popular. The tangy ratatouille relish is very easy to make.

Serves 4
2 shallots, chopped
450g/1lb lean minced (ground) beef
30ml/2 tbsp chopped parsley
30ml/2 tbsp tomato ketchup
1 garlic clove, crushed
1 fresh green chilli, seeded and finely chopped
15ml/1 tbsp olive oil
400g/14oz can ratatouille
4 burger buns
lettuce leaves
salt and ground black pepper, to taste

Preparation: 6 minutes; Cooking: 14 minutes

1 Put the shallots in a bowl with boiling water to cover. Leave for 1–2 minutes, then slip off the skins. Put the shallots on a board and use a small sharp knife to chop them finely.

2 Mix half the shallots with the beef in a bowl. Add the chopped parsley and tomato ketchup, with salt and pepper to taste. Mix well with clean hands.

3 Divide the beef mixture into four. Knead each portion into a ball, then flatten it into a burger.

4 Make a spicy relish by cooking the remaining shallots with the garlic and green chilli in the olive oil for 2–3 minutes, until soft.

5 Add the canned ratatouille to the pan containing the vegetables. Bring to the boil, then lower the heat and simmer for 5 minutes.

6 Meanwhile, preheat the grill (broiler) and cook the burgers for about 5 minutes on each side, until browned and cooked through. Meanwhile, split the burger buns in half. Arrange lettuce leaves on the bun bases, add the burgers and top with warm relish and the bun tops.

Thai-style Beef Energy 286kcal/1200kJ; Protein 27.4g; Carbohydrate 14.7g, of which sugars 14.4g; Fat 13.5g, of which saturates 3.5g; Cholesterol 57mg; Calcium 19mg; Fibre 2.6g; Sodium 615mg.
Home-made Burgers Energy 484kcal/2021kJ; Protein 27.9g; Carbohydrate 30.2g, of which sugars 7.7g; Fat 28.8g, of which saturates 9.3g; Cholesterol 68mg; Calcium 120mg; Fibre 2.2g; Sodium 473mg.

Russian Hamburgers

These tasty hamburgers can be made very quickly and yet still taste divine. Serve them solo, with a tomato sauce and vegetables, or just slide them into buns.

Serves 4
2 thick slices white bread,
   crusts removed
45ml/3 tbsp milk
450g/1lb finely minced (ground)
   beef, lamb or veal
1 egg, beaten
30ml/2 tbsp plain
   (all-purpose) flour
30ml/2 tbsp sunflower oil
salt and ground black pepper
tomato sauce, pickled vegetables
   and crispy fried onions,
   to serve

Preparation: 6 minutes; Cooking: 12–14 minutes

1 Cut the bread into chunks and crumb in a food processor, or by using a metal grater. Put the breadcrumbs in a bowl and spoon over the milk. Leave to soak for 3 minutes.

2 Add the minced meat, egg, salt and pepper and mix all the ingredients together thoroughly.

3 Divide the mixture into four equal portions and shape into ovals, each about 10cm/4in long and 5cm/2in wide. Coat each with the flour.

4 Heat the oil in a frying pan and fry the burgers for 6–7 minutes on each side. Serve with a tomato sauce, pickled vegetables and fried onions.

> **Variations**
> • These burgers are quite plain. For extra flavour, add freshly grated nutmeg to the mixture, or a little chopped onion fried in oil.
> • Serve with spicy corn relish. Heat 30ml/2 tbsp oil and fry 1 onion, 2 crushed garlic cloves and 1 seeded and chopped red chilli until soft. Add 10ml/2 tsp garam masala and cook for 2 minutes, then mix in 320g/11¼oz canned whole kernel corn and the grated rind and juice of 1 lime.

Corned Beef & Egg Hash

This is traditional family fare at its very best. Warm and comforting, and made in minutes, it will become a firm favourite very quickly.

Serves 4
30ml/2 tbsp vegetable oil
25g/1oz/2 tbsp butter
1 onion, finely chopped
1 green (bell) pepper, seeded
   and diced
2 large firm boiled potatoes, diced
350g/12oz can corned
   beef, cubed
1.5ml/¼ tsp grated nutmeg
1.5ml/¼ tsp paprika
4 eggs
salt and ground black pepper
parsley, deep-fried in oil, to garnish
sweet chilli sauce or tomato
   sauce, to serve

Preparation: 4–5 minutes; Cooking: 12–15 minutes

1 Heat the oil and butter together in a large frying pan. Add the onion and fry for 3–4 minutes until softened.

2 In a bowl, mix together the green pepper, potatoes, corned beef, nutmeg and paprika. Season well. Add to the pan and toss gently to distribute the cooked onion. Press down lightly and fry without stirring for about 3–4 minutes until a golden brown crust has formed on the underside.

3 Stir the mixture through to distribute the crust, then repeat the frying twice, until the mixture is well browned.

4 Make four wells in the hash and carefully crack an egg into each. Cover and cook gently for about 4–5 minutes until the egg whites are set.

5 Sprinkle with deep-fried parsley and cut into quarters. Serve hot with sweet chilli sauce or tomato sauce.

> **Cook's Tip**
> Put the can of corned beef into the refrigerator to chill for about half an hour before using.

Russian Hamburgers Energy 384kcal/1597kJ; Protein 26g; Carbohydrate 13g, of which sugars 1g; Fat 25.7g, of which saturates 9g; Cholesterol 116mg; Calcium 56mg; Fibre 0.4g; Sodium 183mg.
Corned Beef Hash Energy 421kcal/1758kJ; Protein 30.9g; Carbohydrate 17g, of which sugars 5.4g; Fat 26.2g, of which saturates 10.6g; Cholesterol 277mg; Calcium 65mg; Fibre 1.7g; Sodium 871mg.

Beef Stroganoff

This is one of the most famous fast meat dishes, consisting of tender strips of steak in a tangy sour cream sauce. Serve it with chips or on a bed of noodles.

Serves 4

450g/1lb fillet steak (beef tenderloin) or rump (round) steak, trimmed and tenderized with a rolling pin or meat mallet

15ml/1 tbsp sunflower oil
25g/1oz/2 tbsp butter
1 onion, sliced
15ml/1 tbsp plain (all-purpose) flour
5ml/1 tsp tomato purée (paste)
5ml/1 tsp Dijon mustard or wholegrain
5ml/1 tsp lemon juice
150ml/¼ pint/⅔ cup sour cream
salt and ground black pepper
fresh herbs, to garnish

Preparation: 3 minutes; Cooking: 12 minutes

1 Using a sharp cook's knife, cut the tenderized steak into thin strips, about 5cm/2in long.

2 Heat the oil and half the butter in a frying pan and fry the beef over a high heat for 2 minutes, or until browned. Remove with a slotted spoon, leaving any juices behind.

3 Melt the remaining butter in the pan and gently fry the onion for 8 minutes, until soft.

4 Stir in the flour, tomato purée, mustard, lemon juice and sour cream. Return the beef to the pan and stir until the sauce is bubbling. Season well and garnish with fresh herbs.

Variation
Mushrooms are often added to beef stroganoff. Buy large open-cap button (white) mushrooms or meaty field or portabello mushrooms, wipe them clean, then slice them thickly. Before cooking the steak, fry the mushrooms in butter for about 4 minutes, during which time they will yield their juice and absorb it again, becoming lovely and juicy. Set aside. Reheat them with the beef in the sauce just before serving.

Beef Strips with Orange & Ginger

Stir-frying is one of the quickest as well as one of the healthiest ways to cook.

Serves 4

450g/1lb rump (round) steak, cut into strips
grated rind and juice of 1 orange

15ml/1 tbsp soy sauce
1 tbsp cornflour (cornstarch)
2.5cm/1in fresh root ginger, finely chopped
10ml/2 tsp sesame oil
1 carrot, cut into small strips
2 spring onions (scallions), thinly sliced

Preparation: 3–4 minutes; Cooking: 6 minutes

1 Place the beef strips in a bowl and sprinkle with the orange rind and juice. Leave to marinate. Drain the liquid and reserve, then mix the meat with the soy sauce, cornflour and ginger. Heat the oil in a wok and stir-fry the beef for 1 minute. Add the carrot and stir-fry for 2–3 minutes. Stir in the spring onions and the reserved liquid, then boil, stirring, until thickened. Serve.

Steak with Pickled Walnut Sauce

This is a traditional Scottish way of cooking beef.

Serves 4

15ml/1 tbsp vegetable oil

75g/3oz/6 tbsp butter
8 slices of beef fillet (filet mignon)
4 onions, sliced
15ml/1 tbsp pickled walnut juice
salt and ground black pepper

Preparation: 2 minutes; Cooking: 15–18 minutes

1 Heat the oil and half the butter in a frying pan and cook the steaks for 4–5 minutes on each side until almost done. Keep the steaks warm while you cook the onions.

2 Melt the remaining butter then add the sliced onions. Increase the heat and stir to brown and soften the onions, scraping the base of the pan. Add the pickled walnut juice and cook for a few minutes. Season to taste with salt and ground black pepper. Serve the beef with the onions and juices on top.

Beef Stroganoff Energy 308kcal/1282kJ; Protein 26.5g; Carbohydrate 5.8g, of which sugars 2.5g; Fat 20.1g, of which saturates 10.2g; Cholesterol 102mg; Calcium 50mg; Fibre 0.4g; Sodium 124mg.
Beef Strips Energy 212kcal/885kJ; Protein 25.7g; Carbohydrate 3.8g, of which sugars 0.3g; Fat 10.5g, of which saturates 4.3g; Cholesterol 65mg; Calcium 7mg; Fibre 0g; Sodium 341mg.
Steak Energy 1960kcal/8144kJ; Protein 173.6g; Carbohydrate 24.4g, of which sugars 17.2g; Fat 130.4g, of which saturates 68g; Cholesterol 668mg; Calcium 124mg; Fibre 4.4g; Sodium 876mg.

Steak with Warm Tomato Salsa

A tangy salsa of tomatoes, spring onions and balsamic vinegar makes a colourful topping for chunky, pan-fried steaks cooked just the way you like them.

Serves 2
2 steaks, about 2cm/¾in thick
4 large plum tomatoes
2 spring onions (scallions)
30ml/2 tbsp balsamic vinegar

Preparation: 2–3 minutes; Cooking: 8 minutes

1 Trim any excess fat from the steaks, then season on both sides with salt and pepper. Heat a non-stick frying pan and cook the steaks for about 3 minutes on each side for medium rare. Cook for a little longer if you like your steak well cooked.

2 Meanwhile, put the tomatoes in a heatproof bowl, cover with boiling water and leave for 1–2 minutes.

3 When the tomato skins start to split, drain and peel them, then halve the tomatoes and scoop out the seeds. Dice the tomato flesh.

4 When the steaks are cooked to your taste, remove from the pan with a fish slice, to drain off any excess oil, and transfer them to plates. Keep the steaks warm on a very low oven temperature while you prepare the salsa.

5 Thinly slice the spring onions and add them to the cooking juices in the frying pan with the diced tomato, balsamic vinegar, 30ml/2 tbsp water and a little seasoning. Stir briefly until warm, scraping up any meat residue. Spoon the salsa over the steaks, dividing it equally between them, and serve.

Cook's Tip
Choose rump (round), sirloin or fillet steak (beef tenderloin). If you prefer to grill (broil) the steak, the timing will be the same as the recipe, though you must take into account the thickness of the meat.

Beef with Blue Cheese Sauce

Celebrations call for special dishes, and this one is more special than most. Roquefort cheese, cream and fillet steak is a rich combination, so keep the rest of the meal simple. Serve this with a selection of freshly roasted vegetables.

Serves 4
25g/1oz/2 tbsp butter
30ml/2 tbsp olive oil
4 fillet steaks (beef tenderloins), cut 5cm/2in thick, about 150g/5oz each

salt and coarsely ground black pepper
fresh flat leaf parsley, to garnish
roast potatoes and Mediterranean vegetables, to serve

For the blue cheese sauce
30ml/2 tbsp brandy
150ml/5fl oz/⅔ cup double (heavy) cream
75g/3oz Roquefort cheese, crumbled

Preparation: 2 minutes; Cooking: 10–12 minutes

1 Heat the butter and oil together in a heavy frying pan over a high heat. Season the steaks well. Fry them for 1 minute on each side, to sear them.

2 Lower the heat slightly and cook for a further 2–3 minutes on each side, or according to your taste. Remove the steaks to a dish, cover with foil and set aside.

3 Reduce the heat and add the brandy, stirring to incorporate the pan juices.

4 Stir in the cream. Bring the sauce to the boil, then cook for 1 minute to reduce a little.

5 Add the crumbled Roquefort cheese and mash it into the sauce using a spoon. Taste for seasoning. Pour into a small sauce jug (pitcher).

6 Serve the steaks on individual heated plates, garnished with flat leaf parsley, and with a little of the Roquefort cheese sauce poured over each one. Offer the remaining sauce separately.

Steak with Salsa Energy 207kcal/872kJ; Protein 33.9g; Carbohydrate 3.4g, of which sugars 3.4g; Fat 6.5g, of which saturates 2.7g; Cholesterol 89mg; Calcium 17mg; Fibre 1.2g; Sodium 100mg.
With Blue Cheese Energy 573kcal/2374kJ; Protein 36.3g; Carbohydrate 0.7g, of which sugars 0.7g; Fat 45.4g, of which saturates 24.4g; Cholesterol 170mg; Calcium 117mg; Fibre 0g; Sodium 341mg.

Pan-fried Steaks with Whisky & Cream

A good steak is always a popular choice for dinner, and top quality meat plus timing are the keys to success. Choose small, thick steaks rather than large, thin ones if you can.

Serves 4
4 x 225–350g/8–12oz sirloin steaks, at room temperature
5ml/1 tsp oil
15g/½oz/1 tbsp butter
50ml/2fl oz/¼ cup whisky
300ml/½ pint/1¼ cups double (heavy) cream
salt and ground black pepper

Preparation: 0 minutes; Cooking: 10–12 minutes

1 Dry the steaks with kitchen paper and season with pepper. Heat a cast-iron frying pan, or other heavy pan, over high heat. When it is very hot, add the oil and butter. Add the steaks to the foaming butter, one at a time, and seal the meat quickly on both sides.

2 Lower the heat to moderate and continue to cook the steaks, allowing 3–4 minutes for rare, 4–5 minutes for medium or 5–6 minutes for well-done steaks.

3 When the steaks are cooked to your liking, transfer them to warmed plates and keep warm. Pour off the fat from the pan and discard. Add the whisky and stir around to scrape off all the sediment from the base of the pan.

4 Allow the liquid to reduce a little, then add the cream and simmer over a low heat for a few minutes, until the cream thickens. Season to taste, pour the sauce around or over the steaks, as you prefer, and serve immediately.

> **Cook's Tips**
> • *Turn the steaks only once during cooking to seal in the juices.*
> • *Serve with fried onions and mushrooms, peas and oven chips (French fries).*

Collops of Beef with Shallots

Caramelized shallots are delicious. The time needed for cooking the steaks will depend upon how thick they are. Rare meat will feel soft to the touch; medium will have some resistance; well done will feel firm.

Serves 4
4 fillet steaks (beef tenderloin)
15ml/1 tbsp olive oil
50g/2oz/¼ cup butter
20 shallots, peeled
5ml/1 tsp caster (superfine) sugar
150ml/¼ pint/⅔ cup beef stock
salt and ground black pepper

Preparation: 0 minutes; Cooking: 10–12 minutes

1 Take the steaks out of the refrigerator well before you need them and dry with kitchen paper. Heat the oil and butter in a large frying pan then cook the steaks allowing 3–4 minutes for rare, 4–5 minutes for medium or 5–6 minutes for well-done meat.

2 Once cooked remove the steaks from the pan and keep warm. Put the shallots in the pan and brown lightly in the meat juices.

3 Add the sugar to the shallots and then stir in the stock. Reduce the heat to low and allow the liquid to evaporate, shaking the pan from time to time to stop the shallots from sticking.

4 The shallots will end up slightly soft, browned and caramelized with a shiny glaze. Season to taste with salt and ground black pepper.

5 Serve the steaks on warmed plates and spoon over the caramelized shallots and juices from the pan.

> **Cook's Tip**
> *Serve with sautéed potatoes. Cook unpeeled baby potatoes in boiling salted water for about 20 minutes until just tender. Drain, cool, then remove the skins. Slice thickly. Heat a mixture of olive oil and butter in a frying pan and cook the potato slices until browned and crisp. Drain on kitchen paper and serve.*

Pan-fried Steaks Energy 806kcal/3345kJ; Protein 65.9g; Carbohydrate 1.3g, of which sugars 1.3g; Fat 56.5g, of which saturates 32.6g; Cholesterol 251mg; Calcium 51mg; Fibre 0g; Sodium 232mg.
Collops of Beef Energy 424kcal/1767kJ; Protein 43.2g; Carbohydrate 6.1g, of which sugars 4.6g; Fat 25.4g, of which saturates 12.5g; Cholesterol 149mg; Calcium 27mg; Fibre 0.9g; Sodium 166mg.

Green Beef Curry with Thai Aubergines

This is a very quick curry so it is essential that you use good-quality meat. Sirloin is recommended, but tender rump or even fillet steak could be used instead.

Serves 4–6

450g/1lb beef sirloin
15ml/1 tbsp vegetable oil
45ml/3 tbsp Thai green
  curry paste
600ml/1 pint/2½ cups
  coconut milk
4 kaffir lime leaves, torn
15–30ml/1–2 tbsp Thai
  fish sauce
5ml/1 tsp palm sugar (jaggery) or
  light muscovado (brown) sugar
150g/5oz small Thai aubergines
  (eggplants), halved
a small handful of fresh Thai basil
2 fresh green chillies, to garnish

Preparation: 2 minutes; Cooking: 16 minutes

1 Trim off any excess fat from the beef. Using a sharp knife, cut it into long, thin strips. This is easiest to do if it is well chilled, so pop it into the freezer first if you have time. Set it aside.

2 Heat the oil in a large, heavy pan or wok. Add the curry paste and cook for 1–2 minutes, until it is fragrant.

3 Stir in half the coconut milk, a little at a time. Cook, stirring frequently, for about 5–6 minutes, until an oily sheen appears on the surface of the liquid.

4 Add the beef to the pan with the kaffir lime leaves, Thai fish sauce, sugar and aubergine halves. Cook for 2–3 minutes, then stir in the remaining coconut milk.

5 Bring back to a simmer and cook until the meat and aubergines are tender. Stir in the Thai basil.

6 Prepare the garnish. Slit the fresh green chillies and scrape out the pith and seeds. Shred the chillies finely. Spoon the curry into a heated dish or on to individual plates. Sprinkle with the finely shredded chillies and serve immediately.

Beef with Peppers & Black Bean Sauce

A spicy, rich dish with the distinctive taste of black bean sauce. This is a recipe that will quickly become a favourite because it is so easy to prepare and quick to cook.

Serves 4

350g/12oz rump (round) steak,
  trimmed and thinly sliced
20ml/4 tsp vegetable oil
300ml/½ pint/1¼ cups
  beef stock
2 garlic cloves, finely chopped
5ml/1 tsp grated (shredded) fresh
  root ginger
1 fresh red chilli, seeded and
  finely chopped
15ml/1 tbsp black bean sauce
1 green (bell) pepper, seeded and
  cut into 2.5cm/1in squares
15ml/1 tbsp dry sherry
5ml/1 tsp cornflour (cornstarch)
5ml/1 tsp granulated (white)
  sugar
45ml/3 tbsp cold water
salt
cooked rice noodles, to serve

Preparation: 6 minutes; Cooking: 7–8 minutes

1 Place the thin slices of rump steak in a bowl. Add 5ml/1 tsp of the oil and stir to coat them thoroughly.

2 Bring the stock to the boil in a pan. Add the beef and cook for 2 minutes, stirring constantly to prevent the slices from sticking together. Lift out the beef slices, put them on a plate and set aside. Strain the stock into a jug (pitcher), cool quickly and refrigerate for use in another recipe.

3 Heat the remaining oil in a wok. Stir-fry the garlic, ginger and chilli with the black bean sauce for a few seconds.

4 Add the pepper squares and a little water. Cook for about 2 minutes more, then stir in the sherry. Add the beef slices to the pan, spoon the sauce over and reheat.

5 Mix the cornflour and sugar to a cream with the water. Pour the mixture into the pan. Cook, stirring, until the sauce has thickened. Season with salt. Serve with rice noodles.

Green Beef Curry Energy 147kcal/619kJ; Protein 18.2g; Carbohydrate 6.4g, of which sugars 6.3g; Fat 5.6g, of which saturates 1.9g; Cholesterol 38mg; Calcium 36mg; Fibre 0.5g; Sodium 341mg.
Beef with Peppers Energy 146kcal/613kJ; Protein 19.3g; Carbohydrate 2.1g, of which sugars 1.1g; Fat 6.4g, of which saturates 1.8g; Cholesterol 52mg; Calcium 5mg; Fibre 0g; Sodium 115mg.

Beef with Chanterelle Mushrooms

The trick here is to use really good beef with no fat and to fry the dried pieces quickly in the hot oil so the outside is well browned and the inside very rare. Chanterelle mushrooms are the most delicious wild mushrooms, yellowy orange in colour and with a shape like inverted umbrellas.

Serves 4

115g/4oz chanterelle mushrooms
2 rump (round) steaks, 175g/6oz
   each, cut into strips
45ml/3 tbsp olive oil
1 garlic clove, crushed
1 shallot, finely chopped
60ml/4 tbsp dry white wine
60ml/4 tbsp double
   (heavy) cream
25g/1oz/2 tbsp butter
salt and ground black pepper
chopped fresh parsley, to garnish

Preparation: 2 minutes; Cooking: 7–8 minutes

1 Clean the mushrooms. If you have collected them from the wild cut off the ends where they have come from the ground and, using kitchen paper, wipe off any leaf matter or moss that may be adhering to them. Trim the mushrooms, then cut them in half through the stalk and cap.

2 Dry the beef thoroughly on kitchen paper. Heat a large frying pan over a high heat then add 30ml/2 tbsp olive oil. Working in batches add the meat to the hot oil in the pan and quickly brown the strips on all sides.

3 Remove the meat, which should still be very rare, from the pan, set aside and keep warm. Add the remaining olive oil to the pan and reduce the heat. Stir in the garlic and shallots and cook, stirring, for about 1 minute.

4 Increase the heat and add the mushrooms. Season and cook until the mushrooms just start to soften. Add the wine, bring to the boil and add the cream. As the liquid thickens, return the beef to the pan and heat through.

5 Remove the pan from the heat and swirl in the butter. Serve on warmed plates, garnished with the parsley.

Calf's Liver with Crisp Onions

Sautéed or creamy mashed potatoes go well with fried calf's liver. Serve with a salad of mixed leaves and fresh herbs, to complement the simple flavours of this main course.

Serves 4

50g/2oz/¼ cup butter

4 onions, thinly sliced
5ml/1 tsp caster (superfine) sugar
4 slices calf's liver, each weighing
   about 115g/4oz
30ml/2 tbsp plain
   (all-purpose) flour
30ml/2 tbsp olive oil
salt and ground black pepper
parsley, to garnish

Preparation: 3–4 minutes; Cooking: 16 minutes

1 Melt the butter in a large, heavy-based pan with a lid. Add the onions and mix well to coat with butter. Cover the pan with a tight-fitting lid and cook gently for 10 minutes, stirring the onions occasionally to prevent them from sticking.

2 Stir in the sugar and cover the pan. Cook the onions for 8 minutes more, or until they are soft and golden. Increase the heat, remove the lid and stir the onions over a high heat until they are deep gold and crisp. Use a slotted spoon to remove the onions from the pan, draining off the fat.

3 Meanwhile, rinse the calf's liver in cold water and pat it dry on kitchen paper. Season the flour, put it on a plate and turn the slices of liver in it until they are lightly coated in flour.

4 Heat the oil in a large frying pan, add the liver and cook for about 2 minutes on each side, or until lightly browned and just firm. Arrange the liver on warmed plates, with the crisp onions. Garnish with parsley and serve with sautéed or mashed potatoes with a little mustard, if you like.

> **Cook's Tip**
> Take care not to cook the liver for too long as this may cause it to become tough and unpalatable.

Beef Energy 415kcal/1725kJ; Protein 29.9g; Carbohydrate 0.7g, of which sugars 0.6g; Fat 31g, of which saturates 14.2g; Cholesterol 122mg; Calcium 21mg; Fibre 0.4g; Sodium 124mg.
Calf's Liver Energy 350kcal/1458kJ; Protein 23.9g; Carbohydrate 19.7g, of which sugars 8.6g; Fat 20.1g, of which saturates 8.5g; Cholesterol 452mg; Calcium 61mg; Fibre 2.4g; Sodium 162mg.

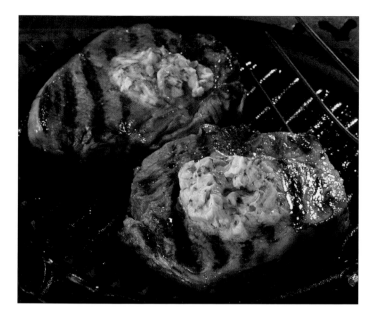

Pan-fried Veal Chops

Veal chops from the loin are an expensive cut and are best cooked quickly and simply so that their subtle flavour and tenderness can be enjoyed to the full. When a cut is costly, buy from a reputable butcher and cook with care.

Serves 2
25g/1oz/2 tbsp butter, softened
15ml/1 tbsp Dijon mustard
15ml/1 tbsp chopped fresh basil
olive oil, for brushing
2 veal loin chops, 2.5cm/1in thick
    (about 225g/8oz each)
ground black pepper
fresh basil sprigs, to garnish

Preparation: 2 minutes; Cooking: 7–9 minutes

1 To make the basil butter, cream the butter with the mustard and chopped basil in a small bowl, then season with pepper.

2 Lightly oil a heavy frying pan or griddle. Set over high heat until very hot but not smoking. Brush both sides of each chop with a little oil and season with a little pepper.

3 Place the chops in the pan or griddle and reduce the heat to medium. Cook for 4–5 minutes, then turn and cook for 3–4 minutes more until done as preferred. Top each chop with half the basil butter and serve, garnished with basil.

Cook's Tip
Veal is coming back into favour in the UK, thanks to more humane farming practices than those of the past, when young, milk-fed animals were confined in crates so that their muscles atrophied to produce white veal. Today's high-welfare veal is rose pink in colour, and comes from calves that live outside for much of the year. Look for meat with the Freedom Food Label.

Variation
The flavour of basil goes well with the veal, but rosemary or parsley in the herb butter would also work well.

Veal Escalopes with Tarragon

These thin slices of veal need little cooking and the sauce is made very quickly as well, so this is the ideal dish to come home to after a busy day at the office.

Serves 4
4 veal escalopes (US scallops)
    about 120–150g/4–5oz each
15g/½oz/1 tbsp butter
30ml/2 tbsp brandy
250ml/8fl oz/1 cup chicken or
    beef stock
15ml/1 tbsp chopped
    fresh tarragon
salt and freshly ground
    black pepper
tarragon sprigs, to garnish

Preparation: 4 minutes; Cooking: 6 minutes

1 Place the veal escalopes between two sheets of clear film (plastic wrap) and pound with the flat side of a meat mallet or roll them with a rolling pin to flatten them out to about 5mm/¼in thickness. Season with salt and ground black pepper.

2 Melt the butter in a large frying pan over a medium-high heat. Add enough meat to the pan to fit easily in one layer (do not overcrowd the pan, cook in batches if necessary) and cook for 1½–2 minutes, turning once. Each escalope should be lightly browned, but must not be overcooked. Transfer to a platter.

3 Add the brandy to the pan, then pour in the stock and bring to the boil. Add the tarragon and continue boiling until the liquid is reduced by half.

4 Return the veal to the pan with any accumulated juices and heat through. Serve immediately, garnished with tarragon sprigs.

Variation
This treatment also works well with turkey escalopes. Pound them between clear film (plastic wrap) until thin and take care not to overcook them, or they will be tough. The sauce can be flavoured with tarragon, as here, or try another fresh herb, such as sage, thyme or marjoram.

Veal Escalopes with Lemon

Popular in Italian restaurants, this dish is very simple to make at home. White vermouth and lemon juice make the perfect sauce for the delicately flavoured meat.

Serves 4
4 veal escalopes (US scallops)
30–45ml/2–3 tbsp plain
  (all-purpose) flour
50g/2oz/¼ cup butter
60ml/4 tbsp olive oil
60ml/4 tbsp Italian dry white
  vermouth or dry white wine
45ml/3 tbsp lemon juice
salt and ground black pepper
lemon wedges, grated lemon rind
  and finely chopped fresh
  parsley, to garnish
salad, to serve

Preparation: 3–4 minutes; Cooking: 15 minutes

1 Put each veal escalope between two sheets of clear film (plastic wrap) and pound with the side of a rolling pin or the smooth side of a meat mallet until the slices are very thin.

2 Cut the pounded escalopes in half or quarters. Season the flour with a little salt and pepper and use it to coat the escalopes on both sides. Shake off any excess seasoned flour.

3 Melt the butter with half the oil in a large, heavy frying pan until sizzling. Add as many escalopes as the pan will hold. Cook over a medium to high heat for about 2 minutes on each side until lightly coloured. Remove with a spatula and keep hot.

4 Add the remaining oil to the pan and cook the remaining veal escalopes in the same way.

5 Remove the pan from the heat and add the vermouth or wine and the lemon juice. Stir vigorously to mix well with the pan juices, then return the pan to the heat.

6 Return all the veal escalopes to the pan. Spoon the sauce over to coat the veal. Heat through for about 2 minutes, shaking the pan occasionally. Serve immediately with a salad, garnished with lemon wedges, grated lemon rind and a sprinkling of finely chopped fresh parsley.

Escalopes of Veal with Cream Sauce

This quick, easy dish is delicious served with buttered tagliatelle and lightly steamed green vegetables. It works just as well with turkey escalopes.

Serves 4
15ml/1 tbsp plain
  (all-purpose) flour
4 veal escalopes (US scallops),
  about 75–115g/3–4oz each
30ml/2 tbsp sunflower oil
1 shallot, chopped
150g/5oz/2 cups oyster
  mushrooms, sliced
30ml/2 tbsp Marsala or
  medium-dry sherry
200ml/7fl oz/scant 1 cup crème
  fraîche or sour cream
30ml/2 tbsp chopped
  fresh tarragon
salt and ground black pepper

Preparation: 2–3 minutes; Cooking: 15–17 minutes

1 Put the flour in a strong plastic bag and season with salt and pepper. Add the veal escalopes and shake the bag to coat them. Remove from the bag and set the meat aside, taking care not to disturb the coating.

2 Heat the oil in a large frying pan and cook the shallot and mushrooms for 5 minutes. Add the escalopes and cook over a high heat for about 1½ minutes on each side. Pour in the Marsala or sherry and cook until reduced by half.

3 Remove the escalopes from the pan. Stir the crème fraîche, tarragon and seasoning into the juices in the pan and simmer gently for 3–5 minutes, or until the sauce is thick and creamy.

4 Return the escalopes to the pan and heat through for 1 minute before serving on heated individual plates with the sauce, noodles and broccoli.

> **Cook's Tip**
> If the escalopes (US scallops) are too thick, put them between pieces of clear film (plastic wrap) and flatten them with a rolling pin or meat mallet. This will help to cut down the cooking time.

Veal with Lemon Energy 360kcal/1498kJ; Protein 29g; Carbohydrate 4.8g, of which sugars 0.6g; Fat 23.5g, of which saturates 8.9g; Cholesterol 92mg; Calcium 16mg; Fibre 0.2g; Sodium 151mg.
Veal with Cream Energy 377kcal/1567kJ; Protein 25.1g; Carbohydrate 5.9g, of which sugars 2.5g; Fat 27.5g, of which saturates 14.9g; Cholesterol 108mg; Calcium 45mg; Fibre 0.8g; Sodium 75mg.

Cantonese Fried Noodles

Chow mein is hugely popular with the Chinese, who believe in turning leftovers into tasty dishes.

Serves 2–3
225g/8oz lean beef steak or pork fillet (tenderloin)
225g/8oz can bamboo shoots, drained
1 leek
25g/1oz Chinese dried mushrooms, soaked for 30 minutes in 120ml/4fl oz/ ½ cup warm water
150g/5oz Chinese leaves (Chinese cabbage)
450g/1lb cooked egg noodles (255g/8oz dried), drained well
90ml/6 tbsp vegetable oil
30ml/2 tbsp dark soy sauce
15ml/1 tbsp cornflour (cornstarch)
15ml/1 tbsp rice wine or medium-dry sherry
5ml/1 tsp sesame oil
5ml/1 tsp caster (superfine) sugar
salt and ground black pepper

Preparation: 5 minutes; Cooking: 12 minutes

1 Slice the beef or pork, bamboo shoots and leek into matchsticks. Drain the mushrooms, reserving 90ml/6 tbsp of the soaking water.

2 Cut off and discard the mushroom stems, then thinly slice the caps. Cut the Chinese leaves into diamond-shaped pieces and sprinkle with salt. Pat the noodles dry with kitchen paper.

3 Heat a third of the oil in a large wok or frying pan and sauté the noodles. After turning them over once, press the noodles evenly against the bottom of the pan with a wooden spatula until they form a flat, even cake.

4 Cook over medium heat for about 4 minutes or until the noodles at the bottom have become crisp.

5 Turn the noodle cake over with a fish slice or metal spatula or invert on to a large plate and slide back into the wok.

6 Cook for 3 minutes more, then slide on to a heated plate. Keep warm.

7 Heat 30ml/2 tbsp of the remaining oil in the wok. Add the strips of leek, then the meat strips and stir-fry for 10–15 seconds.

8 Sprinkle over half the soy sauce and then add the bamboo shoots and mushrooms, with salt and pepper to taste. Toss over the heat for 1 minute, then transfer this mixture to a plate.

9 Heat the remaining oil in the wok and sauté the Chinese leaves for 1 minute. Return the meat and vegetable mixture to the wok and sauté with the leaves for 30 seconds.

10 Mix the cornflour with the reserved mushroom water. Stir into the wok along with the rice wine or sherry, sesame oil, sugar and remaining soy sauce. Cook for about 15 seconds until it has thickened.

11 Divide the noodles among 2–3 serving dishes and pile the meat and vegetables on top.

Pork Kebabs with BBQ Sauce

Use pork fillet for these kebabs because it is lean and tender and cooks quickly.

Serves 4
500g/1¼lb lean pork fillet (tenderloin)
8 large, thick spring onions (scallions)
120ml/4fl oz/½ cup barbecue sauce
1 lemon, cut into wedges, to garnish

Preparation: 3–4 minutes; Cooking: 10 minutes

1 Cut the pork into 2.5cm/1in cubes. Cut the spring onions into 2.5cm/1in-long sticks.

2 Preheat the grill (broiler) to high. Oil the wire rack and spread out the pork cubes on it. Grill (broil) the pork until the juices drip, then dip the pieces in the barbecue sauce and put back on the grill. Grill until cooked through, repeating the dipping process twice more. Set aside and keep warm.

3 Trim the spring onions and gently grill until soft and slightly brown on the outside. Do not dip in the barbecue sauce. Thread about four pieces of pork and three spring onion pieces on to each of eight bamboo skewers.

4 Arrange the skewers on a platter. Squeeze a little lemon juice over each skewer. Serve immediately, offering the remaining lemon wedges separately, so that guests can squeeze the juice over their meat.

> **Variation**
> This is an unusual kebab recipe, in that the cubes of pork are threaded on to the skewers only after cooking. This is because the meat is regularly dipped in glaze, and it is easier to get an all-round coating if the cubes of pork are free. If you prefer to assemble the skewers first and cook them on the barbecue, do so. Use metal skewers, which will not char, and baste frequently with the sauce.

Fried Noodles Energy 695kcal/2894kJ; Protein 35.3g; Carbohydrate 38.7g, of which sugars 7.7g; Fat 45.3g, of which saturates 8.5g; Cholesterol 79mg; Calcium 79mg; Fibre 4.6g; Sodium 1185mg.
Pork Kebabs Energy 192kcal/806kJ; Protein 27.6g; Carbohydrate 9.2g, of which sugars 8.8g; Fat 5.1g, of which saturates 1.8g; Cholesterol 79mg; Calcium 21mg; Fibre 0.6g; Sodium 578mg.

Lemon Grass & Ginger Pork Burgers

Lemon grass lends a fragrant citrus flavour to pork and is enhanced by the fresh zing of ginger. Serve the burgers in burger buns with tomato, crisp lettuce and some chilli sauce. Apricot chutney would also go well with the burgers, or use smooth or chunky apple sauce. Alternatively, dispense with sauce and instead add slices of fried fresh pineapple or canned pineapple rings.

Serves 4
450g/1lb/2 cups minced
   (ground) pork
15ml/1 tbsp grated fresh
   root ginger
1 lemon grass stalk, outer layers
   discarded and centre part
   chopped finely
30ml/2 tbsp sunflower oil
salt and ground black pepper

To serve
juicy tomatoes, thickly sliced
crisp lettuce leaves
chilli sauce

Preparation: 5 minutes; Cooking: 6–8 minutes

1 Put the pork in a bowl and stir in the ginger and chopped lemon grass. Season with salt and pepper. Shape the mixture into four burgers and ideally chill for about 20 minutes.

2 Heat the oil in a large, non-stick frying pan and add the burgers. Fry for 3–4 minutes on each side over a gentle heat, until cooked through.

3 Remove from the pan with a metal spatula and drain on kitchen paper.

4 Serve in burger buns with the sliced tomato, lettuce and chilli sauce, if you like.

Variation
Omit the ginger and lemon grass and add 60ml/4 tbsp grated apple to the pork to make tasty apple-flavoured burgers.

Pork with Cream & Apple Sauce

Tender noisettes of pork in a creamy leek and apple sauce make a great dinner party dish. Use the same white wine as the one you plan to serve with the meal, or try cider.

Serves 4
30ml/2 tbsp plain
   (all-purpose) flour
4 noisettes of pork, firmly tied
25g/1oz/2 tbsp butter
4 baby leeks, finely sliced

5ml/1 tsp mustard seeds,
   coarsely crushed
150ml/¼ pint/⅔ cup dry
   white wine
2 eating apples
150ml/¼ pint/⅔ cup double
   (heavy) cream
30ml/2 tbsp chopped
   fresh parsley
salt and ground black pepper

To serve
red cabbage
fried polenta

Preparation: 2 minutes; Cooking: 18 minutes

1 Place the flour in a bowl and add plenty of seasoning. Turn the noisettes in the flour mixture to coat them lightly and evenly on both sides.

2 Melt the butter in a heavy frying pan and cook the noisettes for 1 minute on each side, turning them with tongs.

3 Add the sliced leeks to the pan and cook for 3 minutes. Stir in the mustard seeds. Pour in the wine. Cook gently for 10 minutes, turning the pork occasionally. Peel the apples, remove the cores, cut in half and slice thinly.

4 Add the sliced apples and double cream to the pan and simmer for 3 minutes, or until the pork is fully cooked and the sauce is thick, rich and creamy. Taste for seasoning, add salt and pepper if needed, then stir in the chopped parsley and serve the pork at once with red cabbage and fried polenta.

Variation
Use thin slices of pork fillet (tenderloin) for even faster cooking.

Pork Burgers Energy 234kcal/974kJ; Protein 21.6g; Carbohydrate 0g, of which sugars 0g; Fat 16.4g, of which saturates 4.7g; Cholesterol 74mg; Calcium 8mg; Fibre 0g; Sodium 74mg.
Pork with Cream Energy 415kcal/1724kJ; Protein 23.1g; Carbohydrate 8.8g, of which sugars 4.4g; Fat 29.5g, of which saturates 17.2g; Cholesterol 128mg; Calcium 45mg; Fibre 1.3g; Sodium 119mg.

Bacon Chops with Apple & Cider Sauce

Either thin bacon or pork chops could be used in this recipe, which brings the traditional ingredients of pork and apples together in an attractive dish.

Serves 4
15ml/1 tbsp oil
4 bacon chops
1 or 2 cooking apples, peeled, cored and sliced
knob (pat) of butter
1 or 2 garlic cloves, finely chopped

5ml/1 tsp sugar
150ml/¼ pint/⅔ cup dry (hard) cider
5ml/1 tsp cider vinegar
15ml/1 tbsp wholegrain mustard
10ml/2 tsp chopped fresh thyme
salt and ground black pepper
sprigs of thyme, to garnish

To serve
mashed potatoes
steamed buttered cabbage

Preparation: 5 minutes; Cooking: 15 minutes

1 Heat the oil in a large heavy frying pan over a medium heat, and cook the chops for 10 minutes, browning well on both sides. Remove the chops from the pan and keep warm.

2 Add the butter and apples to the frying pan and cook until the juices begin to turn brown.

3 Add the garlic and sugar, and cook for 1 minute, then stir in the cider, cider vinegar, mustard and chopped thyme. Boil for a few minutes until reduced to a saucy consistency. Season well.

4 Place the chops on warmed serving plates, spoon over the sauce, garnish with the thyme sprigs and serve.

> **Cook's Tip**
> For the chops to cook through in the time stated, they will need to be fairly thin. For thick pork or bacon chops, cook for about 10 minutes on each side.

Aromatic Pork with Basil

The combination of moist, juicy pork and mushrooms, crisp green mangetouts and fragrant basil in this ginger- and garlic-infused stir-fry is absolutely delicious. Served with simple steamed jasmine rice, it makes a perfect quick supper during the week.

Serves 4
40g/1½oz cornflour (cornstarch)
500g/1¼lb pork fillet (tenderloin), thinly sliced
15ml/1 tbsp sunflower oil

10ml/2 tsp sesame oil
15ml/1 tbsp very finely shredded fresh root ginger
3 garlic cloves, thinly sliced
200g/7oz mangetouts (snow peas), halved lengthways
300g/11oz/generous 4 cups mixed mushrooms, such as shiitake, button (white) or oyster, sliced if large
120ml/4fl oz/½ cup Chinese cooking wine
45ml/3 tbsp soy sauce
a small handful of sweet basil leaves
salt and ground black pepper
steamed jasmine rice, to serve

Preparation: 6 minutes; Cooking: 10–13 minutes

1 Place the cornflour in a strong plastic bag. Season well and add the sliced pork. Shake the bag to coat the pork in flour and then remove the pork and shake off any excess flour. Set aside.

2 Preheat the wok over a high heat and add the oils. When very hot, stir in the ginger and garlic and cook for 30 seconds. Add the pork and cook over a high heat for about 5 minutes, stirring often, until sealed.

3 Add the mangetouts and mushrooms to the wok and stir-fry for 2–3 minutes. Add the Chinese cooking wine and soy sauce, stir-fry for 2–3 minutes and remove from the heat.

4 Just before serving, stir the sweet basil leaves into the pork. Serve with steamed jasmine rice.

> **Cook's Tip**
> When adding the oils to the hot wok, dribble them around the inner rim so that the oil flows down to coat the surface evenly.

Bacon Chops Energy 1140kcal/4760kJ; Protein 105.6g; Carbohydrate 26g, of which sugars 26gg; Fat 64.4g, of which saturates 21.6g; Cholesterol 160mg; Calcium 68mg; Fibre 3.2g; Sodium 536mg.
Aromatic Pork Energy 298kcal/1248kJ; Protein 30.4g; Carbohydrate 14.6g, of which sugars 4.8g; Fat 9.8g, of which saturates 2.4g; Cholesterol 79mg; Calcium 41mg; Fibre 2g; Sodium 903mg.

Pork & Pineapple Coconut Curry

The heat of this curry balances out its sweetness to make a fragrant dish.

Serves 4
400ml/14fl oz coconut milk
10ml/2 tsp Thai red curry paste
400g/14oz pork loin steaks, trimmed and thinly sliced
15ml/1 tbsp Thai fish sauce
5ml/1 tsp palm sugar (jaggery) or light muscovado (brown) sugar
15ml/1 tbsp tamarind juice, made by mixing tamarind paste with warm water
2 kaffir lime leaves, torn
½ medium pineapple
1 fresh red chilli, seeded and finely chopped
lime rind, to garnish

Preparation: 3 minutes; Cooking: 17 minutes

1 Pour the coconut milk into a bowl and let it settle, so that the cream rises to the surface. Scoop the cream into a measuring jug (cup). You should have about 250ml/8fl oz/1 cup. If necessary, add a little of the coconut milk.

2 Pour the coconut cream into a large pan and bring it to the boil over high heat, stirring once or twice.

3 Cook the coconut cream for about 8 minutes, until the cream separates, stirring frequently to prevent it from sticking to the base of the pan. Peel and chop the pineapple.

4 Ladle a little of the coconut cream into a bowl and stir in the red curry paste. Return the mixture to the pan and stir until well mixed. Cook, stirring occasionally, for about 3 minutes, until the paste is fragrant.

5 Add the sliced pork and stir in the fish sauce, sugar and tamarind juice. Cook, stirring constantly, for 2–3 minutes, until the sugar has dissolved and the pork is no longer pink.

6 Add the remaining coconut milk and the lime leaves. Bring to the boil, then stir in the pineapple. Reduce the heat and simmer gently for 3 minutes, or until the pork is fully cooked. Spoon into a large heated bowl or four individual bowls and sprinkle the chilli and strips of lime rind over. Serve immediately.

Sweet & Sour Pork Thai-style

It was the Chinese who originally created sweet and sour cooking, but the Thais also do it very well. This version has a fresher and cleaner flavour than the Chinese version.

Serves 4
350g/12oz lean pork
30ml/2 tbsp vegetable oil
4 garlic cloves, thinly sliced
1 small red onion, sliced
30ml/2 tbsp Thai fish sauce
15ml/1 tbsp sugar
1 red (bell) pepper, seeded and diced
½ cucumber, seeded and very thinly sliced
2 plum tomatoes, cut into wedges
115g/4oz piece fresh pineapple, cut into small chunks
2 spring onions (scallions), cut into short lengths
ground black pepper

To garnish
coriander (cilantro) leaves
spring onions (scallions), shredded

Preparation: 6 minutes; Cooking: 13 minutes

1 Cut the pork into thin strips. This is easier to do if you freeze it for 30 minutes first.

2 Heat the oil in a wok or large frying pan. Add the garlic. Cook over a medium heat until golden, then add the pork and stir-fry for 4–5 minutes. Add the onion slices and toss to mix.

3 Add the fish sauce, sugar and ground black pepper to taste. Toss the mixture over the heat for 3–4 minutes more.

4 Stir in the red pepper, cucumber, tomatoes, pineapple and spring onions. Stir-fry for 3–4 minutes more, then spoon into a bowl. Garnish with the coriander and spring onions and serve.

Cook's Tip
Also known as nam pla, Thai fish sauce is one of the most important ingredients in Thai cuisine. It is made from salted fish, usually anchovies, which are fermented to create the thin liquid that is the base of the sauce. The strong aroma and intense flavour becomes less pronounced with cooking.

Pork Curry Energy 187kcal/790kJ; Protein 22.2g; Carbohydrate 15.3g, of which sugars 15.3g; Fat 4.5g, of which saturates 1.6g; Cholesterol 63mg; Calcium 55mg; Fibre 1.2g; Sodium 449mg.
Sweet and Sour Pork Energy 211kcal/885kJ; Protein 20g; Carbohydrate 12.4g, of which sugars 11.8g; Fat 9.4g, of which saturates 2g; Cholesterol 55mg; Calcium 29mg; Fibre 1.8g; Sodium 68mg.

Pork in Sweet & Sour Sauce

The combination of sweet and sour flavours makes this a popular dish. Crushed mixed peppercorns add extra bite.

Serves 2
1 whole pork fillet (tenderloin), about 350g/12oz
25ml/1½ tbsp plain (all-purpose) flour
30–45ml/2–3 tbsp olive oil
250ml/8fl oz/1 cup dry white wine
30ml/2 tbsp white wine vinegar
10ml/2 tsp sugar
15ml/1 tbsp mixed peppercorns, coarsely ground
salt and ground black pepper
cooked broad (fava) beans tossed with grilled (broiled) bacon, to serve

Preparation: 2–3 minutes; Cooking: 6 minutes

1 Using a sharp knife, cut the pork diagonally into thin slices. Place between two sheets of baking parchment or clear film (plastic wrap) and pound lightly with a meat mallet or rolling pin to flatten them.

2 Spread out the flour in a shallow bowl. Season generously with salt and pepper, add the meat and turn it in the seasoned flour until coated evenly. Alternatively, put the seasoned flour in a strong plastic bag, add the pork and shake to coat.

3 Heat 15ml/1 tbsp of the oil in a wide heavy pan or frying pan and add as many slices of pork as the pan will hold. Fry over a medium to high heat for 2–3 minutes on each side until the pork is crisp and tender. Remove with a fish slice or metal spatula and place on a plate. Keep warm, either by tenting foil over the pork or in a low oven. Fry the remaining pork in the same way, adding more oil to the pan as necessary.

4 Mix the wine, vinegar and sugar in a measuring jug (cup). Pour into the pan and stir over a high heat until reduced.

5 Stir in the peppercorns and return the pork to the pan. Spoon the sauce over the pork until it is evenly coated and heated through. Serve with cooked broad beans tossed with grilled (broiled) bacon.

Pork with Marsala & Juniper

Although most frequently used in desserts, Sicilian Marsala gives savoury dishes a rich, fruity and alcoholic tang, bringing out the flavour of the pork perfectly.

Serves 4
25g/1oz/½ cup dried cep or porcini mushrooms
4 pork escalopes (US scallops)
10ml/2 tsp balsamic vinegar
8 garlic cloves
15g/½ oz/1 tbsp butter
45ml/3 tbsp Marsala
several fresh rosemary sprigs
10 juniper berries, crushed
salt and ground black pepper
noodles and green vegetables, to serve

Preparation: 4 minutes; Cooking: 15 minutes

1 Put the dried mushrooms in a bowl and just cover with hot water. Leave to stand. Bring a small pan of water to the boil and add the garlic cloves. Cook for 10 minutes until soft. Drain, put the garlic in a bowl and set aside.

2 Meanwhile, place the pork escalopes on a board, brush with 5ml/1 tsp of the vinegar and add a generous and even grinding of salt and black pepper.

3 Melt the butter in a large frying pan. Add the pork and fry quickly until browned on the underside. Turn the meat over and cook for another minute.

4 Add the Marsala and rosemary to the pan. Drain the dried mushrooms, saving the juices, and add them to the mixture. Stir in 60ml/4 tbsp of the mushroom juices, then add the garlic cloves, juniper berries and remaining vinegar. Simmer for 3 minutes, season and serve with noodles and vegetables.

> **Cook's Tips**
> • Use good quality butcher's pork, which won't be overwhelmed by the intense flavour of the sauce.
> • Juniper berries are the principal flavouring for gin. When added to meat, they impart a gamey flavour.

Pork with Marsala Energy 282kcal/1176kJ; Protein 32.2g; Carbohydrate 0.9g, of which sugars 0.9g; Fat 15.3g, of which saturates 8g; Cholesterol 118mg; Calcium 13mg; Fibre 0g; Sodium 175mg.
Pork in Sweet and Sour Energy 440kcal/1839kJ; Protein 38.3g; Carbohydrate 11.8g, of which sugars 6.1g; Fat 18.1g, of which saturates 4.1g; Cholesterol 110mg; Calcium 37mg; Fibre 0.3g; Sodium 128mg.

Five-flavour Noodles

The Japanese name for this dish is gomoku yakisoba, meaning five different ingredients; however, you can add as many different ingredients as you wish to make an exciting and tasty noodle stir-fry.

Serves 4
300g/11oz dried Chinese thin egg noodles or 500g/1¼lb fresh soba noodles
200g/7oz lean boneless pork, thinly sliced
22.5ml/4½ tsp sunflower oil
10g/¼oz grated fresh root ginger
1 garlic clove, crushed
200g/7oz green cabbage, roughly chopped
115g/4oz/2 cups beansprouts
1 green (bell) pepper, seeded and cut into fine strips
1 red (bell) pepper, seeded and cut into fine strips
salt and ground black pepper
20ml/4 tsp ao-nori seaweed, to garnish (optional)

For the seasoning mix
60ml/4 tbsp Worcestershire sauce
15ml/1 tbsp Japanese soy sauce
15ml/1 tbsp oyster sauce
15ml/1 tbsp sugar
2.5ml/½ tsp salt
ground white pepper

Preparation: 7–9 minutes; Cooking: 11–13 minutes

1 Cook the noodles according to the instructions on the packet. Drain well and set aside.

2 Cut the pork into 3–4cm/1¼–1½in strips and lay these on a board. Season with plenty of salt and pepper.

3 Heat 7.5ml/1½ tsp of the oil in a large wok or frying pan. Add the seasoned pork strips, stir-fry the pork until just cooked, then remove it from the wok or pan.

4 Wipe the wok or pan with kitchen paper, and heat the remaining oil in it. Add the ginger, garlic and cabbage and stir-fry for 1 minute. Add the beansprouts, stir until softened, then add the peppers and stir-fry for 1 minute more.

5 Return the pork to the pan and add the noodles. Stir in all the ingredients for the seasoning mix and stir-fry for 2–3 minutes. Serve immediately, sprinkled with ao-nori seaweed (if using).

Fried Pork with Scrambled Egg

When you need a tasty meal before going out for the evening, this quick-to-prepare and easy rice dish, with just a little meat, is the answer. Use regular rice, if you like, but that will take longer.

Serves 4
2 x 250g/9oz sachets quick-cook rice
45ml/3 tbsp vegetable oil
1 onion, chopped
15ml/1 tbsp chopped garlic
115g/4oz pork, cut into small cubes
2 eggs, beaten
30ml/2 tbsp Thai fish sauce
15ml/1 tbsp dark soy sauce
2.5ml/½ tsp caster (superfine) sugar

For the garnish
4 spring onions (scallions), finely sliced
2 fresh red chillies, sliced
1 lime, cut into wedges

Preparation: 5 minutes; Cooking: 12 minutes

1 Cook the rice according to the instructions on the packet. Spread out and leave to cool.

2 Heat the oil in a wok or large frying pan. Add the onion and garlic and cook for about 2 minutes, until softened.

3 Add the pork to the softened onion and garlic. Stir-fry until the pork changes colour and is cooked.

4 Add the eggs and cook until scrambled into small lumps.

5 Add the rice and continue to stir and toss, to coat it with the oil and prevent it from sticking.

6 Stir in the fish sauce, soy sauce and sugar and mix well. Continue to fry until the rice is thoroughly heated. Spoon into warmed individual bowls and serve, garnished with sliced spring onions, chillies and lime wedges.

Variation
Substitute sliced field (portabello) mushrooms for the pork.

Five-flavour Noodles Energy 425kcal/1799kJ; Protein 28.2g; Carbohydrate 62.6g, of which sugars 9.4g; Fat 8.6g, of which saturates 2.6g; Cholesterol 67mg; Calcium 82mg; Fibre 4.4g; Sodium 844mg.
Fried Pork Energy 602kcal/2512kJ; Protein 18.8g; Carbohydrate 101.3g, of which sugars 1.1g; Fat 12.8g, of which saturates 2.2g; Cholesterol 113mg; Calcium 45mg; Fibre 0.2g; Sodium 323mg.

Fusilli with Sausage

Getting sausages, pasta and tomato sauce ready at the right moment takes a bit of juggling, but the result is a delicious dish that every member of the family is bound to love.

Serves 4
400g/14oz spicy pork sausages
30ml/2 tbsp olive oil
1 small onion, finely chopped
2 garlic cloves, crushed
5ml/1 tsp paprika
5ml/1 tsp dried mixed herbs
5–10ml/1–2 tsp chilli sauce
1 large yellow (bell) pepper, seeded and cut into strips
400g/14oz can Italian plum tomatoes
250ml/8fl oz/1 cup vegetable stock
300g/11oz/2¾ cups dried fusilli
salt and ground black pepper
freshly grated Pecorino or Parmesan cheese, to serve

Preparation: 4–5 minutes; Cooking: 12–15 minutes

1 Grill (broil) the sausages for 10–12 minutes until they are browned on all sides.

2 Meanwhile, heat the oil in a large pan, add the onion and garlic and cook for 3 minutes. Add the paprika, herbs and chilli sauce to taste, then the yellow pepper. Cook for 3 minutes more, stirring occasionally.

3 Pour in the canned tomatoes, breaking them up with a wooden spoon, then add salt and pepper to taste and stir well. Cook over a medium heat for 10–12 minutes, adding the vegetable stock gradually. At the same time, add the pasta to a large pan of lightly salted boiling water and cook for 10–12 minutes, until *al dente*.

4 While the tomato sauce and pasta are cooking, drain the cooked sausages on kitchen paper, and, when cool enough to touch, cut each one diagonally into 1cm/½in pieces.

5 Add the sausage pieces to the sauce and mix well. Drain the pasta and add it to the pan of sauce. Toss well, then divide among four warmed bowls, sprinkled with the grated Pecorino or Parmesan cheese.

Spaghetti Carbonara

This Italian classic, flavoured with pancetta and a garlic-and-egg sauce that cooks around the hot spaghetti, is popular worldwide. It makes a great last-minute supper.

Serves 4
30ml/2 tbsp olive oil
1 small onion, finely chopped
1 large garlic clove, crushed
8 slices pancetta or rindless smoked streaky (fatty) bacon, cut into 1cm/½in pieces
350g/12oz dried spaghetti
4 eggs
90–120ml/6–8 tbsp crème fraîche
60ml/4 tbsp freshly grated Parmesan cheese, plus extra to serve
salt and ground black pepper

Preparation: 3 minutes; Cooking: 15–17 minutes

1 Heat the oil in a large pan, add the onion and garlic and fry gently for about 5 minutes until softened. Add the pancetta or bacon to the pan. Cook for 10 minutes, stirring often.

2 Meanwhile, cook the spaghetti in a large pan of lightly salted boiling water for 10–12 minutes.

3 Put the eggs, crème fraîche and grated Parmesan in a bowl. Stir in plenty of black pepper, then beat together well.

4 Drain the pasta thoroughly, tip it into the pan with the pancetta or bacon and toss well to mix. Turn off the heat under the pan, then immediately add the egg mixture and toss thoroughly so that it cooks lightly and coats the pasta.

5 Season to taste, then divide the pasta among four warmed bowls and sprinkle with ground black pepper. Serve immediately, with extra grated Parmesan handed around separately in a bowl.

> **Variation**
> Instead of beating the eggs with crème fraîche, use double (heavy) cream or sour cream, if you prefer.

Fusilli Energy 709kcal/2970kJ; Protein 20.9g; Carbohydrate 72.2g, of which sugars 10.5g; Fat 39.5g, of which saturates 13.3g; Cholesterol 47mg; Calcium 74mg; Fibre 4.6g; Sodium 774mg.
Spaghetti Energy 708kcal/2966kJ; Protein 30.7g; Carbohydrate 66.6g, of which sugars 4.2g; Fat 37.5g, of which saturates 15.5g; Cholesterol 261mg; Calcium 250mg; Fibre 2.8g; Sodium 824mg.

Tortellini with Ham

This is a very easy recipe that can be made quickly from store-cupboard ingredients. It is therefore ideal for an after-work supper or a casual lunch for friends.

Serves 4
2 tbsp olive oil
1 small onion, finely chopped
115g/4oz cooked ham, diced
150ml/¼ pint/⅔ cup passata (strained tomatoes)
100ml/3½fl oz/scant ½ cup panna da cucina or double (heavy) cream
250g/9oz fresh tortellini alla carne (meat-filled tortellini)
75g/3oz/1 cup freshly grated Parmesan cheese
salt and ground black pepper

Preparation: 5 minutes; Cooking: 12 minutes

1 Heat the oil in a large pan, add the onion and cook over low heat, stirring frequently, for about 5 minutes, until softened. Add the ham and cook, stirring occasionally, until it darkens.

2 Add the passata to the pan along with 150ml/¼ pint/⅔ cup water. Stir well, then add salt and pepper to taste. Bring to the boil, lower the heat and simmer the sauce for a few minutes, stirring occasionally, until it has reduced slightly. Stir the cream into the sauce and heat gently without boiling.

3 Meanwhile, bring a large pan of lightly salted water to the boil. Add the meat-filled tortellini, stir and cook for about 3 minutes, until it is tender.

4 Drain the pasta well and add it to the sauce. Add a handful of grated Parmesan to the pan. Stir, toss well and taste for seasoning. Serve in warmed bowls, topped with the remaining Parmesan cheese.

Cook's Tip
Keep a couple of cans of passata in the storecupboard and some vacuum-packed tortellini in the refrigerator and this dish is a doddle.

Fettuccine with Ham & Peas

This simple dish makes a very good first course for six people, or a main course for three to four. Despite its simplicity, it makes an ideal impromptu supper.

Serves 3–6
50g/2oz/¼ cup butter
1 small onion, finely chopped
200g/7oz/1¾ cups fresh or frozen peas
100ml/3½ fl oz/scant ½ cup chicken stock
2.5ml/½ tsp sugar
175ml/6fl oz/¾ cup dry white wine
350g/12oz fresh fettuccine
75g/3oz piece cooked ham, cut into bitesize chunks
115g/4oz/1⅓ cups freshly grated Parmesan cheese
salt and ground black pepper

Preparation: 4 minutes; Cooking: 8–10 minutes

1 Melt the butter in a medium frying pan, add the onion and cook over a low heat for about 5 minutes until softened but not coloured. Add the peas, stock and sugar, then stir in salt and freshly ground pepper to taste.

2 Bring the mixture to the boil, then lower the heat and simmer for 3–5 minutes or until the peas are tender. Add the wine, increase the heat and boil until the wine has reduced.

3 Meanwhile, cook the pasta in a large pan of lightly salted boiling water for about 3 minutes. When it is almost ready, add the ham to the sauce, with about a third of the Parmesan. Heat through, stirring, then taste for seasoning.

4 Drain the pasta and tip it into a large warmed bowl. Pour the sauce over the pasta and toss well. Serve immediately, sprinkled with the remaining Parmesan.

Cook's Tip
If you want to make this with dried pasta it will take a little longer, but if you start cooking the pasta before making the sauce, it won't take too much more time.

Tortellini Energy 509kcal/2118kJ; Protein 19.9g; Carbohydrate 26.2g, of which sugars 4.1g; Fat 36.8g, of which saturates 17.5g; Cholesterol 85mg; Calcium 353mg; Fibre 1.9g; Sodium 696mg.
Fettuccine Energy 414kcal/1738kJ; Protein 19.4g; Carbohydrate 48.6g, of which sugars 4g; Fat 15.1g, of which saturates 8.6g; Cholesterol 44mg; Calcium 259mg; Fibre 3.4g; Sodium 413mg.

Pasta with Ham & Asparagus

Tagliatelle dressed with a creamy asparagus sauce is the basis for this sustaining salad. If you've spent the morning gardening or playing sport, this is a great lunch you won't have to wait for.

Serves 4
450g/1lb asparagus
450g/1lb dried tagliatelle
225g/8oz cooked ham, in 5mm/
  ¼ in-thick slices, cut into fingers
2 hard-boiled eggs, sliced
50g/2oz Parmesan cheese
salt and ground black pepper

For the dressing
50g/2oz cooked potato
75ml/5 tbsp olive oil
15ml/1 tbsp lemon juice
10ml/2 tsp Dijon or
  wholegrain mustard
120ml/4fl oz/½ cup
  vegetable stock

Preparation: 5 minutes; Cooking: 12 minutes

1 Snap the asparagus spears; they will break naturally at the point where the tender top meets the base. Discard the tough woody ends. Cut the spears in half.

2 Bring a pan of salted water to the boil and cook the thicker halves for 12 minutes, adding the tips after 6 minutes.

3 Meanwhile, cook the pasta in a large pan of lightly salted boiling water for 10–12 minutes.

4 Drain the asparagus. Reserve the tips. Purée the remainder of the asparagus with the potato, olive oil, lemon juice, mustard and vegetable stock to make a smooth dressing.

5 Drain the pasta, toss with the asparagus sauce and cool slightly. Divide among four pasta plates. Top with the ham, hard-boiled eggs and asparagus tips. Shave Parmesan cheese over the top.

Variation
Use sliced chicken instead of the ham, or thin slices of softer Italian cheese, such as Fontina or Asiago.

Pan-fried Gammon with Cider

Gammon and cider are a delicious combination, since the sweet, tangy flavour of cider complements the gammon perfectly. Serve with mustard mashed potatoes and a dark green vegetable, such as steamed Savoy cabbage, green beans or lightly cooked Brussels sprouts.

Serves 4
4 gammon (smoked or cured
  ham) steaks, 225g/8oz each
150ml/¼ pint/⅔ cup dry
  (hard) cider
45ml/3 tbsp double (heavy) cream
30ml/2 tbsp sunflower oil
salt and ground black pepper
flat leaf parsley, to garnish
mustard mashed potatoes,
  to serve

Preparation: 1 minute; Cooking: 7–10 minutes

1 Heat the oil in a large frying pan until hot. Neatly snip the rind on the gammon steaks to stop them curling up and add them to the pan.

2 Cook the steaks for 3–4 minutes on each side, then pour in the cider. Allow to boil for a couple of minutes, then stir in the cream and cook for 1–2 minutes, or until thickened. Season with salt and pepper, and serve immediately.

Variation
The Irish dish, champ, makes a great alternative to mustard mashed potatoes: Cook 900g/2lb peeled potatoes in boiling salted water until tender. Meanwhile heat 120ml/4fl oz/½ cup creamy milk with 6 finely chopped spring onions (scallions). Mash the potatoes with the milk and onions and 50g/2oz/ ¼ cup butter. Pile the champ in a dish, make a well in the middle, and place another 50g/2oz/¼ cup butter in the well.

Cook's Tip
Cooking gammon (smoked or cured ham) in a liquid is a good way of ensuring it stays moist and soft-textured.

Ham and Pasta Energy 699kcal/2941kJ; Protein 35.4g; Carbohydrate 88.2g, of which sugars 6.6g; Fat 25.2g, of which saturates 6.3g; Cholesterol 140mg; Calcium 228mg; Fibre 5.3g; Sodium 852mg.
Gammon Energy 429kcal/1784kJ; Protein 39.6g; Carbohydrate 1.2g, of which sugars 1.2g; Fat 28.4g, of which saturates 10.1g; Cholesterol 67mg; Calcium 24mg; Fibre 0g; Sodium 1985mg.

Bacon, Pumpkin & Parmesan Pasta

The sweet flavour of pumpkin is nicely balanced by the Parmesan in this creamy pasta sauce, while fried garlic breadcrumbs provide a welcome crunch.

Serves 4
800g/1¾lb fresh pumpkin flesh, cut into small cubes
300g/11oz dried tagliatelle
65g/2½oz/5 tbsp butter
1 onion, sliced
115g/4oz rindless smoked back bacon, diced

15ml/1 tbsp olive oil
2 garlic cloves, crushed
75g/3oz/1½ cups fresh white breadcrumbs
150ml/¼ pint/⅔ cup single (light) cream
50g/2oz/⅔ cup freshly grated Parmesan cheese
freshly grated nutmeg
30ml/2 tbsp chopped fresh parsley
15ml/1 tbsp chopped fresh chives
salt and ground black pepper
sprigs of flat leaf parsley, to garnish

Preparation: 4 minutes; Cooking: 14 minutes

1 Bring two pans of lightly salted water to the boil. Place the pumpkin cubes in one pan and the pasta in the other. Cook for 10–12 minutes, stirring both pans several times.

2 Meanwhile, heat one-third of the butter in a separate large pan. Fry the onion and bacon for 5 minutes.

3 Melt the remaining butter with the oil in a frying pan. Add the garlic and breadcrumbs. Fry gently until the crumbs are golden brown and crisp. Drain on kitchen paper, spoon into a dish and keep warm for topping the pasta.

4 Drain the pumpkin and add it to the onion and bacon mixture, with the cream. Heat without stirring until bubbles appear on the surface and the cream is just below boiling point.

5 Drain the pasta, add to the pan and heat through. Stir in the Parmesan, nutmeg, chopped parsley, chives and seasoning. Spoon into a warmed bowl or individual pasta bowls, sprinkle with the garlic breadcrumbs and garnish with the sprigs of flat leaf parsley. Serve immediately.

Chorizo & Egg Bake

This adaptable dish is a swirl of red, green, yellow and white. You can use different vegetables, but should always include the chorizo for its flavour.

Serves 4
30ml/2 tbsp olive oil
115g/4oz diced smoked bacon or pancetta
2 chorizos, cubed
1 onion, chopped

2 garlic cloves, finely chopped
1 red and 1 green (bell) pepper, seeded and chopped
500g/1¼lb tomatoes, chopped
15–30ml/1–2 tbsp fino sherry
45ml/3 tbsp chopped parsley
8 large (US extra large) eggs
salt, paprika and cayenne pepper

For the garlic crumbs
4 thick slices stale bread
oil, for frying
2 garlic cloves, bruised

Preparation: 4–5 minutes; Cooking: 15 minutes

1 Preheat the oven to 180°C/350°F/Gas 4. Heat the oil in a large pan and fry the diced bacon and chorizo until they yield their fat. Add the onion and garlic and cook gently until softened, stirring.

2 Add the peppers and tomatoes and cook to reduce, stirring occasionally. Add some paprika and stir in the sherry.

3 Divide the mixture among four individual baking dishes. Sprinkle with parsley. Swirl the eggs with a fork, season with salt and cayenne, and pour over the vegetable mixture.

4 Bake the eggs and vegetables for 8 minutes, or until the eggs are just set.

5 Meanwhile make the garlic crumbs. Crumb the bread in a food processor. Heat plenty of oil in a large frying pan, add the garlic cloves for a few moments to flavour it, then remove and discard them. Throw in the breadcrumbs and brown quickly, scooping them out on to kitchen paper with a slotted spoon.

6 Season with a little salt and paprika, then sprinkle the crumbs around the edge of the eggs, when ready to serve.

Bacon Pasta Energy 691kcal/2897kJ; Protein 23.8g; Carbohydrate 76.6g, of which sugars 8.1g; Fat 34.2g, of which saturates 18.1g; Cholesterol 83mg; Calcium 293mg; Fibre 4.8g; Sodium 834mg.
Chorizo Bake Energy 597kcal/2485kJ; Protein 27.3g; Carbohydrate 28g, of which sugars 11.1g; Fat 42.4g, of which saturates 11.7g; Cholesterol 429mg; Calcium 163mg; Fibre 3.2g; Sodium 1116mg.

Pittas with Spiced Lamb Koftas

When you are eating *al fresco*, a bite in the hand is worth two on the plate. Harissa gives the lamb koftas a mildly fiery flavour, easily tamed by a drizzle of yogurt, some cucumber and tomato, and a little mint.

Serves 4
450g/1lb/2 cups minced (ground) lamb
1 small onion, finely chopped
10ml/2 tsp harissa paste
8 pitta breads, salad vegetables, mint and yogurt, to serve
salt and ground black pepper

Preparation: 10 minutes; Cooking: 10 minutes

1 Prepare a barbecue. Soak eight wooden skewers in cold water for 10 minutes.

2 Meanwhile, put the minced lamb in a large bowl and add the finely chopped onion and harissa paste. Mix well to combine, and season with plenty of salt and pepper.

3 Drain the skewers. Divide the spiced lamb mixture into eight equal pieces and mould each piece around a skewer in a sausage shape to make the koftas.

4 Cook the skewered koftas on the barbecue for about 10 minutes, turning occasionally, until cooked through.

5 Warm the pitta breads on the barbecue grill, then split them and open them out to make pitta pockets. Place a kofta in each one, and remove the skewer.

6 Add some cucumber and tomato slices, mint leaves and a drizzle of yogurt to each filled pocket, and serve immediately.

> **Variation**
> *Instead of adding mint leaves and yogurt separately to the pittas, spoon in some tzatziki, made by mixing finely diced cucumber, spring onions (scallions) and crushed garlic with Greek (US strained plain) yogurt.*

Shanghai Noodles with Lap Cheong

Lap cheong are firm, cured waxy pork sausages, available from Chinese food markets. Sweet and savoury, they can be steamed with rice, chicken or pork, added to an omelette or stir-fried with vegetables.

Serves 4
30ml/2 tbsp vegetable oil
115g/4oz rindless back (lean) bacon, cut into bitesize pieces
2 lap cheong, rinsed in warm water, drained and finely sliced
2 garlic cloves, finely chopped
2 spring onions (scallions), roughly chopped
225g/8oz Chinese greens or fresh spinach leaves, cut into 5cm/2in pieces
450g/1lb fresh Shanghai noodles
30ml/2 tbsp oyster sauce
30ml/2 tbsp soy sauce
ground black pepper

Preparation: 8 minutes; Cooking: 8 minutes

1 Heat half the oil in a wok or large frying pan. Add the bacon and lap cheong with the garlic and spring onions. Stir-fry for a few minutes until golden. Using a slotted spoon, remove the mixture from the wok or pan and keep warm.

2 Add the remaining oil to the wok or pan. When hot, stir-fry the Chinese greens or spinach over a high heat for about 3 minutes until it just starts to wilt.

3 Add the noodles and return the lap cheong mixture to the wok or pan. Season with oyster sauce, soy sauce and pepper. Stir-fry until the noodles are heated through.

> **Variation**
> *Use chipolata sausages instead of the lap cheong.*

> **Cook's Tip**
> *You can buy rindless bacon already cut into bitesize pieces. To remove the rind from bacon rashers (strips) cut it off with sharp kitchen scissors, occasionally dipping them in hot water.*

Shanghai Noodles Energy 485kcal/2043kJ; Protein 30.5g; Carbohydrate 60.7g, of which sugars 5.3g; Fat 14.9g, of which saturates 2.8g; Cholesterol 63mg; Calcium 47mg; Fibre 3.2g; Sodium 440mg.
Pittas Energy 609kcal/2568kJ; Protein 35.3g; Carbohydrate 83.8g, of which sugars 5.4g; Fat 17g, of which saturates 7.3g; Cholesterol 87mg; Calcium 230mg; Fibre 3.8g; Sodium 737mg.

Kofta Lamb Burgers

For a quick and easy supper, simply slide these spicy little burgers into cones made by rolling warmed tortillas. A dollop of thick yogurt or crème fraîche wouldn't go amiss either.

Serves 4
450g/1lb minced (ground) lamb
1–2 large slices French bread, very finely crumbed
1/2 bunch fresh coriander (cilantro), finely chopped
5 garlic cloves, chopped
1 onion, finely chopped
juice of 1/2 lemon
5ml/1 tsp ground cumin
5ml/1 tsp paprika
15ml/1 tbsp curry powder
a pinch each of ground cardamom, turmeric and cinnamon
15ml/1 tbsp tomato purée (paste)
cayenne pepper or chopped fresh chillies (optional)
1 egg, beaten (optional)
salt and ground black pepper
flat bread and salads, to serve

Preparation: 8 minutes; Cooking: 10 minutes

1 Put the lamb, crumbed bread, coriander, garlic, onion, lemon juice, spices, tomato purée, cayenne pepper or chillies and seasoning in a large bowl. Mix well. If the mixture does not bind together, add the beaten egg and a little more bread.

2 Divide the mixture into four large or eight small rounds. With wet hands, shape into burgers.

3 Heat a heavy non-stick frying pan, add the burgers and cook for about 10 minutes, until browned. Turn carefully once or twice, but make sure that they do not fall apart. Serve hot with flat bread and salads.

Variations
• Mix a handful of raisins or sultanas (golden raisins) into the meat mixture before shaping it into burgers.
• Serve in conventional burger buns, splitting them and toasting them under a hot grill (broiler) before filling.
• Try these with coleslaw for a substantial snack.

Pan-fried Mediterranean Lamb

This Mediterranean dish makes a simple weekday meal.

Serves 4
8 lean lamb cutlets (US rib chops)
1 onion, thinly sliced
2 red (bell) peppers, seeded and sliced
400g/14oz can plum tomatoes
1 garlic clove, crushed
45ml/3 tbsp chopped fresh basil
30ml/2 tbsp chopped pitted black olives
salt and ground black pepper
pasta, to serve (optional)

Preparation: 2 minutes; Cooking: 18 minutes

1 Trim any excess fat from the lamb, then cook in a non-stick frying pan, without any added fat, turning frequently, for 2 minutes, until golden brown all over. Add the onion and red peppers to the pan. Cook, stirring, for 1 minute to soften, then add the plum tomatoes, garlic and fresh basil leaves.

2 Cover and simmer for 15 minutes, or until the lamb is tender. Stir in the olives, season to taste and serve hot.

Cumin- & Coriander-rubbed Lamb

When summer sizzles, turn up the heat a little more with these spicy lamb chops. If you have time, marinate the chops for an hour – they will taste even better.

Serves 4
30ml/2 tbsp ground cumin
30ml/2 tbsp ground coriander
30ml/2 tbsp olive oil
8 lamb chops
salt and ground black pepper

Preparation: 3 minutes; Cooking: 10 minutes.

1 Prepare a barbecue or preheat the grill (broiler). Mix the cumin, coriander and oil in a bowl, beating with a spoon until a smooth paste is formed. Season with salt and pepper. Rub the mixture all over the lamb chops. Cook the chops for 5 minutes on each side, until lightly charred on the outside but still pink in the centre. Serve immediately.

Kofta Lamb Burgers Energy 298kcal/1249kJ; Protein 24.2g; Carbohydrate 16.5g, of which sugars 2.6g; Fat 15.5g, of which saturates 7.1g; Cholesterol 87mg; Calcium 57mg; Fibre 1.1g; Sodium 242mg.
Pan-Fried Lamb Energy 637kcal/2634kJ; Protein 23.9g; Carbohydrate 9.9g, of which sugars 9.3g; Fat 56g, of which saturates 27.3g; Cholesterol 117mg; Calcium 33mg; Fibre 2.8g; Sodium 272mg.
Cumin Lamb Energy 494kcal/2059kJ; Protein 55.6g; Carbohydrate 0g, of which sugars 0g; Fat 30.1g, of which saturates 12.6g; Cholesterol 220mg; Calcium 18mg; Fibre 0g; Sodium 150mg.

Barbecued Lamb with Red Pepper Salsa

Vibrant red pepper salsa brings out the best in succulent lamb steaks to make a dish that looks as good as it tastes. Serve a selection of salads and crusty bread with the lamb.

Serves 6
6 lamb steaks
about 15g/½oz/½ cup fresh
   rosemary sprigs
2 garlic cloves, sliced

60ml/4 tbsp olive oil
30ml/2 tbsp maple syrup
salt and ground black pepper

For the salsa
200g/7oz red (bell) peppers,
   roasted, peeled, seeded
   and chopped
1 garlic clove, crushed
15ml/1 tbsp chopped chives
30ml/2 tbsp extra virgin olive oil
fresh flat leaf parsley, to garnish

Preparation: 3 minutes; Cooking: 4–10 minutes

1 Place the lamb steaks in a shallow dish that will hold them all in one layer. Season with salt and pepper. Pull the leaves off the rosemary and sprinkle them over the meat.

2 Add the slices of garlic, then drizzle the olive oil and maple syrup over the top. Cover and chill until ready to cook. If you have time, the lamb steaks can be left to marinate in the refrigerator for 12 hours or up to 24 hours.

3 Prepare a barbecue or preheat the grill (broiler). Make sure the steaks are liberally coated with the marinating ingredients, then cook them over the hot barbecue or under the grill for 2–5 minutes on each side. The cooking time willl depend on the heat of the barbecue coals and the thickness of the steaks as well as the result required – rare, medium or well cooked.

4 While the lamb steaks are cooking, mix together all the ingredients for the salsa in a bowl. Serve the salsa spooned on to the plates with the meat or in a small serving dish on the side. Garnish the lamb with sprigs of flat leaf parsley and pass around a cool, crisp salad – iceberg lettuce would be ideal.

Sweet & Sour Lamb

Buy lamb loin chops from your butcher and ask him to French trim them for you. Serve the chops with a hot sauce based on their marinade and with steamed carrots and green beans on the side.

Serves 4
8 French-trimmed lamb loin chops
90ml/6 tbsp balsamic vinegar
30ml/2 tbsp caster
   (superfine) sugar
30ml/2 tbsp olive oil
salt and ground black pepper

Preparation: 3 minutes; Cooking: 8–10 minutes

1 Put the lamb chops in a shallow, non-metallic dish and drizzle over the balsamic vinegar.

2 Sprinkle with the sugar and season with salt and black pepper. Turn the chops to coat in the mixture, then cover with clear film (plastic wrap) and chill for 10 minutes.

3 Heat the olive oil in a large frying pan and add the chops, reserving the marinade. Cook for 3–4 minutes on each side.

4 Pour the marinade into the pan and leave to bubble for about 2 minutes, or until reduced slightly. Remove from the pan and serve immediately.

> **Variations**
> Use sherry vinegar instead of balsamic in the marinade. Mint and lamb are good companions, and adding a little chopped fresh mint to the marinade will also give good results.

> **Cook's Tip**
> Lamb loin chops are sold as a rack of lamb, which is also known as a guard of honour, but they are chined (have the backbone removed) to leave cutlets that can be easily separated. French-trimmed chops are those that have had the skin removed as well as the backbone.

Barbecued Lamb Energy 390kcal/1627kJ; Protein 44.1g; Carbohydrate 2.1g, of which sugars 2g; Fat 22.8g, of which saturates 6.8g; Cholesterol 158mg; Calcium 33mg; Fibre 0.5g; Sodium 106mg.
Sweet and Sour Lamb Energy 258kcal/1077kJ; Protein 19.7g; Carbohydrate 7.9g, of which sugars 7.9g; Fat 16.7g, of which saturates 6g; Cholesterol 76mg; Calcium 12mg; Fibre 0g; Sodium 87mg.

Lamb Steaks with Redcurrant Glaze

Good and meaty, but thin enough to cook quickly, lamb leg steaks are a good choice for the cook short on time. The redcurrant and rosemary glaze looks gorgeous especially with a fresh redcurrant garnish.

Serves 4

4 large fresh rosemary sprigs
4 lamb leg steaks
75ml/5 tbsp redcurrant jelly
30ml/2 tbsp raspberry or
    red wine vinegar

Preparation: 2–3 minutes; Cooking: 10 minutes

1 Reserve the tips of the rosemary sprigs and finely chop the remaining leaves. Rub the chopped rosemary, salt and pepper all over the lamb to infuse it with flavour.

2 Preheat the grill (broiler). Heat the redcurrant jelly gently in a small pan with 30ml/2 tbsp water and a little seasoning. Stir in the raspberry or red wine vinegar.

3 Place the lamb steaks on a foil-lined grill (broiling) rack and brush with a little of the redcurrant glaze. Cook under the grill for about 5 minutes on each side, until deep golden, brushing frequently with more redcurrant glaze.

4 Transfer the lamb to warmed plates. Tip any juices from the foil into the remaining glaze and heat through gently. Pour the glaze over the lamb and serve with peas and new potatoes, garnished with the reserved rosemary sprigs.

Cook's Tip
This is a good recipe for the barbecue. Wait until the fierce heat has subsided and the coals are dusted with white ash, then place the rosemary-rubbed steaks directly on the grill rack. Brush frequently with the glaze as they cook. If you grow your own rosemary, try sprinkling some over the coals. As the oil in the herb warms, the scent of rosemary will perfume the air and stimulate the appetite.

Fried Lamb Meatballs

Meatballs cook quickly; the only fiddly bit is shaping them. Mixing everything together with your hands is very satisfying and also the most efficient way of preparing them.

Serves 4

2 medium slices of bread,
    crusts removed
500g/1 1/4lb minced (ground)
    lamb or beef
1 onion

5ml/1 tsp each dried thyme
    and oregano
45ml/3 tbsp chopped fresh
    flat leaf parsley, plus extra
    to garnish
1 egg, lightly beaten
salt and ground black pepper
lemon wedges, to serve (optional)

For frying
25g/1oz/1/4 cup plain
    (all-purpose) flour
30–45ml/2–3 tbsp vegetable or
    light olive oil

Preparation: 10–15 minutes; Cooking: 5 minutes

1 Soak the slices of bread in a shallow bowl of water for 5 minutes or until softened. While the bread is soaking, grate or very finely chop the onion.

2 Drain the bread in a colander. Using clean hands, squeeze it dry and put it in a large bowl. Add the meat, onion, dried herbs, parsley, egg, salt and pepper to the bread. Mix together, preferably using your hands, until well blended.

3 Shape the meat mixture into individual balls about the size of a walnut, and roll them in the flour to give them a light dusting, shaking off any excess coating.

4 Heat the oil in a large frying pan. When it is hot, add the meatballs and fry for about 5 minutes, shaking the pan, turning them frequently, until they are cooked through and look crisp and brown.

5 Using a slotted spoon, lift out the meatballs and drain on a double sheet of kitchen paper, to get rid of the excess oil. Sprinkle with the remaining chopped parsley and serve with lemon wedges, if you like.

Lamb Steaks Energy 362kcal/1518kJ; Protein 34.4g; Carbohydrate 13g, of which sugars 13g; Fat 19.6g, of which saturates 9.1g; Cholesterol 133mg; Calcium 16mg; Fibre 0g; Sodium 156mg.
Lamb Meatballs Energy 411kcal/1710kJ; Protein 28.4g; Carbohydrate 13g, of which sugars 1.5g; Fat 27.6g, of which saturates 9.7g; Cholesterol 123mg; Calcium 66mg; Fibre 1.1g; Sodium 192mg.

Warm Lamb & Noodle Salad

This Thai-inspired salad combines thin slices of lamb with lightly cooked fresh vegetables and rice noodles, all tossed together with a deliciously fragrant dressing.

Serves 4

30ml/2 tbsp red Thai curry paste
60ml/4 tbsp sunflower oil
750g/1lb 11oz lamb neck (US shoulder or breast) fillets, thinly sliced
250g/9oz sugar snap peas
500g/1¼lb medium or thick fresh rice noodles

1 red (bell) pepper, seeded and very thinly sliced
1 cucumber, cut into very thin slices with a vegetable peeler
6–7 spring onions (scallions), sliced diagonally
a large handful of fresh mint leaves

For the dressing
15ml/1 tbsp sunflower oil
juice of 2 limes
1 garlic clove, crushed
15ml/1 tbsp golden caster (superfine) sugar
15ml/1 tbsp fish sauce
30ml/2 tbsp soy sauce

Preparation: 10 minutes plus marinating; Cooking: 7–9 minutes

1 In a shallow dish, mix together the red curry paste and half the oil. Add the lamb slices and toss to coat. Cover and leave to marinate in the refrigerator for up to 24 hours.

2 Blanch the sugar snap peas in a wok of lightly salted boiling water for 1–2 minutes. Drain, refresh under cold water, drain again thoroughly and transfer to a large bowl.

3 Put the noodles in a separate bowl and pour over boiling water to cover. Soak for 5–10 minutes, until tender, then drain well and separate. Add the noodles to the sugar snap peas, then add the red pepper, cucumber and spring onions.

4 Heat a wok over a high heat and add the remaining sunflower oil. Stir-fry the lamb in two batches for 3–4 minutes, or until cooked through, then add to the bowl of salad ingredients.

5 Place all the dressing ingredients in a screw-top jar, screw on the lid and shake well. Pour over the warm salad, sprinkle over the mint and toss to combine. Serve immediately.

Devilled Kidneys on Brioche Croûtes

The trick with lamb's kidneys is not to overcook them, so this recipe is a gift for the quick cook. Cream tames the fiery sauce, making a mixture that tastes great on croûtes or as a filling for tartlets.

Serves 4
8 mini brioche slices
25g/1oz/2 tbsp butter

1 shallot, finely chopped
2 garlic cloves, finely chopped
115g/4oz/1½ cups mushrooms, halved
1.5ml/¼ tsp cayenne pepper
15ml/1 tbsp Worcestershire sauce
8 lamb's kidneys, halved and trimmed
150ml/¼ pint/⅔ cup double (heavy) cream
30ml/2 tbsp chopped fresh parsley

Preparation: 5 minutes; Cooking: 12–14 minutes

1 Preheat the grill (broiler) and toast the brioche slices until golden brown on both sides. Keep warm.

2 Melt the butter in a frying pan. Add the shallot, garlic and mushrooms and cook for 5 minutes, or until the shallot has softened. Stir in the cayenne pepper and Worcestershire sauce and simmer for 1 minute.

3 Add the kidneys to the pan and cook for 3–5 minutes on each side. Finally, stir in the cream and simmer for about 2 minutes, or until the sauce has heated through.

4 Remove the brioche croûtes from the wire rack and place on warmed plates. Top with the kidneys. Sprinkle with chopped parsley and serve with salad.

Cook's Tip
If you can't find mini brioches, you can use a large brioche instead. Slice it thickly and stamp out croûtes using a 5cm/2in round cutter. If you prefer, the brioche croûtes can be fried rather than toasted. Melt 25g/1oz/2 tbsp butter in a frying pan and fry the croûtes until crisp and golden on both sides.

Warm Lamb Salad Energy 820kcal/3418kJ; Protein 46g; Carbohydrate 76.4g, of which sugars 9.4g; Fat 36g, of which saturates 11.7g; Cholesterol 143mg; Calcium 55mg; Fibre 4.1g; Sodium 709mg.
Devilled Kidneys Energy 575kcal/2412kJ; Protein 37.7g; Carbohydrate 40.7g, of which sugars 13.2g; Fat 30.3g, of which saturates 16.3g; Cholesterol 623mg; Calcium 122mg; Fibre 2g; Sodium 599mg.

Chicken Omelette Dippers

Have you got a reluctant eater in the family? Not any more. Children love these protein-packed chicken omelette rolls. You might have to ration the ketchup dip, however.

Serves 4
1 skinless chicken thigh, about
    115g/4oz, boned and cubed
40ml/8 tsp butter
1 small onion, chopped
½ carrot, diced
2 shiitake mushrooms,
    stems removed and
    caps chopped finely
15ml/1 tbsp finely chopped
    fresh parsley
225g/8oz/2 cups cooked long
    grain white rice
30ml/2 tbsp tomato ketchup,
    plus extra to serve
6 eggs, lightly beaten
60ml/4 tbsp milk
2.5ml/½ tsp salt, plus extra
    to season
ground black pepper

Preparation: 3 minutes; Cooking: 16 minutes

1 Season the chicken. Melt 10ml/2 tsp butter in a frying pan. Fry the onion for 1 minute, then add the chicken and fry until cooked. Add the mushrooms and carrot, stir-fry over a medium heat until soft, then add the parsley. Set aside. Wipe the pan with a wad of kitchen paper.

2 Melt 10ml/2 tsp butter in the frying pan, add the rice and stir well. Mix in the fried ingredients, ketchup and black pepper. Stir well, adding salt to taste. Keep the mixture warm.

3 Beat the eggs with the milk in a bowl. Stir in the salt, and add pepper. Melt 5ml/1 tsp of the remaining butter in an omelette pan. Pour in a quarter of the egg mixture and stir it briefly with a fork, then allow it to set for 1 minute. Top with a quarter of the rice mixture, spreading it evenly over the omelette.

4 There are two ways of shaping the omelette. Either just flip it over the filling, then cut in half to make wedges, or roll the omelette around the filling and cut in half. Keep the filled omelette hot in a low oven while cooking three more. Serve two wedges or rolls per person, on individual plates, with a bowl of ketchup for dipping.

Fiery Chicken Wings with Blood Oranges

This is a great recipe for the barbecue – it is quick and easy, and best eaten with the fingers. The oranges can be cooked separately or with the wings. Their flavour is great with chicken.

Serves 4
60ml/4 tbsp fiery harissa
30ml/2 tbsp olive oil
16–20 chicken wings
4 blood oranges, quartered
icing (confectioners') sugar
a small bunch of fresh coriander
    (cilantro), chopped
salt

Preparation: 3 minutes; Cooking: 10 minutes

1 Mix the harissa with the olive oil in a small bowl, or, if using home-made harissa (see Cook's Tip below), simply measure the required amount into a bowl.

2 Add a little salt and stir to combine. Brush this mixture over the chicken wings so that they are well coated. Cook the wings on a hot barbecue or under a hot grill (broiler) for 5 minutes on each side, turning them over with tongs.

3 Once the wings begin to cook, dip the orange quarters lightly in icing sugar and grill (broil) them for a few minutes, until they are slightly burnt but not blackened. If you thread them on to skewers, it will be easier to turn them under the heat.

4 Serve the chicken wings immediately with the oranges, sprinkled with a little chopped fresh coriander.

> **Cook's Tip**
> Try making your own harissa if you have a blender. You will need 6–8 dried red chillies, 2 crushed garlic cloves, 2.5ml/½ tsp salt, 5ml/1 tsp ground cumin, 2.5ml/½ tsp ground coriander and 120ml/4fl oz/1 cup olive oil. Blend to a paste. To store, spoon into a jar and cover with olive oil. It will keep for 1 month.

Dippers Energy 316kcal/1322kJ; Protein 18g; Carbohydrate 21.5g, of which sugars 3.7g; Fat 18.4g, of which saturates 8.1g; Cholesterol 338mg; Calcium 80mg; Fibre 0.5g; Sodium 322mg.
Chicken Wings Energy 658kcal/2758kJ; Protein 61.9g; Carbohydrate 21.8g, of which sugars 20.7g; Fat 36.7g, of which saturates 10.1g; Cholesterol 264mg; Calcium 163mg; Fibre 2.6g; Sodium 866mg.

Chicken with Lemon & Garlic

These chicken strips make an unusual first course for four, and only need to be cooked at the last moment. Serve them as a main course for two with fried or baked potatoes.

Serves 2–4

2 skinless chicken breast fillets

30ml/2 tbsp olive oil
1 shallot, finely chopped
4 garlic cloves, finely chopped
5ml/1 tsp paprika
juice of 1 lemon
30ml/2 tbsp chopped fresh
  parsley
salt and ground black pepper
fresh flat leaf parsley, to garnish
lemon wedges, to serve

Preparation: 3 minutes; Cooking: 3–5 minutes

1 Remove the little fillet from the back of each breast portion. If the breast still looks fatter than a finger, bat it with a rolling pin to make it thinner. Slice all the chicken meat into strips.

2 Heat the oil in a large frying pan. Stir-fry the chicken strips with the shallot, garlic and paprika over a high heat for about 3 minutes until cooked through.

3 Add the lemon juice and parsley and season with salt and pepper to taste. Serve immediately on warmed plates, with lemon wedges. Garnish with flat leaf parsley.

Variation

For a variation on this dish, try using strips of turkey breast or pork fillet. They need slightly longer cooking. The whites of spring onions (scallions) can replace shallots, and the chopped green tops can be used instead of parsley.

Cook's Tip

Chicken breast fillets have a little fillet strip that easily becomes detached. Collect these in a bag or container in the freezer. You won't miss them and will soon have sufficient for this dish.

Chicken Croquettes

Croquettes are very popular snacks and there are many different variations. This one is based on béchamel sauce, which is perfect for taking on different flavours such as ham or chopped peppers.

Serves 4

25g/1oz/2 tbsp butter
25g/1oz/¼ cup plain
  (all-purpose) flour
150ml/¼ pint/⅔ cup milk

15ml/1 tbsp olive oil, plus extra
  for deep-frying
1 boneless chicken breast portion
  with skin, diced
1 garlic clove, finely chopped
1 small egg, beaten
50g/2oz/1 cup stale white
  breadcrumbs
salt and ground black pepper
fresh flat leaf parsley,
  to garnish
lemon wedges, to serve

Preparation: 2 minutes; Cooking: 12 minutes

1 Melt the butter in a pan. Add the flour and cook gently, stirring, for 1 minute. Gradually stir in the milk and cook until smooth and thick. Cover the surface closely to prevent the formation of a skin, and set aside.

2 Heat the oil in a medium frying pan and fry the piece of chicken with the garlic for 5 minutes.

3 When the chicken is lightly browned and cooked through, tip the contents of the frying pan into a food processor and process until finely chopped. Tip the mixture into the sauce and stir to combine. Season with plenty of salt and pepper to taste, then set aside to cool completely.

4 Once cooled and firm, shape the mixture into eight small sausage shapes. Dip each one in beaten egg, then roll in breadcrumbs to coat.

5 Heat the oil in a large pan, until a cube of bread dropped in the oil browns in 1 minute. Lower the croquettes into the oil and cook for 4 minutes until crisp and golden. Lift out using a slotted spoon and drain on kitchen paper. Serve with lemon wedges and garnish with fresh flat leaf parsley.

Chicken with Lemon Energy 139kcal/580kJ; Protein 18.6g; Carbohydrate 1.5g, of which sugars 1.1g; Fat 6.5g, of which saturates 1g; Cholesterol 53mg; Calcium 33mg; Fibre 0.8g; Sodium 50mg.
Chicken Croquettes Energy 286kcal/1195kJ; Protein 13.9g; Carbohydrate 16.4g, of which sugars 2.2g; Fat 18.9g, of which saturates 5.8g; Cholesterol 89mg; Calcium 80mg; Fibre 0.5g; Sodium 189mg.

Caramelized Chicken Wings

These caramelized chicken wings are irresistible.

Serves 2–4
75ml/5 tbsp sugar

30ml/2 tbsp vegetable oil
25g/1oz fresh root ginger, grated
12 chicken wings, split in two
chilli oil, for drizzling
mixed pickled vegetables, to serve

Preparation: 0 minutes; Cooking: 18 minutes

1 Heat the sugar with 60ml/4 tbsp water in a heavy pan until it forms a golden syrup. Heat the oil in a wok and stir-fry the ginger until fragrant. Add the chicken wings, brown them and continue to stir-fry for 5–6 minutes. Pour in the syrup and coat the chicken.

2 Cover and cook for 12 minutes, until the chicken is tender. Drizzle chilli oil over and serve with the mixed pickled vegetables.

Chicken Livers in Sherry

This delicious little tapas dish is particularly good eaten with bread or toast.

Serves 4
225g/8oz chicken livers, thawed
   if frozen
15ml/1 tbsp olive oil
1 small onion, finely chopped

2 small garlic cloves,
   finely chopped
5ml/1 tsp fresh thyme leaves
30ml/2 tbsp sweet oloroso sherry
30ml/2 tbsp crème fraîche or
   double (heavy) cream
2.5ml/½ tsp paprika
salt and ground black pepper
fresh thyme, to garnish

Preparation: 3–4 minutes; Cooking: 5 minutes

1 Trim any green spots and sinews from the chicken livers. Heat the oil in a frying pan and fry the onion, garlic, chicken livers and thyme for 3 minutes.

2 Stir the sherry into the livers, add the crème fraîche and cook briefly. Season with salt, pepper and paprika, garnish with thyme and serve immediately.

Crispy Five-spice Chicken

Strips of chicken fillet, with a spiced rice flour coating, become deliciously crisp and golden when fried. They make a great meal when served on stir-fried vegetable noodles.

Serves 4
200g/7oz thin egg noodles
30ml/2 tbsp sunflower oil
2 garlic cloves, very thinly sliced
1 fresh red chilli, seeded
   and sliced
½ red (bell) pepper, very
   thinly sliced

2 carrots, peeled and cut into
   thin strips
300g/11oz Chinese broccoli or
   Chinese greens, roughly sliced
45ml/3 tbsp hoisin sauce
45ml/3 tbsp soy sauce
5ml/1 tsp caster (superfine) sugar
4 skinless chicken breast fillets,
   cut into strips
2 egg whites, lightly beaten
115g/4oz/1 cup rice flour
15ml/1 tbsp five-spice powder
salt and ground black pepper
vegetable oil, for frying

Preparation: 5 minutes; Cooking: 10–12 minutes

1 Cook the noodles in a pan of salted boiling water according to the packet instructions, drain and set aside.

2 Heat the sunflower oil in a wok, then add the garlic, chilli, red pepper, carrots and broccoli or greens and stir-fry over a high heat for 2–3 minutes.

3 Add the sauces and sugar to the wok and cook for a further 2–3 minutes. Add the drained noodles, toss to combine, then remove from the heat, cover and keep warm.

4 Dip the chicken strips into the egg white. Combine the rice flour and five-spice powder in a shallow dish and season. Add the chicken strips to the flour mixture and toss to coat.

5 Heat about 2.5cm/1½in oil in a clean wok. When hot, shallow-fry the chicken for 3–4 minutes until crisp and golden.

6 To serve, divide the noodle mixture between warmed plates or bowls and top each serving with the chicken.

Chicken Wings Energy 393kcal/1641kJ; Protein 30.5g; Carbohydrate 14.4g, of which sugars 14.4g; Fat 24.1g, of which saturates 6.3g; Cholesterol 134mg; Calcium 16mg; Fibre 0g; Sodium 91mg.
Chicken Livers Energy 119kcal/494kJ; Protein 10.3g; Carbohydrate 1.5g, of which sugars 1.1g; Fat 7.1g, of which saturates 2.8g; Cholesterol 222mg; Calcium 13mg; Fibre 0.2g; Sodium 46mg.
Five-spice Chicken Energy 574kcal/2419kJ; Protein 49.6g; Carbohydrate 68g, of which sugars 9.4g; Fat 12.3g, of which saturates 2.5g; Cholesterol 120mg; Calcium 83mg; Fibre 5.1g; Sodium 1210mg.

Spicy Fried Noodles with Chicken

This is a wonderfully versatile dish as you can adjust it to include your favourite ingredients.

Serves 4

225g/8oz egg thread noodles
60ml/4 tbsp vegetable oil
2 garlic cloves, finely chopped
175g/6oz pork fillet (tenderloin), sliced into thin strips
1 skinless chicken breast fillet, sliced into thin strips
115g/4oz/1 cup peeled cooked prawns (shrimp)

45ml/3 tbsp fresh lemon juice
45ml/3 tbsp Thai fish sauce
30ml/2 tbsp soft light brown sugar
2 eggs, beaten
1/2 fresh red chilli, seeded and finely chopped
50g/2oz/2/3 cup beansprouts
60ml/4 tbsp roasted peanuts, chopped
3 spring onions (scallions), cut into 5cm/2in lengths and shredded
45ml/3 tbsp chopped fresh coriander (cilantro)

Preparation: 6 minutes; Cooking: 8–10 minutes

1 Bring a large pan of lightly salted water to the boil, add the noodles and cook, then leave for 5 minutes.

2 Meanwhile, heat 45ml/3 tbsp of the oil in a wok or large frying pan, add the garlic and cook for 30 seconds. Add the pork and chicken and stir-fry until lightly browned, then add the prawns and stir-fry for 2 minutes. Stir in the lemon juice, then add the fish sauce and sugar. Stir-fry until the sugar has dissolved.

3 Drain the noodles and add to the wok or pan with the remaining 15ml/1 tbsp oil. Toss all the ingredients together. Pour the beaten eggs over the noodles and stir-fry until almost set, then add the chilli and beansprouts.

4 Divide the roasted peanuts, spring onions and coriander leaves into two equal portions, add one portion to the pan and stir-fry for about 2 minutes.

5 Transfer the noodles to a serving platter. Sprinkle on the remaining roasted peanuts, spring onions and chopped coriander and serve immediately.

Orange Chicken Salad

With their tangy flavour, orange segments are the perfect partner for tender chicken in this tasty rice salad. To appreciate all the flavours fully, serve the salad at room temperature. It makes the perfect dish for a hot summer day and could even be packed for a picnic. Keep the toasted nuts separate and add them at the last minute, or they will become soft.

Serves 4

3 large seedless oranges
175g/6oz/scant 1 cup long grain rice
10ml/2 tsp strong Dijon mustard
2.5ml/1/2 tsp caster (superfine) sugar
175ml/6fl oz/3/4 cup vinaigrette
450g/1lb cooked chicken, diced
45ml/3 tbsp chopped fresh chives
75g/3oz/3/4 cup almonds or cashew nuts, toasted
salt and ground black pepper
mixed salad leaves, to serve

Preparation: 5 minutes; Cooking: 15 minutes

1 Pare one of the oranges thinly, removing only the rind, not the white pith. Put the pieces of orange rind in a pan and add the rice.

2 Pour in 475ml/16fl oz/2 cups water, add salt and bring to the boil. Cover and cook over very low heat for 15 minutes, until the rice is tender and the water has been absorbed.

3 Meanwhile, peel the oranges, removing all the white pith. Working over a plate to catch the juices, separate them into segments. Tip in the orange juice from the plate and add to the vinaigrette with the mustard and sugar, whisking to combine. Check the seasoning.

4 When the rice is cooked, remove it from the heat and discard the pieces of orange rind. Spoon the rice into a bowl, let it cool slightly, then add half the dressing. Toss well, then set aside to cool completely.

5 Add the chicken, chives, toasted nuts and orange segments to the cooled rice. Pour over the remaining dressing and toss gently to combine. Serve on a bed of mixed salad leaves.

Spicy Fried Noodles Energy 605kcal/2537kJ; Protein 39.8g; Carbohydrate 52.1g, of which sugars 11.5g; Fat 27.9g, of which saturates 5.5g; Cholesterol 226mg; Calcium 83mg; Fibre 3.1g; Sodium 1052mg.
Orange Chicken Salad Energy 642kcal/2679kJ; Protein 35.6g; Carbohydrate 49.5g, of which sugars 14.1g; Fat 33.7g, of which saturates 4.7g; Cholesterol 79mg; Calcium 118mg; Fibre 3.5g; Sodium 278mg.

Pan-fried Chicken with Pesto

Warm pesto accompanying pan-fried chicken makes a deliciously quick meal. Serve with baby carrots and celery, braised in stock in a separate pan while the chicken is cooking. Mashed potato makes the most of the delicious sauce. For a lighter meal, serve the pan-fried chicken with couscous and a salad of baby spinach leaves with lemon dressing.

Serves 4
15ml/1 tbsp olive oil
4 chicken breast portions, skinned
fresh basil leaves, to garnish

For the pesto
90ml/6 tbsp olive oil
50g/2oz/1/2 cup pine nuts
50g/2oz/2/3 cup freshly grated
   Parmesan cheese
50g/2oz/1 cup fresh basil leaves
15g/1/2oz/1/4 cup fresh parsley
2 garlic cloves, crushed
salt and ground black pepper

Preparation: 2–3 minutes; Cooking: 18 minutes

1 Heat the 15ml/1 tbsp oil in a frying pan. Add the chicken breasts and cook gently for about 15 minutes, turning several times with tongs until they are tender, lightly browned and thoroughly cooked.

2 Meanwhile, to make the pesto, place all the ingredients in a food processor and process until smooth and well mixed.

3 Remove the chicken from the pan, cover and keep hot. Reduce the heat slightly, then add the pesto to the pan and cook gently, stirring constantly, for a few minutes, or until the pesto has warmed through.

4 Put the cooked chicken on a warmed platter or individual plates, pour the warm pesto over the top, then garnish with basil leaves and serve immediately.

> **Cook's Tip**
> Save time by using bought pesto instead of fresh, or use a prepared bruschetta topping. An Italian tomato and herb one would be delicious, or try a French onion and garlic blend.

Greek-style Chicken

The sauce for the chicken is based on avogolemono, an exquisite egg and lemon mixture which is one of Greece's gifts to good cooks everywhere. It tastes great with the fennel.

Serves 4
4 skinless chicken breast fillets
plain (all-purpose) flour,
   for dusting
30–45ml/2–3 tbsp olive oil

1–2 onions, chopped
1/4 fennel bulb, chopped (optional)
15ml/1 tbsp chopped fresh
   parsley, plus extra to garnish
7.5ml/1 1/2 tsp fennel seeds
75ml/5 tbsp dry Marsala
120ml/4fl oz/1/2 cup
   chicken stock
300g/11oz/2 1/4 cups petits pois
   (baby peas)
juice of 1 1/2 lemons
2 egg yolks
salt and ground black pepper

Preparation: 3–4 minutes; Cooking: 15 minutes

1 Season the chicken with salt and pepper, then dust generously with flour. Shake off the excess flour; set aside.

2 Heat 15ml/1 tbsp oil in a pan, add the onions, fennel (if using), parsley and fennel seeds. Cook for 3 minutes, then add the remaining oil and the chicken to the pan and cook over a high heat for 5–6 minutes on each side, until lightly browned and cooked through. Remove from the pan and set aside.

3 Deglaze the pan by pouring in the Marsala and cooking over a high heat until reduced to about 30ml/2 tbsp, then pour in the stock. Add the peas and return the chicken and onion mixture to the pan. Cook over a very low heat while you prepare the egg mixture.

4 In a bowl, beat the lemon juice and egg yolks together, then slowly add about 120ml/4fl oz/1/2 cup of the hot liquid from the chicken and peas, stirring well to combine. Return the mixture to the pan and cook over a low heat, stirring, until the mixture thickens slightly. (Do not allow the mixture to boil or the eggs will curdle and spoil the sauce.) Serve the chicken immediately, sprinkled with a little extra chopped fresh parsley.

Pan-fried Chicken Energy 480kcal/1998kJ; Protein 43.2g; Carbohydrate 1g, of which sugars 0.9g; Fat 33.8g, of which saturates 6.4g; Cholesterol 118mg; Calcium 192mg; Fibre 1.1g; Sodium 232mg.
Greek-style Chicken Energy 301kcal/1260kJ; Protein 41.6g; Carbohydrate 10.4g, of which sugars 3.3g; Fat 8.4g, of which saturates 1.5g; Cholesterol 105mg; Calcium 34mg; Fibre 4.3g; Sodium 96mg.

Chicken Stuffed with Ham & Cheese

Breasts of chicken stuffed with smoked ham and Gruyère, coated in egg and breadcrumbs, make a tasty treat few can resist.

Serves 4

4 skinless, boneless chicken breast portions, about 130g/ 4½oz each
4 very thin smoked ham slices, halved and rind removed
about 90g/3½oz Gruyère cheese, thinly sliced
plain (all-purpose) flour, for coating
2 eggs, beaten
75g/3oz/¾ cup natural-coloured dried breadcrumbs
5ml/1 tsp dried thyme
75g/3oz/6 tbsp butter
60ml/4 tbsp olive oil
salt and ground black pepper
mixed leaf salad, to serve

Preparation: 6–8 minutes; Cooking: 10–12 minutes

1 Slit the chicken breasts about three-quarters of the way through, then open them up and lay them flat. Place a slice of ham on each cut side of the chicken, trimming to fit if necessary so that the ham does not hang over the edge.

2 Top with the Gruyère slices, making sure that they are well within the ham slices. Fold over the chicken and reshape, pressing well to seal and ensuring that no cheese is visible.

3 Spoon the flour for coating into a shallow bowl. Pour the beaten eggs into another shallow bowl and mix the breadcrumbs with the thyme and seasoning in a third bowl.

4 Toss each stuffed breast in the flour, then coat in egg and breadcrumbs, shaking off any excess.

5 Place half the butter and half the oil in one pan, and the remaining half measures in the other, and heat separately.

6 When the fat stops foaming, gently slide in the coated breasts, two in each pan. Shallow fry over a low to medium heat for about 5 minutes each side, turning over carefully with a spatula. Drain on kitchen paper for a few seconds to soak up the excess fat. Serve immediately with the mixed leaf salad.

Soy Sauce & Star Anise Chicken

Although the chicken cooks quickly, it does benefit from being marinated first. This only takes a moment and ensures that there is no last-minute work to do when guests arrive.

Serves 4

4 skinless chicken breast portions
2 whole star anise
45ml/3 tbsp olive oil
30ml/2 tbsp soy sauce
ground black pepper

Preparation: 3–4 minutes plus marinating; Cooking: 16 minutes

1 Put the chicken breast fillets in a shallow, non-metallic dish and add the star anise.

2 In a small bowl, whisk together the oil and soy sauce and season with black pepper to make a marinade.

3 Pour the marinade over the chicken and stir to coat each breast fillet all over. Cover the dish with clear film (plastic wrap) and set aside for as much time as you have. If you are able to make it ahead, leave the chicken in the marinade for around 6–8 hours as the flavour will be improved. Place the covered dish in the refrigerator.

4 Cook the chicken under a hot grill (broiler), turning occasionally. It will need about 8 minutes on each side. Place each piece of chicken on a warmed plate and serve immediately.

Variation
If you prefer, cook on a barbecue. When the coals are dusted with ash, spread them out evenly. Remove the chicken breasts from the marinade and cook for 8 minutes on each side, spooning over the marinade from time to time, until the chicken is cooked through. The chicken can also be cooked on top of the stove on a ridged grill (broiler) pan or griddle. Get the pan very hot first, add the chicken and turn the pieces after a few minutes so that they are branded in a criss-cross fashion.

Chicken Stuffed Energy 599kcal/2496kJ; Protein 41.8g; Carbohydrate 14.8g, of which sugars 0.8g; Fat 41.5g, of which saturates 18.4g; Cholesterol 220mg; Calcium 222mg; Fibre 0.4g; Sodium 698mg.
Star Anise Chicken Energy 237kcal/992kJ; Protein 36.2g; Carbohydrate 0.6g, of which sugars 0.6g; Fat 9.9g, of which saturates 1.6g; Cholesterol 105mg; Calcium 9mg; Fibre 0g; Sodium 624mg.

Crumbed Chicken with Caper & Herb Mayonnaise

The contrast between crisp crumb and tender chicken is what makes this so successful. Caper mayonnaise is traditional but mayo flavoured with wasabi would be good too.

Serves 4
4 skinless chicken breast fillets,
    each weighing about 200g/7oz
juice of 1 lemon
5ml/1 tsp paprika
plain (all-purpose) flour,
    for dusting
1–2 eggs
dried breadcrumbs, for coating
about 60ml/4 tbsp olive oil
salt and ground black pepper
lemon wedges (optional),
    to serve

For the mayonnaise
120ml/4fl oz/½ cup mayonnaise
30ml/2 tbsp pickled capers,
    drained and chopped
30ml/2 tbsp chopped fresh
    parsley

Preparation: 4 minutes; Cooking: 12 minutes

1 Skin the chicken fillets. Lay them outside down and, with a sharp knife, cut horizontally, almost through, from the rounded side. Open them up like a book. Press gently, to make a roundish shape the size of a side plate. Sprinkle the surface of the chicken with lemon juice and paprika.

2 Set out three shallow bowls. Sprinkle flour over one, seasoning it well. Beat the egg with a little salt and pour into the second. Sprinkle the third with dried breadcrumbs. Dip the fillets first into the flour on both sides, then into the egg, then into the breadcrumbs to coat them evenly.

3 Put the mayonnaise ingredients in a bowl and mix well.

4 Heat the oil in a heavy frying pan over a high heat. Fry the breast portions two at a time, turning after 3 minutes, until golden on both sides. Add more oil for the second batch if needed. Serve immediately, on individual plates, with the mayonnaise and lemon wedges, if using.

Chicken Salad

This warm salad combines pan-fried chicken, spinach, tomatoes and spring onions with a delicious, light and tasty nutty dressing.

Serves 4
45ml/3 tbsp olive oil
30ml/2 tbsp hazelnut oil
15ml/1 tbsp white wine vinegar
1 garlic clove, crushed
15ml/1 tbsp chopped fresh
    mixed herbs
225g/8oz baby spinach leaves
250g/9oz cherry tomatoes, halved
1 bunch spring onions (scallions),
    chopped
2 chicken breast fillets, skinned
    and cut into thin strips
salt and ground black pepper

Preparation: 8 minutes; Cooking: 10 minutes

1 First make the dressing. Place 30ml/2 tbsp of the olive oil, the hazelnut oil, vinegar, garlic and herbs in a small bowl or jug (pitcher) and whisk together until thoroughly mixed. Set aside.

2 Trim any long stalks from the spinach leaves, then place in a large serving bowl with the tomatoes and spring onions, and toss with two spoons until thoroughly mixed.

3 Heat the remaining 15ml/1 tbsp olive oil in a large frying pan, add the chicken and fry over a high heat for 7–10 minutes, or until cooked through and lightly browned.

4 Scatter the chicken pieces over the salad, give the dressing a quick whisk to blend, then drizzle it over the salad and gently toss all the ingredients together to mix. Season and serve.

Cook's Tip
A battery-operated milk frother is great for making dressings.

Variation
This salad can also be served cold, if you need to make it in advance or have some cooked chicken breast to use up.

Crumbed Chicken Energy 582kcal/2428kJ; Protein 51.5g; Carbohydrate 10.3g, of which sugars 0.8g; Fat 37.6g, of which saturates 6g; Cholesterol 210mg; Calcium 43mg; Fibre 0.5g; Sodium 369mg.
Chicken Salad Energy 292kcal/1218kJ; Protein 20.9g; Carbohydrate 13.8g, of which sugars 10.3g; Fat 17.4g, of which saturates 2.8g; Cholesterol 56mg; Calcium 120mg; Fibre 2.1g; Sodium 163mg.

Chicken & Broccoli

Gorgonzola makes a tangy dressing that goes well with both chicken and broccoli. Serve for a lunch or supper dish, with crusty Italian bread.

Serves 4
175g/6oz broccoli florets, divided into small sprigs
225g/8oz/2 cups fresh farfalle
2 large cooked chicken breast fillets

For the dressing
90g/3½oz Gorgonzola cheese
15ml/1 tbsp white wine vinegar
60ml/4 tbsp extra virgin olive oil
2.5 5ml/½–1tsp finely chopped fresh sage, plus extra sage sprigs to garnish
salt and ground black pepper

Preparation: 8–10 minutes; Cooking: 5–6 minutes

1 Cook the broccoli florets in a large pan of salted boiling water for 3 minutes. Using a slotted spoon, transfer to a colander, rinse under cold running water, then spread out on kitchen towels to drain and dry.

2 Add the pasta to the broccoli cooking water, then bring back to the boil and cook for 2–3 minutes, until *al dente*.

3 When cooked, drain the pasta into a colander, rinse under cold running water until cold, then leave to drain and dry, shaking the colander occasionally.

4 Remove the skin from the cooked chicken breast fillets and cut the meat into bitesize pieces.

5 Make the dressing. Put the cheese in a large bowl and mash with a fork, then whisk in the wine vinegar followed by the oil and sage, and salt and pepper to taste.

6 Add the pasta to the bowl of dressing. Toss to coat all the shapes, then add the chicken and broccoli. Toss again, more gently this time, then season with salt and pepper to taste. Spoon on to a large platter or divide among individual plates, garnish with sage and serve.

Chicken with Basil & Chilli

This quick and easy chicken dish from Thailand owes its spicy flavour to fresh chillies and its pungency to Thai basil, which has a lovely aroma with hints of liquorice.

Serves 4–6
45ml/3 tbsp vegetable oil
4 garlic cloves, thinly sliced
2–4 fresh red chillies, seeded and finely chopped

450g/1lb skinless chicken breast fillets, cut into bitesize pieces
45ml/3 tbsp Thai fish sauce
10ml/2 tsp dark soy sauce
5ml/1 tsp granulated (white) sugar
10–12 fresh Thai basil leaves
2 fresh red chillies, seeded and finely chopped, and about 20 deep-fried Thai basil leaves, to garnish

Preparation: 7–8 minutes; Cooking: 9–11 minutes

1 Heat the oil in a wok or large, heavy frying pan. Add the garlic and chillies and stir-fry over a medium heat for 1–2 minutes until the garlic is golden. Take care not to let the garlic burn, otherwise it will taste bitter.

2 Add the pieces of chicken to the wok or pan, in batches if necessary, and stir-fry until the chicken changes colour.

3 Stir in the fish sauce, soy sauce and sugar. Stir-fry the mixture for 3–4 minutes, until the chicken is cooked and golden brown.

4 Stir in the fresh Thai basil leaves. Spoon the mixture on to a warm platter, or into individual dishes. Garnish with the chopped chillies and deep-fried Thai basil and serve.

Cook's Tip
To deep-fry Thai basil leaves, first make sure that the leaves are completely dry. Heat vegetable or groundnut (peanut) oil in a wok or deep-fryer to 190°C/375°F. Add the leaves and deep-fry them briefly until they are crisp and translucent – this will take only about 30–40 seconds. Lift out the leaves using a slotted spoon or wire basket and leave them to drain on kitchen paper before using.

Chicken and Broccoli Energy 472kcal/1977kJ; Protein 25.3g; Carbohydrate 42.5g, of which sugars 2.5g; Fat 23.5g, of which saturates 6.8g; Cholesterol 52mg; Calcium 151mg; Fibre 2.8g; Sodium 310mg.
Chicken with Basil Energy 138Kcal/576kJ; Protein 18.3g; Carbohydrate 1.9g, of which sugars 1.8g; Fat 6.4g, of which saturates 0.9g; Cholesterol 53mg; Calcium 6mg; Fibre 0.1g; Sodium 579mg.

Chicken with Cashew Nuts

This popular Chinese dish is quick and easy to make and can be enjoyed to the full by using good-quality organic products that are full of flavour.

Serves 4

350g/12oz skinless chicken breast fillets
pinch of ground white pepper
15ml/1 tbsp dry sherry
300ml/½ pint/1¼ cups chicken stock

15ml/1 tbsp sunflower oil
1 garlic clove, finely chopped
1 small carrot, cut into cubes
½ cucumber, about 75g/3oz, cut into 1cm/½in cubes
50g/2oz/½ cup drained canned bamboo shoots, cut into 1cm/½in cubes (optional)
5ml/1 tsp cornflour (cornstarch)
15ml/1 tbsp soy sauce
25g/1oz/¼ cup dry-roasted cashew nuts
2.5ml/½ tsp sesame oil
noodles, to serve

Preparation: 10 minutes; Cooking: 7–8 minutes

1 Cut the chicken into 2cm/¾in cubes. Place the cubes in a bowl, stir in the white pepper and sherry, cover with clear film (plastic wrap) and marinate for 10 minutes.

2 Bring the stock to the boil in a large pan. Add the chicken and cook, stirring, for 3 minutes. Drain, reserving 90ml/6 tbsp of the stock, and set the chicken aside on a plate.

3 Heat the sunflower oil in a large non-stick frying pan until it is very hot, add the finely chopped garlic and stir-fry for a few seconds.

4 Add the cubed carrot and cucumber to the frying pan with the bamboo shoots, if using, and continue to stir-fry the vegetables over a medium heat for 2 minutes.

5 Stir in the chicken and reserved stock. Put the cornflour in a cup or small bowl and stir in the soy sauce. Add the mixture to the pan. Cook, stirring, until the sauce thickens slightly.

6 Finally, add the cashew nuts and sesame oil. Toss to mix thoroughly, then serve with noodles.

Chicken & Lemon Grass Curry

Quick-cook curries work well in a wok, especially if you use an electric one.

chopped roasted peanuts and chopped fresh coriander (cilantro), to garnish

Serves 4

45ml/3 tbsp vegetable oil
2 garlic cloves, crushed
500g/1¼lb skinless chicken thighs, boned and chopped into small pieces
45ml/3 tbsp Thai fish sauce
120ml/4fl oz/½ cup chicken stock
5ml/1 tsp granulated (white) sugar
1 lemon grass stalk, chopped into 4 sticks and lightly crushed
5 kaffir lime leaves, rolled into cylinders and thinly sliced across, plus extra to garnish

For the curry paste

1 lemon grass stalk, coarsely chopped
2.5cm/1in piece fresh galangal, peeled and coarsely chopped
2 kaffir lime leaves, chopped
3 shallots, coarsely chopped
6 coriander (cilantro) roots, coarsely chopped
2 garlic cloves
2 fresh green chillies, seeded and coarsely chopped
5ml/1 tsp shrimp paste
5ml/1 tsp ground turmeric

Preparation: 5 minutes; Cooking: 14 minutes

1 Make the curry paste. Place all the ingredients in a large mortar, or food processor. Pound or process to a paste.

2 Heat the vegetable oil in a wok or large, heavy frying pan, add the garlic and cook over a low heat, stirring frequently, until golden brown. Add the curry paste and stir-fry with the garlic for about 30 seconds more.

3 Add the chicken pieces to the pan and stir until thoroughly coated with the curry paste. Stir in the Thai fish sauce and chicken stock, with the sugar, and cook for 2 minutes more.

4 Add the lemon grass and lime leaves, reduce the heat and simmer for 10 minutes. If the mixture begins to dry out, add a little more stock or water.

5 Spoon the curry into four dishes, garnish with the lime leaves, peanuts and coriander and serve immediately.

Chicken with Cashews Energy 153kcal/645kJ; Protein 22.9g; Carbohydrate 5.1g, of which sugars 2.8g; Fat 4.3g, of which saturates 0.9g; Cholesterol 61mg; Calcium 14mg; Fibre 0.7g; Sodium 342mg.
Chicken Curry Energy 229Kcal/959kJ; Protein 31.3g; Carbohydrate 4.3g, of which sugars 3.4g; Fat 9.7g, of which saturates 1.4g; Cholesterol 94mg; Calcium 32mg; Fibre 0.5g; Sodium 397mg.

Curried Chicken Noodles

Chicken or pork can be used to provide the protein in this tasty dish. It is so quick and easy to prepare and cook, it makes the perfect snack for busy people who find themselves with little spare time.

Serves 2
30ml/2 tbsp vegetable oil
10ml/2 tsp magic paste
1 lemon grass stalk, finely chopped
5ml/1 tsp Thai red curry paste
90g/3½oz skinless chicken breast fillet or pork fillet (tenderloin), sliced into slivers
30ml/2 tbsp light soy sauce
400ml/14fl oz/1⅔ cups coconut milk
2 kaffir lime leaves, rolled into cylinders and thinly sliced
250g/9oz medium egg noodles
90g/3½oz Chinese leaves (Chinese cabbage), shredded
90g/3½oz spinach or watercress (leaves), shredded
juice of 1 lime
small bunch fresh coriander (cilantro), chopped

Preparation: 5 minutes; Cooking: 10 minutes

1 Heat the oil in a wok or large, heavy frying pan. Add the magic paste and lemon grass and stir-fry over a low to medium heat for 4–5 seconds, until they give off their aroma.

2 Stir in the curry paste, then add the chicken or pork. Stir-fry over a medium to high heat for 2 minutes, until the chicken or pork is coated in the paste and seared on all sides.

3 Add the soy sauce, coconut milk and sliced lime leaves. Bring to a simmer, then add the noodles. Simmer for 4 minutes. Add the Chinese leaves and watercress. Stir, then add the lime juice. Spoon into a warmed bowl and sprinkle with coriander.

> **Cook's Tip**
> *Magic paste is a mixture of crushed garlic, coriander (cilantro) root and white pepper. It is extensively used in Thai cooking, and is available in jars from supermarkets and Asian stores.*

Crème Fraîche & Coriander Chicken

This is an any-occasion main course dish that can be turned around in minutes. Be generous with the coriander leaves, as they have a wonderful flavour, and a fragrance all of their own.

Serves 4
6 skinless, boneless chicken thigh portions
60ml/4 tbsp crème fraîche
1 small bunch fresh coriander (cilantro), roughly chopped
15ml/1 tbsp sunflower oil
salt and ground black pepper

Preparation: 8 minutes; Cooking: 8 minutes

1 Using a sharp cook's knife or cleaver, cut each chicken thigh into three or four pieces.

2 Heat the oil in a large frying pan, add the chicken and cook for about 6 minutes, turning occasionally.

3 Add the crème fraîche to the pan and stir until melted, then allow the mixture to bubble for 1–2 minutes.

4 Add the chopped coriander to the chicken and stir to combine. Season with salt and ground black pepper to taste, spoon into a heated dish or onto individual plates and serve immediately.

> **Variations**
> • *Cream cheese can be used instead of crème fraîche. Use the full-fat variety and mix it with a little cream or milk to thin it before adding it to the pan containing the cooked boneless chicken thighs. Stir constantly until it has melted.*
> • *This recipe uses boneless chicken thighs, but boneless breast portions can be used instead. Simply cut into bitesize pieces and cook in the frying pan for 5–6 minutes, until just tender.*

> **Cook's Tip**
> *Make sure the chicken thighs are fully cooked before serving.*

Curried Chicken Energy 702kcal/2965kJ; Protein 28.7g; Carbohydrate 101.6g, of which sugars 14.2g; Fat 23g, of which saturates 4.9g; Cholesterol 69mg; Calcium 187mg; Fibre 4.7g; Sodium 1564mg.
Coriander Chicken Energy 249kcal/1041kJ; Protein 32.1g; Carbohydrate 0.7g, of which sugars 0.6g; Fat 13.1g, of which saturates 5.6g; Cholesterol 174mg; Calcium 44mg; Fibre 0.6g; Sodium 143mg.

Penne with Chicken & Broccoli

Crisp-tender, lightly cooked broccoli gives this dish colour and crunch.

Serves 4
400g/14oz/3½ cups dried penne
115g/4oz/scant 1 cup broccoli
   florets, divided into tiny sprigs
50g/2oz/¼ cup butter
2 chicken breast portions, skinned
   and cut into thin strips
2 garlic cloves, crushed
120ml/4fl oz/½ cup dry
   white wine
200ml/7fl oz/scant 1 cup panna
   da cucina or double
   (heavy) cream
90g/3½oz Gorgonzola cheese,
   rind removed, finely diced
salt and ground black pepper
freshly grated Parmesan cheese,
   to serve

Preparation: 3–4 minutes; Cooking: 12–14 minutes

1 Bring two pans of lightly salted water to the boil. Add the penne to one pan and cook over a medium heat for 10–12 minutes or until tender.

2 Meanwhile, plunge the broccoli into the second pan of salted boiling water. Bring back to the boil and boil for 2 minutes, then drain in a colander and refresh under cold running water. Shake well to remove the surplus water and set aside to drain.

3 While the pasta is cooking, melt the butter in a large frying pan and add the chicken and garlic, with salt and pepper to taste. Stir well. Fry over a medium heat, stirring frequently, for 3 minutes, or until the chicken becomes white.

4 Pour the wine and cream over the chicken mixture in the pan, stir to mix, then simmer, stirring occasionally, for about 5 minutes, or until the sauce has reduced and thickened and the chicken is cooked through.

5 Add the broccoli, increase the heat and toss to heat it through and mix it with the chicken. Taste for seasoning.

6 Drain the pasta and add it to the sauce. Add the Gorgonzola and toss well. Serve in warmed bowls and sprinkle each portion with grated Parmesan.

Chicken Fried Rice

This stir-fry is based on cooked rice, so is ideal for using up yesterday's leftovers. Any rice will do, but jasmine has the best flavour, especially if cooked in coconut milk.

Serves 4
30ml/2 tbsp groundnut (peanut) oil
1 small onion, finely chopped
2 garlic cloves, chopped
2.5cm/1in piece fresh root ginger,
   peeled and grated
225g/8oz skinless chicken breast
   fillets, cut into 1cm/½in dice
450g/1lb/4 cups cold cooked
   white long grain rice
1 red (bell) pepper, seeded
   and sliced
115g/4oz/1 cup drained canned
   whole kernel corn
5ml/1 tsp chilli oil
5ml/1 tsp hot curry powder
2 eggs, beaten
salt
spring onion (scallion) shreds,
   to garnish

Preparation: 4–5 minutes; Cooking: 10–12 minutes

1 Heat the oil in a wok. Add the onion and stir-fry over a medium heat for 1 minute, then add the garlic and ginger and stir-fry for 2 minutes more.

2 Push the onion mixture to the sides of the wok, where it will keep warm but not cook, add the chicken to the centre and stir-fry for 2 minutes. Add the rice and toss well. Stir-fry over a high heat for about 3 minutes more, until the chicken is cooked through.

3 Stir in the sliced red pepper, corn, chilli oil and curry powder, with salt to taste. Toss over the heat for 1 minute. Stir in the beaten eggs and cook for 1 minute more, while the eggs lightly cook. Garnish with the spring onion shreds and serve.

Cook's Tip
If you don't have any cold cooked rice in the refrigerator, you can still make this stir-fry if you have a couple of pouches of instant or express long grain or basmati rice in the cupboard. This type of rice cooks in under 2 minutes. Cool it quickly.

Penne Energy 951kcal/3982kJ; Protein 47.8g; Carbohydrate 80.2g, of which sugars 8.6g; Fat 48.8g, of which saturates 28.5g; Cholesterol 165mg; Calcium 324mg; Fibre 10.2g; Sodium 433mg.
Fried Rice Energy 356kcal/1500kJ; Protein 21g; Carbohydrate 46.4g, of which sugars 6.3g; Fat 10.9g, of which saturates 2.5g; Cholesterol 135mg; Calcium 46mg; Fibre 1.4g; Sodium 150mg.

Spiced Chicken Risotto with Mint

A classic risotto must be stirred for around 20 minutes. This quick version is a good alternative.

Serves 4

250g/9oz skinless chicken breast fillets, diced
3 garlic cloves, chopped
5ml/1 tsp ground turmeric
30–45ml/2–3 tbsp olive oil
2 medium carrots, diced
seeds from 6–8 cardamom pods

500g/1¼ lb/2½ cups long grain rice
250g/9oz tomatoes, chopped
750ml/1¼ pints/3 cups chicken stock

For the lemon and mint relish

3 tomatoes, diced
1 bunch or large handful fresh mint, chopped
5–8 spring onions (scallions), thinly sliced
juice of 2 lemons

Preparation: 3–5 minutes; Cooking: 15–17 minutes

1 Mix the diced chicken with half the garlic and the turmeric. Heat a little of the oil in a pan, add the chicken and fry until the chicken has cooked through thoroughly. Remove from the pan and set aside.

2 Add the remaining oil, garlic and cardamom seeds with the carrots and rice. Stir-fry for 1–2 minutes.

3 Add the tomatoes and chicken stock to the pan and bring to the boil. Cover and simmer for about 10 minutes. Meanwhile, make the relish by mixing all the ingredients in a bowl.

4 When the rice is almost cooked, fork in the chicken and heat through. Serve with the relish.

Variations
• Use the same quantity of pumpkin or butternut squash in place of the carrots.
• To make a vegetarian version, omit the chicken and add a drained 400g/14oz can of chickpeas to the rice just before the end of cooking.

Chicken & Basil Coconut Rice

For this dish, the rice is partially boiled before being simmered with coconut so that it fully absorbs the flavour of the chillies, basil and spices.

Serves 4

350g/12oz/1¾ cups Thai fragrant rice, rinsed
30–45ml/2–3 tbsp groundnut (peanut) oil
1 large onion, finely sliced into rings
1 garlic clove, crushed

1 fresh red chilli, seeded and finely sliced
1 fresh green chilli, seeded and finely sliced
generous handful of basil leaves
3 skinless, boneless chicken breast fillets, about 350g/12oz, finely sliced
5mm/¼in piece of lemon grass, pounded or finely chopped
50g/2oz piece of creamed coconut dissolved in 600ml/ 1 pint/2½ cups boiling water
salt and ground black pepper

Preparation: 3–5 minutes; Cooking: 15–17 minutes

1 Bring a pan of lightly salted water to the boil. Add the rice to the pan and boil for about 6 minutes, until partially cooked. Tip into a colander and drain thoroughly.

2 Meanwhile, heat the oil in a frying pan and fry the onion rings for 5 minutes until golden and crisp. Lift out the rings with a slotted spoon, drain on kitchen paper and set aside.

3 Fry the garlic and chillies in the oil remaining in the pan for 2–3 minutes, then add the basil leaves and fry briefly until they begin to wilt. Remove a few leaves and set them aside for the garnish, then add the chicken slices with the lemon grass and fry for 2–3 minutes until golden.

4 Add the rice. Stir-fry for a few minutes to coat the grains, then pour in the coconut liquid. Cook for 4–5 minutes or until the rice is tender, adding a little more water if necessary.

5 Adjust the seasoning. Pile the rice into a warmed serving dish, scatter with the fried onion rings and basil leaves, and serve immediately.

Spiced Risotto Energy 600kcal/2511kJ; Protein 26g; Carbohydrate 105.9g, of which sugars 5.3g; Fat 7.4g, of which saturates 1.1g; Cholesterol 44mg; Calcium 73mg; Fibre 1.8g; Sodium 55mg.
Chicken Rice Energy 492kcal/2368kJ; Protein 16.1g; Carbohydrate 30.5g, of which sugars 8.7g; Fat 43.7g, of which saturates 18.2g; Cholesterol 95mg; Calcium 187mg; Fibre 8.5g; Sodium 1197mg.

Chicken & Pineapple Rice

This way of presenting rice not only looks spectacular, it also tastes so good that it can easily be served solo.

Serves 4
75g/3oz/¾ cup natural peanuts
1 large pineapple
45ml/3 tbsp groundnut (peanut) or sunflower oil
1 onion, chopped
1 garlic clove, crushed

2 chicken breast fillets, about 225g/8oz, cut into strips
225g/8oz/generous 1 cup Thai fragrant rice, rinsed
600ml/1 pint/2½ cups chicken stock
1 lemon grass stalk, bruised
2 thick slices of ham, cut into julienne strips
1 fresh red chilli, seeded and very finely sliced
salt

Preparation: 0 minutes; Cooking: 13–14 minutes

1 Dry-fry the peanuts by spreading them out in a non-stick frying pan and shaking over a medium heat until golden. When cool, grind one-sixth of them in a coffee or herb mill and chop the remainder.

2 Cut a lengthways slice of pineapple, slicing through the leaves, then cut out the flesh to leave a neat shell. Chop 115g/4oz of the pineapple into cubes, saving the remainder for another dish or for eating as a dessert.

3 Heat the oil in a pan and fry the onion and garlic for 3–4 minutes until soft. Add the chicken strips and stir-fry over a medium heat for a few minutes until evenly brown.

4 Add the rice to the pan. Toss with the chicken mixture for a few minutes, then pour in the stock, with the lemon grass and a little salt. Bring to just below boiling point, then lower the heat, cover the pan and simmer gently for 10 minutes until both the rice and the chicken pieces are tender.

5 Stir the chopped peanuts, the pineapple cubes and the ham into the rice, then spoon the mixture into the pineapple shell. Garnish by sprinkling the ground peanuts and the sliced chilli over the top and serve immediately.

Gingered Duck with Tamari

Duck takes very little time to cook on a griddle and tastes great with a tamari and mirin glaze.

Serves 4
4 large duck breast fillets, total weight about 675g/1½lb
5cm/2in piece fresh root ginger, finely grated

½ large cucumber, peeled
12 Chinese pancakes
6 spring onions (scallions), finely shredded

For the sauce
105ml/7 tbsp tamari
105ml/7 tbsp mirin
25g/1oz/2 tbsp sugar
salt and ground black pepper

Preparation: 4–5 minutes; Cooking: 13 minutes

1 Make four slashes in the skin of each duck breast fillet, then lay them skinside up on a plate. Squeeze the grated ginger over. Rub the juice all over the duck. Cut the cucumber in half, scoop out the seeds and chop the flesh. Set aside.

2 To make the sauce, mix the tamari, mirin and sugar in a heavy pan and heat gently together until the sugar has dissolved. Increase the heat and simmer for 4–5 minutes, or until the sauce has reduced by about one-third and become syrupy.

3 Heat a griddle on the stove over a high heat until a few drops of water sprinkled on to the surface evaporate instantly. Sear the duck breasts, placing them skinside down.

4 When the fat has been rendered, and the skin is nicely browned, remove the duck from the pan. Drain off the fat and wipe the pan clean. Reheat it, return the duck flesh side down, and cook over a medium heat for 3 minutes.

5 Brush on a little of the sauce, turn the duck over, brush the other side with sauce and turn again. This should take about 1 minute, by which time the duck should be cooked rare. Let the duck rest for a few minutes before slicing each breast across at an angle. Meanwhile, wrap the pancakes in foil and warm them in a steamer for about 3 minutes. Serve with the duck, sauce, spring onions and cucumber.

Chicken Rice Energy 124kcal/522kJ; Protein 12.6g; Carbohydrate 12.9g, of which sugars 11g; Fat 2.9g, of which saturates 0.5g; Cholesterol 32mg; Calcium 26mg; Fibre 1.8g; Sodium 32mg.
Gingered Duck Energy 436kcal/1829kJ; Protein 38g; Carbohydrate 23.3g, of which sugars 11g; Fat 21.6g, of which saturates 2.2g; Cholesterol 186mg; Calcium 113mg; Fibre 0.7g; Sodium 1615mg.

Skewered Duck with Poached Eggs

This combination of marinated duck, chanterelle mushrooms and poached eggs is quite delicious, and can easily be prepared within 20 minutes.

Serves 4
3 skinless duck breast fillets, thinly sliced
30ml/2 tbsp soy sauce

30ml/2 tbsp balsamic vinegar
30ml/2 tbsp groundnut (peanut) oil
25g/1oz/2 tbsp unsalted (sweet) butter
1 shallot, finely chopped
115g/4oz/1½ cups chanterelle mushrooms
4 eggs
50g/2oz mixed salad leaves
salt and ground black pepper
extra virgin olive oil, to serve

Preparation: 8 minutes; Cooking: 11 minutes

1 Toss the duck in the soy sauce and balsamic vinegar. Cover and marinate for 8–10 minutes. Soak 12 bamboo skewers in water to help prevent them from burning later.

2 Meanwhile, melt the butter in a frying pan and cook the finely chopped shallot until softened but not coloured. Add the chanterelle mushrooms and cook over a high heat for about 5 minutes, stirring occasionally. Leave the pan over a low heat while you cook the duck.

3 Preheat the grill (broiler). Thread the duck slices on to the skewers, pleating them neatly. Place on a grill pan and drizzle with half the oil. Grill (broil) for 3 minutes, then turn the skewers and drizzle with the remaining oil. Grill for 3 minutes more, or until the duck is cooked.

4 Poach the eggs while the duck is cooking. Half fill a frying pan with water, add salt and heat until simmering. Break the eggs one at a time into a cup before tipping carefully into the water. Poach the eggs gently for about 3 minutes, or until the whites are set. Use a slotted spoon to transfer the eggs to a plate.

5 Arrange the salad leaves on serving plates, then add the chanterelles, duck and poached eggs. Drizzle with olive oil, season and serve.

Stir-fried Duck with Pineapple

The fatty skin on duck makes it ideal for stir-frying: as soon as the duck is added to the hot pan the fat runs, creating delicious crisp skin and tender flesh when cooked.

Serves 4
250g/9oz fresh sesame noodles
2 duck breasts, thinly sliced

3 spring onions (scallions), cut into strips
2 celery sticks, cut into matchstick strips
1 fresh pineapple, peeled, cored and cut into strips
300g/11oz carrots, peppers, beansprouts and cabbage, shredded
90ml/6 tbsp plum sauce

Preparation: 5 minutes; Cooking: 10 minutes

1 Bring a pan of water to the boil and add the noodles. Cook for approximately 3 minutes, then drain and set aside.

2 Meanwhile, heat a wok. Add the duck and stir-fry for 2 minutes, until crisp. Drain off all but 30ml/2 tbsp of the fat. Add the spring onions and celery and stir-fry for 2 minutes. Remove the ingredients from the wok and set aside.

3 Add the pineapple strips and mixed vegetables to the wok and stir-fry for 2 minutes.

4 Add the cooked noodles to the wok with the plum sauce, then replace the duck mixture.

5 Stir-fry the duck mixture for about 2 minutes more, or until the noodles and vegetables are hot and the duck is cooked through. Serve at once.

> **Cook's Tip**
> *Fresh sesame noodles can be bought from large supermarkets – you'll find them in the chiller cabinets alongside fresh pasta. If they aren't available use fresh egg noodles instead and cook according to the instructions on the packet. For extra flavour, add a little sesame oil to the cooking water.*

Skewered Duck Energy 269kcal/1125kJ; Protein 29.3g; Carbohydrate 1.8g, of which sugars 1.3g; Fat 18.2g, of which saturates 6.3g; Cholesterol 327mg; Calcium 53mg; Fibre 0.7g; Sodium 412mg.
Stir-fried Duck Energy 455Kcal/1927kJ; Protein 28.3g; Carbohydrate 69g, of which sugars 22.6g; Fat 11g, of which saturates 1.4g; Cholesterol 110mg; Calcium 81mg; Fibre 5.7g; Sodium 143mg.

Duck & Sesame Stir-fry

For a special family meal that is a guaranteed success, this is ideal. It tastes fantastic and cooks fast, so you'll be eating in no time.

Serves 4
250g/9oz boneless duck meat
15ml/1 tbsp sesame oil
15ml/1 tbsp vegetable oil

4 garlic cloves, finely sliced
2.5ml/½ tsp dried chilli flakes
15ml/1 tbsp Thai fish sauce
15ml/1 tbsp light soy sauce
120ml/4fl oz/½ cup water
1 head broccoli, cut into
  small florets
coriander (cilantro) and 15ml/
  1 tbsp toasted sesame seeds,
  to garnish

Preparation: 3 minutes; Cooking: 5–7 minutes

1 Cut all the duck meat into bitesize pieces. Heat the oils in a wok or large, heavy frying pan and stir-fry the garlic over a medium heat until it is golden brown – do not let it burn. Add the duck to the pan and stir-fry for a further 2 minutes, until the meat begins to brown.

2 Stir in the chilli flakes, fish sauce, soy sauce and water. Add the broccoli and continue to stir-fry for about 2 minutes, until the duck is just cooked through.

3 Serve on warmed plates, garnished with coriander and the toasted sesame seeds.

Cook's Tip
Broccoli has excited interest recently since it is claimed that eating this dark green vegetable regularly can help to reduce the risk of some cancers. Broccoli is a source of protein, calcium, iron and magnesium, as well as vitamins A and C.

Variation
Pak choi (bok choy) or Chinese flowering cabbage can be used instead of broccoli.

Chinese Duck Curry

The duck is best marinated for as long as possible, although it tastes good even if you only have time to marinate it briefly.

Serves 4
4 duck breast portions, skin and
  bones removed
30ml/2 tbsp five-spice powder
30ml/2 tbsp sesame oil
grated rind and juice of 1 orange

1 medium butternut squash,
  peeled and cubed
10ml/2 tsp Thai red curry paste
30ml/2 tbsp Thai fish sauce
15ml/1 tbsp palm sugar or light
  muscovado (brown) sugar
300ml/½ pint/1¼ cups
  coconut milk
2 fresh red chillies, seeded
4 kaffir lime leaves, torn
small bunch coriander (cilantro),
  chopped, to garnish

Preparation: 3 minutes plus marinating; Cooking: 17 minutes

1 Cut the duck meat into bitesize pieces and place in a bowl with the five-spice powder, sesame oil and orange rind and juice. Stir well to mix all the ingredients and coat the duck in the marinade. Cover and marinate for at least 10 minutes.

2 Meanwhile, cook the squash in boiling water for 10 minutes, until just tender. Drain and set aside.

3 Pour the marinade from the duck into a wok and heat until boiling. Stir in the curry paste and cook for 1 minute, until well blended and fragrant. Add the duck and cook for 3 minutes, stirring constantly, until browned on all sides.

4 Add the fish sauce and palm sugar and cook for 1 minute more. Stir in the coconut milk until the mixture is smooth, then add the cooked squash, with the chillies and lime leaves. Simmer gently, stirring frequently, for 2 minutes, then spoon into a dish, sprinkle with the coriander and serve.

Cook's Tip
Save time by buying prepared butternut in bags from the supermarket. Small cubes are best, since they cook quickly.

Duck Stir-fry Energy 165kcal/686kJ; Protein 17.4g; Carbohydrate 2.3g, of which sugars 2g; Fat 10.6g, of which saturates 1.8g; Cholesterol 69mg; Calcium 72mg; Fibre 2.9g; Sodium 345mg.
Duck Curry Energy 295kcal/1241kJ; Protein 31.4g; Carbohydrate 13.3g, of which sugars 10g; Fat 10.5g, of which saturates 2.3g; Cholesterol 165mg; Calcium 65mg; Fibre 1.8g; Sodium 546mg.

Jungle Curry of Guinea Fowl

This is a traditional wild food country curry from the north-central region of Thailand.

Serves 4
1 guinea fowl or similar game bird
15ml/1 tbsp vegetable oil
10ml/2 tsp green curry paste
15ml/1 tbsp Thai fish sauce
2.5cm/1in piece fresh galangal, peeled and finely chopped
15ml/1 tbsp fresh green peppercorns
3 kaffir lime leaves, torn
15ml/1 tbsp whisky, preferably Mekhong
300ml/½ pint/1¼ cups chicken stock
50g/2oz snake beans or yard-long beans, cut into 2.5cm/1in lengths (about ½ cup)
225g/8oz/3¼ cups chestnut mushrooms, sliced
1 piece drained canned bamboo shoot, about 50g/2oz, shredded
5ml/1 tsp dried chilli flakes, to garnish (optional)

Preparation: 7 minutes; Cooking: 6–7 minutes

1 Cut up the guinea fowl, remove and discard the skin, then take all the meat off the bones. Chop the meat into bitesize pieces and set aside.

2 Heat the oil in a wok or frying pan and add the curry paste. Stir-fry over a medium heat for 30 seconds, until the paste gives off its aroma.

3 Add the fish sauce and the guinea fowl meat and stir-fry until the meat is browned all over. Add the galangal, peppercorns, lime leaves and whisky, then pour in the stock.

4 Bring to the boil. Add the vegetables, return to a simmer and cook gently for 2–3 minutes, until they are just cooked. Spoon into a dish, sprinkle with chilli flakes, if you like, and serve.

> **Cook's Tip**
> Fresh green peppercorns are simply unripe berries. They are sold on the stem and look rather like miniature Brussels sprout stalks. Look for them at Thai supermarkets.

Spiced Quail with Mixed Leaf & Mushroom Salad

Quail is at its best when the breast meat is removed from the carcass, so that it cooks quickly and can be served rare.

Serves 4
8 quail breasts
50g/2oz/¼ cup butter
5ml/1 tsp paprika
salt and ground black pepper

For the salad
60ml/4 tbsp walnut oil
30ml/2 tbsp olive oil
45ml/3 tbsp balsamic vinegar
25g/1oz/2 tbsp butter
75g/3oz/generous 1 cup chanterelle mushrooms, sliced if large
25g/1oz/3 tbsp walnut halves, toasted
115g/4oz mixed salad leaves

Preparation: 5 minutes; Cooking: 9 minutes

1 Preheat the grill (broiler). Arrange the quail breasts on the grill rack, skin sides up. Dot with half the butter and sprinkle with half the paprika and a little salt.

2 Grill (broil) the quail breasts for 3 minutes, then turn them over and dot with the remaining butter, then sprinkle with the remaining paprika and a little salt.

3 Grill for a further 3 minutes, or until cooked. Transfer the quail breasts to a warmed dish, cover and leave them to stand while you prepare the salad.

4 Make the dressing first. Whisk the oils with the balsamic vinegar, then season and set aside. Heat the butter in a medium pan until foaming and cook the chanterelles for about 3 minutes, or until just beginning to soften. Add the walnuts and heat through. Remove the pan from the heat.

5 Thinly slice the cooked quail breasts and arrange them on four individual serving plates with the warmed chanterelle mushrooms and walnuts and mixed salad leaves. Drizzle about half the oil and vinegar dressing over the salad and serve warm, with the remaining dressing served separately.

Guinea Fowl Energy 321kcal/1345kJ; Protein 42.2g; Carbohydrate 1.1g, of which sugars 0.7g; Fat 50.4g, of which saturates 12.8g; Cholesterol 240mg; Calcium 91mg; Fibre 1.5g; Sodium 305mg.
Quail Energy 443kcal/1837kJ; Protein 25.6g; Carbohydrate 0.9g, of which sugars 0.8g; Fat 37.5g, of which saturates 12.3g; Cholesterol 110mg; Calcium 24mg; Fibre 0.7g; Sodium 176mg.

Chilli Cheese Tortilla with Fresh Tomato & Coriander Salsa

Good warm or cold, this is like a sliced potato quiche without the pastry base, and is well spiked with chilli. It makes a satisfying lunch.

Serves 4
45ml/3 tbsp sunflower or olive oil
1 small onion, thinly sliced
2–3 fresh green jalapeño chillies, seeded and sliced
200g/7oz cold cooked potato, thinly sliced
150g/5oz/1¼ cups grated Cheddar cheese

6 eggs, beaten
salt and ground black pepper
fresh herbs and chilli, to garnish

For the salsa
500g/1¼lb fresh, flavoursome tomatoes, peeled, seeded and finely chopped
1 fresh mild green chilli, seeded and finely chopped
2 garlic cloves, crushed
45ml/3 tbsp chopped fresh coriander (cilantro)
juice of 1 lime
2.5ml/½ tsp salt

Preparation: 6–7 minutes; Cooking: 12 minutes

1 Make the salsa by mixing all the ingredients in a bowl. Mix well, cover and set aside.

2 Heat 15ml/1 tbsp of the oil in a large frying pan and gently fry the onion and jalapeños for 5 minutes, stirring until softened. Add the potato and cook for 5 minutes until lightly browned, keeping the slices whole. Using a slotted spoon, transfer the vegetables to a warm plate.

3 Wipe the pan with kitchen paper, then add the remaining oil and heat until really hot. Return the vegetables to the pan. Sprinkle the cheese over the top and season.

4 Pour in the beaten egg, making sure that it seeps under the vegetables. Cook over a low heat, stirring, until set.

5 Serve the chilli cheese tortilla hot or cold. It looks good cut in wedges and piled up on the plate, with the salsa alongside. Garnish with fresh herbs and chilli.

Frittata with Leeks & Red Pepper

Similar to a quiche, but without the crust, this frittata incorporates a mixture of lightly spiced vegetables in an egg custard.

Serves 3–4
30ml/2 tbsp olive oil
1 large red (bell) pepper, seeded and diced
2.5–5ml/½–1 tsp ground toasted cumin

3 leeks, about 450g/1lb, thinly sliced
150g/5oz small spinach leaves
45ml/3 tbsp pine nuts, toasted
5 large (US extra large) eggs
15ml/1 tbsp chopped fresh basil
15ml/1 tbsp chopped fresh flat leaf parsley
salt and ground black pepper
watercress, to garnish
50g/2oz Parmesan cheese, grated, to serve

Preparation: 5 minutes; Cooking: 14 minutes

1 Heat a frying pan and add the oil. Add the red pepper and cook over a medium heat, stirring occasionally, for 3–4 minutes, until soft and beginning to brown. Add 2.5ml/½ tsp of the cumin and cook for another 1–2 minutes.

2 Stir in the leeks, then part-cover the pan and cook gently for about 5 minutes, until the leeks have softened and collapsed. Season with salt and ground black pepper.

3 Add the spinach. Cover the pan and leave the spinach to wilt in the steam for 2 minutes, then stir to mix it into the vegetables. Add the pine nuts and stir to mix well.

4 Preheat the grill (broiler). Beat the eggs with salt, pepper, the remaining cumin, basil and parsley. Add to the pan and cook over a gentle heat until the bottom of the omelette sets and turns golden brown. Pull the edges of the omelette away from the sides of the pan as it cooks and tilt the pan so that the uncooked egg runs underneath.

5 Flash the frittata under the hot grill to set the egg on top, but do not let it become too brown. Cut the frittata into wedges and serve warm, garnished with watercress and sprinkled with grated Parmesan.

Tortilla Energy 375kcal/1563kJ; Protein 19.3g; Carbohydrate 13.5g, of which sugars 5.7g; Fat 27.1g, of which saturates 10g; Cholesterol 315mg; Calcium 305mg; Fibre 2.6g; Sodium 589mg.
Frittata Energy 323kcal/1342kJ; Protein 17.6g; Carbohydrate 7.1g, of which sugars 6.2g; Fat 25.3g, of which saturates 6g; Cholesterol 250mg; Calcium 281mg; Fibre 4.2g; Sodium 280mg.

Pea & Mint Omelette

Serve this deliciously light omelette with crusty bread and a green salad for a fresh lunch. When they are in season, use freshly shelled peas instead of frozen ones.

Serves 2
50g/2oz/¹/₂ cup frozen peas
4 eggs
30ml/2 tbsp chopped fresh mint
a knob (pat) of butter
salt and ground black pepper

Preparation: 2 minutes; Cooking: 8–10 minutes

1 Break the eggs into a large bowl and mix with a fork until just combined; do not beat. Season well with salt and pepper and set aside.

2 Bring a large pan of salted water to the boil over high heat. Add the peas and cook them for 3–4 minutes until tender.

3 Drain well in a colander and add to the eggs in the bowl. Stir in the chopped fresh mint and swirl with a spoon until thoroughly combined.

4 Heat the butter in a medium frying pan until foamy. Pour in the egg mixture and cook over a medium heat for 3–4 minutes, drawing in the cooked egg from the edges from time to time, until the mixture is set underneath, but remains slightly moist on the surface of the omelette.

5 Finish off cooking the omelette under a hot grill (broiler) until set and golden. Carefully fold the omelette over, cut it in half and serve immediately.

> **Variation**
> *When young broad (fava) beans are in season, use them instead of peas. Shell the beans and cook them in boiling salted water for 3–4 minutes until just tender. Meanwhile, grill (broil) 3–4 rashers (strips) of bacon. Add the beans to the egg mixture instead of the peas and crumble the bacon over the omelette when it is almost cooked.*

Spicy Omelette

The accusation that egg dishes can be a bit bland could never be levelled at this spicy, vegetable-rich dish. It comes from India, where it is often served for breakfast.

Serves 4–6
30ml/2 tbsp vegetable oil
1 onion, finely chopped
2.5ml/¹/₂ tsp ground cumin
1 garlic clove, crushed

1 or 2 fresh green chillies, finely chopped
a few coriander (cilantro) sprigs, chopped, plus extra, to garnish
1 firm tomato, chopped
1 small potato, cubed and boiled
25g/1oz/¹/₄ cup cooked peas
25g/1oz/¹/₄ cup cooked corn, or drained canned corn
2 eggs, beaten
25g/1oz/¹/₄ cup grated Cheddar or Red Leicester cheese
salt and ground black pepper

Preparation: 6–7 minutes; Cooking: 10 minutes

1 Heat the vegetable oil in a wok or large frying pan, and fry the onion, cumin, garlic, chillies, chopped coriander, tomato, potato cubes and corn for 2–3 minutes until the ingredients are well blended but the potato and tomato are still firm. Season with salt and ground black pepper.

2 Increase the heat and pour in the beaten eggs. Reduce the heat, cover and cook until the bottom of the omelette is golden brown.

3 Sprinkle the omelette with the grated cheese. Place under a hot grill (broiler) and cook until the egg sets completely and the cheese on the surface has melted.

4 Slide the omelette onto a plate. Cut in wedges and place on a serving plate. Garnish with sprigs of coriander and serve with salad for a light lunch or supper.

> **Variation**
> *You can use any vegetable with the potatoes. Try adding thickly sliced mushrooms instead of the corn.*

Pea Omelette Energy 208kcal/865kJ; Protein 14.6g; Carbohydrate 3.3g, of which sugars 0.6g; Fat 15.7g, of which saturates 5.8g; Cholesterol 391mg; Calcium 79mg; Fibre 1.2g; Sodium 172mg.
Spicy Omelette Energy 93kcal/388kJ; Protein 4g; Carbohydrate 3.7g, of which sugars 1.2g; Fat 7.1g, of which saturates 1.9g; Cholesterol 67mg; Calcium 46mg; Fibre 0.6g; Sodium 104mg.

Soufflé Omelette with Mushrooms

A soufflé omelette makes an ideal meal for one, especially with this delicious filling, but be warned – when others smell it cooking they are likely to demand their share.

Serves 1
2 eggs, separated
15g/½oz/1 tbsp butter
flat leaf parsley or coriander
    (cilantro) leaves, to garnish

For the mushroom sauce
15g/½oz/1 tbsp butter
75g/3oz/generous 1 cup button
    (white) mushrooms,
    thinly sliced
15ml/1 tbsp plain
    (all-purpose) flour
85–120ml/3–4fl oz/⅓–½ cup
    semi-skimmed (low-fat) milk
5ml/1 tsp chopped fresh parsley
salt and ground black pepper

Preparation: 5 minutes; Cooking: 13–15 minutes

1 To make the mushroom sauce, melt the butter in a pan or frying pan and add the sliced mushrooms. Fry gently for 4–5 minutes, stirring occasionally. The mushrooms will exude quite a lot of liquid, but this will rapidly be reabsorbed.

2 Stir in the flour, then gradually add the milk, stirring all the time. Cook until the sauce boils and thickens. Add the parsley, if using, and season with salt and pepper. Keep warm.

3 Make the omelette. Beat the egg yolks with 15ml/1 tbsp water and season with a little salt and pepper. Whisk the egg whites until stiff, then fold into the egg yolks. Preheat the grill (broiler) for at least 3 minutes.

4 Meanwhile, melt the butter in a large frying pan. Pour in the egg mixture. Cook over a gentle heat for 2–4 minutes.

5 Place the frying pan under the grill and cook for a further 3–4 minutes until the top of the omelette has puffed up and has turned a golden brown colour.

6 Slide the omelette on to a warmed serving plate, pour the mushroom sauce over the top and fold the omelette in half. Serve, garnished with parsley.

Mexican Tortilla Parcels

Seeded green chillies add just a flicker of fire to the spicy tomato filling in these parcels, which are perfect as a main course or snack.

Serves 4
675g/1½lb tomatoes
60ml/4 tbsp sunflower oil
1 large onion, finely sliced
1 garlic clove, crushed
10ml/2 tsp cumin seeds
2 fresh green chillies, seeded
    and chopped
30ml/2 tbsp tomato purée
    (paste)
1 vegetable stock (bouillon) cube
200g/7oz can corn, drained
15ml/1 tbsp chopped fresh
    coriander (cilantro)
115g/4oz/1 cup grated
    Cheddar cheese
8 wheat tortillas
fresh coriander (cilantro),
    shredded lettuce and sour
    cream, to serve

Preparation: 5 minutes; Cooking: 14 minutes

1 Peel the tomatoes: place them in a heatproof bowl, add boiling water to cover and leave for 30 seconds. Lift out with a slotted spoon and plunge into a bowl of cold water. Leave for 1 minute, then drain. Slip the skins off the tomatoes and chop.

2 Heat half the oil in a frying pan and fry the onion with the garlic and cumin seeds for 5 minutes, until the onion softens. Add the chillies and tomatoes, then stir in the tomato purée. Crumble the stock cube over, stir well and cook gently for 5 minutes, until the chilli is soft but the tomato has not completely broken down. Stir in the corn and fresh coriander and heat gently to warm through. Keep warm.

3 Sprinkle grated cheese in the middle of each tortilla. Spoon some tomato mixture over the cheese. Fold over one edge of the tortilla, then the sides and finally the remaining edge, to enclose the filling completely.

4 Heat the remaining oil in a frying pan and fry the filled tortillas for 1–2 minutes on each side until golden and crisp. Lift them out carefully with tongs and drain on kitchen paper. Serve immediately, with coriander, shredded lettuce and sour cream.

Soufflé Omelette Energy 838kcal/3514kJ; Protein 45.5g; Carbohydrate 53.7g, of which sugars 42.1g; Fat 51.4g, of which saturates 28.3g; Cholesterol 497mg; Calcium 1150mg; Fibre 1.3g; Sodium 707mg.
Tortilla Parcels Energy 576kcal/2424kJ; Protein 17.5g; Carbohydrate 79.3g, of which sugars 12.2g; Fat 22.5g, of which saturates 7.8g; Cholesterol 28mg; Calcium 339mg; Fibre 5g; Sodium 656mg.

Vegetable & Egg Noodle Ribbons

Serve this elegant, colourful dish with a tossed green salad as a light lunch. Use fresh pasta noodles for optimum speed and maximum flavour.

Serves 4
1 large carrot, peeled
2 courgettes (zucchini)
50g/2oz/¼ cup butter
15ml/1 tbsp olive oil

6 fresh shiitake mushrooms, finely sliced
50g/2oz/½ cup frozen peas, thawed
350g/12oz fresh broad egg ribbon noodles
10ml/2 tsp chopped fresh mixed herbs, such as marjoram, chives and basil
salt and ground black pepper
25g/1oz Parmesan cheese, to serve (optional)

Preparation: 3 minutes; Cooking: 7 minutes

1 Using a vegetable peeler, carefully slice thin strips from the carrot and the courgettes.

2 Heat the butter with the olive oil in a large frying pan. Stir in the carrots and shiitake mushrooms; fry for 2 minutes. Add the courgettes and peas and stir-fry until the courgettes are cooked, but still crisp. Season with salt and pepper.

3 Meanwhile, cook the noodles in a large pan of boiling water until just tender. Drain the noodles well and tip them into a bowl. Add the vegetables and toss gently to mix.

4 Sprinkle over the fresh herbs and season to taste. If using the Parmesan cheese, grate or shave it over the top. Toss lightly and serve in the large bowl or in individual pasta bowls.

> **Variation**
> When fresh young green peas are in season, use them instead of the frozen peas. Their flavour is incomparable and they need very little cooking. To obtain 50g/2oz podded peas you will need to buy at least double that weight in pods. Mangetouts (snow peas) would also taste good in this noodle dish.

Sesame-tossed Asparagus with Noodles

Tender asparagus spears tossed with sesame seeds and served on a bed of crispy, deep-fried noodles makes a lovely dish for casual entertaining.

Serves 4
15ml/1 tbsp sunflower oil
350g/12oz thin asparagus spears, trimmed
5ml/1 tsp salt
5ml/1 tsp ground black pepper
5ml/1 tsp golden caster (superfine) sugar

30ml/2 tbsp Chinese cooking wine or sherry
45ml/3 tbsp light soy sauce
60ml/4 tbsp vegetarian oyster sauce
10ml/2 tsp sesame oil
60ml/4 tbsp toasted sesame seeds

For the noodles
50g/2oz dried bean thread noodles or thin rice noodles
sunflower oil, for frying

Preparation: 2–3 minutes; Cooking: 7–8 minutes

1 First make the crispy noodles. Fill a wok one-third full of oil and heat to 180°C/350°F (or until a cube of bread, dropped into the oil, browns in 15 seconds). Add the noodles, small bunches at a time, to the oil; they will crisp and puff up in seconds. Using a slotted spoon, remove from the wok and drain on kitchen paper. Set aside.

2 Heat a clean wok over a high heat and add the sunflower oil. Add the asparagus and stir-fry for 3 minutes.

3 Put four bowls to warm so that they are ready for serving.

4 Add the salt, pepper, sugar and wine or sherry to the wok with the soy sauce and oyster sauce. Stir-fry for 2–3 minutes. Add the sesame oil, toss and remove from the heat.

5 To serve, divide the crispy noodles between four warmed plates or bowls and top with the asparagus and juices. Sprinkle over the toasted sesame seeds and serve immediately.

Vegetable Ribbons Energy 500kcal/2100kJ; Protein 13.9g; Carbohydrate 68.1g, of which sugars 5.6g; Fat 21g, of which saturates 9.1g; Cholesterol 53mg; Calcium 62mg; Fibre 4.9g; Sodium 242mg.
Asparagus with Noodles Energy 131kcal/547kJ; Protein 4.6g; Carbohydrate 16.5g, of which sugars 6.9g; Fat 5.6g, of which saturates 0.6g; Cholesterol 0mg; Calcium 31mg; Fibre 2g; Sodium 1047mg.

Fried Bananas with Egg & Tomato Rice

Arroz a la cubana, garnished with fried eggs and bananas, is popular in the Canary Islands and Catalonia. It makes an easy and substantial supper dish.

Serves 4
850ml/28fl oz/3½ cups water
2 whole and 1 chopped
    garlic cloves
120ml/4fl oz/½ cup olive oil
300g/11oz/1½ cups long
    grain rice

15g/½ oz/1 tbsp butter
4 small bananas or 2 large
    bananas, halved lengthways
4 large (US extra large) eggs
salt and paprika

For the tomato sauce
30ml/2 tbsp olive oil
1 onion, chopped
2 garlic cloves, finely chopped
2 x 400g/14oz cans tomatoes
4 thyme or oregano sprigs
ground black pepper

Preparation: 4 minutes; Cooking: 16 minutes

1 Put the measured water in a pan with the two whole garlic cloves and 15ml/1 tbsp of the oil. Bring to the boil, add the rice and cook for 10 minutes until the rice is cooked and the liquid has been absorbed.

2 Meanwhile, make the tomato sauce. Heat the oil in a pan, add the onion and garlic and fry gently, stirring, until soft. Stir in the tomatoes and herb sprigs and simmer for 5 minutes. Season to taste. Remove the herb sprigs and keep the sauce warm.

3 Heat a pan with 30ml/2 tbsp of the oil and gently fry the chopped garlic clove. Tip in the rice, stir, season well, then turn off the heat and cover the pan.

4 Heat the butter in a frying pan with 15ml/1 tbsp of the oil. Fry the bananas briefly on both sides. Keep them warm.

5 Add the remaining oil to the pan and fry the eggs. Season with salt and paprika. Serve with the rice, tomato sauce and fried bananas.

Ensaladilla

Also known as Russian salad, this mixture of cooked and raw vegetables in a rich garlic mayonnaise makes a useful vegetarian dish.

Serves 4
8 new potatoes, scrubbed
    and quartered
1 large carrot, diced
115g/4oz fine green beans,
    cut into 2cm/¾in lengths
75g/3oz/¾ cup peas
½ Spanish (Bermuda) onion,
    chopped
4 cornichons or small
    gherkins, sliced

1 small red (bell) pepper, seeded
    and diced
50g/2oz/½ cup pitted black
    olives
15ml/1 tbsp drained
    pickled capers
15ml/1 tbsp freshly squeezed
    lemon juice
30ml/2 tbsp chopped fresh fennel
    or parsley
salt and ground black pepper

For the aioli
2–3 garlic cloves, finely chopped
2.5ml/½ tsp salt
150ml/¼ pint/⅔ cup
    mayonnaise

Preparation: 10 minutes; Cooking: 8 minutes

1 Make the aioli. Put two or three garlic cloves, depending on their size, in a mortar. Add the salt and crush to a paste. Whisk or stir into the mayonnaise.

2 Cook the potatoes and diced carrot in a pan of boiling lightly salted water for 5 minutes, until almost tender.

3 Add the beans and peas to the potatoes and carrot and cook for 2 minutes, or until all the vegetables are tender but the beans still retain some crunch. Drain and transfer to a bowl of iced water to cool quickly.

4 Drain the vegetables, place them in a large bowl and add the onion, cornichons or gherkins, red pepper, olives and capers. Stir in the aioli and pepper and lemon juice to taste.

5 Toss the vegetables and aioli together until well combined, check the seasoning and chill well. Serve garnished with fennel or parsley.

Fried Bananas Energy 725kcal/3071kJ; Protein 11.5g; Carbohydrate 88.2g, of which sugars 25.9g; Fat 35.4g, of which saturates 7.5g; Cholesterol 198mg; Calcium 67mg; Fibre 3.2g; Sodium 112mg.
Ensaladilla Energy 395kcal/1636kJ; Protein 5.2g; Carbohydrate 25.6g, of which sugars 8.1g; Fat 30.9g, of which saturates 4.8g; Cholesterol 28mg; Calcium 68mg; Fibre 4.9g; Sodium 472mg.

Nutty Spinach with Spring Onions

Lightly cooked spinach with a little onion, olive oil, raisins and pine nuts is a typical Italian-Jewish combination. It makes a tasty and quick-to-prepare supper dish that the whole family will enjoy. This would also make a good accompaniment.

Serves 4
60ml/4 tbsp raisins
1kg/2¼ lb fresh spinach
   leaves, washed
45ml/3 tbsp olive oil
6–8 spring onions (scallions),
   thinly sliced or 1–2 small yellow
   or white onions, finely chopped
60ml/4 tbsp pine nuts
salt and ground black pepper

Preparation: 4 minutes; Cooking: 10 minutes

1 Put the raisins in a small bowl and pour over boiling water to cover. Cover the bowl and stand for about 10 minutes until the raisins have plumped up, then drain.

2 Meanwhile, steam or cook the spinach in a very large pan over a medium to high heat, with only the water that clings to the leaves after washing, for 1–2 minutes until the leaves are bright green and wilted. Remove from the heat, tip into a colander and drain well. Leave to cool.

3 When the spinach has cooled, put it on a board and chop it roughly with a sharp knife.

4 Heat the oil in a frying pan over a low to medium heat, then lower the heat further and add the spring onions or onions. Fry for about 5 minutes, or until soft.

5 Add the spinach, raisins and pine nuts. Raise the heat and cook for 2–3 minutes to warm through. Season with salt and ground black pepper to taste and serve hot or warm.

Cook's Tip
Pine nuts can turn rancid quickly, so always buy them in small quantities. Freeze any leftover amounts for use in later dishes.

Sweet Peppers Stuffed with Two Cheeses

This is a delicious barbecue starter to cook before the grill tastes too strongly of meat. Alternatively, use a disposable barbecue.

Serves 4
4 sweet romano peppers,
   preferably in mixed colours,
   total weight about 350g/12oz
90ml/6 tbsp extra virgin olive oil
200g/7oz mozzarella cheese
10 drained bottled sweet cherry
   peppers, finely chopped
115g/4oz ricotta salata
30ml/2 tbsp chopped fresh
   oregano leaves
24 black olives
2 garlic cloves, crushed
salt and ground black pepper
dressed mixed salad leaves and
   bread, to serve

Preparation: 5 minutes; Cooking: 12–14 minutes

1 Prepare a barbecue. Split the peppers lengthways and remove the seeds and membrane. Rub 15ml/1 tbsp of the oil all over the peppers. Place them hollow side uppermost. Slice the mozzarella and divide it among the pepper halves.

2 Sprinkle over the chopped cherry peppers, season lightly and crumble the ricotta salata over the top, followed by the oregano leaves and olives. Mix the garlic with the remaining oil and add a little salt and pepper. Spoon about half the mixture over the filling in the peppers.

3 Once the flames have died down, rake the coals to one side. Position a lightly oiled grill (broiler) rack over the coals to heat. When the coals are medium to hot, or with a moderate coating of ash, place the filled peppers on the section of grill rack that is not over the coals.

4 Cover with a lid, or improvise with a wok lid or tented heavy-duty foil. Cook for 6 minutes, then spoon the remaining oil mixture over the filling, replace the lid and continue to grill (broil) for 6–8 minutes more, or until the peppers are lightly charred and the cheese has melted. Serve with a dressed green or leafy salad and bread.

Spinach Energy 271kcal/1119kJ; Protein 9.6g; Carbohydrate 12g, of which sugars 11.7g; Fat 20.7g, of which saturates 2.1g; Cholesterol 0mg; Calcium 437mg; Fibre 6g; Sodium 357mg.
Sweet Peppers Energy 371kcal/1532kJ; Protein 13.1g; Carbohydrate 6.6g, of which sugars 6.3g; Fat 32.6g, of which saturates 12.2g; Cholesterol 41mg; Calcium 203mg; Fibre 2g; Sodium 484mg.

Stuffed Sweet Peppers

This is an unusual recipe in that the stuffed peppers are steamed rather than baked. The technique is speedy and the result is beautifully light and tender.

Serves 4
3 garlic cloves, finely chopped
2 coriander (cilantro) roots, finely chopped
400g/14oz/3 cups button (white) or field (portabello) mushrooms, quartered
5ml/1 tsp Thai red curry paste
1 egg, lightly beaten
15–30ml/1–2 tbsp light soy sauce
2.5ml/½ tsp sugar
3 kaffir lime leaves, finely chopped
4 yellow (bell) peppers, halved lengthways and seeded

Preparation: 5 minutes; Cooking: 15 minutes

1 In a mortar or spice grinder pound or blend the garlic with the coriander roots. Scrape into a bowl.

2 Put the mushrooms in a food processor and pulse briefly until they are finely chopped. Add to the garlic mixture in the bowl, then stir in the curry paste, egg, soy sauce, sugar and lime leaves until thoroughly mixed.

3 Place the pepper halves in a single layer in a steamer basket. Spoon the mixture loosely into the pepper halves.

4 Bring the water in the steamer to the boil, then lower the heat to a simmer. Steam the peppers for 15 minutes, or until the flesh feels tender when tested with a knife tip.

5 Lift out the pepper halves, taking care not to disturb the filling, and place them on a serving platter. They can be eaten hot, at room temperature or cold.

> **Variation**
> Use red, orange or even green (bell) peppers if you prefer, or a combination. This recipe can easily be doubled or trebled to serve more guests.

Mixed Bean & Tomato Chilli

The only talent this dish requires of the cook is the ability to open a can, chop a chilli and stir a sauce. It's ideal for those days when your energy levels are zero and you need food fast to restore your vitality.

Serves 4
400g/14oz jar tomato and herb sauce
2 x 400g/14oz cans mixed beans, drained and rinsed
1 fresh red chilli
large handful of fresh coriander (cilantro), finely chopped
120ml/4fl oz/½ cup sour cream

Preparation: 2–3 minutes; Cooking: 12 minutes

1 Seed and thinly slice the chilli, then put it into a pan.

2 Pour the tomato sauce and mixed beans into the pan. Set some of the finely chopped coriander aside for the garnish and add the remainder to the tomato and bean mixture. Stir the contents of the pan to mix all the ingredients together.

3 Bring the mixture to the boil, then quickly reduce the heat, cover and simmer gently for 10 minutes. Stir the mixture occasionally and add a dash of water if it starts to dry out.

4 Ladle the chilli into warmed individual bowls and top with sour cream. Sprinkle with coriander and serve.

> **Cook's Tip**
> If you can't find cans of mixed beans, use one can of borlotti beans and one of kidney beans.

> **Variation**
> This chilli is great just as it is, served with chunks of bread, but you may want to dress it up a bit occasionally. Try serving it over a mixture of long grain and wild rice, piling it into split pitta breads or using it as a filling for baked potatoes. Serve with yogurt or crème fraîche instead of sour cream.

Stuffed Peppers Energy 89kcal/374kJ; Protein 5.1g; Carbohydrate 10.6g, of which sugars 9.9g; Fat 3.2g, of which saturates 0.8g; Cholesterol 48mg; Calcium 27mg; Fibre 3.5g; Sodium 563mg.
Chilli Energy 309kcal/1302kJ; Protein 16.7g; Carbohydrate 43.7g, of which sugars 14.1g; Fat 8.7g, of which saturates 4.2g; Cholesterol 18mg; Calcium 193mg; Fibre 12.4g; Sodium 1202mg.

Bean Feast with Salsa

This is a very quick and easy recipe using canned beans, although it could be made with dried beans.

Serves 4

15ml/1 tbsp olive oil
1 small onion, finely chopped
3 garlic cloves, finely chopped
1 fresh red Ancho chilli, seeded and finely chopped
1 red (bell) pepper, seeded and coarsely chopped
2 plum tomatoes, chopped
2 bay leaves
10ml/2 tsp chopped fresh oregano
10ml/2 tsp ground cumin
5ml/1 tsp ground coriander
2.5ml/½ tsp ground cloves
15ml/1 tbsp soft dark brown sugar

400g/14oz can red kidney beans, rinsed and drained
400g/14oz can flageolet (small cannellini) beans, rinsed and drained
400g/14oz can borlotti beans, rinsed and drained
300ml/½ pint/1¼ cups vegetable stock
salt and ground black pepper
fresh coriander (cilantro), to garnish

For the salsa

1 ripe avocado, diced
45ml/3 tbsp fresh lime juice
1 small red onion, chopped
1 small fresh hot green chilli
5 ripe plum tomatoes, peeled
45ml/3 tbsp chopped fresh coriander (cilantro)

Preparation: 6 minutes; Cooking: 4 minutes

1 Heat the oil and fry the onion for 3 minutes, until transparent. Add the garlic, chilli, pepper, herbs and spices.

2 Stir well and cook for a further 3 minutes, then add the sugar, beans and stock, and cook for 8 minutes. Season with salt and plenty of ground black pepper.

3 To make the salsa, mix the avocado with the lime juice in a bowl. Add the onion. Slice the chilli, discarding the seeds. Chop the tomatoes.

4 Add the chilli, tomatoes and coriander to the avocado. Season with black pepper and stir to mix. Spoon the beans into a warmed serving dish or into four serving bowls. Serve with the tomato and avocado salsa and garnish with coriander.

Parsnip, Carrot & Chèvre Cheese Fricassee

This excellent vegetarian main course also makes a fine accompaniment for roast or grilled meats or fish.

Serves 4–6

4 parsnips
4 carrots
1 red onion, sliced
30ml/2 tbsp pine nuts or flaked (sliced) almonds, lightly toasted
sprigs of tarragon, to garnish

For the sauce

40g/1½oz/3 tbsp unsalted (sweet) butter
40g/1½oz/⅓ cup plain (all purpose) flour
300ml/½ pint/1¼ cups milk
130g/4½oz chèvre (goat's cheese)
15ml/1 tbsp chopped fresh or 2.5ml/½ tsp dried tarragon
salt and ground black pepper

Preparation: 5 minutes; Cooking: 13–14 minutes

1 Cut the parsnips and carrots into sticks. Put them in a pan and add the onion. Season, cover with cold water and bring to the boil.

2 Lower the heat and simmer for 10 minutes or until the vegetables are just tender. Drain, reserving 200ml/7fl oz/ scant 1 cup of the cooking water in a measuring jug (cup). Put the vegetables in a dish and keep hot.

3 Make the sauce. Melt the butter in a clean pan and stir in the flour. Cook for 1 minute, stirring, then gradually whisk in the reserved vegetable water and the milk. Heat, whisking, until the sauce boils and thickens. Lower the heat and simmer the sauce gently for 2 minutes.

4 Remove the sauce from the heat and stir in the chèvre, tarragon and salt and pepper.

5 Pour the sauce over the vegetables and sprinkle with the pine nuts or almonds. Garnish with the sprigs of tarragon and serve. Triangles of wholemeal (whole-wheat) toast make a good accompaniment.

Bean Feast Energy 463kcal/1955kJ; Protein 24.1g; Carbohydrate 72.3g, of which sugars 28.3g; Fat 10.5g, of which saturates 2g; Cholesterol 0mg; Calcium 268mg; Fibre 23.8g; Sodium 1196mg.
Fricassee Energy 268kcal/1118kJ; Protein 9.5g; Carbohydrate 21.8g, of which sugars 10.7g; Fat 16.5g, of which saturates 8.3g; Cholesterol 37mg; Calcium 145mg; Fibre 5.1g; Sodium 209mg.

Simple Rice Salad

Sometimes called confetti salad, this features brightly coloured chopped vegetables served in a well-flavoured dressing. Chill it well if you intend to take it on a picnic and transport it in a chiller bag. Unpack only when ready to serve.

Serves 6
275g/10oz/1½ cups long
 grain rice
1 bunch spring onions (scallions),
 finely sliced

1 green (bell) pepper, seeded and
 finely diced
1 yellow (bell) pepper, seeded and
 finely diced
225g/8oz tomatoes, peeled,
 seeded and chopped
30ml/2 tbsp chopped fresh flat leaf
 parsley or coriander (cilantro)

For the dressing
75ml/5 tbsp mixed olive oil and
 extra virgin olive oil
15ml/1 tbsp sherry vinegar
5ml/1 tsp strong Dijon mustard
salt and ground black pepper

Preparation: 6 minutes; Cooking: 10–12 minutes

1 Cook the rice in a large pan of lightly salted boiling water for 10–12 minutes, until tender but still *al dente*. Be careful not to overcook the rice or it will become soggy.

2 Drain the rice well in a sieve (strainer), rinse thoroughly under cold running water and drain again. Leave the rice to cool while you prepare the ingredients for the dressing.

3 Meanwhile, make the dressing by whisking all the ingredients together. Transfer the rice to a bowl and add half the dressing to moisten it and cool it further.

4 Add the spring onions, peppers, tomatoes and parsley or coriander with the remaining dressing, and toss well to mix. Season with salt and pepper to taste.

Cook's Tip
If cooked rice is not eaten immediately, cool it quickly and keep it in the refrigerator, then reheat until piping hot.

Mushroom Stroganoff

This creamy mixed mushroom sauce tastes great and is ideal for a dinner party. Serve it with toasted buckwheat, brown rice or a mixture of wild rices. Ribbon noodles also make a good accompaniment. Cook them in boiling water or stock and toss them in a little olive oil.

Serves 8
25g/1oz/2 tbsp butter
900g/2lb/8 cups mixed
 mushrooms, cut into
 bitesize pieces
350g/12oz/1¾ cups white long
 grain rice
350ml/12fl oz/1½ cups white
 wine sauce
250ml/8fl oz/1 cup sour cream
chopped chives, to garnish

Preparation: 3 minutes; Cooking: 15–17 minutes

1 Melt the butter in a large, heavy pan and add the mushrooms. Cook over a medium heat until the mushrooms give up their liquid. Continue cooking until they are tender and beginning to reabsorb the pan juices and brown.

2 Meanwhile, bring a large pan of lightly salted water to the boil. Add the rice, partially cover the pan and cook over a medium heat for 13–15 minutes until the rice is just tender.

3 Add the wine sauce to the cooked mushrooms in the pan and bring to the boil, stirring. Stir in the sour cream and season to taste. Drain the rice well, spoon on to warm plates, top with the sauce and garnish with chives.

Cook's Tip
Although you can make this with regular button (white) mushrooms, it is especially delicious with wild mushrooms such as ceps or oyster mushrooms. When wild fungi are plentiful, in the autumn, farmers' markets are a good source. You may even be able to find more unusual specimens such as chicken of the woods, chanterelles, cauliflower fungus, morels or wood blewits. If you pick wild mushrooms yourself, make sure you know exactly what you are doing – mistakes can be deadly.

Stroganoff Energy 556kcal/2316kJ; Protein 13.3g; Carbohydrate 80.4g, of which sugars 7.2g; Fat 21.7g, of which saturates 11.4g; Cholesterol 51mg; Calcium 96mg; Fibre 2.5g; Sodium 897mg.
Rice Salad Energy 276kcal/1150kJ; Protein 4.6g; Carbohydrate 41.9g, of which sugars 5.2g; Fat 9.9g, of which saturates 1.4g; Cholesterol 0mg; Calcium 29mg; Fibre 1.7g; Sodium 8mg.

Mexican Tomato Rice

Versions of this dish – a relative of Spanish rice – are popular all over South America. It is a delicious medley of rice, tomatoes and peas. Fresh chillies make it a hot favourite but can be omitted if preferred.

Serves 4

400g/14oz can chopped tomatoes in tomato juice

30ml/2 tbsp vegetable oil, or preferably olive oil

½ onion, roughly chopped

2 garlic cloves, roughly chopped

500g/1¼lb/2½ cups long grain rice

750ml/1¼ pints/3 cups vegetable stock

2.5ml/½ tsp salt

3 fresh chillies

150g/5oz/1 cup frozen peas

ground black pepper

Preparation: 3 minutes; Cooking: 17 minutes

1 Pour the tomatoes and the can juices into a food processor or blender, and process until smooth.

2 Heat the oil in a large, heavy pan, add the onion and garlic and cook over a medium heat for 2 minutes until softened. Stir in the rice and stir-fry for 1–2 minutes.

3 Add the tomato mixture and stir over a medium heat for 3–4 minutes until all the liquid has been absorbed.

4 Stir in the stock, salt, whole chillies and peas. Bring to the boil. Cover and simmer for about 6 minutes, stirring occasionally, until the rice is just tender.

5 Remove the pan from the heat, cover it with a tight-fitting lid and leave it to stand in a warm place for 5 minutes.

6 Remove the chillies and serve in bowls, sprinkled with black pepper. The chillies can be used as a garnish, if you like.

Variation
To save time, use passata instead of blended canned tomatoes.

Aubergine, Mint & Couscous Salad

Packets of flavoured couscous are available in most supermarkets – you can use whichever you like, but garlic and coriander is particularly good for this recipe. Fruity couscous with almonds would also work well.

Serves 2

1 large aubergine (eggplant), cut into chunks

30ml/2 tbsp olive oil

115g/4oz packet couscous flavoured with garlic and coriander (cilantro)

30ml/2 tbsp chopped fresh mint

salt and ground black pepper

Preparation: 3 minutes; Cooking: 6 minutes

1 Preheat the grill (broiler) to high. Toss the aubergine chunks with the olive oil. Season with salt and pepper to taste and spread them on a non-stick baking sheet. Grill (broil) for 5–6 minutes, turning occasionally, until golden brown.

2 Meanwhile, prepare the flavoured couscous according to the instructions on the packet.

3 Stir the grilled aubergine and chopped fresh mint into the garlic and coriander couscous, toss thoroughly and serve immediately.

Cook's Tip
At one time, it was essential to degorge aubergines (eggplant) to remove excess liquid and render them less bitter. This process involved layering the aubergine slices or chunks in a colander, salting them and leaving them to stand for a while, before rinsing and drying them. Today, new varieties are sweeter and less dense, so salting is seldom needed.

Variation
For extra colour and flavour, add tomato to the salad. Grill (broil) about six baby plum tomatoes alongside the aubergine (eggplant).

Mexican Rice Energy 552kcal/2305kJ; Protein 12.7g; Carbohydrate 108.3g, of which sugars 4.8g; Fat 7g, of which saturates 1g; Cholesterol 0mg; Calcium 43mg; Fibre 3g; Sodium 10mg.
Couscous Salad Energy 251kcal/1044kJ; Protein 4.8g; Carbohydrate 32.5g, of which sugars 2g; Fat 12.1g, of which saturates 1.7g; Cholesterol 0mg; Calcium 53mg; Fibre 2g; Sodium 5mg.

Lemony Couscous Salad

This popular salad mixes olives, almonds and courgettes with fluffy couscous and adds a herb, lemon juice and olive oil dressing. It has a deliciously delicate flavour.

Serves 4
275g/10oz/1⅔ cups couscous
550ml/18fl oz/2½ cups boiling
   vegetable stock
2 small courgettes (zucchini)
16–20 black olives
25g/1oz/¼ cup flaked (sliced)
   almonds, toasted

For the dressing
60ml/4 tbsp olive oil
15ml/1 tbsp lemon juice
15ml/1 tbsp chopped fresh
   coriander (cilantro)
15ml/1 tbsp chopped fresh
   parsley
a good pinch of ground cumin
a good pinch of cayenne pepper

Preparation: 10 minutes; Cooking: 0 minutes

1 Place the couscous in a bowl and pour over the boiling stock. Stir with a fork and then set aside for 10 minutes until all the stock has been absorbed and the couscous has fluffed up.

2 Meanwhile, trim the courgettes and cut them into pieces about 2.5cm/1in long. Slice into fine julienne strips with a sharp knife. Halve the black olives, discarding the pits.

3 Fluff up the couscous with a fork, then carefully mix in the courgettes, olives and almonds.

4 Whisk the olive oil, lemon juice, coriander, parsley, cumin and cayenne in a bowl. Stir into the salad and toss gently. Transfer to a large serving dish and serve.

Variation
A tomato dressing would also suit this salad. Combine 2 crushed garlic cloves and 15ml/1 tbsp white wine vinegar in a bowl. Add salt, pepper and a pinch of sugar. Whisk in 60ml/ 4 tbsp olive oil, then add 4 chopped spring onions (scallions) and 8 quartered cherry tomatoes.

Couscous with Halloumi

Couscous is very often considered a side dish, but here it plays a leading role and is topped with griddled sliced courgettes and halloumi – a mild cheese from Cyprus.

Serves 4
30ml/2 tbsp olive oil, plus extra
   for brushing
1 large red onion, chopped
2 garlic cloves, chopped
5ml/1 tsp mild chilli powder
5ml/1 tsp ground cumin
5ml/1 tsp ground coriander
5 cardamom pods, bruised
3 courgettes (zucchini), sliced
   lengthways into ribbons
225g/8oz halloumi cheese, sliced
1 bay leaf
1 cinnamon stick
275g/10oz/1⅔ cups couscous
50g/2oz/¼ cup whole shelled
   almonds, toasted
1 peach, stoned (pitted) and diced
25g/1oz/2 tbsp butter
salt and ground black pepper
chopped fresh flat leaf parsley,
   to garnish

Preparation: 5 minutes; Cooking: 10–12 minutes

1 Heat the oil in a large heavy pan, add the onion and garlic and sauté for 3–4 minutes until the onion has softened, stirring occasionally. Stir in the chilli powder, cumin, coriander and cardamom pods, and leave the pan over a low heat to allow the flavours to mingle.

2 Meanwhile, brush the courgettes lightly with oil and cook them on a hot griddle or under a hot grill (broiler) for 2–3 minutes, until tender and slightly charred. Turn the courgettes over, add the halloumi and continue cooking for a further 3 minutes, turning the halloumi over once.

3 While the vegetables are cooking, pour 300ml/½ pint/1¼ cups water into a large pan and add the bay leaf and cinnamon stick. Bring to the boil, remove from the heat and immediately add the couscous. Cover and allow to swell for 2 minutes.

4 Add the couscous to the spicy onion mixture, with the almonds, peach and butter. Toss over the heat for 2 minutes, then remove the whole spices, arrange the couscous on a plate and season well. Top with halloumi and courgettes. Sprinkle with parsley and serve.

Lemony Couscous Energy 319kcal/1322kJ; Protein 6.6g; Carbohydrate 36.9g, of which sugars 1.4g; Fat 16.9g, of which saturates 2.1g; Cholesterol 0mg; Calcium 68mg; Fibre 1.8g; Sodium 286mg.
With Halloumi Energy 515kcal/2138kJ; Protein 19.9g; Carbohydrate 42.7g, of which sugars 6.1g; Fat 30.3g, of which saturates 12.5g; Cholesterol 46mg; Calcium 290mg; Fibre 2.9g; Sodium 264mg.

Summer Vegetable Kebabs with Harissa

This would be lovely for lunch for guests to nibble while waiting for more filling barbecue fare.

Serves 4
60ml/4 tbsp olive oil
juice of ½ lemon
1 garlic clove, crushed
5ml/1 tsp ground coriander
5ml/1 tsp ground cinnamon
10ml/2 tsp clear honey
2 aubergines (eggplants), part peeled and cut into chunks
2 courgettes (zucchini), cut into chunks

2–3 red or green (bell) peppers, seeded and cut into chunks
12–16 cherry tomatoes
4 small red onions, quartered
5ml/1 tsp salt

For the harissa and yogurt dip
450g/1lb/2 cups Greek (US strained plain) yogurt
30–60ml/2–4 tbsp harissa
a small bunch of fresh coriander (cilantro), finely chopped
a small bunch of mint, finely chopped
salt and ground black pepper

Preparation: 7 minutes; Cooking: 8–10 minutes

1 Preheat the grill (broiler) or prepare a barbecue. Mix the olive oil, lemon juice and garlic in a bowl. Add ground coriander, cinnamon, honey and salt.

2 Add the aubergine and courgette chunks, with the peppers, cherry tomatoes and onion quarters. Stir to mix, then thread on to skewers, so that they are just touching each other.

3 Cook the kebabs under the grill or over the coals, turning occasionally until the vegetables are browned all over.

4 Meanwhile, make the dip. Put the yogurt in a bowl and beat in harissa to taste. Add most of the coriander and mint, reserving a little to garnish, and season well.

5 As soon as the kebabs are cooked, serve on a bed of couscous and sprinkle with the remaining coriander. Spoon yogurt dip on the side. Serve the rest separately.

Tofu & Pepper Kebabs

A simple coating of ground, dry-roasted peanuts pressed on to cubed tofu provides plenty of additional flavour along with the peppers. Use metal or bamboo skewers for threading.

Serves 4
250g/9oz firm tofu
50g/2oz/½ cup dry-roasted peanuts
2 red and 2 green (bell) peppers
60ml/4 tbsp sweet chilli dipping sauce

Preparation: 6–8 minutes; Cooking: 10–12 minutes

1 Pat the tofu dry on kitchen paper and then cut it into small cubes. Grind the peanuts in a blender or food processor and transfer to a plate.

2 Preheat the grill (broiler) to medium. Using a sharp knife, halve and seed the red and green peppers, and cut them into large chunks. Turn the tofu cubes in the ground nuts to coat thoroughly on all sides.

3 Thread the chunks of pepper on to four large skewers with the tofu cubes and place on a foil-lined grill rack. Grill (broil) the kebabs, turning frequently, for 10–12 minutes, or until the peppers and peanuts are beginning to brown.

4 Serve on a large platter. These are intended to be eaten in the hand so have paper napkins and wipes handy.

Variation
Give the kebabs a fruity flavour by threading slices of nectarine or chunks of pineapple on to the skewers with the peanut-coated cubes of tofu and the red and green (bell) peppers.

Cook's Tip
Chilli sauces vary from fairly mild to searingly hot, while some are quite sweet and are best mixed with lime juice.

Vegetable Kebabs Energy 305kcal/1267kJ; Protein 9.9g; Carbohydrate 24.8g, of which sugars 22.6g; Fat 19.1g, of which saturates 6.6g; Cholesterol 16mg; Calcium 230mg; Fibre 5.2g; Sodium 181mg.
Tofu Kebabs Energy 175kcal/730kJ; Protein 10g; Carbohydrate 12.9g, of which sugars 11.4g; Fat 9.6g, of which saturates 1.6g; Cholesterol 0mg; Calcium 339mg; Fibre 3.6g; Sodium 108mg.

Stir-fried Crispy Tofu

Vegetarian guests often draw the short straw at dinners where meat eaters are in the majority. Serve this and there'll be envious looks at the table.

Serves 1–2
250g/9oz deep-fried tofu cubes
30ml/2 tbsp groundnut (peanut) oil

15ml/1 tbsp Thai green curry paste
30ml/2 tbsp light soy sauce
2 kaffir lime leaves, sliced
30ml/2 tbsp sugar
150ml/¼ pint/⅔ cup vegetable stock
250g/9oz asparagus, trimmed and sliced into 5cm/2in lengths
30ml/2 tbsp roasted peanuts, finely chopped

Preparation: 3–4 minutes; Cooking: 12 minutes

1 Preheat the grill (broiler) to medium. Place the tofu cubes in a grill (broiling) pan and grill (broil) for 2–3 minutes, then turn them over and continue to cook until they are crisp and golden brown all over. Watch them carefully: they must not burn.

2 Heat the oil in a wok or heavy frying pan. Add the green curry paste and cook over a medium heat, stirring constantly, for 1–2 minutes, until it gives off its aroma.

3 Stir the soy sauce, kaffir lime leaves, sugar and vegetable stock into the wok or pan and mix well. Bring to the boil, then reduce the heat to low so that the curried stock is just simmering.

4 Add the asparagus and simmer gently for 5 minutes. Meanwhile, chop each piece of tofu into four, then add to the pan with the peanuts.

5 Toss to coat all the ingredients in the sauce, then spoon into a warmed dish and serve immediately.

Variation
Substitute slim carrot batons, baby leeks or small broccoli florets for the asparagus, if you like.

Tofu & Green Bean Red Curry

This is one of those versatile recipes that should be in every cook's repertoire. This version uses green beans, but other types of vegetable work equally well.

Serves 4–6
600ml/1 pint/2½ cups coconut milk
15ml/1 tbsp Thai red curry paste
10ml/2 tsp palm sugar (jaggery) or honey

225g/8oz/3¼ cups button (white) mushrooms
115g/4oz green beans, trimmed
175g/6oz firm tofu, rinsed, drained and cut into 2cm/¾in cubes
4 kaffir lime leaves, torn
2 fresh red chillies, seeded and sliced
fresh coriander (cilantro) leaves, to garnish

Preparation: 2–3 minutes; Cooking: 7 minutes

1 Pour about one-third of the coconut milk into a wok or pan. Cook until it starts to separate and an oily sheen appears on the surface of the hot liquid.

2 Add the red curry paste and palm sugar or honey to the coconut milk. Mix thoroughly, then add the mushrooms. Stir and cook for 1 minute over medium heat.

3 Stir in the remaining coconut milk. Bring back to the boil, then add the green beans and tofu cubes. Simmer gently for 4–5 minutes more, stirring occasionally.

4 Stir in the kaffir lime leaves and sliced red chillies. Spoon the tofu and green bean curry into a serving dish, garnish with the coriander leaves and serve immediately.

Cook's Tip
Unless there are compelling health reasons, do not use low-fat coconut milk for this curry. The flavour of the full-cream product is superior. If you buy the canned product and have some left over, freeze it in ice cube trays – handy for future sauces.

Stir-fried Tofu Energy 551kcal/2287kJ; Protein 37.3g; Carbohydrate 7.8g, of which sugars 5.2g; Fat 41.4g, of which saturates 2.8g; Cholesterol 0mg; Calcium 1894mg; Fibre 3.1g; Sodium 1203mg.
Tofu Curry Energy 59kcal/250kJ; Protein 3.8g; Carbohydrate 7.5g, of which sugars 7.1g; Fat 1.8g, of which saturates 0.4g; Cholesterol 0mg; Calcium 188mg; Fibre 0.8g; Sodium 291mg.

Indian Mee Goreng

This is a truly international noodle dish combining Indian, Chinese and Western ingredients. It is a delicious treat for lunch or supper, or any time of day.

Serves 4
450g/1lb fresh yellow egg noodles
60–90ml/4–6 tbsp vegetable oil
115g/4oz fried tofu or 150g/5oz firm tofu
2 eggs
30ml/2 tbsp water
salt and ground black pepper
1 onion, sliced
1 garlic clove, crushed
15ml/1 tbsp light soy sauce
30–45ml/2–3 tbsp tomato ketchup
15ml/1 tbsp chilli sauce
1 large cooked potato, diced
4 spring onions (scallions), shredded
1–2 fresh green chillies, seeded and thinly sliced (optional)

Preparation: 6 minutes; Cooking: 8–9 minutes

1 Bring a large pan of water to the boil, add the fresh egg noodles and cook for just 2 minutes. Drain the noodles, rinse under cold water, drain again and set aside.

2 If using fried tofu, cut each cube in half, refresh it in a pan of boiling water, then drain well and set aside. Heat 30ml/2 tbsp of the oil in a large frying pan. If using plain tofu, cube it, fry until brown, then set aside.

3 Beat the eggs with 30ml/2 tbsp water and seasoning. Add to the frying pan and cook, without stirring, until set. Flip over, cook the other side, then slide it out of the pan, roll up and slice thinly.

4 Heat the remaining oil in a wok and fry the onion and garlic for 2–3 minutes. Add the drained noodles, soy sauce, ketchup and chilli sauce. Toss well over medium heat for 2 minutes, then add the diced potato. Reserve a few spring onion shreds for garnish and stir the rest into the noodles with the chilli, if using, and the tofu.

5 When hot, stir in the omelette slices. Serve on a hot platter, garnished with the remaining spring onion.

Sesame Noodles

This is one of those quick, comforting dishes that become family favourites.

Serves 4
450g/1lb fresh egg noodles
½ cucumber, sliced lengthways, seeded and diced
4–6 spring onions (scallions)
a bunch of radishes, about 115g/4oz
225g/8oz mooli (daikon), peeled
115g/4oz/2 cups beansprouts, rinsed and drained
60ml/4 tbsp groundnut (peanut) oil or sunflower oil
2 garlic cloves, crushed
45ml/3 tbsp toasted sesame paste
15ml/1 tbsp sesame oil
15ml/1 tbsp light soy sauce
5–10ml/1–2 tsp sweet chilli sauce, to taste
15ml/1 tbsp rice vinegar
120ml/4fl oz/½ cup vegetable stock
5ml/1 tsp sugar, or to taste
salt and ground black pepper
roasted cashew nuts, to garnish

Preparation: 10 minutes; Cooking: 4 minutes

1 Cook the fresh noodles in boiling water for 1 minute then drain well. Rinse the noodles in fresh water and drain again.

2 Place the cucumber in a colander or sieve (strainer), sprinkle with salt and leave to drain over a bowl for 10 minutes.

3 Meanwhile, cut the spring onions into fine shreds. Cut the radishes in half and slice finely. Coarsely grate the mooli. Rinse the cucumber, drain, pat dry and mix with all the vegetables in a salad bowl. Toss gently.

4 Heat half the oil in a wok or frying pan and stir-fry the noodles for about 1 minute. Using a slotted spoon, transfer the noodles to a large serving bowl and keep warm.

5 Add the remaining oil to the wok. When hot, fry the garlic to flavour the oil. Remove from the heat. Stir in the sesame paste, with the sesame oil, sauces, vinegar and chicken stock.

6 Add a little sugar and season to taste. Warm through but do not overheat. Pour the sauce over the noodles and toss well. Garnish with the cashew nuts and serve with the vegetables.

Mee Goreng Energy 478kcal/2010kJ; Protein 16.8g; Carbohydrate 64.2g, of which sugars 5.1g; Fat 18.9g, of which saturates 3.2g; Cholesterol 86mg; Calcium 323mg; Fibre 2.9g; Sodium 466mg.
Sesame Noodles Energy 633kcal/2658kJ; Protein 17.6g; Carbohydrate 84.5g, of which sugars 5.3g; Fat 27.2g, of which saturates 5g; Cholesterol 34mg; Calcium 139mg; Fibre 5.7g; Sodium 484mg.

Buckwheat Noodles with Goat's Cheese

This good, fast supper dish combines the earthy flavour of buckwheat with the nutty, peppery taste of rocket leaves. Both these ingredients are offset by the deliciously creamy goat's cheese, and the fried hazelnuts add a slightly salty note and a contrast in texture.

Serves 4
350g/12oz buckwheat noodles
50g/2oz/¼ cup butter
2 garlic cloves, finely chopped
4 shallots, sliced
75g/3oz/¾ cup hazelnuts, lightly
    roasted and roughly chopped
large handful rocket (arugula)
    leaves
175g/6oz goat's cheese, crumbled
salt and ground black pepper

Preparation: 0 minutes; Cooking: 8–10 minutes

1 Bring a large pan of lightly salted water to a rolling boil and add the noodles. Cook until just tender.

2 Meanwhile, heat the butter in a large frying pan. Add the garlic and shallots and cook for 2–3 minutes, stirring all the time, until the shallots are soft. Do not let the garlic brown. Drain the noodles well.

3 Add the hazelnuts to the pan and fry for about 1 minute. Add the rocket leaves and, when they start to wilt, toss in the noodles and heat through.

4 Season with salt and pepper. Add the goat's cheese, spoon into a large dish and serve immediately.

Cook's Tip
The best-known buckwheat noodles are the Japanese soba, which are usually sold dried in bundles of fine strands. Soba are much darker than wheat noodles. There is also a dark green variety called cha-soba (tea soba), which is made from buckwheat with the addition of green tea.

Vegetarian Fried Noodles

The combination of omelette strips, potatoes and noodles in this typically South-east Asian dish results in a very substantial meal.

Serves 4
2 eggs
5ml/1 tsp chilli powder
5ml/1 tsp ground turmeric
60ml/4 tbsp vegetable oil
1 large onion, finely sliced
2 fresh red chillies, seeded and
    finely sliced

15ml/1 tbsp soy sauce
2 large cooked potatoes, cut into
    small cubes
6 pieces fried tofu, sliced
225g/8oz/4 cups beansprouts
115g/4oz green beans, blanched
    in boiling water for 2 minutes
350g/12oz fresh thick egg
    noodles
salt and ground black pepper
sliced spring onions (scallions),
    to garnish

Preparation: 6–8 minutes; Cooking: 10 minutes

1 Beat the eggs lightly, then strain them into a bowl. Heat a lightly greased omelette pan. Pour in half of the egg to cover the bottom of the pan thinly. When the egg is just set, turn the omelette over and fry the other side briefly. Slide on to a plate, blot with kitchen paper, roll up and cut into narrow strips. Make and slice a second omelette. Set aside.

2 In a cup, mix together the chilli powder and turmeric. Form a paste by stirring in a little water.

3 Heat the oil in a wok or large frying pan. Fry the onion until soft. Reduce the heat and add the chilli paste, sliced chillies and soy sauce. Fry for 2–3 minutes.

4 Add the potatoes and fry for about 2 minutes, mixing well with the chillies. Add the tofu, then the beansprouts, green beans and noodles.

5 Gently stir-fry until the noodles are evenly coated and heated through. Take care not to break up the potatoes or the tofu. Season with salt and pepper. Serve hot, garnished with the reserved omelette strips and spring onion slices.

Buckwheat Noodles Energy 418kcal/1736kJ; Protein 14.4g; Carbohydrate 15g, of which sugars 2.9g; Fat 33.9g, of which saturates 15.2g; Cholesterol 67mg; Calcium 97mg; Fibre 2.2g; Sodium 342mg.
Fried Noodles Energy 696kcal/2923kJ; Protein 28.3g; Carbohydrate 83g, of which sugars 8.2g; Fat 30.3g, of which saturates 4.2g; Cholesterol 121mg; Calcium 813mg; Fibre 5g; Sodium 476mg.

Garganelli with Spring Vegetables

Fresh, brightly coloured spring vegetables both look and taste good when served with pasta.

Serves 4
1 bunch asparagus, about 350g/12oz
4 young carrots
1 bunch spring onions (scallions)
130g/4½oz shelled fresh peas

350g/12oz/3 cups dried garganelli
60ml/4 tbsp dry white wine
90ml/6 tbsp extra virgin olive oil
a few sprigs fresh flat leaf parsley, mint and basil, leaves stripped and chopped
sea salt and ground black pepper
freshly grated Parmesan cheese or premium Italian-style vegetarian cheese, to serve

Preparation: 6–8 minutes; Cooking: 10–12 minutes

1 Trim off and discard the woody part of each asparagus stem, then cut off the tips on the diagonal. Cut the stems on the diagonal into 4cm/1½in pieces. Cut the carrots and spring onions on the diagonal into similar-sized pieces.

2 Bring a large pan of lightly salted water to the boil. Add the carrots, peas, asparagus stems and tips. Bring back to the boil, then reduce the heat and simmer the vegetables for 6–8 minutes, until tender. The asparagus tips will cook quickly, so remove them with a slotted spoon as soon as they are ready.

3 Meanwhile, cook the pasta in salted boiling water for 10–12 minutes, or according to the instructions on the packet, until the garganelli are just tender.

4 Drain the asparagus, carrots and peas and return them to the pan. Add the white wine, olive oil and salt and black pepper to taste, then gently toss over a medium to high heat until the wine has reduced and the vegetables glisten with the olive oil.

5 Drain the garganelli and tip it into a warmed large bowl. Add the vegetables, spring onions and fresh herbs and toss well.

6 Divide the pasta among four warmed individual plates and serve immediately, with freshly grated cheese.

Spinach & Ricotta Gnocchi

The success of this Italian dish lies in not overworking the mixture, to achieve delicious, light mouthfuls. Gnocchi is more usually made with semolina, or with potato, which has been boiled and then put through a ricer, so this is quite an unusual recipe. The spinach not only gives the gnocchi great flavour, but the intense colour looks good, especially on white plates.

Serves 4
900g/2lb fresh spinach
350g/12oz/1½ cups ricotta cheese
60ml/4 tbsp freshly grated Parmesan cheese
3 eggs, beaten
1.5ml/¼ tsp grated nutmeg
45–60ml/3–4 tbsp plain (all-purpose) flour
115g/4oz/½ cup butter, melted
salt and ground black pepper
freshly grated Parmesan cheese, to serve

Preparation: 0 minutes; Cooking: 6–8 minutes

1 Place the spinach in a large pan and cook for 5 minutes, until wilted. Leave to cool, then squeeze the spinach as dry as possible. Put it in a blender or food processor, process to a purée, then transfer to a bowl.

2 Add the ricotta, Parmesan, eggs and nutmeg. Season with salt and pepper and mix together. Add enough flour to make the mixture into a soft dough.

3 Remove from the bowl and place on a clean surface that has been lightly dusted with flour. Using your hands, shape the rolls into sausage shapes, each about 7.5cm/3in long, then dust lightly with flour.

4 Bring a large pan of salted water to the boil. Gently slide the gnocchi into the water and cook for 1–2 minutes, until they float to the surface.

5 Remove the gnocchi with a slotted spoon and transfer to a warmed dish. Pour over the melted butter and toss to coat, then sprinkle with Parmesan cheese. Serve at once, with extra Parmesan in a separate bowl, if you like.

Gnocchi Energy 566kcal/2342kJ; Protein 24.2g; Carbohydrate 15.2g, of which sugars 6.4g; Fat 45.7g, of which saturates 26.4g; Cholesterol 251mg; Calcium 545mg; Fibre 5.1g; Sodium 651mg.
Garganelli Energy 738kcal/3092kJ; Protein 29.5g; Carbohydrate 74g, of which sugars 5.2g; Fat 38.1g, of which saturates 10.4g; Cholesterol 38mg; Calcium 492mg; Fibre 4.3g; Sodium 416mg.

Spaghetti with Lemon

This is the dish when you want a quick bite to eat.

Serves 4
350g/12oz dried spaghetti

90ml/6 tbsp extra virgin olive oil
juice of 1 large lemon
2 garlic cloves, cut into very
   thin slivers
salt and ground black pepper

Preparation: 2–3 minutes; Cooking: 15 minutes

1 Cook the pasta in a large pan of lightly salted boiling water for 10–12 minutes, until tender, then drain well and return to the pan. Pour the olive oil and lemon juice over the cooked pasta, sprinkle in the slivers of garlic and add seasoning to taste. Toss the pasta over a medium to high heat for 1–2 minutes. Serve immediately in four warmed bowls.

Spaghetti with Garlic & Oil

It doesn't get much simpler than this: spaghetti tossed with the very best olive oil, with chilli for a hint of heat and plenty of parsley for a contrasting cool, fresh flavour. If you use fresh pasta, this is one of the quickest dishes there is.

Serves 4
400g/14oz fresh or dried
   spaghetti
90ml/6 tbsp extra virgin olive oil
2–4 garlic cloves, crushed
1 dried red chilli
1 small handful fresh flat leaf
   parsley, roughly chopped
salt

Preparation: 1 minute; Cooking: 4–12 minutes

1 Cook the pasta in a large pan of lightly salted boiling water. Dried pasta will take 10–12 minutes, fresh about 3 minutes. Fresh pasta is ready when it rises to the surface of the water.

2 Meanwhile, heat the oil very gently in a small frying pan. Add the crushed garlic and whole dried chilli and stir over a low heat until the garlic is just beginning to brown. Remove the chilli, which is only used to flavour the oil, and discard.

3 Drain the pasta and tip it into a warmed large bowl. Pour on the oil and garlic mixture, add the parsley and toss vigorously until the pasta glistens. Serve immediately, either in the bowl used for mixing or in individual warmed bowls.

Cook's Tips
• Since the oil is such an important ingredient here, only use the very best cold-pressed extra virgin olive oil.
• Don't use salt in the oil and garlic mixture, because it will not dissolve sufficiently. This is why salt is recommended for cooking the pasta instead.
• In Rome, the home of this dish, grated Parmesan is never served with this dish, nor is it seasoned with pepper.
• In summer, Romans use fresh chillies, which they grow in pots on their terraces and window ledges. As the chilli is mainly used for flavouring, you could use chilli oil instead.

Minty Courgette Linguine

Courgettes and mint are a great combination and are delicious with pasta.

Serves 4
450g/1lb dried linguine
75ml/5 tbsp garlic-infused olive oil

4 small courgettes (zucchini),
   sliced
1 small bunch of fresh mint,
   roughly chopped
salt and ground black pepper

Preparation: 5 minutes; Cooking: 12–15 minutes

1 Cook the pasta in a large pan of lightly salted boiling water for 10–12 minutes.

2 Meanwhile, heat 45ml/3 tbsp of the oil in a large frying pan and add the courgettes. Fry for 2–3 minutes, stirring occasionally, until they are golden.

3 Drain the pasta well and toss with the courgettes and chopped mint. Season with salt and pepper, drizzle over the remaining oil and serve immediately.

Spaghetti with Garlic Energy 498kcal/2097kJ; Protein 12.6g; Carbohydrate 75.3g, of which sugars 3.4g; Fat 18.3g, of which saturates 2.6g; Cholesterol 0mg; Calcium 27mg; Fibre 3.2g; Sodium 3mg.
Spaghetti with Lemon Energy 448kcal/1886kJ; Protein 10.5g; Carbohydrate 64.9g, of which sugars 3g; Fat 18.1g, of which saturates 2.5g; Cholesterol 0mg; Calcium 22mg; Fibre 2.6g; Sodium 3mg.
Linguine Energy 536kcal/2261kJ; Protein 16.2g; Carbohydrate 86.3g, of which sugars 5.9g; Fat 16.4g, of which saturates 2.3g; Cholesterol 0mg; Calcium 86mg; Fibre 4.4g; Sodium 7mg.

Linguine with Sun-dried Tomato Pesto

Tomato pesto was once a rarity, but is becoming increasingly popular. To make it, sun-dried tomatoes are used instead of basil.

Serves 4

25g/1oz/⅓ cup pine nuts
25g/1oz/⅓ cup freshly grated
  Parmesan cheese
50g/2oz/½ cup sun-dried
  tomatoes in olive oil
1 garlic clove, roughly chopped
60ml/4 tbsp olive oil
350g/12oz fresh or dried linguine
ground black pepper
coarsely shaved Parmesan cheese,
  to serve
basil leaves, to garnish

Preparation: 5 minutes; Cooking: 5–16 minutes

1 Put the pine nuts in a small non-stick frying pan and toss over a low to medium heat for 1–2 minutes or until lightly toasted and golden.

2 Tip the nuts into a food processor. Add the Parmesan, sun-dried tomatoes and garlic, with pepper to taste. Process until finely chopped. With the machine running, gradually add the olive oil through the feeder tube until it has all been incorporated evenly and the ingredients have formed a smooth-looking paste.

3 Cook the pasta in a large pan of lightly salted boiling water. Dried pasta will take 10–12 minutes, fresh about 3 minutes. Drain well, reserving a little of the water. Tip the pasta into a warmed bowl, add the pesto and a few spoonfuls of the hot water and toss well. Serve immediately garnished with basil and hand round the Parmesan separately.

> **Cook's Tip**
> You can make this pesto up to 2 days in advance and keep it in the refrigerator. Pour a thin film of olive oil over the pesto in a bowl, then cover the bowl tightly with clear film (plastic wrap).

Pasta with Sun-dried Tomatoes

This is a light, modern pasta dish of the kind served in fashionable restaurants. It is very easy to prepare.

Serves 4–6

15ml/3 tbsp pine nuts
350g/12oz dried paglia e fieno
  (or two different colours
  of tagliatelle)
45ml/3 tbsp extra virgin olive oil
30ml/2 tbsp sun-dried
  tomato paste
2 pieces drained sun-dried
  tomatoes in olive oil, cut into
  very thin slivers
40g/1½oz radicchio leaves,
  finely shredded
4–6 spring onions (scallions),
  thinly sliced into rings
salt and ground black pepper

Preparation: 3 minutes; Cooking: 13–15 minutes

1 Put the pine nuts in a non-stick frying pan and toss over a low to medium heat for 1–2 minutes or until they are lightly toasted and golden. Remove from the pan and set aside.

2 Cook the pasta in two large pans of lightly salted boiling water for 10–12 minutes, using one pan for each colour to keep them separated.

3 While the pasta is cooking, heat 15ml/1 tbsp of the oil in a medium pan or frying pan. Add the sun-dried tomato paste and the sun-dried tomatoes, then stir in 2 ladlefuls of the water used for cooking the pasta. Simmer until the sauce is slightly reduced, stirring constantly.

4 Mix in the shredded radicchio, then taste and season if necessary. Keep on a low heat. Drain the paglia e fieno, keeping the colours separate, and return the pasta to the pans. Add about 15ml/1 tbsp oil to each pan and toss over a medium to high heat until the pasta is glistening with the oil.

5 Arrange a portion of green and white pasta in each of 4–6 warmed bowls, then spoon the sun-dried tomato and radicchio mixture in the centre. Sprinkle the spring onions and pine nuts over the top and serve immediately. Before eating, each diner should toss the sauce ingredients with the pasta.

Linguine Energy 503kcal/2114kJ; Protein 14.4g; Carbohydrate 66.7g, of which sugars 4.7g; Fat 21.7g, of which saturates 3.4g; Cholesterol 6mg; Calcium 102mg; Fibre 3g; Sodium 98mg.
Pasta Energy 309kcal/1302kJ; Protein 8.6g; Carbohydrate 44.9g, of which sugars 3.6g; Fat 11.8g, of which saturates 1.3g; Cholesterol 0mg; Calcium 23mg; Fibre 2.3g; Sodium 16mg.

Pasta with Tomato & Chilli Sauce

This dish comes from Italy, where it is described as all'arrabbiata. This means 'angry' and it describes the heat that comes from the chilli, but if you serve it to someone who hates spices, it may be directed at you.

Serves 4
500g/1¼ lb sugocasa
(see Cook's Tip)
2 garlic cloves, crushed

150ml/¼ pint/⅔ cup dry
white wine
15ml/1 tbsp sun-dried
tomato paste
1 fresh red chilli
300g/11oz/2¾ cups penne
or tortiglioni
60ml/4 tbsp finely chopped fresh
flat leaf parsley
salt and ground black pepper
freshly grated (shredded) Pecorino
cheese, to serve

Preparation: 2–3 minutes; Cooking: 12–14 minutes

1 Mix the sugocasa, garlic, wine, sun-dried tomato paste and whole chilli in a pan and bring to the boil. Reduce the heat, cover the pan and leave the mixture to simmer gently, stirring it occasionally with a wooden spoon.

2 Drop the pasta into a large pan of rapidly boiling salted water. Lower the heat and simmer for 10–12 minutes or until the pasta is just tender, retaining a bit of 'bite'.

3 Remove the chilli from the sauce and add 30ml/2 tbsp of the parsley. Taste for seasoning. If you prefer a hotter taste, chop some or all of the chilli and return it to the sauce.

4 Drain the pasta and tip it into a warmed large bowl. Pour the sauce over the pasta and toss to mix. Serve at once, sprinkled with grated Pecorino and the remaining parsley. Offer more grated Pecorino separately, in a small bowl.

Cook's Tip
Sugocasa resembles passata (bottled strained tomatoes), but is a chunkier mixture; it means 'the sauce of the house'.

Broccoli & Chilli Spaghetti

The contrast between the hot chilli and the mild broccoli is delicious and goes perfectly with spaghetti. Extra flavour and texture are added by sprinkling the finished dish with toasted pine nuts and grated or shaved Parmesan cheese just before serving. For a tangy but less spicy result just exclude the chilli from the recipe.

Serves 4
350g/12oz dried spaghetti
450g/1lb broccoli, cut into
small florets
1 fat red chilli, seeded and
finely chopped
150ml/¼ pint/⅔ cup garlic-infused
olive oil
salt and ground black pepper
freshly grated (shredded)
Parmesan cheese, to serve
handful of toasted pine nuts, to
serve

Preparation: 2–3 minutes; Cooking: 8–10 minutes

1 Bring a large pan of lightly salted water to the boil. Add the spaghetti and broccoli and cook for 8–10 minutes, until both are tender. Drain thoroughly.

2 Using the back of a fork crush the broccoli roughly, taking care not to mash the spaghetti strands at the same time.

3 Meanwhile, warm the oil and finely chopped chilli in a small pan over a low heat and cook very gently for 5 minutes, taking care not to brown the chilli.

4 Pour the chilli and oil over the spaghetti and broccoli and toss together to combine. Season to taste. Divide between four warmed bowls and serve immediately.

Cook's Tip
Cooking the spaghetti and broccoli in the same pan helps the pasta to absorb more of the vegetable's flavour and essential nutrients. To retain more of the nutrients, reserve a small amount of the cooking water and pour over the dish before tossing together all the ingredients.

Pasta with Tomato Energy 681kcal/2856kJ; Protein 25.1g; Carbohydrate 69.7g, of which sugars 7.7g; Fat 35.5g, of which saturates 19g; Cholesterol 91mg; Calcium 264mg; Fibre 4.1g; Sodium 830mg.
Broccoli Spaghetti Energy 396kcal/1678kJ; Protein 17.3g; Carbohydrate 68.3g, of which sugars 6g; Fat 7.9g, of which saturates 0.8g; Cholesterol 0mg; Calcium 114mg; Fibre 5.6g; Sodium 24mg.

Fettucine all'Alfredo

This simple recipe was invented by a Roman restaurateur called Alfredo, who became famous for serving it with a gold fork and spoon. Since those heady days it has become one of the most popular pasta dishes around.

Serves 4
50g/2oz/¼ cup butter
200ml/7fl oz/scant 1 cup double (heavy) cream
50g/2oz/⅔ cup freshly grated Parmesan cheese, plus extra to serve
350g/12oz fresh fettucine
salt and ground black pepper

Preparation: 1–2 minutes; Cooking: 10–12 minutes

1 Melt the butter in a large pan. Add the cream and bring it to the boil. Simmer for 5 minutes, stirring constantly, then add the Parmesan, with salt and ground black pepper to taste, and turn off the heat under the pan.

2 Bring a large pan of lightly salted water to the boil over high heat. Add the pasta and cook for about 3 minutes, or until the fresh fettucine rises to the surface.

3 Turn the heat under the pan of cream to low. Drain the cooked pasta and add it to the pan all at once. Toss until it is coated in the sauce. Taste for seasoning and stir in more salt and pepper if needed. Serve immediately, with extra Parmesan cheese handed around separately.

Cook's Tip
A few drops of oil, added to the pan of water in which the fettucine is cooking, will help to prevent it from boiling over.

Variation
The original recipe for Fettucine all'Alfredo did not contain cream, so the version above is already a slight variation. Some cooks add a little cream cheese, which thickens the coating sauce, or even some mashed blue cheese, such as Gorgonzola.

Linguine with Rocket

This fashionable lunch is very quick and easy to make at home. Rocket has an excellent peppery flavour that combines beautifully with the Parmesan, but watercress leaves, which also have a peppery taste, could be used instead.

Serves 4
350g/12oz dried linguine
120ml/4fl oz/½ cup extra virgin olive oil
1 large bunch rocket (arugula), about 150g/5oz, stalks removed, shredded
75g/3oz/1 cup freshly grated Parmesan cheese

Preparation: 3–5 minutes; Cooking: 11–14 minutes

1 Cook the pasta in a large pan of lightly salted boiling water for 10–12 minutes, then drain thoroughly.

2 Heat about 60ml/4 tbsp of the olive oil in the pasta pan, then add the drained pasta and rocket. Toss over a medium heat for 1–2 minutes, or until the rocket is just wilted, then remove the pan from the heat.

3 Transfer the pasta and rocket to a large, warmed bowl. Add half the freshly grated Parmesan and the remaining olive oil. Add a little salt and black pepper to taste.

4 Toss the mixture quickly to mix all the flavours together and ensure the pasta is well coated with the oil. Serve immediately, sprinkled with the remaining Parmesan.

Cook's Tips
• Linguine is an egg pasta and looks rather like flattened strands of spaghetti.
• Dried pasta cooks in 10–12 minutes, but an even faster result can be obtained by using fresh pasta. Simply add it to a large pan of boiling, lightly salted water, making sure that all the strands are fully submerged, and cook for 2–3 minutes. The pasta is ready when it rises to the top of the pan and is tender to the taste, with a slight firmness in the centre.

Fettucine Energy 697kcal/2912kJ; Protein 16.3g; Carbohydrate 65.8g, of which sugars 3.8g; Fat 42.8g, of which saturates 26g; Cholesterol 108mg; Calcium 199mg; Fibre 2.6g; Sodium 226mg.
Linguine Energy 573kcal/2404kJ; Protein 19g; Carbohydrate 65.4g, of which sugars 3.5g; Fat 28g, of which saturates 6.9g; Cholesterol 19mg; Calcium 311mg; Fibre 3.3g; Sodium 260mg.

Garganelli Pasta with Asparagus & Cream

When fresh asparagus is on sale at the market, this is a wonderful way to serve it. Any type of pasta can be used, but one that mirrors the shape of the asparagus works best.

Serves 4

1 bunch fresh young asparagus, 250–300g/9–11oz
350g/12oz/3 cups dried garganelli
25g/1oz/2 tbsp butter
200ml/7fl oz/scant 1 cup panna da cucina or double (heavy) cream
30ml/2 tbsp dry white wine
90–115g/3½–4oz/1–1⅓ cups freshly grated Parmesan cheese
30ml/2 tbsp chopped fresh mixed herbs, such as basil, flat leaf parsley, chervil, marjoram and oregano
salt and ground black pepper

Preparation: 4–5 minutes; Cooking: 15 minutes

1 Snap off and throw away the woody ends of the asparagus – after trimming, you should have about 200g/7oz asparagus spears. Cut the spears diagonally into pieces about the same length and shape as the garganelli.

2 Blanch the thicker asparagus pieces in a large pan of lightly salted boiling water for 2 minutes, the tips for 1 minute. Using a slotted spoon, transfer the blanched asparagus to a colander, rinse under cold water and set aside.

3 Bring the water in the pan back to the boil, add the pasta and cook for 10–12 minutes.

4 Meanwhile, melt the butter in a heavy pan. Add the cream, with salt and pepper to taste, and bring to the boil. Simmer for a few minutes until the cream reduces and thickens.

5 Stir the asparagus, wine and about half the Parmesan into the sauce. Drain the pasta and return it to the clean pan. Add the sauce and herbs and toss. Serve with the remaining Parmesan, spooned into a small bowl.

Pasta with Fresh Pesto

Bottled pesto is a useful ingredient, but you can make your own in less time than it takes to boil the pasta that accompanies it. Any spare pesto will keep for a few days in the refrigerator. When making pesto in large quantities, put it in jars and pour a thin layer of oil on the surface of each before putting on the lids. This creates a seal that keeps the contents fresh.

Serves 4

400g/14oz/3½ cups dried fusilli
50g/2oz/1⅓ cups fresh basil leaves, plus extra, to garnish
2–4 garlic cloves
60ml/4 tbsp pine nuts
120ml/4fl oz/½ cup extra virgin olive oil
115g/4oz/1⅓ cups freshly grated Parmesan cheese, plus extra to serve
25g/1oz/⅓ cup freshly grated Pecorino cheese
salt and ground black pepper

Preparation: 4 minutes; Cooking: 12–14 minutes

1 Cook the pasta in a large pan of lightly salted boiling water for 10–12 minutes.

2 Meanwhile, put the basil leaves, garlic and pine nuts in a blender or food processor. Add 60ml/4 tbsp of the olive oil. Process until the ingredients are finely chopped, scraping down the sides of the bowl twice.

3 With the motor running, slowly pour the remaining oil in a thin, steady stream through the feeder tube.

4 Scrape the mixture into a large bowl and beat in the cheeses with a wooden spoon. Taste and add salt and pepper if necessary.

5 Drain the pasta well, then add it to the bowl of pesto and toss to coat. Serve immediately, garnished with the fresh basil leaves. Hand shaved Parmesan around separately.

> **Cook's Tip**
> *Fresh Parmesan keeps well in the refrigerator for up to a month.*

Garganelli Energy 716kcal/2994kJ; Protein 22g; Carbohydrate 67g, of which sugars 5g; Fat 41.3g, of which saturates 24.8g; Cholesterol 104mg; Calcium 335mg; Fibre 3.6g; Sodium 298mg.
Pasta with Pesto Energy 783kcal/3279kJ; Protein 27.9g; Carbohydrate 74.7g, of which sugars 3.9g; Fat 43.5g, of which saturates 10.9g; Cholesterol 35mg; Calcium 447mg; Fibre 3.2g; Sodium 385mg.

Pansotti with Walnut Sauce

Recipes don't come much easier than this. Walnuts, garlic oil and cream make a stunningly successful sauce for stuffed pasta. For speed and flavour, use fresh pasta and walnut pieces, which also have the advantage of being cheaper than the whole nuts.

Serves 4

90g/3½oz/scant 1 cup shelled walnuts or walnut pieces
60ml/4 tbsp garlic-flavoured olive oil
120ml/4fl oz/½ cup double (heavy) cream
350g/12oz fresh cheese and herb-filled pansotti or other stuffed pasta

Preparation: 4 minutes; Cooking: 4–5 minutes

1 Put the walnuts and garlic oil in a food processor and process to a paste, adding up to 120ml/4fl oz/½ cup warm water through the feeder tube to slacken the consistency. Spoon the mixture into a large bowl and add the cream. Beat well to mix, then season to taste with salt and black pepper.

2 Cook the stuffed pasta in a large pan of lightly salted boiling water for 4–5 minutes, or according to the instructions on the packet. Meanwhile, put the walnut sauce in a large warmed bowl and add a ladleful of the water the pasta was cooked in to thin it.

3 Drain the pasta and tip it into the bowl of walnut sauce. Toss well, then serve immediately.

Variation
Don't worry if you can't locate pansotti; tortellini will work as well. The best place to buy the pasta is a specialist deli.

Cook's Tip
Walnuts become rancid quite quickly, so you shouldn't store open packets in the pantry for long periods.

Warm Penne with Fresh Tomatoes & Basil

When you're heading off for a family bike ride or a walk on the beach, something light and fresh, but which keeps energy levels topped up over time, is just what you need.

Serves 4

500g/1¼lb/5 cups dried penne
5 very ripe plum tomatoes
1 small bunch fresh basil
60ml/4 tbsp extra virgin olive oil
salt and ground black pepper

Preparation: 2–3 minutes; Cooking: 12–14 minutes

1 Bring a large pan of lightly salted water to the boil. Add the dried penne and cook for 10–12 minutes.

2 Meanwhile, using a serrated knife roughly chop the tomatoes. Tear up the basil leaves.

3 Drain the pasta thoroughly and return it to the clean pan. Toss with the tomatoes, basil and olive oil. Season with salt and freshly ground black pepper and serve immediately.

Variations
• This is one of those good-natured recipes that are capable of infinite variety. Try adding some sliced courgettes (zucchini). Baby vegetables can simply be sliced and added as they are, but courgettes are best when lightly fried in butter and oil.
• A few sun-dried tomatoes in oil, drained and torn into strips, would emphasize the tomato flavour, and would be a particularly good addition if accompanied by sliced black olives.

Cook's Tip
If you cannot find ripe tomatoes, roast those you have to bring out their flavour. Put the tomatoes in a roasting pan, drizzle with oil and roast at 190°C/375°F/Gas 5 for 20 minutes; mash roughly.

Pansotti Energy 702kcal/2931kJ; Protein 14.3g; Carbohydrate 66.1g, of which sugars 4g; Fat 44.1g, of which saturates 13g; Cholesterol 41mg; Calcium 58mg; Fibre 3.3g; Sodium 11mg.
Warm Penne Energy 552kcal/2336kJ; Protein 16.3g; Carbohydrate 96.9g, of which sugars 8.3g; Fat 13.8g, of which saturates 2g; Cholesterol 0mg; Calcium 65mg; Fibre 5.5g; Sodium 19mg.

Tagliatelle with Vegetable Ribbons

Narrow strips of courgette and carrot mingle well with tagliatelle to resemble coloured pasta. Serve with freshly grated Parmesan cheese handed round separately. Children may prefer grated Cheddar or Edam cheese.

Serves 4
2 large courgettes (zucchini)
2 large carrots
250g/9oz fresh egg tagliatelle
60ml/4 tbsp garlic-flavoured
   olive oil
salt and ground black pepper
freshly grated Parmesan cheese,
   to serve

Preparation: 5 minutes; Cooking: 5 minutes

1 With a vegetable peeler, cut the courgettes and carrots into long thin ribbons.

2 Bring a large pan of lightly salted water to the boil, and then add the courgette and carrot ribbons. Bring the water back to the boil and blanch the vegetables for 30 seconds, then remove the courgettes and carrots with a slotted spoon and set them aside in a bowl.

3 Bring the water back to boiling point and cook the pasta for 3 minutes. Drain well and return it to the pan. Add the vegetable ribbons, garlic-flavoured oil and seasoning and toss over a medium to high heat until the pasta and vegetables are glistening with oil. Serve the pasta immediately.

Variation
For a more substantial dish, add 4 vegetarian bacon rashers (strips), grilled (broiled) until crispy, then crumble the rashers on to the pasta.

Cook's Tip
Garlic-flavoured olive oil is used in this dish. Flavoured oils such as chilli or basil are a quick way of adding flavour to pasta.

Farfalle with Gorgonzola Cream

Sweet and simple, this sauce has a nutty tang that comes from the blue cheese. It is also good with long pasta, such as spaghetti, tagliatelle or trenette. Steamed leeks go very well with blue cheeses like Gorgonzola, so cook some separately if you like, and add them when tossing the cooked farfalle with the sauce.

Serves 6
350g/12oz/3 cups dried farfalle
175g/6oz Gorgonzola cheese, any
   rind removed, diced
150ml/¼ pint/¾ cup panna da
   cucina or double (heavy) cream
pinch of sugar
10ml/2 tsp finely chopped fresh
   sage, plus fresh sage leaves
   (some whole, some shredded)
   to garnish
salt and ground black pepper

Preparation: 5 minutes; Cooking: 12–14 minutes

1 Cook the pasta in a large pan of lightly salted boiling water for 10–12 minutes.

2 Meanwhile, put the Gorgonzola and cream in a medium pan. Add the sugar and plenty of ground black pepper and heat gently, stirring frequently, until the cheese has melted. Remove the pan from the heat and let the mixture cool slightly.

3 Drain the cooked pasta well and return it to the pan in which it was cooked. Pour the sauce into the pan with the pasta and gently mix the ingredients together.

4 Add the chopped sage to the pasta and toss over a medium heat until the pasta is evenly coated. Taste for seasoning, adding salt if necessary, then divide among four warmed bowls. Garnish each portion with sage and serve immediately.

Variation
Pine nuts, which are sometimes called pignoli, make a lovely addition to this dish. They can be added just as they are, but will taste even better if spread out in a grill (broiler) pan and toasted under a hot grill for a couple of minutes until browned.

Tagliatelle Energy 397kcal/1663kJ; Protein 11.5g; Carbohydrate 52.4g, of which sugars 8.3g; Fat 17.1g, of which saturates 3.3g; Cholesterol 19mg; Calcium 80mg; Fibre 4.8g; Sodium 127mg.
Farfalle Energy 423kcal/1773kJ; Protein 13.4g; Carbohydrate 43.7g, of which sugars 2.4g; Fat 22.9g, of which saturates 14.1g; Cholesterol 56mg; Calcium 169mg; Fibre 1.7g; Sodium 363mg.

Two Cheese Risotto

This undeniably rich and creamy risotto is just the thing to serve on cold winter evenings when everyone needs warming up. This is a very sociable dish. Invite guests into the kitchen for a chat while you cook.

Serves 3–4
7.5ml/1½ tsp olive oil
50g/2oz/4 tbsp butter

1 onion, finely chopped
1 garlic clove, crushed
275g/10oz/1½ cups risotto rice
175ml/6fl oz/¾ cup dry
  white wine
1 litre/1¾ pints/4 cups
  vegetable stock
75g/3oz/¾ cup fontina
  cheese, cubed
50g/2oz/⅔ cup freshly grated
  Parmesan cheese, plus extra
  shavings to serve
salt and ground black pepper

Preparation: 2 minutes; Cooking: 18 minutes

1 Heat the olive oil with half the butter in a pan and gently fry the onion and garlic for 3 minutes until soft. Add the rice and cook, stirring all the time, until the grains are coated in fat and have become slightly translucent around the edges.

2 Stir in the wine. Cook, stirring, until the liquid has been absorbed, then add a ladleful of hot stock. Stir until the stock has been absorbed, then add the remaining stock in the same way, waiting for each quantity of stock to be absorbed before adding more, and stirring all the time.

3 When the rice is half cooked, after about 9 minutes, stir in the fontina cheese, and continue cooking and adding stock. Keep stirring the rice all the time.

4 When the risotto is creamy and the grains are tender but still have a bit of bite, stir in the remaining butter and the Parmesan. Season, then remove the pan from the heat, cover and leave to rest for 1 minute before spooning into a large bowl or on to individual plates and serving. Shave a little Parmesan over each portion and put the remaining Parmesan, in the piece, on the table with a cheese shaver so guests can add more cheese later, if they like.

Quick Risotto

This is rather a cheat's risotto as it defies all the rules that insist the stock is added gradually. Instead, the rice is cooked quickly in a conventional way, and the other ingredients are simply thrown in at the end. Despite the unconventional cooking method it tastes just as good as a traditional risotto. Chopped cooked ham can be added at the last minute for meat eaters.

Serves 3–4
275g/10oz/1½ cups risotto rice
1 litre/1¾ pints/4 cups
  vegetable stock
115g/4oz/1 cup mozzarella
  cheese, cut into small cubes
2 egg yolks
30ml/2 tbsp freshly grated
  Parmesan cheese
30ml/2 tbsp chopped fresh basil
salt and ground black pepper
fresh basil leaves, to garnish
freshly grated Parmesan cheese,
  to serve

Preparation: 3–4 minutes; Cooking: 16–17 minutes

1 Put the rice in a pan. Pour in the stock, bring to the boil and then cover and simmer for 16–17 minutes until the rice is tender but retains a bit of bite in the centre of the grain.

2 Remove the pan from the heat and quickly stir in the mozzarella, egg yolks, Parmesan and basil. Season well with salt and pepper.

3 Cover the pan and stand for 2–3 minutes to allow the cheese to melt, then stir again. Pile into warmed serving bowls and serve immediately, with extra Parmesan cheese and basil leaves.

Cook's Tip
Making this in the conventional way will not take much longer. Have the stock simmering in a pan. Instead of using egg yolks, melt 50g/2oz/¼ cup butter in a heavy pan. Stir in the rice. Add a ladleful of stock and stir until it has been absorbed. Continue in this fashion, stirring all the time, until all the stock has been added. When the rice is tender, after 18–20 minutes, stir in the remaining ingredients and proceed as in the main recipe.

Quick Risotto Energy 405kcal/1692kJ; Protein 18.3g; Carbohydrate 55.1g, of which sugars 0.2g; Fat 12g, of which saturates 6.5g; Cholesterol 136mg; Calcium 221mg; Fibre 0g; Sodium 425mg.
Two Cheese Risotto Energy 547kcal/2273kJ; Protein 15.1g; Carbohydrate 56.4g, of which sugars 1.2g; Fat 25.1g, of which saturates 13.8g; Cholesterol 57mg; Calcium 312mg; Fibre 0.2g; Sodium 350mg.

Risotto Frittata

Half omelette, half risotto, this makes a delightful light lunch or supper dish.	1 large red (bell) pepper, seeded and cut into thin strips
	175g/6oz/2½ cups button (white) mushrooms, thinly sliced
Serves 4	60ml/4 tbsp freshly grated
250g packet instant risotto, mushroom flavour	Parmesan cheese
40g/1½oz/3 tbsp butter	6–8 eggs
1 small onion, finely chopped	30ml/2 tbsp water
1 garlic clove, crushed	salt and ground black pepper

Preparation: 8 minutes; Cooking: 10 minutes

1 Make the instant risotto, following the instructions on the packet. Timings will vary from 2 minutes for the extra-fast varieties to 12 minutes for 'pronto'.

2 Meanwhile, melt 30ml/2 tbsp of the butter in a large pan. Fry the onion and garlic over low heat for 3–4 minutes until the onion has softened. Add the red pepper strips to the pan and fry for 2–3 minutes, then stir in the mushroom slices. Cook for 4–5 minutes, then stir in the risotto with the Parmesan cheese. Spoon the mixture into a bowl and set aside.

3 Break the eggs into a bowl and add the water. Beat lightly, then add salt and pepper to taste.

4 Preheat the grill (broiler). Melt the remaining butter with the oil in a large omelette pan. Add the risotto mixture. Spread the mixture out to cover the base of the pan evenly.

5 Pour the beaten egg carefully over the risotto mixture in the pan, distributing it as evenly as possible. Cook over a high heat for 1 minute, then lower the heat to medium and cook until the frittata is set underneath, but still slightly moist on top.

6 Put the pan under the grill (broiler) so that the surface of the frittata finishes cooking and turns a golden brown. Loosen it and slide it on to a heated plate. Serve in wedges.

Fiorentina Pizza

An egg adds the finishing touch to this classic Italian spinach pizza; try not to overcook it though, as it's best when the yolk is still slightly soft in the middle.	175g/6oz fresh spinach, stalks removed
	1 pizza base, about 25–30cm/10–12in in diameter
	1 small jar pizza sauce
	freshly grated nutmeg
	150g/5oz mozzarella cheese
Serves 2–3	1 egg
45ml/3 tbsp olive oil	25g/1oz/¼ cup Gruyère cheese, grated
1 small red onion, thinly sliced	

Preparation: 2 minutes; Cooking: 18 minutes

1 Heat 15ml/1 tbsp of the oil and fry the onion until soft. Add the spinach and fry until wilted. Drain any excess liquid.

2 Preheat the oven to 220°C/425°F/Gas 7. Brush the pizza base with half the remaining olive oil. Spread the pizza sauce evenly over the base, using the back of a spoon, then top with the spinach mixture. Sprinkle a little freshly grated nutmeg over the surface of the spinach.

3 Thinly slice the mozzarella and arrange over the spinach. Drizzle over the remaining oil. Bake for 10 minutes, then remove from the oven.

4 Make a small well in the centre of the pizza topping and carefully break the egg into the hole.

5 Sprinkle over the grated Gruyère cheese and return the pizza to the oven for a further 5–10 minutes until crisp and golden. Serve immediately, in wedges.

> **Variation**
> A calzone is like a pizza but is folded in half to conceal the filling. Add the egg with the rest of the pizza topping, fold over the dough, seal the edges and bake for 20 minutes.

Frittata Energy 434kcal/1804kJ; Protein 19.5g; Carbohydrate 34.1g, of which sugars 3.6g; Fat 24.5g, of which saturates 9.5g; Cholesterol 314mg; Calcium 241mg; Fibre 1.4g; Sodium 311mg.
Fiorentina Pizza Energy 503kcal/2100kJ; Protein 20.8g; Carbohydrate 40.3g, of which sugars 5.9g; Fat 29.7g, of which saturates 10.9g; Cholesterol 101mg; Calcium 417mg; Fibre 2.8g; Sodium 668mg.

Courgette & Chèvre Pizza

Cook this tasty pizza at a high temperature to char the vegetables lightly. Dot with goat's milk cheese for an interesting tang.

Serves 2
1 large ready-made, good-quality, crisp pizza base
45ml/3 tbsp drained sun-dried tomatoes in oil
45ml/3 tbsp drained roasted (bell) peppers in oil
1 courgette (zucchini), thinly sliced
1 red onion, thinly sliced
250g/9oz young chèvre (goat's milk cheese), crumbled
15ml/1 tbsp chopped fresh oregano or marjoram
a little extra virgin olive oil, to drizzle
salt and ground black pepper
fresh herbs, to garnish

Preparation: 5 minutes; Cooking: 10–12 minutes

1 Preheat the oven to 220°C/425°F/Gas 7 and place a baking sheet inside the oven to heat up. Put the pizza base on a board. Chop the sun-dried tomatoes and peppers and spread them over the pizza base.

2 Scatter the slices of courgette and onion on top of the tomatoes and peppers, then dot with the crumbled chèvre. Sprinkle with oregano or marjoram, season with salt and pepper to taste and drizzle a little olive oil over the top of the pizza.

3 Place the topped pizza on the hot baking sheet and bake for 10–12 minutes or until the cheese has melted and the vegetables have begun to char. Garnish with herbs, cut into wedges and serve immediately.

> **Variations**
> • A creamy, crumbly blue cheese such as Bleu d'Auvergne or Cashel Blue makes a good alternative to chèvre. A smoked mozzarella would also work well.
> • For a Greek flavour, try lightly sautéed aubergine slices in place of the courgettes and use feta rather than chèvre.

Four Cheese Ciabatta Pizza

Few dishes are as simple – or as satisfying – as this pizza made by topping a halved loaf of ciabatta.

Serves 2
1 loaf ciabatta bread
1 garlic clove, halved
30–45ml/2–3 tbsp olive oil
about 90ml/6 tbsp passata (bottled strained tomatoes) or sugocasa
1 small red onion, thinly sliced
30ml/2 tbsp chopped pitted olives
about 50g/2oz each of four cheeses, one mature/sharp (Parmesan or Cheddar), one blue-veined (Gorgonzola or Stilton), one mild (Fontina or Emmenthal) and a goat's cheese, sliced, grated or crumbled
pine nuts or cumin seeds, to sprinkle
salt and ground black pepper
sprigs of basil, to garnish

Preparation: 4 minutes; Cooking: 10–12 minutes

1 Preheat the oven to 200°C/400°F/Gas 6. Split the ciabatta bread in half. Place on a baking sheet. Rub the cut sides with the garlic, then brush over the oil. Spread both halves with the passata or sugocasa, then add the onion slices and olives. Season to taste with salt and black pepper.

2 Divide the cheeses between the ciabatta halves and sprinkle over the pine nuts or cumin seeds. Bake for 10–12 minutes, until the cheese has melted and the topping is bubbling and golden brown. Cut the pizza into slices and serve immediately, garnished with the sprigs of fresh basil.

> **Variation**
> It is tempting to stick to familiar cheeses when cooking but there is a huge range of regional specialities that are well worth trying. A recipe like this one, which requires particular qualities in the cheeses – mature, blue-veined and mild, plus a goat's cheese – provides the perfect opportunity for trying something new. Visit a cheese shop or a market stall run by an enthusiast and ask for suggestions. You may well discover some as yet undiscovered gems that become firm favourites.

Courgette Energy 711kcal/2963kJ; Protein 35g; Carbohydrate 41.3g, of which sugars 13.4g; Fat 46.3g, of which saturates 23.8g; Cholesterol 116mg; Calcium 260mg; Fibre 3.8g; Sodium 1009mg.
Four Cheese Energy 782kcal/3265kJ; Protein 34g; Carbohydrate 55.8g, of which sugars 6.2g; Fat 47.4g, of which saturates 22.8g; Cholesterol 86mg; Calcium 756mg; Fibre 3.4g; Sodium 1952mg.

Israeli Chopped Vegetable Salad

This colourful and refreshing summer salad is very popular in Israel, where it is often eaten for breakfast, but it can be enjoyed at any time of the day.

Serves 4–6
1 each red, green and yellow (bell) pepper, seeded
1 carrot
1 cucumber
6 tomatoes
3 garlic cloves, finely chopped
3 spring onions (scallions), thinly sliced
30ml/2 tbsp chopped fresh coriander (cilantro) leaves
30ml/2 tbsp each chopped fresh dill, parsley and mint leaves
½–1 hot fresh chilli, chopped (optional)
45–60ml/3–4 tbsp extra virgin olive oil
juice of 1–1½ lemons
salt and ground black pepper

Preparation: 12 minutes; Cooking: 0 minutes

1 Using a sharp knife, finely dice the red, green and yellow peppers, carrot, cucumber and tomatoes and place them in a large mixing bowl. Mix gently to distribute all the ingredients.

2 Add the chopped garlic, sliced spring onions, and chopped coriander, dill, parsley and mint to the chopped vegetables. If using the hot chilli, stir it into the mixture.

3 Pour the olive oil and lemon juice over the vegetables, season with salt and pepper to taste and toss together. Cover with clear film (plastic wrap) and chill before serving.

Cook's Tip
Use a mezzaluna for chopping the herbs quickly and easily.

Variation
This salad lends itself to endless variety: add olives, diced potatoes or beetroot (beet); omit the chilli, vary the herbs or use lime or lemon in place of the vinegar.

Spicy Potato & Olive Salad

This new potato salad is enlivened with cumin and coriander, then dressed in olive oil and a fruity vinegar. It tastes good with cold roast pork or ham.

Serves 4
8 large new potatoes
large pinch of salt
large pinch of sugar
3 garlic cloves, chopped
15ml/1 tbsp vinegar of your choice, such as a fruit variety
large pinch of ground cumin or whole cumin seeds
pinch of cayenne pepper or hot paprika, to taste
30–45ml/2–3 tbsp extra virgin olive oil
30–45ml/2–3 tbsp chopped fresh coriander (cilantro) leaves
10–15 dry-fleshed black Mediterranean olives

Preparation: 5 minutes; Cooking: 10 minutes

1 Chop the new potatoes into chunks. Put them in a pan, pour in water to cover and add the salt and sugar. Bring to the boil, then reduce the heat and boil gently for about 10 minutes, or until the potatoes are just tender.

2 Drain well and leave in a colander to cool. When cool enough to handle, slice the potato chunks and put them in a bowl.

3 Sprinkle the garlic, vinegar, cumin and cayenne or paprika over the salad. Drizzle with olive oil and sprinkle over the chopped coriander and black olives.

Moroccan-style Vegetable Salad

This fresh and invigorating salad has Moroccan origins. The combination of crisp peppers, moist cucumber, spicy chilli and soft potatoes in a herb dressing is a certain winner.

Serves 4–6
1 large cucumber, thinly sliced
2 cold, boiled potatoes, sliced
1 each red, yellow and green (bell) pepper, seeded and thinly sliced
300g/11oz/2⅔ cups pitted olives
½–1 hot fresh chilli, seeded and chopped
3–5 garlic cloves, chopped
3 spring onions (scallions), sliced
60–90ml/4–6 tbsp extra virgin olive oil
15–30ml/1–2 tbsp white wine vinegar
juice of ½ lemon, or to taste
15–30ml/1–2 tbsp chopped fresh mint leaves
15–30ml/1–2 tbsp chopped fresh coriander (cilantro) leaves
salt (optional)

Preparation: 12 minutes; Cooking: 0 minutes

1 Arrange the cucumber, potato and pepper slices and the pitted olives on a serving plate or in a dish.

2 Sprinkle the chopped fresh chilli over the salad and season with salt, if you like. (Olives tend to be very salty.)

3 Sprinkle the garlic, spring onions, olive oil, white wine vinegar and lemon juice over the salad. Cover with clear film (plastic wrap) and chill before serving, sprinkled with the chopped mint leaves and coriander leaves.

Israeli Salad Energy 116kcal/485kJ; Protein 3g; Carbohydrate 12.2g, of which sugars 11.7g; Fat 6.5g, of which saturates 1.1g; Cholesterol 0mg; Calcium 43mg; Fibre 3.8g; Sodium 21mg.
Spicy Potato Energy 238kcal/998kJ; Protein 4g; Carbohydrate 32.6g, of which sugars 2.9g; Fat 11.1g, of which saturates 1.7g; Cholesterol 0mg; Calcium 49mg; Fibre 3.2g; Sodium 448mg.
Moroccan-style Energy 205kcal/847kJ; Protein 2.2g; Carbohydrate 9.5g, of which sugars 6.7g; Fat 17.8g, of which saturates 2.7g; Cholesterol 0mg; Calcium 57mg; Fibre 3.9g; Sodium 1503mg.

Mint & Parsley Tahini Salad

The almost dry flavour of tahini (a creamy sesame seed paste) combines wonderfully with fresh herbs and subtle spices in this refreshing summer salad or light appetizer.

Serves 4–6

115g/4oz/½ cup tahini
3 garlic cloves, chopped
½ bunch (about 20g/¾oz) fresh mint, chopped
½ bunch (about 20g/¾oz) fresh coriander (cilantro), chopped
½ bunch (about 20g/¾oz) fresh flat leaf parsley, chopped
juice of ½ lemon, or to taste
pinch of ground cumin
pinch of ground turmeric
pinch of ground cardamom seeds
cayenne pepper, to taste
salt

To serve

extra virgin olive oil
warmed pitta bread
olives
raw vegetables, such as cherry tomatoes, cucumber and carrots

Preparation: 5 minutes; Cooking: 0 minutes

1 Combine the tahini with the chopped garlic, fresh herbs and lemon juice in a bowl. Taste and add a little more lemon juice, if you like. Stir in a little water if the mixture seems too dense and thick. Alternatively, place the ingredients in a food processor. Process briefly, then stir in a little water if required.

2 Stir in the cumin, turmeric and cardamom to taste, then season with salt and cayenne pepper.

3 To serve, spoon into a shallow bowl or on to plates and drizzle with olive oil. Serve with warmed pitta bread, olives and raw cherry tomatoes, cucumber and carrots.

> **Cook's Tip**
> Tahini is a key ingredient in Middle Eastern cooking, and often features in recipes for hummus. It is made by processing sesame seeds to separate the bran from the kernels. When toasted and ground, these produce an oily paste similar to peanut butter in consistency, which may be light or dark.

Cucumber & Walnut Salad

The combination of cucumbers, garlic and thick yogurt with dill and walnuts makes this cool creamy salad an ideal and quick dish for a hot summer's day.

Serves 6

1 large cucumber
3–5 garlic cloves, finely chopped
250ml/8fl oz/1 cup sour cream
250ml/8fl oz/1 cup yogurt, preferably thick Greek (US strained plain) sheep's milk yogurt
2–3 large pinches of dried dill or 30–45ml/2–3 tbsp chopped fresh dill
45–60ml/3–4 tbsp chopped walnuts
salt
sprig of dill, to garnish (optional)

Preparation: 8 minutes; Cooking: 0 minutes

1 Dice the cucumber finely and place it in a large mixing bowl.

2 Add the garlic, sour cream, yogurt, dill and salt. Mix together, then cover and chill.

3 To serve, pile the mixture into a bowl and sprinkle with walnuts. Garnish with dill, if you like.

> **Variations**
> • Instead of sour cream, use 120ml/4fl oz/½ cup Greek (US strained plain) yogurt mixed with 120ml/4fl oz/½ cup double (heavy) cream.
> • Use fewer garlic cloves if you prefer, although they should not be omitted altogether as they are an essential flavouring.
> • Add spring onions (scallions). Use about four and chop them finely, keeping the white and usable green parts separate. Add the white to the salad and use the green for a garnish.

> **Cook's Tip**
> When made with very thick Greek yogurt, this appetizer can be shaped into balls and served on salad leaves.

Tahini Salad Energy 125kcal/516kJ; Protein 4.3g; Carbohydrate 0.9g, of which sugars 0.7g; Fat 11.6g, of which saturates 1.6g; Cholesterol 0mg; Calcium 180mg; Fibre 2.8g; Sodium 12mg.
Cucumber Salad Energy 263kcal/1085kJ; Protein 5g; Carbohydrate 5.8g, of which sugars 5.7g; Fat 24.6g, of which saturates 12.5g; Cholesterol 53mg; Calcium 141mg; Fibre 0.5g; Sodium 58mg.

Pink Grapefruit & Avocado Salad

Smooth, creamy avocado, zesty pink grapefruit and peppery rocket are perfect partners in this attractive, refreshing salad. The chilli oil adds a spicy note.

Serves 4
2 pink grapefruit
2 ripe avocados
90g/3 ½ oz rocket (arugula)
30ml/2 tbsp chilli oil
salt and ground black pepper

Preparation: 8 minutes; Cooking: 0 minutes

1 Slice the top and bottom off one of the grapefruit, then cut off all the peel and pith from around the side. Working over a small bowl to catch the juices, cut out the segments from between the membranes and place them in a separate bowl.

2 Squeeze any juices remaining in the membranes into the juice bowl, then discard them. Repeat with the remaining grapefruit.

3 Halve, stone (pit) and peel the avocados. Slice the flesh and add it to the grapefruit segments. Whisk a little salt and then the chilli oil into the grapefruit juice.

4 Pile the rocket leaves on to four serving plates and top with the grapefruit segments and avocado. Pour over the dressing, making sure it is evenly distributed, and serve.

Cook's Tips
• Avocados turn brown quickly when exposed to the air, but the acidic grapefruit juice will prevent this. Combine the ingredients as soon as the avocados have been sliced.
• Rocket (arugula) is one of the easiest herbs to grow. Sow successive plantings for a continuous supply of the leaves.

Variation
Pink grapefruit are tangy but not too sharp for this salad, alternatively you could try large oranges for a sweeter flavour.

Salad of Wild Greens & Olives

This simple salad takes only a few minutes to put together. Use as wide a variety of greens as you can find, matching sweet flavours with a few bitter leaves for flavour accent.

Serves 4
115g/4oz wild rocket (arugula)
1 packet mixed salad leaves
¼ white cabbage, thinly sliced
1 cucumber, sliced
1 small red onion, chopped
2–3 garlic cloves, chopped
3–5 tomatoes, cut into wedges
1 green (bell) pepper, seeded and sliced
2–3 mint sprigs, sliced or torn
15–30ml/1–2 tbsp chopped fresh parsley and/or tarragon or dill
pinch of dried oregano or thyme
45ml/3 tbsp extra virgin olive oil
juice of ½ lemon
15ml/1 tbsp red wine vinegar
15–20 black olives
salt and ground black pepper
cottage cheese, to serve

Preparation: 6 minutes; Cooking: 0 minutes

1 In a large salad bowl, put the rocket, mixed salad leaves, sliced white cabbage, sliced cucumber, chopped onion and chopped garlic. Toss gently with your fingers to combine the leaves and vegetables.

2 Arrange the tomatoes, pepper, mint, fresh and dried herbs, salt and pepper on top of the greens and vegetables. Drizzle over the oil, lemon juice and vinegar, stud with the olives and serve with a bowl of cottage cheese.

Variation
This is traditionally served with labneh or yogurt cheese, but tastes good with cottage cheese too. Alternatively, try it with feta, either placing a slab on the salad, or adding cubes.

Cook's Tip
Try to find mixed salad leaves that include varieties such as lamb's lettuce, purslane and mizuna.

Pink Grapefruit Energy 174kcal/719kJ; Protein 2.2g; Carbohydrate 6.8g, of which sugars 6g; Fat 15.4g, of which saturates 2.9g; Cholesterol 0mg; Calcium 62mg; Fibre 3.2g; Sodium 37mg.
Wild Greens Energy 150kcal/619kJ; Protein 3.3g; Carbohydrate 10.4g, of which sugars 9.8g; Fat 10.7g, of which saturates 1.6g; Cholesterol 0mg; Calcium 106mg; Fibre 4.2g; Sodium 338mg.

Turnip Salad in Sour Cream

Often neglected, turnips make an unusual and very tasty accompaniment when prepared in this simple way. For the best results, choose young, tender turnips of the type the French call 'navets' and slice them thinly.

Serves 4
2–4 young, tender turnips, peeled
1/4–1/2 onion, finely chopped
2–3 drops white wine vinegar, or
   to taste
60–90ml/4–6 tbsp sour cream
salt and ground black pepper
chopped fresh parsley or paprika,
   to garnish

Preparation: 5 minutes; Cooking: 0 minutes

1 Thinly slice or coarsely grate the turnips. Alternatively, thinly slice half the turnips and grate the ones that remain. Put in a bowl. Add the onion, vinegar, salt and pepper, toss together then stir in the sour cream. Serve chilled, garnished with a sprinkling of chopped fresh parsley or paprika.

Mushroom Salad

This simple refreshing salad is often served as part of a selection of vegetable salads, or crudités.

Serves 4
175g/6oz button (white)
   mushrooms, trimmed

grated (shredded) rind and juice
   of 1 1/2 lemons
about 30–45ml/2–3 tbsp crème
   fraîche or sour cream
salt and ground white pepper
15ml/1 tbsp chopped fresh
   chives or sliced radishes,
   to garnish

Preparation: 5 minutes; Cooking: 0 minutes

1 Slice the mushrooms thinly and place in a bowl. In a separate bowl mix the lemon rind and juice and the cream, adding a little more cream if needed. Spoon over the mushrooms.

2 Stir gently to mix, then season with salt and pepper. Sprinkle the salad with chopped chives before serving.

Green Leaf Salad with Capers & Stuffed Olives

The best time to make this refreshing salad is in the summer when tomatoes are at their sweetest and full of flavour. It makes a colourful addition to the table.

Serves 4
4 tomatoes
1/2 cucumber
1 bunch spring onions (scallions),
   trimmed

1 bunch watercress
8 stuffed olives
30ml/2 tbsp drained capers

For the dressing
30ml/2 tbsp red wine vinegar
5ml/1 tsp paprika
2.5ml/1/2 tsp ground cumin
1 garlic clove, crushed
75 ml/5 tbsp olive oil
salt and ground black pepper

Preparation: 10 minutes; Cooking: 0 minutes

1 Peel the tomatoes, if you like, although this is not essential, and finely dice the flesh. Put them in a salad bowl.

2 Peel the cucumber, dice it finely and add it to the tomatoes. Chop half the spring onions, add them to the salad bowl and mix lightly. Break the watercress into sprigs. Add to the tomato mixture, with the olives and capers.

3 To make the dressing, mix the wine vinegar, paprika, cumin and garlic in a bowl. Whisk in the oil and add salt and pepper to taste. Pour over the salad and toss lightly. Serve immediately with the remaining spring onions.

Cook's Tip
Stuffed olives are delicious in a salad, and also prove popular when set out in a bowl to serve with drinks. There are several different types on sale, generally using green olives. Fillings include anchovies, pimiento, cheese – including blue cheese – garlic, almonds and lemon. For this recipe, the pimiento or anchovy-stuffed olives would be best.

Turnip Salad Energy 48kcal/198kJ; Protein 1.1g; Carbohydrate 4.1g, of which sugars 3.7g; Fat 3.2g, of which saturates 1.9g; Cholesterol 9mg; Calcium 42mg; Fibre 1.4g; Sodium 14mg.
Mushroom Salad Energy 22kcal/93kJ; Protein 1.1g; Carbohydrate 0.6g, of which sugars 0.5g; Fat 1.8g, of which saturates 1g; Cholesterol 5mg; Calcium 17mg; Fibre 0.7g; Sodium 7mg
Green Leaf Salad Energy 167kcal/692kJ; Protein 2.2g; Carbohydrate 4.3g, of which sugars 4.3g; Fat 15.8g, of which saturates 2.4g; Cholesterol 0mg; Calcium 72mg; Fibre 2.3g; Sodium 305mg.

Spinach & Roast Garlic Salad

Spinach and garlic go wonderfully together, and this simple combination of warm garlic and cold spinach leaves with crunchy pine nuts makes a memorable salad that is perfect for summer.

Serves 4

12 garlic cloves, unpeeled
60 ml/4 tbsp extra virgin olive oil
450g/1lb baby spinach leaves
50g/2oz/½ cup pine nuts,
    lightly toasted
juice of ½ lemon
salt and ground black pepper

Preparation: 3 minutes; Cooking: 15 minutes

1 Preheat the oven to 190°C/375°F/Gas 5. Place the unpeeled garlic cloves in a small roasting pan, add 30 ml/2 tbsp of the oil and stir the cloves around until well coated. Put the pan in the oven and roast the garlic cloves for about 15 minutes, until they are slightly charred around the edges.

2 While still warm, tip the garlic into a salad bowl. Add the spinach, pine nuts, lemon juice, remaining olive oil and a little salt. Toss well and add black pepper to taste. Serve immediately, inviting guests to squeeze the softened garlic cloves out of their skins to eat with the dressed leaves and nuts.

Variation
Garlic is not the only ingredient that goes well with spinach. Pickled lemons are also natural partners. Buy them in jars and rinse well before use. One pickled lemon, finely chopped, will make an excellent addition to this salad and should be added to the spinach leaves with the pine nuts and dressing ingredients.

Cook's Tip
Don't worry about the amount of garlic used in this salad. During roasting, garlic becomes sweet and subtle and loses much of its pungent taste.

Asparagus & Orange Salad

A simple dressing of olive oil and sherry vinegar mingles with the orange and tomato flavours in this asparagus-based salad with great results. This salad is good on its own and even better with prosciutto or some good quality salami. Alternatively, top with strips of grilled bacon.

Serves 4

225g/8oz asparagus, trimmed
    and cut into 5cm/2in pieces
2 large oranges
2 well-flavoured ripe tomatoes,
    cut into eighths
50g/2oz romaine lettuce
    leaves, shredded
30ml/2 tbsp extra virgin olive oil
2.5ml/½ tsp sherry vinegar
salt and ground black pepper

Preparation: 6 minutes; Cooking: 3–4 minutes

1 Cook the asparagus in lightly salted, boiling water for 3–4 minutes, until just tender. Drain in a colander and refresh under cold water. Drain again and set aside.

2 Grate the rind from half an orange and reserve. Peel both oranges and cut into segments, leaving the membrane behind. Squeeze out the juice from the membrane and reserve the juice.

3 Put the asparagus pieces, segments of orange, tomatoes and romaine lettuce leaves into a salad bowl.

4 Mix together the olive oil and sherry vinegar and add 15ml/1 tbsp of the reserved orange juice and 5ml/1 tsp of the grated orange rind, whisking well to combine. Season with a little salt and plenty of ground black pepper. Just before serving, pour the dressing over the salad and mix gently to coat.

Cook's Tip
Sherry vinegar is golden brown with a rounded and full flavour. It is matured in wooden barrels in much the same way as sherry itself. It resembles balsamic vinegar but is less assertive, with a sweet and sour taste that adds interest to sauces, gravies, salads and marinades.

Spinach and Garlic Energy 225kcal/929kJ; Protein 5.9g; Carbohydrate 4.4g, of which sugars 2.4g; Fat 20.6g, of which saturates 2.3g; Cholesterol 0mg; Calcium 195mg; Fibre 3.1g; Sodium 158mg.
Asparagus and Orange Energy 106kcal/442kJ; Protein 3.1g; Carbohydrate 10g, of which sugars 10g; Fat 6.2g, of which saturates 0.9g; Cholesterol 0mg; Calcium 59mg; Fibre 3.1g; Sodium 12mg.

Caesar Salad

This is a well-known and much enjoyed salad invented by a chef called Caesar Cardini. Be sure to use crisp lettuce and add the very soft eggs at the last minute.

Serves 6

175ml/6fl oz/³⁄₄ cup olive oil
115g/4oz French or Italian bread, cut into 2.5cm/1in cubes
1 large garlic clove, crushed or finely chopped
1 cos or romaine lettuce
2 eggs, soft-boiled for 1 minute
120ml/4fl oz/¹⁄₂ cup lemon juice
50g/2oz/²⁄₃ cup freshly grated Parmesan cheese
6 canned anchovy fillets, drained and finely chopped (optional)
salt and ground black pepper

Preparation: 10 minutes; Cooking: 2 minutes

1 Heat 50ml/2fl oz/¹⁄₄ cup of the oil in a large frying pan. Add the bread cubes and garlic. Cook over a medium heat, stirring constantly, until the bread cubes are golden brown all over. Drain well on kitchen paper. Discard the garlic.

2 Tear large lettuce leaves into smaller pieces. Put all the lettuce in a bowl.

3 Add the remaining oil to the lettuce and season with salt and plenty of ground black pepper. Toss well to coat the leaves.

4 Break the eggs on top. Sprinkle with the lemon juice. Toss thoroughly again to combine. Add the Parmesan cheese and anchovies, if using. Toss gently to mix.

5 Sprinkle the fried bread cubes evenly on top of the salad and serve immediately.

Variation
For a tangier dressing, mix 30ml/2 tbsp white wine vinegar, 15ml/1 tbsp Worcestershire sauce, 2.5ml/¹⁄₂ tsp mustard powder, 5ml/1 tsp sugar, salt and pepper in a screw-top jar, then add the oil and shake well.

Watermelon & Feta Salad

The combination of sweet watermelon with salty feta cheese is inspired by Turkish tradition. The salad may be served plain and light, on a leafy base, or with a vinaigrette. It tastes great with grilled food from the barbecue.

Serves 4

4 slices watermelon, chilled
130g/4¹⁄₂oz feta cheese, preferably sheep's milk feta, cut into bitesize pieces
handful of mixed seeds, such as lightly toasted pumpkin seeds and sunflower seeds
10–15 black olives

Preparation: 5 minutes; Cooking: 0 minutes

1 Cut the rind off the watermelon and remove as many seeds as possible. Cut the flesh into triangular-shaped chunks.

2 Mix the watermelon, feta cheese, mixed seeds and black olives together in a serving bowl.

3 Cover the bowl with clear film (plastic wrap) and chill the salad for 30 minutes before serving if possible.

Variation
Although watermelon is usually eaten on its own as a dessert fruit, it also stars in a savoury context, since it is not particularly sweet. It is especially valued for the crisp texture, which is accentuated when the fruit is chilled. In Mediterranean countries, watermelon is often served with a lemon and honey dressing. If this is done ahead of time, and the slices or cubes of watermelon are covered and kept in the refrigerator overnight, the flavour permeates the fruit, which stays delightfully crunchy. Watermelon prepared this way is very good with guinea fowl.

Cook's Tip
The best choice of olives for this recipe are black ones, such as kalamata, other shiny, brined varieties, or dry-cured black olives.

Caesar Salad Energy 782kcal/3251kJ; Protein 49.6g; Carbohydrate 8.6g, of which sugars 1.2g; Fat 62.4g, of which saturates 15.6g; Cholesterol 1342mg; Calcium 354mg; Fibre 1g; Sodium 785mg.
Watermelon Energy 211kcal/884kJ; Protein 8g; Carbohydrate 16g, of which sugars 15g; Fat 13g, of which saturates 5g; Cholesterol 23mg; Calcium 145mg; Fibre 1.1g; Sodium 700mg.

Goat's Cheese Salad

You need a soft goat's cheese with plenty of flavour for this salad. Look out for artisan cheeses at farmers' markets, where you can try before you buy.

Serves 4
175g/6oz mixed salad leaves, such as lamb's lettuce, rocket (arugula), radicchio, frisée or cress

a few fresh large-leafed herbs, such as chervil and flat leaf parsley
15ml/1 tbsp toasted hazelnuts, roughly chopped
15–20 goat's cheese balls or cubes

For the dressing
30ml/2 tbsp hazelnut oil, olive oil or sunflower oil
5–10ml/1–2 tsp sherry vinegar or good wine vinegar, to taste
salt and ground black pepper

Preparation: 8–10 minutes; Cooking: 0 minutes

1 Tear up any large salad leaves. Put all the leaves into a large salad bowl with the fresh herbs and most of the toasted, chopped nuts (reserve a few for the garnish).

2 To make the dressing, whisk the hazelnut, olive or sunflower oil and vinegar together in a bowl, and then season to taste with salt and pepper.

3 Just before serving, toss the salad in the dressing and divide it among four serving plates. Arrange the drained goat's cheese balls or cubes over the leaves, sprinkle over the remaining chopped nuts and serve.

> **Variations**
> • Toasted flaked (sliced) almonds could replace the hazelnuts (teamed with extra virgin olive oil). Stronger-flavoured cheeses work well with walnuts and walnut oil.
> • Mozzarella balls or cubes can be used instead of the goat's cheese, or substitute feta.
> • Pomegranate seeds would look good in this salad, like tiny red jewels among the green of the leaves.

Orange, Onion & Olive Salad

This is a refreshing Moroccan salad for a light summer lunch or to follow a rich main dish, such as a tagine of lamb, or to lighten any spicy meal.

15ml/1 tbsp chopped fresh mint, plus a few extra sprigs
15ml/1 tbsp chopped fresh coriander (cilantro), plus a few extra sprigs
2.5ml/½ tsp orange flower water

Serves 6
5 large oranges
90g/3½oz/scant 1 cup black olives
1 red onion, thinly sliced
1 large fennel bulb, thinly sliced, feathery tops reserved

For the dressing
60ml/4 tbsp olive oil
10ml/2 tsp lemon juice
2.5ml/½ tsp ground toasted coriander seeds
salt and ground black pepper

Preparation: 15 minutes; Cooking: 0 minutes

1 Peel the oranges with a sharp knife, making sure you remove all the white pith, and cut them into 5mm/¼in slices. Remove any pips and work over a bowl to catch all the orange juice. Set the bowl of orange juice aside for the dressing.

2 Stone the olives, if wished. In a bowl, mix the orange slices, onion and fennel with the olives, chopped mint and fresh coriander. Toss lightly to mix.

3 Make the dressing. In a bowl or jug (pitcher), whisk together the olive oil, 15ml/1 tbsp of the reserved fresh orange juice and the lemon juice. Add the ground toasted coriander seeds and season to taste with a little salt and pepper. Whisk thoroughly to mix or use a milk frother.

4 Toss the dressing into the salad and, ideally, leave to stand for 30–60 minutes to allow the flavours to develop fully.

5 Drain off any excess dressing and place the salad on a serving dish. Scatter with the herbs and fennel tops, and sprinkle with the orange flower water. A few orange nasturtiums would make a pretty garnish, if available.

Goat's Cheese Salad Energy 215kcal/893kJ; Protein 11.4g; Carbohydrate 1.5g, of which sugars 1.4g; Fat 18.3g, of which saturates 9.6g; Cholesterol 47mg; Calcium 84mg; Fibre 0.6g; Sodium 302mg.
Orange, Onion Energy 582kcal/2473kJ; Protein 15.2g; Carbohydrate 114.7g, of which sugars 114.5g; Fat 10.4g, of which saturates 1.3g; Cholesterol 0mg; Calcium 646mg; Fibre 24.1g; Sodium 408mg.

Tomato, Mozzarella & Onion Salad

Sweet tomatoes and the heady scent of basil capture the essence of summer in this simple salad. Vine-ripened tomatoes usually have the best flavour. Use local ones if possible.

Serves 6

5 large ripe tomatoes, peeled if liked
2 buffalo mozzarella cheeses, drained and sliced
1 small red onion, chopped

For the dressing

½ small garlic clove, peeled
15g/½oz fresh basil
30ml/2 tbsp chopped fresh flat leaf parsley
25ml/5 tsp small capers in brine, rinsed
2.5ml/½ tsp mustard
75–90ml/5–6 tbsp extra virgin olive oil
5–10ml/1–2 tsp balsamic vinegar
ground black pepper
fresh basil leaves and parsley sprigs, to garnish

Preparation: 15 minutes; Cooking: 0 minutes

1 First make the dressing. Put the garlic, basil, parsley, half the capers and the mustard in a food processor or blender and process briefly to chop. Then, with the motor running, gradually pour in the olive oil through the feeder tube to make a smooth purée with a dressing consistency. Add the balsamic vinegar to taste and season with pepper.

2 Slice the tomatoes. Arrange the tomato and mozzarella slices on a plate. Scatter the onion over and season the salad with a little freshly ground black pepper.

3 Drizzle the dressing over the salad, then scatter the basil leaves, parsley sprigs and remaining capers on top. Leave for 10–15 minutes before serving if possible.

Cook's Tip
When making the dressing, it is a good idea to use the pulse facility for first chopping the garlic, parsley and capers together. Add the mustard and give the ingredients a quick blitz before beginning to pour in the olive oil.

Salad with Omelette Strips & Bacon

Rich duck eggs are delicious in salads as they have a lovely, delicate flavour.

Serves 4

400g/14oz bag of mixed salad leaves
6 streaky (fatty) bacon rashers (strips), rinds removed and chopped
2 duck eggs
2 spring onions (scallions), chopped
few sprigs of coriander (cilantro), chopped
25g/1oz/2 tbsp butter
60ml/4 tbsp olive oil
30ml/2 tbsp balsamic vinegar
salt and ground black pepper

Preparation: 3 minutes; Cooking: 6–7 minutes

1 Warm an omelette pan over a low heat and gently fry the chopped bacon until the fat runs. Increase the heat to crisp up the bacon, stirring frequently. When the bacon pieces are brown and crispy, remove from the heat and transfer to a hot dish to keep warm.

2 Break the duck eggs into a small bowl and add the spring onions and coriander. Season and beat the mixture lightly.

3 Melt the butter in an omelette pan and pour in the beaten eggs. Cook for 2–3 minutes to make an unfolded omelette. Cut into long strips and add to the salad with the bacon.

4 Place the salad leaves in a large bowl. Add the oil, vinegar and seasoning to the omelette pan, heat briefly and pour over the salad. Toss well before serving.

Cook's Tip
Choose a selection of salad leaves, which includes some distinctively flavoured leaves that will add a bite to this salad. A combination that includes rocket, watercress, baby spinach or herbs would be ideal.

Salad with Omelette Energy 301kcal/1246kJ; Protein 12.4g; Carbohydrate 1.8g, of which sugars 1.8g; Fat 27.3g, of which saturates 8.4g; Cholesterol 288mg; Calcium 55mg; Fibre 0.9g; Sodium 664mg.
Tomato, Mozzarella Energy 232kcal/960kJ; Protein 10.3g; Carbohydrate 3.6g, of which sugars 3.3g; Fat 19.7g, of which saturates 8.3g; Cholesterol 29mg; Calcium 206mg; Fibre 1.4g; Sodium 208mg.

Chilli Salad Omelettes with Hummus

These delicate omelettes are filled with salad and served chilled to make a refreshing lunch. Try to include as wide a variety of vegetables as possible.

Serves 6
4 eggs
15ml/1 tbsp cornflour (cornstarch)
15ml/1 tbsp stock or water

115g/4oz/1 cup shredded salad vegetables, such as crisp lettuce, carrot, celery, spring onion (scallions) and peppers
60ml/4 tbsp chilli salad dressing (or add a few drops of chilli sauce to your favourite salad dressing)
60–75ml/4–5 tbsp hummus
4 crisply cooked bacon rashers (strips), chopped
salt and ground black pepper

Preparation: 10 minutes; Cooking: 8 minutes

1 Break the eggs into a bowl. Add the cornflour and stock or water and beat well. Heat a lightly oiled frying pan and pour a quarter of the egg mixture into the pan, tipping it to spread it out to a thin, even layer.

2 Cook the omelette gently to avoid it colouring too much or becoming bubbly and crisp. When cooked, remove from the pan and make a further three omelettes in the same way. Stack between sheets of baking parchment, then cool and chill.

3 When ready to serve, toss the shredded salad vegetables together with 45ml/3 tbsp of the dressing. Spread half of each omelette with hummus, top with the salad vegetables and chopped bacon and fold in half. Drizzle the rest of the dressing over the filled omelettes before serving.

> **Variation**
> These omelettes can be filled with a whole range of ingredients. Try using taramasalata instead of hummus, or fill the omelettes with ratatouille or mixed roasted vegetables.

Summer Salad

Ripe organic tomatoes, mozzarella and olives make a good base for a fresh and tangy pasta salad that is perfect for a light lunch. It travels well so would be good to take to work.

Serves 4
350g/12oz/3 cups dried penne
150g/5oz packet buffalo mozzarella, drained and diced

3 ripe tomatoes, diced
10 pitted black olives, sliced
10 pitted green olives, sliced
1 spring onion (scallion), thinly sliced on the diagonal
1 handful fresh basil leaves

For the dressing
90ml/6 tbsp extra virgin olive oil
15ml/1 tbsp balsamic vinegar or lemon juice
sea salt and ground black pepper

Preparation: 5 minutes; Cooking: 10–12 minutes

1 Cook the pasta for 10–12 minutes, or according to the instructions on the packet. Tip it into a colander and rinse briefly under cold running water, then shake to drain.

2 Make the dressing. Whisk the olive oil and balsamic vinegar or lemon juice in a jug (pitcher) with a little salt and pepper.

3 Place the pasta, mozzarella, tomatoes, olives and spring onion in a large bowl, pour the dressing over and toss together well. Taste for seasoning before serving, sprinkled with basil leaves.

> **Variation**
> Make the salad more substantial by adding sliced peppers, flaked tuna, anchovy fillets or diced ham. Always choose sustainably caught tuna and anchovies.

> **Cook's Tip**
> Mozzarella made from buffalo milk has more flavour than the type made with cow's milk. Look for mozzarella di bufala in your organic store or delicatessen.

Salad Omelettes Energy 173kcal/719kJ; Protein 11.8g; Carbohydrate 5.7g, of which sugars 0.8g; Fat 11.7g, of which saturates 3.1g; Cholesterol 204mg; Calcium 45mg; Fibre 0.6g; Sodium 558mg.
Summer Salad Energy 635kcal/2658kJ; Protein 18.7g; Carbohydrate 67.2g, of which sugars 5.3g; Fat 34.2g, of which saturates 9.1g; Cholesterol 22mg; Calcium 210mg; Fibre 5.5g; Sodium 1845mg.

Country Pasta Salad

Colourful, tasty and nutritious, this is the ideal pasta salad for a summer picnic. All sorts of pasta shapes are now available, including novelties. Any medium-sized shapes are suitable for this salad.

Serves 6
300g/11oz/2¾ cups dried fusilli
150g/5oz fine green beans,
    trimmed and cut into
    5cm/2in lengths
1 potato, about 150g/5oz, diced
200g/7oz cherry tomatoes,
    halved
2 spring onions (scallions),
    finely chopped
90g/3½ oz/scant 1¼ cups
    Parmesan cheese or premium
    Italian-style vegetarian cheese,
    coarsely shaved
6–8 pitted black olives, cut
    into rings
15–30ml/1–2 tbsp capers,
    to taste

For the dressing
90ml/6 tbsp extra virgin olive oil
15ml/1 tbsp balsamic vinegar
15ml/1 tbsp chopped fresh flat
    leaf parsley
sea salt and ground black pepper

Preparation: 4–5 minutes; Cooking: 15–16 minutes

1 Cook the pasta according to the instructions on the packet. Meanwhile, cook the beans and diced potato in a pan of lightly salted boiling water for 5–6 minutes or steam for 8–10 minutes. Drain and leave to cool.

2 Drain the pasta into a colander, rinse under cold running water until cold, then shake the colander to remove as much water as possible. Leave to drain and dry.

3 To make the dressing, put all the ingredients in a large bowl with a little sea salt and ground black pepper to taste and whisk well until the ingredients are well mixed and the dressing has thickened slightly.

4 Add the tomatoes, spring onions, Parmesan, olive rings and capers to the dressing then stir in the cold pasta, beans and potato. Toss well to mix. If you have time, cover with clear film (plastic wrap) and leave to stand for about 30 minutes to allow the flavours to blend. Taste for seasoning before serving.

Pink & Green Salad

There's just enough chilli in this stunning salad to bring a rosy blush to your cheeks.

Serves 4
225g/8oz/2 cups dried farfalle or
    other pasta shapes
juice of ½ lemon
1 small fresh red chilli, seeded
    and very finely chopped
60ml/4 tbsp chopped fresh basil
30ml/2 tbsp chopped fresh
    coriander (cilantro)
60ml/4 tbsp virgin or extra virgin
    olive oil
15ml/1 tbsp mayonnaise
250g/9oz peeled cooked
    prawns (shrimp)
1 avocado
salt and ground black pepper

Preparation: 5 minutes; Cooking: 10–12 minutes

1 Bring a large pan of lightly salted water to the boil and stir in the pasta. Cook it for 10–12 minutes, folllowing the packet instructions, or until it is just tender but retains a bit of bite.

2 Meanwhile, put the lemon juice and chilli in a bowl with half the basil and coriander. Add salt and pepper to taste. Whisk well to mix, then whisk in the oil and mayonnaise until thick. Add the prawns and stir to coat in the dressing.

3 Tip the cooked pasta into a colander, and rinse under cold running water until cold. Leave to drain and dry, shaking the colander occasionally.

4 Halve, stone (pit) and peel the avocado, then cut the flesh into dice. Add to the prawns and dressing with the pasta, toss well to mix and taste for seasoning. Serve immediately, sprinkled with the remaining basil and coriander.

Cook's Tips
• Keep a few chillies in the freezer and you'll never need to worry about getting fresh supplies just when you want them.
• If chillies are not to your taste, add mild peppadews (sweet piquant peppers). They come in bottles and keep well, so it is a good idea to keep some in the refrigerator for recipes like these.

Country Pasta Energy 388kcal/625kJ; Protein 13.5g; Carbohydrate 43.4g, of which sugars 4g; Fat 19g, of which saturates 5.1g; Cholesterol 15mg; Calcium 221mg; Fibre 3.3g; Sodium 547mg.
Pink and Green Energy 420kcal/1761kJ; Protein 19g; Carbohydrate 42.8g, of which sugars 2.6g; Fat 20.3g, of which saturates 3.2g; Cholesterol 125mg; Calcium 112mg; Fibre 3.6g; Sodium 146mg.

Greek Salad

Anyone who has spent a holiday in Greece will have eaten a version of this salad – the Greeks' equivalent of a mixed salad. Its success relies on using only the freshest ingredients, including sun-ripened tomatoes, and a good olive oil. The salad is presented in various ways. Some cooks like to crumble in the feta so that it mixes with all the other ingredients; others place a slice of feta on top.

Serves 6

450g/1lb well-flavoured plum tomatoes
1 small cos or romaine lettuce, trimmed
1 cucumber
4 spring onions (scallions), sliced
200g/7oz feta cheese
50g/2oz/½ cup pitted black olives, halved

For the dressing
90ml/6 tbsp extra virgin olive oil
25ml/1½ tbsp lemon juice
salt and ground black pepper

Preparation: 16 minutes; Cooking: 0 minutes

1 Skin the tomatoes. Cut a small cross in the blossom end of each fruit and place them in a heatproof bowl. Pour over boiling water to cover and leave to stand for 1–2 minutes, or until the skin starts to peel back from the crosses. Drain the tomatoes and slip off the skins. Set aside to cool slightly.

2 Slice the cos or romaine lettuce. Peel the cucumber, cut it in half and remove the seeds with a teaspoon, then chop the cucumber flesh. Slice the spring onions.

3 Place the peeled tomatoes on a chopping board. Using a sharp cook's knife or a serrated knife, cut into quarters and then into eighths. Put them in a bowl and add the lettuce, cucumber and spring onions. Crumble in the feta cheese or leave it whole, placing it on top of the salad. Add the olives.

4 Make the dressing. In a bowl, whisk together the olive oil and lemon juice, then season with salt and ground black pepper, and whisk again. Pour the dressing over the salad. Using salad servers, toss to mix well and serve immediately.

Salad with Feta, Chillies & Parsley

A different take on the feta salad, this time from the Middle East. Colourful vegetables are mixed with lots of fresh parsley and, unusually, grated feta.

Serves 3–4
2 red onions, cut in half lengthways and finely sliced along the grain
1 green (bell) pepper, seeded and finely sliced
1 fresh green chilli, seeded and chopped
2–3 garlic cloves, chopped
1 bunch of fresh flat leaf parsley, roughly chopped
225g/8oz firm feta cheese, rinsed and grated
2 large tomatoes, skinned, seeded and finely chopped
30–45ml/2–3 tbsp olive oil
salt and ground black pepper

To serve
scant 5ml/1 tsp Turkish red pepper flakes or paprika
scant 5ml/1 tsp ground sumac

Preparation: 12 minutes; Cooking: 0 minutes

1 Sprinkle the onions with a little salt to draw out the juice. Leave for about 10 minutes, then rinse and pat dry.

2 Put the onions and green pepper in a bowl with the chilli, garlic, parsley, feta and tomatoes.

3 Add the oil and seasoning and toss well.

4 Tip the salad into a large serving dish and sprinkle with the red pepper or paprika and sumac.

Cook's Tip
Sumac is a spice widely used in Lebanese, Syrian, Turkish and Iranian cuisines. The red berries come from a bush that grows throughout the Middle East. They are picked just before they ripen and are dried for local use and export. When cracked and soaked in water, the berries yield an astringent juice which is a popular souring agent. More often, the berries are ground and the powder used as a rub for meats or an ingredient in salads.

Greek Salad Energy 225kcal/935kJ; Protein 11.2g; Carbohydrate 11.8g, of which sugars 11.1g; Fat 15.1g, of which saturates 8.3g; Cholesterol 39mg; Calcium 249mg; Fibre 3.4g; Sodium 827mg.
Salad with Feta Energy 253kcal/1049kJ; Protein 11.1g; Carbohydrate 13.4g, of which sugars 11g; Fat 17.6g, of which saturates 8.6g; Cholesterol 39mg; Calcium 260mg; Fibre 3.2g; Sodium 824mg.

Avocado, Tomato & Orange Salad

This salad has a feel of the Mediterranean – avocados are grown in many parts of the region and add a delicious flavour and texture to this dish. Take care to find avocados that are fully ripe, but not so ripe that they have developed bruising or are turning black in places. Some stores now sell ready-to-eat avocados.

Serves 4
2 oranges
4 well-flavoured tomatoes
2 small avocados
60ml/4 tbsp extra virgin olive oil
30ml/2 tbsp lemon juice
15ml/1 tbsp chopped
    fresh parsley
1 small onion, sliced into rings
salt and ground black pepper
25g/1oz/¼ cup flaked (sliced)
    almonds and olives, to garnish

Preparation: 5 minutes; Cooking: 0 minutes

1 Peel the oranges and slice into thick rounds. Plunge the tomatoes into boiling water for 30 seconds, then refresh in cold water. Peel off the skins, cut the tomatoes into quarters, remove the seeds and chop roughly.

2 Cut the avocados in half, remove the stones (pits) and carefully peel away the skin. Cut into chunks.

3 In a large bowl, whisk together the olive oil, lemon juice and parsley. Season with salt and pepper. Pour half the dressing into a jug (pitcher). Add the avocados and tomatoes to the dressing remaining in the bowl and toss to coat.

4 Arrange the sliced oranges on a plate and scatter over the onion rings. Drizzle with the rest of the dressing. Spoon the avocados, tomatoes, almonds and olives on top of the salad.

> **Cook's Tip**
> Use avocados that are just ripe for this salad. They should yield to gentle pressure. Avoid any avocados that feel very soft. Unripe avocados will ripen in 4–7 days if stored at room temperature; sooner if bananas are present.

Carrot & Orange Salad

This is a wonderful, fresh-tasting salad with such a fabulous combination of citrus fruit and vegetables that it is difficult to know whether it is a salad or a dessert. It makes a refreshing accompaniment to grilled meat, chicken, fish or prawns.

Serves 4
450g/1lb carrots
2 large navel oranges
15ml/1 tbsp extra virgin olive oil
30ml/2 tbsp freshly squeezed
    lemon juice
pinch of sugar (optional)
30ml/2 tbsp chopped pistachio
    nuts or toasted pine nuts
salt and ground black pepper

Preparation: 5 minutes; Cooking: 0 minutes

1 Peel the carrots and coarsely grate them into a large bowl.

2 Cut a thin slice of peel and pith from each end of the oranges. Place cut side down on a plate and cut off the peel and pith in strips.

3 Holding the oranges over a bowl and using a sharp knife, carefully cut out each segment leaving the membrane behind. Squeeze the juice from the membrane into the bowl.

4 Blend the oil, lemon juice and orange juice in a small bowl to make a light dressing. Season with salt and freshly ground black pepper, and a little sugar, if you like.

5 Toss the oranges with the carrots and pour the dressing over. Sprinkle over the pistachios or pine nuts and serve.

> **Cook's Tips**
> • If you grow your own carrots, and have thinnings available, use them whole in this salad, or look out for bunches of baby carrots at the supermarket. They do not need to be scraped or peeled; just rinsed under cold water.
> • Sultanas or chopped dates can be added to the salad, in which case omit the pinch of sugar.

Carrot and Orange Energy 131kcal/547kJ; Protein 2.7g; Carbohydrate 14.6g, of which sugars 13.9g; Fat 7.3g, of which saturates 1.1g; Cholesterol 0mg; Calcium 65mg; Fibre 4.2g; Sodium 71mg.
Avocado, Tomato Energy 251kcal/1041kJ; Protein 2.7g; Carbohydrate 11.9g, of which sugars 10.9g; Fat 21.7g, of which saturates 3.8g; Cholesterol 0mg; Calcium 60mg; Fibre 4.3g; Sodium 155mg.

Cucumber & Tomato Salad

This salad comes from Bulgaria, where it was traditionally made with the local yogurt. It is claimed that yogurt was first made in Bulgaria and the longevity of some of the country's inhabitants is attributed to eating the dairy food daily.

Serves 4
450g/1lb firm ripe tomatoes
½ cucumber
1 onion
1 small fresh red or green chilli, seeded and chopped, or fresh chives, chopped into 2.5cm/1in lengths, to garnish
crusty bread or pitta breads, to serve

For the dressing
60ml/4 tbsp olive or vegetable oil
90ml/6 tbsp thick Greek (US strained plain) yogurt
30ml/2 tbsp chopped fresh parsley or chives
2.5ml/½ tsp vinegar
salt and ground black pepper

Preparation: 5 minutes; Cooking: 0 minutes

1 Skin the tomatoes by plunging them in boiling water for 1–2 minutes, then drain and plunge into cold water. Skin the tomatoes and seed and chop into even-sized pieces.

2 Chop the cucumber and onion into pieces of similar size to the tomatoes and put them all in a salad bowl.

3 Mix all the dressing ingredients together in a separate bowl and season with salt and pepper to taste. Pour the dressing over the salad and toss all the ingredients together.

4 Sprinkle over black pepper and garnish with the chopped chilli or chives. Serve the salad with chunks of crusty bread or pile into pitta pockets and place these on a plate.

> **Cook's Tip**
> Take care when handling the chillies. Protect your hands by using gloves, if possible. The capsaicin in chillies will burn delicate skin if it comes into contact with it.

Fruit, Vegetable & Noodle Salad

A banana leaf, which can be bought from Asian stores, can be used instead of the mixed salad leaves to line the platter for this wonderful noodle salad.

Serves 6
½ cucumber
2 pears (not too ripe)
1–2 eating apples
juice of ½ lemon
mixed salad leaves
6 small tomatoes, cut in wedges
3 slices fresh pineapple, cored and cut in wedges
3 eggs, hard-boiled and shelled
175g/6oz egg noodles, cooked, cooled and chopped
deep-fried onions, to garnish

For the peanut sauce
2–4 fresh red chillies, seeded and ground
300ml/½ pint/1¼ cups coconut milk
350g/12oz/1¼ cups crunchy peanut butter
15ml/1 tbsp dark soy sauce or dark brown sugar
5ml/1 tsp tamarind pulp, soaked in 45ml/3 tbsp warm water
coarsely crushed peanuts
salt

Preparation: 8–10 minutes; Cooking: 3–5 minutes

1 Make the peanut sauce. Put the ground chillies in a pan. Pour in the coconut milk, then stir in the peanut butter. Heat gently, stirring, until well blended.

2 Simmer gently until the sauce thickens, then stir in the soy sauce or sugar. Strain in the tamarind juice, add salt to taste and stir well. Spoon into a bowl and sprinkle the surface lightly with a few coarsely crushed peanuts.

3 To make the salad, core the cucumber and peel the pears. Cut them into matchsticks. Finely shred the apples and sprinkle them with the lemon juice.

4 Spread a bed of salad leaves on a flat platter, then pile the fruit and vegetables on top.

5 Add the sliced or quartered hard-boiled eggs, the chopped noodles and the deep-fried onions. Serve with the sauce.

Cucumber Energy 156kcal/646kJ; Protein 3g; Carbohydrate 5.8g, of which sugars 5.4g; Fat 13.9g, of which saturates 2.9g; Cholesterol 0mg; Calcium 75mg; Fibre 2.1g; Sodium 32mg.
Fruit, Vegetable Energy 151kcal/645kJ; Protein 3.4g; Carbohydrate 34.3g, of which sugars 33g; Fat 1.1g, of which saturates 0.2g; Cholesterol 0mg; Calcium 78mg; Fibre 4.8g; Sodium 35mg.

Peanut-dressed Crispy Wonton Salad

A traditional Chinese combination, this delicious salad would go as well with conventional chops or steaks as it does as part of an Asian meal. The Tabasco-spiked peanut dressing is particularly good.

Serves 4
8 wonton wrappers
vegetable oil, for deep frying
2 Little Gem (Bibb) lettuces,
    separated into leaves
½ cucumber, halved, seeded and
    cut into 1cm/½in dice
2 ripe tomatoes, peeled, seeded
    and cut into 1cm/½in dice
1 hard-boiled egg, shelled and
    roughly chopped
50g/2oz/½ cup roasted peanuts,
    roughly chopped

For the peanut dressing
15ml/1 tbsp smooth
    peanut butter
120ml/4fl oz/½ cup
    coconut milk
5ml/1 tsp sugar
juice of 1 lime
dash of Tabasco sauce
salt and ground black pepper

Preparation: 7 minutes; Cooking: 8–10 minutes

1 Make the peanut dressing by combining the peanut butter, coconut milk and sugar in a small pan. Stir over a low heat, using a wooden spoon, until just blended.

2 Remove the pan from the heat, stir in the lime juice and Tabasco sauce, then season with salt and pepper to taste. Set aside and leave to cool to room temperature.

3 Separate the wonton wrappers, then re-stack them and cut the stack in quarters. Separate the wontons again.

4 Heat the oil in a deep pan or wok. When hot, add the wontons, a few at a time, and fry until browned. Lift them out of the oil using a slotted spoon and drain on kitchen paper. (The wontons colour quickly; don't let them burn.)

5 Arrange the lettuce leaves on serving plates or bowls. Drizzle with the peanut dressing and sprinkle the cucumber, tomatoes, egg and peanuts on top. Lastly, add the wonton crisps and serve immediately.

Sesame & Soba Noodle Salad

This simple but very tasty Chinese warm salad can be prepared and cooked in just a few minutes.

Serves 4
2 smoked garlic cloves,
    roughly chopped
30ml/2 tbsp sesame paste
15ml/1 tbsp dark sesame oil
30ml/2 tbsp soy sauce
30ml/2 tbsp rice wine
15ml/1 tbsp clear honey,
    preferably acacia honey
pinch of five-spice powder
350g/12oz soba or
    buckwheat noodles
4 spring onions (scallions), finely
    sliced diagonally
50g/2oz/⅓ cup beansprouts
7.5cm/3in piece of cucumber,
    cut into matchsticks
toasted sesame seeds
salt and ground black pepper

Preparation: 3 minutes; Cooking: 3–5 minutes

1 Put the smoked garlic, sesame paste, sesame oil, soy sauce, rice wine, honey and five-spice powder in a blender or food processor. Add a pinch each of salt and ground black pepper. Process the mixture until smooth.

2 Cook the noodles in a pan of boiling water until just tender, following the directions on the packet. Drain the noodles immediately and tip them into a bowl.

3 Add the dressing to the noodles, then mix in the spring onions. Toss until coated, then spoon the mixture on to a large platter or into individual bowls. Top with the beansprouts, cucumber and sesame seeds and serve immediately.

> **Variation**
> Egg noodles can be used instead of soba – or even spaghetti.

> **Cook's Tip**
> If you can't find Chinese sesame paste, then use either tahini paste or smooth peanut butter instead.

Crispy Wonton Energy 236kcal/989kJ; Protein 9.4g; Carbohydrate 27.6g, of which sugars 7.4g; Fat 10.6g, of which saturates 2.2g; Cholesterol 48mg; Calcium 93mg; Fibre 3.3g; Sodium 172mg.
Sesame and Soba Energy 386kcal/1622kJ; Protein 10.9g; Carbohydrate 52.9g, of which sugars 8.6g; Fat 16g, of which saturates 3g; Cholesterol 19mg; Calcium 85mg; Fibre 5.1g; Sodium 310mg.

Halloumi & Grape Salad

In Eastern Europe, firm salty halloumi cheese is often served fried for breakfast or supper. In this recipe it is tossed with sweet, juicy grapes which really complement its distinctive sweet and salty flavour.

Serves 4
150g/5oz mixed green
  salad leaves
75g/3oz seedless grapes
250g/9oz halloumi cheese
45ml/3 tbsp olive oil
fresh young thyme leaves or dill,
  to garnish

For the dressing
60ml/4 tbsp olive oil
15ml/1 tbsp lemon juice
2.5ml/½ tsp caster (superfine)
  sugar
salt and ground black pepper
5ml/1 tsp chopped fresh thyme
  or dill

Preparation: 2 minutes; Cooking: 3–4 minutes

1 To make the dressing, mix together the olive oil, lemon juice and sugar. Season with salt and ground black pepper. Stir in the thyme or dill and set aside.

2 Toss together the salad leaves and the green and black grapes, then transfer to a large serving plate.

3 Thinly slice the cheese. Heat the oil in a frying pan. Add the cheese and fry briefly until turning golden on the underside. Turn with a fish slice or metal spatula and cook the other side.

4 Arrange the cheese over the salad. Pour over the dressing and garnish with thyme or dill.

> **Variations**
> • Add a few fresh mint leaves to the salad leaves, or some young sorrel leaves. Sorrel has a lovely lemony flavour but is high in oxalic acid, so don't use too much.
> • Substitute physalis for the grapes. These little golden fruits have a delicious sweet-sour flavour which would be an excellent foil for the salty halloumi cheese.

Warm Halloumi & Fennel Salad

Halloumi is a robust cheese that holds its shape when cooked on a griddle or barbecue. During cooking it acquires the distinctive griddle marks that look so effective. It tastes good with the aniseed-flavoured fennel and the herbs.

Serves 4
200g/7oz halloumi cheese,
  thickly sliced
2 fennel bulbs, trimmed and
  thinly sliced
30ml/2 tbsp roughly chopped
  fresh oregano
45ml/3 tbsp lemon-infused olive oil
salt and ground black pepper

Preparation: 13 minutes; Cooking: 6 minutes

1 Put the halloumi, fennel and oregano in a bowl and drizzle over the lemon-infused oil. Season with salt and black pepper to taste.

2 Cover the bowl with clear film (plastic wrap) and set aside for 10 minutes.

3 Place the halloumi and fennel on a hot griddle pan or over the barbecue, reserving the marinade, and cook for about 3 minutes on each side, until charred.

4 Divide the halloumi and fennel among four serving plates and drizzle over the reserved marinade. Serve immediately.

> **Variation**
> *Instead of fennel, use young heads of chicory (Belgian endive). Remove any discoloured leaves. Trim the ends slightly. Using a small knife, cut out the bitter core at the base of each endive head. Slice the endive heads thinly.*

> **Cook's Tip**
> *If you have time, chill the halloumi and fennel mixture for about 2 hours before cooking, so it becomes infused with the dressing.*

Halloumi and Grape Energy 215kcal/889kJ; Protein 10.2g; Carbohydrate 1.8g, of which sugars 1.7g; Fat 18.6g, of which saturates 8.1g; Cholesterol 29mg; Calcium 205mg; Fibre 2.4g; Sodium 209mg.
Warm Halloumi Energy 212kcal/876kJ; Protein 10g; Carbohydrate 1.4g, of which sugars 1.3g; Fat 18.6g, of which saturates 8.1g; Cholesterol 29mg; Calcium 199mg; Fibre 1.8g; Sodium 206mg.

Warm Broad Bean & Feta Salad

This recipe is loosely based on a typical medley of fresh-tasting Greek salad ingredients – broad beans, tomatoes and feta cheese. It's lovely as a starter, served warm or cold. It is the sort of dish that would go down very well at a party, so next time you are invited to one of those occasions where every guest brings a contribution, this would be an ideal choice.

Serves 4–6
900g/2lb broad beans, shelled, or 350g/12oz shelled frozen beans
60ml/4 tbsp olive oil
75g/3oz plum tomatoes, halved, or quartered if large
4 garlic cloves, crushed
115g/4oz firm feta cheese, cut into large, even-sized chunks
45ml/3 tbsp chopped fresh dill, plus extra to garnish
12 black olives
salt and ground black pepper

Preparation: 4 minutes; Cooking: 6–8 minutes

1 Cook the fresh or frozen broad beans in lightly salted boiling water until just tender. Drain and refresh, then set aside.

2 Meanwhile, heat the oil in a heavy frying pan and add the tomatoes and garlic. Cook until the tomatoes are beginning to colour and the garlic is pungent.

3 Add the feta to the pan and toss the ingredients together for 1 minute. Mix with the drained beans, dill, olives and salt and pepper. Serve garnished with chopped dill.

Variations
• *For a special treat, pop the shelled broad beans out of their skins and use only the bright green beans inside. This is a bit of a fiddly business, and doesn't yield much in terms of weight of beans, but as a bonus, the appearance and flavour is superb.*
• *Instead of broad beans, use extra-fine green beans, French beans or even runner beans. A mixture of green and yellow beans would look good, when the latter are in season.*
• *Use tiny cocktail tomatoes instead of plum tomatoes.*

Warm Salad with Poached Eggs

Soft poached eggs, chilli, hot croûtons and cool, crisp salad leaves make a lively and unusual combination. This simple salad is perfect for a mid-week supper. Poached eggs are delicious with salad leaves as the yolk runs out when the eggs are pierced and combines with the dressing in the most delightful way.

Serves 2
½ small loaf wholemeal (whole-wheat) bread
45ml/3 tbsp chilli oil
2 eggs
115g/4oz mixed salad leaves
45ml/3 tbsp extra virgin olive oil
2 garlic cloves, crushed
15ml/1 tbsp balsamic or sherry vinegar
50g/2oz Parmesan cheese, shaved
ground black pepper

Preparation: 2–3 minutes; Cooking: 10–12 minutes

1 Carefully cut the crust from the wholemeal loaf and discard. Cut the bread into neat slices and then into 2.5cm/1in cubes.

2 Heat the chilli oil in a large frying pan. Add the bread cubes and cook for about 5 minutes, tossing the cubes occasionally, until they are crisp and golden brown all over.

3 Meanwhile, bring a pan of water to the boil. Break each egg into a measuring jug (cup) and carefully slide into the water, one at a time.

4 Gently poach the eggs in the simmering water for about 4 minutes until they are lightly cooked.

5 Meanwhile, divide the salad leaves between two plates. Using a slotted spoon, remove the croûtons from the pan and arrange them over the leaves.

6 Wipe the pan clean with kitchen paper. Then heat the olive oil in the pan, add the garlic and vinegar and cook over high heat for 1 minute. Pour the warm dressing over the salads.

7 Place a poached egg on each salad. Top with thin Parmesan shavings and a little ground black pepper. Serve immediately.

Warm Broad Bean Energy 175kcal/727kJ; Protein 7.9g; Carbohydrate 8g, of which sugars 2g; Fat 12.6g, of which saturates 3.9g; Cholesterol 13mg; Calcium 109mg; Fibre 4.3g; Sodium 471mg.
Warm Salad Energy 697kcal/2907kJ; Protein 25.9g; Carbohydrate 41.3g, of which sugars 2.8g; Fat 49g, of which saturates 11.5g; Cholesterol 215mg; Calcium 408mg; Fibre 6.3g; Sodium 914mg.

Bean Salad with Tuna & Onion

This makes a great first course or even a light main meal if served with a green salad, some garlic mayonnaise and plenty of warm, crusty bread for mopping up the tasty tarragon dressing.

Serves 4
2 x 300g/11oz cans
  cannellini beans
200–250g/7–9oz fine French
  beans, trimmed
1 large red onion, very thinly sliced
45ml/3 tbsp chopped fresh flat
  leaf parsley

200–250g/7–9oz good-quality
  canned tuna in olive oil,
  drained
200g/7oz cherry tomatoes,
  halved
salt and ground black pepper
a few onion rings, to garnish

For the dressing
90ml/6 tbsp extra virgin olive oil
15ml/1 tbsp tarragon vinegar
5ml/1 tsp tarragon mustard
1 garlic clove, finely chopped
5ml/1 tsp grated lemon rind
a little lemon juice
pinch of caster sugar (optional)

Preparation: 6 minutes; Cooking: 3–4 minutes

1 Drain the cans of beans into a colander and rinse them under cold running water. Drain again and set aside.

2 Meanwhile, whisk all the dressing ingredients apart from the lemon juice and sugar in a bowl. Season to taste with salt, pepper, lemon juice and sugar, if liked.

3 Blanch the French beans in plenty of boiling water for 3–4 minutes. Drain, refresh under cold water and drain again.

4 Place both types of beans in a bowl. Add half the dressing and toss to mix. Stir in the onion and half the chopped parsley, then season to taste with salt and pepper. Flake the tuna into large chunks with a knife and toss it into the beans with the tomato halves.

5 Arrange the salad on four individual plates. Drizzle the remaining dressing over the salad and scatter the remaining chopped parsley on top. Garnish with a few onion rings and serve immediately, at room temperature.

Salad Niçoise

Made with the freshest of ingredients, this classic salad makes a simple yet unbeatable summer dish.

Serves 4
115g/4oz French beans, trimmed
  and cut in half
115g/4oz mixed salad leaves
1/2 small cucumber, thinly sliced
4 ripe tomatoes, quartered
50g/2oz can anchovies, drained

and halved lengthways
4 eggs, hard-boiled
1 tuna steak, about 175g/6oz
olive oil, for brushing
1/2 bunch small radishes, trimmed
50g/2oz/1/2 cup small black olives
salt and ground black pepper

For the dressing
90ml/6 tbsp extra virgin olive oil
2 garlic cloves, crushed
15ml/1 tbsp white wine vinegar

Preparation: 6 minutes; Cooking: 8–10 minutes

1 To make the dressing, whisk together the oil, garlic and vinegar and season to taste with salt and pepper. Set aside.

2 Cook the French beans in a pan of boiling water for 2 minutes until just tender, then drain.

3 Mix together the salad leaves, sliced cucumber, tomatoes and French beans in a large, shallow bowl. Halve the anchovies lengthways and shell and quarter the eggs.

4 Preheat the grill (broiler). Brush the tuna steak with olive oil and sprinkle with salt and black pepper. Grill (broil) for 3–4 minutes on each side until cooked through. Cool, then flake.

5 Scatter the flaked tuna, anchovies, quartered eggs, radishes and olives over the salad. Pour over the dressing and toss together lightly to combine. Serve at once.

Variation
Opinions vary on whether salad Niçoise should include potatoes but, if you like, include a few small cooked new potatoes and some chopped celery.

Bean Salad Energy 266kcal/1112kJ; Protein 27.3g; Carbohydrate 2.3g, of which sugars 2.3g; Fat 16.6g, of which saturates 3g; Cholesterol 32mg; Calcium 40mg; Fibre 0.7g; Sodium 55mg.
Salad Niçoise Energy 351kcal/1457kJ; Protein 21.7g; Carbohydrate 5.3g, of which sugars 5g; Fat 27.3g, of which saturates 5g; Cholesterol 210mg; Calcium 114mg; Fibre 2.6g; Sodium 876mg.

Black Olive, Sliced Tomato & Sardine Salad

The combination of ingredients in this salad – sardines, olives, tomatoes and wine vinegar – brings a real burst of flavour to a delightful light summer dish. The sardines are best cooked under a preheated hot grill. They need very little cooking; 2 minutes on each side will do it.

Serves 6
8 large firm ripe tomatoes
1 large red onion
60ml/4 tbsp white wine vinegar
90ml/6 tbsp good olive oil
18–24 small sardines, cooked
75g/3oz/¾ cup pitted black
 olives, well drained
salt and ground black pepper
45ml/3 tbsp chopped fresh
 parsley, to garnish

Preparation: 4 minutes; Cooking: 0 minutes

1 Slice the tomatoes into 5mm/¼in slices. Using a sharp knife, slice the onion thinly.

2 Arrange the tomatoes on individual plates, overlapping the slices, then top with the red onion.

3 Mix together the wine vinegar, olive oil and seasoning, and spoon over each plate of salad.

4 Top each salad with 3–4 sardines and a few black olives. Sprinkle the chopped parsley over the top.

Cook's Tip
You may not need all the vinegar as the juice from the tomatoes will contribute some acidity.

Variation
This recipe works equally well if the sardines are replaced with 6 shelled and halved hard-boiled eggs.

Spicy Squid Salad

This tasty, colourful salad is a refreshing way of serving squid. The ginger and chilli dressing is added while the squid is still hot, and flavours the shellfish and beans.

Serves 4
450g/1lb squid
300ml/½ pint/1¼ cups fish stock
175g/6oz green beans, trimmed
 and halved
45ml/3 tbsp fresh coriander
 (cilantro) leaves
10ml/2 tsp granulated (white)
 sugar
30ml/2 tbsp rice vinegar
5ml/1 tsp sesame oil
15ml/1 tbsp light soy sauce
15ml/1 tbsp vegetable oil
2 garlic cloves, finely chopped
10ml/2 tbsp finely chopped fresh
 root ginger
1 fresh chilli, seeded and chopped

Preparation: 8–10 minutes; Cooking: 5–7 minutes

1 Prepare the squid. Holding the body in one hand, gently pull away the head and tentacles. Discard the head then trim and reserve the tentacles. Remove the transparent quill from inside the squid and peel off the purplish skin on the outside.

2 Cut the body of the squid open lengthways and wash thoroughly. Score criss-cross patterns on the inside, then cut into 7.5 x 5cm/3 x 2in pieces.

3 Bring the fish stock to the boil in a wok or pan. Add all the squid pieces, then lower the heat and cook for about 2 minutes until they are tender and have curled. Drain.

4 Bring a pan of lightly salted water to the boil. Cook the beans for 3–5 minutes, until they are crisp-tender. Drain, refresh under cold water, then drain again. Mix the squid and beans in a bowl.

5 In another bowl, mix the coriander leaves, sugar, rice vinegar, sesame oil and soy sauce. Pour the mixture over the squid and beans, and toss lightly, using a spoon, to coat.

6 Heat the vegetable oil in a wok or small pan. When it is very hot, stir-fry the garlic, ginger and chilli for a few seconds, then pour the dressing over the squid mixture. Toss gently and serve.

Black Olive Energy 94kcal/393kJ; Protein 7.7g; Carbohydrate 3.4g, of which sugars 3.2g; Fat 5.6g, of which saturates 1.4g; Cholesterol 21mg; Calcium 29mg; Fibre 0.1g; Sodium 52mg.
Spicy Squid Energy 143kcal/602kJ; Protein 18.2g; Carbohydrate 5.4g, of which sugars 3.6g; Fat 5.6g, of which saturates 0.9g; Cholesterol 253mg; Calcium 32mg; Fibre 1g; Sodium 124mg.

Seafood Salad

This is a very pretty arrangement of fresh mussels, prawns and squid rings served on a colourful bed of salad vegetables. Don't be tempted to chill the salad or the delicate flavours will be blunted.

Serves 6
115g/4oz prepared squid rings
12 fresh mussels, scrubbed and
    beards removed
1 large carrot
6 crisp lettuce leaves
10cm/4in piece cucumber,
    finely diced
115g/4oz cooked, peeled
    prawns (shrimp)
15ml/1 tbsp drained
    pickled capers

For the dressing
30ml/2 tbsp freshly squeezed
    lemon juice
45ml/3 tbsp virgin olive oil
15ml/1 tbsp chopped fresh parsley
salt and ground black pepper

Preparation: 3 minutes; Cooking: 4–6 minutes

1 Put the squid rings into a metal sieve (strainer) or vegetable steamer. Place the sieve or steamer over a pan of simmering water, cover with a lid and steam the squid for 2–3 minutes until it just turns white. Cool under cold running water and drain on kitchen paper.

2 Discard any open mussels that do not close when tapped. Cover the base of a large pan with water, add the mussels, then cover and steam for a few minutes until they open. Discard any mussels that stubbornly remain shut.

3 Using a swivel-style vegetable peeler, cut the carrot into wafer-thin ribbons. Tear the lettuce into pieces and arrange on a serving plate. Scatter the carrot ribbons on top, then sprinkle over the diced cucumber.

4 Arrange the mussels, prawns and squid rings over the salad and scatter the capers over the top.

5 Make the dressing. Put all the ingredients in a small bowl and whisk to combine. Drizzle half the dressing over the salad. Serve at room temperature with the remaining dressing.

Prawn & Rice Noodle Salad

The Thai-inspired dressing adds a superb flavour to the noodles and prawns. This delicious salad can be served warm or cold.

Serves 4
200g/7oz rice vermicelli or stir-fry
    rice noodles
8 baby corn cobs, halved
150g/5oz mangetouts (snow peas)
15ml/1 tbsp vegetable oil
2 garlic cloves, finely chopped
2.5cm/1in piece fresh root ginger,
    peeled and finely chopped
1 fresh red or green chilli, seeded
    and finely chopped
450g/1lb raw peeled tiger prawns
    (jumbo shrimp)
4 spring onions (scallions),
    very thinly sliced
15ml/1 tbsp sesame seeds,
    toasted
1 lemon grass stalk, thinly
    shredded, to garnish

For the dressing
15ml/1 tbsp chopped chives
15ml/1 tbsp Thai fish sauce
5ml/1 tsp soy sauce
45ml/3 tbsp groundnut (peanut) oil
5ml/1 tsp sesame oil
30ml/2 tbsp rice vinegar

Preparation: 10 minutes; Cooking: 7 minutes

1 Put the rice vermicelli or noodles in a wide heatproof bowl, pour over boiling water and leave for 5 minutes. Drain, refresh under cold water and drain again. Tip back into the bowl.

2 Boil or steam the corn cobs and mangetouts for about 3 minutes; they should still be crunchy. Refresh under cold water and drain. Now make the dressing. Mix all the ingredients in a screw-top jar, close tightly and shake well to combine.

3 Heat the oil in a large frying pan or wok. Add the garlic, ginger and red or green chilli and cook for 1 minute. Add the tiger prawns and stir-fry for about 3 minutes, until they have just turned pink. Stir in the spring onions, corn cobs, mangetouts and sesame seeds, and toss lightly to mix.

4 Tip the contents of the pan or wok over the rice vermicelli or noodles. Pour the dressing on top and toss well. Garnish with lemon grass and serve immediately.

Seafood Salad Energy 91kcal/379kJ; Protein 7.5g; Carbohydrate 1.5g, of which sugars 1g; Fat 6.2g, of which saturates 0.9g; Cholesterol 84mg; Calcium 29mg; Fibre 0.4g; Sodium 86mg.
Prawn Salad Energy 546kcal/2279kJ; Protein 25.2g; Carbohydrate 78.4g, of which sugars 6.8g; Fat 14.6g, of which saturates 1.7g; Cholesterol 110mg; Calcium 408mg; Fibre 3.3g; Sodium 665mg.

Prawn Noodle Salad

A refreshing salad with all the tangy flavour of the sea. Instead of prawns, try squid, scallops, mussels or crab.

Serves 4
115g/4oz cellophane noodles, soaked in hot water until soft
16 cooked prawns (shrimp), peeled
1 small green (bell) pepper, seeded and cut into strips
½ cucumber, cut into strips
1 tomato, cut into strips
2 shallots, finely sliced
salt and ground black pepper
coriander (cilantro) leaves, to garnish

For the dressing
15ml/1 tbsp rice vinegar
30ml/2 tbsp Thai fish sauce
30ml/2 tbsp fresh lime juice
pinch of salt
2.5ml/½ tsp grated fresh root ginger
1 lemon grass stalk, finely chopped
1 fresh red chilli, seeded and finely sliced
30ml/2 tbsp roughly chopped fresh mint
few fresh tarragon sprigs, roughly chopped
15ml/1 tbsp chopped chives

Preparation: 8–10 minutes; Cooking: 1 minute

1 Make the dressing by combining all the ingredients in a small bowl or jug (pitcher) and whisking well.

2 Drain the noodles, then plunge them in a pan of boiling water for 1 minute. Drain in a colander, rinse under cold running water, shake the colander and drain again well.

3 In a large bowl, combine the noodles with the prawns, pepper, cucumber, tomato and shallots. Lightly season with salt and pepper, then toss with the dressing.

4 Spoon the noodles on to individual plates, arranging the prawns on top. Garnish with a few coriander leaves and serve.

> **Cook's Tip**
> As the prawns (shrimp) are the prime ingredient of this salad, buy the largest and juiciest ones you can afford.

Pasta Salad with Roquefort & Peppered Salami

This pasta dish is easy to make and would be perfect for a picnic or packed lunch.

Serves 4
225g/8oz/2 cups dried fusilli
275g/10oz jar charcoal-roasted peppers in oil
115g/4oz/1 cup pitted black olives
4 sun-dried tomatoes in oil, drained and quartered
115g/4oz Roquefort cheese, crumbled
10 slices peppered salami, cut into strips
115g/4oz packet mixed leaf salad
30ml/2 tbsp white wine vinegar
30ml/2 tbsp chopped fresh oregano
2 garlic cloves, crushed
salt and ground black pepper

Preparation: 3–4 minutes; Cooking: 10–12 minutes

1 Bring a large pan of lightly salted water to the boil and cook the pasta over high heat for 10–12 minutes.

2 Meanwhile, drain the peppers and reserve 60ml/4 tbsp of the oil for the dressing. Cut the peppers into long, fine strips and mix them with the olives, sun-dried tomatoes and Roquefort in a large bowl.

3 Drain the pasta thoroughly in a colander and rinse with cold water, then drain again. Stir it into the pepper mixture along with the strips of peppered salami.

4 Divide the salad leaves among four individual bowls and spoon the pasta salad on top. Whisk the reserved oil with the vinegar, oregano, garlic and seasoning to taste. Spoon this dressing over the salad and serve at once.

> **Variation**
> Use slices of cold roast chicken instead of the salami and cubes of Brie in place of the Roquefort cheese.

Prawn Noodle Salad Energy 103kcal/438kJ; Protein 11g; Carbohydrate 15g, of which sugars 13g; Fat 0.5g, of which saturates 0.1g; Cholesterol 110mg; Calcium 54mg; Fibre 0.7g; Sodium 109mg.
Pasta Salad Energy 429kcal/1797kJ; Protein 17.8g; Carbohydrate 46.7g, of which sugars 6.6g; Fat 20.3g, of which saturates 8.9g; Cholesterol 37mg; Calcium 188mg; Fibre 3.9g; Sodium 1341mg.

Pan-fried Chicken Liver Salad

This Florentine salad uses vin santo, a delicious sweet dessert wine from Tuscany, but this is not essential – any dessert wine will do, or a sweet or cream sherry.

Serves 4
75g/3oz fresh baby spinach
   leaves, washed and dried

75g/3oz lollo rosso leaves, washed,
   dried and torn into pieces
75ml/5 tbsp olive oil
15g/½oz/1 tbsp butter
225g/8oz chicken livers, trimmed
   and thinly sliced
45ml/3 tbsp vin santo
50–75g/2–3oz fresh Parmesan
   cheese, shaved into curls
salt and ground black pepper

Preparation: 4 minutes; Cooking: 6 minutes

1 Put the spinach and lollo rosso leaves into a large bowl, season with salt and ground black pepper to taste and toss gently with salad servers or two spoons to mix.

2 Heat 30ml/2 tbsp of the oil with the butter in a large heavy frying pan. When foaming, add the chicken livers and toss over medium to high heat for 5 minutes, or until the livers are browned on the outside but still pink in the centre. Remove the pan from the heat.

3 Remove the livers from the pan with a slotted spoon, drain them on kitchen paper, then place them on top of the seasoned spinach and lollo rosso leaves.

4 Return the pan to medium heat, add the remaining oil and the vin santo and stir until sizzling. Pour the hot dressing over the leaves and livers and toss to coat. Put the salad in a serving bowl and sprinkle over the Parmesan shavings. Serve the salad at once, while the livers are still warm.

> **Cook's Tip**
> If you can't find baby spinach leaves, you can use older spinach, but discard any tough leaves along with the stalks and tear the remainder into pieces. Or use any other baby leaves.

Chicken, Vegetable & Chilli Salad

This Vietnamese salad is full of surprising textures and flavours. Serve as a light lunch dish or for supper with crusty French bread.

Serves 4
225g/8oz Chinese leaves
   (Chinese cabbage)
2 carrots, cut in matchsticks
½ cucumber, cut in matchsticks
2 fresh red chillies, seeded and
   cut into thin strips

1 small onion, sliced into fine rings
4 pickled gherkins, sliced into fine
   rings, plus 45ml/3 tbsp of the
   liquid from the jar
50g/2oz/½ cup peanuts,
   lightly ground
225g/8oz cooked chicken, sliced
1 garlic clove, crushed
5ml/1 tsp granulated (white)
   sugar
30ml/2 tbsp cider or white
   wine vinegar
salt

Preparation: 14 minutes; Cooking: 0 minutes

1 Discard any tough outer leaves from the Chinese leaves, then stack the remainder on a board. Using a sharp knife, cut them into shreds that are about the same width as the carrot matchsticks. Put the Chinese leaves and carrots in a bowl.

2 Spread out the cucumber matchsticks in a colander and sprinkle with salt. Stand the colander on a plate and set aside for 12–15 minutes, to extract the excess liquid.

3 Mix the chillies and onion rings in a small bowl. Add the sliced gherkins and peanuts. Rinse the salted cucumber thoroughly, drain well and pat dry with kitchen paper.

4 Add the cucumber matchsticks to the salad bowl and toss together lightly. Stir in the chilli mixture. Arrange the chicken on top. In a bowl, whisk the gherkin liquid with the garlic, sugar and vinegar. Pour over the salad, toss lightly and serve.

> **Cook's Tip**
> Add extra cider or white wine vinegar to the dressing for a sharper taste. If it is too tart, add extra sugar.

Pan-fried Chicken Energy 277kcal/1146kJ; Protein 16g; Carbohydrate 0.7g, of which sugars 0.6g; Fat 22.5g, of which saturates 6.9g; Cholesterol 234mg; Calcium 220mg; Fibre 0.8g; Sodium 255mg.
Chicken, Vegetable Energy 167kcal/700kJ; Protein 17.8g; Carbohydrate 9.1g, of which sugars 7.7g; Fat 6.9g, of which saturates 1.4g; Cholesterol 39mg; Calcium 47mg; Fibre 2.9g; Sodium 50mg.

Spicy Sichuan Noodle Salad

Subtly spiced but quite hot dishes are the keynote of western Chinese cuisine – fresh or dried chillies usually play a major role but are balanced.

Serves 4
350g/12oz thick noodles
175g/6oz cooked chicken,
  shredded
50g/2oz/½ cup roasted
  cashew nuts
salt and ground black pepper

For the dressing
4 spring onions (scallions), chopped
30ml/2 tbsp chopped
  coriander (cilantro)
2 garlic cloves, chopped
30ml/2 tbsp smooth peanut butter
30ml/2 tbsp sweet chilli sauce
15ml/1 tbsp soy sauce
15ml/1 tbsp sherry vinegar
15ml/1 tbsp sesame oil
30ml/2 tbsp olive oil
30ml/2 tbsp chicken stock or water
10 toasted Sichuan peppercorns,
  ground

Preparation: 6 minutes; Cooking: 4–6 minutes

1 Cook the noodles in a pan of boiling water until just tender, following the directions on the packet. Drain, rinse under cold running water and drain well.

2 While the noodles are cooking, combine all the ingredients for the dressing in a large bowl and whisk together well.

3 Add the noodles, shredded chicken and cashew nuts to the dressing, toss gently to coat.

4 Season to taste, and serve at once.

> **Variations**
> • Substitute cooked turkey or pork for the chicken for a change.
> • Make a vegetarian version of this noodle salad by dropping the cooked chicken in favour of baby corn cobs, halved lengthways, mangetouts (snow peas) cut in strips, and strips of red (bell) pepper. For extra crunch, drain some canned water chestnuts and slice them into the salad. Use vegetable stock instead of chicken stock in the dressing.

Warm Chorizo & Spinach Salad

Spanish chorizo sausage contributes an intense spiciness to any ingredient with which it is cooked. In this hearty salad, spinach has sufficient flavour to compete with the chorizo and the combination works very well.

Serves 4
225g/8oz baby spinach leaves
90ml/6 tbsp extra virgin olive oil
150g/5oz chorizo sausage,
  very thinly sliced
30ml/2 tbsp sherry vinegar
salt and ground black pepper
warm crusty bread, to serve

Preparation: 2–3 minutes; Cooking: 3 minutes

1 Pour the oil into a large frying pan and add the sausage. Cook gently for 3 minutes, until the sausage slices start to shrivel slightly and colour.

2 Add the spinach leaves and remove the pan from the heat. Toss the spinach in the warm oil until it just starts to wilt. Add the sherry vinegar and a little seasoning. Toss all the ingredients together briefly, then serve the salad warm.

> **Cook's Tip**
> Chorizos, of which there are over 50 varieties, are named after the choricero chilli that gives them both spiciness and colour. Red chorizos, made in links, contain minced (ground) meat, which is mottled with fat. They must be cooked and are usually fried or boiled. The longer varieties are usually sweeter, while some small round ones are hot and spicy. The second type of chorizo, and the one featured in the recipe above, is cured, so needs no further cooking.

> **Variations**
> • Watercress or rocket (arugula) could be used instead of the spinach, if you prefer.
> • For an added dimension, use a flavoured olive oil – rosemary, garlic or chilli oil would work perfectly.

Spicy Sichuan Energy 536kcal/2256kJ; Protein 24.1g; Carbohydrate 71.3g, of which sugars 5.4g; Fat 19.1g, of which saturates 2.7g; Cholesterol 34mg; Calcium 57mg; Fibre 3.9g; Sodium 205mg.
Warm Chorizo Energy 273kcal/1127kJ; Protein 8g; Carbohydrate 2g, of which sugars 2g; Fat 26g, of which saturates 6g; Cholesterol 0mg; Calcium 96mg; Fibre 1.2g; Sodium 300mg.

Bacon Salad with Camembert

Fried apples and bacon are perfect partners. Here they are heaped over crisp lettuce to make an irresistible salad. A warm tangy cheese dressing adds the finishing touch.

Serves 4
30ml/2 tbsp olive oil
50g/2oz diced streaky (fatty) bacon slices, preferably dry-cured

1 eating apple, cored and chopped
2 small heads cos or romaine lettuce
a squeeze of lemon juice
salt and ground black pepper

For the dressing
150ml/¼ pint/⅔ cup sour cream
15ml/1 tbsp cider
50g/2oz Camembert or similar cheese, chopped
a dash of cider vinegar

Preparation: 5 minutes; Cooking: 4–5 minutes

1 Heat 15ml/1 tbsp of the olive oil in a large frying pan and add the diced streaky bacon. Cook over a medium heat until crisp and golden. Add the apple and cook gently for 1–2 minutes until golden brown and softened.

2 Having removed any torn or damaged leaves, tear the cos or romaine lettuce carefully into bitesize pieces.

3 To make the dressing, heat the ingredients together in a small pan over a low heat until smooth and creamy.

4 Toss the lettuce with the remaining oil and the lemon juice, season, then divide among four plates. Heap the warm apple and bacon on top, then drizzle over the dressing.

> **Variations**
> • For a slightly tangier topping, replace the Camembert with a mild and creamy blue cheese, such as Cambozola.
> • Substitute a firm but ripe pear for the apple, or use an Asian or Nashi pear, which has a distinctly different texture to a European or American pear, and is always crisp.

Warm Salad of Ham, Eggs & New Potatoes

With a lightly spiced nutty dressing, this warm ham salad is as delicious as it is fashionable, and an excellent choice for a casual summer supper with friends.

Serves 4
225g/8oz new potatoes, halved if large
50g/2oz green beans
115g/4oz baby spinach leaves

2 spring onions (scallions), sliced
4 eggs, hard-boiled and quartered
50g/2oz cooked ham, cut into strips
juice of ½ lemon
salt and ground black pepper

For the dressing
60ml/4 tbsp olive oil
5ml/1 tsp ground turmeric
5ml/1 tsp ground cumin
50g/2oz/⅓ cup shelled hazelnuts

Preparation: 3 minutes; Cooking: 15–17 minutes

1 Cook the potatoes in a pan of lightly salted boiling water for 10–15 minutes, or until tender. Meanwhile, cook the beans in a separate pan of lightly salted boiling water for 2 minutes.

2 Drain the potatoes and beans in a colander and put them in a bowl. Toss with the spinach and spring onions.

3 Arrange the hard-boiled egg quarters on the salad and sprinkle the strips of ham over the top. Drizzle with the lemon juice and season with plenty of salt and pepper.

4 Heat the dressing ingredients in a large frying pan and continue to cook, stirring frequently, until the nuts turn golden. Pour the hot, nutty dressing over the salad, toss to coat the potatoes, beans and leaves, and serve immediately.

> **Variation**
> An even quicker salad can be made by using a 400g/14oz can of mixed beans and pulses instead of the potatoes. Drain and rinse the beans and pulses, then drain again.

Bacon Salad Energy 190kcal/785kJ; Protein 5.9g; Carbohydrate 3.5g, of which sugars 3.5g; Fat 16.7g, of which saturates 8.4g; Cholesterol 42mg; Calcium 76mg; Fibre 0.5g; Sodium 244mg.
Warm Salad Energy 318kcal/1319kJ; Protein 12.4g; Carbohydrate 11g, of which sugars 2.2g; Fat 25.4g, of which saturates 4g; Cholesterol 198mg; Calcium 106mg; Fibre 2.3g; Sodium 268mg.

Crunchy Salad with Black Pudding

Highly flavoured black pudding is a spicy sausage enriched with blood. This puts some people off, which is a pity as it has a great flavour. It is the star of this simple salad.

Serves 4

250g/9oz black pudding (blood sausage), sliced
1 focaccia loaf, plain or flavoured with sun-dried tomatoes, garlic and herbs, cut into chunks
45ml/3 tbsp olive oil
1 cos or romaine lettuce, torn into bitesize pieces
250g/9oz cherry tomatoes, halved

For the dressing

juice of 1 lemon
90ml/6 tbsp olive oil
10ml/2 tsp French mustard
15ml/1 tbsp clear honey
30ml/2 tbsp chopped fresh herbs, such as coriander (cilantro), chives and parsley
salt and ground black pepper

Preparation: 4 minutes; Cooking: 8–12 minutes

1 Dry-fry the black pudding in a large, non-stick frying pan for 5–10 minutes, or until browned and crisp, turning occasionally. Remove the black pudding from the pan using a slotted spoon and drain on kitchen paper. Set the black pudding aside and keep warm.

2 Cut the focaccia into chunks. Add the oil to the juices in the frying pan and cook the focaccia cubes in two batches, turning often, until golden on all sides. Lift out the focaccia chunks and drain on kitchen paper.

3 Mix together all the focaccia, black pudding, lettuce and cherry tomatoes in a large bowl. Mix together the dressing ingredients and season with salt and pepper. Pour the dressing over the salad. Mix well and serve at once.

> **Variation**
> If black pudding (blood sausage) isn't your thing, try this recipe with spicy chorizo or kabanos sausages instead. Cut them into thick diagonal slices before cooking.

Asparagus, Bacon & Leaf Salad

As an accompaniment, this excellent salad turns a plain roast chicken or simple grilled fish into an interesting meal, or makes an appetizing first course or light lunch. Sweeten the French dressing with honey for the best flavour.

Serves 4

500g/1¼lb medium asparagus spears
130g/4½ oz thin-cut smoked back (lean) bacon
250g/9oz mixed leaf salad or frisée lettuce leaves
100ml/3½fl oz/scant ½ cup French dressing

Preparation: 5 minutes; Cooking: 6 minutes

1 Trim off any tough stalk ends from the asparagus and cut the spears into three, setting the tender tips aside. Heat a 1cm/½in depth of water in a frying pan until simmering.

2 Reserve the asparagus tips and cook the remainder of the spears in the water for about 3 minutes, until almost tender. Add the tips and cook for 1 minute more. Drain and refresh under cold, running water.

3 Place the bacon in a frying pan without adding any butter or oil. Heat it gently until the fat runs, then increase the heat and fry the bacon until it is golden and crisp. Drain on kitchen paper and then set it aside to cool slightly. Use kitchen scissors to snip it into bitesize pieces.

4 Place the frisée or mixed leaf salad in a bowl and add the bacon. Add the asparagus and a little black pepper to the salad. Pour the dressing over and toss the salad lightly, then serve before the leaves begin to wilt.

> **Cook's Tip**
> A wide range of different salad leaves is readily available – frisée has feathery, curly, slightly bitter-tasting leaves and is a member of the chicory family. Frisée leaves range in colour from yellow-white to yellow-green and are very pretty.

Crunchy Salad Energy 641kcal/2674kJ; Protein 15.1g; Carbohydrate 55g, of which sugars 8.1g; Fat 41.6g, of which saturates 9.4g; Cholesterol 43mg; Calcium 196mg; Fibre 3.2g; Sodium 1001mg.
Asparagus, Bacon Energy 259kcal/1068kJ; Protein 9.5g; Carbohydrate 3.6g, of which sugars 3.5g; Fat 23g, of which saturates 4.6g; Cholesterol 17mg; Calcium 53mg; Fibre 2.7g; Sodium 519mg.

Spinach with Raisins & Pine Nuts

Raisins and pine nuts are frequent partners in recipes, especially ones that originate in the Iberian peninsula. Here, tossed with wilted spinach and croûtons, they make a delicious snack or main meal accompaniment.

Serves 4
50g/2oz/⅓ cup raisins
1 thick slice crusty white bread
45ml/3 tbsp olive oil
25g/1oz/⅓ cup pine nuts
500g/1¼lb young spinach,
    stalks removed
2 garlic cloves, crushed
salt and ground black pepper

Preparation: 10 minutes; Cooking: 4–5 minutes

1 Put the raisins in a small bowl with boiling water and leave to soak for 10 minutes.

2 Meanwhile, cut the crusts from the slice of bread and discard them. Cut the bread into neat cubes. Heat 30ml/2 tbsp of the oil in a large frying pan and fry the bread until golden. Drain on kitchen paper and set aside.

3 Heat the remaining oil in the pan. Fry the pine nuts until beginning to colour. Add the spinach and garlic and cook quickly, turning the spinach until it has just wilted.

4 Toss in the raisins and season lightly with salt and pepper. Transfer to a warmed serving dish. Scatter the spinach mixture with croûtons and serve hot.

> **Cook's Tip**
> Make sure that the oil in the frying pan is hot when adding the bread cubes, so that they are quickly sealed on all sides.

> **Variation**
> Use the leaves of Swiss chard or spinach beet instead of the spinach, cooking them for a little longer if necessary.

Green Lima Beans in a Sauce

Make the most of lima beans or broad beans by teaming them with tomatoes and fresh chillies in this simple accompaniment.

Serves 4
450g/1lb fresh lima beans or
    broad (fava) beans
30ml/2 tbsp olive oil
1 onion, finely chopped
2 garlic cloves, crushed
400g/14oz can plum tomatoes,
    drained and chopped
25g/1oz/about 3 tbsp drained
    pickled jalapeño chilli slices,
    chopped
salt
fresh coriander (cilantro) and
    lemon slices, to garnish

Preparation: 2–3 minutes; Cooking: 16–17 minutes

1 Bring a pan of lightly salted water to the boil. Add the lima beans or broad beans and cook for 15 minutes, or until the beans are just tender.

2 Meanwhile, heat the olive oil in a frying pan, add the onion and garlic and sauté until the onion is translucent. Tip in the tomatoes and continue to cook, stirring, until the mixture thickens to become a rich, flavoursome sauce.

3 Add the chilli slices and cook for 1–2 minutes. Season the sauce with salt to taste but do not add pepper.

4 Drain the beans and return them to the pan. Pour over the tomato mixture and stir over the heat for a few minutes. If the sauce thickens too quickly add a little water.

5 Spoon the mixture into a serving dish, garnish with the coriander and lemon slices and serve.

> **Cook's Tip**
> Pickled jalapeño chillies are often hotter than roasted chillies – taste one before adding to the recipe and adjust the quantity to suit your taste. Alternatively, use mild pickled chillies or sweet piquant peppers such as peppadews.

Spinach with Raisins Energy 206kcal/855kJ; Protein 5.8g; Carbohydrate 15.5g, of which sugars 11.1g; Fat 13.8g, of which saturates 1.6g; Cholesterol 0mg; Calcium 228mg; Fibre 3.4g; Sodium 218mg.
Green Lima Beans Energy 170kcal/714kJ; Protein 10.1g; Carbohydrate 18.7g, of which sugars 6.3g; Fat 6.6g, of which saturates 1g; Cholesterol 0mg; Calcium 79mg; Fibre 8.7g; Sodium 19mg.

Green Beans with Eggs

This is an unusual way of cooking green beans, but tastes delicious. Try this dish for a light supper or as an accompaniment to a simple roast. Served solo, it is a good source of protein and would make a quick, easy and attractive-looking vegetarian meal.

Serves 6
300g/11oz string beans, topped, tailed and halved
30ml/2 tbsp vegetable oil
1 onion, halved and thinly sliced
3 eggs
salt and ground black pepper
50g/2oz/½ cup grated Monterey Jack or mild Cheddar cheese
strips of lemon rind, to garnish

Preparation: 4 minutes; Cooking: 13–14 minutes

1 Bring a pan of water to the boil, add the beans and cook for 5–6 minutes or until tender. Drain in a colander, rinse under cold water to preserve the bright colour, then drain the beans once more, shaking the colander several times.

2 Heat the oil in a frying pan and fry the onion slices for 3–4 minutes until soft and translucent. Break the eggs into a bowl and beat them with seasoning.

3 Add the egg mixture to the onion. Cook slowly over a moderate heat, stirring constantly so that the egg is lightly scrambled. The egg should be moist throughout. Do not overcook; the consistency must be creamy.

4 Add the beans to the pan and cook for a few minutes until warmed through. Tip the mixture into a heated serving dish, sprinkle with the grated cheese and lemon rind and serve.

> **Variations**
> • *Freshly grated Parmesan can be used instead of the Monterey Jack or Cheddar cheese for a sharper flavour.*
> • *Garnish with strips of red (bell) pepper instead of lemon rind for a more colourful finish, or use a mixture of peppers.*
> • *For a more substantial dish, add cooked spaghetti.*

Spiced Turnips, Spinach & Tomatoes

Sweet baby turnips, tender spinach and ripe tomatoes make tempting partners in this simple but very tasty Eastern Mediterranean vegetable stew. It is quite substantial as it stands, but could be served with rice, couscous or simply with a loaf of olive or sun-dried tomato bread.

Serves 6
450g/1lb plum tomatoes
2 onions
60ml/4 tbsp olive oil
450g/1lb baby turnips, peeled
5ml/1 tsp paprika
2.5ml/½ tsp sugar
60ml/4 tbsp chopped fresh coriander (cilantro)
450g/1lb fresh young spinach
salt and ground black pepper

Preparation: 3–4 minutes; Cooking: 12–14 minutes

1 Plunge the tomatoes into a bowl of boiling water for 30 seconds or so, then refresh in a bowl of cold water. Drain, peel away the tomato skins and chop the flesh roughly.

2 Slice the onions. Heat the olive oil in a large frying pan or sauté pan and gently fry the onion slices for about 5 minutes until golden. Ensure that they do not blacken.

3 Add the baby turnips, tomatoes and paprika to the pan with 60ml/4 tbsp water and cook until the tomatoes are pulpy. Cover the pan with a lid and continue cooking until the baby turnips have softened.

4 Stir in the sugar and coriander, then add the spinach and a little salt and ground black pepper. Cook the mixture for a further 2–3 minutes until the spinach has wilted. The dish can be served warm or cold.

> **Variations**
> • *Try this with celery hearts instead of baby turnips. It is also good with fennel or drained canned artichoke hearts.*
> • *Not everyone likes the flavour of coriander (cilantro). If you are not a fan, use chopped fresh parsley instead.*

Green Beans Energy 126kcal/519kJ; Protein 6.7g; Carbohydrate 2.7g, of which sugars 1.9g; Fat 9.8g, of which saturates 3.3g; Cholesterol 104mg; Calcium 106mg; Fibre 1.4g; Sodium 102mg.
Spiced Turnips Energy 94kcal/391kJ; Protein 3.7g; Carbohydrate 9.7g, of which sugars 8.7g; Fat 4.8g, of which saturates 0.7g; Cholesterol 0mg; Calcium 177mg; Fibre 4.6g; Sodium 124mg.

Stir-fried Asparagus with Chilli, Galangal & Lemon Grass

Wherever it is grown, asparagus is popular and much sought after. This tasty recipe comes from Vietnam, where asparagus was introduced by French colonists.

Serves 2–4
30ml/2 tbsp groundnut
   (peanut) oil
2 garlic cloves, finely chopped
2 fresh red chillies, seeded and
   finely chopped

25g/1oz fresh galangal or root
   ginger, finely shredded
1 lemon grass stalk, trimmed and
   finely sliced
350g/12oz fresh asparagus
   stalks, trimmed
30ml/2 tbsp tuk trey or
   fish sauce
30ml/2 tbsp soy sauce
5ml/1 tsp sugar
30ml/2 tbsp unsalted roasted
   peanuts, finely chopped
1 small bunch fresh coriander
   (cilantro), finely chopped

Preparation: 8 minutes; Cooking: 3–5 minutes

1 Heat a large wok and add the oil. Stir in the garlic, chillies, galangal or ginger and lemon grass and stir-fry until golden.

2 Add the asparagus and stir-fry for a further 1–2 minutes, until it is just tender but not too soft.

3 Stir in the tuk trey or fish sauce with the soy sauce and sugar. Stir in the peanuts and coriander and serve immediately.

Cook's Tip
To prepare an asparagus stalk, snap the stem. It will break between the usable tender section and the woody base.

Variation
This recipe also works well with broccoli, green beans and courgettes (zucchini), cut into strips.

Caramelized Mushrooms with Allspice & Herbs

Button mushrooms caramelize beautifully in their own juice, but still keep their moistness and nutty flavour. They are usually served as a side dish for grilled lamb chops or liver, or as a hot or cold meze dish with chunks of bread to mop up the tasty cooking juices, but they are also good served on toasted bread as a light lunch with a salad. Use whatever herbs and spices you have available.

Serves 4
45ml/3 tbsp olive oil
15ml/1 tbsp butter
450g/1lb button (white)
   mushrooms, wiped clean
3–4 garlic cloves, finely chopped
10ml/2 tsp allspice berries,
   crushed
10ml/2 tsp coriander seeds
5ml/1 tsp dried mint
1 bunch each of fresh sage and
   flat leaf parsley, chopped
salt and ground black pepper
lemon wedges, to serve

Preparation: 2–3 minutes; Cooking: 15 minutes

1 Heat the oil and butter in a wide, heavy pan, then stir in the mushrooms with the garlic, allspice and coriander. Cover and cook for about 10 minutes, shaking the pan from time to time, until the mushrooms start to caramelize.

2 Remove the lid and toss in the mint with some of the sage and parsley. Cook for a further 5 minutes, until most of the liquid has evaporated, then season with salt and pepper.

3 Tip the mushrooms into a serving dish and sprinkle the rest of the sage and parsley over the top. Serve hot or at room temperature, with lemon wedges for squeezing.

Cook's Tip
Button (white) mushrooms are ideal for this recipe as they don't release much liquid into the pan and caramelize beautifully. Don't wash the mushrooms before cooking, just wipe with a clean dish towel and keep them whole.

Stir-fried Asparagus Energy 117kcal/482kJ; Protein 5g; Carbohydrate 3.3g, of which sugars 2.7g; Fat 9g, of which saturates 1g; Cholesterol 0mg; Calcium 30mg; Fibre 2g; Sodium 535mg.
Caramelized Mushrooms Energy 125kcal/517kJ; Protein 2.8g; Carbohydrate 1.2g, of which sugars 0.8g; Fat 12.2g, of which saturates 3.3g; Cholesterol 8mg; Calcium 58mg; Fibre 2.5g; Sodium 37mg.

Sautéed Herb Salad with Chilli & Lemon

Firm-leafed fresh herbs, such as flat leaf parsley and mint, tossed in a little olive oil and seasoned with salt, are fabulous with spicy kebabs or beef steaks.

Serves 4
1 large bunch of flat leaf parsley
1 large bunch of mint
1 large bunch of fresh coriander (cilantro)
1 bunch of rocket (arugula)
1 large bunch of spinach leaves, about 115g/4oz
60–75ml/4–5 tbsp olive oil
2 garlic cloves, finely chopped
1 fresh green or red chilli, seeded and finely chopped
½ preserved lemon, finely chopped
salt and ground black pepper
45–60ml/3–4 tbsp Greek (US strained plain) yogurt, to serve

Preparation: 4–5 minutes; Cooking: 2 minutes

1 Roughly chop the herbs and put them in a bowl. Trim the rocket and spinach, discarding any tough stems or tattered leaves. Add them to the herbs and mix well.

2 Heat the olive oil in a wide, heavy pan. Stir in the garlic and chilli, and fry until they begin to colour. Toss in the herbs and leaves and cook gently, until they begin to wilt.

3 Spoon into a serving bowl, add the preserved lemon and season to taste. Serve warm with yogurt.

Cook's Tip
This is the perfect recipe for anyone with a herb garden. Pick the herbs immediately before preparing them, if possible. If you must pick them sooner, stand the stems in a jar of water.

Variation
Flavour the yogurt with crushed garlic, if you like.

Broccoli with Soy Sauce & Sesame Seeds

The best way to cook broccoli is to fry it quickly in a wok, so that the rich colour and crunchy texture are retained. Soy sauce and sesame seeds add to the flavour of this tasty dish.

Serves 2
225g/8oz purple-sprouting broccoli
15ml/1 tbsp sesame seeds
15ml/1 tbsp olive oil
15ml/1 tbsp soy sauce
salt and ground black pepper

Preparation: 2 minutes; Cooking: 3–4 minutes

1 Using a sharp knife, cut off and discard any thick stems from the broccoli and cut the broccoli into long, thin florets.

2 Spread out the sesame seeds in a small frying pan and dry-fry over a medium heat until toasted. Do not leave them unattended as they will readily burn and acquire a nasty, bitter taste if left just a fraction too long.

3 Heat the olive oil in a wok or large frying pan and add the broccoli. Stir-fry for 3–4 minutes, or until tender, adding a splash of water if the pan becomes too dry.

4 Add the soy sauce to the broccoli, then season with salt and ground black pepper to taste. Add the sesame seeds and toss to combine. Tip the broccoli mixture into a warmed serving bowl or individual bowls and serve immediately.

Variation
Purple-sprouting broccoli has been used for this recipe. This vegetable is at its best when in season during early spring, so finding a good crop may not always be easy during the rest of the year. When it is not available, an ordinary variety of broccoli, such as calabrese, will also work very well. Or you could substitute the broccoli altogether with Chinese leaves, which offer just as much crunch.

Sautéed Herb Salad Energy 142kcal/585kJ; Protein 3.6g; Carbohydrate 3.1g, of which sugars 2.7g; Fat 12.9g, of which saturates 2.1g; Cholesterol 2mg; Calcium 216mg; Fibre 4.4g; Sodium 82mg.
Broccoli with Soy Sauce Energy 135kcal/558kJ; Protein 6.6g; Carbohydrate 2.7g, of which sugars 2.3g; Fat 10.9g, of which saturates 1.7g; Cholesterol 0mg; Calcium 115mg; Fibre 3.5g; Sodium 545mg.

Cabbage with Onions, Bacon & Garlic

Serve this quick, easy and flavoursome dish with goose, turkey or pork, or try it with sausages or chops and creamy mashed potatoes with chives.

Serves 4
25g/1oz/2 tbsp butter or bacon fat or pork fat, or 30ml/2 tbsp olive oil

115g/4oz bacon or pancetta, chopped
1 onion, halved and thinly sliced
5ml/1 tsp caraway seeds or cumin seeds (optional)
2 garlic cloves, finely chopped
1 green cabbage (such as Savoy cabbage), thick stalks removed and leaves shredded
105ml/7 tbsp water
salt and ground black pepper

Preparation: 5 minutes; Cooking: 11–12 minutes

1 Melt the butter or fat or heat the oil in a large frying pan over a gentle heat. Cook the bacon or pancetta and onion gently, until the onion is soft.

2 Increase the heat slightly to medium-low and scatter over the caraway seeds or cumin seeds, if using, then cook, stirring occasionally, until the onion begins to brown.

3 Add the chopped garlic and stir-fry for 2 minutes.

4 Add the cabbage and turn it in the juices to coat, then stir in 5ml/1 tsp salt and the water. Cover tightly and cook over a high heat for 5–6 minutes, stirring once. The cabbage should be tender, but still retain a little crispness. Season to taste with black pepper and serve immediately.

Crispy Cabbage

Like so many brassicas, cabbage is lovely when crisp and horrible when soggy. In this recipe the balance is just right.

Serves 4–6
1 medium green or small white cabbage
30–45ml/2–3 tbsp oil
salt and ground black pepper

Preparation: 2–3 minutes; Cooking: 2–3 minutes

1 Remove the central core from the cabbage as well as any coarse outside leaves and the central rib from the larger remaining leaves.

2 Place the cabbage on a board and shred the leaves finely. Wash under cold running water, drain in a colander, shake well and blot on kitchen paper to dry thoroughly.

3 Heat a wok or wide-based flameproof casserole over a fairly high heat. Heat the oil and add the cabbage. Stir-fry for 2–3 minutes, using one or two wooden spoons to keep the cabbage moving so that it cooks evenly but is still crunchy. Season with salt and pepper and serve immediately.

Cook's Tip
Don't throw away the coarse outer leaves and central rib from the cabbage. They can be used with other vegetables such as onions and carrots to make vegetable stock. As long as the cabbage doesn't dominate, the flavour will be very good.

Variation
For cabbage with a bacon dressing, fry 225g/8oz diced streaky (fatty) bacon in a pan. Set aside while cooking the cabbage. Remove the cabbage from the pan and keep warm with the bacon. Boil 15ml/1 tbsp wine or cider vinegar with the juices remaining in the pan. Bring to the boil and season with ground black pepper. Pour over the cabbage and bacon. This makes a versatile side dish, and is especially good with chicken.

Variations
• Substitute a large leek for the onion and use shredded Brussels sprouts instead of the green cabbage. Omit the seeds.
• For vegetarians, leave out the bacon or pancetta and use strips of sun-dried tomato instead.

Crispy Cabbage Energy 56kcal/230kJ; Protein 1.2g; Carbohydrate 4.2g, of which sugars 4.1g; Fat 3.8g, of which saturates 0.5g; Cholesterol 0mg; Calcium 41mg; Fibre 1.8g; Sodium 6mg.
Cabbage with Onions Energy 151kcal/623kJ; Protein 6.7g; Carbohydrate 7.4g, of which sugars 7g; Fat 10.5g, of which saturates 2.6g; Cholesterol 15mg; Calcium 67mg; Fibre 2.8g; Sodium 452mg.

Stir-fried Brussels Sprouts with Bacon

This is a great way of cooking Brussels sprouts, helping to retain their sweet flavour and crunchy texture. Stir-frying guarantees that there will not be a single soggy sprout. Children who turn up their noses when offered sprouts often enjoy this.

Serves 4
450g/1lb Brussels sprouts, trimmed and washed
30ml/2 tbsp sunflower oil
2 streaky (fatty) bacon rashers (strips), finely chopped
10ml/2 tsp caraway seeds, lightly crushed
salt and ground black pepper

Preparation: 4 minutes; Cooking: 5 minutes

1 Using a sharp knife, carefully cut all the Brussels sprouts into fine shreds.

2 Heat the oil in a wok or large frying pan. Add the shredded sprouts and turn quickly over the heat, season with salt and ground black pepper, then remove and set aside.

3 Use the same wok or pan to cook the chopped bacon. Stir-fry for 1–2 minutes until golden.

4 Return the seasoned sprouts to the pan containing the bacon and stir in the caraway seeds. Cook for a further 1–2 minutes, then serve immediately.

Variation
Instead of seasoning the Brussels sprouts with salt and pepper, add a little soy sauce or mushroom ketchup.

Cook's Tip
Save time on preparation by buying diced bacon or diced pancetta, available ready packaged at the supermarket.

Green Beans with Tomatoes

This recipe is full of the flavours of summer. It relies on first-class ingredients, so use only the best ripe plum tomatoes and green beans that you can buy.

Serves 4
30ml/2 tbsp olive oil
1 large onion, finely sliced
2 garlic cloves, finely chopped
6 large ripe plum tomatoes, peeled, seeded and coarsely chopped
150ml/¼ pint/⅔ cup dry white wine
450g/1lb green beans, sliced in half lengthways
16 pitted black olives
10ml/2 tsp lemon juice
salt and ground black pepper

Preparation: 3–4 minutes; Cooking: 15 minutes

1 Heat the oil in a large frying pan. Add the finely sliced onion and chopped garlic. Cook over a medium heat for about 5 minutes, stirring frequently and lowering the heat if necessary, until the onion has softened but not browned.

2 Add the chopped tomatoes, white wine, beans, olives and lemon juice, and cook over a gentle heat for a further 10 minutes, stirring occasionally, until the sauce has thickened and the beans are tender. Season with salt and pepper to taste and serve immediately.

Variation
The best tomatoes for this recipe are those you harvest from your own garden, with the warmth of the sun still on the fruit. However, when tomatoes are out of season, and the only ones available in the shops have little flavour, it is better to use good quality canned plum tomatoes, either plain or with herbs such as oregano or marjoram. Add a pinch of sugar if necessary.

Cook's Tip
Green beans need little preparation and now that they are grown without the string, you simply trim either end.

Brussels Sprouts Energy 131kcal/545kJ; Protein 5.9g; Carbohydrate 4.6g, of which sugars 3.5g; Fat 10g, of which saturates 2g; Cholesterol 8mg; Calcium 30mg; Fibre 4.6g; Sodium 164mg.
Green Beans Energy 162kcal/672kJ; Protein 4.2g; Carbohydrate 14.4g, of which sugars 11.6g; Fat 8g, of which saturates 1.3g; Cholesterol 0mg; Calcium 80mg; Fibre 5.4g; Sodium 298mg.

Masala Beans with Fenugreek

The secret of this super-fast dish is the spice mixture that coats the vegetables. Cooking is kept to a minimum so that individual flavours are still detectable yet blend beautifully.

Serves 4

1 onion
5ml/1 tsp ground cumin
5ml/1 tsp ground coriander
5ml/1 tsp sesame seeds
5ml/1 tsp chilli powder
2.5ml/½ tsp crushed garlic
1.5ml/¼ tsp ground turmeric
5ml/1 tsp salt
30ml/2 tbsp vegetable oil
1 tomato, quartered
225g/8oz/1½ cups green
   beans, blanched
1 bunch fresh fenugreek leaves,
   stems discarded
60ml/4 tbsp chopped fresh
   coriander (cilantro)
15ml/1 tbsp lemon juice

Preparation: 4–5 minutes; Cooking: 10–12 minutes

1 Roughly chop the onion. Put the ground cumin and coriander, sesame seeds, chilli powder, garlic, turmeric and salt in a bowl and stir to mix.

2 Put the chopped onion and spice mixture into a food processor or blender, and process for 30–45 seconds until you have a rough paste. Pulse the ingredients if possible.

3 In a wok or large, heavy pan, heat the oil over a medium heat and fry the spice paste for about 5 minutes, stirring the mixture occasionally to prevent it from sticking.

4 Add the tomato quarters, blanched green beans, fresh fenugreek and chopped coriander.

5 Stir-fry the contents of the pan for about 5 minutes, then sprinkle in the lemon juice and serve.

> **Variation**
> Instead of fresh fenugreek, substitute 15ml/1 tbsp dried fenugreek, which is available from Indian markets.

Spiced Greens

Here is a really good way to enliven your greens, excellent for crunchy cabbages but also good for kale and other purple sprouting leaves. Using a combination of stir-frying and steaming means that the leaves become beautifully tender but retain the crisp quality that makes this incredibly quick recipe such a winner.

Serves 4

1 medium cabbage, or the
   equivalent in quantity of your
   chosen green vegetable
15ml/1 tbsp groundnut
   (peanut) oil
5ml/1 tsp grated fresh
   root ginger
2 garlic cloves, grated
2 shallots, finely chopped
2 red chillies, seeded and
   freshly sliced
salt and ground black pepper

Preparation: 1 minute; Cooking: 5 minutes

1 Remove any tough outer leaves from the cabbage, then quarter it and remove the core. Shred the leaves.

2 Pour the groundnut oil into a large pan and as it heats stir in the ginger and garlic. Add the shallots and as the pan becomes hotter add the chillies.

3 Add the greens and toss to mix. Cover the pan and reduce the heat to create some steam. Cook, shaking the pan occasionally, for about 3 minutes. Remove the lid and increase the heat to dry off the steam, season with salt and pepper and serve immediately in a heated bowl.

> **Variations**
> Instead of shallots, use a small onion, a few spring onions (scallions) or even a finely chopped leek. The chillies give the dish a certain zing, but can be omitted. For warmth without too much fire, add chopped bottled peppadews (sweet piquant peppers), choosing either the mild or the hot variety, depending on your palate. Sun-dried tomatoes would make a good alternative. Fresh galangal can be used instead of ginger.

Masala Beans Energy 70kcal/289kJ; Protein 1.6g; Carbohydrate 2.7g, of which sugars 2.1g; Fat 6g, of which saturates 0.7g; Cholesterol 0mg; Calcium 47mg; Fibre 2g; Sodium 6mg.
Spiced Greens Energy 77kcal/322kJ; Protein 2.6g; Carbohydrate 9.9g, of which sugars 9.4g; Fat 3.1g, of which saturates 0.5g; Cholesterol 0mg; Calcium 90mg; Fibre 3.9g; Sodium 13mg.

Young Vegetables with Tarragon

This is almost a salad, but the vegetables here are just lightly cooked to bring out their different flavours. The tarragon adds a wonderful depth to this bright, fresh dish. An accompaniment like this one looks good on the plate and appeals to the senses, with its tempting aromas, tasty flavours, interesting textures and cool colours.

Serves 4
50g/2oz/½ cup butter
5 spring onions (scallions),
    quartered lengthways
1 garlic clove, crushed
115g/4oz asparagus tips
115g/4oz mangetouts
    (snowpeas), trimmed
115g/4oz broad (fava) beans
2 Little Gem (Bibb) lettuces
5ml/1 tsp finely chopped
    fresh tarragon
salt and ground black pepper

Preparation: 5 minutes; Cooking: 10 minutes

1 Heat half the butter in a large frying pan. Add the spring onions and the garlic and fry gently over a medium-low heat for 3–4 minutes until the onions soften. Do not let the garlic burn or it will taste bitter.

2 Add the asparagus tips, mangetouts and broad beans. Mix in, covering all the pieces with oil.

3 Pour in just enough water to cover the base of the pan, season with salt and ground black pepper, and bring to the boil. Lower the heat and simmer gently for a few minutes.

4 Cut the lettuces into quarters and add to the pan. Cook for 3 minutes then, off the heat, swirl in the remaining butter and the tarragon. Spoon the vegetable mixture into a heated bowl or individual bowls and serve immediately.

Cook's Tip
This dish is very succesful as a light accompaniment to fish and seafood. Try it with a piece of poached salmon or as a side dish with fried trout. Or top it with cooked prawns (shrimp).

Braised Swiss Chard

Swiss chard is less well known than spinach. First use the leaves for a recipe such as this, then on the next day cook the stalks in the same way as asparagus.

Serves 4
900g/2lb Swiss chard or spinach
15g/½ oz/1 tbsp butter
a little freshly grated nutmeg
sea salt and ground black pepper

Preparation: 6 minutes; Cooking: 3–5 minutes

1 Remove the stalks from the Swiss chard or spinach (and reserve the chard stalks, if you like, for another dish). Wash the leaves well and lift straight into a lightly greased heavy pan; the water clinging to the leaves will be all that is needed for cooking.

2 Cover with a tight-fitting lid and cook over medium heat for about 3–5 minutes, or until just tender, shaking the pan occasionally to prevent the greens from sticking.

3 Drain well, then add the butter and nutmeg and season to taste. When the butter has melted, toss it into the Swiss chard and serve immediately.

Variation
Give this recipe a twist by adding spring onions (scallions) and ginger. Be generous, grating a large knob of ginger and finely chopping at least 6 spring onions. Instead of adding the butter at the end, start by melting it in the pan and frying the ginger and spring onions until the latter soften, then adding the chard.

Cook's Tip
To cook the stalks, trim the bases, wash them and tie in bundles like asparagus. Add to a pan of boiling water, with a squeeze of lemon juice, and cook for about 20 minutes, or until tender but still slightly crisp. Drain and serve with some white sauce or fresh single (light) cream.

Young Vegetables Energy 596kcal/2476kJ; Protein 18.8g; Carbohydrate 24.4g, of which sugars 12g; Fat 48g, of which saturates 29.2g; Cholesterol 116mg; Calcium 220mg; Fibre 14g; Sodium 356mg.
Swiss Chard Energy 336kcal/1388kJ; Protein 25.2g; Carbohydrate 14.4, of which sugars 13.6g; Fat 19.6g, of which saturates 8.8g; Cholesterol 32mg; Calcium 153.2mg; Fibre 18.8g; Sodium 1352mg.

Braised Lettuce & Peas

This light vegetable dish is based on the classic French method of braising peas with lettuce and spring onions in butter, and is delicious served with grilled fish or duck. It is also good as an accompaniment for a vegetarian meal, served with sun-dried tomato sausages or nut roast.

Serves 4

50g/2oz/¼ cup butter
4 Little Gem (Bibb) lettuces, halved lengthways
2 bunches spring onions (scallions), trimmed and cut into pieces
400g/14oz shelled peas (about 1kg/2¼ lb in pods)
120ml/4fl oz/½ cup water
salt and ground black pepper

Preparation: 2–3 minutes; Cooking: 13 minutes

1 Melt half the butter in a wide, heavy pan over a low heat. Add the lettuces and spring onions.

2 Turn the vegetables in the butter, then sprinkle with salt and plenty of ground black pepper. Cover the pan with a tight-fitting lid and cook the lettuces and spring onions very gently for 5 minutes, stirring once.

3 Add the peas and turn them in the buttery juices. Pour in the measured water, then cover and cook over a gentle heat for a further 5 minutes. Uncover and increase the heat to reduce the liquid to a few tablespoons.

4 Stir in the remaining butter and adjust the seasoning. Transfer to a warmed serving dish and serve immediately.

Variations
• For a splash of extra colour, and to add some crunch to the texture, braise about 250g/9oz baby carrots with the lettuce.
• Try a meatier alternative by cooking 115g/4oz chopped smoked bacon or pancetta in the butter in step 1. Use one bunch of spring onions (scallions) and stir in some chopped fresh parsley or chives.

Creamy Leeks with Cheese

This is quite a rich dish that could easily be served as a meal in itself with brown rice or couscous.

Serves 4

4 large leeks or 12 baby leeks, trimmed and washed

15ml/1 tbsp olive oil
150ml/¼ pint/⅔ cup double (heavy) cream
75g/3oz mature (sharp) Cheddar or Monterey Jack cheese, grated
salt and ground black pepper

Preparation: 3–4 minutes; Cooking: 12 minutes

1 If using large leeks, slice them lengthways; leave baby ones intact. Heat the oil in a large frying pan and add the leeks. Season with salt and pepper and cook for about 4 minutes, stirring occasionally, until they become aromatic and the outsides start to turn golden.

2 Preheat the grill (broiler) to high. Pour the cream into the pan, drizzling it over the leeks, and stir until well combined. Lower the heat and allow to bubble gently for a few minutes, but do not overboil as the cream may begin to curdle.

3 Transfer the creamy leeks to a shallow ovenproof dish and sprinkle with the cheese. Grill (broil) for 4–5 minutes, or until the cheese topping is golden brown and bubbling. Serve immediately, while the dish is still piping hot.

Variations
• This recipe works well with all sorts of hard cheeses, from Parmesan and Gran Padano to Red Leicester, Double Gloucester and Caerphilly.
• For a more substantial dish, cook sliced button (white) mushrooms with the leeks, or top the mixture with sliced cherry tomatoes before adding the cheese.
• To make the dish more appealing to meat lovers, add some diced smoky bacon or pancetta to the pan in step 1, after you have fried the leeks for a couple of minutes.

Braised Lettuce Energy 191kcal/790kJ; Protein 8g; Carbohydrate 13.3g, of which sugars 4.2g; Fat 12.3g, of which saturates 6.9g; Cholesterol 27mg; Calcium 52mg; Fibre 5.7g; Sodium 81mg.
Creamy Leeks Energy 322kcal/1330kJ; Protein 7.8g; Carbohydrate 5g, of which sugars 4g; Fat 29.8g, of which saturates 17.1g; Cholesterol 70mg; Calcium 193mg; Fibre 3.3g; Sodium 147mg.

Curried Red Cabbage Slaw

Three shades of red combine in this fresh, crisp slaw. Each contributes a different texture and flavour, from the crunch of cabbage to the satin smoothness of the sweet red pepper.

Serves 4–6
½ red cabbage, thinly sliced
1 red (bell) pepper, chopped
  or very thinly sliced
½ red onion, chopped
60ml/4 tbsp red or white wine
  vinegar or cider vinegar
60ml/4 tbsp sugar, or to taste
120ml/4fl oz/½ cup Greek (US
  strained plain) yogurt or natural
  (plain) yogurt
120ml/4fl oz/½ cup mayonnaise,
  preferably home-made
1.5ml/¼ tsp curry powder
2–3 handfuls raisins
salt and ground black pepper

Preparation: 5 minutes; Cooking: 0 minutes

1 Put the cabbage, pepper and red onion in a bowl and toss to combine. In a small pan, heat the vinegar and sugar until the sugar has dissolved, then pour over the vegetables. Leave to cool slightly.

2 Combine the yogurt and mayonnaise, then mix into the cabbage mixture. Season to taste with curry powder, salt and ground black pepper, then mix in the raisins.

3 Chill the salad before serving, if you have time. Just before serving, drain off any excess liquid and briefly stir the slaw again.

Variations
• If you prefer, ready-made low-fat mayonnaise can be used instead of the Greek yogurt and mayonnaise mixture. Stir the curry powder into the mayonnaise.
• Use a crisp pear instead of the apple. An Asian or Nashi pear is naturally crisp when ripe.
• Substitute dried cranberries for the raisins.
• Omit the curry powder and use a lemon mayonnaise instead.
• If you don't like sweet (bell) pepper, use cucumber instead. Cut one in half and scrape out the seeds before slicing.

Beetroot with Fresh Mint

The lovely, bright colour of beetroot contrasts beautifully with the deep green of mint. The flavours work well together, too, and are enhanced by the sweet balsamic dressing.

Serves 4
4–6 cooked beetroot (beets)
5–10ml/1–2 tsp sugar
15–30ml/1–2 tbsp balsamic
  vinegar
juice of ½ lemon
30ml/2 tbsp extra virgin olive oil
1 bunch fresh mint, leaves
  stripped and thinly sliced
salt

Preparation: 3–4 minutes; Cooking: 0 minutes

1 Slice the beetroot or cut it into even-sized dice with a sharp knife. Put the beetroot in a bowl.

2 Add the sugar, balsamic vinegar, lemon juice, olive oil and a pinch of salt to the diced beetroot and toss lightly.

3 Add half the thinly sliced fresh mint to the salad and toss lightly until well combined. If you have time, chill the salad for about 1 hour. Serve garnished with the remaining thinly sliced mint leaves.

Cook's Tip
Cook the beetroot (beets) yourself in boiling water for 45–60 minutes until they are soft and the skins can easily be slipped off. Avoid buying beetroot that has been cooked in vinegar.

Variations
• To make a spicy version, add harissa to taste and substitute fresh coriander (cilantro) for the mint.
• As an alternative, add a chopped onion and some fresh dill.
• Serve surrounded by slices of pepper salami or chorizo.
• Use sherry or red wine vinegar instead of balsamic.

Red Cabbage Energy 272kcal/1136kJ; Protein 3g; Carbohydrate 27.9g, of which sugars 27.5g; Fat 17.5g, of which saturates 3.4g; Cholesterol 15mg; Calcium 74mg; Fibre 2g; Sodium 120mg.
Beetroot Energy 90kcal/376kJ; Protein 1.9g; Carbohydrate 7.8g, of which sugars 6.7g; Fat 5.9g, of which saturates 0.8g; Cholesterol 0mg; Calcium 45mg; Fibre 1.2g; Sodium 69mg.

Stir-fried Carrots with Mango & Ginger

Ripe, sweet mango tastes wonderful with carrots and ginger in this spicy vegetable dish, which is good enough to serve on its own with plain yogurt and boiled new potatoes or chunks of wholemeal or rustic white bread.

Serves 4–6
15–30ml/1–2 tbsp olive oil
2–3 garlic cloves, chopped
1 onion, chopped
25g/1oz fresh root ginger, peeled and chopped
5–6 carrots, sliced
30–45ml/2–3 tbsp shelled pistachio nuts, roasted
5ml/1 tsp ground cinnamon
5–10ml/1–2 tsp ras el hanout
1 small firm, ripe mango, peeled and roughly diced
a small bunch of fresh coriander (cilantro), finely chopped
juice of ½ lemon
salt

Preparation: 6 minutes; Cooking: 4–5 minutes

1 Heat the olive oil in a heavy frying pan or wok. Stir in the garlic, then the onion and ginger. Fry for 1 minute.

2 Add the carrots, tossing them in the pan to make sure that they are mixed with the flavouring ingredients, and cook until they begin to brown.

3 Roughly chop the roasted pistachio nuts. Add to the pan with the ground cinnamon and ras el hanout, then gently mix in the diced mango.

4 Sprinkle with the chopped coriander, season with salt and pour over the lemon juice. Toss with two spoons to mix, then spoon into a heated dish and serve immediately.

Cook's Tip
Ras el hanout is a traditional spice mix that is widely used across the Middle East and North Africa. It is available in most North African and Arab food stores.

Broad Beans with Bacon

This dish is particularly associated with Ronda, in southern Spain, the home of bull fighting, where broad beans are fed to fighting bulls to build them up. It is also found elsewhere in Spain, where it is known as habas españolas. If you have time, remove the dull skins from the broad beans to reveal the bright green beans beneath.

Serves 4
30ml/2 tbsp olive oil
1 small onion, finely chopped
1 garlic clove, finely chopped
50g/2oz rindless smoked streaky (fatty) bacon, roughly chopped
225g/8oz podded broad (fava) beans, thawed if frozen
5ml/1 tsp paprika
15ml/1 tbsp sweet sherry
salt and ground black pepper

Preparation: 5 minutes; Cooking: 12 minutes

1 Heat the olive oil in a large frying pan or sauté pan. Add the chopped onion, garlic and bacon and fry over a high heat for about 4 minutes, stirring frequently, until the onion is softened and the bacon browned.

2 Add the beans and paprika to the pan and stir-fry for 1 minute. Add the sherry, lower the heat, cover and cook for 7 minutes until tender. Season with salt and pepper to taste and serve hot.

Cook's Tip
Also known as horse beans or fava beans, broad beans are delicious, especially when young. Podding them is a satisfying job, but nature provides an extraordinary amount of packaging, and you will end up with a big bag of fleshy pods. Put these on the compost heap, as they are a good source of nitrogen.

Variation
For a vegetarian version of this dish, fry sun-dried tomatoes with the onion and garlic instead of the chopped bacon.

Stir-fried Carrots Energy 89kcal/371kJ; Protein 1.7g; Carbohydrate 8.2g, of which sugars 7.5g; Fat 5.7g, of which saturates 0.8g; Cholesterol 0mg; Calcium 23mg; Fibre 2.2g; Sodium 47mg.
Broad Beans Energy 140kcal/583kJ; Protein 6.6g; Carbohydrate 8g, of which sugars 1.8g; Fat 8.8g, of which saturates 1.9g; Cholesterol 8mg; Calcium 36mg; Fibre 3.9g; Sodium 163mg.

Cauliflower Cheese

The use of flour to thicken sauces began in France in the 17th century – hence the name 'roux' for the mixture of flour and fat that forms the basis of a white sauce – but cheese sauce made in this way has become a staple of English cookery.

Serves 4
1 medium cauliflower
25g/1oz/2 tbsp butter
25g/1oz/4 tbsp plain
*   (all-purpose) flour*
300ml/½ pint/1¼ cups milk
115g/4oz mature Cheddar or
*   Cheshire cheese, grated*
salt and ground black pepper

Preparation: 2 minutes; Cooking: 10 minutes

1 Trim the cauliflower and cut it into florets. Bring a pan of lightly salted water to the boil, drop in the cauliflower and cook for 5–8 minutes or until just tender. Drain and tip the florets into an ovenproof dish.

2 To make the sauce, melt the butter in a pan, stir in the flour and cook gently, stirring constantly, for about 1 minute (do not allow it to brown). Remove from the heat and gradually stir in the milk.

3 Return the pan to the heat and cook, stirring, until the mixture thickens and comes to the boil. Simmer for 1–2 minutes.

4 Stir in three-quarters of the cheese and season to taste. Spoon the sauce over the cauliflower and scatter the remaining cheese on top. Put under a hot grill (broiler) until the cheese topping bubbles and turns golden brown.

Variations
• *Boost the cheese flavour by adding a little English (hot) mustard to the cheese sauce.*
• *As an alternative to Cheddar or Cheshire cheese, use a blue cheese such as Stilton. You will not need as much.*
• *Cauliflower cheese is delicious with strips of crisp fried bacon, either served on the side or crumbled into the sauce.*

Carrot & Parsnip Purée

Puréed vegetables aren't just for the under-fives. Their creaminess appeals to all ages, and they are ideal partners for crisp vegetables such as lightly cooked green beans. If serving the purée directly on to plates, mould it by using two spoons, taking a scoop with one and sliding it off with the other.

Serves 6–8
350g/12oz carrots
450g/1lb parsnips
a pinch of freshly grated nutmeg
*   or ground mace*
15g/½oz/1 tbsp butter
about 15ml/1 tbsp single (light)
*   cream or crème fraîche*
a small bunch of parsley,
*   chopped, plus extra to garnish*
salt and ground black pepper

Preparation: 3 minutes; Cooking: 15–17 minutes

1 Peel the carrots and slice fairly thinly. Peel the parsnips and cut into bitesize chunks.

2 Boil the carrots and parsnips in separate pans of lightly salted water until tender. Drain them well, then purée them together in a food processor, with the grated nutmeg or mace, a generous seasoning of salt and ground black pepper, and the butter. Whizz until smooth.

3 Transfer the purée to a bowl and beat in the cream or crème fraîche. Add the chopped parsley for extra flavour.

4 Transfer the carrot and parsnip purée to a warmed serving bowl, sprinkle with the remaining chopped parsley to garnish, and serve immediately, as vegetable purées lose heat rapidly.

Cook's Tips
• *Any leftover purée can be thinned to taste with good-quality chicken or vegetable stock and heated to make a quick home-made soup. Add more seasoning if needed.*
• *The carrots can be replaced by a small sweet potato. Peel and dice finely. Boil the sweet potato a little ahead of the parsnips, if possible.*

Carrot and Parsnip Purée Energy 71kcal/298kJ; Protein 1.5g; Carbohydrate 10.7g, of which sugars 6.6g; Fat 2.7g, of which saturates 1.4g; Cholesterol 5mg; Calcium 49mg; Fibre 4g; Sodium 31mg.
Cauliflower Cheese Energy 318kcal/1318kJ; Protein 17.4g; Carbohydrate 4.4g, of which sugars 3.9g; Fat 25.8g, of which saturates 16.3g; Cholesterol 71mg; Calcium 371mg; Fibre 1.8g; Sodium 453mg.

Red Cauliflower

Vegetables are seldom served plain in Mexico. The cauliflower here is flavoured with a simple tomato salsa and fresh cheese. The salsa could be any table salsa; tomatillo is particularly good. The contrast with the texture and mild flavour of the cauliflower makes for a tasty dish which tastes good with triangles of toast, or for a more substantial meal, with sausages.

Serves 6
1 small onion
1 lime
1 medium cauliflower
400g/14oz can chopped
   tomatoes
4 fresh serrano chillies, seeded
   and finely chopped
1.5ml/¼ tsp caster (superfine)
   sugar
75g/3oz feta cheese, crumbled
salt
chopped fresh flat leaf parsley,
   to garnish

Preparation: 4 minutes; Cooking: 10 minutes

1 Chop the onion very finely and place in a bowl. With a zester peel away the zest of the lime in thin strips. Add to the chopped onion in the bowl and mix well.

2 Cut the lime in half and add the juice from both halves to the onion and lime zest mixture. Set aside so that the lime juice can soften the onion. Cut the cauliflower into florets.

3 Tip the tomatoes into a pan and add the chillies and sugar. Heat gently. Meanwhile, place the cauliflower in a pan of boiling water and cook gently for 5–8 minutes until tender.

4 Add the onions to the tomato salsa, with salt to taste, stir in and heat through, then spoon about a third of the salsa into a serving dish and level the surface.

5 Arrange the drained cauliflower florets on top of the salsa and spoon the remaining salsa on top.

6 Sprinkle with the crumbled feta, which should soften a little on contact. Serve the cheese-topped cauliflower immediately, sprinkled with chopped fresh flat leaf parsley.

Cauliflower with Egg & Lemon

Although cauliflower has shrugged off its image as the vegetable most people love to hate, it still needs a bit of a makeover now and then. This recipe is Greek in origin and tastes great.

Serves 4
75–90ml/5–6 tbsp extra virgin
   olive oil

1 medium cauliflower, divided into
   large florets
2 eggs
juice of 1 lemon
5ml/1 tsp cornflour (cornstarch),
   mixed to a cream with a little
   cold water
30ml/2 tbsp chopped fresh flat
   leaf parsley
salt

Preparation: 2–3 minutes; Cooking: 12 minutes

1 Heat the olive oil in a large heavy pan, add the cauliflower florets and sauté over a medium heat until they start to brown.

2 Pour in enough hot water to almost cover the cauliflower, add salt to taste, then cover the pan and cook for 7–8 minutes until the florets are just soft. Remove the pan from the heat and leave to stand, covered, while you make the sauce.

3 Beat the eggs in a bowl, add the lemon juice and cornflour and beat until mixed. Beat in a few tablespoons of the hot liquid from the cauliflower.

4 Pour the egg mixture slowly over the cauliflower, then stir gently. Place the pan over a very gentle heat for 2 minutes to thicken the sauce, but do not allow to boil. Spoon into a warmed serving bowl or individual bowls, sprinkle with parsley and serve immediately.

> **Variation**
> This delightful, summery style of cooking cauliflower is popular in the Mediterranean. It works equally well with a close relative, broccoli. Divide the broccoli into small florets and cook for slightly less time than the cauliflower, until just tender.

Red Cauliflower Energy 81kcal/338kJ; Protein 5.9g; Carbohydrate 5.6g, of which sugars 4.9g; Fat 4g, of which saturates 2.3g; Cholesterol 11mg; Calcium 79mg; Fibre 2.3g; Sodium 230mg.
Cauliflower with Egg Energy 201kcal/833kJ; Protein 7g; Carbohydrate 4.4g, of which sugars 2.7g; Fat 17.5g, of which saturates 3g; Cholesterol 95mg; Calcium 51mg; Fibre 2.2g; Sodium 47mg.

Cauliflower with Garlic Crumbs

This method of cooking cauliflower is very simple and it makes a great accompaniment to any meat or dairy meal. The garlic breadcrumbs add bite and flavour. If you are not keen on garlic it can be omitted and the cauliflower can be topped with grated cheese. Brown the cheese topping under a hot grill.

Serves 4–6
1 large cauliflower, cut into bitesize florets
pinch of sugar
90–120ml/6–8 tbsp olive or vegetable oil
130g/4½ oz/2¼ cups dry white or wholemeal (whole-wheat) breadcrumbs
3–5 garlic cloves, thinly sliced or chopped
salt and ground black pepper

Preparation: 5 minutes; Cooking: 10 minutes

1 Steam or boil the cauliflower in a pan of water, to which you have added the sugar and a pinch of salt, until just tender. Drain the cauliflower in a colander and leave to cool.

2 Heat 60–75ml/4–5 tbsp of the olive or vegetable oil in a pan, add the breadcrumbs and cook over a medium heat, tossing and turning, until browned and crisp. Add the garlic, turn once or twice, then remove from the pan and set aside.

3 Heat the remaining oil in the pan, then add the cauliflower, mashing and breaking it up a little as it lightly browns in the oil. (Do not overcook but just cook lightly in the oil.)

4 Add the garlic breadcrumbs to the pan and cook them, stirring, until well combined and some of the cauliflower is still holding its shape. Season with salt and pepper and spoon into a heated dish. Serve hot or warm.

> **Cook's Tip**
> In Israel, where this dish is popular, it is often eaten with meat or fish wrapped in filo pastry, since the textures and flavours complement each other perfectly.

Caramelized Shallots

Sweet, golden shallots are good with all sorts of main dishes, including poultry or meat. They are traditionally served with baked ham or gammon and taste great with a roast rib of beef. Try them with roasted chunks of butternut squash or pumpkin.

Serves 4–6
50g/2oz/¼ cup butter
500g/1¼ lb shallots or small onions, peeled with root ends intact
15ml/1 tbsp golden caster (superfine) sugar
30ml/2 tbsp red or white wine, Madeira or port
salt and ground black pepper

Preparation: 3 minutes; Cooking: 17 minutes

1 Heat the butter in a large frying pan and add the shallots or onions in a single layer. Cook gently, turning occasionally, for about 5 minutes, until they are lightly browned all over.

2 Sprinkle the sugar over the browned shallots and cook gently, turning the shallots in the juices, until the sugar melts and then gradually begins to caramelize.

3 Pour the wine, Madeira or port over the caramelized shallots and increase the heat. Let the mixture bubble for 4–5 minutes.

4 Add 150ml/¼ pint/⅔ cup water and seasoning. Cover and cook for 5 minutes, then remove the lid and cook until the liquid evaporates and the shallots are tender and glazed. Taste and add more salt and pepper if needed, before serving.

> **Cook's Tips**
> • Leaving the root ends of the shallots intact helps to ensure that they do not separate or unravel during cooking, but remain whole. They also look more presentable served in this way.
> • Shallots can be quite costly, so look out for small onions of the type used for pickling, for a cheaper alternative.
> • Substitute half the wine with balsamic vinegar or sherry vinegar for a more piquant result.

Cauliflower Energy 204kcal/852kJ; Protein 5.5g; Carbohydrate 19.3g, of which sugars 2.7g; Fat 12.2g, of which saturates 1.7g; Cholesterol 0mg; Calcium 46mg; Fibre 2g; Sodium 172mg.
Caramelized Shallots Energy 96kcal/399kJ; Protein 1.3g; Carbohydrate 5.4g, of which sugars 5.4g; Fat 7.5g, of which saturates 1.1g; Cholesterol 0mg; Calcium 22mg; Fibre 1.2g; Sodium 9mg.

Squash & New Potatoes with Sour Cream

This is an Israeli dish of fresh vegetables and fragrant dill, tossed in a rich, buttery sour cream sauce. It looks and tastes delicious, and is an easy to make all-in-one accompaniment.

Serves 4

400g/14oz mixed squash, such as green courgettes (zucchini), and small yellow squash
400g/14oz tiny, baby new potatoes
pinch of sugar
40–75g/1½–3oz/3–5 tbsp butter
2 bunches spring onions (scallions), thinly sliced
1 large bunch fresh dill, finely chopped
300ml/½ pint/1¼ cups sour cream or Greek (US strained plain) yogurt
salt and ground black pepper

Preparation: 5 minutes; Cooking: 14 minutes

1 Cut the squash into pieces about the same size as the potatoes. Put the potatoes in a pan and add water to cover, with the sugar and salt. Bring to the boil, then simmer for about 10 minutes, until almost tender. Add the squash and continue to cook until the vegetables are just tender, then drain.

2 Melt the butter in a large pan; fry the spring onions until just wilted, then gently stir in the dill and vegetables.

3 Remove the pan from the heat and stir in the sour cream or yogurt. Return to the heat and heat gently until warm. Season with salt and pepper and serve.

Cook's Tip
This is a very good recipe for anyone who regularly has an organic vegetable box delivered. When squash are in season you may well receive some unfamiliar varieties. The recipe works particularly well with courgettes (zucchini) and patty pan or custard squash, but is also good with winter varieties like pumpkin, butternut or turban squash.

Luffa Squash with Mushrooms, Spring Onions & Coriander

Winter gourds, such as pumpkins, bitter melons, luffa squash and a variety of other squash that come under the kabocha umbrella, are popular ingredients for soups and braised vegetable dishes, especially in Asia.

Serves 4

750g/1lb 10oz luffa squash, peeled
30ml/2 tbsp groundnut (peanut) or sesame oil
2 shallots, halved and sliced
2 garlic cloves, finely chopped
115g/4oz/1½ cups button (white) mushrooms, quartered
15ml/1 tbsp mushroom ketchup
10ml/2 tsp soy sauce
4 spring onions (scallions), cut into 2cm/¾ in pieces
fresh coriander (cilantro) leaves and thin strips of spring onion (scallion), to garnish

Preparation: 6–7 minutes; Cooking: 6 minutes

1 Cut the luffa squash diagonally into 2cm/¾in-thick pieces. Heat the oil in a large wok or heavy pan. Stir in the halved shallots and garlic, stir-fry until they begin to colour and turn golden, then add the mushrooms.

2 Add the mushroom and soy sauces, and the squash. Reduce the heat, cover and cook gently for a few minutes until the squash is tender. Stir in the spring onion pieces, garnish with coriander and spring onion strips, and serve.

Cook's Tip
Also known as silk gourd or Chinese okra, luffa looks like a long, skinny courgette (zucchini) or a very large okra pod. The most common variety is ridged down its length and is dark green in colour. It has a mild, delicate taste, very similar to cucumber, and is a popular ingredient in stir-fries. Young luffa will not need peeling, but if the skin is tough it is best to peel it completely. Unlike cucumber, it is never eaten raw.

Squash and Potatoes Energy 328kcal/1361kJ; Protein 6.7g; Carbohydrate 22.3g, of which sugars 7.3g; Fat 24.1g, of which saturates 14.8g; Cholesterol 66mg; Calcium 122mg; Fibre 2.7g; Sodium 107mg.
Luffa Squash Energy 194kcal/800kJ; Protein 3g; Carbohydrate 19g, of which sugars 3g; Fat 12g, of which saturates 2g; Cholesterol 0mg; Calcium 31mg; Fibre 5.1g; Sodium 100mg.

Grilled Radicchio & Courgettes

Radicchio is often grilled or barbecued in Italian cooking to give it a special flavour. Combined with courgettes, it makes a quick and tasty side dish.

Serves 4
2–3 firm heads radicchio, round or long type, rinsed
4 courgettes (zucchini)
90ml/6 tbsp olive oil
salt and ground black pepper

Preparation: 2–3 minutes; Cooking: 8–10 minutes

1 Preheat the grill (broiler) or prepare a barbecue. Using a sharp knife, cut the radicchio in half through the root section or base. Cut the courgettes into 1cm/½in diagonal slices.

2 When ready to cook, brush the vegetables with the olive oil and add salt and pepper. Cook for 4–5 minutes on each side.

Baked Tomatoes Provençal Style

These tomatoes, epitomizing the flavour of Provence, France, are perfect with roast meat or poultry. You can prepare them a few hours ahead, then cook them while carving the roast. They are particularly good with roast lamb or beef, but can also be served solo, and for a light lunch.

Serves 4
2 large tomatoes
45ml/3 tbsp fresh white breadcrumbs
2 garlic cloves, very finely chopped
30ml/2 tbsp chopped fresh parsley
30–45ml/2–3 tbsp olive oil
salt and ground black pepper
fresh flat leaf parsley sprigs, to garnish

Preparation: 2–3 minutes; Cooking: 8–10 minutes

1 Preheat the oven to 220°C/425°F/Gas 7. Cut the tomatoes in half and arrange them cut side up on a foil-lined baking sheet.

2 In a bowl, mix together the breadcrumbs, garlic and parsley. Stir in salt and pepper to taste, then spoon the mixture over the tomato halves, covering them completely.

3 Drizzle the tomatoes generously with olive oil and bake them for about 8–10 minutes until lightly browned. Transfer carefully to a platter or individual plates and serve immediately, garnished with the parsley sprigs.

Variations
• This is a very versatile recipe. Use wholemeal (whole-wheat) breadcrumbs, if you like, and try adding finely chopped hazelnuts or flaked (sliced) almonds.
• Alternatively, fry finely chopped mushrooms and garlic in a little oil, bind with breadcrumbs and use instead of the dry crumb topping on the tomatoes.
• For an even easier topping, use a bought bread stuffing mix, such as sage and onion, sprinkling it directly over the tomatoes. Drizzle each topped tomato with olive oil, as in the main recipe, before putting them in the oven and baking them.

Griddle Potatoes

This attractive dish has traditionally been made with leftover cooked potatoes that have been boiled in their skins. It makes a tasty accompaniment to grilled meat or fish.

Serves 4–6
2 onions, thinly sliced
450–675g/1–1½lb whole cooked potatoes, boiled in their skins
25g/1oz butter and 15ml/1 tbsp oil, for shallow-frying
salt and ground black pepper

Preparation: 10 minutes; Cooking: 8 minutes

1 Put the onions in a large pan and scald them briefly in boiling water. Refresh under cold water and drain well. Peel the potatoes. Using a sharp knife, slice them thickly.

2 Put a mixture of butter and oil into a large, heavy frying pan and heat well. When the fat is hot, fry the onion until tender. Add the potato slices and brown them together, turning the potato slices to brown as evenly as possible on both sides. Transfer to a dish and season with salt and pepper. Serve hot.

Baked Tomatoes Energy 105kcal/438kJ; Protein 2g; Carbohydrate 11.5g, of which sugars 2.7g; Fat 6g, of which saturates 0.9g; Cholesterol 0mg; Calcium 20mg; Fibre 1.1g; Sodium 92mg.
Grilled Radicchio Energy 195kcal/802kJ; Protein 4.2g; Carbohydrate 4.9g, of which sugars 4.7g; Fat 17.7g, of which saturates 2.6g; Cholesterol 0mg; Calcium 71mg; Fibre 2.5g; Sodium 4mg.
Griddle Potatoes Energy 652kcal/2724kJ; Protein 13.6g; Carbohydrate 105.6g, of which sugars 20g; Fat 22g, of which saturates 13.2g; Cholesterol 52mg; Calcium 194mg; Fibre 10.4g; Sodium 196mg.

Patatas Bravas

There are several variations on this chilli and potato dish, but the most important thing is the spicing, which is made hotter still by adding vinegar. The classic version is made with fresh tomato sauce flavoured with garlic and chilli. The name bravas implies that the potatoes are so hot that it is manly to eat them. Patatas bravas often appear on tapas menus and are good with drinks.

Serves 4
675g/1½lb small new potatoes
75ml/5 tbsp olive oil
2 garlic cloves, sliced
3 dried chillies, seeded
   and chopped
2.5ml/½ tsp ground cumin
10ml/2 tsp paprika
30ml/2 tbsp red or white
   wine vinegar
1 red or green (bell) pepper,
   seeded and sliced
coarse sea salt, for sprinkling
   (optional)

Preparation: 4 minutes; Cooking: 15 minutes

1 Scrub the potatoes and put them into a pan of lightly salted water. Bring to the boil and cook for 10 minutes, or until almost tender. Drain and leave to cool slightly. Peel, if you like, then cut the potatoes into neat, even-sized chunks.

2 Heat the oil in a large frying or sauté pan and fry the potatoes, turning them frequently, until golden.

3 Meanwhile, crush together the garlic, chillies and cumin using a mortar and pestle. Mix the paste with the paprika and wine vinegar, then add to the potatoes with the sliced pepper and cook, stirring, for 2 minutes. Scatter with salt, if using, and serve hot as a tapas dish or cold as a side dish.

Variations
Patatas bravas means fierce potatoes. They are meant to be fiery but the flavour can be moderated by reducing the amount of chilli. Although classically vegetarian, they are often served with chorizo or with chunks of roast pork. Try making them with sweet potatoes for a tasty change.

Colcannon

This traditional Irish dish is especially associated with Halloween, when it is likely to be made with curly kale and would have a ring hidden in it – predicting marriage during the coming year for the person who found it. At other times during the winter green cabbage is more often used.

Serves 3–4
450g/1lb potatoes, peeled
   and boiled
450g/1lb curly kale or
   cabbage, cooked
milk, if necessary
50g/2oz/¼ cup butter, plus extra
   for serving
1 large onion, finely chopped
salt and ground black pepper

Preparation: 5 minutes; Cooking: 10 minutes

1 Mash the potatoes and spoon them into a large bowl. Chop the kale or cabbage, add it to the potatoes and mix. Stir in a little milk if the mash is too stiff, and season with salt and ground black pepper.

2 Melt a little butter in a frying pan over a medium heat and add the onion. Cook for 3–4 minutes until softened. Remove and mix well with the potato and kale or cabbage.

3 Add the remainder of the butter to the hot pan. When it is very hot, turn the potato mixture on to the pan and spread it out in an even layer.

4 Fry the potato mixture until golden brown, then cut it roughly into pieces and continue frying until these are crisp and brown.

5 Spoon the colcannon into a large bowl or individual bowls, and add a generous knob of butter to each. Serve immediately. As the butter melts, guests fork it in to the cabbage mixture.

Cook's Tip
It is delicious with pork chops or sausages or can simply be served with fried eggs.

Patatas Bravas Energy 256kcal/1070kJ; Protein 3.3g; Carbohydrate 30g, of which sugars 4.9g; Fat 14.4g, of which saturates 2.2g; Cholesterol 0mg; Calcium 14mg; Fibre 2.4g; Sodium 20mg.
Colcannon Energy 1224kcal/5124kJ; Protein 21.6g; Carbohydrate 162.4g, of which sugars 54.4g; Fat 58.4g, of which saturates 35.2g; Cholesterol 144mg; Calcium 416mg; Fibre 23.6g; Sodium 508mg.

Fried Plantains

These simple and tasty treats from the Caribbean are the perfect accompaniment to highly spiced and seasoned foods. Their sweet flavour provides an interesting contrast.

Serves 4
4 ripe plantains
75g/3oz/6 tbsp butter
10ml/2 tsp vegetable oil
strips of spring onion (scallion)
*   and red (bell) pepper,*
*   to garnish*

Preparation: 2 minutes; Cooking: 10–12 minutes

1 Peel the plantains, cut them in half lengthways, then cut them in half again. Melt the butter with the oil in a large frying pan.

2 Add the plantains to the pan in a single layer and fry for 8–10 minutes, turning halfway through. Drain on kitchen paper. Spoon into a heated dish and garnish with strips of spring onion and red pepper. Serve immediately.

Variation
Fried plantains are very good on their own, or with a generous scoop of sour cream, crème fraîche or thick yogurt, but also taste great with black beans. Soak 450g/1lb/2½ cups black turtle beans in water overnight. Next day, drain the beans and put them in a pan. Cover with cold water. Add a 115g/4oz piece of gammon or uncooked ham and a bay leaf. Bring to the boil, then simmer and cook for 1 hour or until the beans are tender. In a separate pan, fry 2 crushed garlic cloves in 30ml/2 tbsp oil until aromatic. Add two ladles of cooked beans and fry for 2–3 minutes, breaking up the beans. Tip the refried beans back into the pan and season. Simmer gently for 10 minutes, then serve.

Cook's Tip
Ripe plantains have dark, almost black skins. Do not use green, under-ripe plantains, which are very hard and which will not soften, no matter how long you cook them for.

Corn with Cream

In Mexico, this would be made with heavy cream, the American equivalent of double cream, but the sauce has a better consistency when made with full-fat soft cheese. The jalapeños give the somewhat bland corn kernels a bit of a kick, but could be omitted in favour of diced sweet pepper or even peppadews.

Serves 6
4 corn cobs
50g/2oz/¼ cup butter
1 small onion, finely chopped
115g/4oz/⅔ cup drained pickled
*   jalapeño chilli slices*
130g/4½ oz/⅔ cup full-fat
*   soft cheese*
25g/1oz/⅓ cup freshly grated
*   Parmesan cheese, plus*
*   shavings, to garnish*
salt and ground black pepper

Preparation: 2 minutes; Cooking: 11–13 minutes

1 Strip off the husks from the corn and pull off the silks. Place the cobs in a bowl of water and use a vegetable brush to remove any remaining silks. Stand each cob in turn on a board and slice off the kernels, cutting as close to the cob as possible.

2 Melt the butter in a pan, add the chopped onion and fry for 4–5 minutes, stirring occasionally, until the onion has softened.

3 Add the corn kernels and cook for 4–5 minutes, until they are just tender. Chop the jalapeños finely and stir them into the corn mixture until evenly distributed.

4 Stir in the soft cheese and the grated Parmesan. Cook over a low heat until both cheeses have melted and the corn kernels are coated in the mixture. Season to taste, tip into a heated dish and serve, topped with Parmesan shavings.

Cook's Tip
To save time, use 350g/12oz/2 cups frozen corn kernels. Thaw before adding to the fried onion mixture. Alternatively, use canned whole kernel corn. Drain it well and just let it heat up in the onion mixture before adding the cheese.

Fried Plantains Energy 205kcal/861kJ; Protein 1.2g; Carbohydrate 29.5g, of which sugars 5.8g; Fat 10g, of which saturates 5.5g; Cholesterol 21mg; Calcium 11mg; Fibre 1.3g; Sodium 65mg.
Corn with Cream Energy 328kcal/1367kJ; Protein 7.6g; Carbohydrate 27.7g, of which sugars 10.4g; Fat 21.6g, of which saturates 12.8g; Cholesterol 45mg; Calcium 126mg; Fibre 1.5g; Sodium 463mg.

Wilted Spinach with Rice & Dill

This is a delicious dish that can be made in little time and with little effort.

Serves 5

675g/1½lb fresh spinach, trimmed of any hard stalks
105ml/7 tbsp extra virgin olive oil
1 large onion, chopped
juice of ½ lemon
150ml/¼ pint/⅔ cup water
115g/4oz/generous ½ cup long grain rice
45ml/3 tbsp chopped fresh dill, plus extra sprigs to garnish
salt and ground black pepper

Preparation: 5 minutes; Cooking: 15 minutes

1 Thoroughly wash the spinach in cold water and drain. Repeat four or five times until the spinach is completely clean and free of grit, then drain it completely in a colander. Brush off the excess water with kitchen paper.

2 Heat the olive oil in a large pan and sauté the onion until translucent. Add the spinach and stir for a few minutes to coat all the leaves with the olive oil. As soon as the spinach looks wilted, add the lemon juice and the measured water and bring to the boil.

3 Add the rice and half of the dill, then cover and cook gently for about 10 minutes, or until the rice is cooked to your taste. If it looks too dry, add a little hot water.

4 Spoon into a serving dish and sprinkle the sprigs of dill over the top. Serve hot or at room temperature.

Variation
This is equally good with chard or spring greens.

Cook's Tip
This dish is ideal to accompany fried or barbecued fish or chickpea rissoles. It can also be eaten as a first course.

Saffron Rice with Cardamoms

The addition of aromatic green cardamom pods, cloves, milk and saffron gives this dish both a delicate flavour and colour. It is the perfect dish to accompany a simple chicken or lamb curry and would also go well with a spicy vegetable dish or dhal.

Serves 6

450g/1lb/2⅓ cups basmati rice, soaked
750ml/1¼ pints/3 cups water
3 green cardamom pods
2 cloves
5ml/1 tsp salt
45ml/3 tbsp semi-skimmed (low-fat) milk
2.5ml/½ tsp saffron strands, crushed

Preparation: 6 minutes; Cooking: 10 minutes

1 Drain the rice and place it in a pan. Pour in the water.

2 Add the cardamoms, cloves and salt. Stir, then bring to the boil. Lower the heat, cover the pan tightly and simmer the rice for about 5 minutes so that it starts to cook.

3 Meanwhile, place the milk in a small pan. Add the saffron strands and heat gently.

4 Add the saffron milk to the rice and stir. Cover again and continue cooking over a low heat for 5–6 minutes. Remove from the heat without lifting the lid. Leave the rice to stand for 5 minutes before serving.

Cook's Tips
• The saffron milk can be heated in the microwave. Mix the milk and saffron strands in a suitable jug (pitcher) or bowl and warm them for 1 minute on Low.
• The rice can be coloured and flavoured with a generous pinch of ground turmeric instead of saffron. The effect will not be as subtle, but the results will still be very satisfactory.
• Just before serving the rice, remove the cardamom pods and whole cloves, or warn guests to look out for them.

Wilted Spinach Energy 325Kcal/1,343kJ; Protein 7.8g; Carbohydrate 29.9g, of which sugars 5.6g; Fat 19.2g, of which saturates 2.7g; Cholesterol 0mg; Calcium 327mg; Fibre 4.8g; Sodium 242mg.
Saffron Rice Energy 348kcal/1452kJ; Protein 6.7g; Carbohydrate 71g, of which sugars 0.9g; Fat 3.6g, of which saturates 2g; Cholesterol 8mg; Calcium 21mg; Fibre 0.2g; Sodium 515mg.

Pilau Rice with Whole Spices

This fragrant rice dish makes an excellent accompaniment to any Indian meal.

Serves 4
generous pinch of saffron
  strands
600ml/1 pint/2½ cups
  chicken stock
50g/2oz/¼ cup butter

1 onion, chopped
1 garlic clove, crushed
½ cinnamon stick
6 green cardamom pods
1 bay leaf
250g/9oz/1¼ cups basmati rice
50g/2oz/⅓ cup sultanas
  (golden raisins)
15ml/1 tbsp sunflower oil
50g/2oz/½ cup cashew nuts

Preparation: 2 minutes; Cooking: 17 minutes

1 Add the saffron strands to a jug (pitcher) of hot chicken stock. Stir well to release the colour, and set aside.

2 Heat the butter in a pan and fry the chopped onion and crushed garlic for 5 minutes. Stir in the cinnamon stick, cardamoms and bay leaf and cook for a further 2 minutes.

3 Add the rice and cook, stirring, for 2 minutes more. Pour in the saffron-flavoured stock and add the sultanas. Bring to the boil, stir, then lower the heat, cover with a tight-fitting lid and cook gently for about 8 minutes or until the rice is tender and all the liquid has been absorbed.

4 Meanwhile, heat the oil in a frying pan and fry the cashew nuts until browned. Drain on kitchen paper. Scatter the browned cashew nuts evenly over the rice.

Cook's Tip
Don't be tempted to use black cardamoms in this dish. They are coarser and more strongly flavoured than green cardamoms and are only used in highly spiced dishes that are cooked for a long time. When using cardamoms of any colour, make sure they are fresh or the dish will taste musty.

Special Fried Rice

More colourful and elaborate than other fried rice dishes, special fried rice is almost a meal in itself and is ideal for a midweek supper. It is satisfying without being stodgy.

Serves 4
50g/2oz/⅓ cup cooked peeled
  prawns (shrimp)

3 eggs
5ml/1 tsp salt
2 spring onions (scallions),
  finely chopped
60ml/4 tbsp vegetable oil
115g/4oz lean pork, finely diced
15ml/1 tbsp light soy sauce
15ml/1 tbsp Chinese rice wine
  or dry sherry
450g/1lb/6 cups cooked rice
115g/4oz green peas

Preparation: 3 minutes; Cooking: 7 minutes

1 Pat the prawns dry with kitchen paper. Put the eggs in a bowl with a pinch of the salt and a few pieces of spring onion. Beat well.

2 Heat half the oil in a wok, add the pork and stir-fry until golden. Add the prawns and cook for 1 minute, then add the soy sauce and rice wine or sherry. Remove the mixture from the wok, cover with foil and keep warm.

3 Heat the remaining oil in the wok and lightly scramble the eggs. Add the rice and stir with chopsticks to make sure that each grain of rice is separated.

4 Add the remaining salt and spring onions, the stir-fried prawns, pork and peas. Toss well over the heat to combine, spoon into a bowl and serve either hot or cold.

Cook's Tips
• The weight of rice increases about two and a half times after cooking. When a recipe calls for cooked rice, use just under half the weight in uncooked rice to achieve the desired amount.
• This is a good way of using up leftover roast pork or chicken. Add it with the prawns as it will only need to be heated through, unlike the raw pork, which must be fully cooked.

Pilau Rice Energy 302kcal/1258kJ; Protein 5.8g; Carbohydrate 46.4g, of which sugars 1g; Fat 10.1g, of which saturates 1.1g; Cholesterol 0mg; Calcium 49mg; Fibre 0.8g; Sodium 2mg.
Fried Rice Energy 343kcal/1872kJ; Protein 14.5g; Carbohydrate 51g, of which sugars 4.4g; Fat 20.9g, of which saturates 3.1g; Cholesterol 113mg; Calcium 48mg; Fibre 1.1g; Sodium 58mg.

Stir-fried Noodles with Beansprouts

A classic Chinese noodle combination that makes a marvellous accompaniment to a variety of both Eastern and Western dishes, this is great with seafood.

Serves 4
175g/6oz dried egg noodles
15ml/1 tbsp vegetable oil

1 garlic clove, finely chopped
1 small onion, halved and sliced
225g/8oz/2⅔ cups beansprouts
1 small red (bell) pepper, seeded and cut into strips
1 small green (bell) pepper, seeded and cut into strips
2.5ml/½ tsp salt
1.5ml/¼ tsp ground white pepper
30ml/2 tbsp light soy sauce

Preparation: 5 minutes; Cooking: 9–13 minutes

1 Bring a pan of water to the boil. Cook the noodles for 4 minutes until just tender or according to the instructions on the packet. Drain, refresh under cold water and drain again.

2 Heat the oil in a non-stick frying pan or wok. When the oil is very hot, add the garlic, stir briefly, then add the onion slices. Cook, stirring, for 1 minute, then add the beansprouts and peppers. Stir-fry for 2–3 minutes.

3 Stir in the cooked noodles and toss over the heat, using two spatulas or wooden spoons, for 2–3 minutes or until the ingredients are well mixed and have heated through.

4 Add the salt, pepper and soy sauce and stir thoroughly before serving the noodle mixture in heated bowls.

Cook's Tip
Non-stick woks are a good way of minimizing the amount of fat required for cooking. However, they cannot be heated to the very high temperatures that stir-frying meat usually requires. This dish is an ideal candidate for an electric wok. Preheat it before adding the oil, pouring it around the inner rim so that it flows down to coat the surface. Use a high temperature for the initial stir-frying, but turn it down when reheating the noodles.

Spicy Avocado Salsa

Nachos or tortilla chips are the perfect accompaniment for this classic Mexican dip, which not only tastes deliciously fresh but also takes just minutes to prepare. It makes a very good filling for cocktail tomatoes which have been halved and hollowed out.

Serves 4
2 ripe avocados
2 fresh red chillies, seeded
1 garlic clove
1 shallot
30ml/2 tbsp olive oil, plus extra to serve
juice of 1 lemon
salt
flat leaf parsley, to garnish

Preparation: 5 minutes; Cooking: 0 minutes

1 Halve the avocados, remove their stones (pits) and, using a spoon, scoop out their flesh into a bowl. Mash the flesh well with a large fork or a potato masher.

2 Finely chop the chillies, garlic and shallot, then stir into the mashed avocado with the olive oil and lemon juice. Taste the mixture and add a little salt if required.

3 Spoon the mixture into a small serving bowl. Drizzle a little olive oil over the surface and scatter with a few flat leaf parsley leaves. Serve immediately, or the guacamole may discolour.

Variations
• Add a diced tomato to the guacamole for extra colour and flavour, or stir in some chopped sun-dried tomatoes.
• Use the juice of 2 limes instead of the lemon, if you prefer.

Cook's Tip
The lemon juice prevents the avocado flesh from discolouring once it is exposed to the air. However, even with lemon juice in a recipe, it is still sensible to prepare avocado dishes shortly before they are to be eaten rather than hours in advance.

Noodles Energy 244kcal/1030kJ; Protein 8g; Carbohydrate 39.9g, of which sugars 7.8g; Fat 7g, of which saturates 1.5g; Cholesterol 13mg; Calcium 34mg; Fibre 3.5g; Sodium 352mg.
Avocado Salsa Energy 151kcal/623kJ; Protein 1.2g; Carbohydrate 2.4g, of which sugars 1.3g; Fat 15.2g, of which saturates 2.9g; Cholesterol 0mg; Calcium 10mg; Fibre 2g; Sodium 4mg.

Yogurt Dip

This is a less rich version of a classic mayonnaise and is much easier to make. It tastes quite creamy, thanks to the small amount of mayonnaise in the mixture, and serves not only as a dip but also as a salad dressing.

Makes about 210ml/7fl oz/ scant 1 cup
150ml/¼ pint/⅔ cup natural (plain) yogurt
30ml/2 tbsp mayonnaise
30ml/2 tbsp milk
15ml/1 tbsp chopped fresh parsley
15ml/1 tbsp chopped fresh chives

Preparation: 2 minutes; Cooking: 0 minutes

1 Put all the ingredients together in a bowl. Season to taste with salt and ground black pepper and mix well. If not serving immediately, cover the bowl and place the dip in the refrigerator until required.

Artichoke & Cumin Dip

This dip is so easy to make and is unbelievably tasty. Serve with olives, hummus and wedges of pitta bread as part of a selection of snacks for an informal party in the summertime.

Serves 4
2 x 400g/14oz cans artichoke hearts, drained
2 garlic cloves, peeled
2.5ml/½ tsp ground cumin
olive oil
salt and ground black pepper

Preparation: 2 minutes; Cooking: 0 minutes

1 Put the artichoke hearts in a food processor with the garlic and ground cumin, and add a generous drizzle of olive oil. Process to a smooth purée and season with plenty of salt and ground black pepper to taste.

2 Spoon the purée into a serving bowl and serve with an extra drizzle of olive oil swirled on the top and slices of warm pitta bread or wholemeal (whole-wheat) toast fingers and carrot sticks for dipping.

Muhammara

This thick, roasted red pepper and walnut purée is popular in the Middle East. Serve it as a dip with spears of cos or romaine lettuce, wedges of pitta bread and chunks of tomato.

Serves 4
1½ slices Granary (whole-wheat) bread, day-old and toasted
3 red (bell) peppers, roasted, skinned and chopped
2 very mild chillies, roasted, skinned and chopped
115g/4oz/1 cup walnut pieces
3–4 garlic cloves, chopped
15–30ml/1–2 tbsp balsamic vinegar or pomegranate molasses
juice of ½ lemon
2.5–5ml/½–1 tsp ground cumin
2.5ml/½ tsp sugar, or to taste
105ml/7 tbsp olive oil, preferably extra virgin
salt

Preparation: 8 minutes; Cooking: 0 minutes

1 Break the Granary bread into small pieces and place in a food processor or blender with all the remaining ingredients except the extra virgin olive oil. Blend together until the ingredients are finely chopped.

2 With the motor running, slowly drizzle the extra virgin olive oil into the food processor or blender and process until the mixture forms a smooth paste. Tip the muhammara into a serving dish. Serve at room temperature.

Variation

For a quick and easy variation on the muhammara theme, make red pepper hummus. Drain a 400g/14oz can of chickpeas in a colander, rinse them gently under cold water and drain again. Tip into the bowl of a food processor. Scoop out 2 roasted red peppers from a jar or can, remove any seeds, then add them to the food processor with 1 crushed garlic clove, 15ml/1 tbsp tahini, 2.5ml/½ tsp ground cumin and 2.5ml/½ tsp mild chilli powder. Whizz these ingredients together, then scrape the mixture into a bowl and add salt, pepper and lemon juice to taste. Serve at room temperature.

Yogurt Dip Energy 315kcal/1308kJ; Protein 9.9g; Carbohydrate 14g, of which sugars 13.7g; Fat 25.1g, of which saturates 4.5g; Cholesterol 26mg; Calcium 383mg; Fibre 1.5g; Sodium 282mg.
Artichoke Dip Energy 76kcal/315kJ; Protein 1.6g; Carbohydrate 3.9g, of which sugars 3.5g; Fat 6.2g, of which saturates 1g; Cholesterol 0mg; Calcium 18mg; Fibre 3.5g; Sodium 4mg.
Muhammara Energy 444kcal/1833kJ; Protein 6.8g; Carbohydrate 15.5g, of which sugars 9.9g; Fat 39.8g, of which saturates 4.6g; Cholesterol 0mg; Calcium 62mg; Fibre 3.7g; Sodium 69mg.

Chilli Bean Dip

Substantial enough to serve for supper on a baked potato, this creamy bean dip also tastes great with triangles of lightly toasted pitta bread or a bowl of crunchy tortilla chips. Serve it warm to enjoy it at its best. If the flavours are too fiery, use sweet peppers instead of green chillies and omit the red chilli strips.

Serves 4

2 fresh green chillies
2 garlic cloves
1 onion
30ml/2 tbsp vegetable oil
5–10ml/1–2 tsp hot chilli powder
400g/14oz can kidney beans
75g/3oz/³⁄₄ cup grated
  (shredded) mature (sharp)
  Cheddar cheese
1 fresh red chilli, seeded
salt and ground black pepper

Preparation: 2–3 minutes; Cooking: 9–10 minutes

1 Slit the green chillies and use a sharp knife to scrape out and discard the seeds. Chop the chilli flesh finely, then crush the garlic and finely chop the onion.

2 Heat the oil in a large pan or wok and add the garlic, onion and green chilli mixture. Stir in the chilli powder. Cook gently for 5 minutes, stirring, until the onions have softened and are transparent, but not browned.

3 Drain the kidney beans, reserving the liquid in which they were canned. Set aside 30ml/2 tbsp of the beans and purée the remainder in a food processor or blender.

4 Spoon the puréed beans into the pan or wok and stir in 30–45ml/2–3 tbsp of the reserved can liquid. Heat gently, stirring to mix all the ingredients well.

5 Stir in the reserved whole kidney beans and the Cheddar cheese. Cook gently for 2–3 minutes, stirring regularly until the cheese melts. Add salt and pepper to taste.

6 Cut the red chilli into tiny strips. Spoon the dip into four individual serving bowls and sprinkle the chilli strips over the top. Serve warm.

Melting Cheese Dip

This is a classic fondue in true Swiss style. It should be served with cubes of crusty, day-old bread, speared on long-handled forks, but it is also good with chunks of spicy, cured sausage such as chorizo, or with batons of carrot or celery.

Serves 2

1 garlic clove, finely chopped
150ml/¹⁄₄ pint/²⁄₃ cup dry
  white wine
150g/5oz Gruyère cheese
5ml/1 tsp cornflour (cornstarch)
15ml/1 tbsp Kirsch
salt and ground black pepper
bread or chorizo cubes, to serve

Preparation: 3 minutes; Cooking: 7 minutes

1 Place the garlic and wine in a small pan and bring gently to the boil. Lower the heat and simmer for 3–4 minutes.

2 Coarsely grate the cheese and stir it into the wine. Continue to stir as the cheese melts.

3 Blend the cornflour to a smooth paste with the Kirsch and pour into the pan, stirring. Bring to the boil, stirring continuously until the sauce is smooth and thickened.

4 Add salt and pepper to taste. Serve immediately in heated bowls or transfer to a fondue pan and keep hot over a spirit burner. Garnish with black pepper and serve with bread or chorizo cubes.

Cook's Tips

• In the 1960s this was a favourite centrepiece for a dinner party, usually kept warm in a pottery pot set over a burner. Using long-handled forks, guests speared cubes of bread and dunked them in the cheese, twirling the forks until the bread was thoroughly coated. This activity could be hazardous and cubes of bread were often lost. When this happened, the individual concerned had to pay a forfeit.
• Gruyère is a tasty cheese that melts incredibly well. Don't substitute other cheeses in this dip.

Chilli Bean Dip Energy 240kcal/1002kJ; Protein 12.3g; Carbohydrate 20.3g, of which sugars 5.4g; Fat 12.3g, of which saturates 4.8g; Cholesterol 18mg; Calcium 219mg; Fibre 6.6g; Sodium 527mg.
Melting Cheese Dip Energy 390kcal/1617kJ; Protein 19.4g; Carbohydrate 3.3g, of which sugars 0.6g; Fat 24.6g, of which saturates 16.3g; Cholesterol 73mg; Calcium 562mg; Fibre 0.1g; Sodium 547mg.

Orange, Tomato & Chive Salsa

Fresh chives and sweet oranges provide a very cheerful combination of flavours. An unusual salsa, this is a very good accompaniment for grilled meats, such as lamb or pork kebabs. It also tastes good with grilled halloumi.

Serves 4
2 large, sweet oranges
1 ripe beefsteak tomato,
   or 2 plum tomatoes
bunch of fresh chives
1 garlic clove
30ml/2 tbsp extra virgin olive oil
   or grapeseed oil
sea salt

Preparation: 6–8 minutes; Cooking: 0 minutes

1 Slice the base off one orange so that it will stand firmly on a chopping board. Using a large sharp knife, remove the peel by slicing from the top to the bottom of the orange. Prepare the second orange in the same way.

2 Working over a bowl, segment each orange in turn. Slice towards the middle of the fruit, and slightly to one side of a segment, and then gently twist the knife to release the orange segment. Repeat. Squeeze any juice from the remaining membrane so that it falls into the bowl.

3 Roughly chop the orange segments and add them to the bowl with the collected orange juice.

4 Halve the tomato and use a teaspoon to scoop the seeds into the bowl. With a sharp knife, finely dice the flesh and add to the oranges and juice in the bowl.

5 Hold the bunch of chives neatly together and use a pair of kitchen scissors to snip them into the bowl.

6 Thinly slice the garlic and stir it into the orange mixture. Pour over the olive oil, season with sea salt and stir well to mix. Serve the salsa in the bowl in which it was made, or spoon into four individual bowls. It can also be spooned into the empty orange shells for serving. This involves slightly more difficult preparation but looks very effective.

Thousand Island Dip

This variation on the classic Thousand Island Dressing is far removed from the original version, but can be served in the same way – with shellfish laced on to bamboo skewers for dipping or with a simple mixed salad.

Serves 4
4 sun-dried tomatoes in oil
4 plum tomatoes, or 2 beefsteak
   tomatoes

150g/5oz/²⁄₃ cup mild soft
   cheese, or mascarpone or
   fromage frais
60ml/4 tbsp mayonnaise
30ml/2 tbsp tomato purée (paste)
30ml/2 tbsp chopped
   fresh parsley
1 lemon
Tabasco sauce, to taste
5ml/1 tsp Worcestershire sauce
   or soy sauce
salt and ground black pepper

Preparation: 6 minutes; Cooking: 0 minutes

1 Drain the sun-dried tomatoes and cut them into small pieces. Cut a cross in the blossom end of each fresh tomato, place them in a heatproof bowl and pour over boiling water. Leave for 1–2 minutes, then lift them out and peel off the skins. Chop the flesh finely. Put the sun-dried tomatoes and chopped fresh tomatoes in separate bowls and set aside.

2 Put the soft cheese in a bowl. Beat it until it is creamy, then gradually beat in the mayonnaise. Add the tomato purée in the same way.

3 Stir in the parsley and sun-dried tomatoes, then the fresh tomatoes. Mix well so that the dip is evenly coloured.

4 Grate (shred) the lemon finely and add the rind to the dip. Mix well. Squeeze the lemon and add the juice to the bowl, with Tabasco sauce to taste. Stir in the Worcestershire sauce or soy sauce, and salt and pepper to taste.

5 Spoon the dip into a serving bowl, swirling the surface attractively. Cover with clear film (plastic wrap) and chill in the refrigerator until ready to serve.

Orange Salsa Energy 91kcal/380kJ; Protein 1.3g; Carbohydrate 9.3g, of which sugars 9.3g; Fat 5.7g, of which saturates 0.8g; Cholesterol 0mg; Calcium 49mg; Fibre 2g; Sodium 7mg.
Thousand Island Dip Energy 194kcal/805kJ; Protein 4.7g; Carbohydrate 5.7g, of which sugars 5.6g; Fat 17.1g, of which saturates 5.2g; Cholesterol 27mg; Calcium 11mg; Fibre 1.2g; Sodium 184mg.

Tsatziki

You can serve this reduced-fat version of the classic Greek dip with strips of pitta bread toasted on the barbecue, or you could use vegetable sticks. The tangy cucumber makes it a light, refreshing snack for warm summer days. Instead of serving it solo, with pitta, try it as an accompaniment to grilled fish.

Serves 4
I mini cucumber
4 spring onions (scallions)
I garlic clove
200ml/7fl oz/scant I cup
    low-fat Greek (US strained
    plain) yogurt
45ml/3 tbsp chopped fresh mint
salt and ground black pepper
fresh mint sprig, to garnish
    (optional)
toasted pitta bread, to serve

Preparation: 4–5 minutes; Cooking: 0 minutes

I Using a sharp knife, trim the ends from the cucumber, then cut it lengthways into 5mm/¼in slices. Dice these neatly.

2 Trim the spring onions and garlic, then chop both very finely.

3 Beat the yogurt in a bowl until smooth, if necessary, then gently stir in the chopped cucumber, spring onions, garlic and mint until well combined.

4 Add salt and plenty of ground black pepper to taste, then transfer the mixture to a serving bowl. Chill in the refrigerator until ready to serve, then garnish with a small mint sprig.

5 Serve the dip with slices of pitta bread that have been toasted on the barbecue or under a hot grill (broiler).

Cook's Tip
It isn't necessary to peel the cucumber for this dip; in fact it looks better with the contrast of dark green outer skin and paler inner flesh. If you prefer to remove the peel, do so, but then cut the cucumber in half lengthways and scrape out the seeds with a teaspoon before dicing the flesh.

Tahini Sauce

Made of sesame seeds, spiced with garlic and lemon juice, this is Israel's most famous sauce. It makes a delicious dip and, when thinned with water, can be spooned over falafel.

Serves 4–6
150–175g/5–6oz/⅔–¾ cup
    tahini
3 garlic cloves, finely chopped
juice of I lemon
1.5ml/¼ tsp ground cumin
small pinch of ground coriander

small pinch of curry powder
50–120ml/2–4fl oz/¼–½ cup
    water
cayenne pepper
sea salt

For the garnish
15–30ml/1–2 tbsp extra virgin
    olive oil
chopped fresh coriander (cilantro)
    or flat leaf parsley
handful of olives and/or pickled
    vegetables
a few chillies or a hot pepper
    sauce

Preparation: 5 minutes; Cooking: 0 minutes

I Put the tahini in a bowl and add the finely chopped garlic cloves. Mix together well. Stir in the lemon juice, cumin, ground coriander and curry powder.

2 Slowly add the water to the tahini, beating all the time. The mixture will thicken at first, then become thin. Season with cayenne pepper and salt.

3 To serve, spoon the tahini on to a serving plate, individual plates or into a shallow bowl. Drizzle over the oil and sprinkle with the chopped fresh coriander or flat leaf parsley. Surround with the olives and/or pickled vegetables and the chillies, if using. If you do not wish to serve fresh chillies, offer hot pepper sauce to those who want to spice up the mixture.

Cook's Tip
Tahini sauce forms the basis of many of the salads and dips popular in Middle Eastern cuisine. Buy tahini from Middle Eastern shops and delis. It looks like peanut butter.

Tsatziki Energy 76kcal/316kJ; Protein 3.7g; Carbohydrate 3.7g, of which sugars 2.9g; Fat 5g, of which saturates 3.4g, Cholesterol 8mg; Calcium 95mg; Fibre 0.3g; Sodium 36mg.
Tahini Energy 175kcal/725kJ; Protein 5.2g; Carbohydrate 1.2g, of which sugars 0.3g; Fat 16.7g, of which saturates 2.4g; Cholesterol 0mg; Calcium 184mg; Fibre 2.5g; Sodium 7mg.

Chilli Sauce

Hot with chillies, pungent with garlic, and fragrant with exotic cardamom, this spicy sauce can be served with rice, couscous and soup. It also goes well with roast chicken or vegetable dishes.

Makes about 475ml/16fl oz/ 2 cups

5–8 garlic cloves, chopped
2–3 medium-hot chillies, such as jalapeño, seeded and chopped
5 tomatoes, diced
1 small bunch coriander (cilantro), roughly chopped
1 small bunch flat leaf parsley, chopped
30ml/2 tbsp extra virgin olive oil
10ml/2 tsp ground cumin
2.5ml/½ tsp ground turmeric
2.5ml/½ tsp curry powder
seeds from 3–5 cardamom pods
juice of ½ lemon
sea salt
a few sprigs of parsley or coriander, to garnish

Preparation: 7 minutes; Cooking: 0 minutes

1 Put all the sauce ingredients except the salt in a food processor or blender. Process until finely chopped, then season with salt if necessary.

2 Pour the sauce into a bowl, cover and chill. Garnish with chopped herbs before serving. The sauce can be covered and stored in the refrigerator for 3–4 days.

Variations
• To make a spicy dip, put 400g/14oz chopped fresh tomatoes, or a mixture of chopped fresh and canned tomatoes, in a bowl. Stir in 120ml/4fl oz/½ cup of the chilli sauce, or to taste, and season with salt, if necessary. Spread the dip on to wedges of flat bread, or serve in a bowl with raw vegetables for dipping.
• To make a spicy tomato relish, soak 30ml/2 tbsp fenugreek seeds in cold water for at least 2 hours and preferably overnight. Drain, then grind the seeds in a spice grinder or pound them in a mortar with a pestle until they form a smooth paste. In a bowl, combine the paste with 15ml/1 tbsp of the chilli sauce and 2 diced tomatoes. Season with salt and black pepper to taste.

Garlic Mayonnaise

Fresh wet organic garlic is available in spring and summer, but try to use dried, cured bulbs for this mouthwatering creamy mayonnaise as they have a more pungent flavour. For a delightful change, use smoked garlic, which will subtly alter the flavour.

Serves 4–6

2 large egg yolks
pinch of dried mustard
about 300ml/½ pint/1¼ cups mild olive oil
15–30ml/1–2 tbsp lemon juice, white wine vinegar or warm water
2–4 garlic cloves
sea salt and ground black pepper

Preparation: 6–8 minutes; Cooking: 0 minutes

1 Make sure the egg yolks and oil have come to room temperature before you start. Place the yolks in a bowl with the mustard and a pinch of salt, and whisk together to mix.

2 Gradually whisk in the oil, one drop at a time. When almost half the oil has been fully incorporated, start to add it in a slow, steady stream, whisking all the time.

3 As the mayonnaise thickens, thin it with a few drops of lemon juice or vinegar, or a few teaspoons of warm water.

4 When the mayonnaise is as thick as soft butter, stop adding oil. Season the mayonnaise to taste and add more lemon juice or vinegar as required.

5 Crush the garlic with the blade of a knife and stir it into the mayonnaise. For a slightly milder flavour, blanch the garlic twice in plenty of boiling water, then purée the cloves before beating them into the mayonnaise.

Watchpoint
The very young, the elderly, pregnant women and those in ill-health or with a compromised immune system are advised against consuming raw eggs or dishes containing them.

Chilli Sauce Energy 160kcal/673kJ; Protein 4.7g; Carbohydrate 19.7g, of which sugars 18.2g; Fat 7.6g, of which saturates 1.3g; Cholesterol 0mg; Calcium 78mg; Fibre 6g; Sodium 79mg.
Garlic Mayonnaise Energy 323kcal/1330kJ; Protein 1.2g; Carbohydrate 0.6g, of which sugars 0.1g; Fat 35.2g, of which saturates 5.3g; Cholesterol 67mg; Calcium 9mg; Fibre 0.1g; Sodium 3mg.

Fresh Fruit Salad

Oranges are an essential ingredient for a successful and refreshing fruit salad, which can include any fruit in season. A colourful combination takes just minutes to make and is always popular, whether served for dessert or for a healthy breakfast.

Serves 6
2 apples
2 oranges
2 peaches
16–20 strawberries
30ml/2 tbsp lemon juice
15–30ml/1–2 tbsp orange
  flower water
icing (confectioners') sugar,
  to taste (optional)

Preparation: 6 minutes; Cooking: 0 minutes

1 Peel and core the apples and cut into thin slices. Remove the pith and peel from the oranges and cut each one into segments. Squeeze the juice from the membrane and retain.

2 Blanch the peaches by immersing them for 1 minute in a bowl of boiling water. Peel and slice thickly.

3 Hull the strawberries, and halve any big ones. Place them in a large bowl with the sliced apples, orange segments and sliced peaches.

4 Mix the lemon juice, orange flower water and any reserved orange juice in a jug (pitcher). Taste and add a little icing sugar to sweeten, if you like. Pour the fruit juice over the salad, toss gently to mix, and serve.

Cook's Tips
• The easiest way to remove the pith and peel from an orange is to cut a thin slice from each end of the orange first, using a sharp knife. Stand the fruit upright and it will then be easy to cut off the remaining peel and pith.
• Orange flower water gives the salad a lovely, delicate flavour. If you are serving it for a special occasion, add a little Cointreau or other orange liqueur, if you like.

Dried Fruit Salad

This dessert doesn't take long to prepare, but must be made ahead of time, to allow the dried fruit to plump up and flavours to blend. It is also good for breakfast.

Serves 4
115g/4oz/½ cup ready-to-eat
  dried apricots, halved
115g/4oz/½ cup ready-to-eat
  dried peaches, halved
750ml/1¼ pints/3 cups water

1 pear
1 apple
1 orange
115g/4oz/1 cup mixed
  raspberries and blackberries
1 cinnamon stick
50g/2oz/¼ cup caster
  (superfine) sugar
15ml/1 tbsp clear honey
30ml/2 tbsp lemon juice

Preparation: 6 minutes; Cooking: 12 minutes; Make ahead

1 Place the dried apricots and peaches in a large pan and pour in 600ml/1 pint/2½ cups of the water.

2 Peel and core the pear and apple, then dice. Remove peel and pith from the orange and cut into wedges. Add all the cut fruit to the pan with the raspberries and blackberries.

3 Pour in the remaining water. Add the cinnamon stick, stir in the sugar and honey, and heat gently, stirring until the sugar and honey have dissolved. Bring to the boil. Cover and simmer for 10 minutes, then remove the pan from the heat.

4 Stir in the lemon or lime juice. Leave to cool completely, then transfer the fruit and syrup to a bowl, cover with clear film (plastic wrap) and chill for 1–2 hours before serving.

Variation
Swap the fruits around, using dried apples and pears and fresh apricots and peaches instead of the combination suggested in the recipe. Cranberries and blackcurrants are delicious alternatives to the raspberries and blackberries.

Fresh Fruit Salad Energy 42kcal/180kJ; Protein 1.1g; Carbohydrate 9.8g, of which sugars 9.8g; Fat 0.1g, of which saturates 0g; Cholesterol 0mg; Calcium 28mg; Fibre 1.9g; Sodium 5mg.
Dried Fruit Salad Energy 190kcal/811kJ; Protein 3.3g; Carbohydrate 46g, of which sugars 46g; Fat 0.5g, of which saturates 0g; Cholesterol 0mg; Calcium 75mg; Fibre 6g; Sodium 13mg.

Fragrant Fruit Salad

Organic summer fruits make a delicious seasonal fruit salad. Any combination of fruits can be used, although this exotic choice is particularly suitable for a dinner party.

Serves 6
130g/4½oz/scant ¾ cup unrefined sugar
thinly pared rind and juice of 1 lime
30ml/2 tbsp brandy
5ml/1 tsp instant coffee granules or powder dissolved in 30ml/ 2 tbsp boiling water
1 small pineapple
1 papaya
2 pomegranates
1 medium mango
2 passion fruits or kiwi fruit
fine strips of pared lime rind, to decorate

Preparation: 10–12 minutes; Cooking: 6 minutes

1 Put the sugar and lime rind in a small pan with 150ml/¼ pint/⅔ cup water. Heat gently until the sugar dissolves, then bring to the boil and simmer for 5 minutes.

2 Cool rapidly, then strain into a large serving bowl, discarding the lime rind. Stir in the lime juice, brandy and dissolved coffee.

3 Using a sharp knife, cut the plume and stalk ends from the pineapple. Peel and cut the flesh into bitesize pieces. Add to the bowl. Discard the central core.

4 Halve the papaya and scoop out the seeds. Cut away the skin, then slice the papaya. Halve the pomegranates and scoop out the seeds. Add to the bowl.

5 Cut the mango lengthways into three pieces, along each side of the stone. Peel the skin off the flesh. Cut into chunks and add to the pineapple, papaya, pomegranate seeds and syrup in the bowl. Stir gently to mix the ingredients.

6 Halve the passion fruits and scoop out the flesh using a teaspoon or peel and chop the kiwi fruit. Add to the bowl and serve, decorated with strips of pared lime rind.

Minted Pomegranate Yogurt with Grapefruit Salad

Ruby red or salmon pink, the jewel-like seeds of the pomegranate make any dessert look beautiful. Here they are stirred into yogurt to make a delicate sauce for a fresh-tasting grapefruit salad. The flecks of green are finely chopped fresh mint, which complement the citrus flavours perfectly.

Serves 3–4
300ml/½ pint/1¼ cups Greek (US strained plain) yogurt
2–3 ripe pomegranates
small bunch of fresh mint, finely chopped
clear honey or caster (superfine) sugar, to taste (optional)

For the grapefruit salad
2 red grapefruits
2 pink grapefruits
1 white grapefruit
15–30ml/1–2 tbsp orange flower water

To decorate
handful of pomegranate seeds
fresh mint leaves

Preparation: 8 minutes; Cooking: 0 minutes; Make ahead

1 Put the yogurt in a bowl and beat well. Cut open the pomegranates and scoop out the seeds, removing and discarding all the bitter pith.

2 Fold the pomegranate seeds and mint into the yogurt. Sweeten with a little honey or sugar, if using, then chill.

3 Peel the red, pink and white grapefruits, cutting off and discarding all the pith. Cut between the membranes to remove the segments, holding the fruit over a bowl to catch the juices.

4 Discard the membranes and mix the fruit segments with the reserved juices. Sprinkle with the orange flower water and add a little honey or sugar, if using. Stir gently then decorate with a few pomegranate seeds.

5 Decorate the chilled yogurt with a sprinkling of pomegranate seeds and mint leaves, and serve with the grapefruit salad.

Fruit Salad Energy 218kcal/930kJ; Protein 1.4g; Carbohydrate 49.8g, of which sugars 49.8g; Fat 0.4g, of which saturates 0g; Cholesterol 0mg; Calcium 60mg; Fibre 4.4g; Sodium 10mg.
Pomegranate Energy 188kcal/784kJ; Protein 8.8g; Carbohydrate 18g, of which sugars 18g; Fat 10.5g, of which saturates 5.2g; Cholesterol 0mg; Calcium 202mg; Fibre 3.6g; Sodium 82mg.

Citrus Fruit Flambé

A fruit flambé makes a dramatic finale for a dinner party. Topping this refreshing citrus fruit dessert with crunchy pistachio praline makes it extra special.

Serves 4
4 oranges
2 ruby grapefruit
2 limes

50g/2oz/¼ cup butter
50g/2oz/⅓ cup light muscovado
  (brown) sugar
45ml/3 tbsp Cointreau
fresh mint sprigs, to decorate

For the praline
oil, for greasing
115g/4oz/½ cup caster
  (superfine) sugar
50g/2oz/½ cup pistachio nuts

Preparation: 5 minutes; Cooking: 8–10 minutes; Make ahead

1 First, make the pistachio praline. Brush a baking sheet lightly with oil. Place the caster sugar and nuts in a small heavy pan and cook over a low heat, swirling the pan occasionally until all the sugar has melted completely.

2 Continue to cook over a fairly low heat until the nuts start to pop and the sugar has turned a dark golden colour. Pour on to the oiled baking sheet and set aside to cool. Using a sharp knife, chop the praline into rough chunks.

3 Cut all the rind and pith from the citrus fruits. Holding each fruit in turn over a large bowl, cut between the membranes so that the segments fall into the bowl, with any juice.

4 Heat the butter and muscovado sugar together in a heavy frying pan until the sugar has melted and the mixture is golden. Strain the citrus juices into the pan and continue to cook, stirring occasionally with a wooden spoon, until the juice has reduced and is fairly thick and syrupy.

5 Add the fruit segments and warm through without stirring. Pour over the Cointreau and set it alight. As soon as the flames die down, spoon the fruit flambé into serving dishes. Scatter some praline over each portion and decorate with sprigs of fresh mint.

Mango Stacks with Tangy Raspberry Coulis

This makes a very healthy yet stunning dessert – it is low in fat and contains no added sugar. However, if the raspberries are a little sharp, add a pinch of sugar to the purée to sweeten it.

Serves 4
3 filo pastry sheets, thawed
  if frozen
50g/2oz/¼ cup butter, melted
2 small ripe mangoes
115g/4oz/⅔ raspberries, thawed
  if frozen

Preparation: 10 minutes; Cooking: 5 minutes

1 Preheat the oven to 200°C/400°F/Gas 6. Lay the filo sheets on a clean work surface and cut out four 10cm/4in rounds from each.

2 Brush each round with the melted butter and lay the rounds on two baking sheets. Bake for 5 minutes, or until crisp and golden. Place on wire racks to cool.

3 Peel the mangoes, remove the stones and cut the flesh into thin slices. Put the raspberries in a food processor with 45ml/ 3 tbsp water and process to a purée.

4 Place a pastry round on each of four serving plates. Top with a quarter of the mango and drizzle with a little of the raspberry purée. Repeat until all the ingredients have been used, ending with a layer of mango and a drizzle of raspberry purée.

Variation
Use sliced nectarines or peaches instead of the mangoes.

Cook's Tip
Always place a dish towel or some clear film (plastic wrap) over the filo sheets you are not working with to prevent them from drying out, becoming brittle and cracking.

Fruit Flambé Energy 446kcal/1872kJ; Protein 4.8g; Carbohydrate 65.2g, of which sugars 64.8g; Fat 17.4g, of which saturates 7.4g; Cholesterol 27mg; Calcium 127mg; Fibre 4.4g; Sodium 155mg.
Mango Stacks Energy 186kcal/779kJ; Protein 2.2g; Carbohydrate 21.7g, of which sugars 11.9g; Fat 10.7g, of which saturates 6.7g; Cholesterol 27mg; Calcium 36mg; Fibre 3.1g; Sodium 79mg.

Fresh Fig Compote

Lightly poaching figs in a vanilla and coffee syrup brings out their wonderful flavour, especially if the dessert is left to stand for an hour or so before being served. Do not put the compote in the refrigerator.

Serves 4–6

400ml/14fl oz/1²/₃ cups brewed coffee
115g/4oz/¹/₂ cup clear honey
1 vanilla pod
12 slightly under-ripe fresh figs
Greek (US strained plain) yogurt, to serve (optional)

Preparation: 3 minutes; Cooking: 8 minutes; Make ahead

1 Choose a frying pan with a lid, large enough to hold the figs in a single layer. Pour in the coffee and add the honey.

2 Split the vanilla pod lengthways and scrape the seeds into the pan. Add the vanilla pod, then bring to the boil over high heat. Continue to boil the syrup until it has reduced to about 175ml/6fl oz/³/₄ cup. Pour into a bowl and cool quickly.

3 Wash the figs and pierce the skins several times with a sharp skewer. Cut in half and add to the syrup. Lower the heat, cover and simmer for 5 minutes. Remove the figs from the syrup with a slotted spoon and set aside to cool.

4 Strain the syrup over the figs. Allow to stand at room temperature for 1 hour before serving with yogurt, if liked.

Cook's Tips
- *Rinse and dry the vanilla pod; it can be used several times. If placed in a jar of sugar, it will impart a delightful flavour.*
- *Figs come in three main varieties – red, white and black – and all three are suitable for cooking. Naturally high in sugar, they are sweet and succulent and complement well the stronger flavours contributed by the freshly brewed coffee and vanilla.*
- *To cool the syrup quickly, place the bowl in a larger bowl filled with iced water. Stirring speeds the cooling process.*

Grapefruit in Honey & Whisky

Create a simple yet elegant dessert by arranging a colourful fan of pink, red and white grapefruit segments on a plate and pouring over a sweet whisky sauce. This dessert is perfect after a rich meal.

Serves 4

1 pink grapefruit
1 red grapefruit
1 white grapefruit
50g/2oz/¹/₄ cup sugar
60ml/4 tbsp clear honey
45ml/3 tbsp whisky
mint leaves, to decorate

Preparation: 4 minutes; Cooking: 14 minutes; Make ahead

1 Cut a thin slice of peel and pith from each end of the grapefruit. Place the cut side down on a plate and cut off the peel and pith in strips. Remove any remaining pith. Cut out each segment leaving the membrane behind. Put the grapefruit segments into a shallow bowl and set aside.

2 Put the sugar and 150ml/¹/₄ pint/²/₃ cup water into a heavy pan. Bring to the boil, stirring constantly, until the sugar has completely dissolved, then reduce the heat and simmer, without stirring, for 10 minutes, until thickened and syrupy. Do not cover the pan.

3 Heat the honey in a small pan and boil until it becomes a slightly deeper colour and begins to caramelize. Remove the pan from the heat and carefully add the whisky, standing back in case the mixture spits. Using a match or taper, carefully ignite, if you like, then pour the mixture into the sugar syrup.

4 Bring the syrup to the boil, and pour over the grapefruit segments. Cover and leave until cold. To serve, put the grapefruit segments on to four serving plates, alternating the colours. Pour over some of the syrup and decorate with the mint leaves.

Variation
The whisky can be replaced with brandy or an orange liqueur such as Cointreau, Grand Marnier or Van der Hum.

Fresh Fig Compote Energy 147kcal/628kJ; Protein 1.7g; Carbohydrate 36g, of which sugars 35.8g; Fat 0.6g, of which saturates 0g; Cholesterol 0mg; Calcium 103mg; Fibre 3g; Sodium 27mg.
Grapefruit in Honey Energy 154kcal/649kJ; Protein 1.1g; Carbohydrate 32.7g, of which sugars 32.7g; Fat 0.1g, of which saturates 0g; Cholesterol 0mg; Calcium 35mg; Fibre 1.6g; Sodium 6mg.

Chocolate & Banana Fool

This delicious dessert has a lovely flavour. It is quite rich, so it is a good idea to serve it with some dessert biscuits, such as shortbread, biscotti or vanilla wafers.
Serves 4

115g/4oz plain (semisweet) chocolate, broken into small pieces
300ml/½ pint/1¼ cups ready-made fresh custard
2 bananas

Preparation: 3 minutes; Cooking: 2 minutes

1 Put the chocolate pieces in a heatproof bowl and melt in the microwave on high power for 1–2 minutes. Stir, then set aside. If you do not have a microwave, put the chocolate in a heatproof bowl and place it over a pan of water that has boiled and then been removed from the heat. Leave until melted, stirring frequently to ensure that the liquid chocolate is perfectly smooth.

2 Pour the custard into a bowl and gently fold in the melted chocolate to make a rippled effect.

3 Peel and slice the bananas and stir these into the chocolate and custard mixture. Spoon into four glasses. If you have time, chill for at least 30 minutes before serving.

Variation
For a lovely contrast in texture, fry wholemeal (whole-wheat) breadcrumbs in butter with a little sugar until crisp. When cool, layer the crunchy crumbs with the chocolate custard and fruit.

Cook's Tip
Good-quality bought custard is ideal for this dessert. Don't be tempted to use anything but the best chocolate, though, or the flavour will be compromised. Look for a bar that contains at least 70 per cent cocoa solids. A flavoured chocolate such as pistachio or orange takes the dessert into another dimension.

Lemon Posset

This old-fashioned dessert was once considered a remedy for the common cold. It is certainly worth suffering a sniffle if it means you get to sample its superb citrus and cream flavour.

Serves 4
600ml/1 pint/2½ cups double (heavy) cream
175g/6oz/scant 1 cup caster (superfine) sugar
grated rind and juice of 2 unwaxed lemons

Preparation: 2 minutes; Cooking: 8–10 minutes

1 Pour the cream into a heavy pan. Add the sugar and heat gently until the sugar has dissolved, then bring to the boil, stirring constantly. Add the lemon juice and rind, reserving a little of the rind for decoration, and stir constantly over a medium heat until it thickens.

2 Pour the mixture into four heatproof serving glasses. Cool, then chill in the refrigerator until just set. Serve the posset decorated with a few strands of lemon rind, and with a selection of dessert biscuits (cookies), if you like. Rich, buttery shortbread is ideal.

Variation
To intensify the lemon flavour of this lovely old-fashioned dessert even more, swirl a spoonful of lemon curd or lemon cheese on the surface just before serving. Physalis make a suitable and very stylish accompaniment.

Apple & Rose Petal Snow

This is a lovely, light and refreshing dessert, which is ideal to make when the trees in the orchards are groaning with apples. The rose petals give a delicate fragrance, which is heightened by the use of rose water. Other edible petals such as honeysuckle, lavender and geranium could also be used.

Serves 4
2 large cooking apples
150ml/¼ pint/⅔ cup thick apple juice
30ml/1 tbsp rose water
2 egg whites
75g/3oz/generous ⅓ cup caster sugar, or to taste
a few rose petals from an unsprayed rose
crisp biscuits (cookies) or brandy snaps, to serve

Preparation: 5 minutes; Cooking: 3–4 minutes

1 Peel and chop the apples and cook with the apple juice until soft. Strain, then add the rose water and leave to cool.

2 Whisk the egg whites until peaking, then gently whisk in the sugar. Gently fold together the apple and egg whites. Stir in most of the rose petals.

3 Spoon the snow into four glasses and chill. Serve topped with the remaining petals and crisp biscuits or brandy snaps.

Chocolate Fool Energy 268kcal/1127kJ; Protein 4.1g; Carbohydrate 42.1g, of which sugars 38.1g; Fat 9.6g, of which saturates 4.9g; Cholesterol 3mg; Calcium 81mg; Fibre 1.4g; Sodium 33mg.
Lemon Posset Energy 917kcal/3801kJ; Protein 2.7g; Carbohydrate 48.5g, of which sugars 48.5g; Fat 80.6g, of which saturates 50.1g; Cholesterol 206mg; Calcium 98mg; Fibre 0g; Sodium 36mg.
Apple and Rose Petal Snow Energy 113kcal/483kJ; Protein 1.7g; Carbohydrate 28.1g, of which sugars 28.1g; Fat 0.1g, of which saturates 0g; Cholesterol 0mg; Calcium 16mg; Fibre 0.9g; Sodium 33mg.

Rhubarb & Ginger Trifles

Choose a good-quality jar of rhubarb compote for this recipe; try to find one with large, chunky pieces of fruit. Alternatively, for even more zing, use rhubarb and ginger jam, or whole-fruit apricot jam.

Serves 4

12 gingernut biscuits
  (gingersnaps)
50ml/2fl oz/¼ cup rhubarb
  compote
450ml/¾ pint/scant 2 cups extra
  thick double (heavy) cream

Preparation: 3–4 minutes; Cooking: 0 minutes

1 Put the ginger biscuits in a strong plastic bag and knot it tightly to seal. Bash the biscuits with a rolling pin or meat mallet until roughly crushed. The biscuits can also be crumbed in a food processor but use the pulse button and watch closely as it is important they are only crushed and not reduced to fine crumbs.

2 Set aside two tablespoons of crushed biscuits in a bowl and divide the rest among four glasses.

3 Spoon the rhubarb compote on top of the crushed biscuits, then top with the cream. Place in the refrigerator and chill for about 30 minutes.

4 To finish, sprinkle the reserved crushed biscuits over the trifles and serve immediately.

Variations
• *Try this with hazelnut biscuits (cookies) and gooseberry compote for a delicious change.*
• *Instead of using individual glasses, use a straight-sided glass bowl. Dribble ginger wine over the layer of crushed biscuits.*
• *Add a layer of custard. Good-quality bought custard is fine.*
• *Use choc chip cookies instead of gingernuts (gingersnaps) and crumble a chocolate flake bar over the top of the dessert.*
• *Amaretti biscuits or ratafias also work well and are particularly good with apricot compote.*

Blueberry Meringue Crumble

Imagine the most appealing flavours of a blueberry meringue dessert – fresh tangy fruit, crisp sugary meringue and vanilla-scented cream – all served in a tall glass for easy eating. For a patriotic pudding, add a layer of cooked cranberries or raspberries and celebrate the red, white and blue. This is a fun way to mark a national day.

Serves 3–4

150g/5oz/1¼ cups fresh
  blueberries, plus extra
  to decorate
15ml/1 tbsp icing
  (confectioners') sugar
250ml/8fl oz/1 cup vanilla
  iced yogurt
200ml/7fl oz/scant 1 cup full
  cream (whole) milk
30ml/2 tbsp lime juice
75g/3oz meringues,
  lightly crushed

Preparation: 4 minutes; Cooking: 0 minutes

1 Put the blueberries and sugar in a blender or food processor with 60ml/4 tbsp water and blend until smooth, scraping the mixture down from the side once or twice, if necessary.

2 Transfer the purée to a small bowl and rinse out the blender or food processor bowl to get rid of any remaining juice.

3 Put the iced yogurt, milk and lime juice in the blender and process until thoroughly combined. Add half of the crushed meringues and process again until smooth.

4 Carefully pour alternate layers of the milkshake, blueberry syrup and the remaining crushed meringues into tall glasses, finishing with a few chunky pieces of meringue.

5 Drizzle any remaining blueberry syrup over the tops of the meringues and decorate with a few extra blueberries. Serve.

Variation
Iced yogurt is used to provide a slightly lighter note than ice cream, but there's nothing to stop you using ice cream instead.

Ginger Trifles Energy 695kcal/2874kJ; Protein 3.6g; Carbohydrate 27.1g, of which sugars 14.1g; Fat 64.3g, of which saturates 39.4g; Cholesterol 154mg; Calcium 98mg; Fibre 0.6g; Sodium 124mg.
Meringue Crumble Energy 164kcal/691kJ; Protein 6.2g; Carbohydrate 30.8g, of which sugars 30.8g; Fat 2.7g, of which saturates 1.6g; Cholesterol 8mg; Calcium 197mg; Fibre 1.2g; Sodium 96mg.

Blackcurrant Fool

The strong flavour and deep colour of this fruit makes it especially suitable for fools and ices, although this adaptable recipe can be made using other soft fruits too. Try it with raspberries, redcurrants or loganberries.

Serves 6
350g/12oz/3 cups blackcurrants
45ml/3 tbsp water
about 175g/6oz/scant 1 cup
   caster (superfine) sugar
5ml/1 tsp lemon juice
300ml/½ pint/1¼ cups double
   (heavy) cream

Preparation: 5 minutes; Cooking: 5 minutes; Make ahead

1 Put the blackcurrants into a small pan with the measured water and cook over a low heat until soft. Remove from the heat, add the sugar according to taste and stir until dissolved.

2 Cool slightly, then liquidize (blend) to make a purée. Leave to cool completely. Add the lemon juice and stir well.

3 Whip the double cream until it is fairly stiff and, using a metal spoon, carefully fold it into the blackcurrant purée, losing as little volume as possible.

4 Turn the mixture into a serving dish or six individual serving glasses, smooth the surface and leave to set. Cover with clear film (plastic wrap). Chill in the refrigerator until ready to serve.

Cook's Tip
Freeze blackcurrants on the stalks and they will come off easily.

Variation
To make an easy no-stir blackcurrant ice cream, turn the completed fool into a freezerproof container. Cover and freeze (preferably at the lowest setting). Transfer from the freezer to the refrigerator 10–15 minutes before serving to allow the ice cream to soften. Serve with whipped cream and biscuits.

Cool Chocolate Float

Chocolate milkshake and scoops of chocolate and vanilla ice cream are combined here to make the most meltingly delicious dessert drink ever.

Serves 2
115g/4oz plain (semisweet)
   chocolate, broken into pieces

250ml/8fl oz/1 cup milk
15ml/1 tbsp caster
   (superfine) sugar
4 large scoops classic vanilla
   ice cream
4 large scoops dark (bittersweet)
   chocolate ice cream
a little lightly whipped cream
grated chocolate or chocolate
   curls, to decorate

Preparation: 6 minutes; Cooking: 2 minutes

1 Put the chocolate in a heavy pan and add the milk and sugar. Heat gently, stirring with a wooden spoon until the chocolate has melted and the mixture is smooth. Pour into a bowl and set in a larger bowl of iced water to cool quickly.

2 Blend the cooled chocolate mixture with half of both ice creams in a blender or food processor until the mixture resembles chocolate milk.

3 Scoop the remaining ice cream alternately into two tall glasses: vanilla then chocolate.

4 Using a dessertspoon, drizzle the chocolate milk over and around the ice cream in each glass, so that it dribbles down in swirls. Top with lightly whipped cream and sprinkle over a little grated plain chocolate or some chocolate curls to decorate. Serve the floats immediately.

Variations
• You can experiment with all kinds of flavours of ice cream. Try substituting banana, coconut or toffee flavours for the chocolate and vanilla ice cream if you prefer.
• The health-conscious cook might prefer to substitute frozen yogurt, but for best results, make sure it is a creamy variety.

Fool Energy 1516kcal/6324kJ; Protein 6g; Carbohydrate 140.8g, of which sugars 140.8g; Fat 107.6g, of which saturates 66.8g; Cholesterol 276mg; Calcium 300mg; Fibre 8.4g; Sodium 60mg.
Float Energy 990kcal/4149kJ; Protein 17.7g; Carbohydrate 115.4g, of which sugars 110.4g; Fat 52.3g, of which saturates 32g; Cholesterol 83mg; Calcium 518mg; Fibre 1.5g; Sodium 262mg.

Whisky Trifle

This luxuriously rich trifle is made the old-fashioned way, with real sponge cake, fresh fruit and rich egg custard, but with whisky rather than the usual sherry flavouring.

Serves 6–8
1 x 15–18cm/6–7in sponge cake
225g/8oz raspberry jam
150ml/¼ pint/⅔ cup whisky
450g/1lb ripe fruit, such as pears, bananas and strawberries

300ml/½ pint/1¼ cups whipping cream
flaked almonds, to decorate

For the custard
450ml/¾ pint/scant 2 cups full cream (whole) milk
1 vanilla pod (bean) or a few drops of vanilla essence (extract) (optional)
3 eggs
25g/1oz/2 tbsp caster (superfine) sugar

Preparation: 12 minutes; Cooking: 5 minutes

1 To make the custard, put the milk into a pan with the vanilla pod, if using, and bring almost to the boil. Remove the pan from the heat. Whisk the eggs and sugar together lightly. Remove the pod. Gradually whisk the milk into the egg mixture.

2 Rinse out the pan with cold water, return the mixture to it and stir over low heat until it thickens enough to cover the back of a wooden spoon; do not allow the custard to boil.

3 Turn the custard into a mixing bowl and add the vanilla essence, if using. Cover the custard and set aside.

4 Halve the sponge cake horizontally, spread with the raspberry jam and make a sandwich. Using a sharp knife, cut it into slices and use them to line a large glass serving bowl.

5 Sprinkle with the whisky. Peel and slice the fruit, then spread it out over the sponge to make an even layer. Pour the custard on top, cover with clear film (plastic wrap) to prevent a skin forming, and leave to cool and set. Chill until required. Before serving, whip the cream and spread it over the set custard. Decorate with the almonds.

Pineapple & Rum Cream

When pineapple is heated, the flavour intensifies and the gorgeous sweet juices caramelize. Add rum and cream and you have a dream of a summer dessert for the grown-ups.

Serves 4
25g/1oz/2 tbsp butter
115g/4oz pineapple, roughly chopped
45ml/3 tbsp dark rum
300ml/½ pint/1¼ cups double (heavy) cream

Preparation: 4 minutes; Cooking: 4 minutes

1 Heat the butter in a frying pan and add the pineapple. Cook over a moderate to high heat until the pineapple is starting to turn golden at the edges.

2 Add the rum and allow to bubble for 1–2 minutes, then remove from the heat and set aside.

3 Pour the cream into a bowl and beat until soft. Fold the pineapple and rum mixture evenly through the cream, then spoon carefully into four glasses and serve immediately.

Cook's Tip
A ripe pineapple has a lovely perfume. The leaves on top should be glossy and healthy-looking, and the skin should be free from bruising. To prepare the pineapple, cut off the plume, then cut a slice off the base so the fruit will stand upright. Cut off the skin in wide diagonal strips, removing the black eyes, which have a peppery taste. Any that remain should be gouged out. Slice or dice the fruit, removing the hard central core if necessary.

Variation
Although a sumptuous dessert in its own right, this fruity alcoholic cream also works very well as a topping. Spoon over vanilla or rum-and-raisin ice cream for an extra special touch to a simple dessert.

Whisky Trifle Energy 4260kcal/17754kJ; Protein 72.6g; Carbohydrate 348g, of which sugars 255.6g; Fat 259.2g, of which saturates 86.4g; Cholesterol 1026mg; Calcium 1164mg; Fibre 13.8g; Sodium 2016mg.
Pineapple Cream Energy 455kcal/1876kJ; Protein 1.4g; Carbohydrate 4.2g, of which sugars 4.2g; Fat 45.5g, of which saturates 28.3g; Cholesterol 116mg; Calcium 43mg; Fibre 0.4g; Sodium 55mg.

Pineapple Baked Alaska

Most children love the surprise of this classic pudding – hot meringue with ice-cold ice cream inside. Here's a new variation, with coconut and pineapple.

Serves 3–4
3 large (US extra large) egg whites
150g/5oz/³/4 cup caster (superfine) sugar
25g/1oz desiccated (dry unsweetened shredded) coconut
175–225g/6–8oz piece of ready-made cake, such as ginger or chocolate
6 slices ripe, peeled pineapple
500ml/17fl oz/2¼ cups vanilla ice cream, in a brick
a few cherries or figs, to decorate

Preparation: 5 minutes; Cooking: 5–7 minutes

1 Preheat the oven to 230°C/450°F/Gas 8. Whisk the egg whites in a grease-free bowl until stiff, then whisk in the sugar until the mixture is stiff and glossy. Fold in the coconut.

2 Slice the cake into two thick layers so that each has the same rectangular shape as the ice cream.

3 Cut the pineapple into triangles or quarters, cutting it over the cake to catch any drips. On a baking sheet, arrange the fruit on top of one slice of cake. Top with the ice cream and then the second layer of cake.

4 Spread the meringue over the cake and ice cream, and bake in the oven for 5–7 minutes, or until turning golden. Serve immediately, topped with fruit.

> **Cook's Tips**
> • Do not use soft-scoop ice cream for this dessert as it will soften too quickly when heated in the oven.
> • When covering the cake and ice cream with the meringue, spread it carefully to ensure that no part of the pudding underneath is exposed, or the ice cream will melt in the oven.

Summer Fruit Brioche

Scooped-out individual brioches make perfect containers for the fruity filling in this stylish but simple dessert. If small brioches are not available, serve the fruit on slices cut from a large brioche. Any summer fruits can be used in this dessert – try raspberries, sliced peaches, nectarines, apricots, or pitted cherries. Serve with single cream poured over.

Serves 4
300g/11oz/2½ cups small ripe strawberries, halved
30ml/2 tbsp caster (superfine) sugar
115g/4oz/²/3 cup raspberries
4 individual brioches

Preparation: 4 minutes; Cooking: 2–3 minutes

1 Put the strawberries in a pan with the sugar and add 60ml/4 tbsp water. Heat very gently for about 1 minute, until the strawberries are softened but still keep their shape. Remove the pan from the heat, stir in the raspberries lightly and carefully and leave for a couple of minutes to cool.

2 Preheat the grill (broiler). Slice the tops off the brioches and use a teaspoon to scoop out their centres, leaving a 1cm/½in-thick case. Lightly toast them, turning once and watching them carefully, as they will brown very quickly.

3 Place the hot toasted brioches on plates and pile the warm fruit mixture into them. Add plenty of juice to saturate the brioches and allow it to flood the plates. Place any extra fruit on the plates, around the brioches, and serve immediately.

> **Variations**
> • Use bought meringue shells instead of brioche cases. Let the berry fruit mixture cool before spooning it into the shells, and serve with whipped cream.
> • Instead of poaching the berries lightly in a syrup made from sugar and water, use raspberry jam, melting it with a little water and a dash of lemon juice.

Baked Alaska Energy 667kcal/2808kJ; Protein 10.8g; Carbohydrate 104.6g, of which sugars 93.9g; Fat 25.7g, of which saturates 9.8g; Cholesterol 33mg; Calcium 215mg; Fibre 2.3g; Sodium 317mg.
Fruit Brioche Energy 340kcal/1431kJ; Protein 5.1g; Carbohydrate 57.5g, of which sugars 41g; Fat 11.5g, of which saturates 6.4g; Cholesterol 0mg; Calcium 55mg; Fibre 2.2g; Sodium 291mg.

Summer Berries in Warm Sabayon Glaze

This luxurious combination consists of summer berries under a light and fluffy sauce flavoured with liqueur. The topping is lightly grilled to form a crisp, caramel crust.

4 egg yolks
50g/2oz/¼ cup vanilla sugar or
  caster (superfine) sugar
120ml/4fl oz/½ cup liqueur,
  such as Cointreau, Kirsch or
  Grand Marnier, or a white
  dessert wine
a little icing (confectioners') sugar,
  sifted, and mint leaves, to
  decorate (optional)

Serves 4
450g/1lb/4 cups mixed summer
  berries, or soft fruit

Preparation: 9 minutes; Cooking: 2 minutes

1 Arrange the fruit in four heatproof ramekins. Preheat the grill (broiler) using the maximum setting.

2 Put the egg yolks in a large heatproof bowl and add the sugar and liqueur or wine. Whisk lightly to mix. Place over a pan of hot water and whisk constantly until thick, fluffy and pale.

3 Pour equal quantities of the sabayon sauce over the fruit in each dish. Place under the grill for 1–2 minutes until just turning brown. Watch closely – the sabayon must not burn.

4 Dust the fruit with icing sugar and sprinkle with mint leaves just before serving, if you like. You could also add an extra splash of liqueur, or serve a glass of liqueur on the side.

> **Variations**
> • If you prefer to omit the alcohol, use grape, mango or apricot juice for flavouring instead of the liqueur.
> • Poached apricots can be used instead of the berry fruits, in which case toast some sliced almonds in a dry frying pan and use them to decorate the top of the desserts before serving. Hazelnuts could be used instead.

Fresh Summer Berries with Coffee Sabayon

For a light and deliciously refreshing finale, serve a platter of fresh summer fruit with a fluffy coffee sauce, which has the added advantage of being delightfully easy to make.

5 egg yolks
75g/3oz/scant ½ cup caster
  (superfine) sugar
50ml/2fl oz/¼ cup brewed coffee
30ml/2 tbsp coffee liqueur,
  such as Tia Maria, Kahlúa
  or Toussaint
strawberry or mint leaves,
  to decorate (optional)
30ml/2 tbsp icing (confectioners')
  sugar, to dust

Serves 6
900g/2lb/6–8 cups mixed
  summer berries such as
  raspberries, blueberries and
  strawberries (hulled and halved,
  if large)

Preparation: 3 minutes; Cooking: 4 minutes

1 Arrange the mixed summer berries on a serving platter or individual plates and decorate with strawberry or mint leaves, if you like. Dust with icing sugar.

2 Whisk the egg yolks and caster sugar in a bowl over a pan of simmering water until the mixture begins to thicken.

3 Gradually add the coffee and liqueur, pouring in a thin, continuous stream and whisking all the time.

4 Continue whisking until the sauce is thick and fluffy. Spoon into a wide-mouthed jug (pitcher) and serve warm, or allow to cool, whisking occasionally, and serve cold with the fresh mixed summer berries.

> **Cook's Tip**
> Ensure that the water doesn't get too hot when making the sauce, or it may curdle.

Berries in Glaze Energy 235kcal/984kJ; Protein 3.9g; Carbohydrate 27.1g, of which sugars 27.1g; Fat 5.6g, of which saturates 1.6g; Cholesterol 202mg; Calcium 48mg; Fibre 1.3g; Sodium 18mg.
Berries with Coffee Energy 219kcal/919kJ; Protein 3.9g; Carbohydrate 29.7g, of which sugars 29.7g; Fat 5.6g, of which saturates 1.6g; Cholesterol 202mg; Calcium 50mg; Fibre 1.2g; Sodium 20mg.

Strawberry & Passion Fruit Coulis

A fresh fruit coulis tastes heavenly with all kinds of desserts and it transforms ice cream, crème fraîche or yogurt into something special. The sweet and delectable flavours of strawberry and passion fruit make a perfect sauce for a sundae of frozen yogurt.

Serves 4
175g/6oz/1½ cups strawberries, hulled and halved

1 passion fruit
10ml/2 tsp icing (confectioners') sugar (optional)

To serve
175g/6oz/1½ cups strawberries, hulled and halved
2 ripe peaches, stoned (pitted) and chopped
8 scoops (about 350g/12oz) vanilla or strawberry frozen yogurt

Preparation: 4–5 minutes; Cooking: 0 minutes

1 Purée the strawberries in a food processor. Scoop out the passion fruit pulp and add it to the coulis. Sweeten the mixture with a little icing sugar, if necessary.

2 Spoon half the strawberries and half the chopped peaches into four tall sundae glasses.

3 Add a scoop of vanilla or strawberry frozen yogurt. Set aside a few choice pieces of fruit for decoration, and use the rest to make a further layer on the top of each sundae. Top each sundae with a final scoop of frozen yogurt.

4 Pour the strawberry and passion fruit coulis over, and decorate the sundaes with the reserved strawberries and pieces of peach. Serve immediately.

> **Variation**
> You can make a coulis with any berry fruit with or without the passion fruit. Raspberries are particularly fine because they have a delicate and sweet flavour.

Gooseberry Fool

Blackberries, raspberries, blackcurrants or rhubarb work well in place of gooseberries. When using young pink rhubarb there is no need to sieve the cooked fruit, so give step 2 a miss.

Serves 4
450g/1lb gooseberries, trimmed and cut into short lengths
125g/4½ oz/¼ cup caster (superfine) sugar, or to taste
300ml/½ pint/1¼ cups double (heavy) cream

Preparation: 4 minutes; Cooking: 10 minutes

1 Put the gooseberries into a pan with 30ml/2 tbsp water. Cover and cook gently for about 10 minutes until the fruit is soft. Stir in the sugar to taste.

2 Tip the fruit into a nylon sieve (strainer) and press it through, using the back of a serving spoon. Leave the purée to cool.

3 Put the cream in a bowl and whip it until it is stiff enough to hold soft peaks. Stir in the gooseberry purée without over-mixing (it looks pretty with some streaks).

4 Spoon the mixture into serving glasses. If you have time, chill the desserts in the refrigerator for 30 minutes before serving, to give the flavours a chance to blend.

> **Variations**
> • *Gooseberry and banana fool* Mash 4 ripe bananas with 15ml/1 tbsp caster (superfine) sugar. Stir this into the gooseberry purée until thoroughly mixed, then add the whipped cream and spoon the mixture into serving glasses.
> • *Mango and redcurrant fool purée* Ripe mango (or use canned mango slices) with lightly cooked redcurrants. Proceed as in the main recipe and decorate the desserts with tiny sprigs of fresh redcurrants.
> • *Apricot fool* For the most intense flavour, use dried apricots. Cook them in a little water until soft, purée in a food processor or blender, and flavour with honey and lime juice.

Fruit Coulis Energy 126kcal/534kJ; Protein 4.8g; Carbohydrate 26.6g, of which sugars 26.6g; Fat 0.8g, of which saturates 0.4g; Cholesterol 4mg; Calcium 150mg; Fibre 1.7g; Sodium 63mg.
Gooseberry Fool Energy 517kcal/2147kJ; Protein 2.6g; Carbohydrate 37.3g, of which sugars 37.3g; Fat 40.7g, of which saturates 25.1g; Cholesterol 103mg; Calcium 85mg; Fibre 2.7g; Sodium 21mg.

White Chocolate Snowballs

These little spherical cakes are particularly popular during the Christmas season. They're simple to make, yet utterly delicious and bursting with creamy, buttery flavours. Make a big batch when family and friends are due to visit.

Makes 16

200g/7oz white chocolate
25g/1oz/2 tbsp butter, diced
90g/3½ oz/generous 1 cup desiccated (dry unsweetened shredded) coconut
90g/3½ oz syrup sponge or Madeira cake, crumbled
icing (confectioner') sugar, for dusting

Preparation: 8 minutes; Cooking: 3 minutes

1 Break the chocolate into pieces and put in a heatproof bowl with the butter. Rest the bowl over a pan of gently simmering water and stir frequently until melted. Remove the bowl from the heat and set aside for a few minutes.

2 Meanwhile, put 50g/2oz/⅔ cup of the coconut on a plate and set aside. Add the cake to the melted chocolate with the remaining coconut. Mix well to form a chunky paste.

3 Take spoonfuls of the mixture and roll into balls about 2.5cm/1in in diameter and immediately roll them in the reserved coconut. Place the balls on baking parchment and leave to set at room temperature. If you put them in the refrigerator they may get too hard, so take them out at least half an hour before serving.

Cook's Tips
• You'll need to shape the mixture into balls as soon as you've mixed in the coconut and cake; the mixture sets very quickly and you won't be able to shape it once it hardens.
• If you like, make them in advance of a special tea as they will keep well in the refrigerator for a few days.
• Roll each ball of paste around a glacé (candied) cherry if you like, so that each snowball has a surprise in the centre.

Warm Zabaglione

Light as air and highly alcoholic, this warm custard is a much-loved Italian pudding. It is traditionally made with Marsala, but Madeira or sweet sherry can be used instead.

Serves 4

4 egg yolks
50g/2oz/¼ cup caster (superfine) sugar
60ml/4 tbsp Marsala, Madeira or sweet sherry
amaretti, to serve

Preparation: 0 minutes; Cooking: 5–7 minutes

1 Place the egg yolks and sugar in a large heatproof bowl, and whisk with an electric beater until the mixture is pale and has thickened considerably.

2 Gradually add the Marsala, Madeira or sherry to the egg mixture, 15ml/1 tbsp at a time, whisking well after each addition.

3 Place the bowl over a pan of gently simmering water and continue to whisk for 5–7 minutes, until the mixture becomes thick; when the beaters are lifted they should leave a thick trail on the surface of the mixture. Do not underbeat the mixture, or the zabaglione will be likely to separate.

4 Pour into four warmed, stemmed glasses and serve immediately with amaretti for dipping.

Variation
To make a chocolate version of this dessert, whisk in 30ml/2 tbsp unsweetened cocoa powder with the wine or sherry and serve dusted with cocoa powder and icing (confectioners') sugar.

Cook's Tip
Zabaglione is also delicious served as a sauce with cooked fruit. Try serving it with poached pears, grilled (broiled) peaches or baked bananas to create a really special dessert.

Snowballs Energy 133kcal/554kJ; Protein 1.6g; Carbohydrate 10.9g, of which sugars 9.7g; Fat 9.5g, of which saturates 6.6g; Cholesterol 3mg; Calcium 38mg; Fibre 0.8g; Sodium 46mg.
Warm Zabaglione Energy 131kcal/548kJ; Protein 3g; Carbohydrate 14.1g, of which sugars 14.1g; Fat 5.5g, of which saturates 1.6g; Cholesterol 202mg; Calcium 31mg; Fibre 0g; Sodium 12mg.

Hot Chocolate Zabaglione

Once you've tasted this slinky, sensuous dessert, you'll never look at cocoa in quite the same way again. The Marsala makes it rather expensive – and fairly alcoholic – so this is an indulgence that is strictly adults only. Make it when the children are safely tucked up in bed.

Serves 6
6 egg yolks
150g/5oz/²⁄₃ cup caster
   (superfine) sugar
45ml/3 tbsp unsweetened
   cocoa powder
200ml/7fl oz/scant 1 cup
   Marsala
unsweetened cocoa powder or
   icing (confectioners') sugar,
   for dusting

Preparation: 2 minutes; Cooking: 5–7 minutes

1 Half fill a medium pan with water and bring to simmering point. Select a heatproof bowl which will fit over the pan, place the egg yolks and sugar in it, and whisk until the mixture is pale and all the sugar has dissolved.

2 Add the cocoa and Marsala, then place the bowl over the simmering water. Whisk with a hand-held electric mixer until the mixture is smooth, thick and foamy.

3 Pour quickly into tall heatproof glasses, dust lightly with cocoa or icing sugar and serve immediately, with chocolate cinnamon tuiles or amaretti biscuits.

Cook's Tips
Use the best cocoa powder you can find. There are a couple of Fairtrade products that are particularly good, and it is worth paying a little extra. Cocoa powder is made from cocoa solids, the residue when chocolate liquor is pressed to extract the cocoa butter. To neutralize the acids, some cocoa is treated with alkali. The cocoa that results is called Dutch-processed. If this is used for cakes, it is important to use baking powder as a raising agent, since bicarbonate of soda (baking soda) will not react unless one of the other ingredients is sufficiently acidic.

Honey Baked Figs with Hazelnut Ice Cream

Figs baked in a lemon grass-scented honey syrup have the most wonderful flavour, especially when served with a good-quality ice cream dotted with roasted hazelnuts. If you prefer to avoid nuts, because you don't like them or because a guest has an allergy, use plain rich vanilla or toffee ice cream instead.

Serves 4
1 lemon grass stalk,
   finely chopped
1 cinnamon stick, roughly broken
60ml/4 tbsp clear honey
200ml/7fl oz/scant 1 cup water
75g/3oz/³⁄₄ cup hazelnuts
8 large ripe dessert figs
400ml/14fl oz/1²⁄₃ cups
   good-quality vanilla ice cream
30ml/2 tbsp hazelnut
   liqueur (optional)

Preparation: 4 minutes; Cooking: 16 minutes

1 Preheat the oven to 190°C/375°F/Gas 5. Make the syrup by mixing the lemon grass, cinnamon stick, honey and measured water in a small pan. Heat gently, stirring until the honey has dissolved, then bring to the boil. Simmer for 2 minutes.

2 Meanwhile, spread out the hazelnuts on a baking sheet and grill (broil) under a medium heat until golden brown. Shake the sheet occasionally, so that they are evenly toasted.

3 Cut the figs into quarters, leaving them intact at the bases. Stand in a baking dish, pour the syrup over, cover tightly with foil and bake for 13–15 minutes until the figs are tender.

4 While the figs are baking, remove the ice cream from the freezer and let it soften slightly. Chop the hazelnuts roughly and beat the softened ice cream briefly with an electric beater, then fold in the toasted hazelnuts until evenly distributed.

5 To serve, puddle a little of the syrup from the figs on to each dessert plate. Arrange the figs on top and add a spoonful of ice cream. At the very last moment before serving, spoon a little hazelnut liqueur over the ice cream, if you like.

Hot Zabaglione Energy 627kcal/2635kJ; Protein 11.9g; Carbohydrate 82.6g, of which sugars 80.3g; Fat 19g, of which saturates 6.7g; Cholesterol 537mg; Calcium 127mg; Fibre 2.4g; Sodium 222mg.
Honey Baked Figs Energy 433kcal/1816kJ; Protein 7.8g; Carbohydrate 53.6g, of which sugars 52.1g; Fat 21.2g, of which saturates 7g; Cholesterol 24mg; Calcium 227mg; Fibre 4.2g; Sodium 88mg.

Coffee Crêpes with Peaches

Juicy golden organic peaches and cream conjure up the sweet taste of summer. Here they are delicious as the filling for these light buckwheat crêpes.

Serves 6
75g/3oz/²/₃ cup plain (all-purpose) flour
25g/1oz/¹/₄ cup buckwheat flour
1 egg, beaten
200ml/7fl oz/scant 1 cup milk
15g/¹/₂ oz/1 tbsp butter, melted
100ml/3¹/₂ fl oz/scant ¹/₂ cup brewed coffee, cooled
sunflower oil, for frying

For the filling
6 ripe peaches
300ml/¹/₂ pint/1¹/₄ cups double (heavy) cream
15ml/1 tbsp brandy
225g/8oz/1 cup crème fraîche
65g/2¹/₂ oz/generous ¹/₄ cup caster (superfine) sugar

Preparation: 5 minutes; Cooking: 15 minutes

1 Sift the flours into a mixing bowl. Make a well in the middle and add the beaten egg, half the milk and the melted butter. Gradually mix in the flour, beating until the mixture is smooth, then beat in the remaining milk and the coffee.

2 Heat a drizzle of sunflower oil in a 15–20cm/6–8in crêpe pan. Pour in just enough batter to cover the base of the pan thinly, swirling the pan to spread the mixture evenly. Cook for 2 minutes, then flip the crêpe over and cook the other side.

3 Slide the crêpe out of the pan on to a plate. Continue making crêpes until all the mixture is used, stacking and interleaving them with baking parchment.

4 To make the filling, slice the peaches thickly. Whip the cream and brandy together until soft peaks form. Beat the crème fraîche with the sugar until smooth. Beat 30ml/2 tbsp of the cream into the crème fraîche, then fold in the remainder.

5 Place six of the crêpes on individual serving plates. Spoon a little of the brandy cream on to one half of each crêpe and top with peach slices. Gently fold the crêpe over and dust with a little sifted icing sugar, if you like. Serve immediately.

Fruit-filled Soufflé Omelette

This impressive dish is surprisingly quick and easy to make. The creamy omelette fluffs up in the pan, is flopped over to envelop its fruit filling and then slid out on to the plate.

Serves 2
75g/3oz/³/₄ cup strawberries, hulled
45ml/3 tbsp Kirsch, brandy or Cointreau
3 eggs, separated
30ml/2 tbsp caster (superfine) sugar
45ml/3 tbsp double (heavy) cream, whipped
a few drops of vanilla extract
25g/1oz/2 tbsp butter
icing (confectioners') sugar, sifted

Preparation: 5 minutes; Cooking: 4–5 minutes

1 Cut the strawberries in half and place in a bowl. Pour over 30ml/2 tbsp of the liqueur and set aside to macerate.

2 Beat the egg yolks and sugar together until pale and fluffy, then fold in the whipped cream and vanilla extract. Whisk the egg whites until stiff, then carefully fold in the yolks.

3 Melt the butter in an omelette pan. When sizzling, pour in the egg mixture and cook until set underneath, shaking occasionally. Spoon on the strawberries and liqueur and, tilting the pan, slide the omelette so that it folds over.

4 Carefully slide the omelette on to a warm serving plate, spoon over the remaining liqueur, and serve dredged with icing sugar. Cut the omelette in half, place on plates and serve.

> **Cook's Tip**
> *You can give your omelette a professional look by marking sizzling grill lines on top. Protecting your hand with an oven glove, hold a long, wooden-handled skewer directly over a gas flame until it becomes very hot and changes colour. Sprinkle the top of the omelette with icing (confectioners') sugar, then place the hot skewer on the sugar, which will caramelize very quickly.*

Soufflé Omelette Energy 434kcal/1802kJ; Protein 10.2g; Carbohydrate 18.4g, of which sugars 18.4g; Fat 30.7g, of which saturates 16.4g; Cholesterol 343mg; Calcium 70mg; Fibre 0.4g; Sodium 189mg.
Coffee Crêpes Energy 578kcal/2403kJ; Protein 6.5g; Carbohydrate 36.3g, of which sugars 23.1g; Fat 45.7g, of which saturates 28.8g; Cholesterol 150mg; Calcium 123mg; Fibre 2.1g; Sodium 63mg.

Tropical Fruit Gratin

This out-of-the-ordinary gratin is strictly for grown-ups. A colourful combination of fruit is topped with a simple sabayon before being flashed under the grill. The contrast between the hot, creamy topping and the cool, juicy fruit is the secret of its undeniable success.

Serves 4
2 tamarillos
½ sweet pineapple
1 ripe mango
175g/6oz/1½ cups blackberries
120ml/4fl oz/½ cup sparkling white wine
115g/4oz/½ cup caster (superfine) sugar
6 egg yolks

Preparation: 8 minutes; Cooking: 10 minutes

1 Cut each tamarillo in half lengthways, then into thick slices. Cut the rind and core from the pineapple and take spiral slices off the outside to remove the eyes. Cut the flesh into chunks. Peel the mango and cut the flesh from the stone (pit) in slices.

2 Divide all the fruit, including the blackberries, among four 14cm/5½in gratin dishes set on a baking sheet and set aside. Heat the wine and sugar in a pan until the sugar has dissolved. Bring to the boil and cook for 5 minutes.

3 Put the egg yolks in a large heatproof bowl. Place the bowl over a pan of simmering water and whisk until pale. Slowly pour on the hot sugar syrup, whisking all the time, until the mixture thickens. Preheat the grill (broiler).

4 Spoon the mixture over the fruit. Place the baking sheet holding the dishes on a low shelf under the hot grill until the topping is golden. Serve the gratin hot.

> **Variation**
> *Boiling drives off the alcohol in the wine, but children do not always appreciate the flavour. Substitute orange juice if making the gratin for them. White grape juice or pineapple juice would also work well.*

Chocolate & Orange Pancakes

Flip for these fabulous baby pancakes in a rich creamy orange liqueur sauce.

Serves 4
115g/4oz/1 cup self-raising (self-rising) flour
30ml/2 tbsp unsweetened cocoa powder
2 eggs
50g/2oz plain (semisweet) chocolate, broken into squares
200ml/7fl oz/scant 1 cup milk
finely grated rind of 1 orange

30ml/2 tbsp orange juice
butter or oil for frying
60ml/4 tbsp chocolate curls, for sprinkling

For the sauce
2 large oranges
30ml/2 tbsp unsalted (sweet) butter
45ml/3 tbsp light muscovado (brown) sugar
250ml/8fl oz/1 cup crème fraîche
30ml/2 tbsp Grand Marnier
chocolate curls, to decorate

Preparation: 6–8 minutes; Cooking: 12–14 minutes

1 Sift the flour and cocoa into a bowl and make a well in the centre. Add the eggs and beat well, gradually incorporating the surrounding dry ingredients to make a smooth batter.

2 Mix the chocolate and milk in a pan. Heat gently until the chocolate has melted, then beat into the batter until smooth and bubbly. Stir in the orange rind and juice.

3 Heat a large heavy frying pan and grease it. Drop large spoonfuls of batter on to the hot surface, leaving room for spreading. When the pancakes are lightly browned underneath and bubbly on top, flip them over to cook the other side. Slide on to a plate and keep hot while making more.

4 Make the sauce. Grate the rind of 1 orange into a bowl and set aside. Peel both oranges, taking care to remove all the pith, then slice the flesh fairly thinly. Heat the butter and sugar in a wide, shallow pan over a low heat, stirring until the sugar dissolves. Stir in the crème fraîche and heat gently. Heat the pancakes and orange slices in the sauce for 1–2 minutes, then spoon over the liqueur. Sprinkle with the reserved orange rind. Scatter over the chocolate curls and serve.

Gratin Energy 300kcal/1270kJ; Protein 6.2g; Carbohydrate 52.8g, of which sugars 52.7g; Fat 8.7g, of which saturates 2.4g; Cholesterol 302mg; Calcium 119mg; Fibre 4.6g; Sodium 22mg.
Pancakes Energy 752kcal/3131kJ; Protein 12.1g; Carbohydrate 58.1g, of which sugars 35.5g; Fat 53.2g, of which saturates 27g; Cholesterol 185mg; Calcium 282mg; Fibre 3.9g; Sodium 304mg.

Syrupy Brioche Slices with Vanilla Ice Cream

Keep a few individual brioche buns in the freezer to make this super dessert. For a slightly tarter taste, use finely grated lemon rind and juice instead of orange rind. For an everyday version of this simple dessert, use sliced currant buns – hot cross buns are an excellent vehicle for the spicy orange syrup – or even slices of raisin bread or fruity date loaf.

Serves 4
butter, for greasing
finely grated rind and juice of
 1 orange, such as Navelina or
 blood orange
50g/2oz/¼ cup caster
 (superfine) sugar
90ml/6 tbsp water
1.5ml/¼ tsp ground cinnamon
4 brioche buns
15ml/1 tbsp icing
 (confectioners') sugar
400ml/14fl oz/1²⁄₃ cups vanilla
 ice cream

Preparation: 4 minutes; Cooking: 9–10 minutes

1 Lightly grease a gratin dish and set aside. Put the orange rind and juice, sugar, water and cinnamon in a heavy pan. Heat gently, stirring constantly, until the sugar has dissolved, then boil rapidly, without stirring, for 2 minutes, until the mixture has thickened and is syrupy.

2 Remove the orange syrup from the heat and pour it into a shallow heatproof dish. Preheat the grill (broiler). Cut each brioche vertically into three thick slices. Dip one side of each slice in the hot syrup and arrange in the gratin dish, syrupy sides down. Reserve the remaining syrup. Grill (broil) the brioche under medium heat until lightly toasted.

3 Using tongs, turn the brioche slices over and dust well with icing sugar. Grill for about 3 minutes more, or until they are just beginning to caramelize around the edges.

4 Transfer the hot brioche to serving plates and top with scoops of vanilla ice cream. Spoon the remaining syrup over them and serve immediately.

Passion Fruit Soufflés

If you shun soufflés because you imagine them to be difficult, try these delightfully easy desserts based on bought custard. They are guaranteed to rise every time.

Serves 4
softened butter, for greasing
200ml/7fl oz/scant 1 cup ready-
 made fresh custard
3 passion fruit
2 egg whites

Preparation: 3–4 minutes; Cooking: 8–10 minutes

1 Preheat the oven to 200°C/400°F/Gas 6. Grease four 200ml/7fl oz/scant 1 cup ramekin dishes with the butter.

2 Pour the custard into a large mixing bowl. Cut the passion fruits in half. Using a teaspoon, carefully scrape out the seeds and juice from the halved passion fruit so that they drop straight on to the custard. Beat the mixture with a metal spoon until well combined, and set aside.

3 Whisk the egg whites in a clean, grease-free bowl until stiff, and fold a quarter of them into the custard.

4 Carefully fold the remaining egg whites into the custard, then spoon the mixture into the ramekin dishes. Place the dishes on a baking sheet and bake for 8–10 minutes, or until the soufflés are well risen. Serve immediately.

Variation
Flavour the ready-made fresh custard with a little lemon curd, if you like. Lemon goes very well with passion fruit, and the slightly less sweet combination works well in these simple soufflés.

Cook's Tip
Run the tip of the spoon handle around the inner rim of the soufflé mixture in each ramekin before baking to ensure that the soufflé rises evenly when baked in the oven.

Syrupy Brioche Energy 399kcal/1681kJ; Protein 8.5g; Carbohydrate 65.5g, of which sugars 42.5g; Fat 12g, of which saturates 7.2g; Cholesterol 25mg; Calcium 174mg; Fibre 1.3g; Sodium 252mg.
Passion Fruit Soufflés Energy 59kcal/249kJ; Protein 3.1g; Carbohydrate 8.8g, of which sugars 7.1g; Fat 1g, of which saturates 0g; Cholesterol 1mg; Calcium 48mg; Fibre 0.4g; Sodium 53mg.

Hot Mocha Rum Soufflés

These superb hot mocha soufflés always rise beautifully. Serve them as soon as they are cooked for a fantastic finale to a dinner party.

Serves 6

25g/1oz/2 tbsp unsalted (sweet)
    butter, melted
65g/2½oz/generous ½ cup
    unsweetened cocoa powder
75g/3oz/⅓ cup caster
    (superfine) sugar
60ml/4 tbsp strong black coffee
30ml/2 tbsp dark rum
6 egg whites
icing (confectioners') sugar,
    for dusting

Preparation: 3–4 minutes; Cooking: 12–15 minutes

1 Preheat the oven with a baking sheet inside to 190°/375°F/ Gas 5. Grease six 250ml/8fl oz/1 cup soufflé dishes by brushing the interiors all over with melted butter.

2 Mix 15ml/1 tbsp of the cocoa with 15ml/1 tbsp of the caster sugar in a bowl. Tip the mixture into each of the dishes in turn, rotating them so that they are evenly coated.

3 Put the remaining cocoa in a bowl. Add the strong black coffee and then stir in the dark rum.

4 Whisk the egg whites in a clean, grease-free bowl until they form firm peaks. Whisk in the remaining caster sugar. Stir a generous spoonful of the whites into the cocoa mixture to lighten it, then fold in the remaining whites.

5 Spoon the mixture into the prepared dishes, smoothing the tops. Place on the hot baking sheet, and bake in the hot oven for 12–15 minutes or until well risen. Serve the soufflés immediately, dusted with icing sugar.

> **Cook's Tip**
> *When serving the soufflés at the end of a dinner party, prepare them just before the meal is served. Pop in the oven as soon as the main course is finished and serve freshly baked.*

Fried Bananas with Sugar & Rum

Children love fried bananas, but this Caribbean version with rum delivers an extra kick and is strictly for grown-ups. Fried bananas can be incredibly sweet, but the lime juice cuts through the sweetness with delicious and satisfying results.

Serves 4

50g/2oz/¼ cup caster
    (superfine) sugar
45ml/3 tbsp rum
65g/2½oz/5 tbsp unsalted
    (sweet) butter
grated rind and juice of 1 lime
4 bananas, peeled
vanilla ice cream, to serve

Preparation: 2–3 minutes; Cooking: 12 minutes

1 Place the sugar, rum, butter, grated lime rind and lime juice in a large heavy frying pan over a low heat. Cook for a few minutes, stirring occasionally with a wooden spoon, until the sugar has completely dissolved.

2 Add the bananas to the pan, turning to coat them in the sauce. Cook over a medium heat for 5 minutes on each side, or until the bananas are golden. Remove from the heat and cut the bananas in half. Serve two pieces of banana per person with a scoop of vanilla ice cream and a generous drizzle of the hot sauce.

> **Variations**
> • *Rum is the traditional spirit for this delicious dessert, but brandy can be used instead. Alternatively, try this with an orange liqueur such as Grand Marnier or Cointreau, and substitute grated orange rind and juice for the lime.*
> • *Use half a pineapple instead of bananas. Peel a fresh pineapple, quarter it, then slice each quarter into wedges.*

> **Cook's Tip**
> *Avoid using bananas that are too ripe, otherwise they may break apart in the pan before they get a chance to colour.*

Rum Soufflés Energy 148kcal/619kJ; Protein 5g; Carbohydrate 14.3g, of which sugars 13.1g; Fat 5.8g, of which saturates 3.6g; Cholesterol 9mg; Calcium 23mg; Fibre 1.3g; Sodium 190mg.
Fried Bananas Energy 385kcal/1616kJ; Protein 5.9g; Carbohydrate 53.9g, of which sugars 29.7g; Fat 17.7g, of which saturates 5.8g; Cholesterol 48mg; Calcium 59mg; Fibre 3g; Sodium 22mg.

Flambéed Bananas with Caribbean Coffee Sauce

This dessert has all the flavour of the Caribbean: bananas, dark sugar, coffee and rum. The bananas become beautifully tender, with a sweet, sticky sauce that is delicious, whether you enjoy it alone or with ice cream.

Serves 4–6

6 bananas
40g/1½ oz/3 tbsp butter
50g/2oz/¼ cup soft dark
  brown sugar
50ml/2fl oz/¼ cup strong
  brewed coffee
60ml/4 tbsp dark rum
vanilla ice cream, to serve

Preparation: 3–4 minutes; Cooking: 7–8 minutes

1 Peel the bananas and cut in half lengthways. Melt the butter in a large frying pan over a medium heat. Add the bananas and cook for 3 minutes, turning halfway through cooking time, taking care not to break them. They will be quite soft.

2 Sprinkle the sugar over the bananas, then add the coffee. Continue cooking, stirring occasionally, for 2–3 minutes, or until the bananas are tender and covered in the sticky sauce. Pour the rum into the pan and bring to the boil. With a long match or taper and tilting the pan, ignite the rum. As soon as the flames subside, serve the bananas with vanilla ice cream.

Variation
Espresso is the best coffee for this intensely flavoured sauce. Partner it with a coffee liqueur instead of rum, if you like. Toussaint is a good choice. Not as sweet as some of the other coffee liqueurs, it gives the sauce impressive depth.

Cook's Tip
These hot bananas taste equally good served with coconut or coffee ice cream. Alternatively, try them with thick, creamy yogurt.

Steamed Custard in Nectarines

Steaming nectarines or peaches brings out their natural colour and sweetness, so this is a good way of making the most of underripe or less flavourful fruit from the market.

Serves 6

6 nectarines
1 large (US extra large) egg
45ml/3 tbsp light muscovado
  (brown) sugar or palm sugar
30ml/2 tbsp reduced-fat
  coconut milk

Preparation: 15 minutes; Cooking: 5–10 minutes; Make ahead

1 Cut the nectarines in half. Using a teaspoon, scoop out the stones (pits) and a little of the surrounding flesh.

2 Lightly beat the egg, then add the sugar and the coconut milk. Beat until the sugar has dissolved.

3 Transfer the nectarines to a steamer and carefully fill the cavities three-quarters full with the custard mixture. Steam over a pan of simmering water for 5–10 minutes. Remove from the heat and leave to cool completely before transferring to plates and serving.

Variations
• *Instead of nectarines, use peaches, skinning them first by dunking them in boiling water until the skins peel back and can easily be removed.*
• *An alternative method of preparation is to chop 3 nectarines and spoon the fruit into six ramekins. Divide the custard among them and steam until set.*
• *Use full-fat coconut milk if you prefer.*

Cook's Tip
Palm sugar, also known as jaggery, is made from the sap of certain Asian palm trees, such as coconut and palmyrah. It is available from Asian food stores. If you buy it as a cake or large lump, grate it before use, so it will dissolve easily.

Flambéed Bananas Energy 200kcal/839kJ; Protein 1.3g; Carbohydrate 32g, of which sugars 29.7g; Fat 5.8g, of which saturates 3.6g; Cholesterol 14mg; Calcium 12mg; Fibre 1.1g; Sodium 42mg.
Steamed Custard Energy 119kcal/507kJ; Protein 3.8g; Carbohydrate 25.2g, of which sugars 25.2g; Fat 1.1g, of which saturates 0.3g; Cholesterol 32mg; Calcium 24mg; Fibre 2.3g; Sodium 20mg.

Semolina Cake

This is a popular Greek treat. It takes very little time to make and uses quite inexpensive ingredients.

Serves 6–8
500g/1¼ lb/2½ cups caster
    (superfine) sugar
1 litre/1¾ pints/4 cups cold water

1 cinnamon stick
250ml/8fl oz/1 cup olive oil
350g/12oz/2 cups coarse
    semolina
50g/2oz/½ cup blanched
    almonds
30ml/2 tbsp pine nuts
5ml/1 tsp ground cinnamon

Preparation: 5 minutes; Cooking: 8 minutes, plus standing

1 Put the sugar in a heavy pan, pour in the water and add the cinnamon stick. Bring to the boil, stirring, until the sugar dissolves, then boil without stirring for about 4 minutes.

2 Meanwhile, heat the oil in a separate, heavy pan. When it is almost smoking, add the semolina gradually and stir continuously until it turns light brown.

3 Lower the heat, add the almonds and pine nuts and brown together for 2–3 minutes, stirring continuously. Take the semolina mixture off the heat and set aside.

4 Remove the cinnamon stick from the hot syrup using a slotted spoon and discard it.

5 Protecting your hand with an oven glove or dish towel, carefully add the hot syrup to the semolina mixture, stirring all the time. The mixture will spit at this point, so stand back.

6 Return the pan to a gentle heat and stir until all the syrup has been absorbed and the mixture looks smooth. Remove the pan from the heat, cover it with a clean dish towel and let it stand for 10 minutes.

7 Scrape the mixture into a 20–23cm/8–9in round cake tin (pan), preferably fluted, and set it aside. When it is cold, unmould it on to a platter and dust it with cinnamon.

Cinnamon Pinwheels

These impressive sweet pastries go well with tea or coffee or as an accompaniment to ice cream and creamy desserts. If you find they turn soft during storage, re-crisp them briefly in the oven. Cinnamon is widely used in both sweet and savoury cooking: here ground cinnamon is used but it is also available as woody sticks. It has a delicious fragrant aroma and gives these simple-to-make pinwheels a warm spicy flavour.

Makes 20–24
50g/2oz/¼ cup caster (superfine)
    sugar, plus a little extra
    for sprinkling
10ml/2 tsp ground cinnamon
250g/9oz puff pastry
beaten egg, to glaze

Preparation: 6 minutes; Cooking: 10 minutes

1 Preheat the oven to 220°C/425°F/Gas 7. Grease a large baking sheet. Mix the sugar with the cinnamon in a small bowl.

2 Roll out the pastry on a lightly floured surface to a 20cm/8in square and sprinkle with half the sugar mixture. Roll out the pastry to a 25cm/10in square so that the sugar is pressed into it.

3 Brush with the beaten egg and then sprinkle with the remaining sugar mixture. Loosely roll up the pastry into a log, brushing the end of the pastry with a little more egg and pressing down to secure the edge in place.

4 Using a sharp knife, cut the log into thin slices and transfer them to the prepared baking sheet. Bake for 10 minutes, until golden and crisp. Sprinkle with more sugar and transfer to a wire rack to cool. Serve alone or with cream.

Cook's Tip
Ground cinnamon in jars rapidly loses its intense fragrance. It is better to buy cinnamon sticks and grind them to a powder just before use. A coffee grinder is ideal for this.

Semolina Cake Energy 660kcal/2776kJ; Protein 6.8g; Carbohydrate 99.8g, of which sugars 65.7g; Fat 28.7g, of which saturates 3.6g; Cholesterol 0mg; Calcium 56mg; Fibre 1.5g; Sodium 10mg.
Cinnamon Pinwheels Energy 47kcal/197kJ; Protein 0.6g; Carbohydrate 6g, of which sugars 2.3g; Fat 2.6g, of which saturates 0g; Cholesterol 0mg; Calcium 12mg; Fibre 0g; Sodium 33mg.

Torrijas

Translated as 'poor knights', these sugared toasts are perfect for almost every occasion. Without the wine, they make a good tea-time snack for children, or to accompany a cup of hot chocolate. As a party dessert they are the equivalent of France's toasted brioche.

Serves 4
120ml/4fl oz/½ cup white wine
2 large eggs
12 thick rounds of stale
*   French bread*
60–90ml/4–6 tbsp sunflower oil
ground cinnamon, and caster
*   (superfine) sugar, for dusting*

Preparation: 4–5 minutes; Cooking: 6 minutes

1 Pour the wine into a shallow dish and dip the bread rounds into it so that they are coated all over.

2 Beat the eggs together in another shallow dish. Dip half the bread rounds into the beaten egg first on one side and then on the other so that they are completely covered.

3 Heat 60ml/4 tbsp oil in a pan until very hot and fry the bread rounds for about 1 minute on each side until crisp and golden. Reserve on kitchen paper, then dip and fry the rest, adding more oil if necessary. Serve the torrijas hot, sprinkled with plenty of ground cinnamon and sugar.

Variation
For an extra-special treat, use panettone or slices of Stollen instead of French bread. Serve with crème fraîche or whipped cream.

Cook's Tip
These toasts are often enjoyed at Spanish festivals and are a typical dish from Madrid (although variations can be found all over Europe). Milk can be used in place of white wine, if liked, making them suitable for children.

Nutty Nougat

This chewy sweet is made from egg white whisked together with a hot sugar syrup. Nuts and candied fruits are traditionally added but other fruits, such as dried apricots or glacé cherries, can also be used.

Makes about 500g/1¼lb
225g/8oz/generous 1 cup sugar
225g/8oz/1 cup clear honey or
*   golden (light corn) syrup*
1 large (US extra large) egg white
115g/4oz/1 cup flaked (sliced)
*   almonds or chopped pistachio*
*   nuts, roasted*

Preparation: 8–10 minutes; Cooking: 5–6 minutes

1 Line an 18cm/7in square tin with rice paper and set aside.

2 Place the sugar, honey or golden syrup and 60ml/4 tbsp water in a large heavy pan and heat gently until the sugar has totally dissolved, stirring frequently with a wooden spoon.

3 Bring the syrup to the boil and boil gently to the soft crack stage, or 151°C/304°F on a sugar thermometer.

4 Meanwhile, whisk the egg white until very stiff, but not crumbly, then slowly drizzle the syrup into the egg white while whisking constantly with an electric whisk.

5 Quickly stir in the nuts and pour the mixture into the prepared tin. Leave to cool but, before the nougat becomes too hard, cut it into squares.

Cook's Tips
• *If you do not have a sugar thermometer, test the syrup by adding a few drops of it to a cup of iced water. Leave for a few seconds and then pour the water away. The syrup will have congealed. If it is brittle enough to snap, the syrup is ready.*
• *If you make this nougat on a very warm day, you will find it takes longer to firm up and you will need to wait a little longer before cutting. It may help to take it out of the tin and cut it into squares as soon as it has set.*

Torrijas Energy 419kcal/1763kJ; Protein 12.2g; Carbohydrate 56.3g, of which sugars 3g; Fat 15.7g, of which saturates 2.4g; Cholesterol 95mg; Calcium 138mg; Fibre 2.4g; Sodium 652mg.
Nougat Energy 2250kcal/9511kJ; Protein 29.2g; Carbohydrate 415g, of which sugars 411.9g; Fat 64.2g, of which saturates 5.1g; Cholesterol 0mg; Calcium 408mg; Fibre 8.5g; Sodium 115mg.

Chocolate & Prune Bars

Wickedly self-indulgent and very easy to make, these fruity chocolate bars will keep for 2–3 days in the refrigerator – if they don't all get eaten as soon as they are ready. For an adult treat, soak the prunes in brandy before use.

Makes 12 bars
250g/9oz good quality
  milk chocolate
50g/2oz/¼ cup unsalted
  (sweet) butter
115g/4oz digestive biscuits
  (graham crackers)
115g/4oz/½ cup ready-to-eat
  prunes

Preparation: 4–5 minutes; Cooking: 0 minutes; Chill ahead

1 Break the chocolate into small pieces and place in a heatproof bowl. Add the butter and melt in the microwave on High for 1–2 minutes. Stir to mix and set aside. (Alternatively, place the chocolate pieces and butter in a bowl over a pan of gently simmering water and leave until melted, stirring frequently.)

2 Put the biscuits in a plastic bag and seal, then bash into small pieces with a rolling pin. Alternatively, break up the biscuits in a food processor but do not let them become too fine. Use the pulse button or process in short bursts.

3 Roughly chop the prunes and stir into the melted chocolate with the biscuits. Spoon the mixture into a 20cm/8in square cake tin (pan) and smooth out any lumps with the back of the spoon. Chill for 1–2 hours until set. Remove the cake from the refrigerator and, using a sharp knife, cut into 12 bars.

Variations
• Use dark (bittersweet) chocolate instead of milk chocolate. Fruit and nut chocolate makes for particularly rich-tasting bars.
• Any firm sweet biscuit (cookie) can be used. Gingernuts (gingersnaps) are delicious, especially if preserved or candied ginger is added with or instead of the prunes.
• Substitute dried apricots or peaches for the prunes. This variation works well with orange-flavoured chocolate.

Cinnamon & Orange Tuiles

The aroma of cinnamon and orange evokes a feeling of Christmas. These chocolate-dipped tuiles are perfect for festive occasions.

finely grated rind of 1 orange
50g/2oz/½ cup plain
  (all-purpose) flour
75g/3oz/6 tbsp butter, melted

Makes 15
2 egg whites
90g/3½ oz/½ cup caster
  (superfine) sugar
7.5ml/1½ tsp ground cinnamon

For the dipping chocolate
75g/3oz Belgian plain
  (semisweet) chocolate
45ml/3 tbsp milk
75–90ml/5–6 tbsp double
  (heavy) or whipping cream

Preparation: 4 minutes; Cooking: 12–14 minutes; Make ahead

1 Preheat the oven to 200°C/400°F/Gas 6. Line two very large baking trays with baking parchment.

2 Whisk the egg whites until softly peaking, then whisk in the sugar until smooth and glossy. Add the cinnamon and orange rind, sift over the flour and fold in with the melted butter. When well blended, stir in 15ml/1 tbsp of recently boiled water.

3 Place 4–5 teaspoons of the mixture on each tray, well apart. Flatten out and bake, one tray at a time, for 6–7 minutes until just turning golden. Cool for a few seconds then remove from the tray with a fish slice or metal spatula and immediately roll around the handle of a wooden spoon. Place on a rack to cool.

4 To make the dipping chocolate, melt the chocolate slowly in the milk until smooth, then stir in the cream. Dip one or both ends of the biscuits in the chocolate and cool.

Cook's Tip
If you haven't made these before, cook only one or two at a time until you get the hang of it. If they harden too quickly to allow you time to roll them, return the baking sheet to the oven for a few seconds, then try rolling them again.

Anglesey Shortbread

Originating in Aberffraw, a village on Anglesey, these biscuits are called 'Teisen Berffro' in Welsh. They are made by pressing the dough into a queen scallop shell prior to baking. They do, of course, taste just as good without the marking.

Makes 12

100g/3½ oz/½ cup butter, softened
50g/2oz/¼ cup caster (superfine) sugar, plus extra for sprinkling
150g/5½ oz/1¼ cups plain (all-purpose) flour

Preparation: 6–7 minutes; Cooking: 10 minutes

1 Preheat the oven to 200°C/400°F/Gas 6. Line a baking sheet with baking parchment.

2 Put the butter and sugar into a bowl and beat until light and fluffy. Sift the flour over and stir it in until the mixture can be gathered into a ball of soft dough.

3 Knead the dough, working it back and forth so that the warmth of your hand keeps the dough soft and pliable. Divide and shape it into 12 balls.

4 Sprinkle the inside of a scallop shell with sugar, and gently press a ball of dough into it, spreading it evenly so the shell is filled. Invert on to the paper-lined sheet, pressing it down to flatten the base and to mark it with the impression of the shell.

5 Lift the shell off, carefully prising out the dough. Alternatively, press or roll the dough balls into plain biscuits (cookies) measuring about 5cm/2in across.

6 Put into the hot oven and cook for about 10 minutes until set. Traditionally, they should not be allowed to brown, but they look very attractive and taste delicious with crisp golden edges.

7 Sprinkle with a little extra sugar, transfer to a wire rack and leave to cool completely.

All Butter Cookies

These biscuits or cookies are known as refrigerator biscuits as the mixture is chilled until it is firm enough to cut neatly into thin biscuits. The dough can be frozen and when thawed enough to slice, can be freshly baked, but do allow a little extra cooking time.

Makes 28–30

275g/10oz/2½ cups plain (all-purpose) flour
200g/7oz/scant 1 cup unsalted (sweet) butter
90g/3½ oz/scant 1 cup icing (confectioners') sugar, plus extra for dusting
10ml/2 tsp vanilla extract

Preparation: 5–7 minutes; Cooking: 8–10 minutes; Chilling: 1 hour

1 Put the flour in a food processor. Add the butter and process until the mixture resembles coarse breadcrumbs. Add the icing sugar and vanilla, and process until the mixture comes together to form a dough. Knead lightly and shape into a thick sausage, 30cm/12in long and 5cm/2in in diameter. Wrap and chill for at least 1 hour, until firm.

2 Preheat the oven to 200°C/400°F/Gas 6. Grease two baking sheets. Using a sharp knife, cut 5mm/¼ in thick slices from the dough and space them slightly apart on the baking sheet.

3 Bake for 8–10 minutes, alternating the position of the baking sheets in the oven halfway through cooking, if necessary, until the biscuits are cooked evenly and have just turned pale golden around the edges. Leave for 5 minutes, then transfer to a wire rack to cool. Serve dusted with icing sugar.

> **Cook's Tips**
> • *These cookies do not spread much when baked, so can be spaced fairly close together on the baking sheets. Leave a little room between them, though, or they will be more difficult to lift off once they have cooled slightly.*
> • *Transfer the cooked cookies to the wire rack with a spatula. They will still be softish at this stage but will firm up on cooling.*

Shortbread Energy 121kcal/506kJ; Protein 1.2g; Carbohydrate 14.1g, of which sugars 4.6g; Fat 7g, of which saturates 4.4g; Cholesterol 18mg; Calcium 21mg; Fibre 0.4g; Sodium 51mg.
Cookies Energy 84kcal/350kJ; Protein 0.8g; Carbohydrate 9.6g, of which sugars 3.3g; Fat 4.9g, of which saturates 3.1g; Cholesterol 12mg; Calcium 14mg; Fibre 0.3g; Sodium 36mg.

Index